KU-450-694

Controlling Corruption

The Politics of Corruption

Series Editor: Robert Williams
Professor of Politics
University of Durham, UK

1. Explaining Corruption
   Robert Williams

2. Corruption in the Developing World
   Robert Williams and Robin Theobald

3. Corruption in the Developed World
   Robert Williams, Jonathan Moran and Rachel Flanary

4. Controlling Corruption
   Robert Williams and Alan Doig

Wherever possible, the articles in these volumes have been reproduced as originally published using facsimile reproduction, inclusive of footnotes and pagination to facilitate ease of reference.

For a list of all Edward Elgar published titles visit our site on the World Wide Web at http://www.e-elgar.co.uk

Controlling Corruption

Edited by

Robert Williams

Professor of Politics
University of Durham, UK

and

Alan Doig

Professor of Public Services Management
Liverpool Business School, Liverpool John Moores University, UK

THE POLITICS OF CORRUPTION 4

An Elgar Reference Collection
Cheltenham, UK • Northampton, MA, USA

Published by
Edward Elgar Publishing Limited
Glensanda House
Montpellier Parade
Cheltenham
Glos GL50 1UA
UK

Edward Elgar Publishing, Inc.
136 West Street
Suite 202
Northampton
Massachusetts 01060
USA

A catalogue record for this book is available from the British Library.

Library of Congress Cataloguing in Publication Data

Controlling corruption / edited by Robert Williams and Alan Doig.
— (The politics of corruption ; 4)
Includes bibliographical references and index.
1. Political corruption. 2. Political corruption—Prevention. I. Williams, Robert, 1946 Sept. 10– II. Doig, Alan. III. Series.

JF1081+
364.1'323—dc21 00–044233

ISBN 1 84064 492 3
1 84064 115 0 (4 volume set)

Printed and bound in Great Britain by Biddles Ltd, *www.biddles.co.uk*

Contents

Acknowledgements

The editors and publishers wish to thank the authors and the following publishers who have kindly given permission for the use of copyright material.

Frank Cass & Co. Ltd for articles: Robert Wade (1984), 'The System of Administrative and Political Corruption: Canal Irrigation in South India', *Journal of Development Studies*, **18** (3), April, 287–328; John Toye and Mick Moore (1998), 'Taxation, Corruption and Reform', *European Journal of Development Research*, **10** (1), June, 60–84; Stephen P. Riley (1998), 'The Political Economy of Anti-Corruption Strategies in Africa', *European Journal of Development Research*, **10** (1), June, 129–59.

Comparative Politics for article: Kate Gillespie and Gwenn Okruhlik (1991), 'The Political Dimensions of Corruption Cleanups: A Framework for Analysis', *Comparative Politics*, **24** (1), October, 77–95.

Institute for Criminal Justice Ethics, New York, USA for article: James B. Jacobs and Frank Anechiarico (1992), 'Blacklisting Public Contractors as an Anti-Corruption and Racketeering Strategy', *Criminal Justice Ethics*, **11** (2), Summer/Fall, 64–76.

Institute for Social and Economic Change, Bangalore, India for article: S.N. Sangita (1995), 'Institutional Arrangement for Controlling Corruption in Public Life: Karnataka Experience', *Indian Journal of Public Administration*, **XLI** (1), January–March, 45–67.

Johns Hopkins University Press for article: Peter Eigen (1996), 'Combatting Corruption Around the World', *Journal of Democracy*, **7** (1), January, 158–68.

Kluwer Academic Publishers BV for articles: Kenneth M. Gibbons (1986), 'Canada's Task Force on Conflict of Interest', *Corruption and Reform*, **1**, 51–6; Judith A. Truelson (1987), 'Blowing the Whistle on Systematic Corruption: On Maximizing Reform and Minimizing Retaliation', *Corruption and Reform*, **2** (1), 55–74; Peter N. Grabosky (1990), 'Citizen Co-Production and Corruption Control', *Corruption and Reform*, **5** (2), 125–51; Michael M. Atkinson and Maureen Mancuso (1992), 'Edicts and Etiquette: Regulating Conflict of Interest in Congress and the House of Commons', *Corruption and Reform*, **7** (1), 1–18; Mark Findlay and Andrew Stewart (1992), 'Implementing Corruption Prevention Strategies Through Codes of Conduct', *Corruption and Reform*, **7** (1), 67–85; Louis M. Seagull (1994/95), 'Whistleblowing and Corruption Control: The GE Case', *Crime, Law and Social Change*, **22** (4), 381–90; Angela Gorta and Suzie Forell (1995), 'Layers of Decision: Linking Social Definitions of Corruption and Willingness to Take Action', *Crime, Law and Social Change*, **23** (4), 315–43; Adriana Alberti (1996), 'Political Corruption and the Role of Public Prosecutors in Italy', *Crime, Law and Social Change*, **24** (4), 273–92; Alan Doig (1998), 'Dealing with Corruption: The Next

Steps', *Crime, Law and Social Change*, **29** (2–3), 99–112; Petter Langseth and Bryane Michael (1998), 'Are Bribe Payments in Tanzania "Grease" or "Grit"?', *Crime, Law and Social Change*, **29** (2–3), 197–208; Peter Poerting and Werner Vahlenkamp (1998), 'Internal Strategies Against Corruption: Guidelines for Preventing and Combating Corruption in Police Authorities', *Crime, Law and Social Change*, **29** (2–3), 225–49.

MCB University Press for article: Frederick Stapenhurst and Petter Langseth (1997), 'The Role of the Public Administration in Fighting Corruption', *International Journal of Public Sector Management*, **10** (5), 311–30.

Oxford University Press for article: Simon Coldham (1995), 'Legal Responses to State Corruption in Commonwealth Africa', *Journal of African Law*, **39** (2), 115–26.

Sage Publications, Inc. for articles: Max J. Skidmore (1996), 'Promise and Peril in Combating Corruption: Hong Kong's ICAC', *Annals of the American Academy of Political and Social Science*, **547**, September, 118–30; Craig W. Thomas (1998), 'Maintaining and Restoring Public Trust in Government Agencies and Their Employees', *Administration and Society*, **30** (2), May, 166–93.

Virginia Journal of International Law for article: Lucinda A. Low, Andrea K. Bjorklund and Kathryn Cameron Atkinson (1998), 'The Inter-American Convention Against Corruption: A Comparison With the United States Foreign Corrupt Practices Act', *Virginia Journal of International Law*, **38** (243), Spring, 243–92.

John Wiley & Sons Ltd for articles: Alan Doig (1995), 'Good Government and Sustainable Anti-Corruption Strategies: A Role for Independent Anti-Corruption Agencies?', *Public Administration and Development*, **15** (2), May, 151–65; Robert Klitgaard (1997), 'Cleaning Up and Invigorating the Civil Service', *Public Administration and Development*, **17** (5), December, 487–509.

World Bank for articles: Susan Rose-Ackerman (1996), *Redesigning the State to Fight Corruption: Transparency, Competition, and Privatization*, Private Sector Development Department, Note No. 75, April, 1–4; Petter Langseth, Rick Stapenhurst and Jeremy Pope (1997), *The Role of a National Integrity System in Fighting Corruption*, EDI Working Papers, 400/142, Shelf No. E1976, 1–23, 25–27, 29–31, 33–35; Kenneth M. Dye and Rick Stapenhurst (1998), *Pillars of Integrity: The Importance of Supreme Audit Institutions in Curbing Corruption*, EDI/World Bank Institute Working Papers, 1–17, 19–21, 23–25.

Every effort has been made to trace all the copyright holders but if any have been inadvertently overlooked the publishers will be pleased to make the necessary arrangement at the first opportunity.

In addition the publishers wish to thank the Library of the London School of Economics and Political Science and the Library of Indiana University at Bloomington, USA, for their assistance in obtaining these articles.

Introduction

Robert Williams

Corruption is ancient and modern. History is replete with cases of bribery and nepotism but the academic study of corruption is primarily a late twentieth century phenomenon. While historians have recorded the details of individual scandals and *cause célèbres*, the dominant perspective has been one which sees corruption as a deviant and probably transitory activity. Individual scoundrels and scandals attracted attention and lent colour to otherwise mundane accounts of economic and political history. At the same time, the rise and fall of political machines in the USA and the elimination of rotten boroughs and other forms of electoral malpractice in the UK also attracted critical attention. The supposition was that corruption, like adolescence, is a phase which countries go through before they reach maturity. Thus corruption was either linked to the demonization of particular individuals or seen as a particular stage or point on the path to modernity.

The study of corruption was transformed by the success of the independence movements of the 1950s and 1960s. The winds of change which blew through Africa and Asia created a large number of newly independent states. The study of the politics of underdeveloped, less developed, developing countries and now the South (the nomenclature shifted over time) became a social science industry and, it was widely noted, corruption was a major problem. The key question was whether corruption in such countries was different from or similar to corruption in developed countries. The developed countries had apparently experienced corrupt phases before getting corruption under control through a combination of political, judicial and administrative reforms. From this perspective, corruption was associated with forms of political and economic immaturity which educational and social progress would overcome. But subsequent events combined to render this sanguine interpretation and prognosis both inadequate and inaccurate.

It became clear that the corruption experienced in some newly independent states was pervasive and deep seated. It was simultaneously appreciated that the 'take off' phase of economic growth seen as necessary for political and social development had not materialized. Development was seen as the cure for all manner of social and economic ills and, without it, what was once seen as a transitional phase looked more like a permanent condition. Economic 'take off' in a global economy dominated by powerful industrialized states proved more difficult than was once envisaged. It was no longer legitimate to assume that development would resolve the multiple problems besetting the South and, if development was stalled, it was necessary to tackle the specific problems directly.

But just as the perception that corruption was a major problem in developing countries emerged, confidence in its decline in developed countries began to evaporate. The incidence of political scandals was hard to reconcile with the belief that corruption was a problem which had been solved. The implosion of the Italian political system after the 'tangentopoli' revelations revealed how deep seated a problem corruption still is in some developed states.

The last bastion of self righteousness was Britain where, as late as the 1970s and 1980s, public figures ritually extolled the high ethical standards that prevailed in British public life. When scandals did occur, they were attributed to the odd 'rotten apple' in an otherwise wholesome barrel. But the 'cash for questions' affair in the early 1990s set off a chain of events which proposed substantial structural reform in British government and politics. The corruption eruption is therefore a global rather than a regional phenomenon.

The perception of corruption has radically changed. Where it was once seen as deviant, peripheral and transitory, it is now seen as common, deep rooted and permanent. But is this only a problem of perception or does it signify a decline in standards of behaviour? Are corruption scandals the exceptions that prove the rule or only the tip of an iceberg? Is the multilateral action against corruption in the 1990s evidence of a timely response to a freshly perceived phenomenon or a sign of institutional panic borne of years of policy neglect?

Like poverty, corruption has always been with us. Like prosperity for all, absolute integrity in public life is rhetorical or idealistic rather than practical and real. Eliminating corruption completely from public life is an impossible dream. But electorates and citizenry in both North and South seem increasingly intolerant of corruption and its associated costs and consequences. Allegations of corruption have demonstrated a unique capacity to generate demonstrations and riots against regimes in many parts of the world. And just as the dispossessed of the world are angered by corruption, the priority and attention it attracts in the international agencies and financial institutions have reached unprecedented heights. The World Bank, the United Nations, US Aid and the UK Department for International Development are all parts of the consensus which argues that corruption is a major cause of poverty and a serious obstacle to development. The consensus further holds that something must be done, new policies devised and programmes of action implemented. This represents a significant shift in both policy and priorities. Before the late 1980s, corruption was seen by donor bodies as something regrettable but probably inescapable. In some cases, the geopolitical role of dictators such as Mobutu in Zaire was seen as important enough to condone the massive corruption associated with their regimes. The end of the Cold War removed the need to support every anti-communist regime, however brutal or corrupt, and produced a sea change in the attitudes and policies of the World Bank and other bodies. What was once perceived as undesirable but tolerable is now seen as completely unacceptable. Governments which have not responded to international calls for firm action against corruption, for example, Kenya, have found their flows of international assistance being reduced or even cut off.

Thus we see that interest in corruption has increased dramatically in a number of ways; corruption in the South has been identified as a major problem and many governments are taking active steps to combat it. Contrary to some expectations, corruption in the North has not declined or disappeared and there are heightened levels of political and public interest in confronting it. The international donor community has now recognized corruption as a serious obstacle to development. If corruption has always been with us, it has rarely attracted the intensity of global attention it now receives.

Fatalists would say that, because corruption has always been with us, it always will be. Its causes are rooted in basic human weaknesses such as greed, and therefore attempts to control corruption are largely futile. But this ignores the fact that levels of corruption vary dramatically from country to country. Greed may be a constant factor in human life but political and economic structures and processes clearly play important roles in determining to what extent this vice can be exercised. In terms of corruption, Denmark is very different from Nigeria but, more interestingly, so is Botswana. There can be striking differences in the incidence of corruption within continents, within regions, between adjacent states and even within states. In some states in the USA corruption is a way of life, while in others it is virtually unknown. The same observation could be made about corruption in local authorities in the UK.

Corruption not only varies from place to place but also from time to time. In every state's history, there are periods when corruption appears to be peculiarly high and others when its incidence seems to decline. The ebb and flow of corruption is difficult to predict but what is certain is that claims to have won the 'war against corruption' or to have found the cure for the 'cancer of corruption' are at least premature and probably misconceived. Corruption offers no grounds for complacency and experience of tackling corruption suggests that success is usually temporary and partial.

The 'corruption eruption' has given the subject a much higher profile in both the academic and policy-making worlds. Whereas corruption experts were once few in number and had difficulty in persuading publishers and journals to publish their research, the flow of publications on corruption has now turned into a raging torrent. It has become very difficult, even for specialists, to monitor, let alone read, everything written about corruption in newspapers, magazines, journals, books, think tank papers and the official reports, inquiries and publications of national and international governmental bodies.

This new collection of articles is therefore extremely timely. Corruption is a jungle and there is an urgent need for an authoritative guide to the flora and fauna. It would be a bold individual who laid claim to expert status in all aspects of corruption and, when invited to edit this collection, the need for specialist help was apparent. By a fortuitous piece of timing, the research group investigating corruption and anti-corruption strategies on behalf of the UK Department for International Development had just begun its work and assistance from my research colleagues, Alan Doig, Rachel Flanary, Jon Moran and Robin Theobald, was quickly forthcoming. The task was more challenging than originally anticipated because the literature is now substantial. Much of the literature is unsatisfactory in that there are significant problems of gaps, overlaps and duplication. In terms of geographical coverage, corruption has been extensively researched in some countries, patchily studied in others and hardly considered at all in still others. In dividing the material, it was difficult to arrive at criteria that allowed a clear demarcation between the volumes. Corruption seems to be a subject which invites varying mixtures of theory and empiricism, micro and macro analysis, explanation and prescription, and case studies and comparative analysis.

The first volume in this collection, *Explaining Corruption*, is more conceptual than empirical. But despite the giant lava flow of publications from the 'corruption eruption', the literature on this aspect of corruption still generates more heat than light. Many contributions appear ideological in character and corruption remains a highly contested concept. We still lack firmly grounded theories of corruption and the shortage of analytically informed empirical inquiries continues. Too many participants in the contemporary corruption debate content themselves with resurrecting tired clichés about the topic or with slaying long-dead dragons. In selecting material for this collection, two criteria have been employed; first, the contributions say something important, different or interesting about corruption. This is not to say that the editor necessarily agrees with what is said but rather indicates that the articles are intellectually provocative and stimulating and should be read by all serious students of corruption. The second and related criterion is that the article marks a particular point or phase in the study of corruption or has influenced the ways in which academics and policy analysts have subsequently thought about corruption.

The volume is concerned with the different ways in which scholars have sought to understand corruption and the range of theories and perspectives they have used to explain it. Thus it includes articles on definitions, on conceptual classification and distinctions, and on the salience of particular disciplines to the key explanatory problems posed by corruption. Such articles address a variety of deceptively simple questions: What is corruption? What form does it take? How can it be distinguished from similar or related concepts? What are its principal causes? What are its major political and economic consequences? In seeking the answers to these questions, scholars display a spectrum of rival and apparently incompatible theoretical frameworks and analytical approaches. In their attempts to understand and explain the concept, corruption has become something of a disciplinary football to be kicked backward and forward. It began life as a political or philosophical concept but was subsequently given a legal character before being appropriated successively by sociologists, anthropologists and, most recently, by economists. The issue remains of how to judge the outcome of this interdisciplinary competition for conceptual ownership.

This intellectual competition mirrored changes in broader political and ideological struggles. The collapse of the Soviet Empire had profound implications for the international order and patterns of political support. But while the perception of corruption has been dramatically reshaped by these international changes, the ground was already laid in changes in the internal politics of the USA and the UK. Ideological shifts in the USA and UK in the 1980s had implications not merely for the domestic policies of those nations but also for their perceptions of the external world and its problems. Thus, when President Reagan observed that 'government is not the answer to our problems, it is the problem', he pithily encapsulated a cluster of attitudes, ideas and policy strategies. This perception was brought to bear not only on the US budget deficit but on the debt crises of the South. The perceived need to limit the role of the state, to 'downsize' the federal government and to elevate the market and promote the virtues of individual responsibility and self reliance all made their impact on the ways in which international institutions conducted their affairs. Such institutions became more receptive to certain kinds of neo-liberal message which were incorporated into institutional thinking and policy making.

The intellectual ascendancy of neo-liberal thinking and the political dominance of Reagan and Thatcher helped ensure that the new forms of conditionality introduced into foreign assistance programmes would reflect the view that government was often the enemy of development and the prime source of corruption. To some, corruption was the unpleasant but inevitable by-product of the unwarranted distortion of markets by governments. The logic suggested that when the size and role of government were reduced, the opportunities and incentives for corruption would similarly decline. But this framework of analysis ran into a number of problems. In many contexts, there is an absence of other competent players ready to take up the roles previously performed by government. It seems that, if some activities or services are to continue, there is often no alternative to the government performing the role. The key policy prescriptions of neo-liberalism were privatization and de-regulation, and they brought their own crop of corruption-related problems. In many cases, privatization amounted to little more than the licensed theft of state property. To those unable to secure basic services without making an illicit payment, the issue of public or private ownership is largely irrelevant.

There are obvious indications that neo-liberalism has passed its political zenith and, while economists are still prominent in the contemporary corruption literature, their prescriptions have been modified in the light of privatization and de-regulation experience. Some current research suggests that, while corruption is obviously linked to the role and performance of the state, a more appropriate and effective response is not rolling back the state but reforming it. The debate goes on but it is clear that, in different periods, contrasting paradigms have dominated both academic and political discourse.

The first volume is therefore intended to set the scene for the volumes that follow. It identifies the evolution of the theoretical debates, their points of agreement and disagreement, and considers how corruption can best be understood. The range of contributions suggests that corruption is not a simple phenomenon susceptible to monocausal explanation. The intention here is not to resolve the debate but to expose more clearly its origins, development and current parameters.

The second and third volumes offer a global perspective on corruption. *Corruption in the Developing World* includes some selections that are intended to convey how thinking about corruption in such contexts has evolved. Some early contributions sought to explain corruption in terms familiar to students of American politics. Comparisons were made with political machines and with spoils and patronage politics. Max Weber's hitherto neglected concept of patrimonialism was re-discovered and subsequent analysis has conclusively shown that the social and political costs of patrimonial forms of politics have been extremely high for less developed countries. Most of the articles in this volume have been chosen to illustrate the dismal consequences for citizens, governments and the economy of the pervasive illegal appropriation of public resources. In extreme cases, the ravages of corruption have been so damaging as to culminate in acute civil strife and state collapse. The volume begins, however, with an article which demonstrates the scope and potential for corruption by presenting a peasant's eye view of the world and its dangers.

The other readings offer a representative range of case studies as possible given that Latin America is under-represented in the literature in English on corruption. But, even here, the selection illustrates the characteristic problems of institutionalized corruption, drug-related corruption and the transition from dictatorship to democracy, as well as an overview of the continental issues. In comparison, African states are relatively new entities and their political origins render their institutional structures particularly susceptible to abuse and, in extreme cases such as Zaire, this can lead to the effective privatization of the state. In such contexts a growing proportion of the population withdraw or 'exit' into subsistence farming or into the informal economy by means of smuggling, black marketeering and banditry. Corruption in its 'grand' and 'petty' forms plays a major role in the political and economic life of the continent but there are still exceptions and an article is included on Botswana which examines how one state has managed to combine political stability, administrative effectiveness and economic growth with low levels of corruption.

Selecting examples from Asia was a particular challenge given its somewhat imprecise geographical identity and the vast range of societies and states. The choices were made on the rough and ready assumption that it is possible to identify three broad types of Asian state: those which have endured long periods of authoritarian rule in which the military has been the dominant force, such as Indonesia, Thailand and the Philippines; formal democracies, albeit with an authoritarian tinge, such as Malaysia and India; and the command economies in the process of transition, such as the People's Republic of China and Vietnam. The final selections deal with the issue of to what extent certain developmental processes, notably marketization and democratization, exacerbate or ameliorate the problem of corruption in the developing world.

The third volume, *Corruption in the Developed World*, includes articles on Europe, North America, Australia and Japan. The contributions include reflections on corruption and social change, corruption and organized crime, and, in the Italian and Russian cases, reflections on the notion of structural corruption. They offer discussions of the inter-relationship of corruption with political culture and party finance, and with concepts of democracy, accountability and public ethics. While many analysts have principally focused their attention on the less developed states, the corruption scandals which have afflicted most developed states in the past twenty years have stimulated new analyses and revisions of once strongly held convictions about standards of public integrity in the developed world.

In some cases, the source of corruption can be traced to a particular characteristic of the political system; for example, campaign finance practices in the United States or the interweaving of party and state structures in Italy. In other cases, political transformation of the Russian sort has created new incentives and opportunities and has exchanged one kind of corrupt system for another.

Complacency has given way to concern and, across the developed world, anti-corruption reform is high on political agendas. It is no longer possible to tolerate corruption, to shrug one's shoulders and accept that a certain degree of nepotism and fraud is an unavoidable consequence of a particular national political style. Political cultures may vary but, as the European Commissioners discovered in 1999, it is increasingly the norm for common and rigorous standards to be applied. Countries which place a premium on combating corruption in the less developed world find it morally and politically necessary to tackle corruption at home.

The fourth volume in this series, *Controlling Corruption*, reflects the global consensus that corruption is a major problem which has a variety of negative impacts on political, economic and social systems around the world. But the consensus which shares the conviction that something must be done does not extend to agreement on what exactly needs to be done. If corruption is a common problem, are there common solutions? While the Independent Commission Against Corruption in Hong Kong is frequently hailed as a success, attempts to replicate it in very different political and economic contexts are fraught with difficulty.

This volume includes articles from the ever expanding literature on anti-corruption strategies. Anti-corruption strategies can be initiated at a variety of levels; international, regional, national, sub-national and local. The impetus for reform can come from international bodies such as the World Bank and from donor countries in the form of specific assistance and aid conditionality. But reform can also be domestically driven and evidence suggests that, without strong political will and commitment, reform programmes are likely to be cosmetic rather than substantive. But even where political commitment is not wholehearted, the demands and protests emanating from civil society can induce reluctant political leaders to conduct anti-corruption purges.

The articles selected represent different strands of thinking about how best to tackle corruption. Some approaches are holistic, arguing that corruption issues are a sub-set of governance problems and the governance problems are a manifestation of structural and systemic problems of the political economy of particular societies. The aim here is comprehensive reform but, however laudable the aims, it is not yet clear how such grand designs can be implemented. Even if wholesale reform of economies, societies and governance is thought feasible, it is still necessary to determine priorities, to provide co-ordination and to work out the sequencing of reform measures. The costs of anti-corruption strategies need to be identified, as does their impact on the effectiveness of organizations. Research suggests that striving to eliminate corruption completely can be counterproductive when the need to avoid corruption takes priority over achieving the aims and objectives of the organization. Some reformers have more limited ambitions and reject the holistic approach in favour of targeting the most vulnerable parts of state activity; for example, customs services and procurement procedures.

The debate on corruption and anti-corruption strategies continues because it is a complex, multi-faceted phenomenon. Few reforms to date have been completely successful and some have been counterproductive. Anti-corruption strategies are beset by problems of transferability, sustainability, cost effectiveness, sequencing and intent. The choice of strategy has implications for different elements of the government. A focus on investigating corruption has obvious implications for the criminal justice system, its resourcing and independence. If the focus is on prevention rather than retribution, or on attacking the causes rather than the consequences of corruption, different considerations apply. All require state resources, and decisions have to be made about whether the concern is the loss of state income or the diversion of state expenditure into unnecessary and expensive projects. Where low level, 'petty' corruption is concerned, anti-corruption strategies sometimes focus on empowering the public through information and access in order to hold local officials to account. If grand and petty corruption both flourish best in secrecy, openness and transparency are often seen as key elements in anti-corruption strategies. The contributions assembled here do not definitively resolve the above issues but rather offer a range of perspectives and approaches which illustrate the scale and difficulty of the task.

Taken together, the four volumes offer a representative, up-to-date and authoritative guide to the literature on corruption. They do not purport to be comprehensive because the literature has expanded so rapidly in the past ten years. Hard choices had to be made about what to exclude and what the balance should be between academic and policy-related literature and between theoretical and empirical work. The result is four volumes which contain, in the editor's judgement, the most informative, important and influential articles written on corruption in the last third of the twentieth century. The intention is to provide students of corruption with a substantial body of material which shows how the subject has developed and how it is currently understood and explained. Volumes 2 and 3 illustrate and explain the scope, incidence and consequences of corruption in a variety of political settings in the developed and developing worlds. The decision was made to place Russia in the developed world although, sadly, it is recognized that there is now a case for locating it in the developing world.

Corruption differs from many other subjects in that those who study it are often committed to combat it. Volume 4 is therefore dedicated to illustrating the variety of prescriptions that have been presented as ways of controlling corruption. Although the problems which bedevil anti-corruption strategies are, as *Controlling Corruption* shows, considerable, that should not deter reformers. Academics may be content to define, conceptualize, theorize, interpret and explain but detachment is difficult when the pernicious effects of corruption are felt across the globe. Perhaps Karl Marx had corruption as well as class struggle in mind when he wrote that 'philosophers have only interpreted the world, the point is to change it'. But we first need to recognize and understand the enemy before it can be overcome. These volumes are offered as a contribution to that vital process.

Acknowledgement to the Department for International Development (DFID)

All the members of the editorial team worked together on a two year research project funded by DFID on corruption and anti-corruption strategies. We would like to record our appreciation to DFID for its recognition of the seriousness of the global problem of corruption and for its financial and other support for our research. I would like to emphasize that the Introduction and the final selection of articles are the editors' responsibility and do not represent the views or policies of DFID.

Other Acknowledgements

The task of the editorial team was made more manageable by the development of corruption databases and by the establishment of a unique library of articles and reports. Our research colleague, Stephanie McIvor, was largely responsible for this work and, on behalf of the editorial team, I would like to record our thanks to her. I would also like to thank my editorial colleagues, Alan Doig, Robin Theobald, Rachel Flanary and Jonathan Moran, for their invaluable assistance in the editorial process. They do not bear responsibility for the Introduction or the final difficult choice of articles, and the blame for any important omissions is mine.

In Durham, I would like to thank Jean Richardson and Heather Marquette for their timely and crucial help and, last but not least, I would like to thank Edward Elgar for suggesting this collection to me. We first discussed the possibility of publishing a book on corruption almost twenty years ago and, while this is a totally different project, I hope he is as pleased as I am that our conversations have finally borne fruit.

Part I
General

[1]

The Political Dimensions of Corruption Cleanups

A Framework for Analysis

Kate Gillespie and Gwenn Okruhlik

Political corruption has been a pervasive and persistent phenomenon throughout history. It is found today in diverse degrees and forms in all types of political systems. The subject has long been of interest to philosophers, historians, and social scientists, but discussion has intensified significantly since the mid 1960s with the study of modernization and development. There are relatively few efforts, however, to systematically study cleanups, that is, government-announced campaigns to curb or eliminate corruption.

The intent of this essay is to provide a conceptual framework in which we can examine cleanups within and across states. We begin with a synthesis of the abundant work on corruption and an examination of the tangential literature on cleanups. We conclude with several generalizations about the political aspects of cleanups, particularly their political contexts, stimuli, objectives, strategies, and consequences. These generalizations are derived primarily from a survey of twenty-five Middle Eastern and North African states covering a seventeen year period to confirm tentatively the empirical relevance of our propositions. Case examples from elsewhere are cited to illustrate the applicability of our propositions outside the Middle East, although further confirmation awaits more thorough investigation from other regions.

Corruption: A Synthesis

Five major issues are evident in the corruption literature: definition, causes, consequences, context, and types of corrupt activity.

Definition Conceptual definitions require two qualities: they must be general enough to allow cross-cultural comparison yet precise enough to be empirically useful. Meeting both objectives has proven controversial with regards to the concept of corruption. While there is a consensus that corrupt behavior involves misuse of public authority for private gain, debate exists over the criteria used to determine when authority has been misused.[1] Many scholars focus upon violation of the legal codes which regulate public officials.[2] This makes corruption fairly easy to identify and provides a precise standard for comparison among countries. For others, the determinant of corrupt activity is either public opinion[3] or a breach of the public interest.[4] Finally, some definitions of corrupt activity are based on market principles regarding the allocation of scarce resources.[5]

There are problems with each of these standards. Legal codes are not necessarily congruent with societal norms.[6] Public opinion is difficult to utilize as opinions are not necessarily stable, aggregated, or articulated. Scholars who use the public interest as the criterion suggest that a single interpretation of the public interest is available when in reality several contrasting views may exist or none exists at all. Even those definitions expressed in market principles still imply that there exists a difference between the standards applicable to public officials and those applicable to business persons working in a free market without ever specifying how these standards are set.

Causes Explanations of the occurrence of corrupt activity are usually found in the interaction of individual and social structural factors. Corruption has been attributed to human nature,[7] psychocultural ambivalence towards behavioral norms,[8] the transition from colonial status to self-government,[9] socioeconomic inequalities,[10] and the vagaries of organizational arrangements and procedures.[11]

Scholars have also drawn connections between the existence of corruption and the process of modernization.[12] Some argue that levels of corruption reflect differences in the modernization and development of each country. Corruption tends to be most prevalent during the most intense phases of modernization. First, the conflict between modern and traditional codes of behavior render a developing society normless; since no standard is commonly accepted as legitimate, all are suspect. The vacuum created by this conflict opens opportunities for individuals to behave in a manner justified by neither the modern nor the traditional norms. Second, modernization gives rise to corruption because it creates new groups with new resources who want to trade money for political power. Third, the expansion of government authority and regulations multiplies the opportunities for corruption. Finally, corruption is prevalent in those modernizing countries which lack effective political parties, as corruption varies inversely with political organization. Corruption eventually begins to undermine the conditions of its own existence, for it contributes to the growth and strengthening of those institutions which transcend individual interests.[13]

Consequences The most heated debate on corruption concerns whether its effects on the welfare of a society are positive or negative. It was argued for years that corruption must be condemned for its inherent evil and negative consequences on society.[14] This so-called moral or traditional position was disputed in the 1960s by those who contended that corruption may fulfill societal needs that would otherwise go unheeded. Proponents of this position are usually referred to as revisionists or functionalists.[15] Some argue that corruption contributes to economic development because it serves as an instrument for the allocation of scarce resources, makes investment possible, and strengthens the private sector vis-à-vis the public sector by reducing uncertainty. Through corrupt activity, investors can be assured that the government will not intervene in their affairs. As funds are increasingly channeled into investment, greater competition and efficiency will result.[16] Others focus on the contribution of corruption to the development of new and stronger political institutions which have the capacity to serve as a means of channeling demands upon the system in lieu of other alternatives such as violence.[17] Some argue that corruption encourages social integration by allowing otherwise excluded individuals access to public officials and administrative

Kate Gillespie and Gwenn Okruhlik

bureaucracies. Corruption serves as a lubricant which eases the rigid wheels of a bureaucracy.[18]

The revisionist position has since been challenged by those observers who emphasize the dysfunctional consequences of corruption. The postfunctionalists reject the "Godfatherism . . . and condescension" of those who had rationalized and apologized for corruption.[19] They argue that corruption wastes revenues and resources which might be utilized elsewhere,[20] erodes the trust and loyalty granted to political leaders by their followers,[21] and solidifies inequities in the apportionment of goods in favor of certain strata of society.[22]

Several scholars argue that incumbents can utilize corruption to maintain their control of the political arena because it allows manipulation of access to resources, positions, and wealth. Strategic groups must acquiesce in incumbent demands in order to obtain the goods and services they desire. Corruption in these cases is a mechanism for buying political loyalty. The ability to manipulate access fosters dependency on the regime and thereby contributes to the survival of the ruling elites.[23] "Ruling groups . . . use the benefits of political power in an attempt to redress the insecure position they find themselves in. . . . [Thus] mutual back-scratching is inaugurated . . ." between the regimes and the privileged entrepreneurs.[24]

This peculiar relationship has been called "a parasitic symbiosis between the public and private sectors,"[25] in which the business groups become a "parasitic state class"[26] or a "state-dependent bourgeoisie."[27] The point is that the ties between the ruling group and the large-scale or foreign entrepreneurs which are fostered by corruption hinder the development of a private, indigenous, independent bourgeoisie. They also contribute to an increase in the alienation felt by those groups excluded from the advantages of corruption.

Context Attention has turned within the last decade from arguments explicitly about the consequences of corruption to a closer examination of its context, that is, its underlying patterns and structures. Corruption is studied as a process of exchange between parties with each participant having something the other wants or needs. To understand better how this exchange works, analysts focus on its context: the particular conditions necessary for corrupt behavior to occur,[28] the actors and stakes involved,[29] and the internal mechanisms of such an exchange, that is, the means by which it is accomplished.[30] Corruption may not be a single, simple exchange, but a whole series of subtransactions. These works have turned inward to look at the who, what, and how of corrupt activity.

Typologies There have long been attempts to classify corruption according to its diverse characteristics in order to provide some systematic method of approaching so complex a phenomenon. For example, corruption has been ordered by the relationship among its participants, by the judgment of officials and the public, by the type of activity involved, and by political consequences. Parochial and market corruption are differentiated by whether favors are granted on the basis of kinship and affection or an impersonal process which rewards the highest bidder.[31] Endemic, planned, and developmental corruption each reflects different aspects of the relationship between citizenry and state.[32] Black, white, and gray forms of corruption are distinguished by the degree to which the activity is condemned or tolerated by elite and mass opinion.[33] Quasi-corruption, precorruption, corruption, and high

Comparative Politics October 1991

crime encompass a wide range of activity from simple disciplinary violations to treason.[34] Finally, integrative corruption links people in lasting networks of shared interests (not necessarily just or beneficial), whereas disintegrative corruption produces no such networks.[35] Such efforts are important, as they allow us to pursue questions relating specific types of corruption with the public or official response to that activity.

Cleanups: An Emerging Literature

A corrupt exchange in and of itself may not be particularly noteworthy. However, the perception of and response to the corrupt activity among sizable or powerful groups can transform corruption into a politically salient issue. Ironically, very little scholarly attention is focused primarily on the phenomenon of cleanups. When cleanups are addressed, the discussion is usually tangential to a larger work on corruption or limited to a single case study with little attempt to draw generalizations applicable elsewhere. While some scholars have raised pertinent questions regarding the goals, policy orientation, occurrence, and risks of cleanups, they have not pursued extensive cross-national comparison.[36]

What emerges from the literature is a "how to" argument concerning the most effective method to curb or eradicate corruption. Analysts generally advocate a multipronged attack to produce substantial and enduring results, but they focus on one particular type of cleanup measure. The prescribed types of corruption control strategies can be called societal, legal, market, and political.

Societal Strategies Three major emphases are evident in societal strategies: ethical norms, education, and public vigilance. Scholars agree that no cleanup measure can be effective unless it is supported by the ethical norms of society. This implies that society as a whole accepts certain standards of behavior regarding fairness and propriety. When the application of these standards to public servants is marginal or nonexistent, conflict ensues. Corruption thrives in an environment where there is no consensus on what it is. An important corrective, then, is a common standard of morality.[37]

The achievement of such a standard and the eradication of corruption may involve a "fairly low-pitched but steady and continuous educational effort in schools. . . . it should not be a brief and violent campaign; rather a consistent effort that becomes a normal part of the educational process."[38] Through education, states can inculcate a willingness to sacrifice self-interest for the common welfare.

Others argue that the remedy for corruption is public vigilance. The best elements in a society should mobilize to lead a sustained citizen-initiated protest action. The media can be vitally important channels of such a vigorous citizen outcry. A "community justice strategy" would incorporate all of the societal elements to combat corruption by consciously endeavoring to achieve and sustain public concern and scrutiny of public officials.[39]

Legal Strategies The first unified body of law, the Code of Hammurabi from the eighteenth century B.C., specifies legal sanctions against corrupt activity, particularly the bribing of judicial officials.[40] Legal codes which prohibit corrupt activity are now found in almost all states. The activities of civil servants are regulated by a plethora of rules which regard the collection of political funds, the acceptance of bribes or gifts, the disclosure of assets and liabilities, the acquisition of property, and conflicts of interest. Governments sometimes establish ad hoc committees to review existing codes and to suggest new and more effective sanctions against corruption (for example, India's Santhanam Committee established in 1962).[41] This also occurs on a transnational basis, as evident when the International Chamber of Commerce organized a committee of leading government and business representatives to examine the incidence of bribery and extortion in 1977.[42]

Legal sanctions which condemn corruption are unlikely to be effective, though, unless they are strengthened by complementary strategies. The use of independent auditing and investigation would increase the probability of detection and conviction, thus raising the psychic costs of corruption. Special commissions of inquiry should be invested with the capacity to enforce their findings, enabling them to punish political offenders instead of merely gathering facts. Penalties for corruption can be increased.[43] Furthermore, exemplary proceedings against high-ranking officials would underscore the law and the determination of the government to curb corruption.[44]

Market Strategies Several scholars have assessed the relationship between market structure and the incidence of corrupt activity. They suggest that corruption is encouraged by heavy reliance on government intervention in the economy or by excessive bureaucratic overlay. Bureaucratic inertia, commonly found in such situations, results in a disequilibrium between supply and demand for goods and services. Situations where demand outstrips supply are conducive to corrupt activity. Individuals competing to achieve the ends they desire may circumvent official channels by personally attaining the acquiescence or participation of those in authority.

A prescribed strategy to clean up corruption would involve a decreased reliance on legal sanction and bureaucratic regulation. The most efficient way to distribute available resources to achieve the highest productivity is simply to allow market forces to operate unencumbered.[45]

Political Strategies Those who endorse political strategies to curb or eliminate corruption direct their attention to three concerns: authority, access to the political process, and administrative reform.

One tactic is to diffuse authority by placing key decisions in the hands of a committee instead of an individual. To be effective, this diffusion should be coupled with the element of randomness as to which individuals will sit on particular committees, thereby creating an uncertain environment for potential bribe-givers. It has also been suggested that the discretionary powers of public officials be reduced. Opportunities for corruption would be minimized if all laws, not just those pertaining to corruption, were made more arbitrary and precise, allowing nothing to the discretion of authorities. The termination of special privileges that are granted to authorities would facilitate an attempt to curb corruption. Finally, the creation of an ombudsman institution, a permanent authority, would provide the machinery necessary to control the administration.[46]

A broader strategy to clean up corruption concentrates on the expansion of access to the political process. Officials should deliberately maximize public access to the decision-making

Comparative Politics October 1991

process and minimize any private contact between themselves and the parties affected by their decision. Some suggest that substantive participation in the political process by all citizens serves to reinforce a sense of civic virtue and prevents government agencies from becoming isolated. This can destroy factions which consistently subvert the law. The implementation of expanded political participation, though, requires a commitment on the part of the government to utilize additional resources. With regard to elite participation, it has been suggested that electoral laws be reformed to check the costs of competition. Not only do exorbitant costs exclude some people from running for office, but they also introduce opportunities for corruption in the politician's drive to raise the necessary revenue.[47]

Those who advocate administrative reform to combat corruption argue that corrupt behavior may be discouraged by increasing the benefits of noncorrupt behavior, for example, providing increased salaries, pensions, professional training, and other privileges for public servants. The point is to establish a close link between conscientious effort and reward. Also, the frequency of transfers between administrative posts should be reduced since competition for particularly attractive posts tends to make transfers a part of the corruption process.

Those who study corruption as an organizational problem suggest that mutual antagonistic surveillance between government agencies should be encouraged. This two-way vigilance reduces the opportunities for corruption to occur.[48]

The Cleanup Phenomenon

The primary question, then, in the tangential discussions of cleanups concerns the preferred strategy to curb or eliminate corrupt activity. This focus on method has obscured some of the more politically interesting questions. Since the perception of and response to corruption can be more important than the actual occurrence of corrupt activity, we should explicitly address the phenomenon of cleanups.

Past investigations of cleanups are limited and impressionistic. Our framework provides a means to examine systematically cleanups within and across states. We disaggregate the concept of cleanups into five dimensions: political context, stimulus, objective, strategy, and political consequence. First, cleanups are political phenomena. Decisions to initiate them are political, as are their scope and initial targets. It is thus critical that we understand the political context in which they occur. There are five such contexts: postcoup, postrevolution, incumbent, postsuccession, and postelection. Second, cleanups are responses to internal or external stimuli. Internal stimuli include the personal values of the head of state, challenges from a counterelite, and popular discontent arising from socioeconomic conditions. External stimuli include adverse publicity or investigations which originate in another country and major political developments elsewhere. Third, cleanups are political instruments which may be used to achieve several objectives: to delegitimate the previous regime, to purge opposition, to manipulate the political agenda, or to decrease the incidence of corruption and thereby legitimate the current regime. Fourth, the strategies by which cleanups are conducted are legal, societal, political, and economic.[49] Fifth, as a consequence of cleanups, the political position of the head of state is either fortified or undermined.

The data upon which our framework rests comprises a survey of scandals and cleanups in twenty-five Middle Eastern and North African states between the years 1970 and 1986.[50] The survey was drawn primarily from a week by week analysis of news items appearing in the *Middle East Economic Digest (MEED)*. *MEED* provides reports and translation of business, economic, and related political news appearing in the media of all twenty-five states. Additional material was collected from *African Research Political Series*, the *Social Science Index*, the *Wall Street Journal Index*, U.S. court and congressional records, and the chronology of *The Middle East Journal*. We identified twenty-four distinct cases of cleanups occurring in sixteen states and coded locales, dates, involvement of government officials, private actors, source of allegation, and scope of involvement (local, international). We followed the progress of each cleanup over time.[51] We also incorporate into our analysis the incidence of cleanups in countries outside of the Middle East to illustrate the pervasiveness of the cleanup phenomenon and the cross-cultural utility of the proposed framework. Several observations regarding the political dimensions of cleanups warrant further discussion.

Political Contexts Heads of state announce and initiate cleanups within various political contests and at various points during their tenure. There are five basic political contexts: postcoup, postrevolution, incumbent, postsuccession, and postelection.[52]

In the past it has been argued that cleanups are essentially a postcoup phenomenon.[53] The possibility of incumbent cleanups was ignored or disparaged by many analysts. For example, cleanups "are not and cannot for political reasons be used as evidence in cases of high-level systemic corruption. It is unlikely that a corrupt regime will investigate itself; it is only possible when there is a change of regime; and then the exercise is politically suspect (as an apologia for the current regime)."[54]

Interestingly, however, empirical evidence illustrates otherwise. The twenty-four observed cleanups were distributed as follows: postcoup, 6; postrevolution, 1; incumbent, 14; postsuccession, 3; and postelection, 0 (see Table 1). The three postsuccession cleanups were continuations of cleanups initiated by prior incumbents.

Table 1 Cleanups in the Middle East

Type:	Post-Coup	Post-Revolution	Succession	Incumbent
1970	Iraq			Morocco
1971	Libya			
1974	Ethiopia			
1975				*Saudi Arabia
1976				Egypt, Iran, Yemen Arab Republic
1977				Syria
1978				Algeria, Iran
1979		Iran	Algeria, Iraq	
1980				Libya
1981	Turkey		Egypt	Ethiopia, Somalia
1983				Sudan
1984	Mauritania			
1985	Sudan			Tunisia
1986				Afganistan

*Technically this cleanup occurred shortly after a succession. However, the cleanup announcement was determined to be coincidental to the death of the prior head of state.
SOURCE: Survey of news sources.

Contrary to existing notions, cleanups may occur, not only immediately following the assumption of power by heads of states, but also long after heads of state have been in power. All cleanups following opposition-forced changes in head of state (postcoup and postrevolution) account for less than one-third of the observed cases. Those following any change in head of state represent less than half of the observed cleanups. More than half of the cleanups in the Middle East between 1970 and 1986 were initiated by an incumbent head of state.

A closer look at the data reveals an even more interesting pattern. In the first five years of the survey, three of the four cleanups followed coups. After 1975, though, we see a sudden, dramatic, and sustained increase in the frequency of incumbent cleanups. They represent two-thirds of all cases. The prior concentration on postcoup cases to explain the entire range of cleanups has biased analysis of the phenomenon.

Political context is a useful point of departure. The next step is to analyze cleanups within each political context according to their stimulus, objective, strategy, and consequence (see Table 2).

Postcoup Cleanups The occurrence of a coup does not necessarily require a broad base of popular support. The new leadership is in a vulnerable position unless it receives the allegiance or acquiescence of the population. Ousted leaders who mount counterattacks can damage the credibility of the new administration during this uneasy, interim period. This threat stimulates postcoup leaders to initiate a cleanup.

Postcoup leaders hope to achieve two objectives: to further discredit the prior leadership and to provide an ex post facto justification of their own assumption of power. Making public the allegations and evidence of corruption serves to demonstrate the hypocrisy of the former administration and the supposed virtue of the new one. These cleanups have a particular strategy: they are initiated immediately after the coup; they are highly publicized; and they are aimed specifically at the highest levels of the prior administration. The targets of postcoup cleanups—the segment(s) of government employees comprising the individuals arrested, indicted, or dismissed as a result of the cleanup—are heads of state, ministers, and their families. The consequence is that these cleanups are perceived to be mere attempts to purge political opposition rather than attempts to confront the corruption issue. The elimination of political opponents may enhance the short-term security of the new leadership, but it engenders popular cynicism in the long run.

In our survey of Middle Eastern states, we observe postcoup cleanups in Iraq (1970), Libya (1971), Ethiopia (1974), Turkey (1981), Mauritania (1984), and Sudan (1985). In all cases the immediate lack of popular support caused postcoup leaders to undertake cleanups to discredit prior leaders and lend legitimacy to themselves. In Sudan, for example, leaders undertook a cleanup to placate the Trade Union Alliance which threatened strikes and civil disobedience to ensure that their demands for reforms were met. In nearly all cases, top level officials including former heads of state were targeted.[55] This is particularly evident in Ethiopia where many ex-ministers we well as Prince Desta, the Emperor's grandson, were executed. Also, the army nationalized all property owned by the Haile Selassie Foundation, from which the royal family and nobility had long benefited. Arrests and trials were usually quick, and in most cases penalties were severe. All coup leaders were successful in retaining

Table 2 Cleanups: Distinguishing Characteristics by Context

Context	Stimuli	Objectives	Strategies	Consequences
Post-Coup	•Elite instability	•Discredit prior leadership •Justify assumption of power	•Immediate initiation •High publicity •High level targets	•Short-term security •Popular cynicism in longer term
Post-Revolution	•Public mandate	•Fulfill mandate •Consolidate power •Manipulate political agenda	•Community justice •New legal codes and commisions •Restructuring of bureaucratic and economic institutions •Return of property from prior leadership	•Consolidation of new leadership •Popular sense of new beginnings
Incumbent	•Societal changes associated with economic development •Channels of information •Major political developments elsewhere	•Political security and acceptance •Manipulate political agenda •Self-preservation	•Legal clarifications and stiffer penalties •Special courts and commissions •Mid-level targets, moderate levels of arrests	•Enhancement of legitimacy •Destabilization
Post-succession	•Need for public recognition and smooth transition	•Public perception of continuity •Consolidate power	•Continue cleanup in progress	•Sense of Continuity •Popular cynicism
Post-election	•Electorate demands •Adverse publicity •Challenges of counter elite	•Facilitate re-election •Consolidate power •Manipulate political agenda	•Enhanced legal restrictions and punishments	•Strengthen allegience to ruling party •Lessen chances of re-election

power in the intermediate term. However, corruption continued to be a problem. In the case of Iraq, Libya, and Ethiopia, the same regimes years later were forced to initiate incumbent cleanups.

This phenomenon of discrediting former leaders and legitimizing oneself but failing to eradicate corruption is noted in postcoup cleanups outside the Middle East. A military coup by Major General Yakubu Gowan ousted a Nigerian civilian regime in 1966. Gowan justified his action by pledging to clean up corruption. The regime survived nearly ten years, but corruption failed to abate. In Indonesia during the same period, a postcoup cleanup failed to eradicate corruption due to a failure to attack corruption at lower levels of government. In Brazil, where a military regime seized power in the 1960s and retained control for two decades, corruption remained similarly pervasive.[56]

Postrevolution Cleanups Underlying any revolution is intense dissatisfaction with the political system. This broad public mandate is the primary stimulus for the initiation of a postrevolution cleanup. Such cleanups have several objectives. They are used to fulfill the popular mandate, which includes the limitation or eradication of corruption among government officials. Cleanups are also instruments used to consolidate the power of revolutionary leaders and offset challengers. In the jostling for position which accompanies revolution, cleanups are rallying cries, symbols of national unity. Finally, cleanups are used to manipulate the political agenda, that is, to divert attention away from economic ills or painful reconstruction. Postrevolution cleanups are not needed to justify one's assumption of power or to delegitimize the prior regime as in postcoup cases.

The very nature of a revolution is such that the proceeding cleanup encompasses all spheres of public activity and utilizes many strategies, for example, the institution of a community justice strategy, rewriting of legal codes, and restructuring of bureaucratic and economic institutions. Moreover, there is an emphasis on the return of currency and property from the prior leadership to the new regime as guardians of the revolution.

Consequently, postrevolution cleanups may contribute to the consolidation of the new leadership, a popular sense of new beginnings, and a possible alleviation of the incidence of corruption. Revolutions are rare, however. Only one postrevolution cleanup is evident in our survey, that of Iran.

In the wake of the Iranian revolution of 1979, arrests and executions for corruption and economic treason were undertaken with relatively little rhetoric by the new Islamic Republic. Cleanup targets comprised high and mid level officials, though many potential targets had already fled the country. The new regime confiscated property in Iran of the former royal family and made major efforts to retrieve similar fortunes overseas. Legal reforms concerning corruption began almost immediately, and Islamic values were introduced into the banking system.

Targeting lower level officials as part of the postrevolution cleanup was slower in coming and relatively contained as well. Nepotism and favoritism remained in the bureaucracy, and foreign companies claimed low level officials commonly approached them for kickbacks. A wider postrevolution cleanup in Iran's case may have been postponed due to strains involved with economic recovery from strikes during the revolution, the removal of many women from the bureaucracy, and the escalating war with Iraq. Furthermore, many bureaucrats shifted their support away from the Shah when he began mass arrests for corruption in 1978. If unable or unwilling to further eradicate corruption, Majlis Speaker Ali Akbar Hashemi Rafsanjani used it to manipulate the political agenda and deflect criticism by accusing counterrevolutionaries of employing corruption to destroy the revolution.

Incumbent Cleanups Incumbent cleanups demand particular attention due to their predominance. Unlike other types, these cleanups are not announced by the head of state immediately upon assumption of power. Rather, they occur during the course of the tenure of the administration. Since the degree of popular support for an incumbent can range from disaffection to approval, the dimensions and intensity of incumbent cleanups are complex and varied.

Unless they are directed solely at the previous administration, cleanups are an inherently risky undertaking. Incumbent cleanups are an admission of inability to control corruption in one's own administration or the prior ignorance (or toleration) of such activity. Neither alternative is attractive to a head of state. What factors are powerful enough to stimulate such risk taking on the part of incumbents? The most important explanation is derived from internal stimuli. Cleanups may reflect the personal values of the head of state, the desire to eradicate corruption, but incumbent cleanups are more often a reflection of societal changes that are associated with economic development. Increased capital flow and the presence of foreign investors may increase the opportunities for corrupt activity to occur. At the same time, cleavages in the social structure lead to less tolerance for corruption and stronger pressure for its limitation, if not elimination.

Other observers have shown that the administration and the state-dependent entrepreneurial groups benefit from corrupt activity only by the exclusion of other groups from the spoils. The middle class is often excluded from the advantages of corruption. Members of the middle class are motivated to pressure the government to control such activity that is detrimental to their well-being. Indeed, by the late 1970s observers noted increasing displeasure among technocrats and small business people regarding corruption.[57]

The peculiar situation we observe is one of increased corruption accompanied by increased pressure on governments to clean up corruption. This is an intriguing paradox: while economic growth may increase corruption, it may also stimulate the discontent to which incumbent cleanups are a response. The differential consequences of modernization on the well-being of various groups in society may account for the opposing effects of the same process. The beneficiaries of corrupt practices sometimes represent specific groups in society. In these cases, corruption reinforces existing societal cleavages and generates antagonism among the excluded populace. Cleanups are likely to occur when the "boundaries" between those who benefit from those who are excluded from the spoils of corruption coincide with other societal divisions (economic, political, and familial, for example) that are exacerbated by a rapid and unequal modernization process.

These phenomena alone may not be adequate to stimulate a cleanup. Societal groups must have access to information. Channels of information to make public and spread the allegations of corruption include opposition leaders, the press, and government leaks. Also, external stimuli serve as catalysts to incumbent cleanups. For example, adverse publicity or investigations which originate in another country may pressure incumbents to resolve the

Comparative Politics October 1991

problem internally. Finally, the repercussions of major political developments elsewhere (revolution, realignment, legal changes) may instigate heads of state to cleanse public life in their own countries.

The objectives of incumbent cleanups are not primarily to discredit the prior government or to purge opposition. Extensive corruption, we have seen, may contribute to feelings of alienation and exclusion among the populace, because it lessens the sense of loyalty and commitment which individuals feel towards their political system. By taking responsibility for the elimination of corruption, the source of such negative attitudes, incumbents seek to build their own political security and acceptance. If perceived to be successful, a cleanup serves to enhance the legitimacy of the incumbent. These cleanups may also be used to manipulate the political agenda, that is, merely to appear to address the problem in order to placate the public or to protect vulnerable political allies by diverting attention elsewhere. Finally, cleanups may be used by incumbents to save themselves when they are seriously threatened. The objective of a last minute incumbent cleanup is self-preservation.

The strategies of incumbent cleanups vary with regard to legal groundwork, level of targets, scope of arrests, and the speed with which they are conducted. They begin as carefully orchestrated events due to their political dangers, that is, guilt by association and loss of political control. They are characterized by legal changes relating to corruption, such as the introduction of stiffer penalties for corruption ranging from fines to death. Clearer restrictions are placed on public servants regarding conflicts of interest. Special courts or commissions may be established to investigate allegations of corruption. Incumbents who want to avoid the appearance of a political purge or manipulation institute these legal changes several months prior to actual arrests or punishments.

The targets of incumbent cleanups vary over time. The arrest and dismissal level of incumbent cleanups is moderate. The initial choice of middle level targets such as deputy ministers or directors of public sector companies reflects the incumbents' dual needs to satisfy the most constituents with regard to anticorruption sentiment and to avoid any close association with corrupt officials. The arrests of a few mid level officials also serves as warning to others yet allows time for adjustment to the new regulations without resorting to sweeping arrests.[58] Heads of state could be destabilized by numerous arrests at lower levels on which they usually depend for acquiescence if not support.

Over time, however, incumbents may lose control of the target level of cleanups. A cleanup can backfire as high level targets are gradually incorporated, even reaching the immediate family of the head of state. Cleanups that begin as carefully designed programs can threaten the incumbent in the end.

Incumbent cleanups that vary in strategy and intensity took place in fourteen of the states we surveyed. Announcement of incumbent cleanups are commonly reiterated over time (we found forty such announcements). Moreover, the intensity of long-running incumbent cleanups ebbs and flows and differs significantly among cases.

Both internal and external stimuli are evident in the survey. Corruption likely grew in absolute terms during this period as a result of the influx of capital to the area either directly to the oil-rich members of OPEC or indirectly through worker remittances to the North African states. Expanding government revenues and purchases and increasing competition for goods and services increased the opportunities for corrupt transactions to occur. Such activity, however, did not go unnoticed.

Kate Gillespie and Gwenn Okruhlik

The Shah's 1978 cleanup in Iran was stimulated by internal opposition. His public admission of corrupt and unjust rule and the cleanup directed at his own family and their business partners seem to have fueled the opposition. Numeri's cleanup of Sudan in 1983 was likewise stimulated by internal fragmentation. The declared cleanup and state of emergency were in response to student riots, national strikes, insurgency in the south, and the increasing activity of the Moslem Brotherhood. Numeri's Islamization program appears to have been a last ditch effort to seize the initiative from the latter. Furthermore, popular unrest can prompt a virulent press campaign against corruption. The Egyptian press consistently reported investigations of a questionable Egyptair-Boeing transaction as well as covering purely local scandals. In cases outside the Middle East (Sierra Leone 1975 and Zambia 1977) cleanups also appear to be responses to internal stimuli.[59]

In Saudi Arabia, the stimulus for the 1975 cleanup appears to be of external origin. The campaign was clearly concerned with commission payments to agents who mediated international business transactions. It was prompted by the hearings of the U.S. Securities and Exchange Commission. Such adverse international publicity could not be easily ignored.

The primary objective sought by both the Shah and Numeri in their panicked cleanups was self-preservation. However, heads of state who wage long-running, relatively constant campaigns against corruption seek another objective. It appears that the Iraqi cleanup sought to integrate corruption control into the fabric of political life. Such objectives may reflect a party ideology or the personal values of a head of state. The succession-cum-incumbent cleanup in Algeria sought to vastly restructure state organizations and to liberalize the economy. In Libya, Qadaffi sought (in addition to quelling his opponents) to fulfill the platform of the Green Book. In Egypt and Tunisia, cleanups attempted to manipulate the political agenda, diverting attention from deteriorating economic conditions.

With regard to strategy, we observe that cleanups in Saudi Arabia, Libya, and Iraq were directed at foreign firms or their intermediaries and were accompanied by legal changes which restricted the behavior of agents. In Egypt, Syria, and the Yemen Arab Republic, the targets were primarily internal actors such as directors of public sector companies and ministry officials. Finally, incumbent cleanups vary with regard to speed. The gradual ebb and flow of long cleanups in many countries contrasts markedly with those begun in a state of emergency (Somalia) or just prior to the fall of the incumbent (Iran and Sudan).

The consequences of last minute cleanups tend to be destabilizing. The acknowledgment of corruption in an already beleaguered administration enhances the appeal of opposition movements. What was argued about Cuba is applicable elsewhere.

> Cuba's system of corruption and bribery was at once one way in which Batista maintained a consensus of support and one source of his downfall; its inequities, irrationalities, and hardships helped to win for Castro's 26th of July movement allies in all layers of society.[60]

It is more difficult to demonstrate that cleanups have actually increased loyalty to the head of state. We can, however, observe that in some cases incumbents have made corruption control a mainstream political concern and made cleanups an almost institutionalized function.

Comparative Politics October 1991

Postsuccession Cleanups These cleanups differ significantly from those following coups, revolutions, and elections where heads of state may attempt to enhance their popularity by publicly pledging to clean up the corruption of the previous administration. A successor attains his or her position through designation by the previous head of state or core elites. Successors are aware that their own legitimacy is intimately linked with that of the prior incumbent. Successors do not initiate new cleanups; rather, they continue the cleanup already in progress. The stimuli for this activity are the successors' need for public recognition and the desire to provide for a smooth transition in leadership. The objective of a postsuccession cleanup is to ensure a public perception of continuity with the previous head of state. Even when the new head of state has been previously designated, intraelite struggles may occur. In these cases, the continuation of a cleanup may also be used to consolidate one's own position and to intimidate contending elites. It is possible to eliminate potential political threats this way, but a specific scandal with a limited number of clearly identified wrongdoers seems more appropriate than does a general cleanup. A limited scandal allows the successor to avoid the acknowledgment of widespread corruption and the risk of discrediting the new administration of a whole.

The peculiar nature of a succession dictates the strategy of such cleanups. The dynamics of postsuccession cleanups are congruent with cleanup activities initiated by the former head of state. Successors avoid implicating their predecessor in any scandal because their close association may prove self-threatening. Investigations are generally limited to middle level officials.

Postsuccession cleanups essentially provide a sense of continuity, for better or worse. If they are used to oust potential threats, the successor risks popular cynicism. Because postsuccession cleanups follow, as well as turn into, incumbent cleanups, their internal dynamics are quite similar.

The survey revealed three succession cleanups: Chadli Benjedid's succession to Hourari Boumedienne in Algeria, Saddam Hussein's succession to Bakr Sidqi in Iraq, and Husni Mubarak's succession to Anwar Sadat in Egypt. All three succession cleanups followed incumbent cleanups. In all cases, the prior head of state was not targeted. Although Mubarak conceded to overwhelming documentation and parliamentary pressure and allowed members of Sadat's family to be tried for corruption, he warned opposition to keep criticism within bounds. Targets were more commonly mid level officials, particularly minor ministers. During the Algerian cleanup a number of higher level officials came under scrutiny. In the instance of the former minister of foreign affairs under Boumedienne, Chadli was suspected of using the issue of corruption to purge potential opposition, thus hurting the public credibility of the cleanup.

Postelection Cleanups Postelection cleanups vary with the legitimacy of the electoral process itself and with the degree of popular support demonstrated for the new leaders, which can range from landslide victories to the bare elections of fragile coalitions of interests. They are stimulated by the demands of the electorate and the enunciation of party priorities. They are fueled by adverse publicity in the various media. When the new government is a vulnerable coalition of interests, postelection cleanups may also be stimulated by the challenges of the counterelite.

The primary objectives of postelection cleanups are to fulfill campaign promises, retain the allegiance of the constituency, facilitate reelection, and in the case of tenuously elected elites to consolidate their power. Of course they can also be used to manipulate the political agenda and avoid campaign promises by focusing attention elsewhere. In elections with clear winners and losers, cleanups are not needed to discredit prior officials—that has already been accomplished. However, cleanups may be used by postelection coalition governments to discredit former officials and to purge potential political threats.

The key strategy utilized in these cleanups is the enactment of legal restrictions of corrupt activity and punishments for offenders. Except in the case of a coalition government or those elected by a thin margin, speed is not particularly important. Public officials use the media to publicize the cleanup, just as they used it during the campaign.

Postelection cleanups that are perceived to be successful will strengthen allegiance to the ruling party or parties. However, perceived failure to make good on promises to contain corruption may lessen chances of reelection. While no postelection cleanups were discerned in the survey, other cases illustrate these points.

Prime Minister Lee Kuan Yew's postelection cleanup in Singapore beginning in 1959 is commonly judged successful in both decreasing corruption significantly and strengthening allegiance to the ruling party. The cleanup's strategies included the promulgation of more comprehensive anticorruption laws, increased penalties for corruption, and an independent anticorruption agency that was eventually placed directly under the prime minister's office. The prime minister himself was strongly committed to the cleanup and served as an example of exemplary conduct. Concomitantly, the salaries and working conditions of government employees were raised to decrease the temptation and rationalization of illicit gain.[61]

Corruption has become a major issue in recent elections, but two well-publicized postelection cleanups have proven less successful than Singapore's experience.[62] In the Mexican election of 1982 the ruling party of long standing chose a nominee who won easily against weak opposition. Although the new technocratic president, Miguel de la Madrid, sought "moral renovation" within the government and enacted new laws and procedures to curb corruption, he failed to target high level officials and was increasingly perceived as being ambivalent towards corruption.[63] Consequently, corruption was a key issue in the 1988 Mexican presidential election, which was the closest in decades. Although the ruling party retained control, it did so under accusations of widespread fraud. In an attempt to reestablish credibility, consolidate power, and possibly divert attention from Mexico's growing economic problems, President Carlos Salinas de Gortari immediately initiated arrests within the state's most venerable corrupt enclaves.[64] A similar scenario can be observed in the case of Rajiv Ghandi's postelection cleanup in India. He increasingly lost credibility as his administration failed to attack corruption at high levels. In the wake of this failure, corruption at lower levels may have even increased. November 1989 elections failed to deliver a majority of votes to Ghandi's Congress Party, and he was replaced as prime minister by an opposition leader.[65]

The Philippine elections in 1985 differed from those in Singapore, Mexico, and India. Despite allegations of incumbent vote rigging, the opposition ultimately assumed power after an election specifically called in the wake of scandals involving President Ferdinand Marcos. President Marcos fled the country, and the pursuant legislation, commissions, confiscations, and attempts to regain currency and property from the prior regime more resembled postrevolution Iran or postcoup Ethiopia than other postelection cleanups.[66]

Summary and Conclusion

Cleanups are important political phenomena and as such deserve more systematic treatment than they have thus far received. The suggested framework—a disaggregation of cleanups into political context, objective, stimulus, strategy, and consequence—provides a means to examine cleanups within and across states.

Cleanups occur within an identifiable political context: postcoup, postrevolution, incumbent, postsuccession, and postelection. Incumbent cleanups are more prevalent than previously believed. The stimuli to a cleanup are mostly of internal origin. Cleanups are likely to occur when existing societal cleavages are reinforced by the exclusionary nature of corrupt activity. Cleanups are political instruments that are used by heads of state to fortify their position. Strategies are predominantly of the political and legal variety, but enforcement of such sanctions varies markedly by political context and over time. The speed and intensity with which a cleanup is conducted reflects the political insecurity of the head of state. Cleanups which follow opposition-forced changes in the head of state occur more quickly and with greater intensity. Moreover, they target the highest levels of officials. Incumbents and successors purposely avoid the upper echelons and target mostly mid and low level officials.

Whether or not cleanups actually reduce the incidence of corrupt transactions remains unclear. Only breaches of ethical and moral standards are likely to be reported, not observation of such standards. Cleanups still have political consequences even if their impact on corruption itself is not obvious. These consequences are favorable overall to incumbents, successors, and electoral heads of state whose political positions are reasonably secure. This is especially the case if cleanups are integrated into mainstream political life, are institutionalized, and occur on a relatively steady basis. The primary benefits for postcoup and postrevolution heads of state are the short-term weeding out of specific opposition leaders and the diversion of attention from more pressing socioeconomic problems.

The political consequences of cleanups are very often negative for the head of state whose position is already insecure. This is particularly true for vulnerable heads of state who initiate last minute, dramatic cleanups. They only provide fuel to opposition movements. Cleanups can take on a life of their own even if they begin as carefully orchestrated events: heads of state can lose control of the target level. As the level spirals ever upward, they and their families are threatened. Smokescreen cleanups—last gasps of a beleaguered head of state—only engender popular cynicism.

These observations warrant further exploration in both comparative and in-depth single case studies. A survey of this breadth—twenty-five countries over seventeen years—can not fully explain the diversity of cleanups among states nor describe the complexity of a cleanup within each individual state. Nevertheless, these observations reveal the deeply comparative nature of domestic politics. Cleanups are a tool by which elites attempt to fulfill that most basic of political instincts, self-preservation. The increasing occurrence of incumbent cleanups together with their inherent risks indicates that corruption is no more condoned in developing countries than in developed countries. The prevalence of the cleanup phenomenon suggests that people, in the long run, hold a government accountable for its activities.

NOTES

1. For further discussion, see Arnold J. Heidenheimer, *Political Corruption: Readings in Comparative Analysis* (New York: Holt, Rinehart & Winston, 1970), pp. 3–9.

2. For example, "corruption is behavior which deviates from the formal duties of a public role (elective or appointive) because of private-regarding (personal, close family, private clique) wealth or status gains. . . . ," in Joseph S. Nye, "Corruption and Development: A Cost-Benefit Analysis," *American Political Science Review*, 61 (June 1967), 417–427.

3. For example, "a political act is corrupt when the weight of public opinion determines it so," in Barry Rundquist and Susan Hansen, "On Controlling Official Corruption: Elections vs. Laws," unpublished manuscript, 1976, noted in John Peters and Susan Welch, "Political Corruption in America: A Search for Definitions and a Theory," *American Political Science Review*, 72 (September 1978), 975–984.

4. For example, "a corrupt act violates responsibility toward at least one system of public or civic order. . . . violations of common interest for special advantage are corrupt," in Arnold Rogow and Harold Lasswell, *Power, Corruption, and Rectitude* (Englewood Cliffs: Prentice-Hall, 1963), p. 132.

5. For example, "corruption is the use of illegal market mechanisms in allocative decisions set aside for the democratic political system," in Susan Rose-Ackerman, *Corruption: A Study in Political Economy* (New York: Academic Press, 1978), pp. 1–2. See also, Robert Tilman, "Emergence of Black Market Bureaucracy: Administration, Development and Corruption in the New States," *Public Administration Review*, 28 (September-October 1968), 437–444.

6. See Graeme C. Moodie, "On Political Scandals and Corruption," *Government and Opposition*, 15 (Spring 1980), 208–222.

7. Lord Action, in Rogow and Lasswell's discussion of the power-corruption thesis, ch. 1.

8. See Ledivina V. Carino, "Bureaucratic Norms, Corruption and Development," *Philippine Journal of Public Administration*, 19 (October 1975), 278–292.

9. See Jose Veloso Abueva, "The Contribution of Nepotism, Spoils, and Graft to Political Development," *East-West Center Review*, 3 (June 1966), 45–54; Stanislav Andreski, "Kleptocracy as a System of Government in Africa," in *The African Predicament* (New York: Atherton Press, 1968), pp. 92–109; Gunnar Myrdal, *Asian Drama: An Inquiry into the Poverty of Nations* (New York: Twentieth Century Fund, 1968), p. 206; M. McMullan, "A Theory of Corruption," *The Sociological Review*, 9 (July 1961), 181–201; and Victor T. LeVine, *Political Corruption: The Ghana Case* (Stanford: Hoover Institution Press, 1975), pp. 82–86.

10. See J. Patrick Dobel, "The Corruption of a State," *American Political Science Review*, 72 (September 1978), 958–973. The discussion is based on the work of Aristotle, Machiavelli, Rousseau, Plato, and Thucydides.

11. See Stephen G. Bunker and Lawrence E. Cohen, "Collaboration and Competition in Two Colonization Projects: Toward a General Theory of Official Corruption," *Human Organization*, 42 (Summer 1983), 106–114.

12. This discussion is taken from Samuel P. Huntington, "Modernization and Corruption," in Arnold J. Heidenheimer, Michael Johnston, and Victor T. LeVine, eds., *Political Corruption: A Handbook* (New Brunswick: Transaction, 1989), pp. 377–388. Also, see J. C. Scott, "Corruption, Machine Politics, and Political Change," *American Political Science Review*, 63 (December 1969), 1142–1158, and Heidenheimer, *Political Corruption*.

13. For a critique of the modernization thesis, see Anne Deysine, "Political Corruption: A Review of the Literature," *European Journal of Political Research*, 8 (December 1980), 447–462.

14. See Ronald Wraith and Edgar Simpkins, *Corruption in Developing Nations* (London: Allen and Unwin, 1963); also, Myrdal.

15. For review, see Gabriel Ben-Dor, "Corruption, Institutionalization, and Political Development: The Revisionist Theses Revisited," *Comparative Political Studies* (April 1974), 63–83; Simcha B. Werner, "The Development of Political Corruption: A Case Study of Israel," *Political Studies*, 31 (December 1983), 620–639; and Heidenheimer, *Political Corruption*, pp. 479–486.

16. Economic arguments are found in Nathaniel Leff, "Economic Development through Bureaucratic Corruption," *American Behavioral Scientist*, 8 (November 1964), 8–14, and David Bayley, "The Effects of Corruption in a Developing Nation," *Western Political Quarterly*, 19 (December 1966), 719–732.

17. For example, see Huntington and Abueva.

18. See Bayley, Scott, and Nye for administrative or integrative arguments.

19. J. R. Shackleton, "Corruption: An Essay in Economic Analysis," *Political Quarterly* (January-March 1978), 25.

20. See Carino and Nye.

21. Simcha Werner, "New Directions in the Study of Administrative Corruption," *Public Administration Review*, 43 (March-April 1983), 146–154.

22. John Waterbury, "Corruption, Political Stability, and Development: Comparative Evidence from Egypt and Morocco," *Government and Opposition*, 11 (Autumn 1976), 426–445.

23. For an excellent discussion, see ibid.

24. Robin Cohen, in Morris Szeftel, "Corruption and the Spoils System in Zambia," in Michael Clark, ed., *Corruption: Causes, Consequences and Control* (London: Frances Pinter, 1983), p. 184.

25. See Waterbury, p. 439.

26. Stephen Riley, "The Land of Waving Palms: Political Economy, Corruption Inquiries and Politics in Sierra Leone," in Clarke, ed., p. 204.

27. Robert Dowse, "Conceptualizing Corruption," book review in *Government and Opposition*, 12 (Summer 1977), 254.

28. For example, see Peters and Welch; Bernard Schaffer, "Access: A Theory of Corruption and Bureaucracy," *Public Administration and Development*, 6 (October-December 1986), 357–376; and Moodie.

29. Michael Johnston, "The Political Consequences of Corruption: A Reassessment," *Comparative Politics*, 18 (July 1986), 459–477. Also, Philip Oldenburg, "Middlemen in Third-World Corruption: Implications of an Indian Case," *World Politics*, 39 (July 1987), 508–535.

30. Robert Wade, "The Market for Public Office: Why the Indian State Is Not Better at Development," *World Development*, 13 (April 1985), 467–497.

31. James Scott, *Comparative Political Corruption* (Englewood Cliffs: Prentice Hall, 1972), p. 88.

32. John Waterbury, "Endemic and Planned Corruption in a Monarchical Regime," *World Politics*, 25 (July 1973), 533–555.

33. Heidenheimer, *Political Corruption*, pp. 26–28.

34. L. Michael Hager, "Bureaucratic Corruption in India: Legal Control of Maladiminstration," *Comparative Political Studies*, 6 (July 1973), 197–219.

35. Johnston; Waterbury.

36. See Waterbury, Johnston, and Clarke.

37. For discussion of ethical norms, see Eva Etzioni-Halevy, *Political Manipulation and Administrative Power* (London: Routledge and Kegan Paul, 1979), pp. 187–191; John B. Monteiro, *Corruption: Control of Maladministration* (Bombay: Manaktalas and Sons, 1966), pp. 96–105; and Ralph Braibanti, "Refelctions on Bureaucratic Corruption," *Public Administration*, 40 (Winter 1962), 114–116.

38. McMullen, p. 199. See also, Dobel, p. 972, for the role of education.

39. For discussion of public vigilance, see Monteiro, Halaya, Myrdal, and Clarke. "Community justice strategy" is Werner's phrase in "New Directions in the Study of Administrative Corruption," p. 152.

40. See Shaukat Ali, *Corruption: A Third World Perspective* (Lahore: Aziz Publishers, 1985), pp. 2–6.

41. Krushina Singh Padhy, *Corruption in Politics* (Delhi: B. R. Publishing Corporation, 1986).

42. "International Chamber of Commerce: Commission on Ethical Practices and Recommendations to Combat Extortion and Bribery in Business Transactions," *International Legal Materials*, 17 (March 1978), 417–421 (report adopted by the 131st Session of the ICC, November 29, 1977).

43. John A. Gardiner and Theodore R. Lyman, "The Logic of Corruption Control," in Heidenheimer et al., eds., p. 827.

44. These legal strategies are suggested by Shackleton, pp. 35–36; Padhy, p. 213; and McMullen, p. 199.

45. For market strategies, see Dowse, Leff, Rose-Ackerman, and Tilman. Also see John Macrae, "Underdevelopment and the Economics of Corruption: A Game Theory Approach," *World Development*, 10 (August 1982), 677–687.

46. For strategies dealing with authority, see Wade, p. 488, Shackleton, pp. 36–37, and Malya, pp. 129–137.

47. For access strategies, see Oldenburg, p. 527; Dobel, p. 972; Tevfik Nas, Albert Price, and Charles Weber, "A

Policy-Oriented Theory of Corruption," *American Political Science Review*, 80 (March 1986), 116–117; and Robert Wade, "The System of Administrative and Political Corruption: Canal Irrigation in South India," *Journal of Development Studies*, 18 (April 1982), 321.

48. For administrative strategies, see Bunker and Cohen; Leslie Palmier, *The Control of Bureaucratic Corruption: Case Studies in Asia* (New Delhi: Allied Publishers, 1985), pp. 271–281; Wade; and Shackleton.

49. One could argue that religious strategies constitute a fifth category. However, as religion may permeate all aspects of society, it will be incorporated into the aforementioned four categories.

50. Our survey of these states comprises Afghanistan, Algeria, Bahrain, Cyprus, Egypt, Ethiopia, Iran, Iraq, Jordan, Kuwait, Lebanon, Libya, Mauritania, Morocco, Oman, Qatar, Saudi Arabia, Somalia, Sudan, Syria, Tunisia, Turkey, United Arab Emirates, Yemen Arab Republic, and the Democratic People's Republic of Yemen. Israel was not covered in *MEED* and was excluded from the formal survey. A scandal is defined as a publicized incident of alleged corruption with corruption referring to the use of public authority for private benefit in a way that constitutes a breach of law. Virtually all 200 observed incidents involved public officials or employees misappropriating state funds or accepting bribes from individuals or companies in exchange for preferential treatment. For further discussion of scandals in relation to corruption, see Graeme C. Moodie, "On Political Scandals and Corruption," in Heidenheimer et al., eds. pp. 873–886.

51. For further description and documentation of these cleanups, see Kate Gillespie and Gwenn Okruhlik, "Cleaning Up Corruption in the Middle East," *The Middle East Journal*, 42 (Winter 1988), 59–82.

52. Coup refers to a change in national leadership preceded by violence, or the threat of violence, which is initiated by a relatively limited number of participants who already possess institutional bases of power. In all our cases these bases were military. A revolution refers to a change in the national leadership, institutional structure, and supporting myths of a state initiated by widespread popular participation. Incumbents are heads of state whose tenure in office exceeds the preliminary transition period which follows their assumption of power. A succession refers to the transfer of power upon the death or resignation of the head of state to a successor who has been designated by the national leadership. An election refers to the designation of national leadership through formal voting procedures.

53. See, for example Nye, "Corruption and Development," and Neil H. Jacoby, Peter Nehemkis, and Richard Eells, *Bribery and Extortion in World Business* (New York: Macmillan, 1977), pp. 156–157.

54. Riley, in Clarke, p. 195.

55. Turkey (1981) was an exception. For a discussion of the peculiarities of the Turkish case, see Gillespie and Okruhlik, p. 62.

56. Jacoby, Nehemkis, and Eells, pp. 156–157; Klitgaard, p. 1; and Leslie Palmier "Bureaucratic Corruption and Its Remedies," in Clarke, ed., p. 215.

57. Gillespie and Okrulik, p. 65; and Waterbury, "Endemic and Planned Corruption."

58. Penalizing higher officials to set an example for the rank and file was used successfully in a micro setting by Efren Plana in his cleanup of the Bureau of Internal Revenue in the Philippines. See Klitgaard, p. 55.

59. Riley in Clarke, ed., p. 196; and Szeftel in Clarke, ed., pp. 171–173.

60. James O'Connor, quoted in Whitehead in Clarke, ed., p. 159.

61. Klitgaard, pp. 122–133.

62. For example, see Clara Germani, "Drug Corruption Is Main Issue in Bahamian Election," *The Christian Science Monitor*, June 18, 1987, pp. 9 and 13; and Julia Michaels, "Brazilians Say 'No' to Corruption," *The Christian Science Monitor*, Mar, 9, 1989, p. 3.

63. T. Elaine Carey, "Mexico's 'Moral Renovation' Plan Fizzles," *The Christian Science Monitor*, Apr. 23, 1986, p. 7; and Klitgaard, p. 2.

64. Stephan Baker, "Salinas Goes after Another Monster," *Business Week*, Mar. 6, 1989, p. 42; and Brook Larmer, "Mexico's Corruption Clampdown," *The Christian Science Monitor*, Apr. 13, 1989, pp. 1–2.

65. Anthony Spaeth, "Ghandi's Growing Unpopularity Raises the Prospect of a Change in Government," *The Asian Wall Street Journal Weekly*, Apr. 17, 1989, p. 22; and *The New York Times*, Nov. 30, 1989, p. A12.

66. Peter Grier, "Marcos Faces Growing Assault on His Alleged US Financial Assets," *The Christian Science Monitor*, Mar, 12, 1986, pp. 1 and 30; Calyton Jones, "Filipino Panel Recovers $1 Billion of Marcos Assets in 100 Days," *The Christian Science Monitor*, June 11, 1986, p. 12; and John Templeton and Paula Dwyer, "Suddenly, a Swiss Bank Account Isn't What It Used to Be," *Business Week*, Apr. 7, 1986, pp. 37–38.

[2]

FIELD REPORTS

COMBATTING CORRUPTION AROUND THE WORLD

Peter Eigen

Peter Eigen *is chairman of Transparency International, a Berlin-based research and advocacy body devoted to battling global corruption. He has worked for 25 years in economic development, mainly as a manager of programs in Africa and Latin America for the World Bank.*

In the spring of 1990, representatives of the World Bank stationed in Africa met in Swaziland to discuss an urgent request articulated by African leaders in their famous *Long-Term Perspective Study*: "Support better governance."[1] As the World Bank representative in Kenya, I agreed to talk about corruption as a powerful enemy of good governance. I described its enormous reach and its crippling effect on social, economic, and political development. I then proposed a plan of action that had evolved from lengthy discussions with many colleagues and friends in Nairobi. Clearly, most people are against corruption. Why not, then, channel this opposition into the construction of an effective coalition promoting transparency? The timing was propitious: international corruption had reached crisis-level proportions, and many countries that were undergoing political transition were in desperate need of stronger integrity systems.

The initial reaction of the meeting participants was enthusiastic. It was agreed that the World Bank should develop an anticorruption agenda for itself and for its partners, the idea being that the absence of corruption is an important element of an environment conducive to development. I agreed to spearhead the initiative. Soon after the meeting, however, doubts emerged about the Bank's readiness to take this step. Would this constitute a violation of the political abstinence prescribed by the Bank's charter, stirring up a political hornet's nest? Although there was much encouragement within the institution, it fell short of the consensus needed for the Bank to back such an effort. Yet some of us remained determined to take action. Something had to be done, and something could be done. At the end of the Cold War, the time was right.

Unable to act within an existing intergovernmental framework, and feeling a need to draw the private sector and other nongovernmental actors into the necessary dialogue, I and some of my colleagues decided to proceed with the venture independently. This approach had the added advantage of avoiding the scent of conditionality that would have come with the World Bank's playing a dominant role. We wanted a movement driven by the demand for transparency that was then emanating from a number of nations in the global South and East that were in transition economically, socially, and often politically.

In sounding out friends and colleagues, we received an overwhelmingly positive response from a wide cross-section of African society, including academia, the business sector, the media, and the donor community. Corruption had become so widespread that many people had come to accept it as an unavoidable fact of life. Yet underneath that outer resignation we found considerable hope that corruption could be eliminated—revealing the truth of the saying that evil thrives on the apathy of the good.

The initial working group arranged meetings in Eschborn (near Frankfurt), Kampala (Uganda), London, and Washington, D.C. Soon, supporters from other continents joined in the deliberations. Gradually, some fundamental concepts emerged: the organization would work alongside governments and citizens' groups and would focus on developing systems to fight corruption on a step-by-step basis. It was clear that there were no quick or easy solutions to the problem; the struggle would take years.

In early 1993, the nonprofit organization Transparency International (TI) was formally launched in Berlin. In discussions among more than 70 concerned individuals from every corner of the globe—including a newly constituted advisory council of more than 20 people—the initial resolutions of the founders were confirmed: TI's mandate, it was declared, would be to rid society of corruption, defined as the misuse of public power for private gain. In the South, such corruption derails well-intentioned economic-development projects. In the East, it undermines political and economic transitions before the benefits of more open systems can be experienced. The focus of TI, it was decided, would be on large-scale corruption affecting developing countries, regardless of the origin of the illicit transactions.

It was also decided that TI would take a balanced approach, avoiding one-sided assignations of responsibility. Exporters from developed countries with strong anticorruption laws often conform to and even manipulate the shady business practices of the less-developed regions in which they trade. Consider the now-famous statement made in a May 1994 BBC interview by Lord Young, chairman of Cable & Wireless and former U.K. minister for trade and industry: "Now, when you're talking about kickbacks, you're talking about something that's illegal in [the United Kingdom], and of course, you wouldn't dream of doing. . . . But there are parts of the world I've been to where we all know it happens. And if you want to be in business, you have to do [it]."

This "cultural argument"—that corruption is an accepted practice among developing countries—is one of the strongest barriers to rooting out the phenomenon. Because TI has limited resources, it focuses its efforts on a particular segment of global corruption: that pertaining to public projects in the developing world. In dozens of these countries, vast sums of money are involved. Typically, public officials accept payoffs from commercial contractors to funnel public funds to the projects of the contractors' choice; this often diverts investment away from the most worthy projects (such as construction of schools and hospitals) toward others of negligible social value. The biggest victims are members of the local community, who end up saddled with uneconomic "white elephants."

While it is easy to point the finger of blame at corrupt public officials, no less at fault are businesspeople from highly developed industrial states whose thirst for export orders leads them to flout the laws of the developing countries. Behind these companies, rewarding them with tax breaks, stand the same Western governments that provide aid to developing countries to improve their standards of governance.

Far-Reaching Effects

Corruption has far graver consequences than the mere funneling of scarce resources into the pockets of unethical civil servants. As former U.S. congressman John Brademas has pointed out, corruption is "a major obstacle to the advance of democracy and economic growth. . . . By undermining trust in political institutions and public officials and by distorting government policy against the best interests of the majority, corruption impairs the process of democracy. The effects of corruption are especially pernicious in emerging democracies, for the abuse of public office subverts popular confidence in the very idea of self-government."[2] Corruption gives rise to oligarchy. It allows leaders to cling to power while resisting governmental reform, curbing personal freedom, and abusing basic human rights. Corruption hinders the creation of free markets. The magnitude of bribes, rather than the quality of products or services, determines what sells. Hence corruption is conducive to fundamental mistakes in project selection and project design—often with catastrophic consequences for both society and the environment.

This process hinders the growth of competitiveness, frustrates efforts to alleviate poverty, and makes real economic progress impossible. A self-perpetuating cycle can develop, with a broad expectation of corruption causing an increase in its incidence. Such a system rewards the unscrupulous and demoralizes the honest. A "brain drain" often follows, as people who reject the system emigrate to countries in which they will be rewarded for their skills and productivity.

Corruption is more likely to become systematic in the developing countries, with their relatively weak administrations and political institutions. Pay scales there are generally very low. Civil servants may be expected to extort petty bribes in order to supplement their income. They may have an "arrangement" whereby part of their work is privatized—that is, contracted out to their own private consulting firms. Similarly, education-department officials often find that the only way they can afford to send their children to school is for their wives to have businesses selling school textbooks. Such businesses, however, have only one customer: the education department.

Without intending any harm, these people help construct a corrupt system for which everyone ultimately pays the price. All too often, a corrupt environment channels resources to nonproductive areas such as the police, the armed forces, and other organs of social control and repression as the elites move to protect their positions and wealth. In a vicious circle, corruption and autocratic rule feed upon each other and become mutually dependent.

Coping with corruption is usually not a simple matter of enforcement, for the casualties of corruption often include the integrity system itself. A society may be plagued by corrupt judges, lawyers, and prosecutors; corrupt police officers and investigators; corrupt auditors; and, above all, corrupt political leaders who see the judicial system not as a check on their own power, but as a tool for perpetuating it.

Even if a given country's judicial system is not entirely corrupt, laws may be widely flouted with near impunity. Most countries have laws prohibiting bribery—with severe penalties prescribed for infractions by corrupt politicians and officials—and clear guidelines for how public servants should behave. Yet their effect is often minimal. In any attempt at reform, three truths must be kept in mind: First, the mere passage of legislation is unlikely to be effective unless it is accompanied by a raft of practical measures that maximize accountability and transparency, and minimize situations in which corruption is prone to occur. Second, the overall objective must be to change the general perception of corruption from a "low-risk, high-profit" activity to a "high-risk, low-profit" activity. Third, reform of anticorruption measures—like reform in all other areas—should be undertaken in ways that conform to international human rights standards, particularly with regard to due process and fair trials.

Effective reform, then, requires a legal framework that can and will be implemented, and a range of administrative measures in support of the overall process. Experience shows that corruption can be curbed by limiting the opportunity for it to occur, by bolstering outside monitoring by independent agents, and by reducing the benefits that corrupt behavior yields to both recipients and payers of bribes. The overall strategy, in other words, must be one of prevention, with prosecution and punishment eventually coming to play supporting rather than leading roles. An anticorruption program must include the following:

1) a clear and demonstrable commitment on the part of political leaders to the eradication of corruption, from whatever source;

2) the adoption of comprehensive anticorruption legislation and its enforcement by a strong and independent agency of manifest integrity;

3) the identification of the areas of governmental activity most prone to corruption, and a review of relevant procedures;

4) a compensation review to ensure that salaries of civil servants and political leaders are commensurate with the responsibilities of their posts and are as comparable as possible with salaries in the private sector; and

5) a review of legal procedures and remedies to ensure that they constitute an effective deterrent (for example, contracts induced by corruption should be rendered null and void).

Civil society has an important role to play in any battle against corruption. The general public must be made aware of what constitutes corruption. A free press can contribute significantly by exposing specific cases as well as educating the public about preventive measures. Open political debate and accountability are also important. Ultimately, society must affirm and defend its own values, rather than leaving this important function to those in power. In most countries, no matter how developed, there is currently a broad sentiment of impotence regarding the problem of corruption—a feeling of not knowing where to begin.

The Transparency International Approach

The overall approach that TI takes to fighting corruption is threefold. First, the organization builds broad coalitions against corruption. It seeks to minimize confrontation and political wrangling, preferring to work cooperatively with governments and citizens' groups. While sharing the ultimate humanitarian goals of the human rights group Amnesty International, TI has a sharply contrasting methodology. As mentioned above, it is not intent on investigating individual cases, exposing villains, or casting blame. It seeks to strengthen anticorruption systems, both in the developed countries—which are the primary source of illicit payments—and in the developing world, where the blandishments of private promoters often corrupt public officials and pervert their decision making. Rather than monitor gray-zone transactions itself, TI seeks to increase the overall likelihood of detection and to improve mechanisms of deterrence. To this end, TI will work with any government that demonstrates a resolve to attack corruption as well as sufficient credibility to indicate that a plan of action will be implemented.

The second pillar of TI is its system of national chapters. Recognizing that there is no universal recipe for transparency, TI relies on these national chapters to tailor anticorruption programs to their own societies. As of November 1995, TI had or had in the making 50 national chapters, the majority of which are located in the South. While free to define their own mandates and work programs, all TI chapters must follow two important rules of conduct. First, they must not investigate and expose individual cases of corruption. Such activity would undermine TI's efforts to build coalitions that can strengthen anticorruption systems through professional and technical improvements. The ultimate goal is practical change in laws, institutions, and policies so as to reduce the incidence of corruption. Second, they must avoid partisan politics, which could damage TI's credibility and ultimately hinder achievement of its goals.

The third essential element of TI's strategy is its gradualist approach. Instead of sweeping programs of reform, TI implements focused and specific plans of action in an incremental process. Often, the prevalence of corruption discourages individual firms or even entire nations from taking the first step toward transparency. When everyone pays bribes, no one wants to be the first to stop, thereby losing business to competitors. As an answer to this problem, TI has developed a concept called "Islands of Integrity," whereby competing firms in a specific market enter into an Anti-Bribery Pact (ABP). The mechanism was first implemented in the energy sector of Ecuador, as discussed below.

In each country, TI aims to function as a catalyst. Typically, a program begins with an agreement among government officials and prominent citizens that their country would benefit from a visit by TI representatives. TI first holds discussions with senior government officials (often including the head of government) to explain the nature of the mission and TI's mandate. These meetings provide a sound basis for constructive dialogue between the government and civil society on a potentially divisive issue.

Discussions then broaden to include relevant segments of civil society—typically business leaders, journalists, religious figures, academics, nongovernmental activists, and members of chambers of commerce and other professional bodies—to test the interest in and feasibility of forming a national chapter. These discussions also help to identify prospective leaders of such a chapter, who should be of outstanding character and clearly independent of government.

The TI team normally concludes its mission with a final round of talks with government leaders. TI then prepares a diagnostic report detailing its impressions of the situation and prospects for reducing corruption, as well as setting forth a tentative plan of action. The report is distributed to government officials and civic leaders. So far, such missions have been sent to Bangladesh, Benin, Ecuador, Mali, Russia, South Africa, Tanzania, and Uganda. In cases where there is sufficient interest, TI may send one or more follow-up missions. These teams often include technical experts who can elaborate on the recommendations for improvement of the country's integrity system.

Two Operational Examples

Two examples of ongoing operational work illustrate TI's approach: 1) implementation of the "Islands of Integrity" concept for a particular contract in Ecuador, and 2) preparation of an analytical guide to strengthening integrity systems, the "National Integrity Blueprint" (NIB).

1) "Islands of Integrity" in Ecuador. In 1994, the national chapter of TI in Ecuador oversaw the first implementation of the "Islands of Integrity" scheme, which focused on a large project in the energy sector. After two TI missions to the country in 1993, the Ecuadorian government announced in an April 1994 letter to procurement officials that: 1) for all future public works projects, companies bidding for contracts had to commit themselves in writing to avoiding all forms of corruption and notifying the government of all commissions paid in connection with these contracts; 2) certified copies of that document, called an Anti-Bribery Pact, would form part of the package of bidding documents and would be covered by the bid security (normally, a bank guarantee or "bid bond," meant to assure performance); and 3) the government would introduce special safeguards to give credibility to the ABP, and would work closely with citizens' groups—including the Ecuador chapter of TI—to ensure the sustainability of the campaign.

The letter instructed procurement officials "to require all bidders in projects involving international procurement of systems, equipment, or services to submit a signed statement that they will not offer or give a bribe to any public official in connection with such bids." Each competing firm was asked to pledge that it would

- not offer or give bribes or any other form of inducement to any public official in connection with its bid;

- not permit anyone (whether its employee or an independent commission agent) to do so on its behalf;

- make full disclosure in its bid of the beneficiaries of payments relating to the bid (both already made and those proposed to be made in the event of a successful bid) to any person other than an employee of the corporation—including any bonus payments which may be made to employees;

- formally undertake to issue instructions to all of its employees, agents or other representatives in Ecuador, directing them to comply with the laws of Ecuador and in particular not to offer or to pay bribes or other corrupt inducements to officials (whether directly or indirectly).

In order to ensure a strong personal commitment, the letter required a signature from both the chief executive officer of the firm and the manager or legal representative of the Ecuador subsidiary. Because complex legislative procedures were required before signing the ABP could become mandatory, compliance was voluntary at the time of the system's initial implementation.

Four bidders in a 1994 refinery-rehabilitation project with an estimated cost of US$160 million agreed that signing an ABP would be to their mutual benefit.[3] Procurement took place without reports of bribery. Currently, bidders on a proposed oil-pipeline project estimated to cost US$600 million are scheduled to enter into an ABP. The financial viability of the pipeline has been questioned, however, and the project may be postponed or shelved. Moreover, recent political controversies that have led to the resignation of the country's vice president—who was a strong supporter of TI—make further legislative progress in the near future unlikely.

The "Islands of Integrity" concept is being recommended in one form or another to most countries that have entered into relationships with TI. In all cases, it is essential that the ABP be placed on firm legal ground, with provisions for serious consequences in cases of violation, such as the invalidation of contracts, payment of damages to the state as well as competitors, and loss of bid security. This would lend credibility to the ABP as a strong anticorruption device. The ABP can be a bridge out of the prisoner's dilemma in which many commercial interests are caught, in which they realize that if they stop offering bribes while their competitors continue, they stand to lose substantial business.

2) The "National Integrity Blueprint." Although there is no universal prescription for preventing corruption, TI is developing a "National Integrity Blueprint" as a guide for countries that are developing anticorruption legislation and institutions. The blueprint, scheduled for completion in early 1996, will serve as a reference for governments and policy makers, and as a resource for TI national chapters.

The NIB takes a holistic approach, dealing with all the major elements that make up the integrity system of a society—the laws, institutions, and practices through which just and honest government is promoted and protected. Drawing from the experience of countries around the world, it describes the best available models and provides analytical tools with which to review existing systems, pinpoint their weaknesses, and identify programs for addressing those weaknesses effectively. Among the integrity instruments covered by the NIB are procurement practices and public financial management, administrative reform, auditing and bookkeeping practices, the judiciary, and policy regarding public information and education. The importance of civil society in bringing about change is a central theme of the blueprint.

A request for help from the Russian parliament provided an early opportunity to test the effectiveness of the draft blueprint, and to learn important lessons in the process—lessons that will be reflected in the final version. In Namibia, we were able to put the draft NIB to work in preparing for the attorney-general draft legislation regarding disclosure of assets and income. This draft legislation formed part of a general framework providing for privileges and immunities of parliament and parliamentarians. Although both these exercises were positive experiences, their mixed practical impact underscores the importance of a strong and structured civil society to the success of anticorruption efforts.

Parallel Developments

In the international arena, the issue of corruption has recently moved to center stage. Naturally, TI is not the only organization battling this increasingly global phenomenon. There have been a number of important developments during the last few years. In May 1994, the Organization for Economic Cooperation and Development (OECD) recommended that its member countries take a coordinated approach against their nationals' bribery of foreign officials. A working group has been assigned to translate six clusters of recommended measures into action; a consensus regarding the best course to take is already emerging from this effort. TI actively supports the work of the OECD, and hopes that the World Trade Organization will eventually incorporate the corruption issue into its mandate for free trade.

Several important regional efforts to control corruption are also under way. The Council of Europe is actively pursuing the establishment of a binding anticorruption convention among its members, as mandated by a ministerial conference it held in Malta in mid-1994. At the Summit of the Americas in December 1994 in Miami, 35 democratically elected heads of government from throughout the Western Hemisphere decided to launch a regional plan to combat corruption at the highest levels; the Organization of American States is following up on the resolution. A first indication of major change in Africa came in November 1994, when a ministerial conference on combatting corruption was held in

Pretoria, South Africa. There, a regional group was established to monitor corruption and foster creative efforts to contain it. Nongovernmental organizations have been invited to participate in these efforts.

At the same time, the private sector has begun to address corruption through self-regulation. The International Chamber of Commerce is now working to revive its Code of Conduct and increase its effectiveness by developing improved corporate codes and compliance models. Controlling corruption has become a major element of the "good governance" agenda of international development organizations; it was recently identified as a key challenge for the World Bank by its new president, James Wolfensohn.

In 1995, TI published its first Corruption Index, which ranked 41 countries on the basis of how corrupt they were perceived to be by international businesspeople. The list caused a sensation, with countries either pleased or dismayed, depending on how they fared. But corruption is too complicated and broad a phenomenon to be perceived in black-and-white terms. Countries that ranked high in the survey, such as New Zealand, Denmark, and Singapore, cannot claim moral superiority to the countries that ranked at the bottom of the scale, such as Indonesia and China. As emphasized above, corruption is a global practice that often taints international business transactions involving many parties. There are deep-seated problems in every part of the world. The even-handed, pragmatic approach of TI has reflected this reality.

When TI was launched in 1993, none of its founders could have anticipated how quickly it would be accepted as an idea whose time had come. TI has made a difference. It has won recognition—in governmental as well as nongovernmental circles, in developed as well as in developing countries—as an effective weapon against international corruption. Of course, it is understood that TI has embarked on a long and tortuous road. There have been setbacks. But there is a new feeling in the air that discussion of corruption is no longer taboo. More importantly, the first real success stories can now be told.

Today, anticorruption coalitions are forming in many areas of the globe. There is enormous demand for TI's involvement in countries from Argentina to Russia, from South Africa to Bangladesh. Tangible support has come from private firms, nongovernmental organizations (NGOs), universities, the media, development organizations, governments, and individuals around the world. With its strong base of technical and human resources, TI is poised to expand its program of shaping anticorruption strategies.

The Challenges Ahead

Despite its considerable success, TI—like most NGOs—lacks the funds and personnel to do as much as it would like. Many of its resources are earmarked for specific projects. There is an acute shortage of general institutional support—funds that could be used, for instance, for initial investigative missions to determine governments' true level of interest in curbing corruption. There is little money available with which to undertake research or plan regional initiatives.

TI's budding role in East-Central Europe provides a good illustration of the difficulties: In early 1994, the European Union's PHARE program offered a sizeable grant for an exploratory mission to several countries in transition in the East. A strong team has been assembled. Yet the mission has not been launched, because the institutional resources that would be needed for follow-up, including quality control and support for new national chapters of TI in the region, are not assured. The present resources—both human and financial—of the small headquarters in Berlin are already overextended, and in spite of assistance from a vast network of volunteers, the pace of work is not sustainable.

Corruption has become a major world problem, standing alongside those of overpopulation, environmental degradation, AIDS, and poverty. It calls for a massive, systematic attack at the local, regional, and global levels. Concerned individuals, institutions, corporations, and governments have provided TI with considerable support, without which the organization would not exist. But if the struggle against international corruption is to continue and intensify, it desperately needs more funds, more professional and technical expertise—indeed, more resources of all kinds.

The key player in the process of achieving meaningful and enduring reform is civil society. In the words of Edmund Burke: "In all forms of government the people is the true legislator." In the fight against corruption, the challenge is to equip civil society for its crucial role. We at TI are energetically committed to this goal.

NOTES

Transparency International can be contacted at: Heylstrasse 33, D-10825 Berlin, Germany; phone, 49-30-787-5908; fax, 49-30-787-5707; e-mail, ti@contrib.de (Internet: http://www.is.in-berlin.de/service/ti.html).

1. *Sub-Saharan Africa, From Crisis to Sustainable Growth—A Long-Term Perspective Study* (Washington, D.C.: World Bank, 1989), 192.

2. John Brademas, "Cultural Issues on the Threshold of the Twenty-first Century: The Athens Summit" (draft paper, September 1995).

3. The four consortia were Kellogg-Bufete, Industrial Técnicas Reunidas-Eurocontrol, Raytheon-Tenenge, and Sumitomo-Chiyoda.

[3]

REVISITING ANTI-CORRUPTION STRATEGIES: TILT TOWARDS INCENTIVE-DRIVEN APPROACHES?

DANIEL KAUFMANN

Introduction: Ex post versus Ex ante

With the success of the advocacy movement over the past few years, the first stage of a worldwide anti-corruption drive is coming to an end. That success is now paving the way for the next stage: implementation of concrete and sustainable action programmes. Some programmes have been initiated already, and selected country experiences of the past twenty years are now being evaluated. We argue that in the midst of this crucial crossroads it is imperative to pause for a moment to distill the emerging lessons.[1]

Failure to critically evaluate what strategies are appropriate in the next stage of anti-corruption strategies may only exacerbate the emerging tilt towards ex post measures to tackle corruption: legal and institutional enforcement measures designed to improve detection, enforcement and prosecution of already committed corrupt acts. Indeed, the parallel with the field of public health is pertinent in analysing issues of corruption, and not only because corruption can be seen as an "infectious disease" of sorts (with its issues of contagion and prevalence), but also because of the now well-known advantages of focusing on systemic changes to improve prevention rather than the (requisite) individualised curatory approach.

While *ex post* ("curative") measures would be expected to be a component in any anti-corruption strategy, we argue that excessive focus on such *ex post* legal and institutional enforcement perspective, at the expense of *ex ante* preventive approaches will not be effective. And to design effective systemic changes, the understanding of the role of incentives would need to be elevated significantly. The in-depth focus on the **incentives** driving

---

[1] *Of course, other analysts have warned about the need to pause and think about the problem in some depth years ago. As cited in S. Kpundeh (1997), referring to an analysis of corruption in Africa by Olowu:*

"One of the reasons why governmental corruption has grown to be pervasive in Africa today is primarily because much effort has been spent to remedy the problem rather than to understand it". (Olowu, 1992).

Although the above statement refers specifically to Africa, rhetorical remedies to tackle corruption enacted without looking at the fundamentals have abounded in all regions of the world. The suggestion that it may be time to step back to analyse the root causes of corruption applies universally.

the various agents involved in a potentially corrupt activity leads to particular insights that have been underplayed so far, such as the general role of collective action with the partner business community, and the roles of deregulation, demonopolisation and well-implemented economic reforms.

The tenor of the anti-corruption rhetoric appears to be on the rise among governments in the North and South alike, often as lip service to the increasing activism of civil society, and to the more explicit determination of some in the international community to do something about it. This does not mean that there are no instances of serious efforts against corruption underway in some countries. But in the bandwagon of making pronouncements, passing decrees and creating special governmental anti-corruption units, there are many whose commitment to really address the problem is seriously in doubt.

Let us take the very recent case of Kenya, for instance, where the IMF suspended its lending in August 1997 due to the high prevalence and negative macro-economic consequences of corruption. In October, following mounting pressure from civil society and the international community, the President of Kenya issued pronouncements against corruption. As a follow-up to the President's remarks, the office of the Attorney General issued the following statement:

"The Government has this morning formed an anti-corruption squad to look into the conduct of the anti-corruption commission, which has been overseeing the anti-corruption task-force, which was earlier set to investigate the affairs of a Government ad hoc committee appointed earlier this year to look into the issue of high-level corruption among corrupt Government Officers." (Gado, page 6, The Daily Nation, *October 28, 1997).*

While this may be a particularly extreme example of how not to address the problem of corruption, in recent years many statements and decisions like this one can be compiled from press reports in countries in Asia, Latin America and the former Soviet Union. Unfortunately, when dressed in more sophisticated clothes, efforts like these are often times welcomed by some experts and officials in the international community. After all, the payoff for corrupt politicians engaging in rhetoric ostensibly aimed at "eliminating corruption" is rather high nowadays. And the pressures on the donor community to "show visible results" is also mounting.

Thus, one of the challenges at this juncture is to be able to distinguish between a seriously committed programme to control corruption, and politically convenient rhetoric, on the other. To do so, an understanding of the fundamental causes of corruption, as well as the preparedness and commitment of a government to tackle these fundamentals, is critical. Then, even if there is a sense of commitment to address the problem, the follow-up challenge is to ensure that the strategy design incorporates the appropriate elements, accounting for the *ex ante* role of incentives without undue focus on *ex post* stopgap remedial measures.

Hampering the struggle to control corruption is the emergence and existence of many misconceptions, biases and ambiguities regarding what constitutes the fundamental pillars in an anti-corruption strategy. Here we contribute to this debate by analysing some of these prevailing biases and misconceptions, by providing emerging evidence and results of data analysis on the main determinants of corruption, and by putting forth some principles for designing anti-corruption strategies. We attempt to focus squarely on the fundamentals that may determine the prevalence of corruption in a country – moving away from the (institutional or other) "quick-fixes" currently in vogue.

"Anti-Corruption Struggle": Major Crossroads Today

First, it is important to place the anti-corruption issue in perspective. Credit is due upfront: There has been an enormous success in the anti-corruption advocacy movement over the past few years. Awareness about the corruption problem is far more widespread nowadays, as is the involvement of civil society in many places. There is increasing willingness to take action by the international community in general and by some countries in particular. The role of domestic and international NGOs (such as Transparency International) has been key in raising awareness and involving civil society.

Yet the challenge of addressing corruption is now entering a crucial second stage: design and implementation of strategies and concrete actions which are likely to yield durable results. This requires looking in-depth at the **fundamental** causes of corruption, in an open-minded fashion. Just projecting mechanistically into the future from the successful *awareness-raising* advocacy approach of the recent past is likely to result in counter-productive "biases" during the *implementation* stage. These biases are likely to be compounded by the vested interest of some corrupt governments to *appear* active in addressing corruption and thus adopt politically palatable anti-corruption platforms. At this juncture, some of the major biases to guard against are described below.

• **Anti-Business bias.** Blaming business people has become a useful rationalisation. It stems from the "grease" (and "speed money") literature, as well as the notion of business lobbying interests against criminalisation of bribery abroad. Conventional wisdom is that the whole business sector benefits from its ability to bribe, as it gets around excessive regulations ("grease that oils the wheels of development"). Some even argue that business bribery is beneficial to development. This bias works against the logic of collective action and thus concerted action involving the business sector as an interested party.

• **Tackling-the-symptom bias** (vs. identification of fundamental root cause). For instance, the call to "catch and jail a target number of criminals", to pass another anti-corruption law in the country, etc. The pitfalls of single-mindedly trying to fight a symptom are not exclusive to addressing corruption, of course. There was a time in the past when governments would fight inflation by instituting price control commissions.

• **Ex post (vs. ex ante) bias.** Related to the biases towards tackling symptoms (above) and providing "quick fixes" (below), often for political gain, this bias favoring an excessive focus on institutional and legal enforcement approaches has been at the expense of focussing on the role of systemic changes in *ex ante* incentives to engage in corrupt activities.

• **Quick-fix bias** (vs. importance of indirect effects). It ought to be recognised that it is important to attain some concrete results soon within a pragmatic approach. This is, *inter alia*, important to maintain momentum by civil society. At the same time, there is a danger of counterproductive ("quick-and-dirty") interventions insufficiently thought through. The incentive structure for donors and governing domestic politicians is sometimes similar: to show some quick and visible measures (whether meaningful or not in terms of long-lasting results). But are they addressing the real fundamentals? And if the general public at first does not always clearly see these fundamentals as *directly* and *visibly* associated to corruption, will a bias against focusing on the less visible, more *indirect* (yet crucial) determinants of corruption emerge?

• **Injection bias** (vs. global climate change). Like the failed Development Finance Corporation's institutional response to the perceived lack of term credit in development in the seventies, we may face a similar danger

today in the work to control corruption: injection of resources for "greenfield stand-alone" institutional initiatives, such as watchdog bodies, new charters, etc., which may be detrimental to a more comprehensive change in the environment conducive to corruption.

• **Anti-Counterfactual bias.** Often, mistaken conclusions are derived from analysis devoid of proper counterfactuals and controls. Ascribing success to anti-corruption watchdog bodies in Botswana, Singapore and other heralded cases by focusing on the details of the watchdogs themselves, without considering the impact of fundamental reforms in the broader environment, is one example of this bias.

• **Prose bias** (vs. in-depth use of hard evidence, as input for real action). Long prose, proclamations, pronouncements, exhortations, declarations, conferences and communiqués against corruption abound nowadays. For action, it is imperative to move beyond raising awareness and focus on cold, in-depth analysis of the data and evidence at hand and the appropriate design and real implementation of programmes. In this context, it is a myth that data is virtually impossible to come by in this sensitive area.

• **Mechanistic toolkit bias** (vs. **tailor-making,** carefully considering the particularities of the types and main determinants of corruption in each setting). Recognition that both the forms of corruption as well as the relative importance of the various fundamental determinants of corruption vary across countries is vital in order to design programmes which are relevant to each particular setting.

• **Christmas tree bias** (vs. prioritisation – following identification of main causes of corruption in a country). This is a mistaken notion that an "ideal" programme ought to be so fine-tuned and comprehensive so as to contain many scores of measures and initiatives.

• **Anti-economic reforms bias.** It is often argued that economic reforms accentuate corruption. Others implicitly suggest that they are a neutral tool in addressing corruption: oftentimes in writings on corruption, economic reforms do not even appear in the long list of measures suggested to address the problem – or, when it is included, it is as an after-thought. This bias is related to the undue emphasis given to tackling the symptom and to quick-fixes, vs. addressing the fundamentals. Further, this anti-economic reforms bias has been fueled by insufficient attention to the role of incentives in understanding the prevalence of corruption and possible remedies.[2]

The "Grease" and "Speed Money" Arguments Empirically Challenged[3]

{The King} shall protect trade routes from harassment by courtiers, state officials, thieves and frontier guards...{and} frontier officers shall make good what is lost... Just as it is impossible not to taste honey or poison that one may find at the tip of one's tongue, so it is impossible for one dealing with government funds not to taste, at least a little bit, of the King's wealth.

—*From the treatise* The Arthashastra, *by Kautilya (chief minister to the king in ancient India), circa 300 B.C.–150 A.D.*

[2] *To be sure, there is an academic literature that has looked at the role of incentives (starting with Rose-Ackerman, 1978, and more recently Shleifer and Vishny, Ades and Di Tella, Besley, Root, Bardhan, and others). However, the role of incentives is still underplayed in empirical work, and particularly in the design of anti-corruption strategies.*

[3] *Much of the discussion in the next few sections is drawn from the author's recent piece in* Foreign Policy. *See also forthcoming paper by Kaufmann and Wei "Does 'Grease Money' Speed Up the Wheels of Commerce?"*

This citation attests to the ancient nature of corruption. Yet it also illustrates that even then corruption was regarded as corrosive to the development of the state and that specific measures were therefore needed in response. The king's adviser perceptively hinted at the link between illiberal trade, bureaucratic harassment at the border and corruption. And he understood that corruption encompassed far more than bribery: the theft of public revenues was explicitly addressed.

By contrast, in more recent times a revisionist view has held that corruption may not be inconsistent with development and at times may even foster it.[4] These contemporary versions wrap corruption in a cloud of ambiguity. Ambiguity, for example, is said to cloud corruption's meaning in different cultures, implying that what is viewed as corruption in the West would be interpreted differently within the customs of emerging economies. Ambiguity also characterises the revisionist assessment of corruption's effects on economic growth, fueled by the fact that some of the Asian tigers experienced until recently both phenomenal growth and high levels of corruption. Finally, ambiguity emerges in discussions of the effects of market reforms on corruption.

A central theme of the "grease-the-wheels" argument is that bribery can be an efficient way of getting around burdensome regulations and ineffective legal systems. This rationale has not only inspired sophisticated academic models but has legitimised the behavior of private companies that are willing to pay bribes to get business. On closer examination this argument is full of holes. First, it ignores the enormous degree of discretion that many politicians and bureaucrats can have, particularly in corrupt societies. They have discretion over the creation, proliferation and interpretation of counter-productive regulations. Thus, instead of corruption being the grease for the squeaky wheels of a rigid administration, it becomes the fuel for excessive and discretionary regulations. This is one mechanism whereby corruption feeds on itself.

In addition to some academic writings, one school of "corruption apologists" argues that bribery can enhance efficiency by cutting the considerable time needed to process permits and paperwork. The problem with this "speed money" argument lies in the presumption that both sides will actually stick to the deal, and there will be no further demands for bribes. In India, one high-level civil servant who had been bribed could not process an approval any faster given the multiple bureaucrats involved in the process, yet he willingly offered his services to slow the approval process for rival companies.

Even in societies where myriad counterproductive regulations have been created in order to extract bribes, there should be a core of laws and regulations that serve productive social objectives. Simple and transparent building codes, sensible environmental regulations, clear regulations to assure the soundness of the banking system and stringent regulations on the trading of nuclear materials are necessary in any society. The corruption "grease" argument is particularly insidious in this context, since bribes will serve to override such regulations and harm social aims.[5] For instance, illegal logging in tropical rainforests can be the result of illicit payments to officials. Another factor that contributes to bribery is politicians' discretion in limiting the access of potential competitors to the market of the briber – as in scandals in the energy sector in Russia and Ukraine. Unprecedented amounts of "grease"

[4] *In the late 1970s, Nathaniel Leff argued, for example, that "corruption may introduce an element of competition into what is otherwise a comfortably monopolistic industry....{and} payment of the highest bribes {becomes} one of the principal criteria for allocation....Hence, a tendency toward efficiency is introduced into the system." Likewise economist Francis Lui, in a 1985 issue of the Journal of Political Economy, asserted that "bribing strategies...minimise the average value of the time costs of the queue... {and the official}... could choose to speed up the service when bribery is allowed." See also the recent writings by Prof. David Li.*

in these cases strengthen gigantic monopolistic structures. The corrupt practices inherent in poorly supervised financial systems, as well as insider lending, have contributed to macroeconomic crises in Albania, Bulgaria, and, very recently, some countries in East Asia.

Are Poorer Countries Corrupt While Richer Countries are Clean?

"Cultural relativist" rationales that explain away the differences in corruption across countries are being discredited (and are seen as paternalistic). Even in traditional settings, the cultural norms of gift-giving are distinguishable from what would be regarded as abusive corrupt practices anywhere. The view that controlling corruption comes about only when a country is fully industrialized is also being challenged. While there is a correlation between the country's level of development and the degree to which it is experiencing administrative and bureaucratic corruption, it is also the case that there are large variations in the incidence of corruption among groups of countries at similar stages of development. The data goes even further: The Transparency International corruption index has ranked Chile, the Czech Republic, Malaysia, Poland, and South Africa as "cleaner" than industrialised countries such as greece and Italy. Further, these corruption perception indices focus on administrative/bureaucratic corruption and do not incorporate measures of political corruption (where some OECD countries do not fare very well); nor do they measure the propensity of industrialised countries' investors to bribe abroad.

More generally, the determinants of corruption in developing countries are manifold and complex. Institutions (including the rule of law and protection of property rights), civil liberties, governance (including the rule of law and protection of property rights), civil liberties, governance (including the degree of professionalisation of the civil service), and economic policies, as well as other specifics about the country (such as the country size) appear to matter, as suggested in our ongoing empirical research (Kaufmann and Sachs, forthcoming). Special emphasis in this chapter is given to the understanding the effects of economic policies on corruption, yet we underscore that other factors also play a very important role. Further, the economic and noneconomic factors are not independent of each other. For instance, the implementation of economic reforms often strengthens those constituencies that spearhead legal and institutional reforms.

Bribing and rent-seeking also exact a significant economic cost. Talent is misallocated, as the jobs with the potential to collect lucrative graft attract people who otherwise would accept the more modest financial rewards of truly productive occupations. Poor technological decisions are taken by corrupt bureaucrats, who tend to favor nonstandard, complex and expensive capital-intensive projects that make it easier to skim significant sums. A large defense or infrastructure contract may thus be favored over the construction of hundreds of primary schools and health

[5] *A sophisticated economic variation of the "grease is positive" argument is the notion that bribery allows supply and demand to operate. This view maintains that under competitive bidding for a government procurement contract the highest briber will win—and the lowest-cost firm will be able to afford the highest bribe. That is theoretically elegant, but wrong. First, by focusing solely on bribery, this argument fails to take into account that corruption represents a theft of public resources, impairing macroeconomic stability. And the recipient of the bribe will tend to siphon these funds into overseas accounts. Nigeria, for example, has seen billions siphoned out of its budget over the past decades. Second, it is wrong to presume that the highest bidding capability stems from cost-efficiency; instead, it is often associated with substandard quality. Furthermore, the politician rarely subjects the object of an illegal payoff to competitive bidding; rather, he will select whom to trust to get bribes discreetly, given the need for secrecy in the corrupt partnership. In Ukraine, a construction firm submitted a bid of US$10 per square meter for tiling a major public building; the official disqualified it immediately, because the contractor had "dared" to submit a bid for less than the "minimum" bidding cost of US$30 per square meter. The winner of the bid was hardly the most cost-effective firm! Further, viewing bribes as a mechanism for equalising supply and demand also misses the fact that many public goods ought not to be allocated to the highest bidder; the aim of antipoverty programmes is to allocate resources according to the needs of the recipients. Finally, the supply-and-demand view of corruption presumes that the briber gets the good once he has paid for it. This is often not the case, for corrupt transactions cannot be enforced through a court of law.*

clinics. Even more detrimental to development are the many unproductive "white elephant" projects that enrich public officials and suppliers – the recent commission of four incinerators in Lagos, none of which works properly, is one example. Further, enormous time is lost by entrepreneurs and officials engaged in corrupt activities. Queuing, negotiating, ensuring the secrecy of the deals and illicit payments and guarding against the ever-present risk of non-delivery of the promised signatures and permits are time-intensive activities – as is the frequent need to renegotiate or pay an additional bribe to another bureaucrat. All of these activities come at the expense of productively running firms and governments.

Indeed, evidence from various countries indicates that a positive relationship exists between the extent of bribery and the amount of time that an enterprise's manager spends with public officials. A 1996 enterprise survey showed that firm owners in Ukraine who pay high bribes have to spend almost one-third *more time* with bureaucrats and politicians than firm owners who pay little in bribes (Kaufman). Those high-bribing firms also need to spend 75 staff weeks per year of (nonowner) administration time in dealing with officials, as compared with a yearly average of 22 staff weeks for low-bribing firms. Moreover, using cross-country data for 3,000 firms in 59 countries we observe that in countries with *higher* incidence of bribery firms tend to spend a *higher* share of management time with bureaucrats (see Figure 1). Also, for the world at large, the evidence from over 1500 firms in 49 countries surveyed in 1996 is to the effect that where *bribing* is *more* prevalent, the costs of capital and investing for firms tend to be *higher* (Figure 2).[6]

Figure 1. Management Time Spent with Bureaucrats vs. Corruption

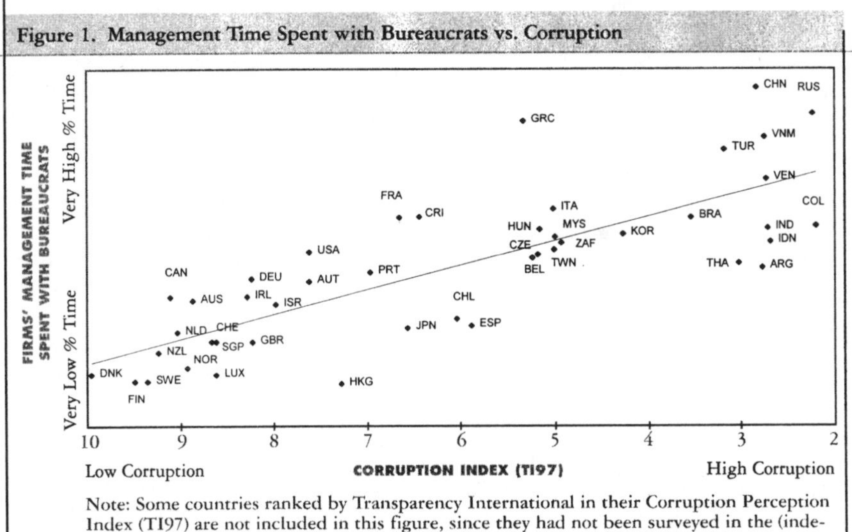

Note: Some countries ranked by Transparency International in their Corruption Perception Index (TI97) are not included in this figure, since they had not been surveyed in the (independent) data set on firms management time (from GCS97). Thus, this figure is not intended to reflect full rankings of either variable.

[6] *On the analytic and empirical details on the positive statistical association between cost of capital and management time spent with bureaucrats, on the one hand, and incidence of bribes, on the other (challenging the "grease" and "speed money" arguments), see Kaufmann and Wei, forthcoming.*

Figure 2. Cost of Capital vs. Bribery

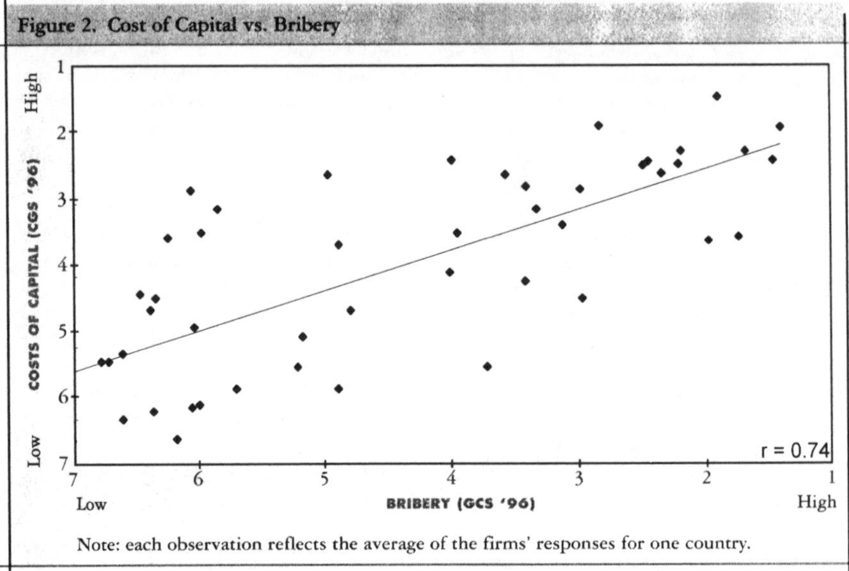

Note: each observation reflects the average of the firms' responses for one country.

In terms of understanding the complex interactions between regulatory interventions, regulatory discretion and the extent and costs of bribery, the data provides insights. From various data sets it is also calculated that in settings with higher regulatory and state-bureaucratic *interference* in business, the incidence of corrupt practices is significantly higher. Further, the higher the degree of regulatory *discretion*, the higher the incidence of bribery of officials (see Figure 3). Surveys carried out in some countries of the former Soviet Union show that *high* and *discretionary* regulations and taxes are associated with the need to pay high bribes in order to survive. That situation generates a high cost of doing business. Bribery as a strategy, on balance, does not reduce the firms' management time "captured" by local politicians and bureaucrats, nor does it reduce their costs of investing. To the contrary, bribery is fueled by bureaucratic discretion in imposing regulations, fees, licenses, taxes and tariffs.

Data and research showing the deleterious effects of corruption on growth have been mounting. A recent study found that a corrupt country is likely to achieve aggregate investment levels of almost 5 per cent less than a relatively uncorrupt country and to lose about half a percentage point of gross domestic product growth per year.[7] And there is evidence that corruption slows foreign direct investment; investing in a relatively corrupt country, as compared with an uncorrupt one, is equivalent to an additional 20 per cent ("private") tax on the investment.[8] The statistical relationship between corruption and lower foreign investment is valid across all regions. Contrary to conventional

[7] *Mauro (1996)*

[8] *Wei (1997)*

wisdom, there is no evidence that foreign investors are any less susceptible to corruption in East Asian economies than in other countries in the world.[9]

The evidence is therefore emerging quite clearly: Corruption is negatively associated with developmental objectives everywhere. Opportunistic bureaucrats and politicians who try to maximise their take without regard for the impact of such practices on the "size of the overall pie" may account for the particularly adverse impact corruption has in some countries of Africa, Asia and the former Soviet Union.[10] Indeed, surveying high-level officials from the public sector and civil society in emerging economies offers complementary evidence. Public sector corruption was rated as the most severe developmental obstacle facing their country, and no significant differences exist across regions. Everywhere, policy-making elites opined that corruption, far from being a lubricant of development, was a most formidable impediment to it (see last box and figures 5-7 in this paper).

Figure 3. Corruption Index vs. Regulatory Discretion

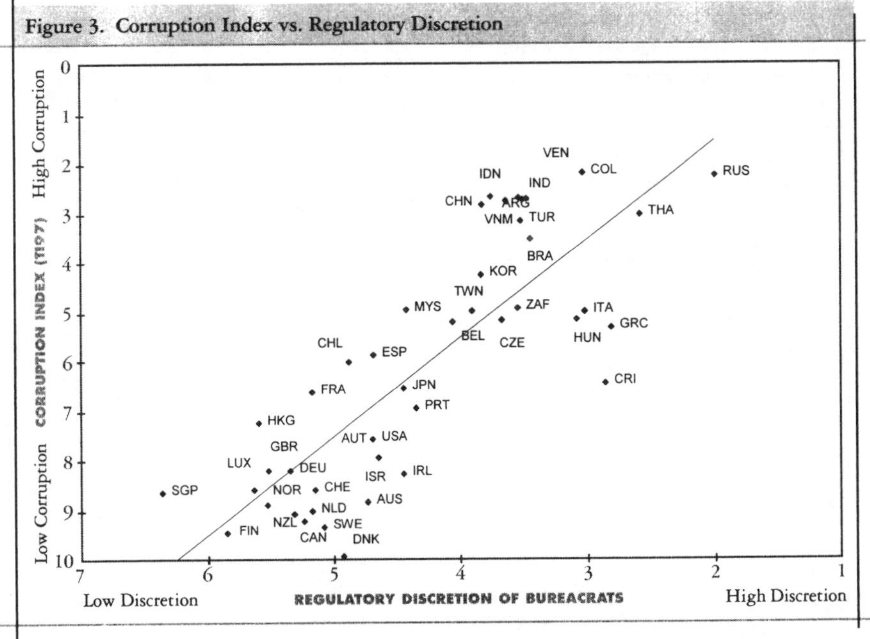

[9] *This finding also challenges the contention that the East Asian experience shows that corruption does not hurt investment and growth. That argument ignores the reality that corruption is only one of a number of factors explaining growth and development; even the few East Asian countries that are considerably corrupt have developed a credible rule of law, maintained decent macroeconomic management in the past, and prevented corrupt practices from encroaching on their export-oriented policies. Further, while they may have grown fast until recently, the Asian countries where corruption and vested interests permeated lending decisions, or more generally, encroached into the integrity of the financial sector and their balance of payments position, are now paying a very high macro-economic cost.*

[10] *Kaufmann, Daniel and Jeffrey Sachs, "Determinants of Worldwide Corruption" Forthcoming, 1998.*

Systemic Changes in Incentives: Do Reforms Fuel Corruption?

In recent years, academics and commentators in the mass media have argued that in transition economies (particularly in the countries of the former Soviet Union and Eastern Europe), and in some emerging country markets, liberalisation and privatisation have significantly increased corruption. They maintain that these reforms respond to the vested interests of corrupt élites. Even highly respected academics are ambivalent on this particular issue, advising extreme caution in initiating economic reforms when legal institutions are not yet well developed. And in the Winter 1996–97 issue of *Foreign Policy*, Robert Leiken wrote that "where corruption is systemic, market and administrative reforms ... may even become counter-productive ... Loosening government controls can facilitate illicit ... economic activity. Moreover, bureaucrats have been known to compensate for lost revenues by exacting new 'fees' in other areas".

The problem with such perspectives is that what passes for economic reform often is not. Half-baked, poorly designed, inadequately implemented market reforms may indeed boost corruption. Well-designed and properly executed market reforms do not. A public monopoly that, through obscure insider deals, becomes a private monopoly controlled by few uncontested shareholders (as happened in pre-reform Argentina) are certainly not an example of progress in the fight against corruption. Instead, a public monopoly, when demonopolised and followed by privatisation through an international, transparent bidding process, will improve matters. Thanks to deregulation and trade liberalisation, bureaucrats cannot extract as many bribes as before, and stiff competition will become less a source of corruption. Yet, lowering import tariffs does little to curb corruption if the rules that give customs officials the discretion to decide the amount of import tax on each container or to revoke an import permit are not changed. Further, counter-factuals are often ignored: analysts who see market reforms as sources of corruption often fail to consider the increasing amount of corruption that would occur in the absence of well-implemented economic reforms. A lack of economic reform can help to perpetuate

Figure 4. Unofficial Economy in Transition

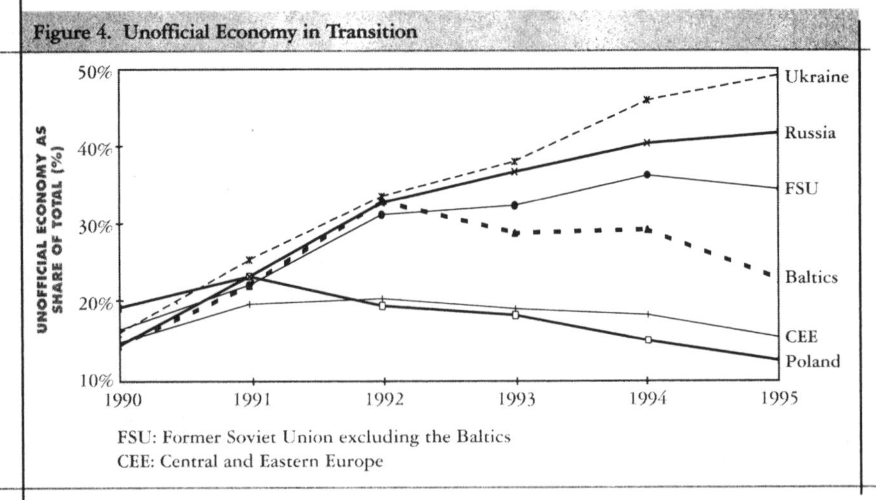

FSU: Former Soviet Union excluding the Baltics
CEE: Central and Eastern Europe

corruption, since élite interests become more entrenched as their financial might accumulates through monopolistic structures. In fact, this "war chest" becomes a major weapon to impede or distort reforms. Through this vicious circle, the costs of reform delays can increase substantially over time.

By contrast, fewer regulatory and trade interventions, macroeconomic stability, and moderate, simple tax regimes with little discretion will do much to reduce the opportunities for corruption. Evidence is found that less regulations, reduced regulatory discretion by bureaucrats and politicians, moderate, single and uniform tax regimes, trade openness and product competition reduce corruption. Survey responses from élites in emerging economies also reject the notion that economic reform fuels corruption. The vast majority of respondents report that corruption would be ameliorated by further economic reform in the areas of deregulation and liberalisation, the budget and the tax regime, and privatisation.

Market Reforms in Eastern Europe

Market reforms are frequently blamed for increased corruption in the former communist countries of Central and Eastern Europe. But with further empirical investigation of these economies a different picture emerges. While most of the economies in Central and Eastern Europe and the Baltics implemented far-reaching economic reforms (macrostabilisation, privatisation, liberalisation, deregulation and the development of market institutions) through the first half of the 1990s, many in the former Soviet Union (FSU) lagged behind. The extend of underground activities has diverged markedly. As illustrated in Figure 4 on the Evolution of the Unofficial Economy in Transition, countries that implemented comprehensive economic and institutional reforms have quickly reversed the initial boom in the underground economy when communism began to falter. At the same time, incomplete reforms that create either opportunities for discretionary decisions by government officials or monopolistic structures further fuel pre-existing corruption. This has been the experience of a number of countries in the FSU.

What has driven much of the economy underground in the less reformist economies? Enterprise surveys shed light on this question. Consider the share of the enterprise owner's (or senior manager's) time that is spend dealing with public officials instead of productively running their firms. In Chile, El Salvador and Uruguay, that share is 8 to 12 percent; in Lithuania, 15 percent; while in Russia and Ukraine (which have the largest unofficial economies in nonwar transition countries) it amounts to 30 to 40 percent of their time. The inordinate amount of time spent with officials is the result of the myriad regulations and licenses that are required for a firm to operate and trade. Considerable bargaining also occurs over highly discretionary and onerous tax regimes. Firms are forced to bribe in order to cut their tax and regulatory burdens – so they can survive.

Finally, empirical evidence indicates that privatisation can also help in the transition. Privatisation transactions have on balance been less corrupt than others (and some privatisation methods in particular have been found to result in less corruption over time), and most countries that delayed privatisation saw the relative size of their underground economy skyrocket.

Considering Incentive-driven Approaches to Control Corruption

The fatalist camp often points out the dearth of successes in anti-corruption drives. More generally, they stress that few countries have significantly reduced corruption in less than a century. Recently, Hong Kong and Singapore are countries that shifted – and quickly – from being very corrupt to being relatively clean. Much earlier, Britain needed many decades to improve its relatively corrupt structures.

Yet the *relative* successes are ignored in this absolutist approach to the issue: countries have managed to reduce the incidence of corruption relatively quickly, even if they are far from rendering it irrelevant. In addition to Hong Kong and Singapore, Botswana has shown improvements over the past dozen years or so; and the Philippines, Poland and Uganda, to name a few, have also scored some successes recently.

Anti-corruption Watchdog Institutions: Crucial substitutes to revamp of incentives?

What are the most common features of these successes? Anti-corruption bodies, such as the Independent Commission Against Corruption in Hong Kong and smaller institutional variations thereof in Botswana, Chile, Malaysia and Singapore are usually credited with much of the progress in fighting corruption. By contrast, often the broader and *complementary economic and institutional reforms* that have taken place simultaneously get insufficient credit. Indeed, countries like Uganda until recently may have exemplified relative success through a broader institutional approach: the Museveni government, which came to power in 1986, implemented a strategy that encompassed economic reforms and deregulation, reforming the civil service, strengthening the auditor general's office, empowering a reputable inspector general to investigate and prosecute corruption and implementing an anti-corruption public information campaign. More recently, however, with a tapering off in the broader institutional and economic reform arena it appears that corruption control has also suffered somewhat – in spite of the continuous valiant efforts of the reputable anti-corruption watchdog body. Similarly in Tanzania the courageous watchdog agency has not been able to ensure concrete progress on its own. And the case of Botswana appears to be an example of sound economic and public sector management policies early on, rather than the "later-in-the-day" advent of an anti-corruption agency.

The survey responses of elites in emerging economies provide a sobering perspective. Most respondents did not think highly of such anti-corruption bodies (see Figure 7). To be credible, they felt such institutions had to go hand in hand with a good example set by a honest leadership, and the need to be independent from political interference. Otherwise, anti-corruption bodies are easily rendered useless or, worse, misused for political gain. Further, respondents emphasised the importance of complementary economic reforms; there is no point in creating anti-corruption agencies where bureaucrats and politicians intervene at will to apply regulatory restrictions. This suggests that an in-depth analysis of the evidence on anti-corruption agencies in many countries which considers the broader institutional, public sector and economic environment (and utilises "counter-factuals" in the analysis) is long overdue, and may shed light consistent with the responses of the surveyed elites in emerging economies.

Indeed, the cleanup of the Philippine tax system in the 1970s, under the charismatic and squeaky-clean leadership of Judge Efren Plana, and the ongoing overhaul of Argentina's bloated social security system (ANSES) could be regarded as strong illustrations of effective institutional reform. In both cases the process included the immediate firing of corrupt personnel, the professionalisation of the staff, new control systems, and modern incentive and performance assessment systems. Even then, broader reforms played an important role. In the Philippines, tax reforms were implemented simultaneously with the institutional revamping of the bureau of internal revenue, tax rates were simplified and exemptions were significantly reduced. These measures severely curtailed the incentives and discretion to extract bribes. In the case of Argentina, competition is aiding in the internal cleanup and reform effort: ANSES is ceasing to be the state monopoly provider of social security; instead, private pension institutions are being set up.

Many of the other "institutional" success stories, in places such as Botswana, Chile, Hong Kong, Malaysia, Poland, Singapore and Uganda, have also involved economic liberalisation and reduced discretionary regulations. The much-heralded case of Singapore, for instance, often underplays the crucial economic liberalisation measures of the early-to-mid eighties, while the Hong Kong success in addressing police corruption must take into account the impact of legalisation of off-track betting.

The evidence emerging from some countries in the former Soviet Union is also telling. The leadership of Ukraine has repeatedly ordered various stand-alone "institutional" initiatives to address the corruption problem. New decrees have been passed, anti-corruption campaigns have been launched, and special units have been created. Yet at the same time economic regulations continue to proliferate. For instance, the Kiev province recently decreed that any firm selling goods within the fourteen counties of the province must have a special trading permit for such intra-province transactions. No anti-corruption drive can succeed in such a policy framework.

More Attention to Incentives, More Reform, Less Corruption

The evidence clearly points to promoting economic reform as a way of addressing corruption. The economic reform agenda in many countries is far from finished, and its anti-corruption potential often has been underemphasised and even maligned.

In designing reform programmes, it is important to identify the discretionary control

Figure 5. Respondents' View on Impediments to Development in their Countries

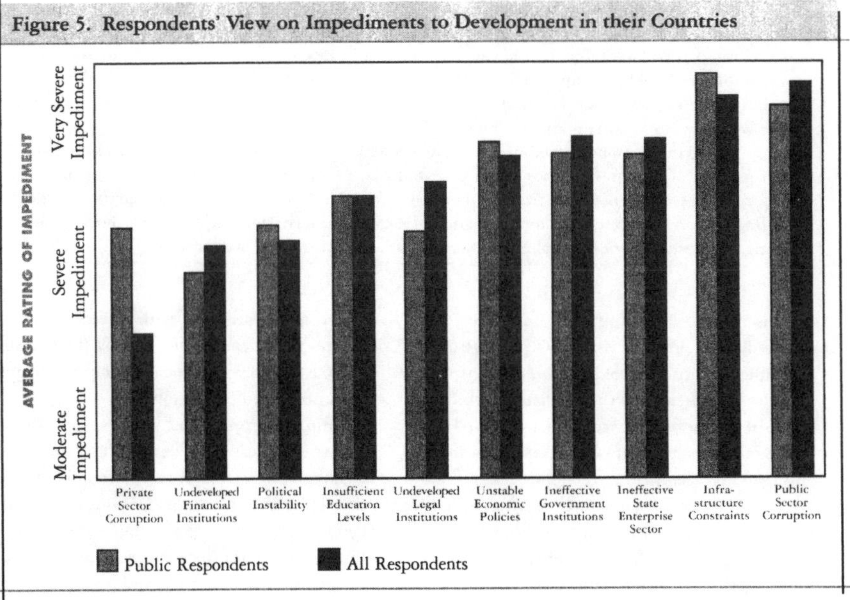

rights at the disposal of politicians and bureaucrats. The majority of politicians are clean, civic-minded citizens, but a significantly corrupt minority can take a large toll on an economy. Typically, the main activities in need of reform are those that involve discretion, including the issuance of licenses, permits, quantitative import restrictions (quotas), passports, customs and border-crossing documentation, and banking licenses; the implementation of price controls; the blocking of entry to new firms and investors and the provision of monopoly power; the awarding of public procurement contracts; the granting of subsidies, soft credits, tax exemptions and inflated pensions and the allowing of tax evasion; the imposition of foreign-exchange controls resulting in multiple exchange rates, the over-invoicing of imports and the flight of capital; the allocation of real estate, grain storage facilities, telecommunications and power infrastructure; the discretionary application of socially desirable regulations such as those that apply to public health and the environment; and the maintenance of obscure or secret budgetary accounts as well as other "leakages" from the budget to private accounts.

What Do Elites in Developing Countries Think About Corruption?

The author surveyed 150 members of the élite from 63 developing and formerly communist countries. Almost one-half of the respondents thought that corruption has increased in their country over the past 10 years, and another one-third believed that it had stayed roughly the same. Corruption in the public sector was seen as significantly more prevalent than in the private sector. When asked to rate the severity of possible impediments to development and growth in their country among a list of 11 choices, public sector corruption was rated as the most severe obstacle (see Figure 5).

The survey respondents support the notion that corruption and lack of economic reform go hand in hand. They are of the view that their country ought to have made more progress in implementing economic reforms, and they blame corrupt interests as one important reason for inaction (Figure 6). At the same time, they believe that economic reforms – particularly deregulation and liberalisation, modernising the budget and the tax regime, and privatisation – can play a key role in alleviating corruption (see Figure 7).

While the respondents emphasised the domestic causes of corruption, many also regard the propensity of foreign investors and traders to bribe in their countries as at least as great a problem. A majority believes that OECD member states should implement anti-corruption measures targeting their traders and investors abroad, and also that international institutions should make curbing corruption a priority and a precondition of assistance to their countries.

The discretionary control rights of officials can be sharply curtailed through a package of economic reforms. Where some regulations ought to stay because of their social desirability, transparent market mechanisms can be used to limit abuses (auctions of pollution quotas, for example). Yet many other economic regulations need to disappear altogether. Conventional economic reforms can have a significant impact via macroeconomic stabilisation, which removes the discretion to provide subsidies and soft credits; via privatisation, with its depoliticisation of state-owned enterprises; and by the building of a constituency that favours competition and broad market liberalisation. Yet simply reforming macroeconomic policies is insufficient. Further emphasis must be placed on fuller liberalisation, microeconomic deregulation, tax reform (creating a simple and non-discretionary regime, with moderate and uniform tax rates, eliminating exemptions and with determined enforcement), government and budget reform

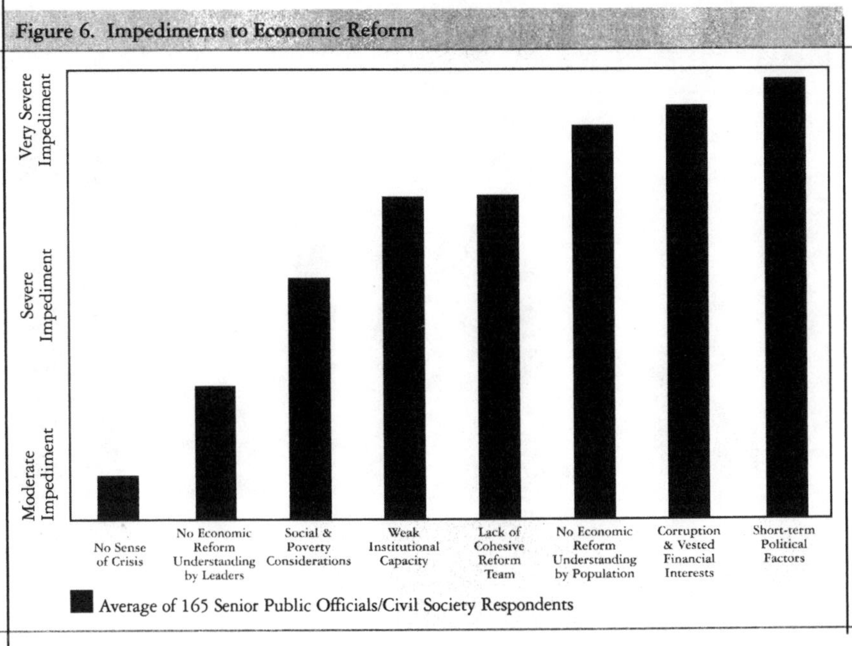

Figure 6. Impediments to Economic Reform

(establishing transparent, financially sound revenue and expenditure mechanisms), and, over the long haul, broader institutional reform (revamping customs and eliminating redundant ministries and agencies) and civil service and legal reform. Setting up an improved civil service pay system, with adequate salary incentives and enforceable penalties for malfeasance, is also critical. Countries that have established a system of rewards for civil servants that are competitive with the private sector have also reduced corruption. Many countries also need to give additional focus to developing the financial sector, because market-determined interest rates, improved banking supervision by independent central banks, transparent accounting standards, reserve-requirement compliance (where owners put their own equity at real risk) and effective payment systems all reduce the opportunities for fraud-driven financial crises. They also limit the loopholes through which money-laundering grows out of control.

These pillars of the next stage of reform – government and regulatory reform – have been neglected in many developing and transition economies. The "state of the art" in these fields is not as advanced as in macrostabilisation or trade liberalisation, where the "jury has long passed a verdict" on what to do and how to do it. Along with recognising that corruption is a symptom of deep-seated institutional and economic fundamentals, emerging countries and the international community need to elevate the priority of these reform areas. The payoff on these difficult and time-consuming measures will be substantial: virtually all economic, deregulation and government-reform measures would help not only to curb corruption but also to sustain national growth strategies.

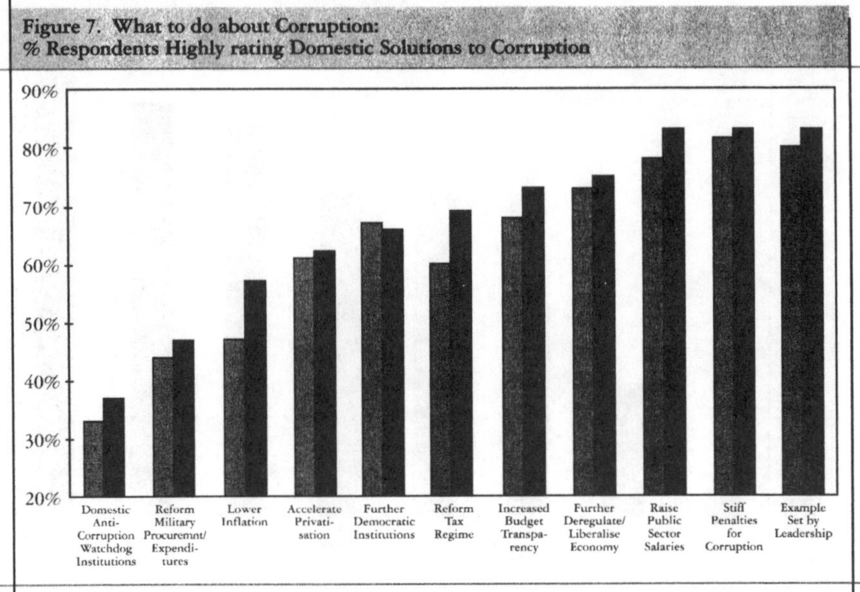

Figure 7. What to do about Corruption: % Respondents Highly rating Domestic Solutions to Corruption

Implications for Design and Implementation of Anti-Corruption Strategies

In terms of the specific details of an anti-corruption strategy in a particular country, we refrain from providing long lists of solutions. The field is still in its infancy in understanding the fundamental causes of corruption and is distilling incipient lessons from experience of what works and what doesn't. Furthermore, the specifics of an anti-corruption strategy may vary significantly from setting to setting. Nonetheless, while the ongoing learning process is underway, some implications and principles for the design of anti-corruption strategies emerge. We briefly put these forth next.

The Underutilised Potential of Evidence and Data Analysis

It is increasingly evident that for a rigorous anti-corruption programme design, which is responsive to country specifics, it is imperative to gather and analyse in-depth country-specific data, as well as lessons from a comparative perspective. Data related to corruption exists, and for a country-specific, in-depth focus, further information can be gathered through appropriate survey tools, for the specific setting under review.

A. Types of data on corruption and bribery

Depending on the particular setting being studied, and whether the corruption issue is to be analysed comparatively across countries or more in-depth within one country, different approaches to data gathering and analysis will be called for. A number of tools are at the disposal of the analyst nowadays.

a. **Firm-level surveys:** both cross-country comparative business surveys on perception of bribery and corruption, and country-specific in-depth surveys gathering hard data on bribery and its correlates.

b. **Service delivery surveys.**
c. **Citizen polls.**
d. **Indices based on expert assessments.**
e. **Procurement prices** of standard and essential publicly provided good: generic medicine; standard school lunch.
f. **Balance of payment** analysis: official exports statistics vs. data from importing country.
g. **Unofficial/Black Economy** estimates.
h. **Composite Corruption Perception Index such as with Transparency International (TI).**

Each tool has its own advantages and drawbacks, and requires some expertise in question design, eliciting reliable answers and data, and data interpretation and analysis.

B. Data on potential variables determining corruption in a particular country

Equally important is to gather information and perform analysis on the main correlates of corruption within a country (and comparatively as well). Among the key variables needed for the analysis:

a. Rule of law and protection of property rights
b. Regulations/regulatory discretion/ bureaucratic red tape
c. Economic policies
d. Political variables (fracture politics, length of leader in power, democracy, etc.)
e. Civil Liberties (and ability of civil society to play a role)
f. Professionalism and incentives of civil service
g. Education/literacy
h. Natural resources
i. Size
j. Ethnolinguistic fragmentation
k. Income per capita
l. Income distribution
m. Financial and accounting systems

Conclusions: Some Principles in Design of Anti-Corruption Programmes

From our analysis, some design principles emerge, which shy away from tailor-made tool kits to be applied in any setting, and also deviate from exclusive focus on *ex post* legal and institutional detection and enforcement measures.

A. **Forms of corruption vary** from country to country: Identify the most important types and forms of corruption for an action programme relevant to a particular country.

B. **Determinants of corruption vary:** Even for a given form of corruption, the importance of different *determinants* will vary from setting to setting. Country-specific understanding is imperative.

C. **Focus on priorities and fundamentals:** Identification of a *small* number of key fundamental determinants of main types of corruption in the country (vs. "Christmas Tree" approach) for implementation in the short-to-medium term. It may be warranted to implement a "20/80" identification approach: which 20% of key measures upfront may deliver (close to) 80% of results? Too often the reverse has been the case; a large number of (non-fundamental) measures delivering meager results.

D. **A Role for a complementary "injection"?:** Where fundamentals are seriously tackled, a selective complementary intervention (such as a watchdog body or a new Charter) *may* make sense if appropriate circumstances are in place (vs. such stand-alone interventions without tackling the fundamentals). It will be vital to identify the intervention (or institutional initiative) which best complements the reforming of fundamentals (under C above).

E. Temporary **"amnesia" about corruption could be useful?**: The Underestimated Power of Indirect Measures. The importance of stepping back and taking distance from corruption-as-a-symptom-of-weakness in the state, and reviewing what the main determinants for weak statehood in a particular setting are, ought to be emphasised. Reform of the Public Sector and Public Finances, as well as improved civil liberties of financial regulations, would be examples of the power of addressing the problem of corruption indirectly.[11]

F. **Open-minded policy advice:** Some of the conventional economic policy advice given in the past needs revisiting. Tax policy is prime example: reduction to more moderate rates, simplicity, uniformity, elimination of discretion, exemptions, loopholes, etc. if needed in many settings. Further, the powerful and complex role of *incentives* in addressing corruption needs to be emphasised more.

G. **Logic of collective action:** It is in the interest of various stakeholders, including the business sector, for collective action credibly pre-committing against bribing. This has concrete implications for policy formulation, such as non-bribery pledges, criminalisation of bribery abroad, etc.

H. **Innovation on public procurement, project execution and concessions:** Role of Incentives, and Price Surveys and Audits. New methodological approaches to procurement need to be explored and are likely to offer large benefits in ameliorating corruption. The important role of incentives in eliciting transparent bidding processes (and without obscure posterior "renegotiations") is also important in the context of public procurement.

I. **Continuing innovations of civil society in helping implement anti-corruption strategies:** Civil society, wherever it is active, is likely to be a major ally in resisting corruption, as eivdenced in the recent successes of some NGOs. However, there are many settings where civil society has not been allowed to operate. Furthering civil liberties in these countries will be important. At the same time, in a number of settings where civil society has been active, misguided advocacy has not necessarily been conducive to action on the fundamental roots of corruption. Calls for conviction of a particular politician may be a useful complement to a broad-based anti-corruption strategy, but in itself it will accomplish little. Therefore, at this juncture it may be wise to engage in an open-minded discourse with civil society on some prevailing (and potentially harmful) "biases", "myths" and misconceptions that have emerged in addressing corruption. In particular, the role of civil society in diagnosing and raising awareness of the sources and forms of corruption (i.e. through the implementation of service delivery or similar governance surveys) in their country ought to be supported.

In concluding, we emphasise the common denominator throughout the empirical and strategic suggestions provided to address corruption: better understanding and incorporation into anti-corruption strategies of the role of *incentives*, and further focus on systemic changes that alter *ex ante* such incentives to engage in corrupt practices.

[11] *Indeed, we would expect that as an increased awareness of the importance of the literature and empirics of the "corruption-as-symptom" approach takes hold, and thus additional focus is given on the fundamental roots behind corruption, the field of public economics will increasingly incorporate concepts, models and empirics from the corruption literature.*

References

Ades, Alberto and Rafael di Tella. "The Causes and Consequences of Corruption: A Review of Recent Empirical Contributions." IDS Bulletin, 27, no. 2, 1996.

Anderson, Annelise. "The Red Mafia: A Legacy of Communism," in Lazear, Edward P., (ed.) *Economic Transition in Eastern Europe and Russia: Realities of Reform*, Stanford, CA: The Hoover Institution Press, 1995.

Brunetti, A. G. Kisunko, et al. "Institutional Obstacles to Doing Business." Region-by-region results from a worldwide survey of the private sector," World Bank Policy Research Working Paper, No. 1759, 1997.

The Daily Nation (newspaper), October 28, 1997. Nairobi, Kenya

Frydman, Roman and Andrzej Rapaczynski. "Markets and Institutions in Large-Scale Privatisation." *In Reforming Central and Eastern European Economies*, edited by V. Corbo, F. Coricelli, and J. Bossak, The World Bank, 1991.

Frydman, Roman, Cheryl W. Gray, and Andrzej Rapaczynski (eds.). "Capitalism with a Comrade's Face," *Corporate Governance in Central Europe and Russia*, Budapest: Central European Press, 1996.

Frye, Timothy and Andrei Shleifer. "The Invisible Hand and the Grabbing Hand." *American Economic Review*, 1997.

Grossman, Sanford J. and Oliver D. Hart. "The Costs and benefits of Ownership: A Theory of Vertical and Lateral Integration." *Journal of Political Economy,* 94:691-719 (1986).

Hart, Oliver D. and John Moore. "Property Rights and the Nature of the Firm." *Journal of Political Economy*, 98:1119-1159 (1990).

Huntington, Samuel P. *Political Order in Changing Societies*, New Haven: Yale University Press, 1968.

Johnson, Simon, Daniel Kaufmann, and Pablo Zoido-Lobaton. "Corruption and the Unofficial Economy." *American Economic Review* (AEA) 1998 Proceedings forthcoming.

Johnson, Simon, Daniel Kaufmann, and Andrei Shleifer. "The Unofficial Economy in Transition." Brookings Panel on Economic Activity, Washington, D.C., 1998.

Johnston, M. "Cross-Border Corruption: Points of Vulnerability and Challenges for Reform" UNDP-PACT and OECD Development Centre Workshop on Corruption and Integrity Improvement Initiatives in the Context of Developing Economies, Paris, 1997.

Kaufmann, Daniel. 1997. "The Missing Pillar of a Growth Strategy for Ukraine: Institutional and Policy Reforms for Private sector Development." In *Ukraine: Accelerating the Transition to Market*, ed. P. Cornelius and P. Lenain, International Monetary Fund: Washington.

Kaufmann, Daniel and Jeffrey Sachs. "Determinants of Worldwide Corruption," forthcoming (1998).

Kaufmann, Daniel. "Corruption: The Facts," in *Foreign Policy*, Summer 1997, Washington, D.C.

Kaufmann, Daniel. "Accelerating Ukraine's Transition to a Market Economy: Credible Macroeconomic Adjustment and Systemic Reforms" (Presentation to IMF/World Bank Seminar, Washington: July 9, 1996)

Kaufmann, Daniel and Paul Siegelbaum. "Privatisation and Corruption in Transition Economies." *Journal of International Affairs*, 50(2): 419-458 (1997).

Klitgaard, Robert. *Controlling Corruption.* Berkeley, CA: University of California Press, 1988.

Kpundeh, Sahr J. "Political Will in Fighting Corruption." UNDP-PACT and OECD Development Centre Workshop on Corruption and Integrity Improvement Initiatives in the Context of Developing Economies, Paris, 1997.

Leff, Nathaniel. "Economic Development Through Bureaucratic Corruption." *American Behavioral Scientist*, 1976.

Leiken, Robert "Controlling the Global Corruption Epidemic," in *Foreign Policy*, Winter, 1996-1997.

Malia, Martin. "The Nomenklatura Capitalists: Who's Running Russia Now?" *The New Republic* 212(21): 17-22 (1995).

Mauro, Paolo. "Corruption and Growth." *The Quarterly Journal of Economics*, 1996.

Rose-Ackerman, Susan. "Corruption and Development." Paper presented at the World Bank ABCDE Conference, 1997.

Wei, Shang-Jin. "How Taxing is Corruption on International Investors." Unpublished manuscript, 1997.

World Development Report. *The State in a Changing World.* The World Bank, Washington, D.C., 1997.

[4]

The Role of a National Integrity System in Fighting Corruption[1]

Structural adjustment focused attention on the need for more effective and efficient public service institutions and use of public resources. The post-structural adjustment era has seen this effectiveness and efficiency linked to a number of other issues: (a) to capacity development where state institutions without the requisite capacity and expertise cannot adjust to a market economy; (b) to results-oriented management, emphasizing the importance of monitoring performance and measuring results; and (c) to public participation in the adjustment process, underscoring the need to tap into the valuable resources and creativity of civil society, while at the same time helping to strengthen the political legitimacy of the state.

A significant issue, however, has been ignored until recently: the promotion of national integrity (see Diagram 1). All of these issues—capacity development, results orientation, public participation, and the promotion of national integrity—need to be addressed holistically if the delivery of public services is to be both efficient and effective and is to contribute to sustainable development. It is the thesis of this paper that the promotion of national integrity is an integral part of this process since corruption inhibits the performance of public institutions and the optimal use of resources. As this paper explains, levels of national integrity need to be enhanced, and corruption reduced, if efforts to promote sustainable and equitable development are not to be undermined.

Corruption engenders wrong choices. It encourages competition in bribery, rather than in quality and price of goods and services. It inhibits the development of a healthy marketplace. Above all, it distorts economic and social development and nowhere with greater damage than in developing countries. Too often, corruption means that the world's poorest must pay for the corruption of their own officials and of companies from developed countries, although they are least able to afford its costs. Moreover, available evidence shows that if corruption is not contained, it will grow. Once a pattern of successful bribes is institutionalized, corrupt officials have an incentive to demand larger bribes, engendering a "culture" of illegality that in turn breeds market inefficiency.[2]

The argument is not simply a "moral" or "cultural" one. Forms of grand corruption need to be contained for practical reasons. Faced with the challenge of maintaining or improving standards of living, no country can afford the inefficiency that accompanies corruption. Emerging democracies, in particular, brave considerable political risks if corruption is not contained, as the corrupt can greatly weaken the authority and capacity of the fledgling state. While apologists for corruption may argue that corruption can help grease the wheels of a slow-moving and over-regulated economy, evidence indicates that it increases the costs of goods and services, promotes unproductive investments, and leads to a decline in the quality of infrastructure services.[3]

2 *Petter Langseth, Rick Stapenhurst, and Jeremy Pope*

Diagram 1: Capacity Building, Results Orientation, and Integrity: The Building Blocks for Improved Public Service Delivery

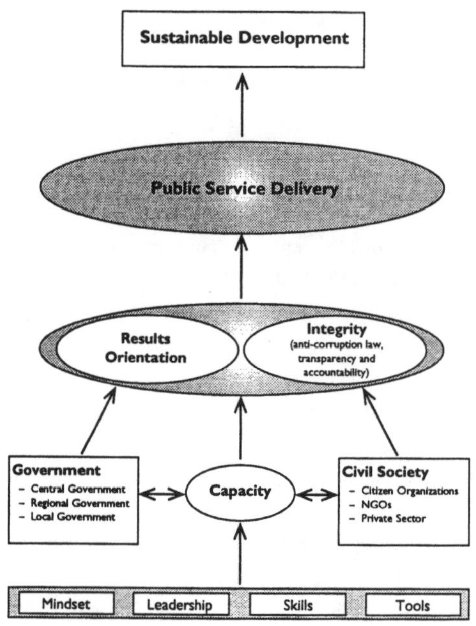

Corruption reports unfold in the news media on a daily basis and clearly demonstrate that it is not something that is exclusively, or even primarily, a problem of developing countries. Recent events in Europe and North America have shown all too clearly that corruption is not a topic on which the developed countries have any moral high ground.

Corruption depends on three factors: the overall level of public benefits available, the risk inherent in corrupt deals, and the relative bargaining power of the briber and the person being bribed.[4] As a single transaction, corruption takes place where there is a meeting of opportunity and inclination. The strategies to contain it, therefore, should address both elements. Opportunities can be minimized through systematic reform, and inclination reduced through effective enforcement and deterrent mechanisms.

Such mechanisms, when designed as part of a national effort to reduce corruption, comprise an integrity system. This system of checks and balances, designed to manage conflicts of interest in the public sector, limits situations in which conflicts of interest arise or have a negative impact on the common good. This involves both prevention and penalty. An integrity system embodies a comprehensive view of reform, addressing corruption in the public sector through government processes (leadership codes, organizational change) and through civil society participation (the democratic process, private sector, media). Thus, reform is initiated and supported not only by politicians and policy makers, but also by members of civil society.

After offering some definitions and examining conceptual issues, this paper analyzes the main costs of corruption and the reasons for its existence and growth. The balance of the paper outlines the principal elements of a national integrity system founded on a holistic approach bringing together various methods and actors. Insights gleaned from joint EDI/Transparency International workshops held in Uganda, Tanzania, and Jordan contribute substantially to this paper; in these workshops participants sought to identify key actors in the promotion of national integrity.[5] The paper concludes by reflecting on ways of managing anti-corruption efforts.

The nature of societies and the challenges they face vary greatly. An integrity system requires country-specific design.

1. What is Corruption?

Corruption is, in its simplest terms, the abuse of entrusted power for personal gain or for the benefit of a group to which one owes allegiance. The word "corruption" is commonly applied to situations of dishonesty in general, but for the purposes of this paper, "corruption" involves behavior on the part of officials in the public sector, whether politicians or civil servants, in which they improperly and unlawfully enrich themselves or those close to them by the misuse of the public power entrusted to them.[6]

Corruption may be divided into two categories: "petty," or survival, corruption practiced by civil servants who may be grossly underpaid and depend on small rents from the public to feed their families and pay school fees, and the "grand corruption" of high public officials who make decisions involving large economic rents.

Corruption occurs in all countries, regardless of levels of social and economic development. In general, it is most likely to occur where public and private sectors meet, and especially where public officials have a direct responsibility for the provision of a public service or the application of specific regulations or levees. This includes, for example, public procurement and contracting, licensing activities, such as the granting of import or export permits, and the rezoning of land and the collection of revenue, whether through taxation or customs duties.

For corruption to take place, the following elements must be present: a public official, discretionary power, a misuse of that public power by the public official, and a benefit (whether in money or in kind) resulting to that official.[7] There are two general cases: the first where services or contracts are provided "according-to-rule"; the second where transactions are "against-the-rule." In the first situation, an official receives private gain illegally for doing something which he or she is ordinarily required to do by law (a phenomenon often described as "grease" payments as they expedite a procedure that would have been carried out any way). In the second situation, the bribe is paid to obtain services which the official is prohibited from providing (e.g., granting contracts that would not otherwise be awarded).[8] Each situation requires different solutions, investigated below in Section 4.

The significance and impact of corruption varies considerably across the world. In this regard, it is often suggested that corruption is part of the "culture" of many countries ("cultural relativism"). Yet, the fact people in a particular country may tolerate demands for small payments in return for official services (e.g., the issuing of permits, licenses) does not necessarily imply that they approve of it; it may simply be that they "perceive it as the most workable way of obtaining things they want or need...[a] perception that may gradually be undermined by rising prices... or dashed more abruptly if consumers come to believe that the underlying scarcities are artificially contrived or that more desirable alternative processes are really possible."[9]

In some cases, corruption may reflect practices introduced to a culture by external influences.[10] Some Asian countries might be beset by corruption, yet certain historians have noted that this phenomenon originated, nor with the locals, but with the colonizing Dutch East India company. The company's men "were underpaid and exposed to every temptation that was offered by the combination of a weak native organization, extraordinary opportunities in trade, and an almost complete absence of checks from home or in Java...Officials became rich by stealing from the company."[11] The same author writes, "Corruption was introduced into [the Philippines] during the Spanish colonial period." In Singapore after World War II, "the British Army officers in charge of local purchases had probably never before been exposed to the type of temptations ...whatever resistance there was in them melted away with mercurial speed."[12] See also Yoong Siew-Yah (1973).

There are significant differences in perceptions and practices between various cultures. What some accept as reasonable and appropriate will differ widely. These differences, however, may have more to do with how business is conducted (through the giving of presents and of hospitality) than with attempts to "buy" favorable decisions. There is a clear distinction between "reciprocity" and reciprocities classified as bribes.[13]

2. The Costs of Corruption

At the conceptual level, there are many costs associated with corruption. However, it is hardly surprising that there is little hard evidence on the incidence and magnitude of corruption. Surveys of businesspeople indicate that the problem varies widely across countries and that even within countries, some public agencies (for example, customs and tax collection) are more prone to corruption than others. Surveys also indicate that, where corruption is endemic, it imposes a disproportionately high cost on small businesses.[14] Most important, the heaviest cost is typically not in the bribes themselves but rather in the underlying economic distortions they trigger.[15]

Once a pattern of successful payoffs is institutionalized, corrupt officials have an incentive to raise the size of bribes demanded and to search for alternative ways to extract payments. Officials may refuse to serve clients unless a bribe is paid. They may design a major procurement project at too large a scale and with too much specialized equipment as a way of generating large bribes and keeping them hidden. They may accept payments to reveal secret information on tenders and privatization projects and to favor insiders. All of these examples risk imposing large costs on society.

2.1 Market Misallocation and Inefficiency

There are many costs associated with corruption. It produces market inefficiency because the need to pay bribes is an entry barrier to the market. This point is well summarized by David Gould and Jose Amaro-Reyes, who state that:

> Corruption, it is also argued, leads to economic inefficiency and waste, because of its effect on the allocation of funds, on production, and on consumption. Gains obtained through corruption are unlikely to be transferred to the investment sector, for example, as ill-gotten money is either used in conspicuous consumption or is transferred to foreign bank accounts. Such transfers represent a capital leakage to the domestic economy. Furthermore, corruption generates allocative inefficiency...corruption lowers the general welfare of the populace. Finally, the gains from corruption tend to draw labor away from productive, non-cor-

rupt activities. Moreover, since corruption affects recruitment and promotion patterns, the most efficient employees may not be recruited at all and the allocation of positions may be inefficient.

Based on an analysis of benefits and costs, they conclude corruption "...has a deleterious effect on administrative efficiency and political economic development.[16] Corruption introduces other kinds of inefficiencies into public sector contracting. Such costs of corruption can be summarized in three categories:

a) Waste of resources:

- if corruption takes the form of a kickback, it serves to diminish the total amount available for public purposes.
- corruption results in a substantial loss in productive effort: the prospect of payoffs can lead officials to create artificial scarcity and red tape.
- corruption represents a rise in the price of administration (the taxpayer must pick up the costs of bribery).

b) Distortion of allocation:

- corruption causes decisions to be weighed in terms of money, not human need. Public housing, for instance, is designed for the poorest families, not those who can pay the most.
- a corrupt act represents a failure to achieve public sector objectives (e.g., corruption in appointments induces inefficiency and waste; corruption in the allocation of scarce university places results in best use not being made of a scarce opportunity, etc.).

c) Failure to lead by example:

- perceived by the people, corruption in government lowers respect for constituted authority and so the legitimacy of government; moreover, if the elite politicians and senior civil servants are widely believed to be corrupt, the public will see little reason why they, too, should not misbehave.[17]

Recent econometric research suggests there is a negative association between high levels of corruption and economic growth.[18] Case study materials from around the world indicates that illegal payoffs can increase the cost and lower the quality of public works projects sometimes by as much as 30–50 percent.[19]

It is extremely difficult to calculate the economic damage produced by corruption owing to the secrecy surrounding illicit payments systems. Initial studies suggest that corruption-related costs to the world economy have reached significant levels, estimated at several billions of US dollars per year.[20] Other sources, however, sug-

Box 1: A Cemetery of White Elephants...

"A cemetery of white elephants, still-born projects and drained of funds, Africa is larded with abandoned motorways eaten away by the savannah, factories that went down the drain barely a year after opening, rail lines impassable due to a lack of maintenance, hydroelectric dams that have been abandoned owing to non-profitability." I. Remil Godeau in *Jeune Afrique*, July 1994.

As Dieter Frisch, former Director General of Development of the European Commission, notes, "[t]here are ruins of factories in the name of development all over Africa that either never began operation or never achieved economic utilization of their capacities, or else operated at a loss that forced the state to subsidize them. When one traces the entire network through, it is discovered in a majority of cases that the state structure protects the unprofitable operations. There is more than a presumption of corruption because for what other reason could such anti-developmental decisions have been taken?" From Frisch (1994), "The Effects of Corruption on Development."

gest that these estimates are very conservative, and speculate that the "commissions" paid by arms dealers alone to be at least US$2 billion a year.[21] They also report that French revenue authorities do not questions commissions of up to 15 percent of the global total of a contract.[22]

Dieter Frisch, former Director-General of Development at the European Commission, has observed that because corruption raises the cost of goods and services, it may contribute to the debt of a country (and carries with it recurring debt-servicing costs). Sub-standard goods are provided and inappropriate or unnecessary technology is acquired as a result of corruption. As a consequence, when a country increases its indebtedness to carry out projects that are not economically viable, the additional debt includes not merely the 10–20 percent extra cost due to corruption; rather the entire investment, all 100 percent, can be attributed to dishonest decisions to proceed with unproductive and unnecessary projects[23] (see Box 1).

In a corrupt environment, resources may be directed towards non-productive areas—the police, the armed forces and other organs of social control—as the elite move to protect themselves, their positions and their material wealth. Resources otherwise available for socio-economic development will be diverted into security expenditure. This in turn can cause the weakening of market institutions as rent-seeking, rather than investment, be comes the major objective of policymakers.

3. Why Corruption Flourishes

The sources of corruption are numerous and complex. Poverty, some say, is at the root of the problem; without poverty there would be no corruption. But even if poverty is an underlying cause, it cannot be the only one. If poverty were the cause of corruption, then it would be hard to explain why industrialized countries are beset by scandals, very few of which involve anyone who might be categorized as "poor."

Corrupt leaders unquestionably deepen the poverty of their people. Public expenditure decisions are fueled by private gain and subsidized by bribes with scant regard for the good of the country or its people. Corruption can thus be seen as a cause of poverty, not only a result of it.

In the poorest countries—often those with corrupt elites—there is a manifest failure by government to pay a living wage to public servants. Frequently the state is wholly unable to afford to do so. Thus, as is described in further detail below, inadequate remuneration for public officials is widely regarded as being a contributing cause of corruption at least at the petty level, if not throughout the system.[24]

3.1 Systemic Bureaucratic Corruption

Systemic corruption occurs where corruption has become an integral part of the system, that is, the system cannot function without it. Systemic corruption is the nemesis of anti-corruption reformers, and a new government may find itself impotent in reforming the very system it must rely on to govern.

This type of ingrained corruption tends to flourish in situations where public sector wages fall below a living wage (see Box 2). Several consequences can ensue. First, civil servants cease to place any value on the job they hold. Individuals may feel forced to augment their income from outside sources (second jobs, absenteeism, moonlighting). Second, if the salary differentials from promotions are low, any salary increase would be unlikely to reflect adequately the work and responsibility that accompany such a promotion. This leads to low motivation for merit-based advancement.

Third, unnecessary or extended foreign travel may be undertaken by government elites. Windfalls coming from foreign travel are seen as an unofficial (and tax free) way of bringing in come up to an acceptable level. Fourth, "ghosts" will appear on the state payroll. Persons who are deceased or retired will continue to be paid, and fictitious names will appear so that as much as a quarter of those on the public payroll are actually non-existent.[25]

These four categories of behavior can be regarded as petty corruption. No one is getting very rich; rather, it is a strategy for survival. These civil servants are victims, as well as perpetuators, of a systemically corrupt government. The result of their behavior, however, can be cumulative and costly.

Other activities typically classified under "petty corruption" include:

- revenue officials practicing extortion by threatening to levy surcharges on tax payers or importers unless bribes are paid, in which case unjustifiably low tax assessments are made or goods are passed for importation without payment of any duty at all;
- law enforcement officials extorting money for their own benefit by threatening to impose penalties unless bribes are paid (which are frequently less than the penalty the offense would attract if it went to court);
- providers of public services (e.g., drivers' licenses, market stall permits, passport control) insisting on payments to speed up service or prevent delays; and
- superiors in the public service charging "rents" from their subordinates, requiring them to raise set sums each week or month and to pass these upwards.

More alarming are abuses of bureaucratic discretionary power, usually occurring in rigid systems with multiple sources of monopoly power. A planned economy, where many prices are below market-clearing levels, provides incentives for payoffs as a way to allocate scarce goods and services. Transactions that would be legal trades in market economies are illegal payoffs in these systems. In addition to selling goods and services to the highest bribe bidders, public servants can have incentives to create even more bottlenecks as a way of extracting higher payoffs.

Officials, for example, might create delays or introduce costly conditions. The fundamental problem is not simply the existence of controlled

Box 2: Systemic Corruption in Hospitals

Describing his own experience, Stanislav Andreski notes: "I have known hospitals...where the patients had to pay nurses to bring them a chamber pot; where the doctors (who were receiving a salary from the state and were supposed to treat the sick free of charge) would only look at those patients who had given them money, and saw first those who had paid most, regardless of whose condition was most urgent. Those in charge of the dispensary stole the medicaments and then sold them either to the patients on the premises or to the traders. The doctors did the same, taking the medicaments for use in their own private consulting rooms. Patients unable to pay got injections of colored water. Many who did pay were cheated and got exactly the same." He adds that the people guilty of such deeds were not "monsters": often their salaries were delayed or did not come at all, many owed substantial sums to pay for their training or as bribes for their appointments, and even if the medicaments available were dispensed properly, the staff could only attend to a tiny fraction of those in need. Further more, "a person whose probity and sense of duty shows his colleagues in a bad light risks being slandered or pushed out."

From *The African Predicament: A Study in the Pathology of Modernization* (London Michael Joseph, 1968), p. 96.

prices set below the market-clearing level, but also the monopoly power of state officials who are not threatened with entry by more efficient and lower-priced competitors.[26]

Other activities associated with bureaucratic discretionary power include:

- ministers "selling" their discretionary powers;
- officials taking percentages on government contracts, which are then often paid into foreign bank accounts;[27]
- officials receiving excessive "hospitality" from government contractors and benefits in kind, such as scholarships for the education of children at foreign universities;
- officials contracting government business to themselves, either through front companies and "partners" or even openly to themselves as "consultants";
- political parties using the prospect of power, or its continuation, to levy large rents on, say, international businesses in return for government contracts (which may be dressed up as a "donation" to a designated "charity") .

Some suggest that systemic bureaucratic corruption was perhaps most widespread throughout the former Soviet bloc, where the state of the economy gave officials an incentive to exploit their positions for private gain and gave their customers and clients an incentive to make payoffs. Corruption was common because the formal rigidity of the system was not supported by an impartial legal system capable of enforcing rules. Instead, ultimate authority was exercised by senior managers who often had their own reasons for bending or changing the rules. Subordinates could not appeal to "the law" as a reason for resisting the demands of their superiors.[28]

Stories of the United States' "robber barons" in the 1920s are invoked to argue that "cowboy capitalism" is just a transition stage that must be endured on the way to a more mature market economy. The danger, however, is that corruption can become so widespread that it can undermine and destroy the transition stage itself. Even if corruption is a by-product of economic growth under some conditions, this does not imply that it facilitates growth or that it does not have other negative political and social consequences.

3.2 Private Sector Involvement

Private sector companies, be they domestic or international, feel the pressure to bribe. These firms provide two main justifications for their actions. First, in certain countries, it is often perceived to be very difficult for anyone to win a major government or parastatal contract without paying a large bribe. This is normally done through a representative who receives a percentage commission when the business is secured. A company then may justify its action not only on the ground of "business necessity" but also that it is merely conforming to local practice.

Second, although any form of bribery may be thought to be legally wrong, off-shore bribery is generally condoned "because everybody does it." It may even be morally defended on the grounds that the resulting business is saving jobs—regardless of the fact that it may be costing jobs elsewhere. Illegal payments made by companies in order to obtain foreign contracts are tolerated, if not actively encouraged, in many industrialized countries. The reason is that winning export orders creates employment opportunities at home and improves the balance of trade.

It is increasingly apparent that companies engaging in practices of "grand corruption" can unwittingly bring into the organization certain deleterious repercussions of this behavior. For example, a corporation that instructs and trains staff to evade laws and to launder bribes as "commission" may well find those same staff cutting into the benefits for individual gain, thereby stealing from the corporation .

4. Establishing a National Integrity System

The ultimate goal of establishing a national integrity system is to make corruption a "high risk" and "low return" undertaking. As such, it is designed to prevent corruption from occurring in the first place. And because corruption tends to be a systemic problems, the primary emphasis is on changing systems, rather than blaming individuals.

An overview of some of the past successes and failures in combating corruption reveals the following problems:

(i) the limits of power at the top: an incoming administration may wish to tackle corruption effectively, but inherits a corrupt bureaucracy that impedes efforts for change;

(ii) the absence of commitment at the top: without demonstrated commitment there is a lack of moral authority to enforce laws and to punish the corrupt, an absence of confidence among rule-enforcers that enforcement actions against powerful people will be supported by the top leadership, and an absence of public belief that the leadership is serious;[29]

(iii) overly ambitious promises leading to unrealistic and unachievable expectations and a loss of public confidence;

(iv) reforms that are "piecemeal" and uncoordinated: no-one "owns" the reforms, and no one is committed to seeing that the reforms are implemented and kept up to date;

(v) reforms that rely too much upon the law or too much on enforcement: this leads to repression, abuses of enforcement power and the emergence of further corruption);

(vi) reforms that "overlook" those at the top and focus only on the "small fry":

Box 3: The Seven Principles of Public Life

Selflessness: Holders of public office should take decisions solely in terms of the public interest. They should not do so in order to gain financial or other materials benefits for themselves, their family, or their friends.

Integrity: Holders of public office should not place themselves under any financial or other obligation to outside individuals or organization that might influence them in formance of their official duties.

Objectivity: In carrying out public business, including making public appointments, awarding contracts, or recommending individuals for rewards and benefits, holders of public office should make choices on merit.

Accountability: Holders of public office are accountable for their decisions and actions to the public and must submit themselves to whatever scrutiny is appropriate to their office.

Openness: Holders of public office should be as open as possible about all the decisions and actions that they take. They should give reasons for their decisions and restrict information only when the wider public interest clearly demands.

Honesty: Holders of public office have a duty to declare any private interests relating to their public duties and to take steps to resolve any conflicts arising in a way that protects the public interest.

Leadership: Holders of public office should promote and support these principles by leadership and example.

From the "First Report of the Committee on Standards in Public Life" (London: HMSO, 1995).

if the law is applied unfairly and unevenly, it soon ceases to have any legitimacy or deterrent effect;

(vii) the failure to establish institutional mechanisms that will outlive the leaders of the reforms; and

(viii) the failure of government to draw in the actors best able to assist it from civil society and the private sector.

Country strategies vary a great deal, but worldwide the policy responses to corruption typically involve one or more of the eight following "pillars" (see Diagram 2):[30]

- public sector anti-corruption strategies;
- "watchdog" agencies;
- public participation in democratic process;
- public awareness of the role of civil society;
- accountability of the judicial process;
- the media;
- the private sector and international business;
- international cooperation.

These pillars are interdependent. If one pillar weakens, an increased load is thrown on to the others. If several weaken, their load will tilt, so that the round ball of "sustainable development" rolls off. Establishing a National Integrity System requires identifying gaps and opportunities for utilizing each of these pillars, as well as catalyzing the work of the government, civil society, donors into a coherent framework of institutional strengthening.

4.1 Public Sector Anti-Corruption Strategies

The responsibility for maintaining standards and minimizing corruption within the public service falls on the public administrator. Criminal law is too blunt to serve as the main instrument for addressing corruption in the public service because: (a) it is concerned only with minimum standards; (b) it emphasizes enforcement rather than prevention; (c) the burden of proof is on the government (in corruption cases, usually only the officials involved know the facts); and (d) it is costly and time-consuming.

If properly conceived, regulations governing conflict of interest in the public service are directed towards erecting and maintaining an administrative and management system to protect the public decision-making process. Rather than detecting and punishing the wrongdoer after the fact, such a system reduces the risk of corruption occurring in the first place. In a well-managed administrative system, the incidence of corrupt practices would be minimized and, where they did occur, swift disciplinary action would be the norm.[31] Focus should be placed, therefore, on reforming public service procedures and systems to make them more accountable to the public interest.

In other words, in an environment of systemic corruption, significant civil service reform will prove elusive if corruption is ignored. In fact, the result could be a reformed but more efficiently corrupt system. Corruption must be faced from the onset of the reform process and dealt with as an integral part of the process.

4.1.1 Ethical Codes

Fighting corruption requires a clear ethical commitment by political leaders to combat corruption wherever it occurs. One promising extension of this principle is the establishment of a public sector ethical code in some countries. The code sets out the ethos which should guide those in managerial/leadership positions; it reminds them of their responsibilities to the public and requires declarations of assets and income. (See Box 3). Yet, these codes have not met with great success, due mainly to lack of enforcement. An exception is Papua New Guinea where the code is central to activities of, and enforced by, the Ombudsman's office. Political figures at all levels

Diagram 2: The Pillars of Integrity

* Anti-corruption agencies, Ombudsman, Auditor General

have felt the weight of the Ombudsman's authority, and in a number of cases senior political careers have come to an abrupt end.[32]

Establishing and maintaining ethical codes depends on a number of critical conditions:

- the ethical environment must be accepted by a broad segment of the public sector;
- deviations must be dealt with equally and consistently across the public sector;
- the ethical environment requires political commitment and leadership as well as broad support by civil society.

4.1.2 Improved Remuneration

The inadequacy of public sector salaries contributes greatly to corrupt activities at the level of need, of "petty corruption." Ensuring living wages is crucial to public sector efficiency and effectiveness. Singapore has been conspicuously successful in this endeavor. An anti-corruption strategy was put into place in the country, along with gradual pay raises, fair salary structures, and strict penalties. Now, Singapore's public service salaries are among the highest in the world (see Box 4) and its productivity and effectiveness widely recognized. In common with other countries, there will be occasional Singaporean official who succumbs to the temptations of "grand corruption," but the problem of corruption is fairly under control.[33]

The Government of Uganda has undertaken the challenge of civil service reform with support from the World Bank and substantial bilateral assistance.[34] In the course of this reform, all civil servants' benefits are being "monetarized." Civil servants are now allowed to decide whether they wish to receive benefits or have them replaced with their monetary equivalent. It is hoped that this freedom to create discretionary spending with their "benefits package" will enhance the value they attach to their posts, decrease temptations to accept bribes, and lead to higher standards of service delivery to the public.

Box 4: Improving Government Salaries in Singapore

Prime Minister Lee Kuan Yew, the architect of Singapore's anti-corruption drive, was asked to justify a policy of paying cabinet ministers well when an increase was being discussed in 1985. His reply was that Singapore needed to preserve its most precious assets through an administration that was "absolutely corruption-free" and with "a political leadership that can be subject to the closest scrutiny because it sets the highest standards."

He continued, "It is not easy, because if we lost this, then our reason for existence, our *raison d'être* will disappear. Why does this island survive? Why does it attract banks, computer software, financial services, information services, manufacturing—in preference to many countries better endowed with natural resources, manpower, and markets? Any traveler knows that, because from the moment you hit the airport to the time you get into the taxi, you travel on the road, you know the difference, whether a place works on rules or it bends rules...How do you ensure that a fortuitous, purely accidental group of men who came in 1959 and after 26 years of office have remained stainless?...Every member knows that there is no easy money on the take. That's the way we are. Nobody believes that we spent money to get into this House...I 'm one of the best paid and probably one of the poorest of the Third World prime ministers...There are ways and ways of doing things. And I'm suggesting our way, moving with the market, is an honest, open, defensible, and workable system. You abandon this for hypocrisy, you'll end up with duplicity and corruption. Take your choice."

Quoted in *Straits Times*, 23 March 1985, pp. 14–16. See also John S. T. Quah, "Singapore's Experience in Curbing Corruption," *Political Corruption: A Source Book*, eds. Arnold J. Heidenheimer et al. (New Brunswick: Transaction Publishers, 1989), pp. 848–9.

It is essential, of course, for public servants and the public at large to understand fully the rationale behind any major public sector pay raises, and for them to appreciate that together with the benefit of higher pay comes the responsibility of enhanced account ability. Raising pay with no increases in oversight could simply result in prospective job candidates paying for the privilege of obtaining a government job.

4.1.3 Administrative Reform

Organizational change within the civil service can help minimize the opportunities for corrupt practices. Such measures include:

- improving work methods and procedures to reduce delay;
- increasing the effectiveness of supervision to enable superior officers to check and control the work of their staff;
- carrying out surprise checks on the work of officers;
- instituting in-service training for civil servants at all levels together with the formulation and dissemination of clearly-defined ethical guidelines and rules of conduct;
- developing internal financial management systems that ensure adequate and effective controls over the use of resources;
- providing channels for complaints to enable junior officials to complain about their superiors' corruption;
- rewarding achievement, recognizing good behavior, and acclaiming role models;
- making the necessary security arrangements to prevent unauthorized persons from having access to a department's premises; and
- reviewing the anti-corruption measures taken once in three to five years with the aim of introducing further improvements.[35]

A discretionary element in decision-making contains the potential for abuse. Eliminating discretionary decisions altogether, while resolving the dilemma, would be impossible and impractical. Instead, in those areas where discretion must be maintained, it would be more realistic to reduce the "monopoly power" of bureaucrats by providing rival sources of supply. For example, citizens may apply for a driver's license at any motor vehicle office; businesses may obtain operating licenses from any of several officials or offices. Conversely, police forces could operate in overlapping jurisdictions so that no official can guarantee a lawbreaker he will not be arrested. Such reforms may not end unofficial "charges" but they will at least drive the "price" down. If the level of bribes is low enough, even a modest effort at law enforcement may discourage corrupt officials.[36]

It is possible to limit the scope for abuse more systematically by keeping the areas for discretion narrowly defined and by providing clear, public guidelines for the exercise of this discretion. A good example of the guiding principles of administrative law can be found in Zambia's Lusaka Statement on Government Under the Law (1992) endorsed by Commonwealth Law Ministers in 1993 and by successive meetings of senior judges in various regions (see Annex A).

4.1.4 Disclosure of Income/Assets/Gifts

One of the key instruments for maintaining integrity in the public service is the periodic completion by all in positions of influence of forms stating their income, assets and liabilities. Disclosure of assets and income certainly will not be accurately completed by those taking bribes. However, it will force them to record their financial position and, in so doing, lay an important building block for any subsequent prosecution. However, today's evidence points to the inadequacy of any voluntary or informal system. Corruption can only be reduced if it is made a high risk and a low return undertaking.[37]

To whom should disclosure be made? Disclosure may be made by politicians to the Speaker of Parliament or to the Ombudsman, or publicly to the people at large. The matters to be disclosed will differ from country to country. Clearly this disclosure should cover all significant assets and liabilities, and a few countries insist that they include a copy of the latest income tax return. Some countries extend these requirements to close blood relations, but others will limit disclosure to the official and his or her spouse (although even this is contested, on the grounds that a spouse should be entitled to privacy from his/her partner). In any case, laws must embody what a society regards as fair and reasonable. If not, enforcement will be impossible, therefore serving to undermine the integrity system itself.

The problem does not end with disclosure. There is also the matter of gifts received by those in public office. Gifts can take many forms—a lunch, a ticket to a sports event, an expensive watch, shares in a company, a holiday abroad, perhaps school fees for a child. Some are accept able; others are not. What is unacceptable is excessive hospitality, such as all-expenses paid holidays for a purchasing officer and spouse.[38]

More difficult to classify are such things as lunches or festive presents; though even here the acceptance of seemingly trivial gifts and hospitality over time can lead to situations where an official has unwittingly become ensnared by the "donor." The dividing line usually rests at the point where the gift places the recipient under some obligation to the gift-giver. The acceptable limit will differ from one society to another, but it can be set in monetary terms so that gifts exceeding it must be declared.

Most governments have written rules clarifying what is and is not acceptable for a Minister to accept as a personal benefit. For example, Malawi recently adopted the following guidelines:

> A "casual gift" means any conventional hospitality on a modest scale or an unsolicited gift of modest value offered to a person in recognition or appreciation of his services, or as a gesture of goodwill towards him, and includes any inexpensive seasonal gift offered to staff or associates by public and private bodies or private individuals on festive or other special occasions, which is not in any way connected with the performance of a person's official duty so as to constitute an offense under Part IV [which governs corrupt use of official powers].[39]

4.1.5 Policy and Program Rationalization

Public programs riddled with corruption can sometimes be reformed through redesign and rationalization efforts.[40] The first option, however, is program elimination. Many countries have rules and regulations that, even if honestly administered, serve no broad public purpose. They can and should be discontinued. Other programs might serve a valid function, but are not effective where corruption is endemic.

Second, the program's basic purpose could be retained, but redesigned to make it simpler and easier to monitor. For example, if economic efficiency is a program goal, then reforms could introduce legal, market-based schemes. But simplification will not always reduce corruption if the rules are very rigid. Bureaucratic rigidity frequently breeds illicit behavior on the part of both public servants and suppliers. Thus, simplicity will work only if it is not excessively arbitrary and if senior officials or independent enforcement officials aggressively pursue anti-corruption measures.

Finally, privatization of state-run enterprises and services can reduce the opportunities for corrupt practices, mainly because private sector accounting methods and competitive market pressures reduce corruption and make corruption more difficult to hide. These benefits however, must take into consideration the possible adverse effects of privatization (unemployment of civil servants, risk of private sector monopolies).

Substantive policy reform, involving reform of the regulatory and tax systems and the elimination of unnecessary programs, is a difficult and time-consuming task. It is also an undertaking that must be geared to the needs and problems of a particular country. Attempts to identify sources of corruption in programs and reduce or eliminate them require detailed, country-specific knowledge.

4.1.6 Improved Procurement Procedures

Public service procurement procedures can be improved in the following ways:

- *Procurement should be economical.* It should result in the best quality of goods/services for the price paid, or the lowest price for the stipulated/acceptable quality of goods/services; this does not necessarily mean procurement of the lowest priced or best quality goods available, but the best combination of these factors to meet the particular needs.
- *Contract award decisions should be fair and impartial.* Public funds should not be used to provide favors; standards/specifications must be non-discriminatory; suppliers/contractors should be selected on the basis of their qualifications and the merit of their offers; there should be equal treatment of all in terms of deadlines and confidentiality.
- *The process should be transparent.* Procurement requirements, rules and decision-making criteria should be readily accessible to all potential suppliers/contractors, preferably announced as part of the invitation to bid/make an offer; opening of bids

should be public; and all decisions should be fully recorded.

- *The procurement process should be efficient.* The procurement rules should reflect the value and complexity of the items to be procured; procedures for small value purchases should be simple and fast; as purchase values and complexity increase, more time and more complex rules are required to ensure that principles are observed; "decision making" for larger contracts may require committee and review process, but bureaucratic interventions should be kept to a minimum.
- *Accountability is essential.* Procedures should be systematic and dependable, and records should be maintained that can explain and justify all decisions and actions. Competence and integrity in procurement encourages suppliers and contractors to make their best offers, in turn leading to improved procurement performance. Purchasers that fail to meet high standards of accountability and fairness should be identified quickly as poor partners with which to do business.
- *A sound and consistent framework is required* to establish the basic principles and practices to be observed in public procurement. This can take many forms, but there is increasing awareness of the advantages of a unified Procurement Code setting out the fundamentals and supplemented by more detailed rules and regulations of the implementing agencies. A number of countries are consolidating existing laws that may have developed in haphazard fashion over many years, into such a code.[41]

4.2 "Watchdog" Agencies

A nation serious about fighting corruption may need to establish new institutions to carry out anti-corruption functions. Anti-corruption agencies, the office of the Ombudsman, and supreme audit institutions are reviewed below for the "watchdog" role they might assume.

4.2.1 Anti-Corruption Agencies

In recent years, governments have sought to bolster detection efforts by introducing independent anti-corruption agencies or commissions. Given that prevention is more efficient and effective than prosecution, a small investigative and monitoring unit with appropriate authority—perhaps reporting directly to the legislative body—may be much better placed to ensure that effective preventive steps are identified and taken. To operate successfully, an anti-corruption agency must possess the following:

- committed political backing at the highest levels of government;
- political and operational independence to investigate even the highest levels of government;
- adequate powers of access to documentation and to question witnesses; and
- leadership which is publicly perceived as being of the highest integrity.[42]

It is important that any special powers conferred on an anti-corruption agency conform to international human rights norms, and that the agency itself operate under the law and is accountable to the courts.

From the outset, the shape and independence of a commission may well be determined by how the officeholder is appointed or removed. If the appointing mechanism ensures consensus support for an appointee through parliament, rather than government, and an accountability mechanism exists outside government (e.g., a parliamentary select committee on which all major parties are represented), the space for abuse for non-partisan activities can be minimized.

It is important that the anti-corruption agency have the power to freeze those assets it reasonably suspects may be held on behalf of people under investigation. It may be desirable for the agency to do so prior to getting a court order when speed is of the essence. Without this power, funds can simply be transferred electronically in a matter of minutes. This presupposes the need for a vital tool—a well thought-out and effective system for monitoring the assets, income, liabilities and lifestyles of decision-makers and public service officials.

It is usual for an agency to have the power to seize and impound travel documents to prevent a person from fleeing the country, particularly as its power of arrest arises only when there is reasonable cause to believe that an offense has been committed. It is also customary that the agency have the power to protect informers. In some cases, informers may be junior government officials who complain about the corrupt activities of their supervisors.

If an extravagant lifestyle is only corroborative evidence in support of a charge of actual corruption, it will not be of much use. Where a civil servant in a position to profit personally is enjoying a lifestyle wholly out of line with his or her known income, it is thought in some countries not to be unreasonable for the civil servant to be required to provide an acceptable explanation for his or her wealth.[43]

4.2.2 Ombudsman

The Ombudsman constitutes an office that independently receives and investigates allegations of maladministration. The primary function of the Ombudsman is to examine:

(i) a decision, process, recommendation, act of omission or commission which is contrary to law, rules or regulations, or is a departure from established practice or procedure; is perverse, arbitrary, unjust, biased, oppressive or discriminatory; or, involves the exercise of powers motivated by bribery, jobbery, favoritism, nepotism, and administrative excesses; and

(ii) neglect, inattention, delay, incompetence, inefficiency and ineptitude in the administration or discharge of duties and responsibilities.

As a high-profile, constitutional institution, the office of Ombudsman is potentially better able to resist improper pressure from the Executive than are other bodies. It can perform an auditing function to stimulate information flows to reveal and contain the limits of corruption in government; the confidentiality of these procedures gives the office an added advantage in providing a shield against the possible intimidation of informants and complainants.[44] The office of the Ombudsman also acts to prevent corruption and maladministration. It can recommend improvements to procedures and practices and act as an incentive for public officials to keep their files in order at all times.

Whether under-funded or not, the office of the Ombudsman should be responsible for its own budget and not be subordinate for funding to another, larger department. With a lack of resources to fulfill the mandate of the post, it is often only "the will of the Ombudsman" that sustains the office-holder in the job. This undesirable situation should be addressed when reforming a country's integrity system.

4.2.3 Supreme Audit Institutions

Responsible internal financial management is crucial to national integrity, but supreme audit institutions are in many ways the linchpin of a country's integrity system. As the agency responsible for auditing government income and expenditure, the supreme audit institution acts as a watchdog over financial integrity and the credibility of reported information (as well as 'performance' or 'value-for-money' auditing). While supreme audit institutions can vary from country to country—for example, in Anglo-Saxon countries this institution is the Auditor General, while in many French-speaking countries it is the *cours de comptes*—the functions of the office are not dissimilar:

> the [Auditor General] audits the Appropriation Accounts on behalf of the House of Commons. He is the external auditor of Government, acting on behalf of the taxpayer, through Parliament, and it is on his investigations that Parliament has to rely for assurances about the accuracy and regularity of Government accounts.[45]

The responsibilities of the office of the Auditor General also include ensuring the Executive complies with the will of the Legislature, as expressed through parliamentary appropriations; promotes efficiency and cost effectiveness of government programs; and prevents corruption through the development of financial and auditing procedures designed to reduce the incidence of corruption and increase the likelihood of its detection.

The supreme audit institution is of such significance that it warrants special provisions concerning appointment and removal procedures and the protection of the office-holder's independence from the control of the governing party, politicians, and senior civil servants. Ideally, the issues of selection, accountability and authority can be incorporated into a country's constitution.

To be effective, any external auditor must be devoid of accountability to, or susceptible to pressures from, the clients or institutions being audited. The office should not be a part of, or managed by, a government department it has to audit. To be so would create a systemic conflict of interest and to open the door to forms of "management." The supreme audit institution's clients are parliament (or comparable bodies) and its subjects are the public officials entrusted with public expenditure.

Unfortunately, this office can be particularly vulnerable to pressure from its clients, and in the majority of cases, the Executive. To assure independence, the office should have relative freedom to manage the department's budget and to hire and assign competent professional staff. The latter is important if it is to maintain its ability to match the capability of senior officials in government.

4.3 Public Participation and the Democratic Process

In political systems where elections occur, transparency in the election process is essential. This would include the need for an independent Election Commission (or similar body) and non-partisan polling officials. The commission's role is to ensure the elections are "fair," inasmuch as they follow existing laws and regulations, including such checks as limits on party election campaign spending. To enable a commission to respond to changing circumstances, some countries have given their commissions limited law-making powers.

As a matter of policy, citizens' groups should be able to observe the processes of their own elections. It is unfortunate that a need for international observers should be deemed necessary in many developing countries. This provision may be required until the responsibility for monitoring is accepted by a country's civil society and can be undertaken in a non-partisan manner.

The recent South African experience shows how taking necessary steps to reform parliamentary practices and procedures can prepare a path towards accountability and transparency, thereby restricting corruption in the democratic process. The reform process there centers on rendering the parliamentary process as open to the public and the press as possible, and empowering select committees, particularly the Public Accounts Committee, to hold the Executive accountable. All select committees meet in public, and if they wish to go into a closed session they must publicly debate the reasons for doing so. Parliamentarians have been empowered to call civil servants to account and to have inputs into the detailed scrutiny of budgetary estimates. Not only does the South African constitution guarantee open, fair, and transparent government procurement, but it also ensures access to information and other rights of due process.[46]

4.4 Public Awareness and the Role of Civil Society

Anti-corruption campaigns cannot succeed without public support. If ordinary people and businesses at all levels of society expect to pay bribes and are accustomed to dealing with the state through payoffs, even as a "necessary evil," then a change in attitudes is essential if fundamental, systemic change is to occur.

Several complementary strategies can have an impact. Some countries have engendered public understanding through public awareness programs focused on: the harm done by corruption; the fact that the corrupt are stealing the public's money; the public's rights to services; and the public duty to complain when officials behave corruptly. In this regard, Tanzania conducted a study to ascertain public perceptions of existing levels of corruption and where it is taking place; this provides a baseline against which progress toward reduced corruption can be measured.[47] These studies also serve to give insights into what civil servants regard as being "corrupt," what they are prepared to report or to discipline, and what prevents them from doing so.

The role of civil society is integral to a national integrity system; the notion that state activities can take place in a vacuum simply does not stand up to experience.[48] Civil society encompasses the expertise and networks needed to address issues of common concern, including corruption. And it has a vested interest in doing so: most corruption involves two principal actors, the government and the private sector, with civil society as the major victim.

Civil society organizations' ability to monitor, detect and reverse the activities of the public officials in their midst is enhanced by their proximity and familiarity with local issues. Indeed, this may be the training ground needed to gain the experience and confidence necessary for action at the national level. Of course, in many countries where corruption is rife, civil associations are weak. However, the very involvement of an emerging civil society can, of itself, provide strength and stimulus for its further development.

Civil society can address issues of corruption by drawing on the expertise of accountants, lawyers, academics, NGOs, the private sector, religious leaders and, perhaps most importantly, ordinary citizens. In Australia, workers in some occupations are involved in industry safety inspections, and in New South Wales consumer groups help to identify hazardous products on sale. In New Zealand, tired of abuses of power by private and government monopolies, a loose-knit group of largely commercial interests has come together to create MUMS (Major Users of Monopoly Services). The group acts as a watchdog on businesses ranging from international airlines and telecommunications concerns to pulp-and-paper producers and film production companies.[49]

There are also examples of joint citizen-state action. For example, Neighborhood Watch schemes are now an established feature of many countries, strengthening links between citizens and police. Hong Kong has set up an Independent Commission Against Corruption, with an entire department devoted to community relations and advisory committees.

4.5 Accountability of the Judicial Process[50]

In the common law system of a number of countries, the Attorney General is not only a member of the Executive but is also the Chief Law Officer of the state. As the latter, the Attorney General acts as the "guardian of the public interest"[51] and has extensive powers and discretion with respect to the initiation, prosecution and discontinuance of criminal proceedings. The Attorney General also has primary responsibility to provide legal advice in matters of public administration and government. The proper performance of these functions depends on impartiality and freedom from party political influences; this can be threatened if the Attorney General is subject to Cabinet control and if Parliament is effectively dominated by the Executive.

One of the most blatant abuses by the Executive is the practice of appointing supporters to the courts.[52] The judicial appointment process is a critical one, therefore, though some governments have found that their own supporters develop a remarkable independence of mind once appointed to high office. To combat this independence, the Executive can manipulate the assignment of cases, perhaps through a compliant Chief Justice, to determine which judge hears a case of importance to the government. It is essential that the task of assigning cases be given not to government servants but to the judges themselves, and that the Chief Justice enjoy the full confidence of his or her peers.

At the lower level of the court structure, a variety of corrupt means are used to pervert the justice system. These include influencing the investigation and the decision to prosecute before the case reaches the court; inducing court officials to lose files, delay cases or assign them to corrupt junior judges; corrupting judges themselves (who are often badly paid or who may be susceptible to promises of likely promotion); and bribing opposing lawyers to act against the interests of their clients.

Clearly, these corrupt practices call for action on several fronts. Those responsible for the investigation and prosecution of cases must impose high standards on their subordinates; court officials should be accountable to the judges for their conduct and subject to sanction by the judges where, for example, files are "lost"; and the judiciary itself must insist on high ethical standards within its own ranks, with complaints being carefully dealt with and, where necessary, inspection teams visiting the lower courts to ensure that they are functioning properly.

The ways in which judges are appointed and subsequently promoted are crucial to their independence. They must not be seen as being appointed for political reasons, but solely for reasons of competence and political neutrality. The public must be confident that judges are chosen on merit and for their individual integrity and ability, not as a reward for party service or as a precaution by the Executive to ensure that it will have a friendly face on the bench if the rule of law is violated.

It is implicit in the concept of judicial independence that provision be made for adequate remuneration of the judiciary and that a judge's right to the remuneration not be altered to his or her disadvantage.[53] If judges are not confident that their tenure of office, or their remuneration, is secure, they may be more susceptible to corruption.

It is axiomatic that a judge must enjoy personal immunity from civil damages claims for improper acts or omissions in the exercise of judicial functions. This is not to say that the aggrieved person should have no remedy; rather, the remedy is against the state, not the judge. Judges should be subject to removal or suspension only for reasons of incapacity, or behavior which renders them unfit to discharge their duties.

Situations involving widespread corruption and judicial tampering can be dealt with by establishing commissions of inquiry or by the appointment of a "special prosecutor"—a public office which has been used in the United States with conspicuous success (e.g. the Watergate scandal).

There are several good reasons for having strong recovery mechanisms against corruption in the civil (as opposed to the criminal) law. Civil courts provide a less onerous atmosphere than the criminal courts for dealing with the consequences of corruption. In the civil court, the burden of proof is not as demanding, and in appropriate cases, the burden of disproving assertions can be more effectively and fairly placed on the suspect. Evidence obtained through civil law need only establish guilt via a "balance of probabilities" rather than "beyond a reasonable doubt."

There are several reasons, too, why private citizens should be able to sue in cases of corruption. One reason involves the potential liability of the state for the losses incurred to a citizen or groups of citizens by reason of the actions of a corrupt official. For example, if the state can be shown to have been negligent in its administration, then those who suffer a loss as a result of a corrupt public procurement exercise may well have a substantial claim for compensation.

4.6 Role of the Media

The right to know is linked inextricably to accountability. Informed appraisal of government by the public, press and parliament is a difficult, even impossible, task if government activities and decision-making processes are obscured from public scrutiny.

Legislation is often required. Hence the desirability of Freedom of Information (FOI) legislation.[54] Not only can FOI legislation establish a right of review (e.g., by the Ombudsman), it also can establish practices which must be observed, even by those least willing to do so. It can help reverse the presumption of secrecy. Citizens are given the legal right of access to official documents without having to first prove special interest, and the burden of justifying non-disclosure falls on the government administration. Naturally, documents whose disclosure might actually harm the public interest are exempted (e.g., criminal investigations, budget proposals, and sensitive economic information).

Freedom of information is also enhanced through a free press, which ranks alongside an independent judiciary as one of the twin powers that can serve as a powerful counterforce to corruption in public life. Unlike judges, public prosecutors and Attorneys-General, the privately-owned media is not appointed by politicians; it is sustained by the public. Regardless of ownership, the media should be, and can be, free of the political patronage system.

The degree to which the media is independent is the degree to which it can perform an effective public watchdog function relating to the conduct of public officials. Just as the Legislature should keep the Executive under day-to day scrutiny, the media should diligently monitor both the Legislature and the Executive against corruption. Politicians and civil servants may be more tempted to abuse their positions for private gain when they are confident they run no risk of public exposure and humiliation through the media. Even today, there are many countries that censor the press and jail journalists.

Laws declaring "freedom of expression" require support and enforcement from the courts. An independent judiciary is the handmaiden of a free press. A prerequisite for building a free press, therefore, is a legal system that is independent of political influence and has firm constitutional support for a free press.

Through the responsible judgments of editors and journalists, a culture of freedom of the press develops. This culture is an important guarantor of the ability of the press to operate as a watchdog on public office holders.

Independence of the media is a complex concept. In general terms, it focuses on the notion that journalists should be free of interference from authorities in the responsible pursuit and practice of their profession. In reality, the owners of the media intervene daily in the operations of the journalists under their employ. In many countries, the government itself is the largest media owner, which can undermine the independence of the media.

Where this happens, efforts should be undertaken to strengthen the independence of the media, possibly through the privatization of existing state-controlled media. Diversifying media ownership could ensure that competition within the media stimulates a wider range of perspectives on public policy issues and provides a check on the political power of media magnates.[55]

In numerous countries, laws uphold the notion of a free press, but also include constraints in the form of "reasonable limits" on grounds of national security or individual privacy. There may be times when national security demands temporary limits on the media (to limit hate literature or curb racial and ethnic tensions). The danger is that governments can abuse such discretion.

4. 7 The Role of the Private Sector

The most compelling reason for companies to review their ethical behavior is likely to be that of self-interest. As noted above, a growing body of evidence suggests that companies tolerating corruption abroad by their employees are placing themselves at risk. "Off the books" accounts, secret bank accounts, paying staff while they serve prison terms and using former senior staff as "middlemen" all cultivate an atmosphere in which the bottom line justifies criminal activity. This is inherently dangerous, and it may be only a matter of time before the company itself finds that it is the victim of similar conduct on the part of its employees.

There appears to be considerable scope for international professional associations and federations of private companies to include a mandatory anti-corruption clause in their ethics codes, with expulsion from its membership as the sanction for non-observance. When such an association is strong in terms of worldwide member ship, its members have relatively little to fear from non-members gaining an unfair advantage from bribery.

4.8 International Cooperation

The only country that has made it illegal to pay bribes offshore is the United States.[56] Other countries, somewhat paradoxically, have a dual set of rules, making it illegal to bribe domestically but implicitly condoning bribery offshore. A country must be able not only to extradite corrupt officials when they flee abroad, but also to obtain assistance with finding evidence, taking statements from witnesses, and seizing bank records and company documentation (mutual legal assistance). Even more important, countries need help in locating, freezing or seizing the proceeds of corruption when these are placed in "safe havens" in foreign countries.

There is now an abundance of legal tools that can be used in fighting international corruption. But before they can be used, there are some basic requirements that must be met. If a country's domestic courts are seen as not being independent, or as corrupt, then it is unlikely that courts in other countries will respect its rulings on corruption or extradition. In a word, it is essential that the rule of law prevail and be seen to prevail if foreign mutual legal assistance is to be forthcoming.

It is also important for law enforcement officials to stay abreast of recent international developments. Limited forms of assistance are being offered by some banking centers.[57] For example, the Swiss Government will now provide assistance where a court finds that monies have been stolen, though it will not yet to do so in the pre-trial stages of an investigation.[58]

New approaches to international cooperation on corruption are needed in both developed and developing countries. The following are some measures that can be taken:

- to achieve any meaningful control over international corruption, it is desirable that a country receive judicial cooperation from its major trading partners (e.g., extradition of suspects, search and seizure of evidence), as well as from off-shore banking centers; and
- to gain the necessary levels of international mutual legal assistance, a country's domestic laws should be harmonized with those of the countries with which it is seeking judicial cooperation.

In this regard, an international convention on drugs is helping to set the tone. Led first by Europe, and then by the 52 Commonwealth countries, the international community now subscribes to a UN drugs convention that contains provisions requiring them to provide mutual legal assistance in illicit drug cases, including the location and forfeiture of the proceeds of drug trafficking.

Since 1990, a series of international measures, triggered by the Financial Action Task Force Initiative of the G7, have been undertaken to make the "laundering" of funds having origins in drug trafficking a criminal offense. As a result, at least 40 countries, including nearly all members of the OECD, have implemented legislation and other administrative arrangements to trace the flow of such funds through their banking systems. These arrangements require commercial banks to report to the Central Bank or a national criminal intelligence office on the receipt of deposits which may have criminal origins. With the EU, these arrangements have been embodied in a directive that is binding on member states.

5. Conclusions: Managing Change for National Integrity

The issue of corruption has come to center stage. The economic consequences of pervasive corruption and recent trends toward democratization have increased the pressure on those in public office for accountability and transparency in the performance of their duties.

This paper does not suggest there are easy solutions that can be applied in the fight against corruption; neither does it suggest any country has yet found an ideal model, or indeed that such a model exists. What this paper does argue is that while each country or region is unique in its own history and culture, its political system, and its stage of economic and social development, similarities in a national integrity system do exist and lessons learned are often transferable.

A national integrity system comprises a number of principle elements. Those reviewed in this paper—public sector anti-corruption strategies, watchdog agencies, public awareness and participation, accountability of the courts, roles of the media and the private sector, and international cooperation—can be taken as the pillars on which a national integrity system can be built...and on which sustainable development depends.

Any one of these elements will have only limited impact in the fight against corruption. Ethical codes or new procurement rules, for example, will have little effect unless implemented and enforced by independent agencies; an ombudsman, supreme audit institutions, and anti-corruption agencies are examples of "watchdog" authorities that can perform these functions. Similarly, anti-corruption strategies depend on the active support and vigilance of civil society and the media; a responsible media can be enlisted to raise public awareness of the harmful repercussions of corruption and of citizens' right to expect ethical conduct from civil servants. The elements of a national integrity system are mutually-reinforcing.

While all of these elements do not need to be carried out or strengthened simultaneously, how a national integrity system is initiated and managed can determine the success or failure of reform efforts. It is vital for each country to define the most strategic elements for reform in order to maximize existing opportunities for positive change while providing critical support to weak areas that, left unattended, could undermine the reform program. Moreover, a few successful and substantial measures will demonstrate to the public that government leaders and representatives are seriously fighting corruption.

The broader societal and political context within which reforms are undertaken will condition the effectiveness of a national integrity system. A democratic political framework creates different incentives for corruption than an authoritarian regime. Opportunities for bribery will vary in market and state-run economies.

In all countries, regardless of the stage of development, it is crucial that promotion of a national integrity system and the fight against corruption be as politically-inclusive and citizen-friendly as circumstances allow. This requires:

- a committed political leadership (where possible, on an all-party, non-partisan basis), that shows its commitment by willingly submitting to a comprehensive monitoring of assets, incomes, liabilities and life-styles;
- public involvement and participation in the reform process, with proposed changes debated widely to generate a sense of ownership among the public and reinforce the values embodied in reform;
- participation by civil service unions and other employees' groups; and
- involvement of professional groups as well as community and religious leaders.

Performance targets and monitoring systems are necessary to measure progress towards reduced corruption. To be effective, results-oriented management must create incentive structures and an enabling environment to encourage achievement of civil service reform targets and quality results. These results should be disseminated to the public at large; sharing information with civil society represents a significant step in ensuring transparency and accountability in government. ❧

Annex A: Government Under the Law (The Lusaka Statement), 1992

The statement reads as follows:

An administrative authority, when exercising a discretionary power some countries have found useful to:

(i) pursue only the purposes for which the power has been conferred;

(ii) be without bias and observe objectivity and impartiality, taking into account only factors relevant to the particular case;

(iii) observe the principle of equality before the law by avoiding unfair discrimination;

(iv) maintain a proper balance between any adverse effects which its decision may have on the rights, liberties or interests of persons and the purpose which it pursues;

(v) take decisions within a time which is reasonable having regard to the matters at stake;

(vi) apply any general administrative guidelines in a consistent manner while at the same time taking account of the particular circumstances of each case.

Procedure:

(i) *Availability of guidelines*: Any general administrative guidelines which govern the exercise of a discretionary power some countries have found useful to either be made public or communicated (in an appropriate manner and to the extent necessary) to the person concerned, at his or her request, whether before or after the taking of an act concerning the person;

(ii) *Right to be heard*: In respect of any administrative act of such a nature as is likely to affect adversely his or her rights, liberties or interests, the person concerned should be entitled to put forward facts and arguments and, in appropriate cases, submit evidence which should be taken into account by the administrative authority; in appropriate cases the person concerned should be informed, in due time and in an appropriate manner, of these rights;

(iii) *Access to information*: Upon request, the person concerned should be informed, before an administrative act is taken and by appropriate means, of all factors relevant to the taking of that act;

(iv) *Statement of reasons*: Where an administrative act is of such a nature as to affect adversely the rights, liberties or interests of a person, the person concerned should be informed of the reasons on which it is based either by stating the reasons in the act itself or, upon request, by communicating them separately to the person concerned within a reasonable time;

(v) *Indication of remedies*: Where an administrative act is given in writing and which adversely affects of rights, liberties or interests of the person concerned, it should indicate the specific remedies available to the person as well as any time-limits which may be involved.

Review:

(i) An act taken in exercise of a discretionary power should be subject to judicial review by a court or other competent body; however this does exclude the possibility of a preliminary review by an administrative authority empowered to decide both on legality and on the merits;

(ii) Where no time limits for the taking of a decision in exercise of a discretionary power have been set by law and the administrative authority does not take its decision within a reasonable time, its failure to do so should be open to review by a competent authority;

(iii) A court or other independent body which controls the exercise of a discretionary power should possess such powers of obtaining information as are necessary for the proper exercise of its functions.

Implementation:

In their implementation, the requirements of good and efficient administration, the legitimate interests of third parties and major public interests should be given due weight, but where these requirements make it necessary to modify these principles in particular cases or specific areas of public administration, every endeavour should be made to conform with these principles and to achieve the highest possible degree of fairness.

It is reasonable to assume that a conflict of interest has not occurred where: (a) the duty of the official is so narrow as to leave no room for any personal discretion (e.g., the duties are simply clerical); (b) the economic interest is negligible (e.g., a small number of shares in a large public company); or (c) involvement in the matter has been formal or technical, so that the person formally occupying a position with conflicting duties has not in fact acted in that position (e.g., when an official has asked someone else to act in his or her stead to avoid any appearance of conflict of interest).

Finally there are organizational changes that can be made in the way government does business, in particular, with the public:

- the demystification of government: citizens should be informed of their legal rights in dealing with government. Staff manuals, etc. some countries have found useful to be published and easily accessible to department users and contractors;
- the depersonalization of government: face-to-face contact should be minimized. Random elements could be introduced so that users cannot predict the officials with whom they may be dealing. Under some conditions, staff should be rotated regularly to minimize the scope for unhealthy relationships developing, both between individual staff and the public they are serving. Rotation, however, can sometimes

facilitate systemic corruption when a corrupt superior uses job rotation to punish subordinates unwilling to play the corrupt game; and
- establishing mechanisms for civil society to be involved in a continuous processes of review. Polling the public periodically on its perceptions of government service delivery may be useful. ❧

Endnotes

1. This paper develops some of the concepts in Transparency International's *National Integrity Source Book* (Washington, D.C.: Transparency International, 1996). The Source Book provides greater detail and analysis on certain topics discussed in this paper.
2. See Rose-Ackerman (1996b).
3. See Rose-Ackerman (1996a) and Gould and Amaro-Reyes (1983).
4. See Rose-Ackerman (1996a).
5. Transparency International is a non-profit organization, based in Berlin, with more than 60 chapters worldwide. Its international focus is on corruption in international business transaction and, through its national chapters, fighting corruption at the domestic level.
6. Corruption in the private sector is outside the scope of this paper.
7. See Klitgaard (1988).
8. See Husted (1994).
9. See Johnston (1986).
10. Michael Johnston notes that "a full discussion of the implications of corruption in any given system must be constructed in the context of system-specific factors. The existence of ethnic factions among elites, the extent to which kinship norms mean that citizens and/or officials take a different view of patronage practices than does the law, or the exclusion of certain economic interests from decision-making processes, for example, can all be critical parts of the corruption story in specific settings." *Ibid.*, p. 463.
11. Quoted in Quah (1982).
12. *Ibid.*, quoting from Yoong Siew-Wah (1973).
13. See Noonan (1984). Judge Noonan's classic study of bribes records that reciprocities classified as bribes were censured, among others, in the ancient kingdoms of Egypt, Mesopotamia, and Palestine and, even more harshly, in Cicero's Rome.
14. See Rose-Ackerman (1996a).
15. See, for example, Rose-Ackerman (1996a).
16. See Gould and Amaro-Reyes (1983).
17. This summary draws in part from Bayley (1991).
18. See Mauro (1995).
19. See Wade (1982) and Manzetti and Drake (forthcoming).
20. See Rubin (1982). See also the rough figures suggested by Susan Rose-Ackerman in "Proposal for Research in the Level and Impact of Corruption in International Business," presented at the annual meeting of Transparency International in Milan, 27–28 March 1995.
21. *Le Monde*, 17 March 1995.
22. *Le Monde* also reported that revenue authorities do not uestion commissions of up to 15 percent of the global total of a contract. *Ibid.*
23. See Frisch (1994).

24. The conventional view—which virtually relates poverty to dishonesty—is attacked vehemently by a number of critics, who see this alleged linkage as being little short of a blanket defamation of the poor. "Can a person not be poor yet honest?" they ask. They point to the fact that many officials remain honest. General Obasanjo observes that: "Sharp practices have characterized the banking industry in Nigeria in recent years. Most bank officials were more than well paid, yet their fraudulent and corrupt practices have been outrageous. Contrast these with other officials, much less well paid, who have maintained their integrity and incorruptibility throughout." See *Financial Times* (1994).
25. Computerization has generally and substantially decreased the numbers on the public service payroll—for example, in Uganda.
26. See Shleifer and Vishney (1992) and Montias and Rose-Ackerman (1981).
27. The various ways in which this is done, including public procurement rules laid down by international lending institutions, are described in the *Good Business Guide to Bribery* by George Moody-Stuart (1994).
28. See Rose-Ackerman (1994).
29. The case of Tanzania, where President Mkapa has demonstrated a strong commitment to the fight against corruption, is illustrative.
30. This list reflects the consensus view of participants at EDI/TI seminars and workshops designed to promote national integrity. An alternative taxonomy, covering essentially the same issues, is presented in Rose-Ackerman (1996b).
31. Botswana falls into this category. Though corruption has not been a serious problem, in Botswana, when it did occur, swift remedial action was taken against the culprits and institutional arrangements were tightened and repaired. See *TI Newsletter*, June 1995.
32. See Pope (1996).
33. See Quah (1989).
34. For details, refer to Langseth (1995).
35. See Quah (1989).
36. See Rose-Ackerman (1978).
37. See Atkinson and Mancuso (1992).
38. Such holidays were provided, for example, to purchasing staff at Britain's Ministry of Defense in the early 1990s.
39. Corrupt Practices Act, Section 3.
40. See Rose-Ackerman (1994) and Klitgaard (1991).
41. Several models are available as a starting point, including those of the GATT/World Trade Organization, the United Nations Committee on International Trade Law (UNCITRAL), the European Union, and a host of national codes.
42. Legislation can provide that the head of the agency be appointed either by the leaders of the governing and main opposition political parties, or in the same way as a superior court judge.
43. As is the case, for example, in Hong Kong.
44. See Hatchard (1992).
45. See House of Commons (1981).
46. For details, see the report of the Transparency International mission to South Africa, December 1994 (Transparency International, Berlin).
47. In addition, EDI and CIETinternational have undertaken service delivery surveys in partnership with the governments of Nicaragua, Mali, Tanzania, and Uganda.
48. See the discussion of Coleman (1990) and Tanzi (1994).
49. *The Evening Post* (Wellington, New Zealand), 14 September 1994.
50. It is recognized that this section reflects only the role of the judiciary in Anglo-Saxon countries.
51. This has been a focus of criticism in a num-

ber of countries in Latin America.

52. The authoritative text of the role of the Attorney General in the fifty Commonwealth countries is *Law Officers of the Crown* (Edwards 1964). For a recent review of the position, see the *Report on Review of Independence of the Attorney-General* (Electoral and Administrative Review Commission 1993).
53. In some countries faced with dire economic problems, judges have accepted a reduction in salaries in line with those of all other public servants, but this has usually been done on the basis of the judges "requesting" similar treatment, rather than it being done to them unwillingly.
54. The issue is not one only for developed countries. It has been stressed *inter alia* at the three African conferences on human rights, democracy, and corruption held by the African Leadership Forum in 1994–95, by participants at the EDI/TI Arusha Integrity Workshop (1995) and journalists in training workshops facilitated by EDI and TI in Uganda (1995).
55. It is recognized that there is a difference between government ownership of the media and government control. Even though the media may be privately owned, government control through censorship, moral suasion, and other means can limit the freedom of the media.
56. The Foreign Corrupt Practices Act (1977).
57. Banking centers are under increasing pressure from the international community, in large part because of concerns about drug trafficking and money laundering.
58. See Shleifer and Vishney (1993).

Bibliography

Aboud, Muhammed. 1993. "Watch-Dog Organizations for Upholding Administrative Ethics in Africa: The Case of Tanzania," in Sadig Rasheed and Dele Olowu (eds.), *Ethics and Accountability in African Public Services*. New York: United Nations Economic Commission for Africa and the African Association for Public Administration and Management.

Atkinson, Michael, and Maureen Mancuso. 1992. "Edicts and Etiquette: Regulating Conflict of Interest in Congress and the House of Commons." *Corruption and Reform* 7 (1): 1–18.

Bayley, David. 1991. "The Effects of Corruption in a Developing Nation." *The Western Political Quarterly* 3 (2): 719–24*ff*

Brett, E. A. 1995. "Neutralising the Use of Force in Uganda: The Role of the Military in Politics," *The Journal of Modern African Studies* 33 (1): 129–152.

Chew, D. C. E. 1990. "Internal Adjustments to Falling Civil Salary: Insights from Uganda," *World Development* 18 (7).

Coleman, James. 1990. *Foundations in Social Theory*. Cambridge: Belknap Press.

Edwards, John L. 1964. *Law Officers of the Crown*. London: Sweet & Maxwell.

The Evening Post (New Zealand). 1994. 14 September.

Financial Times. 1994. "Letters to the Editor." 14 October.

Frisch, Dieter. 1994. "The Effects of Corruption on Development." Paper presented to the African Leadership Forum on Corruption, Democracy, and Human Rights in Africa, Cotonou, Benin, 19–21 September.

Frye, Timothy. 1993. "Caveat Emptor: Institutions, Credible Commitment, and Commodity Exchanges in Russia." In David Weimer (ed.), *Institutional Design*. New York: Kluwer.

Gould, David J., and Jose Amaro-Reyes. 1983. "The Effects of Corruption on Administrative Performance: Illustrations from Developing Countries." World Bank Working Paper No. 580. Washington, D.C.: The World Bank.

Government of Australia. 1993. *Report on Review of Independence of the Attorney-General*. Brisbane: Government of Australia.

Government of Tanzania. 1995. "The National Integrity System in Tanzania." A compendium of draft papers from a workshop convened by the Prevention of Corruption Bureau in cooperation with Transparency International, the Economic Development Institute for the World Bank, Coopers and Lybrand and the British Overseas Development Administration.

Government of Uganda. 1994. *National Integrity System in Uganda*

———. 1995. *National Integrity System in Uganda II*.

Hansen, Holger Bernt, and Michael Twaddle (eds.). 1991. *Changing Uganda*. London: James Currey Ltd.

Hatchard, John. 1992. "The Office of the Ombudsman." In *National Human Rights Institutions in the Commonwealth*. London: Commonwealth Secretariat.

House of Commons. 1981. "First Special Report from the Committee of Public Accounts, Session 1980–81." In *The Role of the Comptroller and Auditor-General, Volume I, Report*. London: HMSO.

Husted, Bryan W. 1994. "Honor Among Thieves." *BusinessEthics Quarterly* 1 (1): 17–27.

Johnston, Michael. 1986. "The Political Consequences of Corruption: A Reassessment." *Comparative Politics* July: 467–8.

Kasozi, A. B. K. 1994. *The Social Origins of Violence in Uganda 1964–1985*. Montreal: McGill-Queen's University Press.

Klitgaard, Robert. 1991. "Adjusting to Reality: Beyond 'State versus Market.'" In *Economic Development*. San Francisco: International Center for Economic Growth.

Kpundeh, Sahr J. and Bruce Heilman. Forthcoming. "*Rushwa*: An Examination of Corruption in Tanzania."

Le Monde. 1995. 17 March.

Langseth, Petter. 1995. "Civil Service Reform: Experience from Uganda." World Bank Discussion Paper. Washington, D.C.: The World Bank.

Manzetti, Luigi, and Charles Drake. Forthcoming. "Market Reforms and Corruption in Latin America: New Means for Old Ways." *Review of International Political Economy*.

Mauro, Paolo. 1995. "Corruption and Growth." *Quarterly Journal of Economics* 109: 681–712.

Montias, J. M., and Susan Rose-Ackerman. 1981. "Corruption in a Soviet-Type Economy: Theoretical Considerations." In Steven Rosenfielde (ed.), *Economic Welfare and the Economics of Soviet Socialism: Essays in Honor of Abram Bergson*. Cambridge: Cambridge University Press.

Moody-Stuart, George. 1994. *Good Business Guide to Bribery*. Berlin: Transparency International.

Noonan, John T. 1984. *Bribes*. Berkeley: University of California Press.

Pope, Jeremy. (Ed.) 1996. *The TI Source Book*. Berlin: Transparency International.

Quah, John S. T. 1982. "Bureaucratic Corruption in the ASEAN Countries: A Comparative Analysis of their Anti-Corruption Strategies." *Journal of Southeast Asian Studies* 13 (1): 153–77.

————. 1989. "Singapore's Experience in Curbing Corruption." In A. J. Heidenheimer (ed.), *Political Corruption: A Source Book*. New Brunswick: Transaction Publishers.

Rose-Ackerman, Susan. 1978. *Corruption: A Study in Political Economy*. New York: New York Academic Press.

————. 1994. "Reducing Bribery in the Public Sector." In Duc V. Trang (ed.), *Corruption and Democracy*. Budapest: In stitute for Constitutional and Legislative Policy.

————. 1995. "Proposal for Research on the Level and Impact of Corruption on International Business." Paper presented at the Transparency International Annual Meeting, Milan, Italy, 27–28 March.

————. 1996a. "The Political Economy of Corruption: Causes and Consquences." *Viewpoint* (World Bank) 74 (April).

————. 1996b. "Redesigning the State to Fight Corruption." Viewpoint (World Bank) 75 (April).

Rubin, S. J. 1982. "International Aspects of the Control of Illicit Payments." *Syracuse Jour-*

nal of International Law and Governance 9: 315–321.

Ruzindana, Augustine. 1994. "Combating Corruption in Africa: The Case of Uganda." Paper delivered at the World Bank, Washington, D.C., 2–3 November.

Shleifer, Andrei, and Robert Vishney. 1992. "Pervasive Shortages under Socialism." *Rand Journal of Economics* 23: 237–46.

————. 1993. "Corruption." *Quarterly Journal of Economics* 108: 599–617.

Tanzi, Vittorio. 1994. "Corruption, Governmental Activities, and Markets." IMF Working Paper Washington, D.C.: International Monetary Fund.

Wade, Robert. 1982. "The System of Administrative and Political Corruption: Canal Irrigation in South India." *Journal of Development Studies* 18: 287–327.

Yoong Siew-Wah. 1973. "Some Aspects of Corruption." *National Youth Leadership Training Institute Journal* (January): 55–6.

[5]

Viewpoint

The World Bank April 1996

Note No. 75

Redesigning the State to Fight Corruption

Transparency, competition, and privatization

Susan Rose-Ackerman

A companion Note argued that, with norms of honesty constant, corruption depends on three factors: the overall level of public benefits available, the riskiness of corrupt deals, and the relative bargaining power of briber and bribee. Anticorruption strategies must operate in parallel, by reducing the benefits under the control of officials, increasing the costs of bribery, and limiting the bargaining power of officials. This Note proposes reforms to achieve these objectives, beginning with measures to increase the riskiness of corruption.

Risks and costs of bribery

Government policy can reduce corruption by increasing the benefits of being honest, increasing the probability of detection and punishment, and increasing the penalties levied on those caught. Such measures will usually require substantive law reform to tighten internal controls, strengthen external monitoring, and introduce more transparency.

Civil service reform

Reforming the civil service is an obvious first step. Often the pay structure needs adjustment. If officials are paid much less than those with similar training elsewhere in the economy, people willing to accept bribes will be disproportionately attracted to the public sector. Officials with discretionary control of large benefits may need to be paid much more than the going rate for people with similar skills, to increase their willingness to resist the high bribes they may be offered. But adequate civil service pay is only a necessary condition, not a sufficient one. Paradoxically, an official whose pay is boosted may demand higher bribes—to offset the risk of losing what is now a very desirable job. Thus, the incidence of bribery falls as fewer officials are willing to accept payoffs, but the size of the bribes paid increases.

Civil service reform must therefore include features tied to the marginal benefits of accepting payoffs. There are two parts to such a strategy. The first is to set civil service wages above the going private sector wage, or to grant public employees generous benefits, such as pensions, that they will receive only if they retire in good order. But, again, such reforms may not be sufficient, since they are not tied to the benefits of individual corrupt deals. Once an official steps over the line and begins to take bribes, these policies will encourage him to take ever-higher and more frequent payoffs. If he faces a high probability of losing his job anyway, why not take as much as possible? Thus, a second step is also necessary. Penalties should be tied to the marginal benefits of the payoffs received. The probability of detection and punishment and the level of punishment, given conviction, should increase with the level of peculation.

Furthermore, to be effective, antibribery laws must apply both to those who pay and to those who receive bribes. Convicted public officials should pay a penalty equal to a multiple of bribes received, and penalties for convicted bribers should be tied to their gains (their excess profits, for example), not to the amount paid. One effective deterrent is debarment procedures that prohibit corrupt firms from contracting with the government for a period of years.

Law enforcement and administrative penalties focus on locating corruption after it has occurred. They can deter civil servants from ac-

cepting or extorting payments if they create the perception that corruption carries high risks. The goal is to use a combination of carrots (desirable pay and benefits) and sticks (legal and administrative penalties) to deter payoffs.

External bodies and whistleblower statutes

Outside institutions can complement internal controls. An independent and honest judiciary, from lower-level clerks to judges, is essential for effective legal sanctions. As alternatives or supplements, other independent review and investigative systems have been proposed, such as an anticorruption commission, an ombudsman, or other independent administrative tribunals. Such external review bodies (Hong Kong's Independent Commission against Corruption, for example[1]) can be valuable, but they carry the risk of arbitrariness if they report only to the country's ruler.

Uncovering evidence of corruption is notoriously difficult because both sides to the transaction have an interest in keeping it secret. In fact, reporting the peculations of others can be dangerous. If corruption is systemic, a "whistleblower" risks being disciplined by corrupt superiors and attacked by coworkers, and may even end up being accused of corruption himself. Governments should consider promulgating whistleblower statutes that protect and reward those in the public and private sector who report malfeasance. The United States, for example, has a statute that rewards those who report irregularities in government contracts.

When corruption is systemic, solutions that appear reasonable in other contexts can have perverse effects. For example, some recommend rotating officials so that they are unable to develop the close, trusting relations in which payoffs may be more likely. But if the entire government agency is corrupt, superiors can use their ability to reassign staff to punish those who refuse to play along. A study of corruption in an irrigation system in India found that such practices were common.[2] They have also been observed in corrupt police forces in the United States.

Increased transparency

Those concerned with fighting corruption should support a free press, few constraints on the creation and operation of watchdog and good-government groups, and freedom of information laws. They should oppose restrictive libel laws, especially those that give special protection to public officials. Elected politicians ought not be immune from charges of corruption.

Within the public sector certain structures and systems can make government actions more transparent. Corruption is deterred because it is more difficult to hide. For example, strong financial management systems are essential that audit government accounts and make financial information about the government public. Open and fair procurement regulations are also necessary. Similarly, corruption among politicians can be deterred through campaign finance reform and conflict of interest rules. But restrictions on legal donations must not be so restrictive that they push candidates off the books. Legal controls must be combined with effective methods of financing campaigns from public money or private contributions.

Integrated approach

It is hard to evaluate the relative merits of these options in the abstract, because their costs and benefits depend on the context. But most cannot stand alone. For example, increases in civil service pay and benefits are pointless if credible monitoring systems are not in place to detect wrongdoing. Policies to increase the risks and costs of corruption are usually part of reform strategies designed to reduce the potential benefits. For example, when Mexico reformed its customs service, it not only simplified the underlying regulations, but also improved civil service pay and improved auditing and control.

Reducing discretionary benefits

The most promising anticorruption reforms are those that reduce the discretionary benefits under the control of public officials. This must be done without simply shifting the benefits to private sector elites, where they will show up as monopoly profits.

Less intervention

The first and most obvious way to reduce payoff opportunities is simply to eliminate those programs riddled with corruption—though this is not an option for programs with strong public policy rationales. If the state has no authority to restrict exports or license businesses, there is no opportunity for bribes. If a subsidy program is eliminated, the associated bribes will also disappear. If price controls are lifted, market prices will express scarcity values, not bribes. If a parastatal that is the locus of corrupt payoffs is moved into the private sector, those payoffs will end.

Of course, many regulatory and spending programs have strong justifications and ought to be reformed, not eliminated.

Competition and market forces

In general, any reform that increases the competitiveness of the economy helps reduce corrupt incentives. Policies that lower the controls on foreign trade, remove entry barriers for private industry, and privatize state firms in a way that assures competition, all contribute to the fight against corruption. But deregulation and privatization must be carried out with care. Deregulating in one area may increase corruption elsewhere. For example, a successful effort to reduce corruption in the transport of agricultural products in one African country increased corruption and legal tariffs in neighboring countries on the same transport route.[3] The privatization process can itself be corrupted, as can new regulatory institutions. Rather than bribing the parastatal to obtain contracts and favorable treatment, bidders bribe officials in the privatization authority. This is not to say that privatization and deregulation are not, on balance, desirable in most cases, but only to caution reformers to be aware of the incentives for malfeasance along the way.

Economists have long recommended reforming regulatory laws in such areas as environmental protection by introducing market-based schemes and charging user fees for scarce government services. In addition to improving efficiency, these reforms reduce corrupt incentives. The sale of water and grazing rights, pollution rights, and import and export licenses can limit corruption by replacing bribes with legal payments.

Administrative reforms can also be important in lowering corrupt incentives. One such reform is the introduction of competition within government to reduce the bargaining power of officials. When bribes are paid for benefits such as licenses and permits, overlapping, competitive bureaucratic jurisdictions can reduce corruption. Since clients can apply to any of a number of officials and go to a second one if the first turns them down, no one official has much monopoly power, and, therefore, no one can extract a very large payoff. For qualified clients, bribes will be no larger than the cost of reapplication. Unqualified clients will still pay bribes, but even they will not pay much so long as they too can try another official. This model can be extended to law enforcement, giving police officers who control illegal businesses overlapping enforcement areas. Gamblers and drug dealers will not pay much to an individual policeman if a second one may come along later and also demand a payoff. The system may work better if the law enforcement officers belong to different police forces—local, state, or federal, for example—making collusion among officers less likely.

Clear rules, simple processes

When corruption is difficult to observe, administrative reforms can be designed to make its effects more easily observed. For example, the state might use private market prices as benchmarks to judge public contracts. Clear rules of proper behavior could be established so violations can be spotted even if the bribery itself is not. Procurement decisions could favor standard off-the-shelf items to provide a benchmark and to lower the cost of submitting a bid.

Corruption in the collection of taxes cannot, of course, be solved by failing to collect revenue. In such cases, one solution is to clarify and streamline the necessary laws. The reform of the Mexican customs service, for example, reduced the steps in the customs process from twelve to four, and streamlined the remaining service to reduce delays. Rules should be transparent and publicly justified. A government could move toward simple nondiscretionary tax, spending, and regulatory laws as a way of limiting corrupt opportunities. But the value of such reforms depends on the costs of limiting the flexibility of public officials. Some risk of corruption often needs to be tolerated in exchange for the benefits of a case-by-case approach in administering programs. But even in these cases, transparency and publicity can reduce corrupt incentives.

Many corrupt situations have both winners and losers. The state could introduce ways for the potential losers to protest or to organize ahead of time, or make it hard for corrupt officials to organize themselves or bribe payers. Sometimes bribe payers view themselves as losers who would be better off in an honest world and are potential allies in an anticorruption effort. But when bribery makes both the payer and the recipient better off than they would be in a no-bribery world, control incentives must rest with outsiders (for example, disappointed bidders, taxpayers, consumers). The existence of losers with a large stake in the outcome, such as disappointed bidders, can facilitate efforts to limit corruption.

Conclusions

Some argue that bribes help firms and individuals circumvent government requirements—reducing delays and avoiding burdensome regulations and taxes. Payoffs seem to be nothing more than the grease needed to move the gears of complex machinery. But corruption cannot be limited to situations where the rules are inefficient. Incentives to make and ask for payoffs exist whenever a government official has economic power over a private firm or individual. It does not matter whether the power is justified or unjustified. Once a pattern of successful payoffs is institutionalized, corrupt officials have an incentive to demand larger bribes and seek new ways to extract payments. Therefore, even when illegal payoffs appear to facilitate commerce, governments and private citizens should not respond with tolerance. Instead, they must move vigorously to stem a "culture" of illegality. Illegal markets are always inefficient relative to a well-functioning legal market. Those with scruples will not participate, price information will be poor because of the illegality of the trades, and time and energy must be expended to keep the deal secret and to enforce its terms. In some cases, paying bribes may be more efficient than complying with existing rules, but corruption is always a second-best response to government failures.

Corruption can never be entirely eliminated. Under many realistic conditions, it is simply too expensive to reduce corruption to zero. And a single-minded focus on preventing corruption can impinge on personal freedoms and human rights. Such a focus could produce a government that is rigid and unresponsive. The aim, therefore, should be not complete rectitude, but a fundamental increase in the honesty—and thus the efficiency, fairness, and political legitimacy—of government.

[1] Robert Klitgaard, *Controlling Corruption*, Berkeley: University of California Press, 1988, chapter 4; Jon Quah, "Controlling Corruption in City-States: A Comparative Study of Hong Kong and Singapore," prepared for a conference on "The East Asian Miracle: Economic Growth and Public Policy," Stanford University, Palo Alto, CA, 1993.

[2] Robert Wade, "The System of Administrative and Political Corruption: Canal Irrigation in South India," *Journal of Development Studies* 18: 287–327 (1982).

[3] Glenn Rogers and Sidi Mohammed Iddal, "Reduction of Illegal Payments in West Africa: Niger's Experience," draft discussion paper presented at a workshop on "Good Governance and the Regional Economy in Francophone Africa," sponsored by USAID and IRIS, Dakar, March 1996.

Susan Rose-Ackerman is Henry R. Luce Professor of Law and Political Science at Yale University and a Visiting Research Fellow at the World Bank in the Private Sector Development Department (email: sroseackerman@worldbank.org). She is the author of Corruption: A Study in Political Economy *and is currently working on a book on corruption in developing and transition economies.*

[6]

Crime, Law & Social Change **29:** 99–112, 1998.

Dealing with corruption: the next steps *

ALAN DOIG
Liverpool Business School, Liverpool John Moores University, UK

Abstract. The 1997 White Paper from the British Government's Department for International Development (DFID) was specific in identifying the role of governance now being addressed by international and national donors: "improving governance can ... improve the lives of poor people directly. It is also essential for creating the environment for faster economic growth. Both aspects can be compromised by corruption, which all governments must address. In developing countries it is the poor who bear proportionally the heaviest cost" (DFID, 1997, p. 30). Dealing with corruption is thus a priority both in terms of who it most affects and in terms of which objectives of governance – including participatory and responsive government and economic growth – it constrains. Although it has long held a specialist academic interest, corruption has become the subject of growing practitioner attention which means that the focus on corruption is beginning to move significantly from theory to practice and the practical. While there is substance to the belief that fire-engines cannot be designed without a thorough understanding of the fire they are intended to put out, there is also a sense in which the pervasiveness and tenacity of the current fires of corruption are such that action rather than refining theories and processes is what is now required. To paraphrase an analogy made by a senior British civil servant about the general issue of identifying policy – that corruption "is rather like the elephant – you recognise it when you see it but cannot easily define it" (quoted in Hill, 1997, p. 6) – is also to suggest that, while theorising may help draw up longer-term approaches to dealing with corruption, there is enough information and experience to develop best practice proposals for more immediate implementation and for developmental strategies that link to the longer-term approaches. This article addresses some of the issues of this agenda which seeks to develop, for those actively involved in anti-corruption initiatives, frameworks within which to consider realisable and cost-effective shorter-term anti-corruption strategies.

Introduction

The new development agenda of the late 1990s prioritises the interests of the poor and marginalised in the context of an enabling state and higher ethi-

* This article draws on themes of an 18-month research project on corruption and anti-corruption strategies funded by the British Government's Department for International Development. The project team comprises: Alan Doig (Liverpool John Moores University), Robert Williams (University of Durham), Michael Levi (University of Wales, Cardiff), Mark Hampton (University of Portsmouth), Robin Theobald (University of Westminster), and David Watt (University of Liverpool). The project has three researchers – Jon Moran, Rachel Flanary and Stephanie McIvor – and is based at the Liverpool Business School, Liverpool John Moores University, Liverpool L3 5UZ.

cal standards among donors (UNDP 1997, World Bank 1997, DFID 1997). There is an acceptance that a limited, legitimate, honest, strengthened and transparent state ought to be at the centre of the development process in both developing and transitional countries: "those most likely to succeed will have effective government, enlightened legislation, prudent budgeting and an efficient administration that responds to the needs of poor people" (DFID 1997, p. 30). Evidence of commitment to good government and good governance – where the former is concerned with the structure and performance of the state and the latter is concerned with the ends to which they are put in terms of achieving nation-wide levels of economic, human, environmental and institutional development (Doig 1995) – is an increasingly explicit assumption in programmes for reform and in warnings of possible curtailment of funding to those countries which fail to reform.

Within the commitment to good government, dealing with corruption has become a core component for the reinvigoration of the state's institutional capacity (World Bank 1997), for ensuring society's trust in its leadership (United Nations International Drug Control Programme 1997) and for protecting the fabric of public life (UNDP 1997). The increasing attention given to corruption, however, has "mostly inspired analyses, conferences and writings rather than action in the international arena ... The time is ripe for a revolution: many emerging economies are now prepared for the international community to deliver concrete support in the fight against corruption" (Kaufmann 1997, p. 130).

International agencies and donors governments have all issued statements or policies on corruption. A number, such as DFID, are actively supporting anti-corruption and good government programmes. The next steps concern the systematic development of strategies on how to approach corruption in practice with a particular emphasis on both short and longer-term reform programmes, with the focus of reform to benefit the most disadvantaged members of society. While there is a role for academic discourse on patterns and varieties of corruption that could help work toward an appropriate framework for reform, it is crucial to appreciate that corruption is currently a pervasive and invasive constraint on reform. There is a need for less theorising and more action. There is also a need to appreciate that the study of corruption does not belong to one academic discipline but should draw on a number of perspectives, just as tacking corruption cannot be a discrete activity but must be considered within other government and governance-related reforms or issues which may enhance or dilute specific anti-corruption approaches. It has been argued, for example, that there is "no point in creating anti-corruption agencies where bureaucrats and politicians intervene at will to apply regulatory restrictions" (Kaufmann 1997 p. 124). Similarly it is suggested, in relation to customs activities, that "what standard principal agent models which focus on an individual administration cannot do is to show how national level factors intervene to influence trade policy and the enforcement of procedures within a customs administration" (quoted in Stasavage & Daubree 1997 p. 1). Such arguments illustrate the need for a approach based on the complementarity of reform that is also sensitive to the social, political, cultural and economic contexts in which institutional reforms may take place. Such an approach must be rooted in experience, recognising what is acceptable, realisable and sustainable in terms of impact, cost and length of implementation.

Theories and practicalities: rethinking reform?

The design and practical delivery of anti-corruption programmes should not be over-influenced by definitional and desk perspectives which offer an indiscriminate, broad-brush approach which belies in-country realities or cross-country differences and neglects the sequential linkages between hypothesised goals and the building blocks to achieve them. All reforms with any practical merit should contain a number of core premises: are there any unanticipated or adverse consequences that may arise either from a specific reform or its interrelation with other reforms; which reforms may be supported externally and which must rely on the goodwill or a longer-term, public-interest view by recipients; do the reforms have a sequential awareness in terms of strategic intervention, longer-term sustainability and, crucially, an integral exit strategy?

The enthusiasm for generalised reform proposals often reflect the lack of experience of implementation on the ground at both the macro- and micro-levels and simply ignore the exigencies of political power. It has been argued rightly that "political corruption seems to have been fostered by the *long stay in power of the same political party*" (Della Porta & Meny 1997 p. 172, emphasis in original) but, while one can limit, for example, presidential tenure, a crucial point about the introduction of democracy is the issue of, and basis for, competition. Thus there is "the need for significant, structured political competition" but that "such competition can scarcely solve all problems (because) its benefits depend on a free flow of information (and thus upon civil liberties and a relatively free press), a lack of pervasive violence in everyday life, a viable civil society, and political will and determination among opposition leaders" (Johnston 1997 p. 14). The achievement of this more detailed permutation of components of an almost Dahlian perception of perfect citizenship still passes over the requisite building blocks and possible constraints such as: the motivations that drive national governments; the logistical, sequencing, financial and political complexities that arise between policy intention and delivery; and the possibility that even their apparent achievement is no guarantee of the delivery of what governance is about. The potential of a gap between form and substance is all too possible. The post-reform reality may be, as David Held argues, that, even when citizens of developing countries "may enjoy formal equality, for example, before the law ... for many of them it is rendered virtually meaningless in practice by the absence of satisfactory housing, nutrition and education". (Held 1995 p. 214). Thus, in terms of developing anti-corruption strategies, longer-term objectives should be taken into account for their direction and purpose but it should be emphasised that longer-term reforms may take decades, if not generations to achieve and embed, and will involve major, inter-related societal development (even then there are no certainty of a rooted public service culture or sustained public participation in politics [see Ridley & Doig 1995]).

What is crucial in determining longer-term goals is a clear awareness of such issues as: firstly, the potentially-adverse consequences of certain reforms (democratisation and the drive for party funding, for example); secondly, the sequence of the building blocks of reform (the effectiveness of anti-corruption agencies may be very much dependent on an honest and efficient judicial system which will take much more time and investment to achieve than the establishment of a single institution); thirdly, the inter-relation of specific governance reforms and more general reform (the promotion of an independent press, the access to the material [such as an efficient distribution and transport system, or radios that are not reliant on expensive batteries] and literacy campaigns); fourthly, what is achievable by direct intervention or what *goals* of reform rely on other, less controllable, factors (party competition can be funded but would recipient countries actively work to support an *effective* political opposition in Parliament?); fifthly, the sequence of reform in terms of an overall goal of governance in terms of legitimacy and trust in government (for example, is police corruption a bigger threat than judicial corruption in terms of public perceptions?).

Such issues are equally applicable to the activities of the state itself. The assumption that any "serious" reform effort must "reduce the size of the civil service, pay decent base salaries to those who remain, and establish a merit-based recruitment system, and develop effective sticks and carrots that give officials an incentive both to be honest and to perform efficiently" (Rose-Ackerman 1997 p. 34) may have adverse political and economic consequences in practice unless properly contexualised and unless such consequences are properly identified and planned for. Accounting for ghost workers (and ghost organisations in some countries) is an important audit exercise but rapidly shrinking a workforce untrained in other competencies and without the benefit of any financial compensation (both common features in public sector downsizing in industrialised countries) into an underdeveloped private sector is an important consideration. The implications for state support is another in that, particularly in countries where ideology and linked party machinery is not a significant political factor, patronage networks traditionally secures political loyalty to the state in, for example, African societies, where "political entrepreneurs exercise their talent, weaving the web of constant wheeling and dealing, capable of rationally managing their material and symbolic resources in their own best interests in the interests of the community which has given them fame and influence" (Bayart 1993 p. 217).

At a micro-level, a number of reforms are sometimes suggested such as overlapping jurisdictions, enhanced salaries and better training. Overlapping jurisdictions as a means for reform derive from the literature on rent-seeking and seek to make bribery a zero-sum activity by sharing responsibilities for decisions, thus diluting the monopoly use of discretionary power. Nevertheless, this is primarily related to licensing and regulation activities (it is not a reform easily applied to police or medical work) and may overlook such basic physical issues such as public access and convenience. It certainly contradicts the usual pressure for deregulation. The major focus of either single-source or overlapping jurisdictions is on the officials involved; the reforms are predicated accordingly. They do not build from the perspective of what the public might want from *existing* procedures which may include the certainty of a decision (time-limited), the reason for the decision (transparency), the name of the official who made the decision (responsibility) and the right of redress (accountability). What should form the basis for reform, therefore, is less that of the means (how to deal with the public official) than what is the objective of the reform: how are the public to be better served and, in so doing, transfer the balance of the exercise of the power in favour of the consumer. It is interesting in Wade's article on canal irrigation on South India (1984) that he sets out two proposals to deal with demands for bribes by officials that take this perspective. Firstly he suggests strengthening "the user side of the irrigator-official relation, both by the familiar devise of a user organisation ... *and* by monitoring of the performance of each canal system by an independent monitoring organisation whose reports would be made public ... Opportunities for the exercise of 'voice', if coupled with a non-partisan source of information, could be much more effective in curbing the arbitrary exercise of authority..." (p. 321; emphasis in the original). He also goes on to suggest a technical means of "designing-out" the potential for corruption by opening up availability of, and access to, water at crucial times with more storage reservoirs, "filled according to a pre-determined, well-advertised schedule, and irrigators would themselves have more responsibility for allocating the water to the fields" (p. 321).

The low (or unpaid) salaries of public servants are often given as a major incentive to solicit bribes, particularly when compared to those of the business people and companies with whom they deal. While this is true for certain activities of the public sector it is not for the voluminous contacts between the public and the public servant. Indeed, it may be arguable that the majority of the public have lower (and even less certain) incomes than the public servants they deal with. It is noteworthy that the public may be more interested in punishment rather than salary enhancement as a means of dealing with corrupt officials (Langsweth & Michael, this volume). It could be argued that the public should not be expected to bear the consequences of what is in effect income displacement and that, if officials are not paid or are poorly-paid, then their grievance is with the employer. Requiring the public to pay "salaries" (and officials invariably seek to maximise their income rather than top-up their official salaries) by way of bribes should not necessarily elicit sympathy for the public official. Nor should it necessarily be assumed that the solution lies with resolving the officials' difficulties when it is the quality and availability of a public service that is the issue. Will paying the official, or paying the official more, achieve these ends? Can pay be linked to performance based on the possible criteria given above? Should donors insist on the certainty of administrative expenditure associated with their programme expenditure? Again, how reform is to be effected should reflect context, complementarity, planning and purpose.

Developing a matrix for planning reform

Formulating practical strategies also means strategies which have as their objective "not merely to reduce corruption in an official agency but, at the same time, not to harm the objective for which the agency was deployed in the first place" (Bardhan 1997 p. 36). They also need to take place within the context of the focus on the state and thus upon the "public office", public sector, or institutional dimensions of corruption because "sound and accountable government ... is the foundation of economic growth and poverty elimination allowing poor and disadvantaged people to achieve their civil, political, economic, social and cultural rights" (DFID 1997 p. 30).

There are clearly a number of core questions to be addressed within the context of this process:

> What type or types of corruption are the most damaging in which institutions or countries?
> What are the relationships between corruption and poverty and how can an effective, enabling state act to reduce corruption?

Depending on the assessments under the previous two headings the focus should then be on:

> What forms of anti-corruption strategies are likely to be most effective in the short and long term to minimise corruption, particularly for those members of society most adversely affected directly and indirectly by its consequences?

Any strategy – and a sequential, cross-institution, cross-activity approach (see for an applied example, Klitgaard 1997, Appendix 2: The Beginnings of a Strategy against Corruption in an Unnamed African Country, and Mills 1997) is preferred to avoid divergence and dissonance in terms of agencies' goals and competition for own-government and external donor support – for tackling the causes of corruption, assessing its consequences and then developing anti-corruption measures will require a framework within which to work. Rather than seeking only to define corruption itself or, indeed, the motivations of those involved, the aim must be to try and build an incremental approach that looks to where corruption does the most damage and what measures minimise opportunity or incentive while increasing the likelihood of detection and enforcement of sanctions cost-effectively by profiling its context and environment.

The context should recognise the diversity of transitional or developing countries: "high-income, oil-exporting countries; industrialising economies with strong states and low debt; industrialising countries with weak states and/or debt problems; potential newly industrialising countries; and primary commodity exporters" among whom "common cause is difficult to achieve with such varying profiles and prospects" (Horsman & Marshall 1995 p. 138). It also assesses the position of the transitional or developing states in terms of the global economy, legitimate or illicit: "the often weak and debt-ridden economies of many developing countries leave them vulnerable and dependant on economic forces and relations over which they have little, if any, control. Although the internationalisation of production and finance places many instruments of economic control beyond even the most powerful countries, the position of those at the lower end of the globalisation hierarchy, experiencing the stronger effects of unevenness, is substantially worse" (D. Held 1995 p. 82).

Such recognition provides the basis to begin mapping, on an individual country or institution basis, information to begin addressing the core questions about corruption: "the next logical step for empirical research on corruption is to conduct case studies which will offer more detail of how corruption actually functions than does the cross-country work but which are designed in a rigorous fashion to test specific corruption hypotheses. This could be done either by considering corruption in a country as a whole, or, more plausibly, by investigating corruption within a given institution in a given country..." (Goudie & Stasavage 1997 p. 51). Such an approach has applied validity because, "after careful country assessments are prepared, specific policy and institutional advice will need to be provided" (Gray & Kaufmann 1998 p. 10). Thus an applied research matrix can be developed that seeks to address the core questions through an assessment of the nature, focus and impact of corruption in individual countries from which country- or institution-specific information may be drawn. Such a matrix may draw together information across three general headings:

Component 1. Causes and impact of corruption

1.1 How far are the causes of corruption are influenced by geography, political, economic and cultural factors, and by the relationships between political and administrative processes, and between the public and private sector?

1.2 How far has corruption led to decreased economic development, loss of revenue, and waste or misallocation of state expenditure, and to partial and arbitrary misuse of powers and procedures on the more vulnerable and disadvantaged groups in society, to limited and poorly-targeted public services and to distorted allocative and decision-making processes in favour of specific groups in society?

1.3 What has been the impact of corruption in terms of the performance of the state or institution; has it encouraged or exacerbated inequality, lawlessness, alienation and poverty and led to lack of trust and legitimacy, instability and alienation from the state or institution?

1.4 What patterns of corruption are identified; what types of activity are generally considered corrupt, and why; and which types of corruption have the most adverse effects on which groups in society, and why?

1.5 To what extent has corruption led to discredited disciplined behaviour and the dilution of legitimate social and individual aspirations, and thus nationbuilding, by denying the impartiality and willingness of the state to support those most at risk or threat from its powers and procedures?

1.6 How far has corruption contributed to the "democratic deficit" by reinforcing power structures and encouraging a political culture based on manipulation of personal, financial and ethnic ties rather than openness, a public service culture and the development of social well-being and confidence in the future?

Component 2. The political, economic, institutional, and social environment

2.1 Is the corruption country- or institution-specific and do different political, administrative and economic configurations give rise to differing levels or types of corruption and thus to differing impacts on different groups in society?

2.2 What is the place of corruption in terms of a broader framework of (good or bad) governance, lawlessness and the rule of law, and fundamental human rights, particularly in relation to the poorest?

2.3 Are there certain activities and functions of the state or institution which are more vulnerable than others, and what further impact arises as a consequence of transitional and developmental change, with particular reference to the effects of democratisation, privatisation, structural adjustment, market liberalisation and the shift from public administration to public management?

2.4 How far does a 'soft' or 'hollow' state exist, and how far does the organisation, complexity and relevance of its procedures and regulations – as well as the means for decision-making, adjudication and redress – promote or exacerbate corruption?

2.5 What are the implications of politics as 'business', and officeholding for 'rent-seeking'?

2.6 How far does corruption lead to the diminution of assets or income, distorts taxation in terms of adversely affecting those least able to avoid tax liabilities, and results in decreased economic dynamism which leads to an inability to pay suitable public salaries and fund basic state functions?

2.7 How far is corruption a consequence of change and thus may be transient or how far corruption is entrenched and likely to persist, with consequences for the wider political, economic, institutional and social context?

2.8 What is the likely effect of the wider issues of change, and more specific structural, legal judicial, party political, cultural and political constraints, on the sustainable development and effectiveness over time of anti-corruption measures?

2.9 How far should – and could – anti-corruption measures and agencies underpin wider social, economic, political, legal and judicial developments, including a 'public' sphere, with strong state institutions with sustainable tax income and, in the longer-term, a civil society with strong non-political professional associations, the primacy of a public service ethos over that of patron-client or vertical ethnic relations, a sustainable independent economic sphere, an informed media, a literate public and a monetarised economy?

Component 3. The global economy and the links between corruption, fraud, organised crime, and international illicit capital flows

3.1 To what extent does corruption inhibit (a) general crime reduction, and (b) judicial independence and efficiency?

3.2 How far does corruption affect the state income via the links between corruption, international tax rates and smuggling transit routes, and inhibit competition within the local economy?

3.3 How is crime organised and to what extent is corruption a necessary or sufficient condition for particular forms of criminal behaviour, i.e. what would be the shape of crime if there were more or less corruption, organised crime and money-laundering?

3.4 What is the impact of local and international financial services regulation in inhibiting corruption and money-laundering; and what is the impact of both perceptions and reality of corruption and organised crime upon inward investment, capital formation and accumulation?

3.5 What is the relationship between corruption and crime, and what are the implications of this for development, stability and democratisation; for confidence in law enforcement and the judicial process; and for developments in fraud, money-laundering and the unlawful secret financing of political parties, both nationally and internationally?

3.6 What is the relationship between developments in international and organised crime in terms of how, at what level(s) and with what resources, the state can respond to corruption and organised crime, and what are the international co-operation pre-requisites for effective action?

Conclusion: Designing and delivering realisable reform

Such components are not comprehensive or all-inclusive. They are also a necessary but not sufficient condition for tackling corruption. Rather, they provide the context within which anti-corruption strategies may be proposed and assessed in terms of: what type or types of corruption are the most damaging; what are the relationships between corruption and wider good government and good governance objectives; how can an effective, enabling state be developed and how should it seek to act to reduce corruption; and what forms of anti-corruption strategy are likely to be most effective in the short and long term to minimise corruption, particularly for those most adversely affected by its consequences, directly and indirectly? Countries "serious about fighting corruption will require a detailed country-specific assessment" – including "where corruption is imposing the most costs", in relation to tax and customs revenues, business regulation, state sponsorship of infrastructure projects, institutional reform, political commitment and public involvement – as well as "the experience of other countries – both successful experiments and those that backfired when the nominal anticorruption fighter became corrupt themselves" (Rose-Ackerman 1997). Similarly, the approach to anti-corruption strategies requires planning, a risk and vulnerability assessment ("what kinds of corruption exist, in which functions and agencies, to what degree, who is helped, who is hurt, and what are the conditions that contribute to the corruption"), a strategy that "focuses on corrupt systems, not (just) corrupt individuals" and implementation policies which integrate a number of components, including an institutional focus, a prioritised and collaborative approach, institution strengthening, public support and wider changes to the shape, delivery and performance of the provision of government services and resources through the state or the private sector (Klitgaard 1997). Thus a range of current practices and proposals could be assessed across state activities at all levels, seeking to maximise their impact and their contribution to the overall reform goals. A final component within the matrix could consider strategy issues at individual, organisational and national levels, as follows:

Component 4. Effective anti-corruption strategy issues

4.1 An assessment at citizen level of sustainable, independent and co-ordinated strategies for controlling or minimising small-scale corruption in terms of protection against the extractive and arbitrary nature of the state and its officials, with particular reference to relations between the public and the state, including structural reform (decentralisation and deregulation), legislative sunlight and sunset provisions, suitable and relevant administrative procedures (overlapping and competitive jurisdictions, and multiple providers, benchmarking, one-stop shops, the customerisation of public services and service delivery surveys), quick and effective complaints and redress (hotlines, whistleblowing, Ombudsmen and administrative tribunals), and community oversight (awareness and education, citizens' watchdog groups, the role of the media);

4.2 An assessment at major contract, and senior political and administrative levels, of strategies for controlling or minimising corruption with particular reference to appropriate and policeable laws, codes of conduct, asset and interests registers, state funding of parties, controls on revolving door and patronage appointments, incentive-based performance for officials, the use of expatriate government staffing to advise on the operations of government departments, the use of Build-Own-Transfer/NGO/-PSI firms for procurement and delivery of vulnerable state activities, judicial independence and effective prosecution procedures, the impact of improved financial management systems and bureaucratic procedures, the use of anti-corruption agencies, the impact of strengthening revenue agencies, the roles of agencies such as Auditor-Generals and parliamentary oversight committees, the Ombudsman, police fraud squads, and the roles of inter-agency work (with reference to shared information, training and resources, co-ordination of effort);

4.3 An evaluation at state level of procedures and training within state or public sector institutions in general for promoting a public service culture that also seeks to curtail the opportunities and incentives for, as well as the inhibitors and facilitators of, corruption, including: procedures to oversee assets, information and contracts: the use of risk and impact assessments; risk management and performance measurement systems; recruitment, appointment, and pay issues; the role of the management of quality, reward mechanisms, enclave development and other capacity-building approaches to 'design out' corruption; procedures to increase the risks of detection; and the effectiveness of investigations and sanctions as deterrence.

For most developing countries the short-term goal is to identify the most effective and economical of such measures with a further emphasis on: whether the focus of reform should be on the office or on the officeholder; whether the focus of any anti-corruption strategy should be on protecting state revenue or on investigating evidence of criminal activity such as contract corruption; whether the purpose of anti-corruption activity is retribution – the visible punishment of wrongdoers – or restitution, protecting state funds and seeking to return to the state those funds and related corrupt payments acquired illegally; and how both corruption and its prevention, detection, investigation and prosecution is to be measured (Doig & Riley 1998). The final stage in the planning process in developing a framework for realisable anti-corruption strategies will then seek to integrate international and other donor agencies' current anti-corruption, good government and good governance initiatives, on a country-by-country basis and involving institutional (and inter-institutional) practices, procedures and strategies for the cost-effective prevention, detection, management and prosecution of corruption with an emphasis on the impact of such strategies for alleviating poverty and fostering closer relationships between the state and the public and on the potential for co-ordinated and co-operative approaches to specific institutions and countries.

References

P. Bardhan (1997) "Corruption and Development: A Review of the Issues". *UNDP-PACT and OECD Development Centre Workshop on Corruption and Integrity Improvement Initiatives in the Context of Developing Countries, Paris.*

J.-F. Bayart (1993) *The State in Africa: The Politics of the Belly.* London: Longman.

DFID (1997) *Eliminating World Poverty.* London: HMSO.

D. Della Porta & Y. Meny (1997) *Democracy and Corruption in Europe.* London: Pinter.

A. Doig (1995) "Good Government and Sustainable Anti-Corruption Strategies: A Role for Independent Anti-Corruption Agencies?", *Public Administration and Development,* Vol. 15, No 2.

A. Doig & F.F. Ridley (1996) *Sleaze: Politics, Private Interests and Public Reaction,* Oxford University Press.

A. Doig & S. Riley (1998) "Corruption and Anti-Corruption Strategies: Issues and Case-Studies from Developing Countries" in G.S. Cheema & J. Bonvin (eds.) *Corruption and Integrity Improvement Initiatives in Developing Economies,* OECD, Paris.

A.W. Goudie & D. Stasavage (1997). "Corruption: the Issues". *OECD Development Centre: Technical Paper No. 122.* Paris.

C.W. Gray & D. Kaufmann (1998) "Corruption and Development". *Finance and Development.* March 1998.

M. Johnston (1997) " 'Frontier Corruption': Points of Vulnerability and Challenges for Reform". *UNDP-PACT and OECD Development Centre Workshop on Corruption and Integrity Improvement Initiatives in the Context of Developing Countries, Paris.*

D. Held (1995) *Democracy and the Global Order.* Polity.

M. Hill (1997) *The Policy Process in the Modern State.* London: Prentice Hall/Harvester Wheatsheaf.

M. Horsman & A. Marshall (1995) *After the Nation State.* Harper Collins.

D. Kaufmann (1997) "Corruption: The Facts". *Foreign Policy.* Summer.

R. Klitgaard (1997) "Cleaning Up and Invigorating the Civil Service". *Report for the Operations Evaluation Department, World Bank.*

A. Mills (1997) "Strengthening Domestic Institutions Against Corruption: The OECD/PUMA Ethics Checklist". *UNDP-PACT and OECD Development Centre Workshop on Corruption and Integrity Improvement Initiatives in the Context of Developing Countries, Paris.*

F.F. Ridley & A. Doig (1995). *Sleaze: Politicians, Private Interests and Public Reaction.* Oxford: Oxford University Press.

S. Rose-Ackerman (1997) "Corruption and Development". *World Bank Annual Conference on Development Economics.* Washington, DC.

D. Stasavage & C. Daubree (1997) "Determinants of Customs Fraud: Evidence from Two African Countries". *UNDP-PACT and OECD Development Centre Workshop on Corruption and Integrity Improvement Initiatives in the Context of Developing Countries, Paris.*

United Nations Development Programme [UNDP]. (1997). *Human Development Report.* Oxford: Oxford University Press.

United Nations International Drug Control Programme [UNDCP]. (1997). *World Drug Report,* Oxford: Oxford University Press.

R. Wade (1984) "The System of Administrative and Political Corruption: Canal Irrigation in South India. *Journal of Development Studies.* Vol. 18. No. 3.

World Bank (1997) *World Development Report,* Oxford: Oxford University Press.

Alan Doig is Professor of Public Services Management and the Head of the Unit for the Study of White Crime, Liverpool Business School, Liverpool L3 5UZ. He is author of a number of publications on corruption, fraud and conflict of interest. He has been project manager of training, and organisational design and development, projects for three overseas anti-corruption agencies.

[7]

The Political Economy of Anti-Corruption Strategies in Africa

STEPHEN P. RILEY

In the mid-1990s an international consensus in development discourse has emerged: democratisation, public sector down-sizing, and economic deregulation are desirable goals in themselves, but they also reduce the extensive corruption in monopolistic state agencies. This study examines these issues with reference to the politics and practicalities of anti-corruption strategies in several African societies. It is argued that although down-sizing the state and political liberalisation are desirable goals in many African countries, they are necessary rather than sufficient conditions for the reduction of corruption. Extensive public sector corruption can coexist with democratic or quasi-democratic politics (as in Nigeria in the 1980s). Economic liberalisation can also create opportunities for corruption, through the sales of parastatals in dubious circumstances, and the creation of new, corrupt markets, as can the political liberalisation of previously authoritarian regimes such as Kenya in the 1990s. For short-term anti-corruption strategies to be effective in African societies, more attention needs to be devoted to questions of sequencing, the detail of reform and its sustainability in very poor societies, and the exceptional political and managerial commitment necessary to promote and maintain reform.

INTRODUCTION

Two political upheavals in May 1997 are symptomatic of the condition of contemporary African states. The collapse of Mobutu's kleptocratic regime in Zaïre was closely followed by the overthrow of the democratically elected government in Sierra Leone [*Collins, 1997; Gourevitch, 1997; Riley, 1997*].

Stephen P. Riley, Reader in Politics, School of Humanities and Social Sciences, Staffordshire University, Stoke on Trent ST4 2DE, United Kingdom. He has also taught at the University of Sierra Leone in West Africa and two South African universities: Rhodes University in Grahamstown and the University of Durban-Westville. He is the founding co-editor of *Corruption and Reform: An International Journal/Crime, Law and Social Change* and is currently (1998–99) the research co-ordinator of a British government-funded Department For International Development (DFID) research project on the control of corruption in developing and transitional countries.

Mobutu's replacement by the Democratic Republic of the Congo under Laurent Kabila is evidence of much broader and generally progressive contemporary developments in Africa. Ruled in a malign and authoritarian way for 32 years by Mobutu Sese Seko, Zaïre's state was a mechanism for the self-enrichment of a clique which surrounded the president. Contrary to Western notions of the state, which stress impartiality and the public interest, Zaïre was moulded to serve the interests of the few. For some, the emergence of Kabila's government, along with similar developments elsewhere in central Africa, was a sign that an old, essentially corrupt, pro-western political order was coming to an end. It remains to be seen whether Kabila's new government will have the political will and the external funding to reconstruct a modern economy and polity out of Mobutu's devastation.

An equally significant set of events occurred in the much smaller and economically and politically insignificant west African state of Sierra Leone. It initially appeared that a conventional *coup d'état* had taken place in late May 1997, ousting the short-lived, democratically-elected government of Ahmad Tejan Kabbah. But the rebel soldiers were joined by elements of a brutal insurrectionary force, the Revolutionary United Front (RUF), which had been fighting against all Sierra Leonean governments since 1991 [*Keen, 1997; Riley, 1996*]. The RUF's campaign focused upon the corrupt and inegalitarian politics of the central state since independence in 1961. The significance of this insurrection was that it represented the coming to power of a 'lumpen' or under-class, profoundly alienated by the corrupt politics of all post-independence governments. Extensive systemic corruption and mal-administration has been evident in Sierra Leone for many years [*Kpundeh, 1995; Reno, 1995; Riley, 1983a; Zack-Williams, 1983*]. Widespread, debilitating and diverse forms of public corruption have contributed to the regime's precipitous economic decline since the 1970s [*Luke and Riley, 1989; 1991*]. The result of the emergence of the hybrid military/rebel junta in late May 1997 is an internationally isolated, very unstable, brutal, populist regime, challenged by foreign troops outside the capital of Freetown. Consequently, professional alarmists, such as the writer Robert Kaplan, argue that the apocalyptic scenario of 'The Coming Anarchy', with collapsing states, increasing crime and social crises, is confirmed by these events [*Kaplan, 1994; 1996; 1997*].

Whatever the future for Africa as a whole – which could move towards a more progressive, second 'post-neo-colonial' generation of political leaders, or a gloomier scenario of increased crime, social disorder and weaker states – there is no doubt that minimising corruption needs to be a high priority. Gross, high-level and systemic corruption formed the backdrop to the dramatic events in both Zaïre and Sierra Leone. Reducing the debilitating effects of public sector corruption, and countering the damaging effects of other, diverse forms of corruption, ought to be the focus of attention in the late 1990s. Both internal political factors and the external pressures of aid donors are responsible for highlighting the issue in the late 1990s: in addition to the domestic political turmoil that extensive corruption can help create, international institutions with financial commitments in Africa are now increasingly publicly concerned with its damaging consequences for growth on the continent. The international institutions are also responding to reactions by western governments and publics against the conspicuous consumption associated with systemic corruption in Africa, as in the case of the wealth and lifestyle of Mobutu and his clique.

For these reasons, attempts to reduce and control corruption are politically salient objectives for social reformers and civil society groups, concerned African governments and for a number of aid donors, who have recently developed policies on these issues [*OECD, 1997; UNDP/OECD, 1997*]. Surveying these developments, this paper first examines the current academic and policy debate on anti-corruption strategies, particularly with reference to the policy initiatives of the major international institutions, such as the World Bank. Secondly, it considers the experience of a number of African countries with both developed and cosmetic 'anti-corruption' strategies. States such as Botswana, Mozambique and Tanzania have had relatively low levels of 'grand' corruption until recently; their anti-corruption strategies have taken differing forms. Nigeria, Sierra Leone, Uganda and Zaïre are examples of societies where anti-corruption strategies have existed, but their results have been meagre. A third section of the paper evaluates the new anti-corruption consensus against this African experience and examines the implications for policy. Tables 1 and 2 (below) summarise both the anti-corruption strategies that have emerged since the 1960s and the types of corruption typically found in African political economies.

ANTI-CORRUPTION STRATEGIES: ANCIENT AND MODERN

The growing concern to develop effective and preferably short-term anti-corruption strategies is partly because corruption has profoundly inegalitarian effects; it damages the interests of the poor most, whether the corruption is 'petty' or 'grand' in character [*Moody-Stuart, 1997*]. In Africa, as elsewhere, corruption often has a 'Robin Hood in reverse' character: the losers are likely to be the exceptionally poor, female, and marginalised, whilst the winners are already wealthy and part of an inefficient, swollen state. Most African corruption rewards the already wealthy: usually, it is a form of redistribution from those in poverty to the office-holding and consequently relatively or extremely rich. This corrupt misallocation of resources happens where poverty is a product of unequal wealth distribution and where it is also a consequence of the social exclusion of the poor [*UNDP, 1997; Ward, 1989; World Bank, 1997a*]. Since independence, many African states have not acted in an efficient and enabling way to promote equitable development; instead, through corruption and maladministration, some African states and their agents have reinforced the current unequal distribution of opportunities, undermined basic human rights, and created new inequalities. The overall thrust of recent academic studies has tended to challenge the revisionist standpoint of J. S. Nye and N. Leff that the economic benefits of corruption (in helping capital formation, speeding up development, as well as humanising politics) outweigh the costs (Nye and Leff in Heidenheimer, LeVine and Johnston [*1989*]).

As a result of the obvious damage that corruption has done in many African societies, politicians and public management specialists have made numerous attempts to reduce or minimise the effects of corruption with a series of anti-corruption strategies. Serious attempts to control corruption are often as old as corruption itself. A recent study by Sen [*1997*] points to some early examples, but see also Noonan [*1984*]. In ancient China, many public officials were paid a corruption-preventing allowance to try to ensure their continued honesty. This illustration relates to recent debates about the relationship between the low salary levels of junior civil servants and levels of corruption in Africa. Kautilya, a fourth century BC Indian political analyst, sought to identify forty different ways in which public officials could be corrupt. He also developed a system of spot-checks to reduce corruption, which were accompanied by a rewards and penalties system. Such ancient examples of attempted corruption-control are similar to those developed by public officials and academic analysts in recent years, in the period since the 1960s. Broadly, there are four levels or types of anti-corruption strategy which can be identified in operation in post-independence Africa: international; national; local; and populist [*Theobald, 1990*].

Since the mid-1990s a series of international (Type 1) anti-corruption initiatives has emerged [*OECD, 1997; Kaufmann, 1997; Rose-Ackerman, 1997*], but earlier decades saw African countries themselves develop strategies based upon national and local action (Types 2 and 3), including anti-corruption agencies, public inquiries, inspector-general systems, legal and quasi-legal trials, complaints procedures, and public awareness campaigns [*Clarke, 1983; Doig, 1995; Heidenheimer, LeVine and Johnston, 1989; IRIS, 1996*]. Often a key issue in assessing the effectiveness and sustainability of such strategies is the commitment of the powerful to act effectively to curb corruption [*Klitgaard, 1997; Kpundeh, 1997*]. Populist initiatives (Type 4) such as purges of civil servants and former politicians have not had much success, although the issue of corruption has acquired great political salience in recent years due to the actions of NGOs and activism by lawyers and other public interest groups [*Doig and Riley, 1998; Harsch, 1993; Theobald, 1990; Transparency*

TABLE 1
TYPES OF ANTI-CORRUPTION STRATEGY

1 INTERNATIONAL
- New World Bank and IMF policies
- OECD efforts to criminalise transnational bribery
- Transparency International's interventions

2 NATIONAL
- Procedures and training within state or public sector institutions
- 'Service Culture' approaches
- 'Islands of Integrity'
- Capacity-building to 'design out' corruption
- Legal approaches, including state funding of parties, controls on 'revolving doors' and patronage appointments
- Anti-Corruption agencies
- Auditor-Generals and Parliamentary oversight
- The Police and 'Inter-Agency Co-operation'

3 LOCAL OR 'CITIZEN' LEVEL
- Minimising small-scale corruption by protection against the extractive and arbitrary nature of the state
- 'Structural reform' (e.g. decentralisation and deregulation)
- 'Legislative sunlight' provisions
- New administrative procedures (e.g. overlapping jurisdictions; multiple providers; customerisation of public services and service delivery surveys)
- Complaints and redress
- Community oversight
- The Media

4 POPULIST
- Purges (e.g. of civil servants)
- 'Making Examples' (public humiliations and executions; quasi-official tribunals)
- 'Moral Rearmament' campaigns and the New Citizen

Source: Compiled by the author but drawing upon Theobald [*1990*], Doig [*1995*], Doig and Riley [*1998*].

International, 1996]. The harsh punishment meted out to former public officials in Ghana and Liberia in 1979 and 1980 – which involved populist revolutions (in effect, *coups d'état*), dubious trials and speedy public executions for several former heads of state, such as President William Tolbert of Liberia – illustrates a general paradox: extensive high-level corruption can contribute to profound political upheavals, but the problem of corruption does not disappear with the removal of those key officials identified as corrupt [*Jeffries, 1982*].

More recently, several African countries have adopted public integrity reforms which are associated with the 'New Public Management' approach to governance in western societies (Type 3). These initiatives are often linked to the influence of aid donors or the activities of pressure groups such as Transparency International (TI). Examples include new administrative procedures such as overlapping jurisdictions (where two or more officials are responsible for an administrative action), service delivery surveys (for example in Tanzania and Uganda, in cooperation with the World Bank), and structural reform, where an administrative machine is decentralised or deregulation takes place. However, there are several potential problems with such strategies. For example, decentralisation, a widely touted remedy for many of the African state's contemporary ills, can also create lower-level corruption unless it is accompanied by some of the range of possible anti-corruption strategies. Nevertheless, aid donors and others hope that these reforms will improve public integrity either directly or indirectly.

Many of the less coercive anti-corruption efforts are based upon the manipulation of incentives for, and the potential punishments to be meted out to, public officials. These modern strategies are often accompanied by attempts to improve both recruitment of public officials who are more likely to be honest and better information upon their preferably honest public conduct, although they are based upon earlier academic and policy studies [*Gould, 1980; McKinney and Johnston, 1986; Klitgaard, 1988*]. The anti-corruption strategy proposed is usually based upon a distinctive view of the causes and character of corruption. There are three distinct approaches to contemporary corruption and anti-corruption strategies: economic analyses; mass public opinion perspectives; and institutional viewpoints. Developed since the 1960s, these are outlined and evaluated in a wide variety of publications [*Heidenheimer, LeVine and Johnston, 1989*]. Economic analyses prioritise the principal-agent market relationship to identify corruption and anti-corruption strategies, whereas mass public opinion perspectives examine the social or cultural context of corruption and suggest as a result mass attitudinal change or civic awareness anti-corruption strategies. These two approaches are well established and well regarded, with an extensive academic literature and some policy applications. A third and newer, institutional approach focuses upon the public sector and institutional reform [*Doig, 1995; Stapenhurst and Langseth, 1997*]. This is important because it enables the analyst of corruption to suggest short-term and specific policy recommendations which focus upon low-level corruption. This newer approach has yet to have a major impact upon policy formation.

Instead, much of the debate on anti-corruption strategy has at its roots neo-classical economic theory and its application and concerns. Thus, for example, Klitgaard's approach, which has been widely promoted and applied in Africa in the 1990s, is based upon principal-agent economic analysis, derived from neo-classical or neo-liberal economic theory, and is evaluated by him in a number of widely differing developing country contexts, particularly in Africa and Latin America [*Klitgaard, 1988; 1991; 1997*]. Klitgaard argues that officials are most corrupt where they have wide discretion in their actions, little accountability, and considerable monopoly power. This enables them to charge what economists call rents. The less diplomatic call it corrupt enrichment. According to Klitgaard, rents can be reduced by decreasing state power, limiting the discretion of officials, and by strengthening the controls exercised over public officials, including accountancy units in ministries. Transparency is also an important notion: opening up previously secret public officialdom and helping generate freer public discussion through a free, questioning press, and an active civil society, can also reduce corruption. Klitgaard's work has been very influential and appears to be at the core of the World Bank's recent analyses, along with that of Susan Rose-Ackerman. Only recently have international institutions such as the World Bank concerned themselves publicly with these issues, although the World Bank did publish one interesting earlier study [*Gould and Amaro-Reyes, 1983; Rose-Ackerman, 1997; World Bank, 1997a*].

THE NEW AGENDA

The academic and policy-orientated debate on the effectiveness of anti-corruption strategies has been changed markedly by events in developing countries and in the former Soviet Bloc in the 1980s. Arguments about curbing corruption take place now in a new context: we are in an era of economic reform, structural adjustment and what Samuel Huntington [*1991*] has called the Third Wave of democratisation in developing and transitional countries. A shaky new international consensus on development emerged as the old Soviet Bloc model of one party states and command economies collapsed: in a unipolar world, there is an expectation that the developing countries reform both economically and politically as aid budgets shrink, external debts grow, and the terms of trade in their primary commodity exports deteriorate [*Hoogvelt, 1997; Randel and German, 1997*].

The relevant parts of this new international consensus can be briefly stated. The new development agenda of the late 1990s involves an expectation of sustained efforts in developing and transitional countries towards the goals of market economies and liberal democratic political systems. More recently, this has also involved the prioritising of the interests of the poor and marginalised in the context of an enabling state and higher ethical standards in donors [*OECD, 1997; UNDP, 1997; UNDP/OECD, 1997; World Bank, 1997a*]. Progress towards these goals therefore means serious attempts to secure better governance and substantially less corruption in developing and transitional countries.

Corruption is most obviously defined as public office, public sector, or institutional corruption, rather than corruption in the private sector, or as the product of the activities of multinational corporations, or even corruption in foreign aid allocations. The assumptions are twofold: first, public sector corruption will be reduced if the size of the state is reduced. Secondly, moves towards liberal, pluralist politics, involving a freer press, competitive party politics, and the revival or creation of other independent institutions, such as the judiciary and professional associations, will also reduce corruption by making it vulnerable to exposure. In this way, corruption will be potentially politically damaging.

The new international policy agenda of the late 1990s also involves the following assumptions. A limited, legitimate, honest and transparent state ought to be at the centre of the development process in both developing and transitional countries. All too often it is not, and the public interest is thereby undermined and human rights infringed. In many cases, the state sector is swollen, inefficient, and corrupt; individual and group private interests have priority over the collective good; and public officials have considerable discretion to accumulate private wealth through exploiting their monopolistic, low and irregularly paid positions, often in collusion with indigenous or foreign businessmen. Corruption frequently takes place in societies where there is considerable discretion for public officials, limited accountability, and little transparency in governmental operations; in such societies, civil society institutions are often weak or undeveloped. This new set of assumptions – the new agenda for controlling corruption – has already been questioned and an alternative research agenda has been articulated [*Harriss-White and White, 1996*].

THE WORLD BANK APPROACH

Many of these new assumptions would be shared by the World Bank. Although the Bank has been concerned with corruption in its projects for some time, it has recently developed an approach to public sector and other forms of corruption while acknowledging the Bank's mandate which formally restricts its activities to economic development issues [*Robinson, 1997; Stevens, 1997*]. In 1997 the Bank changed its own working procedures to include special procurement audits. It is also increasing the number of external auditors. But the Bank argues that corruption inside Bank projects is linked to corruption in the societies in which it works. As a result, it has rejected an 'enclave approach', which would improve only the efficiency of its own operations, and instead has sought to tackle corruption as a more systematic issue. A 20-member Bank working group, headed by Mike Stevens, was established in the aftermath of Bank President James Wolfensohn's speech to the World Bank/International Monetary Fund Annual Meetings in October 1996. Wolfensohn's speech, in which he spoke of the 'cancer of corruption', attracted great attention and led to the re-thinking. The Bank working group developed an initiative which argued that, 'for the Bank, tackling corruption is less a matter of new instruments and more a matter of carrying out existing activities, but with a greater focus upon their potential to reduce corruption'. The working group argued that the problem was that 'corruption is a function of policies created by economic rents and of weak institutions'. It was also argued by the working group during its frequent meetings in late 1996 and early 1997 that 'markets discipline participants more effectively than public sector accountability mechanisms generally can' [*Stevens, 1997: 1–2*].

The World Bank's new initiative was published in mid-1997. It highlights the damaging economic costs of corruption in its lenders, and emphasises the debilitating growth of corruption in Sub-Saharan Africa and the transitional economies of Eastern Europe and the former Soviet Union [*World Bank, 1997b; 1997c*]. It builds upon earlier policy reforms such as governance. The Bank argues that the principal way to reduce corruption is to encourage deeper and more thorough economic liberalisation and deregulation in borrowers, although reforming and strengthening public institutions are also regarded as important.

The aim of the Bank is to tie lending more closely to efforts to reduce corruption. The Bank will create a new lending instrument to support improvements in public sector operations. It will also raise this issue in a more open way with borrowers in policy dialogues, and launch pilot anti-corruption schemes in institutions such as tax and customs departments provided that borrowers agree. A recent Bank internal report accepts that 'the evidence of systemic corruption in itself is not a reason to withdraw the Bank's support' [*World Bank, 1997b: 17*]. Nevertheless, the Bank has been examining in detail the ways of using lending to reduce corruption. If corruption is systemic, is affecting the Bank's projects, and a government is unwilling to act to reduce corruption, the Bank now proposes to reduce sharply or stop lending to the government concerned, although it will continue its support for NGOs and civil society organisations. If the Bank regards corruption as systemic in a society, in future it will always raise the issue with the government and discuss the government's active anti-corruption programme. If a government is unwilling to act to reduce corruption, the Bank will be justified in reducing lending.

The World Bank is clearly using Klitgaard's analysis in its perspective upon corruption. According to the Bank, corruption principally occurs where officials are in a monopoly position (and can extract economic rents or unofficial additional income), have large discretion in their actions, and little accountability. The Bank therefore argues that an effective anti-corruption strategy should encourage the reduction of rents (by means of greater economic liberalisation and deregulation), channel and reduce discretion (through public sector reform and institutional strengthening), and increase accountability (by building up institutions such as accountancy units in government, and by encouraging the growth of a more vibrant, questioning civil society).

The internal report, *Report of the Corruption Action Plan Working Group (CAPWG) – Country and International Strategies, OPC Review Draft, May 1997* – hereafter *World Bank, 1997b* and subsequent public documents [*World Bank, 1997a; 1997c*] synthesise evidence from its own internal project reports and from a survey of the Bank's staff in early 1997. Bank staff appear to be divided about the effects of corruption across the world although they are agreed that it is pervasive, growing in most states, transnational in character, and increasingly linked to organised crime. The major problem areas are in sub-Saharan Africa (especially Kenya, Mozambique, Nigeria, and the former Zaïre) and Eastern Europe. The Bank's staff disagree as to whether or not corruption is damaging in East Asia, where extensive corruption (as in South Korea) does not seem to be a barrier to rapid economic growth. The reports argue that the Bank should adopt a more vigorous anti-corruption effort, despite the political sensitivity of the issue [*World Bank, 1997b; 1997c*].

Cynics would argue that the corruption issue is just another means for the Bank to secure its real goal: greater structural adjustment in those states whose adjustment programmes have been stymied by political pressures. The Bank's new policy plays down other means of reducing corruption. It is less enthusiastic about strengthening public institutions and increasing public education and awareness of the issue. In addition, the Bank's recent policies pay little attention to the various types or levels of persistent and entrenched corruption that exist in African political economies.

CORRUPTION AND ANTI-CORRUPTION STRATEGIES IN AFRICA

The Bank's arguments need to be examined against the African experience. Corruption has been a difficult and systemic problem in many African political economies for decades and has had damaging effects in terms of the public reputation of regimes, economic growth and general development objectives. The economic effects of African corruption are difficult to distinguish from maladministration and incompetence, large-scale fraud, organised, disorganised or business crime, and international theft, especially in those African economies in decline in the 1980s and 1990s [*Ellis (ed.), 1996; Ellis, 1996; Levi and Nelken, 1996*]. Although the seriousness of corruption varies over time and across Africa, a consensual view is that gross corruption has had very damaging effects [*IRIS, 1996; Goudie and Stasavage, 1997*]. Corrupt income in Africa is linked to the growth in external debt and global capital flows, and trade in exchange commodities such as diamonds, gold, weapons and illicit drugs. In the early 1990s, Nigeria became a major transhipment centre in the international illicit trade in cocaine and heroin in addition to its continuing problems with high-level public sector corruption. The proceeds of these trades across Africa as well as corrupt income in general is siphoned off into off-shore tax havens and conspicuous consumption [*Naylor, 1987; 1996; Hampton, 1996; Robinson, 1994*]. In such circumstances, aid donors, responsible public officials, and civic organisations have a difficult task in seeking honest conduct and good governance, even when programmes of economic liberalisation, deregulation and public sector reform have been initiated.

In some African states, like the former Zaïre, corruption 'goes beyond shame and almost beyond imagination' [*Delamaide, 1984: 60*]. In other African states, such as Botswana or Tanzania until the 1990s, corruption has been relatively low level, or petty, in form. As a result an important distinction can be made between incidental, systematic and systemic corruption in Africa and its effects (see Table 2). Incidental corruption (Type 1) is a feature of life in almost all African societies, but it can be systematic in many public institutions (such as customs departments, parastatals and other revenue-generating bodies) in African countries, if not systemic in society as a whole [*DeLeon, 1993; Riley, 1983*]. The more damaging forms of corruption can be both endemic and planned [*Waterbury, 1973*]. Incidental corruption is small-scale corruption and usually involves isolated individuals or small numbers of individuals: very junior public officials, such as policemen and soldiers manning road-blocks on provincial roads in Sierra Leone, customs officials at airports and ports in Nigeria, and tax officials in Zaïre [*Gould, 1980; Riley, 1983a; Williams, 1987*]. This petty corruption does not have a huge macro-economic impact but can be profoundly alienating to the public: as citizens and as consumers of public resources. Incidental corruption is also often hard to curb.

In comparison, systematic corruption in Africa (Type 2) involves larger numbers of public officials and an element of organisation and conspiracy. It is typically found in government departments or parastatals such as procurement agencies and marketing boards. Examples would include the produce marketing boards in Nigeria, Uganda and Sierra Leone in the 1960s. In this form, corruption has a larger developmental impact by the extensive diversion of government revenues and the distortion of priorities. As a result, anti-corruption strategies have often focused upon the reform of such institutions, often by sacking those individual officials thought responsible, or by instituting public inquiries such as the 1962 Collier Commission of Inquiry 'into the affairs of certain Statutory Corporations in Western Nigeria', where there was extensive corruption and maladministration in the produce marketing board [*Forrest, 1993; Riley, 1983a*]. Numerous other anti-corruption strategies have been developed to deal with systematic corruption

TABLE 2
TYPES OF CORRUPTION

1 INCIDENTAL
- Small-scale;
- Involving individual and very junior public officials such as policemen, customs and tax officials;
- Little macro-economic cost, but profound public alienation;
- Often hard to curb.

2 SYSTEMATIC
- Larger developmental impact;
- Can affect most or all of a government department, or a parastatal such as procurement agency or marketing board;
- Can have substantial impact upon government revenues and trade diversion;
- Sustained reform effort necessary rather than 'individualised' response.

3 SYSTEMIC
- Wholly corrupt system: Andreski's 'Kleptocracy' or government by theft;
- Huge developmental impact (Jean-Bedel Bokassa's Central African Republic, Macias Nguema's Equatorial Guinea, Moi's Kenya, Mobutu's Zaïre);
- In such circumstances, honesty is 'irrational';
- Reform by fundamental change?

Note: This is an up-dated version of that found in Riley [*1983a: 190–206*]. It also draws upon DeLeon [*1993*].

but they have been ultimately limited in effect. Some forms of systematic corruption concern specific government contracts, such as the famous example of the corruption surrounding the contract which led to a massive over-ordering of external supplies of cement by Nigeria's government in the 1970s. In 1975, the Ministry of Defence ordered 16 million metric tons of cement for supply that year, although the total import capacity of all Nigeria's ports was about 4.5 million metric tons per year. Some observers thought that enough cement had been ordered to cover the entire surface area of Nigeria. Middlemen with connections to the regime made a fortune, and in late 1975 up to 200 cement-laden ships were waiting to off-load in Lagos [*Forrest, 1993; Williams, 1987*]. In this case and other examples of systematic corruption, individuals are often identified by inquiries and press reports as blame-worthy, but a sustained institutional reform effort is necessary rather than simply legal action against individuals.

Systemic corruption (Type 3) is similar to Andreski's [*1968*] notion of 'Kleptocracy: or, Corruption as a System of Government'. Government by theft involves the idea of a wholly corrupt system which is led by a corrupt leadership. Such patterns of corruption have a hugely damaging impact upon development. In such societies, it is irrational to be honest as the diverse forms of corruption are so pervasive. Both Sierra Leone and Zaïre are examples of

African countries where patterns of systemic corruption developed. In Sierra Leone's case, systemic corruption was associated with the personalist rule of President Siaka Stevens (1968–85) during the initially-dominant and later one-party All People's Congress (APC) regime of 1968–92; it rested upon the theft of government revenues and the unusual characteristics of the political economy of Sierra Leone, an economy principally based upon the official and smuggled export trade in alluvial gem diamonds, gold, other minerals and agricultural produce [*Riley, 1983a; Luke and Riley, 1989; 1991*]. From the late 1970s onwards, a huge 'parallel' economy developed, which exceeded the official economy in size, and involved political middle-men and Lebanese and Indian traders. This style of systemic corruption was later conceptualised as a 'shadow state' where corrupt rule existed behind the formal façade of political power [*Reno, 1995*].

The pattern of systemic corruption in Mobutu's Zaïre is probably more well-known, being notorious and based upon a repressive, patrimonial system, an African variant of the European absolutist state [*Callaghy, 1984*]. Similar extensive theft of state resources took place and there is well-documented evidence of how the proceeds of this theft were enjoyed, including expensive properties in western Europe, gifts, luxury travel, and other forms of conspicuous consumption [*Askin and Collins, 1993*]. In Sierra Leone and Zaïre, there have been a variety of reform efforts since the 1960s. Siaka Stevens and Mobutu Sese Seko issued strictures against corruption or promised or initiated reforms, often in response to external criticism of their regimes by aid donors, but such stratagems were of limited effect. In both regimes the problems of systemic corruption and the difficulties of reform were well-known to the donors. In 1979, 18 years before Mobutu's regime finally collapsed, the head of a team of western bankers sent to Zaïre to (unsuccessfully) run the central bank pointed out that it was certain that all reform efforts would fail. Nevertheless, Western support for Mobutu's regime, particularly from the United States, continued until the 1990s [*Collins, 1997; Callaghy, 1984*].

Such donors are now advocating public integrity reforms in African societies which are linked to economic and political liberalisation, as in the case of the World Bank. Harriss-White and White [*1996*] argue that the mid-1990s has seen the emergence of new forms of corruption and new means to combat both its 'old' and 'new' forms. Much contemporary debate rests upon the argument that there is a symmetry between economic and political liberalisation: the free market in economics should be assisted by the free market in politics (in the form of an idealised liberal polity). But there are problems over the compatibility of these goals in the abstract and in the real world of African political economies [*Riley and Parfitt, 1994*].

The relationship between political and economic liberalisation is nowhere near as clear as its advocates suggest and there are major problems concerning the sequencing of such reforms in Africa as elsewhere [*Leftwich, 1996*]. In most African societies, economic reform has preceded political reform. Only African regimes with authoritarian governments, as in Ghana in the 1980s, have been able to sustain economic liberalisation over time. Those regimes which have democratised first have had major problems implementing the economic liberalisation expected of them, as in Zambia from 1991 onwards [*Wiseman, 1995*]. In addition, although a reduced and more efficient state sector is desirable, as is liberal, pluralist politics, the relationship between these goals and the goal of corruption reduction is difficult to disentangle.

Although down-sizing the state and political liberalisation are desirable goals in many African countries, they are necessary rather than sufficient conditions for the reduction of public sector corruption. Extensive public sector corruption can coexist with democratic or quasi-democratic politics in Africa. This was the case in several west African states, including the small enclave state of The Gambia, which had a multi-party system, a relatively free press, and a good human rights record from 1965 until a *coup d'état* in 1994. The ruling Progressive People's Party [PPP] government gradually became enmeshed in a series of high-level corruption scandals as post-coup Public Inquiries demonstrated. West Africa's major oil-producer and most populous state, Nigeria, also suffered from extensive corruption in the early 1980s, when there was a brief period of democratic rule. Under President Shehu Shagari there was substantial commercial and public sector fraud; huge numbers of 'ghost workers' (living workers who claim and receive the salary of imaginary or deceased employees); outright stealing of government property and other assets; and huge illegal transfers overseas. As one contemporary study pointed out, those involved in this massive corruption also covered their tracks: 'the telecommunications building, Africa's tallest building, the ministry of External Affairs and the Accounts Section of the Federal Capital Authority, Abuja, were all burnt following widespread allegations of fraud in these places' [*Falola and Ihonvbere, 1985: 108*].

A series of mysterious – or not so mysterious – fires destroyed the evidence. The civilian government first denied the extent of the corruption and then set up a whole ministry to combat it. No one was prosecuted for the huge frauds and related corruption that was thereby disguised. Although the civilian government did not last long and was replaced by a military regime after a *coup d'état*, its successors have often been as corrupt. A series of anti-corruption strategies were tried by various Nigerian governments but they have been largely ineffectual, even when they have included widespread purges of civil servants in the mid-1970s and an anti-corruption 'War Against Indiscipline' orchestrated by Mohammadu Buhari's military regime in the mid-1980s. At least 10,000 and perhaps up to 12,000 civil servants were dismissed in the aftermath of a *coup d'état* in July 1975, many for vaguely defined offenses including the abuse of office and a decline in productivity. This was during 'Operation Purge the Nation'. The later military government of Buhari also dismissed or retired a larger number of public officials during 1984 and the purge broadened out from the civil service to the police, military and universities [*Williams, 1987; Theobald, 1990*]. Nevertheless, despite these purges and public relations exercises, the public looting and mismanagement of the economy has continued to undermine Nigeria's state sovereignty and contributed to its huge external debt. Even under military regimes publicly committed to probity, and equipped with a range of anti-corruption strategies, private enrichment overtook the public realm.

By comparison, public sector corruption in Tanzania was not a problem in the early years of Tanzania's independence, but in the 1990s growing problems of both petty and grand corruption undermined the economically liberalised, multi-party state. Surprisingly, the regime itself then appointed a Presidential inquiry into corruption [*Mndeme-Musonda, Mjema and Danielson, 1997; Muganda, 1997; Warioba, 1997*]. The Presidential Commission was chaired by J.S. Warioba, a former Prime Minister and first Vice President and had a career civil servant, Alexander Muganda, as both Secretary to the Commission and Director of the existing Prevention of Corruption Bureau. Unlike many such inquiries, the Warioba inquiry took extensive public evidence and reported quickly. It was appointed in January 1996 and reported in December 1996, although its conclusions have not been as rapidly acted upon.

The Warioba report identified 'rampant corruption in the public service' which had escalated at an alarming rate over the past two decades [*Warioba, 1997: 199*]. There was both 'petty' corruption and 'grand' corruption at the highest public levels. Petty corruption was widespread. Muganda argued that it was 'a serious nuisance' and had 'subverted effective service delivery' in Tanzania in the 1990s. It was found in the police and judicial services as in all the social sectors. From the evidence taken in the extensive public hearings of the Commission during 1996, petty corruption affected most members of the public and was the main source of public discontent. Grand corruption was identified in the procurement of goods and services, in the allocation of permits for hunting and mining, and in large public contracts, in particular in road-building and public construction. An assessment of 24 public construction contracts had found substantial cost over-runs: costs had escalated from US$97.4 million to US$154.7 million. In these cases, there was an 'inference of corruption' [*Muganda, 1997: 5*].

The Warioba Commission also addressed the much disputed issue of the causes of corruption. A number of causes for the growth in corruption were identified, including economic deterioration, a decline in public ethics, and the lack of political leadership on the issue. The Warioba Commission accordingly made a number of recommendations to improve public integrity, including proposed amendments to the Leadership Code of Ethics Act, short-term vetting of public officials, disciplinary action against the police and judiciary, and the reinvigoration of the ineffectual Prevention of Corruption Bureau.

This remarkable set of events – very few African governments investigate themselves, though they are very willing to investigate their political opponents – generated an intense debate about the character of corruption in Tanzania. Public discussion of the Commission has focused upon a number of key issues, including the impact of economic liberalisation, the ranking of the causes of corruption examined by the Warioba Commission, the value of the government's Prevention of Corruption Bureau, and questions relating to the outcome of the Commission. It can be concluded that economic liberalisation has significantly contributed to the increase in corruption in Tanzania, although there are many other causes. The Warioba Commission does not rank the causes of corruption in order of severity: all causes are deemed equally important. But unless the causes are clearly identified and ranked, then it is difficult to prioritise effective anti-corruption strategies. Perhaps not surprisingly, there has been slow progress on implementing the Commission's proposals, although some civil servants and politicians have been disciplined or dismissed [*Mndeme-Musonda, Mjema and Danielson, 1997*].

The circumstances surrounding the establishment of the Warioba Commission are worthy of note. 1994 saw many corruption scandals in Tanzania and as a result the government had to react, partly as a consequence of the 1995 elections. These elections also produced many anti-corruption commitments by the politicians involved. The Commission argued that the Prevention of Corruption Bureau was ineffective, but a further problem was the lack of political commitment to give the Bureau the strength and resources to act. Although the Bureau needed complete re-organisation and more power, it was continuously undermined by the clientelistic links between businessmen and decision-makers, particularly prominent ruling-party politicians. The Warioba Commission argued that these links had greatly increased corruption in recent years. In respect of longer-term issues, the Commission argued that law reform was required. Some laws created opportunities for corruption; they had to be amended. A final area of debate generated by the Commission was that of social engineering. Public education, anti-corruption and positive public integrity advertising, as well as general measures to raise public awareness were all required. It was argued that it was important to remind or educate citizens to complain about corrupt acts and to try and prevent politicians from engaging in the bad habits of corruption.

Much of the corruption identified in Tanzania was in the public sector or concerned the character and actions of public officials. However, another important element of corruption is related to the character of African political economies and the attempts of African governments to regulate trade across their boundaries. Customs fraud, which is linked to public sector corruption, is common in many west African states, including Mali and Senegal, which share many similarities such as colonial heritage, state structure and political style, membership of the Franc Zone, and protectionist policies [*Kulibaba, 1997; Meagher, 1997; Stasavage and Daubree, 1997*]. Customs fraud is a complex and difficult instance of corruption to deal with. It can be of various types, including under-declaration of the value of goods, misclassification, and underpayment of taxes due. But in whatever form it occurs, it can have significant economic consequences for such developing states as the revenue base of the state is highly dependent upon the efficient taxation of trade [*Kulibaba, 1997; Luke and Riley, 1989; Meagher, 1997*].

Stasavage and Daubree used standard principal-agent models as a basis for their research, although it was accepted that such models focus upon national level factors and cannot predict for specific customs administrations. Instead, they compare fraud on a product-by-product basis within customs administrations. Their general conclusions are that trade liberalisation had reduced levels of fraud and that pre-shipment inspection 'can be a powerful tool for reducing fraud'. In addition, to reduce customs fraud, donors should support institutional reforms that reduce the discretion of officials and improve monitoring. Customs fraud in many African societies was itself a symptom of specific national political and institutional failures [*Stasavage and Daubree, 1997*].

Customs fraud raises a number of general issues concerning the question of an appropriate anti-corruption strategy, including the irrelevance of the national framework for fighting corruption and the efficacy of pre-shipment inspection companies (such as the Swiss-based Sociéte Generale de Surveillance – SGS) which play a central role in the customs services of several African countries. There is a tension between the costs of such expensive foreign pre-shipment inspection services and the revenue gains for the African state concerned. Considerable controversy concerns the revenue improvements claimed by pre-shipment inspection services, as the revenue gains were in part based upon accompanying reforms in the customs services themselves, particularly improvements in information gathering and assessment and the computerisation of the services [*Stasavage and Daubree, 1997*]. Effective action to reduce customs fraud in states such as Mozambique, as well as Mali and Senegal, is also dependent upon the development of attitudes which support honesty in public conduct, and the reduction of the corrupting influences of foreign businesses [*Hall and Young, 1997; Hanlon, 1996; Stasavage, 1996*].

The issue of customs fraud, like that of corruption in general, is related to the question of low public sector salaries in African states. Other factors aside, the temptation to engage in corruption or ignore business fraud is greater if salaries are exceptionally low or unpaid. However, according to Stasavage and Daubree, the size of public service salaries was less of an issue in Mali and Senegal, when compared with other African countries. Instead, a key problem with the customs services in Mali and Senegal was the lack of funds for non-wage current expenditures, such as basic necessities (including fuel, vehicles, and other administrative costs) for the officials to do their jobs. Low public sector salaries were more of a factor in customs fraud and petty corruption in general in other African countries, including Angola, Côte d'Ivoire, The Gambia, Mozambique, and Sierra Leone [*Reno, 1997a; 1997b; Riley, 1983a; Luke and Riley, 1991; Stasavage and Daubree, 1997*]. But customs fraud and corruption is also related to developments in the wider political economy, including the rise and decline of distinct business groups, and the development of underground economies trading in illicit goods, such as drugs, and the weapons of war. In west Africa, some groups of industrialists and merchants are also losing the political clout to demand protection as economic liberalisation is creating new business groups, which are influencing policy.

Stasavage and Daubree argue that there is a tension between the costs of expensive pre-shipment inspection services and the revenue thereby gained. The improvements secured by pre-shipment inspection services were in part based upon accompanying reforms in the customs services themselves, particularly improvements in information gathering and assessment and the computerisation of the services. This case study, like other research on corruption in government regulation of the economy, points to the need for an integrated, comprehensive approach to reducing corruption which is not dependent upon any particular academic fashion or approach [*Kulibaba, 1997; Meagher, 1997*].

These examples of corruption and attempted corruption control have virtually all taken place in African societies which have liberalised politically in the 1990s. Only Nigeria has resisted the domestic, as well as external, pressures to liberalise and demilitarise its politics. There is thus considerable evidence from these cases that relatively high levels of both petty and grand corruption can coexist with democratic or quasi-democratic politics. A broadly similar coexistence of democratic politics and some high-level public corruption obtains in Zambia where democratisation in 1991 has been followed by economic liberalisation. But Zambia has also been beset by public office corruption. Since 1991, several ministers in Frederick Chiluba's multi-party Cabinet have been implicated in illicit drug smuggling. In Zambia, as elsewhere, economic liberalisation has created opportunities for corruption. The sale of several government parastatals has not been transparent and has left over 80,000 people jobless. Widespread rumours about how Chiluba's ministers and their business cronies have gained from the parastatal sales formed the backdrop to political instability in the aftermath of a contentious election in 1996.[1]

In addition to the impact of economic liberalisation in Zambia, the admittedly imperfect democratisation of previously authoritarian regimes, including Kenya from 1991 onwards, has not led to a substantial reduction in corruption [*Riley, 1992; Wiseman, 1995*]. Many observers would argue that Kenya has in fact seen a growth in corruption in the 1990s, after the moves towards multi-party politics, primarily as a product of the corrupt enrichment of ruling-party politicians and their close associates. For example, much controversy surrounds the fall-out from the so-called 'Goldenberg scandal' of 1992 which involved a gold-exporting scheme backed by senior ruling party members and businessmen. The scheme is alleged to have lost the Kenyan government over US$400 million.

High-level instances of corruption such as these in many African societies have badly damaged or diverted development objectives, undermined long-term economic growth, increased poverty, and contributed to Africa's declining position in world trade. Unlike many Asian states, such as South Korea or Taiwan, where public office corruption has often coincided with high, sustained growth rates, the African cases demonstrate that corruption linked to a top-heavy or swollen state and a predatory ruling group can have extremely debilitating consequences, as seen in polities such as the APC regime in Sierra Leone during the 1970s and 1980s, Moi's Kenya, and Mobutu's Zaïre [*Harriss-White and White, 1996*].

The political realm's centrality in African development, as a rentier state, employer and locus of economic and political power, is part of the explanation for the damaging effects of public sector corruption in Africa. The crimes of the powerful have broad effects: high level corruption has legitimated low level corruption. It can be argued that in these instances of African corruption – whether incidental, systematic or systemic, and whether endemic or planned – the economic and other effects have been profoundly damaging. The brief survey of reform efforts in Africa demonstrates that many strategies have been tried but few have led to consistent and thorough improvements in public integrity. Some of the anti-corruption strategies have been capricious in their effects and some inquiries or campaigns have been politically-motivated or public relations exercises. Recent reforms encouraged by the international institutions have yet to take effect but, given the histories of integrity reform in states such as Nigeria, Sierra Leone and Zaïre, as well as the more promising cases of Botswana and Uganda, the prognosis is not altogether optimistic.

CORRUPTION, ECONOMIC LIBERALISATION AND DEMOCRATISATION IN AFRICA

In many ways, the contemporary debate on corruption, economic liberalisation and democratisation in Africa as elsewhere has been conducted at too high or abstract a level. As Harris-White and White [*1996*] argue, general arguments about the inverse relationship between economic liberalisation and corruption need to be tempered by recent case-study evidence from China and South Korea which suggests that economic liberalisation displaces, refines and may lead to more corruption. In addition, 'far from improving things in the short and medium term, democratization may actually increase the sources and scale of corruption without strengthening countervailing political or institutional capacity'[*ibid.: 3*]. Corruption has been decentralised by democratisation in Thailand and the Philippines. Greater opportunities for corruption are also created.

The debate on corruption, economic liberalisation and democratisation thus needs a more precise focus. There are, in fact, a number of more specific questions that need to be considered which derive from this brief survey of African corruption and recent African attempts to control corruption. First, what type or types of corruption are the most damaging? Secondly, what are the relationships between corruption and poverty and how can an effective, enabling state act to reduce corruption and through this assist in poverty alleviation? Thirdly, what forms of anti-corruption strategy are likely to be most effective in the short and long term?

The implication of the first question is that not all types of African corruption are equally damaging or objectionable. Additionally, some types of corruption may be easier to reduce or minimise in their impact. A small number of minor instances of petty corruption by public officials does not have a major macroeconomic effect, although it can be profoundly alienating for citizens and damages their immediate material circumstances. Other forms of corruption, such as the grand corruption of state elites – in both the mild and the malevolent forms of corruption associated with the Houphouët-Boigny and Mobutu families, in Côte d'Ivoire and Zaïre – have had grossly damaging effects in terms of reputation as well as economic growth.

In Africa, some forms of petty corruption may be tolerable, culturally accepted, or tolerated when compared to the costs of corruption control or eradication. Traditional society figures, such as Paramount Chiefs, are often cited as examples of public officials where gift-giving is culturally tolerated. The widespread incidental corruption involving rural police or military forces who supplement their income by an unofficial tax upon travellers and trade is another, more problematic, case [*Riley, 1983a; 1983b*]. Cultural sensitivity as well as economic analysis is required when developing an anti-corruption approach. Therefore, strategies to deal with different types or levels of corruption have to be developed, and subtlety as well as an appreciation of cultural attitudes is required. Economic liberalisation might remove some petty corruption, by reducing opportunities for junior officials, whereas democratisation has the potential to create a transparency effect and in the longer term reduce larger, more damaging forms of corruption [*Harriss-White and White, 1996*].

The second general question about corruption control illustrates the fact that debates about strategies to control or reduce corruption in African societies have to be considered in the context of the new international development debates of the late 1990s. The relationship between corruption and poverty in African societies is complex and difficult to determine. In the African cases considered, it is evident that corruption is not simply or solely a redistributional system from the poor to the rich. African corruption can also be a result of poverty. This is the case when poorly paid or unpaid public officials ask for and receive corrupt payments because they have to, or when such public officials 'sell' ostensibly free public services such as health care and drug supplies, because of their own poverty.

Many aid donors to Africa would argue that their poverty alleviation objectives in the late 1990s, including literacy programmes and broader educational opportunities, will lead to less corruption. This argument can be developed as follows. African corruption is part of a set of governance problems. One basic issue is the efficient and impartial delivery of public goods to society as a whole; another is the need for the state to secure a stable and equitable resource base to generate growth and development. As part of that society, Africa's poor need sophisticated, sequenced institutional reform and public sector strengthening in the context of a more effective, and empowering, state [*UNDP, 1997; World Bank, 1997a*]. This hypothetical or future state, unlike many current, empirical African states, creates the framework for the delivery of public goods, principally for the poorest citizens. Effective and cost efficient anti-corruption strategies should be considered as part of this broader governance and development goal.

However, corruption and anti-corruption strategies in Africa should also be evaluated in a broader context of social and economic development and societal underdevelopment. The emergence of corruption as an issue is related to the creation of a developed public sphere of life, with a monetised economy, a vigorous civil society and a relatively high degree of socio-cultural homogeneity. Anti-corruption measures are likely to meet with the greatest difficulties in the conditions prevailing in many African societies: a large, peasant-based mainly subsistence sector; a disarticulated and poorly integrated economy; serious primordial divisions; a weak civil society and accordingly high levels of public mistrust [*Ellis (ed.), 1996; Theobald, 1990*]. It is the case that effective corruption control is primarily a product of development which creates wealth, interests and institutions conducive to public integrity [*Khan, 1996*]. Thus these broader social, cultural and historical dimensions of corruption and anti-corruption approaches need to be taken into account in considering this second question. Because there are immense difficulties in securing the effective reduction of corruption in African societies, it is all the more surprising when some successes in corruption control are achieved.

One of the key problems with the attempts by African regimes to control corruption is that diverse strategies have been ineffectively pursued by politically weak governments in exceptionally poor societies. Many approaches, including those at citizen or popular, institutional or procedural, and major contract and senior office-holder levels, have been attempted. But they have often been poorly implemented, partly due to political pressure from individuals and groups with significant interests at stake. In some African societies, procedural or structural reforms, such as those which reduce the arbitrary power of public officials, like customerisation of public services, ought to be considered to limit the opportunities and incentives for corruption whilst raising the risk of detection as well as providing for citizen involvement, complaints and redress. The key issues in assessing anti-corruption strategies are clearly cost, impact, effectiveness and sustainability, whilst also taking into account the relative political and financial strengths of those involved in corruption. What is really needed in the African societies committed to reducing corruption in the late 1990s is a structured and sequenced approach to combatting corruption cost-effectively and in the interests of the citizenry, particularly the poor.

In terms of the relationship between economic and political liberalisation and corruption control, the principal problem with economic liberalisation is that it is essentially a long-term strategy predicated on market forces. It provides no ready means to deliver immediate targeted improvements in public integrity. The problem with political liberalisation is that it will not always appear simultaneously with good governance and may undermine economic liberalisation. In some cases, democratisation has in fact undermined good governance, as was the case in Ghana in the early 1990s when a reforming government was diverted from its original objectives by the desire to win an election. There are also a number of cases where economically liberalising governments have run into difficulties because of the growth of corruption, as in Mozambique and Tanzania, among others [*Hall and Young, 1997; Hanlon, 1996; Mndeme-Musonda, Mjema and Danielson, 1997; Muganda, 1997; Stasavage, 1996*]. Thus it may be the case that the objective of seeking an effective anti-corruption strategy will conflict with the other broader objectives being pursued. Economic liberalisation will not always reduce corruption; nor will the arrival of democratic politics. But combined with institutional reform and political commitment they do provide the foundations upon which a successful anti-corruption campaign can be conducted.

DECIDING A STRATEGY

African reformers – and those in international institutions hoping to minimise corruption in Africa – need to think more about the politics and practicalities of reform efforts rather than relying upon the unpredictable, longer-term effects of economic and political change. Political cunning and real determination is required to deal with the difficult challenge that entrenched corruption presents [*Johnston, 1997*]. Political choices have to be made both by leaderships and by civil society organisations interested in public integrity. The details of the strategy need identifying. Those involved (usually civil servants and politicians, but also journalists and other activists) should identify the types of corruption that exist and their pervasiveness. In Africa in the 1990s, there have been a number of examples of 'workshop' sessions where ideas and suggestions for strategies have been developed, including those run by civil society groups, local and international NGOs, and pressure groups such as Transparency International [*IRIS, 1996*]. A continuing problem is the identification of the structural conditions that have produced the corruption (for example, the type of bureaucracy, its formal rules, and civil service salary levels) rather than a simple identification, condemnation and punishment of the corrupt actors involved. Implementing an effective strategy to highlight the issue of corruption and to try to reduce it involves a number of general issues, relating to timing and sequencing, the consistency of approach, the technical details of the proposed public integrity initiatives and their sustainability, and the ever-present issue of the political or managerial determination and courage to carry through such reforms.

From the point of view of governments, the start of an anti-corruption campaign should be well thoughtout. Few African governments have started by making an example of high-ranking senior officials or politicians. Instead most have issued a general appeal for honesty from civil servants and others or started a public relations campaign. The West African novelist A.K. Armah once compared corruption purges and inquiries in Ghana to unusual fishing nets: the fishing nets caught all the smaller fish but let the bigger fish go free, as was also the case with many corruption inquiries in Sierra Leone in the 1960s and early 1990s [*Armah, 1966; Kpundeh, 1995; Riley, 1983a*]. Making an example of senior figures is a better strategy and will set a good precedent, although the political difficulties involved in this cannot be overestimated. In addition, some African governments have resorted to scapegoats or have been overtly partisan in their official inquiries.

The timing of a strategy also needs to be thought out in connection with economic liberalisation. Losers from structural adjustment are more likely to engage in corruption. Adjustment will alter comparative prices dramatically and will lead to new opportunities and incentives. Thus it is probably better to refine the strategy after an adjustment programme has taken hold, as there are instances where both petty and grand corruption have increased after economic liberalisation. Democratisation can also affect questions of timing and sequencing. A public integrity strategy can be little more than campaign rhetoric, as was the case with campaigners in Nigerian elections. It is of course difficult to distinguish between a merely symbolic and a truly effective plan. But a reforming government with a democratic mandate at least has the popular will behind it. Attempts to improve public integrity must be consistent over time: the stratagem should be well-coordinated and focus upon a particular issue or theme. Some African inquiries have engaged in extensive public consultations or have advocated public education campaigns, as in the case of Tanzania's Warioba Commission which is similar to campaigns in Hong Kong and in the Australian federal states. In order to be consistent, public interest groups should be realistic about what can be achieved. Many African governments, such as Nigeria's in the 1980s, and Sierra Leone's in the early 1990s (which declared a 'war on economic crime'), announced unconvincing, over-ambitious goals that were unrealistic, and doomed to fail. Attempts to control corruption should also operate across the entire political, administrative and business spectrum of activities. An anti-corruption campaign is unlikely to work if it is inconsistent and omits certain public sectors or public officials. Obviously, some areas of government activity (such as customs and taxation divisions) are most prone to corruption but all those who are potentially corrupt or corruptible should feel at risk.

Few African governments or civil society groups have demonstrated the ability to reduce corruption significantly and permanently, although countries such as Botswana have had relatively low levels of grand corruption since independence. However, Botswana has distinctive characteristics, including political stability, sustained economic growth whose benefits are reasonably widely spread, and a relatively unified elite committed to encouraging foreign investment and maintaining public integrity [*Charlton, 1990; Frimpong, 1997; Good, 1994*]. These features are not often found in contemporary Africa. Benin, Burkina Faso, Mali, Uganda and the former Zaïre have taken a series of anti-corruption initiatives recently, including the return of the assets of former heads of state from overseas, and establishing ethics codes and asset declarations procedures [*Harsch, 1997*]. But very few African countries since independence have successfully tackled the problem of corruption.

For reforming governments that seek to deal with corruption, a number of innovations have developed in recent years. These include confidential surveys of private sector businesses with the intention of establishing where corruption exists in the public sector – in customs, public order, procurement, or the wider political system. Such a survey was used in the 1997 World Development Report [*World Bank, 1997a*]. In addition, few African governments or civil society groups utilise the skills of accountants, public finance specialists, or lawyers and their professional organisations. Only recently have African citizen groups started using the services of bodies such as Transparency International (TI). Whilst there are problems with TI, such as the links it has with international institutions and its initially pro-business bias, the advantage of the growth of this organisation is that it can help political leaders and civic organisations who wish to do something about corruption. Public integrity reforms must also be sustainable as well as politically feasible. Politicians have to recognise that they can take action without seriously damaging their own political prospects. In many African societies, they must be able to take the credit and avoid the blame if they are not themselves involved.

Political determination is a crucial aspect of any public integrity strategy. Without a strong commitment to reform and personal examples and commitments from the political leadership, governmental statements of intent, attempted reforms and strategies remain cosmetic devices. There have been many African political leaders who have decried the cost of significant or systemic corruption yet have failed to do anything about it. Obviously, individual politicians, even at the top of political systems, cannot make much of a difference in some cases of systemic corruption. But they can act to demonstrate their own commitment in other cases. They can use their democratic credibility to make some significant changes. Recent studies have suggested examples of how a leader can demonstrate this [*Klitgaard, 1997; Kpundeh, 1997*]. African politicians could demonstrate their commitment to public integrity by dismissing corrupt ministers and announcing the reason for their dismissal, by restructuring law enforcement agencies to fight corruption, and by holding chief enforcement officers accountable for public integrity. It is possible to challenge vested interests. And scandal, as well as clearly illegal cases of corruption, can be used to initiate action, as recent examples in western Europe show [*Levi and Nelken, 1996*].

Democratic politicians, especially in Africa's precarious and fragile newly-liberalised systems of the 1990s, are nervous about taking action where they see no obvious political benefits and fear the political costs. In order for them to act, their political responsibility and determination need to be strengthened. This can include improving the democratic balance in any society [*Johnston, 1997*], creating a public constituency for reform, and enhancing civil society institutions that help the strategy (such as a free press, and the independence of the professions and public agencies). In many African societies, it is also important for civil society groups to humanise corruption: to make clear to all concerned the individual, human costs of misallocations of resources. In

Africa's weak states, with powerful domestic interests opposed to reform, it is obviously hard but necessary to reinforce the political will of democratic politicians to take action on corruption [*Englebert, 1997*].

CONCLUSION

Exceptional political and managerial determination and courage is necessary to enable African states to promote and maintain reform and reduce public sector corruption. This is rarely found, even in the most populist or post-neo-colonial African states. The political and personal risks of a commitment to public integrity are obvious.[2] For many African leaderships, it is much easier to maintain a formal commitment to reform whilst not endangering the interests and corrupt incomes of powerful groups. However, given the new development agenda of the later 1990s, it is also obviously politic for aid-dependent states to take account of these new donor priorities which expect reductions in corruption and better governance. Where African governments do show a determination to improve public integrity, far more attention needs to be given to questions of timing and sequencing, consistency in approach, the details of reform and its sustainability, and the encouragement of the exceptional political and managerial persistence necessary to promote and sustain reform in this area.

In some west African states, including Mali and Senegal, economic liberalisation seems to have helped reduce customs fraud, and the related corruption, when combined with institutional reform and relatively high salaries. In Tanzania, economic liberalisation is part of the explanation for the growth of petty and grand corruption. Some African states have embarked upon comprehensive public integrity initiatives: in Tanzania, the anti-corruption strategy includes expectations of the beneficial effects of long-term growth and literacy efforts, combined with legal reforms and institutional strengthening.

But such ambitious objectives raise important questions about short-term priorities and the inter-relationships between such reform efforts. Almost all the African country experiences examined here raise in one form or another the politics of reform. Does the political leadership have the sustained commitment to improve public integrity or is it engaged in a mere public relations exercise – for citizens and aid donors? In other polities, such as Hong Kong, exceptionally high political commitment, popular support, good administrative organisation and a coherent strategy have yielded results. But there are questions regarding the sustainability and transferability of such an approach to African societies [*Spelville, 1997; UNDP/OECD, 1997*]. Tanzania's recent anti-corruption effort, with its inquiry process, needs to be turned into a sustained political and institutional commitment. In the cases of

Nigeria, Sierra Leone and the former Zaïre we see the political turmoil that gross corruption can cause. There are many anti-corruption institutions in African societies but they are not all like the ICAC in Hong Kong or its institutional near-equivalent in Botswana, or the inspector-general system in Uganda [*Frimpong, 1997; Ruzindana, 1997; Spelville, 1997*].

One obvious if easy generalisation from the experiences of African states is that an ethically motivated and strong leadership is necessary to promote and maintain anti-corruption reform. But African puritans, or African Oliver Cromwells, are hard to find. International institutions, such as the World Bank, have been promoting universal strategies to control corruption, but different African cases demonstrate the difficulties with such universalist solutions [*World Bank, 1997c*]. If elements of a universal strategy are needed, then a number of basic suggestions can be made. In addition to institutional improvements, in almost all African societies the professions should be strengthened – by enhancing their professionalism, independence and technical skills – as part of a strategy to control corruption. Lawyers, accountants, and investigative journalists all need support, from civil society groups and interested individuals, and technical help, including perhaps from external donors. But enhanced professional skills, as well as a commitment to try to control corruption, are more likely to be seen in democratic societies where the pressures of political competition often force politicians to act. Democratisation is thus a necessary but not a sufficient condition for the reduction of corruption. Economic liberalisation is also not a simple panacea for public sector corruption. But reducing the size of the state also reduces the size of the potential corrupt 'take' and enables the public sector to move towards the ideal of an efficient, enabling state. The African experience suggests that sophisticated, well-timed and properly sequenced short-term anti-corruption strategies will contribute to the governance agenda that economic and political liberalisation seek to achieve.

NOTES

1. In early 1997, a popular song on the streets of Lusaka, the capital of Zambia, expressed this mood about Zambia's President and his ruling party: 'Chiluba anaba mupando' (Chiluba stole the seat and should be caged) people sang. The role of folk-song as well as popular sayings and rumours about corruption – what Gunnar Myrdal called the folklore of corruption – has not been frequently studied but is of great importance. In contemporary Mozambique corruption is called '*cabritismo*' (literally 'goatism', from the phrase 'a goat eats where it is tethered'). Similar sayings about voracious goats were expressed about Siaka Stevens and corruption in Sierra Leone.
2. In 1991 Mozambique's Attorney-General raised the issue of corruption in his annual report to parliament. He subsequently received several death threats. In Zaïre in 1979 the head of a team of western bankers sent to run Zaïre's central bank, being critical of Mobutu's kleptocratic ways, was reduced to sleeping with a shotgun under his bed after receiving similar threats from groups of soldiers.

REFERENCES

Andreski, S., 1968, 'Kleptocracy: Or Corruption as a System of Government', in S. Andreski (ed), *The African Predicament*, London: Michael Joseph, pp.92–109.

Armah, A.K., 1966, *The Beautyful Ones Are Not Yet Born*, London: Heinemann.

Askin, S. and C. Collins, 1993, 'External Collusion with Kleptocracy: Can Zaïre Recapture its Stolen Wealth?' *Review of African Political Economy*, No.57, pp.72–85.

Callaghy, T.M., 1984, *The State–Society Struggle: Zaïre in Comparative Perspective*, New York: Columbia University Press.

Charlton, R., 1990, 'Exploring the Byways of African Political Corruption: Botswana and Deviant Case Analysis', *Corruption and Reform*, Vol.5, No.1, pp.1–28.

Clarke, M. (ed.), 1983, *Corruption: Causes, Consequences and Controls*, London: Frances Pinter.

Collins, C., 1997, 'The Congo is Back!', *Review of African Political Economy*, No.72, pp.277–92.

Delamaide, D., 1984, *Debt Shock*, London: Weidenfeld & Nicolson.

DeLeon, P., 1993, *Thinking About Political Corruption*, New York: M.E. Sharpe.

Doig, R.A., 1995, 'Good Government and Sustainable Anti-corruption Strategies: A Role for Independent Anti-corruption Agencies?' *Public Administration and Development*, Vol.15, No.2, pp.151–65.

Doig, R.A. and S.P. Riley, 1998, 'Corruption and Anti-Corruption Strategies: Issues and Case Studies From Developing Countries', in G.S. Cheema and J. Bonvin (eds.), *Corruption and Integrity Improvement Initiatives in Developing Countries*, Paris: OECD.

Ellis, S., 1996, 'Africa and International Corruption: The Strange Case of South Africa and the Seychelles', *African Affairs*, Vol.95, No.380, pp.165–96.

Ellis, S. (ed.), 1996, *Africa Now: People, Policies and Institutions*, London: James Currey.

Englebert, P., 1997, 'The Contemporary African State: Neither African, Nor State', *Third World Quarterly*, Vol.18, No.4, pp.767–76.

Falola, T. and J. Ihonvbere, 1985, *The Rise and Fall of Nigeria's Second Republic, 1979–1984*, London: Zed Press.

Forrest, T., 1993, *Politics and Economic Development in Nigeria*, Boulder, CO: Westview Press.

Frimpong, K., 1997, 'An Analysis of Corruption in Botswana', paper for the UNDP/OECD Development Centre conference on 'Corruption and Integrity Improvement Initiatives in the Context of Developing Economies', Paris, 24–25 Oct.

Good, K., 1994, 'Corruption and Mismanagement in Botswana: A Best-Case Example', *Journal of Modern African Studies*, Vol.32, No.3, pp.499–521.

Gould, D.J., 1980, *Bureaucratic Corruption and Underdevelopment in the Third World: The Case of Zaïre*, New York: Pergamon Press.

Gould, D.J. and J. Amaro-Reyes, 1983, 'The Effects of Corruption on Administrative Performance: Illustrations From Developing Countries', *World Bank Working Paper No.580.*

Goudie, A. and D. Stasavage, 1997, 'Corruption: The Issues', *OECD Technical Paper No.122.*

Gourevitch, P., 1997, 'Continental Shift', *The New Yorker*, 4 Aug., pp.42–55.

Hall, M. and T. Young, 1997, *Confronting Leviathan: Mozambique since Independence*, London: C. Hurst.

Hampton, M., 1996, *The Offshore Interface: Tax Havens in the Global Economy*, Basingstoke: Macmillan.

Hanlon, J., 1996, *Peace without Profit: How the IMF Blocks Rebuilding in Mozambique*, London: James Currey.

Harriss-White, B. and G. White (eds.), 1996, 'Liberalization and the New Corruption', *IDS Bulletin*, Vol.27, No.2.

Harsch, E., 1993, 'Accumulators and Democrats: Challenging State Corruption in Africa', *Journal of Modern African Studies*, Vol.31, No.1, pp.31–48.

Harsch, E., 1997, 'Africans Take On Corruption', *Africa Recovery*, July, pp.26–7.

Heidenheimer, A.J., LeVine, V.T. and M.J. Johnston (eds.), 1989, *Political Corruption: A Handbook*, New Brunswick, NJ: Transaction.

Hoogvelt, A., 1997, *Globalisation and the Postcolonial World*, London: Macmillan.

Huntington, S. P., 1991, *The Third Wave: Democratization in the Late Twentieth Century*, Norman, OK and London: University of Oklahoma Press.

IRIS, 1996, 'Governance and the Economy in Africa: Tools for Analysis and Reform of Corruption', Center for Institutional Reform and the Informal Sector (IRIS), University of Maryland.

Jeffries, R., 1982, 'Rawlings and the Political Economy of Underdevelopment in Ghana', *African Affairs*, Vol.81, No.384, pp.307–17.

Johnston, M. J., 1997, 'What Can be Done About Entrenched Corruption?', paper presented at the Annual World Bank Conference on Development Economics, Washington, DC, April–May.

Kaplan, R.D., 1994, 'The Coming Anarchy', *The Atlantic Monthly*, Feb., pp.44–72.

Kaplan, R.D., 1996, *The Ends of the Earth*, New York: Random House.

Kaplan, R.D., 1997, 'Was Democracy Just a Moment?', *The Atlantic Monthly*, Dec., pp.55–80.

Kaufmann, D., 1997, 'Corruption: The Facts', *Foreign Policy*, No.107, pp.114–31.

Keen, D., 1997, 'Rebellion and Its Functions in Sierra Leone', paper for the conference on 'Identity and Conflict in Africa', University of Leeds, Leeds, 15–17 Sept.

Khan, M.H., 1996, 'A Typology of Corrupt Transactions in Developing Countries', *IDS Bulletin*, Vol.26, No.2, pp.48–55.

Klitgaard, R., 1988, *Controlling Corruption*, Berkeley, CA: University of California Press.

Klitgaard, R., 1991, *Tropical Gangsters*, London: I.B. Tauris.

Klitgaard, R., 1997, 'Cleaning Up and Invigorating the Civil Service', a report for the Operations Evaluation Department, Washington, DC: The World Bank.

Kpundeh, S.J., 1995, *Politics and Corruption in Africa: A Case Study of Sierra Leone*, Langham, MD: University Press of America.

Kpundeh, S.J., 1997, 'Political Will for Anti-Corruption Activities: An Analysis', unpublished paper, May.

Kulibaba, N., 1997, 'Good Governance in Sheep's Clothing: Implementing the Action Plan for Regional Facilitation of the Livestock Trade in West Africa's Central Corridor', Case Study No.3, Implementing Policy Change Project, Washington, DC: United States Agency for International Development.

Leftwich, A. (ed.), 1996, *Democracy and Development: Theory and Practice*, Oxford: Polity Press.

Levi, M. and D. Nelken (eds.), 1996, *The Corruption of Politics and the Politics of Corruption*, Oxford: Blackwell.

Luke, D.F. and S.P. Riley, 1989, 'The Politics of Economic Decline in Sierra Leone', *Journal of Modern African Studies*, Vol.27, No.1, pp.133–42.

Luke, D.F. and S.P. Riley, 1991, 'Economic Decline and the New Reform Agenda in Africa', IDPM Discussion Papers No.28, University of Manchester.

McKinney, J.B. and M.J. Johnston (eds.), 1986, *Fraud, Waste and Abuse in Government: Causes, Consequences and Cures*, Philadelphia, PA: Institute for the Study of Human Issues.

Meagher, K., 1997, 'Informal Integration or Economic Subversion? Parallel Trade in West Africa', in R. Laverne (ed.), *Regional Integration and Cooperation in West Africa*, Trenton, NJ: Africa World Press, pp.165–88.

Mndeme-Musonda, F., Mjema, G. and A. Danielson, 1997, 'Tanzania 1997, The Urge to Merge: The Revival of East African Cooperation', Macroeconomic Report No.7, Stockholm: Swedish International Development Cooperation Agency.

Moodie-Stuart, G., 1997, *Grand Corruption*, Oxford: WorldView.

Muganda, A., 1997, 'The War Against Corruption in Tanzania: An Overview of the Warioba Report', paper for the UNDP/OECD Development Centre conference on 'Corruption and Integrity Improvement Initiatives in the Context of Developing Economies', Paris, 24–25 Oct.

Naylor, R.T., 1987, *Hot Money and the Politics of Debt*, London: Unwin Hyman.

Naylor, R.T., 1996, 'The Underworld of Gold', *Crime, Law and Social Change*, Vol.25, No.3, pp.191–241.

Noonan, J.T. Jr., 1984, *Bribes*, New York: Macmillan.

Organisation for Economic Co-operation and Development (OECD), 1997, 'OECD Actions to Fight Corruption', Paris.

Randel, J. and T. German, 1997, *The Reality of Aid, 1997*, London: Earthscan.

Reno, W., 1995, *Corruption and State Politics in Sierra Leone*, Cambridge: Cambridge University Press.

Reno, W., 1997a, 'African Weak States and Commercial Alliances', *African Affairs*, Vol.96, No.383, pp.165–85.

Reno, W., 1997b, 'Privatising War in Sierra Leone', *Current History*, May, pp.227–30.

Riley, S.P., 1983a, '"The Land of Waving Palms": Corruption Inquiries, Political Economy and Politics in Sierra Leone', in M. Clarke (ed.), *Corruption: Causes, Consequences and Controls*, London: Frances Pinter, pp.190–206.

Riley, S.P., 1983b, 'The Current Political Situation in Sierra Leone', in P.K. Mitchell and A. Jones (eds.), *Sierra Leone Studies at Birmingham: Proceedings of a Symposium*, University of Birmingham, Birmingham, pp.42–63.

Riley, S.P., 1992, 'Political Adjustment or Domestic Pressure? Democratic Politics and Political Choice in Africa', *Third World Quarterly*, Vol.13, No.3, pp.539–51.

Riley, S.P., 1993, 'Post Independence Anti-Corruption Strategies and the Contemporary Effects of Democratisation', *Corruption and Reform*, Vol.7, No.3, pp.249–61.

Riley, S.P., 1996, 'The 1996 Presidential and Parliamentary Elections in Sierra Leone', *Electoral Studies*, Vol.15, No.4, pp.537–44.

Riley, S.P., 1997, 'Sierra Leone: The Militariat Strikes Again', *Review of African Political Economy*, No.72, pp.287–92.

Riley, S.P. and T.W. Parfitt, 1994, 'Economic Adjustment and Democratisation in Africa', in J. Walton and D. Seddon (eds.), *Free Markets and Food Riots: The Politics of Global Adjustment*, Oxford: Blackwell, pp.135–70.

Robinson, J., 1994, *The Laundrymen*, London: Simon & Schuster.

Robinson, M., 1997, Summary Report of the Workshop on Corruption and Development, IDS, University of Sussex, Brighton, 6–7 May.

Rose-Ackerman, S., 1997, 'Corruption and Development', paper presented at the Annual World Bank Conference on Development Economics, Washington, DC, April–May.

Ruzindana, A., 1997, 'The Importance of Leadership in Fighting Corruption in Uganda', in K.A. Elliot (ed.), *Corruption and the Global Economy*, Washington, DC: Institute for International Economics, pp.133–46.

Sen, A. K., 1997, 'On Corruption and Organised Crime', in United Nations Drug Control Programme (UNDCP), *World Drug Report*, Oxford: Oxford University Press, pp.150–3.

Spelville, B. de, 1997, 'A Study of the Policy Initiatives Against Corruption in Hong Kong', Paris: OECD Development Centre.

Stapenhurst, R. and P. Langseth, 1997, 'The Role of the Public Administration in Fighting Corruption', *International Journal of Public Sector Management*, Vol.10, No.5, pp.311–30.

Stasavage, D., 1996, 'Corruption and the Mozambican Economy', Paris: OECD Development Centre.

Stasavage, D. and C. Daubree, 1997, 'Determinants of Customs Fraud in Mali and Senegal', paper for the UNDP/OECD Development Centre conference on 'Corruption and Integrity Improvement Initiatives in the Context of Developing Economies', Paris, 24–25 Oct.

Stevens, M., 1997, 'The World Bank's Approach to Corruption', paper for the Workshop on Corruption and Development, Institute of Development Studies, University of Sussex, Brighton, 6–7 May.

Transparency International (TI), 1996, *National Integrity Systems: The TI Source Book*, Berlin.

Theobald, R., 1990, *Corruption, Development and Underdevelopment*, Basingstoke: Macmillan.

United Nations Development Programme (UNDP), 1997, *Human Development Report*, Oxford: Oxford University Press.

United Nations Development Programme/Organisation for Economic Co-operation and Development – Development Centre (UNDP/OECD), 1997, Report of the conference on 'Corruption and Integrity Improvement Initiatives in the Context of Developing Economies', Paris, 24–25 Oct.

Waterbury, J., 1973, 'Endemic and Planned Corruption in a Monarchical Regime', *World Politics*, Vol.25, No.4, pp.534 –55.

Ward, P. (ed.), 1989, *Corruption, Development and Inequality*, London: Routledge.

Warioba, J.S., 1997, 'Corruption and the State II: Extracts from Joseph Warioba's Report', *Soundings*, No.7, Autumn, pp.198–208.

Williams, R., 1987, *Political Corruption in Africa*, Aldershot: Gower.

Wiseman, J. (ed.), 1995, *Democracy and Political Change in Sub-Saharan Africa*, London: Routledge.

World Bank, 1997a, *World Development Report: The State in a Changing World*, Oxford: Oxford University Press.

World Bank, 1997b, *Report of the Corruption Action Plan Working Group (CAPWG) – Country and International Strategies*, OPC Review Draft, May.

World Bank, 1997c, *Helping Countries Combat Corruption: The Role of the World Bank*, Washington, DC: World Bank.

Zack-Williams, A., 1983, 'A Reflection on the Class Basis of Corruption in Sierra Leone and its Implications for Development', in P.K. Mitchell and A. Jones (eds.), *Sierra Leone Studies at Birmingham: Proceedings of a Symposium*, University of Birmingham, Birmingham, pp.359–62.

Part II
Codes of Conduct/Ethical Controls

[8]

Corruption and Reform 7: 1–18, 1992

Edicts and etiquette: Regulating conflict of interest in Congress and the House of Commons

MICHAEL M. ATKINSON[1] and MAUREEN MANCUSO[2]
[1]*McMaster University, Canada;* [2]*University of Windsor, Canada*

Abstract. Conflict-of-interest issues are a problem common to legislative bodies in virtually all democratic nations. Strategies for controlling these problems, however, can differ significantly, even in nations as similar as the United Kingdom and the United States. While American conflict-of-interest policies rest on written laws and codes of ethics, or "edicts", British MPs are subject to a system of informal, largely unwritten rules, which can be thought of as a system of elite "etiquette". The former have the advantage of specificity and openness, but lead to a concentration on the letter of the law instead of the broader spirit of limits on conflicts of interest, and encourage Members to turn ethics laws into weapons of partisan conflict. The latter are flexible and applicable to diverse situations, and affirm the expectation that MPs should live up to a separate and more demanding set of elite ethical standards; but they are also more open to evasion, may not be vigorously enforced, and may leave the legislative body vulnerable to exploitation from without. Each type of control, however, reflects fundamental aspects of legislators' roles in their respective political systems.

Conflict of interest has become an increasingly prominent issue in the legislatures of many western democracies. Sensitized by scandals, and by the salary expectations of politicians, electorates have begun to demand that ethical issues be addressed directly. In the United States the House of Representatives, for example, agreed to an "ethics package" in 1989 that provided for a significant salary increase in exchange for severe restrictions on honoraria. In the United States and elsewhere, legislatures have begun to grope toward a set of regulations that will meet demands for moral rectitude without placing excessive burdens on elected officials.

Not all legislatures have approached the task in the same manner. Although conflict of interest is a generic problem, there are many ways of addressing it, including ignoring it altogether. Moreover, legislatures experience the problem in different ways. Conflict of interest arises when a private interest influences, or appears to influence, the discharge of public responsibilities.[1] But public responsibilities differ from one system to the next and private interests have different implications for impartiality depending on the role of the legislator in each system. Legislative responses will be tailored to the manner in which the problem presents itself.[2] However, the fact that there is no one best solution to the conflict of interest problem does not imply that all responses are equally sound, that legislatures have nothing to learn from one another, or that it is impossible to compare the regulation of conflict of interest in different settings. The question is: are the strategies adopted suitable for the particular way in which conflict of interest manifests itself?

In this paper we identify key features of two ideal-typical methods currently employed for managing conflicts of interest, and compare their operation in the legislatures of the United States and Britain. The British House of Commons depends primarily upon parliamentary collegiality for conflict regulation. This "etiquette" solution to problems of conflict of interest relies on the effectiveness of internal norms that protect the legislature and its membership from evaluation by outsiders. In the United States Congress, legislative conflicts of interest are addressed primarily through the creation of a system of general, public rules – "edicts." These edicts form the basis for a contract between the representative and the represented. We show how these different approaches are employed to confront the main sources of conflict of interest in both systems: nepotism, financial interests, and outside employment. The final part of the paper evaluates edicts and etiquette drawing attention to their common and unique weaknesses.

Edicts and etiquette: Congress and Commons

The British House of Commons relies heavily on the etiquette approach to conflict of interest. Legislative norms and parliamentary conventions define ethical standards. There is an implicit faith in the ability of the forces of social and cultural evolution to generate efficient social norms. It is assumed that this process functions optimally when unfettered by formal restrictions, because no set of formal rules can possibly anticipate all of the problems associated with reconciling personal and representative responsibilities. As a result the rules governing conduct in the House of Commons are uncodified; there is no single, coherent blueprint for ethical conduct. Instead, it is assumed that MPs will become acquainted with the norms and expectations that bear upon ethical behaviour because these norms are closely connected to all aspects of representation. To codify them would restrict their evolution and deny the legislature the opportunity to exercise some flexibility in their interpretation.

Honour is the foundation of the etiquette solution. In Britain, MPs are encouraged to believe that they belong to a privileged elite, one whose behaviour is governed by a standard not intended for others. With this comes the presumption that legislators have moral insight into public affairs.

Members may choose to ignore moral urgings, but the etiquette system assumes that, at a minimum, they have the ability to recognize the morally correct course of action. The critical moral dictum is the requirement that legislators place the public interest before their own private advantage, but the concept of honour permits representatives to use their discretion in the application of this principle to concrete situations of conflict of interest. No explicit instructions are needed.

The strength of the etiquette approach is its implicit endorsement of the view that the curtailment of conflict of interest depends on legislators acting together in a collegial setting.[3] In all legislatures the tradition of the "honourable gentleman" is reinforced by the aura of collegiality that descends upon those with common backgrounds and shared legislative experience.[4] The etiquette system assumes that it is in the collegiality of the legislative process, not across the divide of the representative and the represented, that ethical standards and expectations are best defined. Thus legislators remain the primary custodians of the system because no one else enjoys the presumption of honourable behaviour. However, a legislature like the House of Commons, in which the etiquette solution is so prominent, is always open to the charge that it coddles its membership and uses tradition as an excuse to avoid punishing transgression.

Legislatures, like the United States Congress, that rely more extensively on edicts have developed a response to conflict of interest that places much less stress on principles of honour, reciprocity and collegiality, and much more stress on legally enforceable restrictions. The collegial resolution of conflict of interest problems gives way to a permanent regulatory edifice in which the legislator's personal legal responsibility for conflicts of interest is emphasized. The key to this edifice is a written set of public rules. These rules emerge from a collegial process, but their purpose is to alert members to the limits of collegial decision-making.

Contract is the foundation of the edict approach. While the House of Commons depends on unwritten understandings, occasionally punctuated by a resolution of the legislature, Congress has adopted formal codes of conduct and statutory prohibitions. The purpose of these edicts is to circumscribe independent behaviour. In exchange for the public's trust, congressmen agree to abide by a set of public rules and to submit to periodic inspection of their behaviour for compliance. This contractual approach to the regulation of conflicts of interest requires an institutionalized system of standards, investigation and sanction. Although legislatures jealously guard their right to determine their own rules, in Congress this independence has been surrendered to some degree so that a more formalized process of investigation can be adopted. Unlike the etiquette system, the response to a conflict situation is not *ad hoc*; once in motion, the regulatory machinery continues

4

under its own power. Moreover, this machinery need not be exclusively under legislative control. While all legislative assemblies seek to retain for themselves primary responsibility for defining and regulating conflict of interest, Congress has provided outsiders with an opportunity to participate in their regulatory efforts. In all systems that rely on edicts the courts, special prosecutors, independent investigators, and ethics commissioners can all conceivably play a part in the resolution of a conflict of interest.

The strength of the edict system is that it makes legislators, and even candidates, aware of the conditions under which they accept public office. Opportunities for misunderstanding are reduced and procedures for handling violations are clearly established. In this fashion the edict system addresses the problem of consent in an institutional setting. It directs attention toward "a proper understanding of which rules actually prevail and a reconciliation of conflicts, inconsistencies, and ambiguities among those prevailing rules."[5]

The sources of conflict of interest

Conflict of interest was described above as a situation in which private interests interfere, or appear to interfere, with the discharge of public responsibilities. The public official who experiences a conflict of interest cannot convincingly claim that he judges an issue entirely on its merits. In some cases, as when legislators seek to capitalize personally on the opportunities that legislative office provides, conflict of interest is the product of venal intent. More often, however, conflict of interest arises in the ordinary course of performing public duties. In these cases legislators find themselves drawn into a situation in which their personal private interests are affected by a public decision in which they are participating. Even when their estimation of the public interest and their own interest happen to coincide, it has been argued that a conflict of interest results because it is no longer possible to presume that the legislator is capable of acting impartially.[6] The elimination of legislative independence is at the heart of the conflict of interest problem.

Legislatures will differ, however, on what constitutes a threat to legislative independence. Legislators play different roles in different systems, exercise more or less power, and work to different public standards. But whether or not threats to independence and impartiality are treated as serious, in each of the circumstances outlined below an argument can be made that legislative independence is compromised. We compare the response of the United States Congress and the British House of Commons to the three most common threats to legislative independence: nepotism, financial interests and outside employment. These legislatures do not rely exclusively on edicts or etiquette, but in their attempt to manage the conflict of interest problem, Congress and the House of Commons display divergent propensities.

Nepotism

Nepotism is essentially favouritism based on familial relationships. Family ties induce elected officials to award contracts and jobs on the basis of kinship rather than merit. In many systems, this is seen as an especially blatant form of conflict of interest, in which familial obligations overwhelm public ones. Moreover, the financial distance between an official and his spouse or children can be almost negligible. In community property legal systems, such as the states of California, Texas, and Washington, payments to one spouse are ordinarily the property of both, and assets of dependent children are almost universally held to belong to the parents. Thus nepotism potentially involves two separate dimensions of conflict: the tug-of-war between kinship and public impartiality, as well as the possibility of effective personal enrichment through the exercise of public authority.

In Britain, however, nepotism is treated as if it were essentially unproblematic. Among parliamentarians, there exist no formal prohibitions against familial favouritism. In fact, the legislative culture of the House of Commons seems to license, if not positively encourage, the hiring of family members to publicly-funded positions. A recent study of MPs' attitudes toward political corruption revealed that only two per cent of those interviewed considered that hiring one's spouse as a secretary created a conflict of interest; indeed, many were unable to conceive of anyone disapproving of such an action.[7] Spouses, even those without secretarial training or skills, are routinely hired, and their employment is defended on the grounds that they are familiar with the member and his or her personal habits, preferences, and opinions.

In contrast, U.S. federal law prohibits all federal officials, including congressmen, from appointing, promoting, or recommending for appointment or promotion any relative, where 'relative' is defined as

> an individual who is related to the public official as father, mother, son, daughter, brother, sister, uncle, aunt, first cousin, nephew, niece, husband, wife, father-in-law, mother-in-law, son-in-law, daughter-in-law, brother-in-law, sister-in-law, stepfather, stepmother, stepson, stepdaughter, stepbrother, stepsister, half brother or half sister.[8]

This law forbids members of Congress from hiring relatives to their own staff or to the staffs of any committees or sub-committees they chair. These restrictions have been upheld by the courts – an extra-legislative player in the ethical game – and have withstood constitutional challenges. The congressional ethics manual goes so far as to note that should a marriage cause a staff member to become the congressman's "relative," he or she may remain on staff, but cannot benefit from future favourable personnel action by the congressman. Moreover, congressmen must certify that their staff conforms to the law before payroll is authorized.

The U.S. system regulates nepotism in a rigidly precise manner. Without deliberate misrepresentation, a congressman cannot award preferment to a family member, even if that person is fully qualified for the position. In Britain, on the other hand, MPs are trusted to appoint qualified staff at their own discretion, and a familial relationship in no way disqualifies even candidates who do not meet the formal job requirements. The argument that spouses or other family members often have special knowledge and sensitivity is widely accepted. It is also tacitly recognized that MPs are entitled to keep their staff allowances "within the family," as some recompense for their low official salaries.

Financial interests

Legislators come to public office with personal financial portfolios. Many of them have ties to family businesses, partnerships, legal or medical practices, property, investments or shareholdings. Conceivably, such interests or holdings could come into conflict with their public duties. Rather than force legislators to forsake such holdings, most legislatures have adopted procedures to avoid such conflicts from occurring. Such procedures vary, however, in terms of their formality, rigor and enforceability.

In the etiquette-based British system, disclosure is the preferred approach to defusing financial conflicts. Disclosure has a long tradition in the British Parliament. As early as the 17th century, disclosure rules were adopted to enable the House to assess the extent of a member's financial interest in an issue being debated in the House or its committees. This tradition currently manifests itself as a resolution of the House, adopted in 1975. Both Ministers and MPs are required to file annual written public declarations of their outside holdings. Members are requested to declare their holdings and interests under a number of specified headings, including property, shares, foreign travel and investments. Value amounts need not be revealed and the British House does not make provisions for the use of trust – blind or frozen. The purpose of disclosure is merely to acknowledge that the holdings exist. Ministers, as specified in the Cabinet document "Questions of Procedure," face the additional requirement to relinquish directorships, and controlling interests in public corporations, and to withdraw from the day-to-day operation of professional firms or partnerships.

The disclosure rules were extended in 1987 to cover House researchers, secretaries, the parliamentary press gallery and officers of all-party groups. The extension was premised on the belief that anyone working for an MP should reveal all pertinent interests that might affect the performance of his or her responsibilities. This additional information is not open to public inspection and is intended for the sole use and information of MPs themselves. Some members have suggested that the provisions be extended even further to apply to their spouses and dependent children, but the House has yet to implement such a measure. On the whole, additions to the Register have been slow in coming. However, in response to the case of Alan Meale MP, members are now required, as of January 1990, to declare any subsidies from corporations or local councils they receive for operating their constituency offices or for obtaining research assistance. It is also anticipated that more stringent restrictions will soon be introduced to prohibit Select Committee Chairmen from being financially involved with firms that conduct business within the domain of their committees.

The member's declaration forms, collected and published as the Register of Members' Interests, are compiled and administered by a Registrar appointed from the Clerk's Office. The operation of the Register and the investigation of problems which arise are entrusted to the Select Committee on Members' Interests, which discusses violations of the Register, applications of the declaration resolution and any new issues which might warrant attention. The Committee does not initiate investigations into the behaviour of individual members. Complaints must originate with an MP or an outsider. Complaints from a member proceed directly to the Committee, while the Registrar sifts through the complaints of outsiders, passing on to the Committee only those he feels are backed by solid evidence. In only two instances to date has there been enough *prima facie* evidence to take the complaint to the committee.[9]

Matters may be changing. In the past, the Committee has been reluctant to punish members who failed to comply with the declaration requirement. It has also declined to investigate those alleged to have submitted false or inaccurate forms. Enoch Powell, for example, was able to ignore the declaration requirement for years without penalty. In March 1990, however, the Committee recommended that John Browne MP be disciplined for failing to disclose fully his outside financial interests in the Register. The House agreed, and ultimately voted to suspend him for twenty sitting days. This action has sent a signal to MPs that the Select Committee intends to take the declaration requirement more seriously. In fact, the Select Committee has recently initiated a review of the Register and the declaration principles by requesting submissions from interested parties.

In the United States, disclosure provisions are found in *The Ethics in*

8

Government Act (1978) and *The Ethics Reform Act* (1989). The rules of both Houses of Congress explicitly state that Senators and Representatives are required to file an annual declaration of their financial holdings. This declaration includes capital gains, interest, dividends – any financial transaction exceeding two hundred dollars. In addition, members are required to declare all liabilities in excess of ten thousand dollars. While the declarations need not reveal exact dollar amounts they must provide an estimation of the value of a member's interests within a specified range. Such provisions extend to senior congressional staff, as well as to spouses and dependent children.

Completed declaration forms are filed by members with the appropriate ethics committee – the Committee on Standards of Official Conduct of the House of Representatives and the Senate Select Committee on Ethics. These committees are now comprised of fourteen members – as specified in *The Ethics Reform Act* – equally divided between Democrats and Republicans. A permanent staff assists committee members in monitoring the declaration forms for compliance and completeness. The committee also serves as an advisory board for members, providing interpretations and opinions to individuals who are unsure of ethical expectations and requirements. Unlike the British case, these committees are empowered to investigate declaration forms they consider inaccurately or falsely complex. They can request additional information or require an informal meeting with the individual involved. If the committee reaches the conclusion that there has been a willful violation of the rules governing declaration, it can ask the Attorney General's Office to bring a civil action against a member with the possibility of a fine of up to ten thousand dollars. In addition, there is a penalty of two hundred dollars for late filing of declaration forms. And whereas the British Select Committee on Members' Interests conducts its inquiries exclusively *in camera*, the investigations of the Congressional Committees are ordinarily held in open public sessions.

Outside employment

For centuries the British House of Commons has served as a meeting place for gentlemen who viewed membership in Parliament as a public service, not a job. Outside employment for MPs was an accepted part of the representative process. Members were expected to represent not only their geographic constituents, but also interests unattached to a specific locale, including economic and professional interests.[10] This type of representation was intended to sharpen parliamentary debate and make it more relevant to the real needs of the nation. For much of Parliament's history, members received little or no payment for their parliamentary services and thus were dependent for their livelihood on sources of income outside the House. This traditional view of parliamentary service has clashed in recent years with the increasing commoditization of the parliamentary position. Whereas members once contributed practical expertise, garnered from involvement in outside pursuits, to the governing process, now many outside involvements threaten to sap Parliament of attention and resources.

Members of Parliament continue to pursue employment outside the House. While increasing constituency demands and expectations, and heavier committee responsibilities, make it difficult for individuals to maintain an active law or medical practice, members have discovered that employment opportunities arising out of their parliamentary position can easily be coupled with their Parliamentary duties. An increasing number of MPs accept retainers to serve as salaried parliamentary advisors or directors of corporations, public relations firms, and interest groups. In some instances, MPs have established their own parliamentary consultancy firms, appointing themselves director or president. Members are thus able to earn additional income by selling their advice on how best to influence the parliamentary process. Some members are willing to provide their clients with parliamentary papers, access to Westminster by way of a research pass, and dinners in the House at which their clients can meet other parliamentarians. These consultancies have proven both lucrative and convenient: they are easily combined with member's parliamentary duties and the routines of legislative life.

In Congress there is almost no scope for outside employment. The nature of the Congressional career and the parameters of Congressional duties conspire to prevent legislators from actively pursuing another occupation. Whereas Parliament routinely sits in the evenings, the congressional timetable occupies most of the day. In Britain, MPs are not obliged to sit on committees and there is no elaborate network of sub-committees to absorb an MP's time. In Congress, by contrast, the sheer weight of demands from colleagues and constituents prevents congressmen from assuming additional employment opportunities.

In addition, most of the employment that British MPs engage in quite regularly has been outlawed by legislation in the United States. Congressmen and their senior staff are expressly forbidden from accepting payment for working or affiliating with a law or other professional firm, serving on a board of directors, and even teaching, without prior consent of the ethics committee. These alternative forms of employment, which flourish in the British system, are expressly prohibited under *The Ethics Reform Act*. Moreover, and perhaps more fundamentally, the modern American public perception of representation requires a full-time commitment. Americans

10

view politics as a profession, not an avocation for public-spirited individuals: they would not tolerate a congressman who, by holding another job, appeared to be a part-time representative.

Before the new ethics package was adopted in December 1989, the most popular way for congressmen to earn additional income was by way of honoraria. These payments for personal appearances and speeches were profitable for members, especially senior, high-profile or outspoken individuals. While a ceiling was placed on the amount that could be earned in this fashion, many congressmen were able to reach the specified limit, with some going over. Under the new ethics provisions, honoraria limits were frozen at 1989 levels; this meant that members could not receive more than $26,850 per year in earned outside income. More importantly, the new legislation stipulates that, beginning in 1991, House members, staff and other federal officials will be prohibited from keeping any honoraria whatsoever. While charitable donations (with a $2,000 limit) may be made in the name of the congressman, personal payments will no longer be acceptable. In addition, no tax benefit is to accrue to a member for these charitable donations. The House of Representatives agreed to these restrictions on honoraria in return for a twenty-five per cent salary increase as of January 1, 1991.

The Senate originally refused this restrictive approach to honoraria, and instead reduced the maximum amount that Senators could make from honoraria (from 40 to 27 per cent of salary). But in early August of 1990, spurred on no doubt by the denunciation of Senator David Durenberger (R. Minnesota) for ethical violations involving efforts to evade honoraria limits, the Senate passed an amendment to their own ethics code prohibiting Senators from accepting honoraria. They also established a global limit on outside earnings of 15 per cent of the senatorial salary. For grumbling Senators these new restrictions were made somewhat more palatable by a salary increase to $98,400 (up from $89,500).

In the areas of financial interests and outside earnings the preference of the British House for an etiquette approach to managing conflict of interest is apparent. The Register of Members' Interests is neither restrictive nor onerous. While some MPs have been much more diligent than others in the extent and completeness of their forms, the declaration requirement only asks MPs to identify their outside interests. The decision to engage in outside employment is an individual one, but Parliament leaves the field wide open. No prohibitions are imposed on the types of outside jobs MPs can engage in, nor are there established limits on the amount of income that can derived from pursuits outside the House. In all of these areas emphasis is thus placed on personal discretion and judgement.

Congress, on the other hand, severely limits the choices open to its members. Congressmen must not only acknowledge that they hold a certain financial interest, they must also specify its approximate value. A combination of legislation, codes and prohibitions make for a much more structured approach to regulating congressmen's interests. Outside income limits are firmly established in both the House and Senate, and most outside employment is explicitly forbidden. In this fashion the edict approach circumscribes the discretionary judgements of individual legislators.

The weakness of etiquette

For those governed by it, the most positive feature of the etiquette system is its treatment of the individual politician. In Britain, politicians are not obliged to undertake elaborate efforts to demonstrate their political independence. There are few legal requirements imposed on would-be MPs that would suggest they are corruptible. Public office is treated as a noble calling. Members of the public may feel entitled to impose a higher standard of behaviour on their representatives than they impose on themselves, but there are no mechanisms that might suggest just what this standard is. Few MPs have the time or the inclination to pursue apparent indiscretions and there is virtually no incentive to raise the conflict of interest question in the abstract.

The main problem with the etiquette system is that it is unable to guarantee consensus on prevailing standards. In the House of Commons MPs do live in a rule-governed order, but the rules on conflict of interest are often so nebulous that it is difficult to imagine how MPs might consent to them. The most that can be said is that by assuming office MPs have given their tacit consent to accept stringent standards.[11] But as to the rules themselves, MPs on their own or in concert with one another must either discover or invent them. This reliance on unstructured collegiality means that no one is responsible for identifying and communicating the critical unwritten rules. There is no institutionalized means of informing members of their duties and precious few opportunities for members to confront the rules directly or test their understanding of them. Under these circumstances, compliance is effectively voluntary, ignorance of the rules becomes a plausible defence, and members are relieved of the moral responsibility that comes with knowledge.

It is possible, of course, that MPs are following an unwritten set of rules known only to them. Indeed, this interpretation is central to the etiquette approach to conflict of interest regulation. Unfortunately, the research that exists on the subject is discouraging to this line of argument. British MPs are in considerable disagreement about what constitutes corrupt behaviour, and they fall into distinct sub-populations, each with differing and conflicting

12

positions on conflict of interest questions.[12] In a similar fashion, British MPs and candidates for parliamentary office are deeply and systematically divided over alternative interpretations of the constitution. Donald Searing warns against exaggerating these divisions, but he also suggests that "too much may be expected of cultural variables like consensus on rules of the game." In his view, "constitutional constraints," among other things, might be required to compensate for the weakness of unwritten rules.[13]

No incident better illustrates the weakness of unwritten rules in Britain than the Poulson scandal uncovered in the 1970s.[14] According to Steven Chibnall and Peter Saunders,[15] the Poulson affair centered on a clash between privately normalized behaviour and an imposed external standard. Poulson and the implicated MPs sought to justify their behaviour by stressing that they were unaware of any external standard that might render their conduct inappropriate. Chibnall and Saunders warn against making too much of these pleas of ignorance. MPs may, in fact, be aware of alternative interpretations of their behaviour, but simply choose to ignore them.

The question then becomes: How plausible is the excuse of ignorance? Where rules of behaviour are institutionalized in law, then negotiation about how to interpret behaviour takes place in the context of a formalized code. MPs must respond to the challenge of powerful outsiders.[16] But in etiquette systems there are few, if any, institutional means of investigating and disciplining unethical conduct. No permanent bodies exist to serve as the focal point of an investigation, to determine reasonable punishment, or to act as the adjudicator in the case of an appeal. To cope with breaches of trust, the British House of Commons typically appoints special committees or boards of inquiry. Normally, such bodies are staffed by legislators themselves. If an investigator is appointed from outside the legislature, a judge or retired (but unblemished) politician is the preferred choice. No set procedure is followed in these cases and accused legislators are generally unaware of available means of recourse.

As to powers of sanction and disciplinary action, special committees of the House frequently serve only in an advisory capacity. They possess the authority to make recommendations but there are no assurances that what is recommended will be adopted. Moreover, no established penalties exist for contravention of the rules. Each case is decided on its merits. Punishment can include expulsion, censure, or the imposition of a fine, although in Britain criminal proceedings are seldom filed against a legislator charged with misconduct. In short, etiquette systems are overwhelmingly reactive. Continuous studies of legislative ethics are rare, institutional responses are *ad hoc*, and very few preventative mechanisms exist.

In Britain, the regulation of conflict of interest among MPs illustrates the key weaknesses of the etiquette system. Although MPs will occasionally be moved to denounce a colleague's behaviour, such an action is usually preceded by repeated unanswered allegations. The recent case of John Browne MP is illustrative. Allegations that Browne had broken House rules by failing to disclose all of his financial holdings and interests surfaced first in May 1987, but it was not until May 1989 that the Select Committee on Member's Interests launched an investigation into the case. The House of Commons is a reluctant disciplinarian. In embracing the etiquette solution to legislative conflict of interest, it employs a set of ill-defined rules which no one is effectively responsible for enforcing.

Britain is not alone in this regard. Traces of etiquette persist in all legislatures. The members of legislative assemblies seldom make a practice of impugning the personal integrity of their colleagues. Initially at least, they prefer to leave allegations of impropriety to outsiders – the media, electoral challengers, legislative officers or the police. Almost everywhere legislators resist the institutionalization of investigative committees. But where the etiquette system is entrenched, these common propensities are seriously aggravated by the fact that no established set of rules can be employed to frame debates on political morality. Under these circumstances, not even personal moral outrage can be relied upon to prompt legislators to challenge one another's conduct.

The weakness of edicts

The need to protect the institution and its members from the accusations of outsiders is particularly acute in legislative systems that embody a strong element of individual representation. Here allegations of impropriety cannot easily be deflected onto the institution as a whole or dismissed as anomalies, rare instances when members broke the unofficial honour code. Where legislators must take personal responsibility for representation, they are inclined to insist on a more precise rendering of expectations.

Recent cases of impropriety in the United States do not revolve around establishing whether or not members know the content of the rules. Not only are the rules codified and readily available to congressmen, but efforts have been made to publicize interpretations of the rules. In 1967, when Senator Thomas J. Dodd (D. Conn.) was accused of having converted campaign funds to his personal use, he was able to appeal to the vagueness of the rules. By 1979, however, when Senator Herman T. Talmadge (D. Georgia) was accused of the same violation, he could no longer make that case. The reform efforts of 1968 and 1977 had left a set of edicts that denied him this avenue and required the Senate to render a judgement.[17] The ignorance defence which is to a large (though decreasing) extent still available to MPs has long been invalidated in Congress.

14

The main weakness of the edict system is that it does not encourage much reflection on the content of these rules. Having overcome the obstacles to producing a body of rules in the first place, legislators are reluctant to then subject them to detailed scrutiny or to evaluate their contribution to political morality. Congressmen, for example, direct their greatest effort toward securing compliance with the formal requirements, and Congress, as a body, has not been marked by an overt willingness to review current practices. The ethics committees, while serving as permanent foci for ethical concerns in Congress, do not engage in sustained discussions of the broader ethos of American politics. Rather they act as interpreters of the prevailing consensus; they advise, monitor, and when required, investigate allegations. Concern is focused not on the implications of the rules, but on their operation.

Thus the debate, if not the rhetoric, over the Keating Five scandal has been for the most part free of any real moral dimension, and has instead concentrated on degrees of compliance. Once Sen. Alan Cranston (D. Calif.) was found to have violated the Senate's general standards of proper behavior and became the target of continued investigation, he employed various procedural maneuvers to stall and delay inquiry. This indicates a view of ethics regulations as mere extensions of the many tactical rules that govern congressional operations, without any aspirational component.

Pressure on Congress to refine and amend its rules has come more from innovations in the executive branch. In addition to the policy leadership shown during the Carter Presidency, Justice Department investigations and periodic reviews of legislative practice by independent bodies have assisted in keeping the question of the adequacy of existing rules in front of committee staff. But recent Congressional reviews have been premised on the *quid pro quo* of salary increases. Congress has by no means led the way in the resolution of conflict of interest dilemmas, and the edict approach that Congress employs has failed conspicuously to guarantee ethical conduct.[18]

The effectiveness of edicts rests on what congressmen believe is the purpose of the rules. So far the rules have not formed the basis of a search for appropriate moral standards in a collegial setting. On the contrary, they have been used to establish a contractual relationship between representatives and the represented. This relationship is enforced to some degree by the legislature, but as befits a system based heavily on liberal views of representation, the ultimate enforcement agency is the electorate. Congressmen undertake to abide by public rules, while constituents are charged with the responsibility of determining whether formal compliance is sufficient.

A preoccupation with interpreting the rules can also foster the attitude that what is not expressly prohibited is acceptable. The gap between the purpose of the rules and the uses to which they are put is most evident in the area of disclosure. The purpose of disclosure is to allow everyone to know that a conflict of interest exists; disclosure does not, in and of itself, resolve that conflict. For many congressmen, however, the primary, putative advantage of disclosure turns on the assumption that conflicts are in some manner rendered less objectionable by virtue of public knowledge.

In the ethics committees of Congress, staff members discourage this view, reminding members of Congress that constituents may have standards that transcend those found in codes of conduct. But this has not dissuaded congressmen from retaining investments in companies directly subject to legislation and appropriation. Congressmen are aware that under present disclosure rules, at least some conflicts of interest are permitted to exist. There is no requirement that these conflicts be resolved, only revealed. Moreover, congressmen are also aware that, more than likely, constituents will remain ignorant of them. Thus the ethics committees confine their review of disclosure statements to matters of form, including internal and temporal consistency. The working assumption is that once these criteria are satisfied, the content of disclosures becomes a matter to be judged by constituents, the wider public, and a vigilant media.

The formalization of ethics has also engendered the remarkably creative use of ethics as a weapon in the partisan struggle. The "mindless cannibalism" decried by departing Speaker Jim Wright in 1989 was, in his view, the spectacle of politicians scrutinizing one another for deviations from the letter of the law, in order to score political points. Such scrutiny would be impossible in an informal system, where the law has no definite "letter". In filing a formal complaint against Wright, Minority Whip Newt Gingrich (R. Georgia) may have portrayed himself as a crusader for rectitude in Congress, but it is more likely that the possibility of throwing the Democratic hierarchy into turmoil was his primary motivation. Of course, the same can be said of the subsequent complaints filed by Democrats against Gingrich (all eventually dismissed).

This phenomenon has further complicated the work of the ethics committees. Accustomed to fighting against norms of collegiality, they now find themselves directly in the path of storms of partisan retribution. In 1990, after recommending the formal reprimand of Barney Franks (D. Mass.) for improperly using his office to assist a male prostitute, House Ethics Committee Chairman Julian Dixon (D. Calif.) argued against harsher punishment with an institutional appeal to resist the temptation to politicize the issue. He cast the vote as a choice between unanimous approval of the report of a bipartisan committee that had studied the case for almost a year, and "GOP demagogues who would throw their colleagues to the wolves." The Committee's recommendation was eventually accepted, but only after a vote on formal censure divided the House along party lines (141–287).[19]

In the United States, legislators are encouraged to focus most of their attention on the rules themselves and very little on general questions of public morality or the standards of conduct expected of elected officials. These latter issues are left to the electoral arena on the assumption that the parties to the representational contract are the ones who should decide whether or not it warrants renewal. Disclosure assists in this regard. It helps shift much of the burden of evaluating conflict of interest from colleagues to constituents, and in so doing relieves Congress as a whole of the responsibility of establishing ethical standards.

Conclusion

We have argued in this paper that the systems designed to manage conflict of interest in Britain and the United States differ in significant ways and that these differences are evident in the major areas of conflict of interest regulation: nepotism, financial interests and outside employment. We have also argued that, as regulatory systems, both edicts and etiquette have serious liabilities. Although both expect individual legislators to make provision for their own autonomy by exercising sound moral judgement, neither system encourages an open discussion of political morality. In Britain ethical dilemmas are buried in a set of implicit understandings; in the United States a relatively elaborate set of written rules has been unable to eliminate even the most egregious lapses of ethical judgement.

Experience suggests that scandal is the most potent proximate cause of change in regulatory systems. Scandal creates a demand for reform that can seldom be completely assuaged by polite reassurances. In Britain, the etiquette system, and the prevailing interpretation of representation which sustains it, has kept conflict of interest scandals to a minimum.[20] But untested, the system becomes increasingly fragile. The pretence that unwritten codes are effective, or that prime ministers can manage all of the problems that arise by meting out political punishment, is losing credibility. Conflict of interest scandals give rise to demands for more and better rules to hem legislators in and establish enforceable contracts. In Canada, for example, a series of conflict of interest cases has led to legislation that would signal the abandonment of a system based primarily on etiquette and a greater reliance on written rules. Strong features of etiquette would remain, but even now very few cling to the view that MPs and ministers need no guidance on ethical matters, or that prime ministers should be expected to enforce uncodified standards.[21]

Scandal has also set the pace for change in the United States where the "post-Watergate morality" pressured Congress into action.[22] Here a long series of financial scandals continue to embarrass individual congressmen and the institution. These scandals, especially those of the 1970s, forced Congress to embrace the edict approach. Since the basic regulatory machinery has been in place, however, congressmen have been reluctant to tamper with it. Until the media and the public insist on an investigation and collective action, congressmen remain very hesitant to sit in judgement on one another. Moreover, without constant pressure from outside sources, congressmen are inclined to limit the reach of existing regulatory provisions. Thus while scandals have required Congress to reconsider some aspects of existing rules, they have not prompted a legislative overhaul or dictated the precise content of reform.

Most legislatures need a combination of conflict of interest legislation, codes of conduct and unwritten rules. They need legislation to establish firm expectations regarding the nature of the representative task, and they need codes and unwritten rules to foster a collegial approach to the resolution of ethical dilemmas. What is required in short, is a culture of trust girded by enforceable rules. An overemphasis on edicts will circumscribe behaviour without providing ethical leadership; an overreliance on etiquette will leave the institution open to exploitation.

Notes

1. Clement Vose, "Conflict of Interest," *International Encyclopedia of the Social Sciences*, vol. 3, p. 242.
2. Michael M. Atkinson and Maureen Mancuso, "Conflict of Interest in Britain and the United States: An Institutional Argument," *Legislative Studies Quarterly*, XVI, November 1991, pp. 471–493.
3. Dennis F. Thompson, *Political Ethics and Public Office* (Harvard University Press, 1987), 96–97.
4. Michael Clarke, *Regulating the City: Competition, Scandal and Reform* (Open University Press, 1986), 4.
5. Geoffrey Brennan and J.M. Buchanan, *The Reason of Rules* (Cambridge University Press, 1985), 98.
6. This may seem a controversial point, but see Canada, Task Force on Conflict of Interest, Michael Starr and Mitchell Sharp, co-chairmen, *Ethical Conduct in the Public Sector*, Ottawa, Supply and Services Canada, 1984; and Mr. Justice W.D. Parker, *Report of the Commission of Inquiry into the Facts of Allegations of Conflict of Interest Concerning the Honourable Sinclair M. Stevens*, Ottawa, Supply and Services Canada, 1987.
7. Maureen Mancuso, *British Legislative Ethics: The View From Westminster*, unpublished D. Phil Thesis (Nuffield College: Oxford University, 1990), 17.
8. 5 U.S.C. §3110.
9. Registrar of Members' Interests, personal communication, January 12, 1991.
10. Anthony King, "The Rise of the Career Politician in Britain and its Consequences," *British Journal of Political Science*, II, 1981, pp. 249–285.
11. Brennan and Buchanan, op. cit, pp. 100–103, and, in the context of legislative ethics, Amy Gutman and Dennis F. Thompson, "The Theory of Legislative Ethics," in Bruce Jennings and Daniel Callahan (eds.) *Representation and Responsibility* (Plenum Press, 1986), 168–169.

18

12. Mancuso, op. cit., pp. 83–86.
13. Donald D. Searing, "Rules of the Game in Britain: Can the Politicians be Trusted?" *American Political Science Review*, 76, June 1982, p. 256, fn. 19.
14. During bankruptcy proceedings, the personal papers of architect John Poulson revealed payments or gifts in kind to large numbers of local councillors and officials, employees of national industries, senior civil servants and MPs. Some of these payments were deemed legitimate, while others were blatant attempts to influence the awarding of contracts.
15. Steven Chibnall and Peter Saunders, "Worlds Apart: Notes on the Social Reality of Corruption," *British Journal of Sociology*, 28, June 1977, pp. 139–153.
16. Ibid, pp. 140–141.
17. Joel Fleishman, "The Disclosure Model and Its Limitations", in *Revising the United States Senate Code of Ethics*, A Hastings Center Report, Special Supplement, The Hastings Center, 1981.
18. Sandra Williams, "Conflict of Interest: The Experience of the American Congress," *The Parliamentarian*, LXIV:3, July 1983, pp. 138–145.
19. Janet Hook, "The Year of Living Carefully: '89 Scandals Color Reports," *Congressional Quarterly Weekly Report*, July 21, 1990.
20. Anthony King, "Sex, Money and Power: Political Scandals in Great Britain and the United States," *Essex Papers in Politics and Government*, 14, June 1984, pp. 20–30.
21. Ian Greene, "Conflict of Interest and the Canadian Constitution: An Analysis of Conflict of Interest Rules for Canadian Cabinet Ministers," *Canadian Journal of Political Science* XXIII:2, June 1990, pp. 233–256.
22. Alan Doig, "Watergate, Poulson, and the Reform of Standards of Conduct," *Parliamentary Affairs* 36, Summer 1983, pp. 324, 331–332.

[9]

Corruption and Reform 7: 67–85, 1992

Implementing corruption prevention strategies through codes of conduct

MARK FINDLAY[1] and ANDREW STEWART[2]

[1]Institute of Criminology, University of Sydney; and [2]Department of Law, University of Sydney, Australia

Abstract. The promulgation of codes of conflict within large organizations may seem a simple and logical first step in combatting corruption, but in fact they raise complex questions. Successful codes draw upon values shared by both managers and employees, and are based on a realistic diagnosis of the causes of corruption within the organization. All too often, however, codes are developed without careful thought about the functions or the organization, and without regard to the ways employees will respond. Worse yet, developing ethical codes can become an end in itself; once promulgated, the codes can become a substitute for anti-corruption action by administrators, and a cover for continuing corruption in the ranks. Using ideas and examples derived from anti-corruption efforts in New South Wales and elsewhere, this article surveys the many problems, and the opportunities, confronting organizational managers seeking to develop codes of ethics.

Introduction

The concept of a code of conduct, as it appears in corruption prevention strategies, could be viewed as rather misleading. While dealing with conduct in some preferred or pre-emptive sense, these frameworks for 'guidelines' bear little resemblance to prescriptive legal codes. In speaking to the International Bar Association meeting on "Transnational Enterprises and International Codes of Conduct", Prof John Jackson made the following observations,[1] regarding the significance of guideline approaches to corruption prevention:

> Since no single agency has a monopoly over code formulation, and since there exists such a wide range of goals and objectives, clearly one danger is the emergence of codes which conflict with each other, either explicitly or implicitly. The different forums for code discussions have different balances of interests ... and respond to different priorities among the goals ... Code formulation often runs around the shoals of fundamental (definitional) disagreements.

68

> The challenge, at least for the near future, is to develop an understanding of policies involved and the design code rules for those portions of those policies which do seem to command agreement or compromise consensus, so that some of the advantages which a code can bring are soon realised. On the other hand, the challenge is also to avoid irreversible commitment to code rule words which could soon be outdated, or which reflect such studied ambiguity in the face of fundamental disagreement that such code words will engender conflict rather [than] help resolve it.

These cautionary comments foreshadow a number of issues which are critical to such 'code of conduct' frameworks as a centre-piece of corruption prevention strategies.

Corruption prevention is as much fraught with definitional complexity as the object of its endeavour. The application of notionally consensual prevention methods to control problems which often arise out of loose, low profile property relations tends to overlook the forces at work with commitments to anything but corruption prevention. What are the attractions of a compliance-based control strategy, and is compulsion to some extent antithetical to a prevention perspective?

The language of 'guidelines', and more broadly of prevention, merits analysis as it is transformed into anti-corruption commitments. The importance of consensus, which formulates the aims underlying this language and these commitments, provides a useful starting point for such an enquiry. This opens out into a consideration of the various structural options which attend on the 'code of conduct' approach to corruption prevention. The significance of compliance management methods, and the operations of an independent audit function, support particular corruption prevention strategies such as those examined in the following discussion of the labour relations ramifications of code strategies.

The aim of corruption prevention

> Vital though it is to extricate the bad apples from the barrel it is equally important to prevent them from getting into the barrel at all. How is this done? By simply ensuring that the system doesn't allow the rotten ones to get in.[2]

In this way does the Independent Commission Against Corruption (ICAC) in Hong Kong quaintly identify the structural priority of its corruption prevention department. Its New South Wales counterpart prefers a pathological metaphor to justify its focus on management:

> Corruption, in whatever form it takes, is invariably described as a disease or sickness in society. As with many diseases it may be possible to cure after it has been identified, but with no certainty either that the cure is complete or that the disease has not done irreparable damage. Most people would agree that it is better to prevent than to cure.[3]

Both of these interpretations of the essential connection between corruption and prevention overlook the utility that corrupt practices may offer an organisation beyond the enrichment of individuals. It is assumed that:

> If corrupt practices exist within an organisation, its normal operations will undoubtedly be jeopardised ... Corruption prevention is therefore an integral part of good management.[4]

Dogmatic assertions such as this may substitute for the realistic ascription to a uniform commitment to corruption prevention at various levels of management. As Klitgaard points out, for developing economies at least, corruption may provide a 'positively useful role'.[5] On the level of management advantage he proposes:

> Corruption may have uses within an organisation. If bureaucratic rules are constraining, the organisation may sometimes benefit from the employees' corrupt circumvention of the rules. A limited amount of employee theft, embezzlement, misreporting of expenses, kickbacks, 'speed money' and so forth may be tactically allowed by top management on the one hand, because controlling these illicit activities would be prohibitively expensive, and on the other hand because such illicit sources of income may in the long run substitute for higher wages. A slush fund within an organisation may function as a contingency fund which top management may flexibly if illicitly allocate to further the organisation's aims.[6]

Beyond the level of critical analysis, it is necessary for policy designers and implementors to recognise the commercial and organisational adaptations emergent through corrupt practice occurring in certain restrictive market situations. If one views the generation of corrupt relationships in terms of a market model,[7] particularly where corruption is perceived by those closest to it as a tariff on the transaction of certain restricted products and services, then prevention and control strategies can be designed to confront the users' (and not simply 'the controller's') appreciation of corruption. The decision as to whether one selects a corrupt resolution of a commercial option will involve some degree of 'cost/benefit analysis'.[8] Corruption control strategies endeavour to influence the cost factor of the equation. Control may also imply

70

the acceptance of some optimum or tolerable level of corruption within particular commercial settings.[9] In estimating optimal levels, the cost of corruption, as against the cost of its removal on the one hand, can be intersected against measures of social cost and the significance of corruption on the other.

Despite the recognition of the cultural (and even organisational) specificity of corruption:

> As a matter of fact most countries and cultures decry most instances of bribery, fraud, extortion, embezzlement, and most forms of kickbacks on public contracts. Over a wide range of 'corrupt' activities there is little argument that they are wrong and socially harmful.[10]

What remains in dispute is whether, or at least to what extent, corruption can and should be prevented and controlled. As Klitgaard reminds us, "blanket statements about the helpfulness or harmfulness of corruption will not aid us in assessing the effects of particular instances we may encounter".[11]

As a preface to selecting a response to corruption, the economic and social significance of the behaviour in question and the proposed responses require examination. To some degree this can be achieved within a framework of the 'costs' of corruption:

Efficiency
- wastes resources;
- creates 'public bads' as compared with 'private goods';
- distorts policy.

Distribution
- reallocates resources to those with power to influence;
- favours monopoly control.

Incentives
- distorts exercise of official discretion;
- creates risks;
- distorts investment.

Reactions
- induces unproductive preventive measures;
- contributes to monopolistic market regulation;
- promotes 'moral panic' threat imagery.

Politics
- breeds popular alienation and cynicism;
- creates regime instability;
- fosters artificial public/private divisioning.

The language of prevention

Corruption is at its heart an ethical problem.[12] It is addressed in political debate as a moral issue:

> The problem with corruption is that it tends to become the Problem of Corruption. Moral issues are usually obscure practical issues, even where the moral question is a relatively small one and the practical matter is very great.[13]

Moving the corruption debate from the level of moralist rhetoric is not assisted by an expansion into the imagery of prevention. There is a sensitive relationship between preventive initiatives and unwarranted intrusions in the name of community protection, which would not necessarily be tolerated within traditional criminal justice control strategies. The language of prevention is as a result often couched in a fashion calculated to avoid the suggestion of overbearing interventionism. Prevention through compliance, through consensus, through solicitation, are central to corruption prevention persuasion:

> Successful corruption prevention work will depend much on the co-operation and whole-hearted involvement of the client organisation's management and staff. This is something which will require nurturing, principally by a demonstration of the contribution the Commission can make by way of its corruption prevention work to good management.[14]

The discourse of consensus and compliance as the incentive for prevention not only suggests some of the problems for any associated strategy, it also limits the 'community' for which it will have relevance. Expectations for agreement with and implication in the prevention of commercial behaviour which is often clandestine and divisive are not always realised in an atmosphere of generous co-operation. Codes of conduct which depend on supportive management, and procedural guidelines for reporting which rely on a path of voluntary communication, mean little or nothing to the recalcitrant staff member or the subversive senior officer. By tying prevention to compliance without confronting the utility of violation, or the

72

necessity of eventual compulsion, the language of corruption prevention sits uncomfortably with the hard issues of implementation.

The actual process of defining corruption and reducing its prevention to words is a problematic endeavour. If honest and trustworthy behaviour can be expected as part of appropriate work practice then why is it necessary to emphasize corruption prevention beyond the realm of common sense and corporate decency? The response statements of standards and obligations enhance clarity, and certainty implies an identifiable interest, both individual and organisational, in such understandings. Specifically, as far as the workplace is concerned the translation of expectations about conduct into written rules has a wider purpose than as a statement of their content. Such codes represent a framework around which issues of content can be contested and the responsibilities inferred from them can be contrasted and apportioned.

Developing corruption prevention policy

> To develop and implement an anti-corruption programme it is necessary to develop a policy based upon an identification of the indicators of (corruption) activities.[15]

Obvious as this sounds, many structural attempts at corruption prevention proceed from a generalised and nonproblematic vision of corruption, a commitment to the power of anti-corruption rhetoric, and an absence of developed thought concerning the complexity of implementation issues. The success of prevention programmes requires that a particular framework of 'corrupt opportunity' be established prior to their specific application as policy options. Such a framework might consider:

Corruption hazards
- sites for corruption;
- signs of corruption;
- systems comfortable with corruption.

Corruption in progress
- corrupt acts and actors;
- invitations towards corruption;[16]
- peer group support, and complicity;[17]
- organisational content;
- institutional reaction.

As Ward and McCormack emphasize in the case of police corruption, "for an anti-corruption policy to be viable and effective, it must be realistic, manageable and continually reinforced".[18] This is even more so for preventive policy, which in practice relies on a general appreciation and acceptance of the utility of compliance, rather than on some token ascription to codes of ethical standards.

As with any policy initiatives which have individual and institutional aims and arms, effective corruption prevention programmes evolve through:

- planning and design;
- publication;
- consultation;
- revision;
- communication;
- modelling and implementation;
- monitoring stages.

Crime prevention programmes sometimes suffer from an under-attention to, or ignorance of, a vital stage in such a developmental process. For example, if communication and consultation is not attempted at *all* major levels of an organisation, and the programme relies on the trusted transfer of information up through a management hierarchy, then the bottleneck in such a transfer may not be identified until it is the reason in practice for the policy's failure.

In addition to such internal structural indicators, due regard in policy development should be given to significant external influences which can impinge on the operation of policy initiatives. Chin and Benne identify three broad strategies for effecting change in human systems:[19]

Rational – empirical
Power – coercive
Normative – re-educative

Underlying the rational-empirical philosophy is the strategy that employees will choose to do what is in their best interest. The measures of such interest are seen to obviously justify such a choice. The power-coercive strategy basically utilizes power arising from formal authority to impose and enforce change. As such the policy depends on endorsement from more traditional processes of compulsion and sanction. The normative-re-educative model relies on a process of participation, collaboration and complicity, to attempt a long lasting and consensual change. The restructuring anticipated is focused on a range of behaviours and structures, individual and organisational. These approaches may be combined to the extent that they are obviously not exclusionary. The code of conduct technique fits best within the third model.

Codes of conduct

Corruption is a product of monopolistic regulation and discretionary benefit allocation, minus accountability. The broadening of accountability (rather than breaking down the monopoly, or the universalisation of the discretion) is identified in prevention strategies as essential to successful corruption prevention:

> If monopoly power and discretionary enforcement remain, consumers can expect to pay too high a price. The key ideas regarding underlying conditions might not be capitalism versus state socialism, or the private sector versus the public sector, but rather competition and accountability.[20]

After all, accountability is one way of generalising organised strategies and structures for the gathering of information. The knowledge and understanding derived from such accountability in process should assist in the assessment of environments for fair competition. Fairness, in turn, will have an effect on corrupt relationships which exist through regulated and monopolistic avenues of opportunity.

Codes of conduct as a structural instrument represent an advertised endeavour to coalesce standards of behaviour in an atmosphere where compromise replaces intimidation. They are formulated in a congruent language where the reality of reward and penalties is kept to the implicit. Codes are also a move away from rule structures which produce monopolistic regulation through a monopolistic application of sanctions, and hence the potential for the process and institutions of prevention and control themselves to become 'tools for corruption'.[21] Codes of conduct are first designed to influence attitudes rather than prescribe behaviour. They propound the official morality. They are the mirror against which communities are to be educated towards an anti-corruption consciousness. Leys describes the 'line of escape' from corruption as "a nucleus of puritans providing pressure for a code of ethics".[22] It is recognised that the formal enunciation of ethics may have an influence on deviant behaviour if the unethical behaviour can be traced to a lack of written policy. At this level the deterrent potential is apparent, and its relationship with compliance is implicit. However, to assume that more 'moral' organisations will be an essential consequence of a code of conduct may not be justified. Organisational culture may, if it conflicts with the ethical model, prevail.

As is the case in New South Wales, codes of conduct against corruption are usually reliant on mechanisms for disclosure and guidelines for reporting.[23] Whether these in turn are endorsed by sanctions against failure to report will depend on the wider commitment to legislative frameworks for anti-corruption mechanisms. Codes of conduct are a convenient mechanism for indicating the obligations of administrators in the task of corruption-free government. The purpose-designed anti-corruption codes usually operate in addition to more general principles of public service and the professional practice guides such as that issued through the International Institute of Administrative Sciences. Many such codes are an amalgam of work directives, standards of professionalism, and common sense:

> Ultimately professionalism in government may mean no more than simply justifying public trust by putting the interests of the citizen and the government above private interests.[24]

However, no matter to what degree a code of conduct embodies universal, simple values, and strives to embody general consensus, its influence on corruption practice relies on 'integrity testing'. Corruption and bribery thrives on secrecy and pretence. Corrupt practices may exist behind the veil of a conduct code, as much as they are challenged by it. Complacency can be the consequence of a code which does not in practice command compliance at all levels of organisation.

The discussion of codes of conduct will be rather impotent if it focuses on consensus over content alone, and vice versa. Compliance implies some consideration of implementation. At the level of implementation conflict will arise when determining responsibility for ensuring compliance. To some extent compliance conditions will influence the structure and tone of a code of conduct, as the code will operate later to effect compliance. Even the selection of a code-based policy reveals attitudes to the essentials of enforcement such as compulsion, reward, deterrence, shaming etc.

Once the content of a code is settled, and its consistency with other competing or overriding standards is assured, the task for policy shifts to mechanisms of implementation within the workplace. In industrial terms, these can be considered from two perspectives: a) how workers and their unions may be expected to react to the introduction of codes of conduct; and b) the sort of pro-active management strategies needed to overcome the problems likely to be thrown up by adverse reaction from the workforce.

Codes of conduct and labour relations

Those charged with 'fighting' corruption and indeed the general public can be forgiven for seeing the issue of corruption prevention in simple terms of right and wrong. Since corruption is a Bad Thing, it is commendable to introduce procedures for identifying and reporting instances of corruption and for preventing such practices occurring or flourishing within organisations – so the reasoning goes. As employers, however, public sector managers are compelled to view corruption prevention not just as a societal issue, but as a matter of human resource management and, in so far as unions become involved, of industrial relations.

At one level, the introduction of a code of conduct is an unequivocally positive move for any organisation. No sensible analysis of employee relations can ignore the need for the explicit formulation of the standards which managers expect of their workforce and for the communication of these standards to both workers and supervisors. There can be little doubt therefore that codes of conduct which seek to detail forms of behaviour which are or are not acceptable in the case of particular types of worker can play a very important educative function. Although the virtue of this function is often expressed negatively ("if workers have been told exactly what not to do they can't turn round later and say they didn't know"), a more positive rationale would be to highlight the effect that formulating such codes has on management, in that it becomes necessary to address in a very careful fashion what constitutes acceptable practice. Anything that enhances communication between management and labour and compels a re-appraisal of standards, at least if it is well done, is a welcome step forward.

However when codes are used for the specific purpose of combatting corruption, difficulties may emerge. It is a truism that corruption within an organisation is likely to be firmly rooted in attitudes and workplace culture. This much has been recognised by the ICAC in New South Wales:[25]

> There are organisational, cultural or systemic factors which inhibit the reporting of corrupt conduct or the timely referral of reports through the appropriate channels to the principal officer. These include:
>
> 1. Cultural antipathy to 'dobbing in your work mates'.
> 2. A tendency at all levels of an organisation to accept long standing practices, even where they may involve or facilitate corrupt conduct. Examples include receipt of gifts, entertainment or favours, and procurement and tendering procedures.
> 3. Immediate supervisor's possible involvement or association with those involved.

4. Disinclination to report if past experience has shown that 'nothing happens' and/or that those who report receive negative treatment, for example being labelled as 'troublemakers'.
5. Insulation of principal officer and senior management from level 4 employees.
6. Lack of clear and appropriate rules for referral and/or action where corrupt conduct is suspected.

> Baseless complaints made to injure the person(s) implicated or to divert attention may be an additional problem.

Unfortunately the bulk of the ICAC's public pronouncements suggest a belief that merely by introducing codes results will begin to be seen. It is as if it is thought that a code *is* compliance, that a channel of communication *is* reporting. Introducing a code is merely the first step: it is at the stage of *implementation* that the task of turning rhetoric into reality becomes more problematic.

The manner of a code's introduction may itself be a crucial factor in determining the likelihood of successful implementation. Broadly speaking, there is a choice here between, on the one hand, imposing a code from above, and on the other hand negotiating with employees and/or unions over its contents or its introduction. The great danger with unilateral imposition is that it may produce from the workforce a hostile reaction or, worse still, no reaction at all. It is interesting to note in this context that in a recent survey, although 49% of Australian workplaces with more than 20 employees were found to have in place a formal procedure for resolving workplace grievances, 40% reported that these mechanisms were rarely or never used in practice, while only 16% reported regular use. The authors of the survey pointed out that in many instances the relevant procedure had been imposed by senior management or had been formulated through collective bargaining or award negotiations occurring away from the workplace.[26] This suggests that informal arrangements worked out between those actually present at the workplace are preferable as a means of dealing with disciplinary matters and other grievances in such a way as to command acceptance and generate regular observance.

The problem in this specific context is that neither the use of informal arrangements nor the sort of compromises which may have to be struck to ensure that a code is accepted and used may be appropriate where corruption is concerned. It can be argued that the very flexibility, deal-making and relaxed attitudes to formal constraints which are best calculated to minimise shop floor hostility and maximise employee co-operation are themselves the classic breeding conditions for corruption in the first place.

78

Nevertheless, negotiation, compromise and informality may be the lesser evil here. It is simply naive to proceed on the basis that fighting corruption is self-evidently a worthy process, or that introducing a code will strengthen the honest, dismay the corrupt and deter the waverers from slipping into evil ways. Put simply, however 'sensible' or 'right-minded' observers might view the introduction of codes of conduct, workers and their representatives may well react very differently.

Common sense and some discussion with union officials in the New South Wales public sector about the issues thrown up by current or proposed codes of conduct suggest the sort of difficulties that may be encountered. In the first place, the introduction of a code may be seen, no matter how irrationally, as a pretext for an attack on working conditions. This is especially likely in a climate where (as at present in New South Wales and in most of the rest of Australia) public sector workers feel very much on the defensive in the face of 'efficiency' reforms and job-shedding programmes. Secondly, there may be a strong suspicion that the entire corruption prevention exercise is more a matter of 'do as I say' rather than 'do as I do'. The belief may exist that while workers are to be targeted by the new mechanisms, supervisors and managers will be subjected to the same restrictions in theory only and that corruption at higher levels within an organisation will continue unchecked. A variation on this point is the general feeling that workers may have that they are being unfairly singled out in the drive to stamp out corruption. Corruption manifests itself in many areas of society, yet so far as government strategies are concerned almost all attention has been focused on the workplace. Even those investigations which have centred on political corruption have usually involved scrutiny of a public official in relation to the discharge of their duties. Thirdly, there may be a belief among professional employees in particular that ethical standards should not be handed down from senior management, but should be internally generated by the professionals themselves as the persons best suited to make realistic decisions as to the issues involved.

Most importantly though, the reaction that most Australian employees are likely to exhibit on hearing of a proposal to introduce a code of practice will almost certainly involve asking "what does this mean I can get charged with?" In other words, despite the intention that codes are, to some extent at least, to operate merely as guidelines to which voluntary compliance is urged, workers and unions will inevitably focus on the disciplinary sanctions that may ensue from a breach of the code, furthering the likelihood of a negative or hostile reaction. This reflects a traditional feature of workplace relations in Australia: the failure of many managers to find methods other than intimidation and discipline by which to promote better behaviour, a higher level of morale and greater productivity from their workers.[27] Against this background, codes may struggle to fulfil their educative function for workers (and managers) more used to punishment and threats.

This problem is likely to be exacerbated where, as appears to be the case in New South Wales at present, codes are introduced without sufficient thought being given as to the consequences of violation of the standards laid down. One response of course may be that the codes are intended to have no legal effect. But if this is so, unions are likely to respond, why bother introducing it? It is pointless for management to argue that this attitude is misplaced. The fact is that a code of conduct will be of no use whatsoever if it is expressed in such vague and general terms as to give no concrete guidance to employees as to how to behave in given situations. As soon as a code takes on a more definite cast, however, it will also become apparent that its provisions may be breached from time to time. It is a perfectly legitimate query for workers or unions to explore the consequences. Indeed, supervisors and middle managers will tend to view the code in exactly the same light.

There can be little doubt that, at least in Australia, codes of conduct do in fact have the potential to create legal consequences for violators. Even if the relevant code is expressly stated not to have legal force, it is more than likely that external review agencies called upon to determine whether workers have committed offenses which would warrant discipline or dismissal will feel impelled to take the code into account in the course of their deliberations. This may happen in one of two ways. A common feature of the statutes which establish the disciplinary framework for public sector workers is the creation of a variety of offenses which are described in very general terms, such as 'misconduct'.[28] It seems reasonable to suppose that in amplifying the content of this sort of vague standard a tribunal would look to the provisions of the code for guidance. Alternatively, a worker disobeying a specific instruction to abide by the provisions of the code might be charged with failing to obey a 'lawful order', the code again being a principal determinant of what may lawfully be ordered.

If this is correct, it becomes apparent that merely by introducing a code, management may effectively be exposing to disciplinary sanctions conduct that was not formerly so exposed. In that light, it would hardly be surprising if workers and unions reacted with some alarm or trepidation. Two comments made by union officials are of some interest in this connection. One asked what 'corruption' was supposed to mean. Was it, he wondered, "like conspiracy – something you're charged with when they can't prove anything specific against you like fraud or taking a secret commission?" Another pointed out the possible use of disciplinary proceedings triggered by the breach of vague ethical requirements as a pretext for getting rid of staff for extraneous reasons such as personality conflict. It is indeed interesting here to note one provision of the recently revised New South Wales Public

80

Service Personnel Handbook, which requires public servants not to cause their fellow workers or members of the public to take offence or suffer embarrassment. The possibilities of a disciplinary charge predicated on a breach of that particular standard are readily apparent, no matter how fanciful the notion might seem.

Obviously then the educative function of any code of conduct needs to be strengthened by addressing the legal consequences of any 'new' ethical standards which are being imposed and by explaining those consequences to the workers affected. This very definitely entails going beyond the practice of having workers sign to say that they have read and understood the contents of the code. Quite apart from the problem of those workers who are illiterate or unable to comprehend what they are reading, it should be obvious that unless accompanied by carefully constructed training and education programs, this will merely be administrative convenience masquerading as communication. More fundamentally, there is a need for a *managerial* strategy which is calculated to secure genuine acceptance by the workforce of ethical and legal norms.

Pro-active management strategies

The foregoing has endeavoured to emphasize the need for a reality of consensus if a code of conduct strategy is to move beyond good intentions. Essential to the emergence of consensus in a traditional industrial environment, where suspicions surrounding the enunciation of work standards are not difficult to identify, is the need for genuine co-operation. Meaningful guideline strategies for corruption prevention depend on their acceptance at all levels of an enterprise, particularly where sections of the enterprise may be set against prevention for reasons of individual financial gain. Having said this, the importance of managerial initiative beyond the simple imposition of another layer of authority and reporting cannot be overemphasized.

Model practice commitments from management

Recognising that content is largely agreed at the upper levels of management and that 'one on one' channels of accountability are expected, an important method to translate compliance down through an organisation is to initiate the implementation of the code within management. The model relevance of the code at this level may avoid the impression that it is little more than another disciplinary tool designed to unilaterally alter conditions of employment.

Employee motivation

The instructional function of the code is evidenced through modelling as well as through specific awareness programmes and retraining. The latter must emphasize the direct utility of the code (and a noncorrupt work environment) in terms of work place priorities. "In this area, precision and subtlety may have to be sacrificed to clarity and enforceability".[29]

Internal reporting procedures

These procedures are essential for the information gathering, and monitoring stages of corruption prevention. Channels of communication through 'one on one' accountability structures help in overcoming the warping influence of organisational culture. A well motivated public service with strong standards of professional integrity can do much to resist the abuse of office so long as its code of professionalism is not distorted by a mistaken sense of solidarity or defensiveness against acknowledgement of professional wrongdoing.

Methods for countering intimidation

Any reporting system depends heavily on the willingness of those who become aware of possible corruption to put their personal security at risk by disclosing information. Harassment or victimisation of 'informants' is plainly then a matter for concern. Whatever the promises of anonymity and confidentiality made to such persons, the risk of their identity becoming known to fellow workers or managers is always likely to appear considerable to them, regardless of the objective circumstances. Any deficiency then in the arrangements for the protection of 'whistleblowers', particularly those who use reporting channels which bypass established hierarchies or lines of authority, may detract significantly from the efficacy of strategies for the reporting of corruption allegations.

At one level this concern can be met by legislative measures to protect such persons, particularly against 'retaliatory discharge' from their employment. Although Australia has been slow to recognise this need by comparison with other countries, Queensland at least has begun to move in the right direction.[30] However while this sort of initiative may help to correct injustices in individual cases, there is only so much that can be done by external regulation to generate the sort of atmosphere within an organisation that will counter or at least minimise intimidation. Much depends on the design of internal processes. Beyond the level of implementation through example, the effective operation of prevention strategies which are not sanction-guaranteed must rely on a responsible structure of accountability.

82

Organisations can be subverted if they operate without clear lines of accountability. Equally, accountability processes can be intimidated if they focus on a vulnerable few. To diffuse responsibility and to avoid the creation of targets in all situations of corrupt opportunity is to counter potential intimidation.

Independent audit function

The debate on this issue is concerned with the necessity of such supervision and its effect on the environment of compliance. Should the audit be favoured, then is it to be internal, external or independent? Operational responsibility for any management audit and integrity inspections can generate jurisdictional contests which extend beyond a concern about corruption. The association between a complaints function and an audit capacity is prominent in corruption prevention policy. The internal and external credibility of the auditors will influence their ability to receive and screen complaints, and provide a supervisory function throughout levels of corruption opportunity and across all positions and managerial relationships within an enterprise. Audit mechanisms can also be applied to the task of exposing the interrelated costs of corruption.

Countering conflicts of interest

An assumption which must underly the introduction of an anti-corruption code of conduct is that beyond those contradictions which will necessarily arise as part of a prevention perspective, the code of conduct will not itself generate conflicts of interest which cannot be resolved through following the code. Conflicts between official duty and private self interest are at the heart of the need for codes of conduct. However, a realistic set of priorities of those forms of self interest which require intervention is necessary if a code is to avoid ridicule. Conflicts which threaten the public good, more than simply the integrity of code policy, are an appropriate focus for regulation. In this respect the criterion for criminalisation of conflicts of interest may be too limiting.

Beyond the rhetoric of good intentions

> The deterrent effects of investigation and prosecution and the direct incapacitation of wrongdoers by their removal from office and incarceration can reduce corruption in government. Yet virtually all practitioners involved in anti-corruption efforts would concede that, no matter how

> draconian or rigourously enforced the penal measures may be, no society can realistically punish more than a small proportion of the officials who abuse their position. If the level of integrity in government is to be improved it will be by managerial, administrative, regulatory and reporting mechanisms. No matter how frequently imposed or personally gratifying they are to anti-corruption authorities, penal sanctions can help to achieve honesty in government only in a well-administered and well-motivated organisation.[31]

The thrust of this paper has been to stress the importance of carefully thought out implementation strategies whenever codes of conduct are introduced to help prevent corruption. Merely settling on the language to be used and informing those directly involved of the code's existence is not enough. It may sound trite, but the point cannot be overemphasized: codes do not implement themselves. The overriding objective must be the formulation of processes that will avoid two pitfalls. One occurs where promulgation of the code exhausts all enthusiasm for prevention, management simply sitting back with the satisfaction of a job well done. In that scenario the code can simply become a cover for inaction, allowing corruption to flourish behind the facade of official concern. The second pitfall occurs at the other extreme, where unilateral and heavy-handed action by management creates an industrial battleground over the issue of disciplinary outcomes. These potential problems can only be overcome by a strong commitment to *communication* at all levels within the organisation as to the policy objectives of the code, the changes it requires to present practices and, perhaps most significantly from the viewpoint of labour relations, the extent to which it will or will not affect the legal and practical norms regulating disciplinary processes and sanctions.

Many of the problems surrounding implementation can be traced to the fact that in most instances both the urge to introduce a code and the creative work on its content are likely to come from persons outside the organisation in question, or at least officials who are above any of the levels of decision-making or performance at which the code will have most effect. This feature can of course be seen as an advantage, in that an externally imposed code is less prone to subversion from the outset by the very practices and people it is seeking to combat. But by the same token, if by the time the code reaches the workplace the only issue is its implementation, the problems described above (inaction at one extreme, industrial confrontation at the other) are more likely to arise. The answer must lie in finding some way of involving those who will be subject to the code during the prior process of formulation. Difficult though it may seem, to some extent at least the independence of the code process must be traded off against considera-

84

tions of efficacy in implementation. Somewhere there will be common ground between the implementors and those at the workplace who are affected by the code. The trick is to identify that ground without sacrificing the fundamental objectives of the code or of the wider programme of corruption prevention of which it forms part: a task that calls for skillful management indeed.

Notes

1. *Codes of Conduct for Transnational Corporations: Signals of Public Expectations*, International Bar Association, Berlin, 1980, p. 1.5.
2. *An Introduction to the Independent Commission Against Corruption*, ICAC, Hong Kong, 1987, p. 19.
3. "Corruption Prevention Strategy" in *Annual Report to 30 June 1990*, Independent Commission Against Corruption (NSW), Sydney, 1990, p. 1.
4. Ibid, p. 2.
5. R. Klitgaard, *Controlling Corruption*, University of California Press, Berkeley, 1986, p. 30.
6. Ibid.
7. See B.L. Bensen and J. Baden, "The political Economy of Governmental Corruption: The Logic of Underground Government" *Journal of Legal Studies*, vol XIV, 1985, pp. 391–410; M. Findlay, "Corruption Control and Monstering: Government Agendas, Community Expectations and the ICAC solution" *Current Issues in Criminal Justice*, vol 2, no 3, 1991, pp. 36–48.
8. J. Nye, "Corruption Prevention and Political Development: A Cost-Benefit Analysis" *American Political Science Review*, June 1967, p. 427.
9. Klitgaard, op cit, pp. 24–27.
10. Ibid, pp. 3–4.
11. Ibid, p. 35.
12. J.T. Noonan, *Bribes*, Macmillan, New York, 1984, pp. 702–703.
13. J.Q. Wilson, "Corruption is Not Always Scandalous" in J.A. Gardiner and D.J. Olson (eds), *Theft of the City: Readings in Corruption in America*, Indiana University Press, Bloomington, 1968, p. 29.
14. ICAC (NSW), op cit, p. 151.
15. R.H. Ward and R. McCormack, *An Anti-Corruption Manual for Administrators in Law Enforcement*, John Jay Press, New York, 1979, p. 65.
15. P.K. Manning and L.J. Redlinger, "Invitational Edges of Corruption: Some Consequences of Narcotic Law Enforcement" in P. Rock (ed), *Drugs and Politics*, Transaction Books, London, 1977, pp. 279–310.
17. T. Baker, "Peer Group Support for Police Occupational Deviance" *Criminology*, vol 15, no 3, 1977, pp. 9–21.
18. Op cit, p. 65.
19. R. Chin and K.D. Benne, "General Strategies for Effecting Changes in Human Systems" in W.G. Bennis, K.D. Benne and R. Chin (eds), *The Planning of Change*, Holt Rinehart & Winston, New York, 1969.
20. Klitgaard, op cit, p. 67.
21. T. Nakata, "Corruption in the Thai Bureaucracy: Who Gets What, How and Why in its Public Expenditures" *Journal of Development Administration*, vol 18, January 1978, p. 104.
22. M.U. Ekpo, *Bureaucratic Corruption in Sub-Saharan Africa: Towards a Search for Causes and Consequences*, University Press of America, Washington DC, 1979, p. 150.

23. *Independent Commission Against Corruption Act* 1988 (NSW), s 11.
24. United Nations Geneneral Secretariat, *Crime Prevention and Criminal Justice in the Context of Development: Realities and Perspectives of International Co-operation; Practical Measures Against Corruption* Eighth UN Congress on the Prevention of Crime and Treatment of Offenders, Havana, 1990, p. 17.
25. *Effective Reporting of Corrupt Conduct Within Government Departments and Agencies,* ICAC, Sydney, 1990, pp. 1–2.
26. R. Callus, A. Morehead, M. Cully and J. Buchanan, *Industrial Relations at Work: The Australian Workplace Industrial Relations Survey,* AGPS, Canberra, 1991, pp. 129–132.
27. See further A. Stewart, "Workplace Disciplinary Rules and Procedures: Australia", International Labour Organisation research paper, 1991 (on file with the authors).
28. See generally G.J. McCarry, *Aspects of Public Sector Employment Law,* Law Book, Sydney, 1988, chs 6–7.
29. United Nations Geneneral Secretariat, op cit, p. 13.
30. See Electoral and Administrative Review Commission (Qld), *Protection of Whistleblowers,* Issues Paper No 10, EARC, Brisbane, 1990.
31. United Nations Geneneral Secretariat, op cit, p. 9.

Part III
Legal/Formal

[10]

Crime, Law & Social Change **24:** 273–292, 1996.

Political corruption and the role of public prosecutors in Italy *

ADRIANA ALBERTI
European University Institute, Badia Feisolana, Italy

Abstract. This paper analyzes the problem of political corruption in Italy and the role public prosecutors have played in unraveling such a phenomenon. The factors that have contributed to fostering systemic corruption as well as those that have contributed to "uncovering" such a system are given careful consideration. The most relevant conclusion is that whereas endogenous forces in the judiciary (prosecutors and judges) – in particular, its low level of institutional autonomy – have prevented it from containing corruption, exogenous forces – which have broken the conditions that had favoured the stability of the so-called "first" Republic – have led prosecutors to engage in massive investigations.

Introduction

Political corruption seems to be more and more a pervasive phenomenon in modern democracies. Recent studies have shown that most western countries suffer from some form of political corruption regardless of the nature of the party or of the coalition in power (de Leon 1993). In advanced democracies corruption has been generally viewed as the manifestation of isolated cases of violations of political norms and public expectations for personal gains (*ibid.*; Ragazzi 1992). Therefore, it has not been given much attention and the question of its possible degeneration into systemic corruption has not been considered.

Italy is an emblematic example of how single cases of corruption have degenerated into systemic corruption and have seriously challenged the legitimacy of its political system. What at the beginning of the 1960s could have been regarded as occasional and random practice has emerged as an endemic and persistent violation of some of the most fundamental values of its democratic regime. Many factors have contributed to the degeneration and development of such a system, and many allowed it to acquire some sort of "stability". Among the latter, the efforts of the Italian judiciary (which

* This article is a revised version of the paper prepared for delivery at the 1994 Workshop on "Corruption and Politics" held at the Instituto Internacional de Sociologia Juridica, Onati (Spain), July 13–14, 1994. I am appreciative to Prof. Giuseppe Di Federico (University of Bologna) for his deep insights of this complex matter and for his very useful comments.

includes also public prosecutors) have not been, until recently, particularly effective in limiting and in containing the development of systemic corruption in Italy. Although most foreign, but also domestic, observers have attributed to public prosecutors the merits – and indeed they have high merits – of having brought to surface what has been called "*tangentopoli*" (the city of bribes), their role in this complex phenomenon is quite controversial.

This article analyses what role public prosecutors have played in Italy in containing and in unraveling systemic corruption, focusing on those factors which limited their scope of action before February 1992 – when the "first"[1] bribes were discovered - and those which started the massive investigations against political corruption. The framework for such an analysis requires the development of four issues.

The first summarizes the difference – important for an understanding of the following three issues – between corruption that occures in many industrialized countries and systemic corruption.

The second concerns the set of conditions that have favoured and promoted the development and consolidation of systemic corruption in Italy. The main questions will focus on: a) the impact of international factors on the party system dynamics and on the electoral behaviour; b) the role of the opposition; c) the nature and role of the Italian state with particular reference to the economic sphere; and d) the role of civil society. The problem of the *mafia* and its supposed collusion with some members of the local and national political class has also played an important role in fostering corrupt behaviours.

The third issue concerns the main characteristics of the Italian prosecutorial system, including an understanding of why prosecutors have delayed in reacting to the spreading of corruption in Italy, in relation to: a) the institutional set-up, powers and prerogatives of public prosecution in Italy; b) the organization of prosecutors' interests through the ANM (National Association of Italian Magistrates); c) the role of the self-governing body of prosecutors and judges (Superior Council of the Judiciary – CSM) and its division in *correnti*[2]; d) the widespread phenomenon of extra-judicial positions occupied by many "magistrates",[3] and e) the relationship between the Italian judiciary and the political system.

The fourth briefly outlines the main factors that have led to the crisis of the so called first Republic and to the action of public prosecutors against corruption.

Corruption and systemic corruption

Political corruption in general terms is a particular way of exercising influence over public decisions, and it implies an interaction and agreement among two or more actors to use the resources they control in ways that violate social and political rules. It is a transaction or exchange (Pasquino 1983) between he who corrupts and he who is corrupted: "political corruption, in other words, is a cooperative form of unsanctioned, usually condemned, policy influence for some type of significant personal gain, in which the currency could be economic, social, political, or ideological remuneration" (de Leon 1993: 25). In brief, it promotes special interest above common interest whereas a system of public or civic order exalts the latter over the former (Rogow and Lasswell 1970).

While corruption – single occasional deviations from public rules for the attainment of personal benefits – may not hold perverse consequences for the general equilibrium of a political system, systemic corruption – where corruption becomes a predominant element in most or all practices of social, economic and political behaviour – has serious effects on the proper functioning of all institutions. Systemic corruption emerges when the actors engaging in corrupt behaviours are not only willing to play the game but are also able to effectively block or neutralize the prevailing system of controls (Zamagni 1994). The most important, though not the only one, is judicial control. As the ultimate guardians of the principle of legality, public prosecutors as well as judges have a crucial role where, if they fail to exert their control over such practices, systemic corruption may widely develop as individual corrupt behaviour is neither condemned nor controlled. Its degree of development depends, in turn, on the structural characteristics of the institutional framework in which they operate; in particular, the degree of the judiciary's substantial autonomy from other political institutions is quite significant in this sense. How strong institutionally the judiciary is, and thus how autonomous it is from undue political pressures in pursuing its goals, determines its capacity to partially keep under control such a phenomenon. If the judiciary is weak, the level of control will be very low. Not only that, but by granting impunity to corrupt practices the judiciary contributes to "legitimizing" political corruption within society. In this respect, the role of society and individuals either in not opposing or in encouraging corruption is a very important element in fostering and giving a certain "stability" to this *modus vivendi*. In fact, the more the electorate is insensitive to corruption the lower the potential costs of political corruption will be (Ragazzi 1992: 96), and the more widespread this phenomenon will become and the greater the threat of the erosion of one of the most fundamental resources of a constitutional democracy: its legitimacy (Pasquino 1983). Whereas up to a certain point civil society might tolerate – or even encourage – cases of individual corruption, the persistent violation of the rules of the democratic game leads to a general dissatisfaction and low consensus over the political system and its institutions (Cazzola 1994). The main effects of systemic corruption are that privileges dominate over fairness; hidden transactions prevail over clear and distinct modes of behaviour; and informal rules and mechanisms, which might be in contrast with legal principles, become widely accepted, distorting the allocation of resources and the primacy of the rule of law.

Once an integral part of the functioning of a system, its effects might last even after the causes that had favoured it cease to exist (Zamagni 1993). The main consequence, and the most difficult to eradicate once systemic corruption has taken over, is the collective demoralization of all actors who have participated or participate, in one form or the other, to such a system. The general feeling that nothing can be done to change the way things are done (i.e. by evading or circumventing rules and procedures in order to achieve desired goals) is reinforced by the fact that not only is it not "wise" not to engage in corrupt behaviours, but also that who does not do so will be, in some way, penalized by the same system. "Some corruption, in fact, proceeds not only by inducement, but by creating an expectation or realization of *avoided loss*" (Rogow and Lasswell 1970). Honesty, thus, is no longer regarded as a profitable "investment" (Zamagni 1993). On the basis of such an assumption, then, it is easier for those who engage in corruptive practices to justify their actions by blaming the system. No one is responsible, yet everyone – given their respective control over some kind of resource and possibility of using it improperly – contributes to the strengthening and self-preservation of systemic corruption. If on the one hand, it is true that systemic corruption leads to the definition of a set of informal rules and incentive structures which may be difficult to elude, on the other hand it is precisely this belief that makes corruption a pervasive mode of behaviour.

The Italian political system and systemic corruption

In order to identify the roots of systemic corruption in Italy it is necessary to understand how the Italian political system has evolved, what conditions have favoured such a development, and how these factors, in turn, have contributed to the spread of political corruption. Since the first years of the Italian Republic the impact of international factors has, among others, certainly played an important and lasting role in shaping the domestic political arena. Italian democracy in the post-war period has been fundamentally shaped by the Cold War and the presence of two strong sub-cultures: the Catholic and the Marxist (Farneti 1983). These two sub-cultures were reflected, at the political level, in the electoral strength of two main parties, the Christian Democrats (DC) and the Communists (PCI), which between them took about 2/3 of the total votes" (Bull and Newell 1992: 203; Farneti 1983). The Communist party, however, never after 1948 took part in any government and the Socialist Party (PSI) did not either until 1963, since they were perceived, both at an international and, to a certain extent, also at a national level, to have an "anti-system" nature (Panebianco 1982). Moreover, an important international aspect also contributed to the "exclusion" of the PCI (and also PSI until 1963) from government in the immediate years after the end of World War II and the devastation of the Italian economy. Because, at that time, Italy needed both political and economic international support, agreements with the American administration were taken in order to alleviate the economic recession. In fact, in 1947 De Gasperi – an Italian Christian Democrat and first prime minister – went to the United States to negotiate funding for the reconstruction of the Italian economy (what later was called the Marshall Plan). The main condition underlying the American administration support was, however, the exclusion of the PCI and PSI from government. As a consequence, when the elections for the first democratic parliament were held in 1948, the DC – who had obtained the absolute majority of seats – subscribed to the American position and formed the first government on the basis of a centrist coalition. Since then, all governments in Italy have had as their lowest common denominator the exclusion of the PCI and of all the other radical forces acting in the Italian political arena (Bull and Newell 1992; Sartori 1976). It meant that the DC, as the largest party, indefinitely governed in alliance with the smaller parties of the centre and later, in 1963, with the Socialist Party (PSI), which had in the meantime become more moderate (Farneti 1983). Thus, external political considerations had an important impact in influencing the composition of the first Italian governments and in shaping the Italian party system dynamics leading to what has been called a polarized pluralism (Sartori 1976). Electoral competition has been conducted for a long time through the opposition of different economic and social value-systems, and the fear of communism has been a very cohesive element in the strategies of moderate parties (Pasquino 1983). On the other hand, the absence of a viable alternative to the DC and its allies (or at least one likely to attract support among large sectors of the Italian electorate and political class) has led to a blocked political system. In other words, Italian democracy has been unable up to 1994 to produce the conditions for a genuine transfer of power to a competing political party.

This situation has been one of the main factors in favouring the development of systemic corruption in that one of the most fundamental mechanisms in a constitutional democracy – to control politicians' activities via *the option of voting them out of government* – has not been politically feasible. The possibilities of politicians' abusing their powers increase enormously in such circumstances because parties know that, whatever their failures to carry through reform, they would remain in power. Squabbling over minor issues was an ineffective substitute for fighting over more fundamental issues which would have undermined coalition solidarity in the long-term (Bull and Newell 1992; Di Palma 1978). In this respect, some scholars, such as Huntington (1993), have even claimed that a system in which there is no alternation in power cannot be considered as truly democratic. Others, however, such as Rouquiè (1985), have maintained that to define a regime as democratic it is sufficient to foresee the possibility of change in power. The latter seems to be a more appropriate definition of democracy, although the former might bear some significant truth as to the consequences of a blocked system, i.e. the erosion in the long run of fundamental democratic principles.

Under certain circumstances, however, the need to exclude a party or parties which might be perceived as anti-democratic may justify a blocked system. Indeed, for a large part of the Italian electorate, as between a stalled democracy (which inevitably leads to corruption) and "communism", the least dangerous element was certainly perceived to be the former. Furthermore, even when the leftist parties had obtained, in certain periods, significant electoral results they have always failed to create a coherent alternative coalition because of their diverse and heterogeneous positions (Farneti 1983). The same has applied to the right wing.

It is important to underline, however, that although the DC and the parties positioned around the centre have always governed in Italy, the governing coalitions they formed have often been precarious. In fact, the latter were based more on tactical considerations (to prevent the extremist parties from being in power) than on shared political platforms (Farneti 1983). This situation has partially been due to the electoral system (until 1993 a pure proportional system) which has always made it difficult for one party to obtain 51% of the seats in Parliament (Mammarella 1990). Thus, parties have been forced to form electoral alliances and coalitions which have led, most of the time, to unstable governments,[4] and to the exchange of ministerial posts and public positions against governmental support.

This condition of "unstable stability" and the lack of alternation in power, which have characterized the Italian political landscape for the past decades, have been among the main factors contributing to the development of what has been called *partitocrazia*. Such a phenomenon, which refers to the pervasive "invasion" of parties in most political and economic institutions (e.g. administrative agencies operating both at the national and local level, public holdings, media, and banks) and to their interference in all spheres of Italian social life (Romano 1992), has been the main channel through which corruption has developed. In particular, parties have had the opportunity to get a strong hold over public resources mainly due to the institutional framework within which they operated. The strong position the State had within the economy; the adoption of distributive policies through an ever growing public debt, the lack of substantial checks on the administration of the *res publica* together with the traditional weakness of the Italian civic culture were all factors which facilitated parties' control over a wide range of resources. Given the particular situation in which Italy found itself after World War II, i.e. the competition between two different value-systems – the communists and the anti-communists – the costs in terms of maintaining the status quo became increasingly high. In order to keep the prevailing system in place, the main governing parties engaged more and more in clientelistic politics using all the resources they had at their disposal. In this respect, they tried to cover the key positions within the system so as to ensure a hold over resources which were crucial for continuing to play the game of politics. It is important to underline, however, that resources were not only used to run the party or for electoral purposes but also for politicians' private benefit.

In sum, one can say that Italian parties became the privileged actors of most economic and political transactions, and public goods were shared among them, according to their respective electoral strength. The parties in the opposition were no exception to this rule. In particular, after 1970 with the implementation of the constitutional provision concerning the establishment of Regions (local government bodies with elected members and bureaucracies), the PCI started to have a greater stake in the control of public resources (such as, for example, the control over USL – Local Public Health Units). This was partly due to the fact that the PCI took part in local governments (alone or with other parties, even with parties which were in the government coalition) adopting the same strategies the governing coalition followed in using public resources. Moreover, since the beginning of the 1960's the parties in the opposition have followed two different strategies, namely one with the parties in power and one with the electorate. Whereas with the electorate they would express their total dissatisfaction for the coalition in power, at a national level, i.e. in Parliament, they would take agreements with the major parties in order to have a stake in the "sharing out" (*lottizzazione*) of public funds and in the administration of public services (Della Porta 1992). Thus, it was often argued that levels of conflict were more apparent than real as was the isolation of the PCI within the system (the Italian parliamentary committee system also gave it more legislative influence than its exclusion from government would imply) (Bull and Newell 1992: 34). The question then of who was responsible for the malfunctioning of the Italian public administration, for the inefficiencies in legislation and for the many cases of corruption could not be easily traced since all political forces contributed to it, without ever wanting to assume their own responsibilities. The continous bargaining over the "partition" of public resources and services between governing and opposition parties had as its main effect to block any form of effective political control. This phenomenon has led to a perverse form of consociational democracy. Whereas a consociational democracy, as described by Lijphart (1988), is a functional expedient to allow parties sharply divided by strong cleavages (i.e. ethnic, linguistic, religious, etc.) to find points of mediation in order to govern, what developed in Italy was quite different. It was basically a way for both governing and opposition parties to have a hold over public resources.[1] It is very important to understand such a distinction as today in Italy the concept of "compromise" and "bargaining" have assumed a very negative connotation. Because the object of the latter was the partition of resources among political parties and not mediation over issues, a quite strong hostility has developed against any form of bargaining, and such a concern reflects itself in the proposals for institutional change. Actually, compromise and bargaining, if transparent and based on a dialogue over policies, are the essential features of politics in all democratic regimes.

In this respect, the division between public and private sphere has seldom been the guiding principle in most of these transactions. In particular, the use parties have made of public funds for personal or/and party gains is just one example, and maybe the most significant, of how little politicians have been able to act in the public interest. The public debt, which in 1992 has reached 102,7% of the GDP (Quadrio-Curzio 1992), has been one of the main devices through which politicians have gained large benefits. State funds have been allocated to public construction projects, to relief programs – especially in the South – and to local industry in exchange of "*tangenti*" (bribes). Whole blocks of votes in national and local elections were guaranteed in exchange for licenses, concessions, and other authorizations (Ferrarotti 1992). All this was favoured by the fact that public works' markets were never under control and subject to mechanisms of transparency (Cazzaniga 1994). Norms concerning town plannings, the awarding of tenders, and the settlements reached in the construction industry were never quite clear (Ferrarotti 1992). Thus, for a long time politicians have been able to use their position and powers.

One of the most important factors which has allowed such a high level of corruption to develop in Italy has also been the centrality of the Italian state in the economic sphere. In fact, although Italy has a "mixed" economy, both private and public, the predominance of the latter over the former has been quite strong. The state has always had a considerable stake in the big industrial groups, and has often subsidised private industries in moments of financial difficulties. Moreover, the state's presence in the Italian economy has grown ever since the 1970s (Ferrarotti 1992), and Italy's public sector is the only one of the major European democracies to have gone on expanding ever since it was created in the Thirties (Romano 1992). To such an increase in size there has not been, however – as easily inferred – a proportional increase in efficiency and in services rendered to the public (Mammarella 1990). Furthermore, not only have there been high deadweight costs in transferring funds, and an incredible amount of resources wasted to engage in corruption, but also servicing the debt has considerably drained the resources of the State.[6]

Although Italy ranks among the most economically developed countries in the world and has a strong industrial economy, it still presents some features of a neo-patrimonialistic state. In such political systems, where everything belongs to the king or to the landlord, the sale of public offices or of monopolistic rights is considered to be acceptable and to be in the legitimate power of the rulers (Ragazzi 1992). Thus, loyalty is given to the person occupying a certain public position rather than to the position itself; it is not rules that count but rather personal relationships. But what differentiates political regimes among them is the different basis on which their legitimacy is constructed. In Italy, although corruption and the use of public positions for personal gains has, to a certain extent, been justified and accepted by large sectors of the electorate, it has never formed the basis for a legitimate use of power. What has failed to develop in Italy is the idea of its identification with a liberal state (Panebianco 1993).

The last element which should be briefly mentioned is the role civil society has played in Italy in the last decades. Although the Italian citizenry has become progressively more alienated from the political system, civil society has not been quite as "innocent" as it wanted to appear after massive investigations were started against politicians and corrupt behaviours (Panebianco 1993). In fact, civil society has intensively interacted with the political society, and this, in turn, has led to a high level of tolerance, consensus and impunity (Caferra 1992; Cazzola 1994). Perhaps one of the main factors that has lowered the level of social control has been the paralysis of judicial controls which have contributed to making corruption an acceptable phenomenon. The costs of not playing by the rules of the game were perceived as being too high for the individual to oppose the system. What is more is that most people not only have not tried to resist such a system, but have also tried, when possible, to take advantage of it. As a result, the surprise that many have shown after the "discovery" of *tangentopoli* cannot be completely justified as most Italians have been aware of the way politics and business were carried out and, to a certain extent, participated to its strengthening although possibly they were not aware of the extent to which corruption had pervaded all institutions and practices. This issue, however, is very complex and to classify behaviours as being a cause or an effect of corruption is quite difficult. Once the system is in place, relationships among the different actors of society become deeply intertwined and of an interacting nature.

To summarize, the lack of alternation in power, the absence of a real opposition, and the widespread use of "consociational" practices among all parties as well as a weak institutional framework (not least, the ineffectiveness of control systems) are all factors which have characterized for many years the Italian political system and which have led to the development of systemic corruption. In the long run, such a system has thrown Italy into its deepest crisis since the end of the second world war.

Corruption and the role of public prosecution in Italy

In order to understand what has made public prosecution's action against corruption "effective" only after 1992 (when massive investigations started in Milan), it is necessary to briefly analyse its institutional set up, powers and prerogatives, and its relationship with the other political institutions, both at a formal and informal level.

Before proceeding into the subject, it might be useful to underline that public prosecutors exercise a very important function in a democratic regime, as they contribute to determining not only what cases will be examined by the court, but also the matters on which the judges will have to decide (Di Federico 1993). In doing so public prosecutors participate more and more in the political function of defining "who gets what, when, and how" in the community (Di Federico 1994). In other words, they contribute indirectly to the definition of a relevant part of public policies in the criminal sector. Thus, given their position and role in the criminal justice system, public prosecutors' decisions bear important consequences on citizens' fundamental rights, such as freedom, security, and respectability as well as on the effectiveness of criminal policies and the respect for legality (Di Federico 1984). In what ways they deal with criminal policies and how effective they are in pursuing cases has an immediate impact on the correct functioning of a democratic regime.

The Italian prosecutorial system is for many aspects atypical, and its institutional set up different from those of other western democracies. First of all, public prosecutors in Italy are institutionally just as independent as judges are. In fact, they form an undifferentiated and interchangeable part of the judiciary ("magistrates" is the term used to indicate the members of both bodies) (Nelken 1992) and enjoy the same guarantees judges do. Thus, they enjoy the same status, have a common training, same modalities of access to the career (public competition), and can easily shift from one position to the other during their permanence in the judiciary. Public prosecutors' formal independence has been inferred from a constitutional provision (art 112) which maintains that they are obliged to prosecute all criminal cases they are aware of with no exceptions (i.e. principle of compulsory action). It has been mainly as a reaction to the previous system that prosecutors' independence has been considered to be an adequate response to previous problems in the administration of justice. In fact, during the authoritarian regime public prosecutors were under the control of the Ministry of Justice. Hence, the founding fathers of the Republic, who took part in the Constituent Assembly, thought that the only way to avoid previous miscarriages of justice was to set up a prosecutorial system which went "in the opposite direction" (Di Federico 1993).

The constitutional principle of compulsory action, however, has not produced the expected results. If this had been the case, then public prosecutors would have acted only under the rule of law and would have exercised their prosecution powers impartially. But since, for many reasons, this principle has shown to be *de facto* unfeasible, prosecutors have assumed, more and more, a growing political role without, in turn, any kind of democratic check on their activities and no form of accountability. The principle of compulsory action has been shown to be unfeasible basically because of the impossibility of pursuing all criminal cases given on the one hand, the increasing number of complexity of cases and on the other, the scarcity of resources available to cope with them. Thus, highly political decisions (in the sense that they have an impact on the authoritative distribution of values) such as whom to prosecute and what charges to impose have not found in Italy any form of control or guidance.

On the contrary, all other democratic countries, having realized the inapplicability of the principle of compulsory criminal action, have made major efforts – with different results – to set some form of democratic control (either direct or indirect) on prosecutors' actions. The problem of controlling prosecutors' actions is not, however, an easy task. In fact, not only is it necessary to control their activities (so as to avoid total discretion and abuses of power), but also to prevent partisan interferences for political reasons on their decisions. A stable equilibrium between these two functional necessities – responsability and autonomy – seems, however, quite difficult to achieve since the trade-off between competing values often leads to precarious solutions.

Nevertheless, to solve this complicated problem in a formalistic and unrealistic way as has been done in the Italian case has not produced satisfactory results. Furthermore, it is important to underline that not only are Italian public prosecutors independent from any political control (they can decide individually what cases to prosecute, whom to prosecute and what charges to set) but also no other actors (e.g. private prosecution) can initiate a criminal proceeding to remedy public prosecutor inaction. Thus, the principle of compulsory action and the monopoly of criminal action have concentrated *de facto* in the hands of public prosecutors a high degree of unchallenged power. Moreover, prosecutors in Italy "initiate proceedings not only on incoming requests from 'outside' (police, other public authorities, citizens, etc.), but also on their own initiative." In other words, "it is quite legitimate for them to start and carry out, with the greatest independence, investigations of any kind, on any citizen, using the various police forces to verify whether the offences they (more or less justifiably) assume to exist have actually been committed" (Di Federico 1994: 6).

Another important feature of the evolution of public prosecution's setup in Italy is that there has been, throughout time, a progressive dismantling of the internal hierarchical structure. It means that while, formally, chief prosecutors had the power to supervise and coordinate the activities of all the members of the office for which they were competent, *de facto* single prosecutors became more and more independent from such a supervision in their investigations. The main reason for this evolution resides in the belief of the Superior Council of the Judiciary – magistrates' self-governing body – that giving more independence to single prosecutors would have enhanced the possibility of achieving the principle of compulsory action. Hence, to a formal external independence, i.e. independence from other democratic institutions, also a substantial internal independence has been "granted" to Italian public prosecutors. The main consequence, however, has been that of producing a widespread and uncontrolled action of prosecutors, amplifying the already existing problem of high discretionality in criminal proceedings initiatives. In other words, what happened was that each prosecutor could independently define criminal policy priorities according to different parameters rather than to general and uniform guidelines. It is worth underlining that precisely because in Italy criminal compulsory action is the guiding principle in initiating criminal proceedings, no body or institution is responsible for the definition of coherent and nation-wide criminal policy priorities.[2]

The only *formal* link between public prosecutors and the political system is operated through the Superior Council of the Judiciary (CSM), which is the self-governing body of both prosecutors and judges. The CSM (which is composed 2/3 of "magistrates" elected by their own peers and 1/3 of distinguished scholars and lawyers, with at least 15 years of practice, elected by Parliament) regulates all matters concerning "magistrates' " training, appointment, promotions, transfers, salaries and disciplinary actions. Therefore, it has a range of powers not found in any other legal system.

One of the basic problems, however, in the way "magistrates' " recruitment is managed is the lack of a consistent and prolonged period of training before entry into the judiciary, and of some form of specialization. This inevitably has produced low levels of professionalism. The lack of professionalism among "magistrates" has, in turn, led to serious criticisms against the CSM and the way it has dealt with the many organizational problems of the judiciary. As for "magistrates' " recruitment and training it is important to highlight that after taking a public exam – which is highly theoretical and not very selective – "magistrates" enter the judiciary, approximately at the age of 26, "and for the following 45 years they do not undertake any other relevant exam to verify their professional skills. Thus, in Italy "magistrates' " personal and professional qualifications are formed almost exclusively on the job (Di Federico 1990), and their advancement in their career has become *de facto* mainly based on seniority.

The fact that a significant period of training for those who want to become "magistrates" is not foreseen in Italy bears important consequences. It is so not only because practical skills are not refined, but also because "magistrates" do not have an opportunity to develop a coherent set of values concerning their professional integrity and ethos (as well as to develop separate identities between prosecutors and judges). This, in turn, does not allow them to adhere to distinct modes of behaviour and to differentiate themselves from other institutions' political dynamics. The lack of professionalism which, in part, derives from the lack of appropriate mechanisms (such as a long period of training or on-going education) necessary to achieve such a goal, has prevented the judiciary from developing into a strong institution (Huntington 1968). By contrast, what has characterized the Italian judiciary has been a low level in terms of stability of institutionalization since prosecutors and judges have not developed a coherent set of internal rules and a strong identification with their respective institutional roles. What they have developed, instead, is a corporatist logic according to which they have tried to oppose any measure which could reduce – or was perceived to reduce – their "privileges" and status of independence, regardless of the fact that such measures could have produced some improvement in the administration of justice. As a consequence, socialization within the judiciary has been based on the protection of career interests rather than on professional standards. This makes a great difference since the former leads to closer relationships with certain political parties (in order to gain their support in opposing undesired provisions) whereas the latter prevents those same undue contacts from developing. Paradoxically, then, a high degree of formal independence combined with a low degree of institutional autonomy has made the Italian judiciary quite dependent on and influenced by the evolution of the political system.

The weakness of the Italian judiciary's autonomy from other institutions has been clearly shown by the deep politicisation of the judiciary's national union (ANM), which has reproduced in its internal composition the same political divisions of Parliament. The division in organized political factions – *correnti* – developed within the magistrates' professional union mainly as a response to ideological conflicts within the judiciary (which reflected those present in the political arena) but also as the outcome of different views, among "magistrates", concerning specific aspects of their career (Guarnieri 1992). The evolution of such factions, among which the first have been *Magistratura Democratica, Magistratura Indipendente* and *Terzo Potere* (aligned according to the political continuum left-right) has been quite articulated and complex. New *correnti* have developed and old ones have disappeared or broken up in two or more factions according to the major evolutions of the political system. Moreover, not only do these *correnti* have their own programme on how to manage the machinery of justice, but also their strength is proportionally[3] represented in the Superior Council of the Judiciary, which as already mentioned is the governing body of the judiciary itself. The importance of these political groupings in influencing the decisions concerning promotions or other aspects of magistrates' careers becomes even more relevant as the traditional internal hierarchy of prosecutors' offices is slowly dismantled. In fact, because the elements for evaluating single magistrates' capacities are fewer and fewer, political considerations rather than professional skills become the main parameters of evaluation. Political factions then become the means through which magistrates articulate their demands to parliament and the government (Guarnieri 1992).

It is important to underline here that although the powers vested in the Minister of Justice are quite contained, he does exercise, in principle (although, *de facto* his role is very limited) some important functions including a) the power to start disciplinary action against "magistrates" (power which is shared with the General Prosecutor at the Court of Cassation), although the disciplinary judgement is decided by the CSM; b) an advisory role in the appointment process of magistrates to directive functions, although the ultimate decision is taken by the CSM; c) the expression of opinions as far as the promotions of magistrates are concerned.

In brief, the composition of the CSM in political groupings which approximately reflect those in parliament, their political ties with the latter, and the abolition of criteria in evaluating "magistrates" are all elements which have led to a peculiar relationship between the judiciary and the other political institutions. Such a relationship has been based more and more on the exchange of favours and on agreements and connections between magistrates and parties, and between factions and parties (Guarnieri 1992).

What led political parties to adopt strategies of a particularistic nature and to try to "have friends" among "magistrates" was the fear of becoming themselves targets of judicial initiatives, given the unchallenged powers prosecutors had in initiating criminal proceedings. Furthermore, in more than one case, prosecutors had used their powers in discretionary and opportunistic ways either to favour or to discredit a particular party (Di Federico, Guarnieri 1990). The most significant tactic adopted by politicians to achieve the desired goal was to "establish links with individual magistrates by offering them rewards of various types such as creating opportunities for extra-judicial activities at national and local levels, including a seat in Parliament" (*ibid.* 34 1990). Furthermore, "they would influence, often together with factions of the judicial corporation "closest" to them ideologically, the assignment of magistrates to various posts and, in particular, the choice of the heads of judicial offices" (*ibid.* 35 1990). "Magistrates", on their part, were so highly politicised themselves, and benefited, in one way or the other, from such a peculiar relationship with the Italian political parties that they were ready to "close an eye" on "minor" details such as corruption in order to maintain their privileges. Not all "magistrates", however, have acted in the same way. In fact, many of them (e.g. Alemi, Palermo, Del Gaudio, etc.) have tried to break such a system but have always been blocked during their investigations either by indirect political pressures on high level judges or by the non cooperation of other colleagues. Thus, it is extremely important to underline that not all members of the judiciary have been inactive, but that it was sufficient to have the key positions "covered" to neutralize most efforts.

Italy after 1992

Within the context of the main conditions which have favoured corruption in Italy, and which – given the peculiar setup of public prosecutors – have also favoured a peculiar relationship between the judiciary (including public prosecutors) and the political system, what has changed after 1992, and what has led public prosecutors to start investigations against politicians? The most relevant conclusion is that whereas internal factors to the judiciary – in particular, its low institutional autonomy – have prevented "magistrates" from containing corruption, external factors – which have broken the conditions that had favoured the stability of the first republic – have led prosecutors to engage in massive investigations. Prosecutors' actions thus have not been the *cause* but rather the *consequence* of the end of those conditions which had favoured systemic corruption in Italy. A number of factors – political, economic and social, national and international – have acted and interacted in the Italian political landscape, weakening the political system and bringing to an end the "first" Republic.

Among the external factors that have contributed to the collapse of the *partitocrazia* in Italy, the end of the Cold War has certainly been one of the most important. The end of the bipolar system has, in fact, deeply affected the electoral dynamics of political competition, and has posed serious challenges to the justification and existence of many parties. Because the Cold War had had such a great influence on the Italian political parties' alignments (although a certain degree of depolarization had already characterized the Italian political system in the last decades), its end has produced significant changes in the political platforms and strategies of most parties. The first and most important effect has been the dissolution of the Communist Party (PCI) and the birth in January 1991 of the Democratic party of the Left (PDS) and of *Rifondazione Comunista* (the hard core of the remainings of the communist party).

The second factor which is worth noting has been a mounting dissatisfaction with the incapacity of the governing coalition to produce significant reforms. Years of discussions over institutional reforms (in particular, over the electoral system) had not led to any major results, and the protraction of ineffective and unstable governments was no longer tolerated by large sectors of the electorate.

The third factor is related to the Italian economic downturn which started at the end of the eighties following the general negative trend of the world economy. In addition to this situation, the European Union's decision to move towards a European Monetary Union prompted the formulation of tough convergence criteria for membership (Bull and Newell 1993).[4] According to some scholars (Majone 1994; Zamagni 1994) the Maastricht constraint has been a concurring factor in changing the attitude of industrialists towards the political class, and more marginally in disclosing important information to prosecutors. In fact, many industrialists – after Maastricht – started realizing that precisely because the public debt had to be lowered by 40% (in order to comply with Maastricht criteria) the cost of bribes paid to politicans could no longer be "financed" by an increase in the debt. Thus, while before industrialists managed altogether to maintain their expected margin of profit, the prospect of having their profits reduced and of undertaking transactions with a "declining" political class lowered their interest in protecting or taking part in the system.

The fourth factor which has contributed to alter the political scenario has been the emergence of new parties and new movements for reform, which acquired some prominence by the late 1980s. "The most significant was the Lombard League (Lega Lombarda) headed by Umberto Bossi. Largely unheard of before 1987 (it was founded in 1984), the League made rapid electoral progress gaining in the 1990 local elections 16.5%. The strength the

Lega acquired was due to its appeal against corruption and the inefficiencies of the centralised State colonised by clientilistic political parties in Rome but subsidised by Northern taxes" (Bull and Newell 1993). Besides this party, other movements (such as *La Rete, Patto Segni*, and very recently *Forza Italia*) started to grow as a reaction to the general dissatisfaction with the Italian political class and its corrupt behaviours.

The fifth factor, which, in turn, has contributed to the emerging of these new political movements has been a change in the social perception of corruption and of the political class legitimacy. The main reason for this shift in attitude has been probably due to the growing dissatisfaction of all citizens with the economic situation, with the increasing state deficiencies, with parties' inability to face the many problems afflicting the Italian political situation, as well as a sense of deep frustration and alienation from politics.

The last factor which has contributed to weakening the Italian political system has been the 1992 national elections. Indeed, such elections "have produced some of the most significant changes in individual party strengths since the second world war. The most striking results were the fall in the DC and PDS shares of the vote; the relevant increase in support for the *Lega*; the breakthrough of the *Rete*, and the failure of the socialists to make any gain from the collapse of communism" (Bull and Newell 1993). What emerged from these elections was a totally new scenario compared to the past since the four governing parties (DC, PSI, PSDI, PLI) lost the overall majority of votes they had enjoyed until then. The Italian political system was then fragmented, and faced its deepest crisis since the end of the war.

At this point, public prosecutors felt "free" to break their informal ties with the political class and undertake investigations in areas not covered before. Prosecutors felt that they had nothing to lose or to gain from supporting a political class which was rapidly declining and losing control over vital resources. Surprisingly enough, the new situation was triggered, almost by accident, by what seemed to be a minor case of corruption: a local politician, Mario Chiesa, who was also the president of a nursing house for old people in Milan, was caught on 17th February 1992 while he was receiving a relatively small amount of money (approximately, £ 2,500) from a manager to whom he had previously granted a tender. While in preventive detention, Chiesa uncovered a much wider and substantial web of political and administrative corruption. His relevations, strongly amplified by the media, elicited a great deal of public support for the initiatives of public prosecutors in the area of political corruption. The example of public prosecutors' investigations in Milan was soon followed by prosecutors throughout Italy in a crescendo of public support.

In brief, one can say that a multiplicity of factors have, in fact, contributed to fostering prosecutors' investigations in areas that had gone untouched. Among the main factors that allowed and reinforced this trend, one can certainly indicate: 1) many managers and politicians, who did not feel any longer protected by the main parties to which they were affiliated, started releasing important information about the prevailing practices within the system in order to avoid severe measures against them, among them prolonged preventive detention; 2) prosecutors started realizing that they could greatly benefit from this new wave of "judicial" activism and become the national heroes of the Italian political landscape, thanks also to the strategic use they were able to make of the media. The perception that has prevailed in the last years in Italian public opinion certainly confirms this new image and the dominant idea, whether true or not, is up to now that the "transition to the second Republic" has been guided and made possible by the action of public prosecutors. Indeed, what one can say is that over the past years public prosecutors, faced with a situation of generalized institutional uncertainty, have played in Italy an ever growing political role influencing, directly or indirectly, the "fortunes" of political parties, politicians and governments.

Concluding remarks

The main conclusion reached in this paper is that public prosecutors, though being institutionally just as independent as judges and ruled by the principle of compulsory action, have *de facto* shown, until 1992, little inclination to prosecute administrative and political corruption obtaining meanwhile from the political class, through legislative innovations, advantages both in terms of their careers and salary increases.[5] Their action against political corruption seems, in other words, to have been limited by the privileged relation they had established with the party system. Far from being a strong institution, and thus autonomous from the political system, prosecutors have not been able to insulate themselves from the evolution of the Italian party system and have been themselves highly politicised. That is to say that the Italian judicial sub-system has been affected, to a certain extent, by the same logic which had characterized the Italian political system, showing in this respect a high degree of permeability.

After February, 1992, and after the April national elections of the same year, many factors – national and international – have weakened the Italian party system, and have opened up more and more spaces for a direct action of the judiciary. In response to Italian public opinion and to a general turmoil, public prosecutors have started what has been called the Italian "peaceful revolution". Nevertheless, we could say that public prosecutors' investigations have not been the cause but rather the consequence of the end of those conditions that had granted stability to the "first Republic" (Panebianco 1993). In fact, only external factors seem to have led the judiciary to act as a "strong" institution and not because prosecutors' powers or prerogatives have changed since 1992.

The fact that many prosecutors have claimed that before 1992 the political conditions were not favorable to their investigations should be interpreted differently than potrayed by "magistrates" themselves. A totally independent judiciary, with prosecutors being able to initiate an investigation of any citizen, cannot ascribe responsibility for their inaction to the political conditions unless they themselves benefited from such a situation or were, in one way or the other, favorable to its maintainance. Of course, this does not mean that all "magistrates" were equally responsible, but certainly some have not made it possible for others – who even began in the past investigations against corruption – to perform correctly their functions.

References

Bull, Martin J. and James L. Newell. "Italian Politics and the 1992 Elections: From Stable Instability to Instability and Change, Parliamentary Affairs Journal, Oxford University Press, 1992.

Caferra, Vito Marino. "La Corruzione Politica" in Arel Informazioni, 1992, pp. 25–28, 38–39, Roma.

Carocci, Giampiero. *Storia d'Italia dall'Unità ad oggi*, Feltrinelli Editore, Milano, 1986.

Cavallari, Alberto. "The European Janus", Geopolitique Review of the International Institute of Geopolitics, Italy a nation in the scales, n. 38, 1992, p. 37–40, Paris.

Cazzaniga, Gianmario. "Sulle cause morali della corruzione". In: L. Barca e S. Trento (eds) *L'Economia della Corruzione*, Editori Laterza, 1994, pp. 33–47, Roma-Bari.

Cazzola, Franco. "La Corruzione Politica", in Arel Informazioni, 1994, pp. 15–17, Roma.

deLeon, Peter. *Thinking about political corruption*, M.E. Sharpe Inc., New York, 1993.

Della Porta, Donatella. *Lo scambio occulto. Casi di corruzione politica in Italia*, il Mulino, Bologna, 1992.

Di Federico, Giuseppe. "Italy: a peculiar case of Judicialization of Politics. In: C.N. Tate and T. Vallinder (eds) The Global Expansion of Judicial Power, New York University press, N.Y., 1995, pp. 233–243.

—"Dilemmi del pubblico ministero: indipendenza, responsabilità, carriera separata da quella del giudice", in Atti del Convegno "La giurisdizione e la cultura della legalità. Le regole del processo penale alla prova", Camera dei Deputati, Roma, 1993.

—"Lottizzazioni Correntizie e Politicizzazione del CSM: quali rimedi?" Quaderni Costituzionali, X, n. 2, 1991, pp. 279–297, Roma.

—"The crisis of the Justice system and the referendum on the judiciary", in Italian Politics: A Review, Vol. 3. In: Leonardi R. and P. Corbetta (eds) Pinter Publishers, London and New York, 1990.

Di Palma, Giuseppe. *Surviving Without Governing: The Italian Parties in Parliament*, University of California Press, 1978.

Farneti, Paolo. *Il sistema dei partiti in Italia 1946–1979*, il Mulino, Bologna, 1983.

Ferrarotti, Franco. "The Italian Enigma", Geopolitique Review of the International Institute of Geopolitics, Italy a nation in the scales, n. 38, 1992, p. 20–23, Paris.

Galli, G. *I partiti politici*, Torino, Utet, 1974.

Gaito, A. (ed.) *Accusa penale e ruolo del pubblico ministero*, Jovene, 1991, pp. 107–208, Napoli.

Guarnieri, Carlo. *Magistratura e Politica in Italia: Pesi senza contrappesi*, Il Mulino, Bologna, 1992.

—"Magistratura e Politica: il caso italiano", Rivista Italiana di Scienza della Politica, XXI, n. 1, Il Mulino, Bologna, 1991.

—*Pubblico ministero e sistema politico*, CEDAM, Padova, 1984.

Huntington, Samuel. "Power, Institutions and Political Modernization", in *Political Order in Changing Societies*, Yale University Press, New Haven, 1968.

—"Modernization and Corruption". In: Heidenheimer Arnold (ed.) *Political Corruption. Readings in Compartive Analysis*, 1970, pp. 492–500, Holt, Rinehart and Winston, Inc., New York.

—*The third wave. Democratization in the late XXth century*, University of Oklahoma Press, 1991.

Lijphart, Arend. *Le Democrazie Contemporanee*, il Mulino, Bologna, 1988.

Mammarella, Giuseppe. L'Italia contemporanea. Storia d'Italia dall'Unità alla Repubblica, il Mulino, Bologna, 1990.

Marzotto, Paolo. "The Price of Irresponsability", Geopolitique Review of the International Institute of Geopolitics, Italy a nation in the scales, 1992, n. 38, pp. 60–62, Paris.

Nelken, David. "The Judicialization of Politics in Italy: Some notes on the relationship between the academic and the political debate", Paper presented at the Interim Meeting of the Research Committee on Comparative Judicial Studies, Forlì, 1992.

Panebianco, Angelo. Modelli di partito. Organizzazione e potere nei partiti politici, Bologna, Il Mulino, 1982.

—"Fare a meno della politica", il Mulino, anno XLII n. 348, 1993, Bologna.

Pasquino, Gianfranco. "Corruzione Politica". In: Dizionario di Politica (eds) N. Bobbio, N. Matteucci, G. Pasquino, UTET, 1983, pp. 261–262, Torino.

Prodi, Romano. "The Public Sector and The Italian Economy", Geopolitique Review of the International Institute of Geopolitics, Italy a nation in the scales, n. 38, 1992, p. 51–55, Paris.

Quadrio-Curzio, Alberto. "Tre livelli di governo per l'economia", il Mulino, anno XLII 1993, n. 348, Bologna.

Ragazzi, G. "Semantica della corruzione". In: *La corruzione politica*, AREL Informazioni, Roma, 1992.

Rogow, Arnold and H.D. Lasswell. "The Definition of Corruption". In: Heidenheimer, Arnold (ed.) *Political Corruption, Readings in Compartive Analysis*, 1970, pp. 54–55, Holt, Rinehart and Winston, Inc., New York.

Romano, Sergio. "The First Republic A Brief History" in Geopolitique Review of the International Institute of Geopolitics, Italy a nation in the scales, 1992, n. 38, pp. 4–8, Paris.

Rouquiè, Alain. *Como renacen las democracias*, EMECE' editores, Buenos Aires, 1985.

Sartori, Giovanni. *Parties and party system*, Cambridge, Cambridge University Press, 1976.

Savona, Paolo. "Living up to Maastricht", Geopolitique Review of the International Institute of Geopolitics, Italy a nation in the scales, 1992, n. 38, p. 40–44, Paris.

Scott, James. *Comparative Public Corruption*, Prentice Hall, Englewood Cliffs N.J., 1972.

Zannotti, Francesca. *La magistratura, un gruppo di pressione istituzionale. L'autodeterminazione delle retribuzioni*, CEDAM, Padova, 1989.

—*Le attività extragiudiziarie dei magistrati ordinari*, CEDAM, Padova, 1981.

Zamagni, Stefano. Relazione presentata al Convegno su "Tangentopoli ed il Sistema Politico Italiano", Istituto Universitario Europeo, Firenze, 1994.

—"Sul processo di generazione della corruzione sistematica" in *L'Economia della Corruzione*, Editori Laterza, 1994, pp. 91–108, Roma-Bari.

[11]

LEGAL RESPONSES TO STATE CORRUPTION IN COMMONWEALTH AFRICA

SIMON COLDHAM*

Few countries in the world can claim to be free from corruption and none of these is to be found in Commonwealth Africa.[1] Even though administrative incorruptibility was one of the boasts of the British colonial service, low-level corruption was common during the colonial period and indeed served to bolster the colonial system.[2] Since African states obtained political independence, levels of corruption have markedly increased, regardless of official ideology or economic approach, and in many countries corruption is both pervasive and endemic. Changes of government are often accompanied and, in the case of military coups, justified by commitments to eradicate the corrupt practices that allegedly characterized the previous regime. Corruption is an obstacle to economic development and to political integration, and most African governments (cynically or not) avow the need to combat it. Pressure on governments to act has increased in recent years and comes from two sources. The emergence of pro-democracy forces has drawn large numbers of people into the arena of political debate and organization and this in turn has led to demands for openness and accountability on the part of government. Moreover, foreign donors and international financial institutions are today less willing to condone corrupt practices on the part of African governments. They stress the importance of good governance and accountability and the need to link economic reconstruction with institutional reform.[3]

If there is widespread agreement on the deleterious effects of corruption,[4] in that it generally results in the inefficient and inequitable allocation of resources, the causes of corruption are more difficult to identify. Its roots may, for example, lie in cultural factors or in social/economic arrangements, and it is arguable that anti-corruption policies that ignore these matters are bound to fail. However, African governments are under pressure to produce quick results, often in the wake of some public scandal, and for that purpose they turn to the law. If a special commission or squad is set up, if a trial is held and a conviction obtained, or if the criminal law is made more draconian, at least the government can give the impression of tackling the problem. In the course of the last three decades there has been a substantial body of legislation in Commonwealth Africa which relates, directly or indirectly, to the prevention of corruption.[5]

---

* My thanks are due to John Hatchard for his valuable comments on an earlier draft of this article.

[1] In the public office sense of the term corruption can be defined as "behaviour which deviates from the formal duties of a public role because of private-regarding (personal, close family, private clique) pecuniary or status gains; or violates rules against the exercise of certain types of private-regarding influence". J. S. Nye, "Corruption and political development: a cost-benefit analysis", (1967) 61 *American Political Science Review* 419. Nye identifies bribery, nepotism and misappropriation as the main types of corrupt behaviour.

[2] See Robert Tignor, "Political corruption in Nigeria before independence", (1993) 31, 2 *Journal of Modern African Studies* 175.

[3] See Ernest Harsch, "Accumulators and Democrats: Challenging State Corruption in Africa", (1993) 31, 1 *Journal of Modern African Studies* 31, at 39–41.

[4] See, for example, Stephen Ouma, "Corruption in public policy and its impact on development: the case of Uganda since 1979", (1991) 11 *Public Administration and Development* 473, at 483 ff.

[5] One of the most recent and most controversial laws has been the Corruption and Economic Crime Act, 1994, of Botswana, noted by E. K. Quansah in (1994) 38, 2 *Journal of African Law*.

In this article I review the ways in which the law has been used to tackle the problem of corruption in Commonwealth Africa. Although reference is made to other jurisdictions, Commonwealth African countries (apart from South Africa) have sufficient in common, in terms of cultural context, political history, legal background and levels of economic development, to be considered together and compared. However, I intend neither to provide a comprehensive picture of all the legislation on the topic nor to attempt a detailed analysis of the legislation that I do mention. The approach is selective and involves the use of particular laws to illustrate general issues. The first section deals with the criminal law and traces the ways in which governments have attempted to use it to deter corrupt practices. The second section deals with the variety of supervisory controls (such as commissions, ombudsmen and so on) introduced to ensure high standards in public life. The final section attempts to assess the effectiveness of law in this field.

Criminal Law

During the colonial period the Penal Codes were the principal source of law dealing with corruption. The Nyasaland/Malawi Penal Code is typical. Chapter X provides for a number of offences involving corruption and abuse of office and Chapter XLI deals with secret commissions and some other corrupt practices. However, since independence many countries have introduced specific anti-corruption legislation to supplement or replace the Penal Code provisions.[6] Most of this legislation, like the Penal Code provisions themselves, is based, directly or indirectly, on United Kingdom law and, in particular, on the Prevention of Corruption Acts 1889–1916.[7] What is interesting, though, is to identify those features of the African statutes which diverge significantly from the parent legislation, both in the creation of new offences and in the treatment of evidentiary, investigatory and enforcement matters.

The mischief at which the Penal Code provisions were directed was corruption in the public service, that is at the bribery of, and extortion and other abuse of office by, public servants in connection with the performance of their duties. However, although bureaucratic corruption remains a serious problem, such a restrictive definition is hard to sustain in countries where large sectors of the economy are bureaucratized or in countries where the ruling party plays a key role in the implementation of policy. Thus, for example, the Tanzanian Act defines "public officer" to include both employees of parastatal organizations and officers of TANU (the Tanganyika African National Union), as the ruling party was then called.[8] The Zambian Corrupt Practices Act, 1980, went even further by covering corrupt practices in the private sector.[9]

Anti-corruption legislation has also sought to provide a comprehensive list of corrupt acts and this has frequently involved the creation of new criminal offences. Thus the Kenyan Prevention of Corruption Act, 1956, makes it an

[6] Malawi is one of the exceptions. It has, however, introduced a special and rigorous regime for the prosecution and punishment of theft in the public service. See Clement Ng'ong'ola, "Controlling theft in the public service: penal law and judicial responses in Malawi", (1988) 32, 1 *Journal of African Law* 72.

[7] See Commonwealth Legal Advisory Service, British Institute of International and Comparative Law, *Prevention of Corruption: A Comparative Study of Selected Commonwealth Legislation*, New Memoranda Series No. 1, December 1987.

[8] Prevention of Corruption Act, 1971 (No. 16 of 1971), s. 2.

[9] Act No. 14 of 1980, s. 27.

offence for a public servant knowingly to accept a gift from any person whom he knows to be concerned in a matter with him in his capacity as a public servant.[10] There is no need for the prosecution to prove that the gift was accepted on account of something done or to be done in the discharge of his official duties, as there was under the Penal Code. Another example is the offence of favouritism created by the Zimbabwean Prevention of Corruption Act, 1985, an offence for which there may be a particular need in societies where access to favours is as much determined by friendship, kinship or ethnic affiliation as by money.[11] Finally, mention should be made of an unusual and controversial provision in the Tanzanian Act which makes it an offence for a public officer to be or to have been in possession of any property, or to have received the benefit of any service, which he may reasonably be suspected of corruptly acquiring or receiving; the burden of proof is on the defendant to show that there was no corruption.[12] The notion that high-living bureaucrats are *prima facie* corrupt certainly accords with popular prejudice throughout Africa.

Presumptions of corruption are fairly common in the African legislation and they perhaps indicate the problems of bringing successful prosecutions in this field. The United Kingdom Prevention of Corruption Act, 1916, section 2 raises such a presumption in the case of transactions involving government contracts, but while some African countries (such as Kenya) simply adopted the same presumption in their anti-corruption laws, others have applied the presumption of corruption to other situations. Two examples may be given. The first is the Zambian Corrupt Practices Act, 1980, which not only introduced the presumption of corruption in a number of different situations but also expressly placed on the accused the burden of proving the contrary, that is the absence of corruption.[13] The constitutionality of this provision was successfully challenged in the courts on the grounds that it infringed the presumption of innocence contained in article 20(2)(a) of the Constitution of Zambia, 1973.[14] Subsequently the Act was amended; the provisions placing a burden of proof on the accused were deleted, but the presumptions of corruption were retained with the addition of the words "in the absence of a satisfactory explanation by the accused".[15] Similar issues are raised by the Botswana Corruption and Economic Crime Act, 1994, which provides that where, in proceedings under the Act, it is proved that the accused offered or accepted a valuable consideration, the valuable consideration shall be presumed to have been offered and accepted as such inducement or reward, unless the contrary is proved.[16] Moreover, section 34(2) creates an "unexplained lifestyle" offence. It seems likely that, as in Zambia, the constitutionality of these provisions will be challenged in the courts as derogating from both the right of protection against self-incrimination (section 10(7) of the Botswana Constitution)

---

[10] Cap. 65, s. 6(1).

[11] Act No. 34 of 1985, s. 4.

[12] S. 9. A similar "unexplained lifestyle" offence is to be found in the Hong Kong Prevention of Bribery Ordinance (Cap. 201), s. 10(1).

[13] Ss. 33 and 46.

[14] *A. M. Simataa and another* v. *Attorney-General*, High Court, 5 November 1986 (No. 1986/HP/448). Another provision in the Act, compelling the accused to give evidence on oath, was struck down in *Mumba* v. *The People* (1984) ZR 38.

[15] Corrupt Practices (Amendment) Act, No. 29 of 1987, ss. 8, 13. This places an evidential burden on the accused.

[16] S. 42. Evidence of property possessed by the accused for which he is unable to account may be taken by the court as corroborating the testimony of a witness that the accused accepted any valuable consideration *and* as showing a corrupt intent. S. 40(1).

and the presumption of innocence (section 10(2)(a)). Although the latter is qualified, as is generally the case in Commonwealth African constitutions, by a provision that the presumption shall not be breached if the law at issue imposes upon the accused the burden of proving particular facts, it is likely that the Botswana courts would interpret such a provision narrowly and as not applying to an essential ingredient of the offence.[17]

African governments have tended to respond to perceived increases in crime levels by the adoption of harsh penal policies, including the extension of corporal and capital punishment and the introduction of minimum and mandatory sentences for certain offences. Post-independence anti-corruption legislation has generally followed this pattern. Maximum sentences for offences involving corruption have been generally increased and in some jurisdictions minimum/mandatory sentences have been introduced. Perhaps the most extreme example comes from Nigeria where large-scale corruption, illustrated by a series of major scandals, played a significant part in the military overthrow of the civilian government in 1983.[18] The coup was followed by a number of decrees dealing with corruption. The Recovery of Public Property (Special Military Tribunals) Act, 1984, provides for the investigation of the assets of any public officer alleged to have engaged in corrupt practices (very broadly defined) and, if a *prima facie* case is made out, for the establishment of a Special Military Tribunal to try the case. On conviction the accused may be sentenced to a term of imprisonment not exceeding 21 years and, where the accused has failed to declare assets in excess of one million *naira*, the sentence is life imprisonment.[19] The jurisdiction of the courts is excluded, but every sentence has to be confirmed by the Supreme Military Council, which has the discretion to reduce the sentence.[20] While the Nigerian legislation is particularly draconian, both the use of minimum/mandatory sentences and the introduction of special courts have occurred elsewhere.[21] There is no evidence that minimum sentences have a deterrent effect in Africa and there is some evidence that the courts do not like them and, where possible, will contrive to avoid having to impose them.[22]

The threat of forfeiture of property is another weapon that can be used to deter corrupt practices, particularly in jurisdictions where the courts are unable or unwilling to impose custodial sentences and where the maximum fine available is likely to be disproportionate to the profit anticipated from the corrupt transaction. African anti-corruption laws generally follow the United Kingdom law in providing for the recovery of sums and so on paid corruptly, but many go further and recognize that forfeiture of an official's assets, coupled perhaps with a modification of the onus of proof regarding the origin of suspect property, can operate as a powerful deterrent to misconduct. Thus, where an "unexplained lifestyle" offence exists, conviction may involve the forfeiture of "unexplained" assets. For example, under the Sierra Leonean Prevention of Corruption Decree,

---

17 This was the approach taken by the Privy Council in *Vasquez* v. *R* [1994] 3 All E.R. 674.

18 Some of these scandals, e.g. the Cement Scandal, the Rice Scandal and the Jaguar Scandal, are discussed in Robert Williams, *Political Corruption in Africa*, Gower, 1987, at 67 ff and 95 ff.

19 Cap. 389, Laws of the Federation of Nigeria 1990, s. 13(1). The tribunal also has the power to forfeit the assets of the accused. S. 6(4).

20 S. 20.

21 See, for example, the Zambian Corrupt Practices Act, 1980 (as amended), s. 35 (five years imprisonment minimum on a second conviction) and the Tanzanian Economic and Organised Crime Act, 1984, which sets up an Economic Crimes Court (ss. 3 and 4) and special rules of investigation and procedure.

22 See Ng'ong'ola, op. cit.

1992, conviction for such an offence carries the possibility of a maximum ten-year sentence of imprisonment *and* the forfeiture of a sum not exceeding the value of the accused's unexplained resources.[23] The Nigerian legislation goes further and makes it an offence for a public officer simply to fail to declare his assets when called upon to do so by a panel set up by the Federal Military Government; on conviction he is liable both to a minimum five-year term of imprisonment and to the forfeiture of his undeclared assets.[24] Severe though such forfeiture provisions may be, their scope is limited in two important ways. In the first place, they do not help where the proceeds of corruption have been diverted abroad.[25] Secondly, the provisions are confined to public officers, and while this is perfectly satisfactory in a situation where an officer extorts payments from unwilling citizens, it robs the remedy of much of its potential in instances of major corruption, where consensual relationships are the rule. It is arguable that here both the individual instigator of bribery and, where appropriate, his employer should be liable to have their assets forfeited; tough forfeiture provisions might, for example, deter a company from offering a bribe in return for a sales or construction contract.[26]

In this section an attempt has been made to survey the principal ways in which the criminal law has been used to combat corruption in Commonwealth Africa. Although at independence most of the legislation was based, directly or indirectly, on United Kingdom legislation, many African governments have introduced reforms which have made the law both more extensive and more rigorous. The creation of new offences, the widespread use of presumptions of corruption, the introduction of severe penalties and the establishment of special courts are perhaps the most significant measures taken in this field,[27] and while this discussion has tended to focus on some of the more controversial reforms, it will have become clear that the use of the criminal law as a weapon in the fight against corruption has been enthusiastically embraced throughout Commonwealth Africa. Its success as such a weapon depends, of course, on all the actors in the criminal justice system (the police, the prosecution authorities,[28] the courts) being both able and willing to play their roles effectively, and this they have often failed to do. This failure can be attributed to an inadequacy of resources, to a policy of concentrating their energies on offences that may be more serious and easier to investigate than "victimless" economic crimes, and to the susceptibility of some of the actors themselves to bribery and improper pressure. It is partly the failure of the criminal justice system to eradicate corruption that has led many governments to establish institutions with either specific responsibility for combating corruption (such as anti-corruption commissions) or general responsibility for ensuring proper standards of public

---

23 Decree No. 6 of 1992, ss. 5 and 8(2)(a).

24 S. 2(3). Where a public officer makes a false declaration, the onus is on him to show that he had reasonable grounds to believe that it was true. S. 2(4).

25 For a discussion of the issue of international co-operation in this field see *Practical Measures against Corruption*, Doc. A/CONF. 144/8 prepared for the Secretariat for the Eighth UN Congress on the Prevention of Crime and the Treatment of Offenders, held in Havana, Cuba in August/September 1990, at 25 ff. Where the proceeds of corruption are transferred to another Commonwealth state, it may be possible to trace, seize and confiscate them under the Commonwealth Scheme relating to Mutual Assistance in Criminal Matters. See *Commonwealth Schemes on Mutual Assistance in the Administration of Justice*, Commonwealth Secretariat, June 1991.

26 Ibid. at 29 ff.

27 Other measures, not discussed in the text, include the application of special rules of evidence in corruption trials.

28 Prosecutions for corruption generally require the consent of the Attorney-General.

administration (such as ombudsmen). A further reason may be that, while the criminal justice system is mobilized in response to a suspected corrupt act, a permanent national institution can play a role in creating an environment where corrupt acts are less likely to occur.

Institutional Controls

Many Commonwealth African countries have established the office of ombudsman. The first, the Tanzanian Permanent Commission of Enquiry, was set up in 1965 and the most recent, the Botswana Ombudsman, in 1995.[29] Their primary function has been to investigate complaints about maladministration and abuse of office on the part of public officials in an informal and confidential manner, and, as a permanent national institution with wide investigative powers and with the opportunity both to develop personal contacts with high-ranking officials and to build up a reputation for independence with the public at large, they have the potential to play an important role in the fight against corruption. On the whole, however, their record has not been particularly impressive, and it is worthwhile rehearsing some of the reasons for their failure to live up to expectations.

One important reason is their lack of independence of the executive. In most countries the ombudsman is appointed by the head of state (sometimes after consultation) for a short term[30] and is answerable to the head of state[31]; moreover the office is a multi-member institution, it does not have an independent budget and it has no power to enforce its recommendations.[32] In these circumstances it may be susceptible to executive pressure in respect of investigations into politically sensitive areas. The dilemma is that where, as in most African states, the executive arm of government is by far the strongest, the ombudsman needs the support of the executive in order to survive, while at the same time it needs to develop a reputation for independence if it is to enjoy the confidence of members of the public. While formal independence is essential, it is also necessary to guard against threats of an informal kind arising from the symbiotic relationship between the ombudsman and the public service. In making its investigations the ombudsman will depend on the co-operation of the public service, which will itself depend on the ombudsman to protect it from unfounded complaints. An

---

29 Ombudsman Act, 1995, noted later in this issue of the *Journal of African Law*. The Ghanaian Commission on Human Rights and Administrative Justice, established in 1993, is a successor to the Ombudsman established in 1980. For a history of the ombudsman in Africa see John Hatchard, "The institution of the ombudsman in Africa with special reference to Zimbabwe", (1986) 35 *I.C.L.Q.* 255 and "The ombudsman in Africa revisited", (1991) 40 *I.C.L.Q.* 937.

30 A signal exception is the Namibian Ombudsman, who is appointed by the President on the recommendation of the Judicial Service Commission and whose tenure and conditions of service are virtually identical to those of judges. Namibian Constitution, Arts. 89–93. The new ombudsman in Ghana, the Commission on Human Rights and Administration of Justice, also enjoys similar terms and conditions of service to those of judges. Constitution of Ghana 1992, Arts. 221–223.

31 Outside Africa the ombudsman is generally linked to the legislature. It is interesting to note that under the proposed Constitution of Uganda the ombudsman will report to Parliament every six months, whereas at present it reports directly to the President and its reports are publishable at the discretion of the President. Moreover it is proposed that the ombudsman should have judicial powers. See Mubiro Musoke, "Human rights, politics, war and the new Constitution of Uganda", (1993) 2 *Uganda Quarterly Review* 49, at 105 ff.

32 Again exceptions are provided by the two most recently established ombudsmen. In Namibia he may recommend a prosecution and in Ghana the Commission on Human Rights and Administration of Justice has broad powers to bring legal proceedings. In most African jurisdictions implementation is ultimately a matter for the head of state.

excessively cosy relationship between the two bodies may arise which could undermine the effectiveness of the ombudsman's operations.[33]

A further reason for the lacklustre record of the ombudsman in Africa lies in the ways in which its powers of investigation are limited. In most countries, for example, it has no independent power to initiate investigations but can only act on complaints submitted to it in writing.[34] In countries where there is illiteracy, suspicion of government or widespread ignorance of legal rights as well as in situations where there is a need for urgent action, this can limit the potential usefulness of the institution. Moreover, there are often restrictions on the sort of organizations that may be investigated. Thus in Zimbabwe the activities of the defence forces, the police, the prison service and the ruling party are specifically excluded, even though (or, possibly, because) abuse of power by these bodies has been common.[35]

The question of resources is obviously crucial. Budget, staffing and transport problems clearly affect performance. Resource constraints have meant that in many countries the ombudsman's constituency is found primarily among the urban population.[36] A measure of decentralization is essential if the ombudsman is to be a truly national institution and to provide effective protection for all citizens.

The ombudsman has the power to investigate corrupt practices by public officials as well as other forms of maladministration and abuse of power. Indeed the Ugandan Inspector-General is specifically charged to combat corruption by examining the practices and procedures of public bodies (including para-statals) "in order to facilitate the discovery of corrupt practices and secure revision of procedures which may be conducive to [such] practices", by investigating allegations of corrupt practices and by fostering public support against corruption.[37] Such duties go far beyond those demanded of the "traditional" ombudsman in Africa and reflect a realization that the eradication of corruption requires more than the creation of machinery for the investigation and disposal of complaints.

The idea that the ombudsman ought to play a pro-active and educative role has recently been accepted in Ghana, where the new Commission on Human Rights and Administrative Justice has a much broader remit than the former

---

33 This seems to have occurred in Nigeria, where the ombudsman, the Public Complaints Commission, infected from the start with a "civil service" outlook, has developed into a huge, wasteful and inefficient bureaucracy itself. See Oluwole Akanle, "Self-restraint or abdication? A note on the investigating powers of the Nigerian Public Complaints Commissioner (the Ombudsman)", (1978) 10 *Zambia Law Journal* 70, and Victor Ayeni, "Nigeria's bureaucratised ombudsman system: an insight into the problem of bureaucratisation in a developing country", (1987) 7 *Public Administration and Development* 309.

34 An exception is the Ugandan Ombudsman, the Inspector-General of Government (established in 1986), which has the power to undertake investigations on its own initiative.

35 The activities of judicial officers are almost invariably excluded in the interest of preserving the independence of the judiciary.

36 Hatchard notes that in Zimbabwe the largest group of complainants has been civil servants complaining about their terms and conditions of service, whereas the Ombudsman of Tanzania (with its predominantly rural population) receives more complaints per head than any other ombudsman in Africa due in part, it would seem, to its practice of travelling around the country informing people of their rights. Hatchard, op. cit. (1986), at 255 and 267.

37 Inspector-General of Government Statute, 1988, s. 7. Unusually for an ombudsman, the Inspector-General is also required to police and promote the protection of human rights and the rule of law in Uganda.

ombudsman.[38] It has special powers of investigation and, a novel and controversial feature, broad powers to bring proceedings; indeed, in a case where a public officer fails to act on its recommendations, it is required to take court action.[39] While purely reactive strategies have the negative virtue of being non-controversial and are less likely to generate accusations of partisanship, the inherently covert and consensual nature of most corruption (particularly large-scale corruption) severely limits their effectiveness.[40] Moreover, lack of enforcement powers, especially in cases where investigations have uncovered evidence of corruption or other criminal activity, further weakens effectiveness, since the executive cannot be compelled to act on the reports. While the grant of enforcement powers to the ombudsman, as in Ghana, could lead to it duplicating the functions of the police and be wasteful of resources, it is arguable that a measure of overlapping and even competition between institutions can itself be a healthy antidote to corruption.

The recognition that the eradication of corruption demands the adoption of a variety of strategies as well as the development of an expertise in the investigation and prosecution of cases involving alleged corruption has led a few countries to establish single-purpose anti-corruption bodies. In 1980, Zambia, which has had an ombudsman since 1974, set up its Anti-Corruption Commission which is headed by a Commissioner who, together with his Deputy, is appointed by and subject to the direction of the President of the Republic. They must both be qualified to be appointed as High Court judges and their tenure and terms of service are similar to those of High Court judges.[41] The Commission, which was loosely modelled on the Hong Kong Independent Commission against Corruption, has educational/advisory functions, preventive audit-type functions intended to eliminate vulnerability to corruption in systems and procedures, and extensive powers of investigation and arrest together with responsibility for conducting prosecutions (subject to the directions of the D.P.P.).[42] It is difficult to assess its performance. By the late 1980s it appears to have decentralized its activities, set up a Community Relations Department and attracted well-qualified personnel. However, its establishment is small in proportion to the number of complaints received and it has few convictions to its credit. A shortage of resources seems to be a major constraint on its effectiveness.[43]

More recently, a similar institution was established in Botswana. The Corruption and Economic Crime Act, 1994, enacted in the wake of a number of major

---

[38] See Joseph Ayee, "Notes on the Commission on Human Rights and Administrative Justice under the 1992 Ghanaian Constitution", (1994) 27, 2 *Verfassung und Recht in Ubersee* 159.

[39] Constitution of Ghana, 1992, art. 218. The Commission must give reasons for not taking or continuing a case.

[40] "Reactive strategies provide no mechanism for exposing the far more costly effects of sophisticated corruption, inviting the cynical conclusion that the system protects the corrupt but powerful official by sacrificing the clumsy petty thief." *Practical Measures against Corruption*, op. cit., at 21.

[41] Corrupt Practices Act, 1980, s. 6.

[42] Ibid. s. 10(1). By contrast the Commission set up in the Gambia under the Evaluation of Assets and Properties and the Prevention of Corrupt Practices Act, 1982, has purely investigative functions, though these are extensive, including the power to investigate the conduct or assets of any public officer.

[43] See, generally, Gatian Lungu, "The implementability of Zambia's Corrupt Practices Act", (1981) 13 *Zambia Law Journal* 1 and John Hatchard and Muna Ndulo, *Readings in Criminal Law and Criminology in Zambia*, James Currey, 1994, at 87 ff.

corruption scandals,[44] established a Directorate on Corruption and Economic Crime.[45] As in Zambia, the Director and Deputy Director are appointed by and answerable to the President, though the Act says nothing about tenure, qualifications or conditions of service.[46] Moreover, as in Zambia, the Directorate has a variety of functions (educational, preventive and investigative) and extensive powers of investigation and arrest.[47] It does not, however, have any independent power to bring a prosecution; if it appears that an offence has been committed under the Act, the Directorate must refer the matter to the Attorney-General.[48] At the time there was no ombudsman in Botswana and it was therefore surprising that the Directorate had not been made responsible for investigating complaints of maladministration generally; on the other hand, it has been criticized for being unaccountable and, in the last analysis, unnecessary, in that it largely duplicates the work of the police.[49]

The Leadership Code is yet another instrument that has been introduced extensively throughout Commonwealth Africa to ensure that high standards in public life are not only observed but seen to be observed by "leaders" (broadly defined). Such codes set out certain rules of conduct designed to prevent conflicts of interest arising and generally to promote transparency in government. The code is either enshrined in the Constitution (such as in Ghana) or contained in a separate statute (such as in the Zambian Corrupt Practices Act), and suspected breaches of the code are subject to investigation by the ombudsman or, as in Tanzania, by a Leadership Code Enforcement Commission. However, Leadership Codes and schemes for the declaration of assets and so on have a poor track record in Africa. Avoidance is easy and enforcement is lax.[50] Thus although the 1979 Constitution of Nigeria required all public servants to declare their assets within six months, by the end of 1983 only the President and Vice-President had complied.[51] Similarly, the leadership code in Zambia seems (at least in the early years) hardly to have been implemented[52] and the scheme for the registration of interests in Botswana has become a "dead letter".[53] In the absence of effective enforcement, leadership codes remain mere statements of ideals and come to be viewed with increasing cynicism.

Conclusions

In this article I have been concerned with the principal *institutionalized* strategies that have been employed by African governments to combat corruption. No

[44] The reason for the Bill, as stated in the Memorandum, was: "Recent events have revealed that corruption and economic crime are increasing on a large scale especially involving the Public Service and other public institutions." For a discussion of some of these events see Kenneth Good, "Corruption and mismanagement in Botswana: a best-case example", (1994) 32, 3 *Journal of Modern African Studies* 499.

[45] S. 3.

[46] Ss. 3, 4 and 22.

[47] Ss. 6–15.

[48] S. 39.

[49] It has been argued that such a body could never be capable of confronting the type of elite corruption experienced in Botswana. See Good, op. cit., at 521.

[50] See Ernest Harsch, "Accumulators and democrats; challenging state corruption in Africa", (1993) 31, 1 *Journal of Modern African Studies* 31 at 45–46, where President Robert Mugabe is quoted as describing ZANU's leadership code in Zimbabwe as a "despicable piece of paper".

[51] See Williams, op. cit., at 110.

[52] See Lungu, op. cit.

[53] See Good, op. cit., at 517.

attempt has been made to provide an exhaustive catalogue of the many and various anti-corruption measures that have been tried. For example, no mention has been made of the number of commissions established *ad hoc*, either in the wake of some scandal (as recently in Botswana) or (more frequently) in the aftermath of a military coup (as recently in Sierra Leone) to investigate allegations of corruption. No mention has been made of the series of attempts made by military governments in Nigeria to "reform" the civil service, whether by the high-handed sacking of tens of thousands of civil servants or by waging moral campaigns (such as the 1983 "War against Indiscipline") or the more considered reforms of 1988.[54] It is obvious that governments have a range of anti-corruption methods at their disposal and may employ several such methods simultaneously. However, the two main legal institutions which are used to combat corruption in nearly all the countries under consideration are the criminal law and the ombudsman or anti-corruption commission, and it is on these that this article has concentrated.

In the 30 or more years that have elapsed since most of these countries attained political independence levels of corruption have risen significantly. In an attempt to do or at least to be seen to be doing something about the problem, governments have relied on law reform, on more law and tougher law. This survey has shown that a variety of steps has been taken to sharpen the deterrent effect of the criminal law. New offences have been created, presumptions of corruption adopted, severe penalties introduced and special courts established. During the same period the powers and duties of ombudsmen and other institutions concerned with standards of public administration have been progressively extended. Enjoying limited accountability, these bodies have been given increasingly broad powers of investigation, arrest and search; in some countries they have the power to institute prosecutions and in Uganda it is proposed that the ombudsman should have the power to determine cases involving corruption, with appeal lying to the Supreme Court. Many of these reforms raise serious human rights issues and it is interesting that the Botswana Corruption and Economic Crime Act, 1994, which contains little that is not to be found in legislation elsewhere in Commonwealth Africa, has received a less than enthusiastic reception. The question is not simply whether certain provisions of the Act are constitutional or not, but whether the Act is necessary at all. The conventional wisdom in much of Commonwealth Africa that increasing levels of corruption can only be tackled by the adoption of tougher penal policies and the extension of the powers and duties of ombudsmen is open to debate.[55]

The fact that corruption continues to be rife in Africa does not, of course, mean that the reforms discussed in this article have been totally ineffective. However, the evidence is not encouraging. In most countries not only are police forces seriously under-resourced in the face of crime rates that are rising generally, but they may be susceptible to corruption themselves. Given that much corruption is consensual and hence hard to detect and to prove, and given that its investigation may be politically sensitive, it would not be surprising if the police devoted their efforts elsewhere. Apart from the politically-motivated "show"

[54] See, generally, H. D. Dlakwa, "Salient features of the 1988 civil service reforms in Nigeria", (1992) 12 *Public Administration and Development* 297. He concludes that these reforms, while laudable enough in principle, are grafted on to the old corrupt social system and have therefore no more chance of being effective than earlier attempts.

[55] It is possible that some of the reforms actually increase opportunities for corruption, in that they establish bureaucratic bodies with limited accountability and broad discretionary powers.

trials that sometimes accompany a military coup, it is usually the "small fish" that are convicted on corruption charges. The others get away.[56]

If the "toughening" of the criminal law has not proved to be a quick-fix solution to the problem of corruption, neither has the broadening of the powers and duties of the ombudsman. Where, as is generally the case in Africa, the ombudsman is appointed by and is accountable solely to the President, there is inevitably the danger that it will be susceptible to executive pressure in deciding whether to pursue a particular investigation or not. There is, further, the danger that a cosy relationship may develop between the ombudsman and the executive which could protect the ombudsman itself from charges of maladministration and abuse of power. *Quis custodiet ipsos custodes?*[57]

The bureaucratization of the state and the concentration of state power in the executive arm of government are common features of the political systems of Commonwealth African states. Many leaders felt that a strong executive was necessary in order to bring about economic and social development. Legislatures have been tamed, the judiciary has been intimidated, the press has been controlled, the universities have been silenced, the unions have been emasculated and important sectors of the economy have been taken over by the state. In this sort of political culture corruption is likely to thrive and although the political leadership may genuinely, like Julius Nyerere (former President of Tanzania), wish to eradicate corruption, it will be reluctant to allow the creation of an independent focus of power, whether this be an ombudsman, an anti-corruption commission or a leadership code commission. However, events of the last few years give grounds for some hope that the strong executive state is beginning to weaken and that state power is being both reduced and redistributed among a variety of institutions. The democratization process has involved large numbers of people in political debate, one-party systems have been abandoned and genuine elections held. New foci of power have emerged as journalists, intellectuals and trade unionists have joined the debate. Most important will be the capacity of the population at large to protest against corruption, to be "sufficiently alert, self-confident and politically aware to ... 'blow the whistle', and determined enough to require effective redress".[58] In these circumstances, the incidence of corruption is likely to decline while the anti-corruption measures discussed in this article are likely to be more effective.

Unfortunately, people who have power are seldom willing to give it up voluntarily. Their motives may sometimes be honourable, but more often they are related to a determination to retain and to continue to enjoy the spoils of office. Where, as in Zaire, for example, there is "presidentialized corruption", where little distinction is made between public and private resources and where the power of the state is used primarily to enrich the President and his coterie, the chance of domestic pressures forcing him from office are slim, and although Commonwealth Africa does not contain a regime that is as endemically corrupt as Zaire, it has had and continues to have its own examples of presidentialized corruption and in these countries only international pressures will compel leaders

[56] See, e.g., Good, op. cit., at 519 ff and Kpundeh, op. cit., at 153.

[57] During the Nkrumah period in Ghana much corruption went undetected because of corruption within the Auditor-General's Department. See Herbert Werlin, "The roots of corruption—the Ghanaian enquiry", (1972) 10, 2 *Journal of Modern African Studies* 247, at 259.

[58] Michael Clarke (ed.), *Corruption: Causes, Consequences and Control*, New York, 1983, at xvi.

to take action.[59] Such pressures could come, for example, from donor-countries linking aid to good governance or from an organization like Transparency International whose international campaign against corruption is supported by a growing number of national chapters in Africa.[60] While law clearly does have a role to play in the fight against corruption, this article has indicated some of the constraints that limit its effectiveness in Commonwealth Africa.

[59] For an account of the measures that the international community might take against corrupt African governments, see Patrick McAuslan, "A new deal for Africa", unpublished paper presented at a conference on Corruption in Africa at the Institute of Commonwealth Studies, University of London, October 1994.

[60] Transparency International's international agenda is (i) to monitor development concerning corruption in international business transactions and to mobilize action to contain it, and (ii) to serve as an international solidarity movement, with national groups supporting each other, by sharing experience and strategies and, where necessary, by providing political support and encouragement. See Jeremy Pope, "Corruption in Africa: the role for Transparency International", paper presented to the African Leadership Forum, Corruption, Democracy and Human Rights in West Africa, at Cotonou, Republic of Benin, 19–24 September 1994.

[12]

Corruption and reform 1: 51–56 (1986)

Notes and comments

Canada's Task Force on Conflict of Interest

KENNETH M. GIBBONS
University of Winnipeg, Canada

The specific backdrop against which the Canadian federal government's Task Force on Conflict of Interests was developed consisted of a number of cases of dubious ethical character which occurred in the late 1970s and early 1980s. One of these cases, the so-called "Gillespie Affair", was cited explicitly in the report as a catalyst in its formation.[1] This incident concerned the efforts of a former Liberal government energy minister, Alastair Gillespie, to arrange a deal between the federal government and his own development company to launch a liquified coal project as part of an oil substitution program. Opposition parties and the media contended that Gillespie's involvement was a clear violation of conflict of interest guidelines then used by the government, particularly as these applied to what are generally known as post-employment restrictions.[2]

Despite the direct reference to the Gillespie Affair, it is unlikely that this one event was extraordinary enough in its own right to have single-handedly precipitated the creation of the Task Force. Rather, it is necessary to view this incident as part of a legion of minor events which, when seen in their cumulative light, created an increasingly cynical view of government in the media if not in public opinion. In one case a Liberal backbencher, who was also a former cabinet minister, was accused of being a paid lobbyist for a firm seeking government contracts, a charge which was upheld in the case of the businessman in question, but which was found unsubstantiated in the case of the Member of Parliament.[3] In other cases a Senator was convicted of influence-peddling and fined $25,000; certain officials of the government-owned airline Air Canada were accused of fraud in the acquisition of a new headquarters building; and a minister was accused of providing government flights for family members on 15 occasions. At the bureaucratic level, there

1. Canada. Task Force on Conflict of Interest. Ethical Conduct in the Public Sector. Ottawa: Canadian Government Publishing Centre, 1984, p. 6.

2. See, for example, PM promises energy deal probe, Winnipeg Free Press, February 17, 1983, p. 1; and Gillespie debate grips Commons, Winnipeg Free Press, February 18, 1983, p. 1.

3. This case also drew lenghty and widespread media coverage. See, for example, Mackasey's day in court, Maclean's, May 30, 1983, p. 15, for a brief summarization of the case.

52

were also lingering effects from the so-called Reisman-Grandy affair, in which ethical questions were raised about the lobbying activities of two former senior civil servants on behalf of Lockheed Aircraft Corporation.[4] The number and regularity of such accusations, justified or not, led a national political columnist to headline one articel, "The litany of Liberal sins".[5]

The choice of a task force as the instrument of policy advice is, especially in this situation, an interesting one. Canada's political heritage combines aspects of its formal British constitutional lineage with a variety of modifications from other sources. While some of these modifications are of European origin, such as the widespread use of the Ombudsman, the largest number of these are drawn from American experience. The reasons for this are, at the general level, obviously related to the physical and cultural proximity of the United States. However, at the specific level, there are certain attractions in using institutional arrangements having an American origin. In the case of task forces, the attraction rests upon the ways in which such bodies are unencumbered by parliamentary traditions which can make governments reluctant to use royal commissions.

Royal commissions, by tradition, are bodies of a temporary nature which consist of members who are neither politicians nor civil servants and traditionally headed by a member of the judiciary. While this relationship to the judiciary was based, in part, on the judiciary's independence from Parliament, it also reflected the nature of these early royal commissions in that they were largely "judicial" inquiries. In more recent times royal commissions have become more important for their policy advice role, hence the frequent choice of commissioners from non-judicial backgrounds. In either case, however, the commissioners are not drawn from the government itself, a limitation which does not apply to task forces. Indeed, the use of government personnel has been a great attraction to Canadian governments.

The Task Force on Conflict of Interest was headed by two Senators, and its staff was frequently seconded from other government agencies. On the other hand, the executive director of the Task Force was a lawyer from private practice who had extensive government experience. Thus the ability to mix public sector and private sector backgrounds on any task force could allow both critical policy analysis and, by including representatives of government in the body, an awareness of the practicalities of reform. Moreover, royal

4. Scrutinizing the Air Canada move, Maclean's, May 16, 1983, p. 17, Minister's family flies free, CBC says, Winnipeg Free Press, June 2, 1983, p. 4, The New Master of Trade, Maclean's, November 18, 1985, p. 15.

5. Allan Fotheringham, The Litany of Liberal Sins, Maclean's, April 25, 1983, p. 64. The "sins" in question did not relate solely to matters of ethical conduct such as conflict of interest, but extended to questions of bad policy judgement also.

commissions are sometimes criticized for offering policy advice for which they will not ultimately be responsible for executing. While the same might also be said of task forces, the presence of government personnel is thought to provide some sensitivity to the problem of policy administration which might otherwise be missing.

Other distinctions between task forces and the more traditional royal commissions can also be made. One is the lack of government control over the cost and duration of royal commissions, leading to the generalized complaint that royal commissions are too costly and time-consuming. Task forces are generally tightly controlled on both counts and, because they do not share the same traditional commitment to public hearings, these controls seem to work. What cannot be calculated in this trade-off is the value of public participation which, though not necessarily absent from task force deliberations, is generally more restricted than in royal commissions.

A final distinction between these two means of policy advice and investigation is that royal commissions are subject to a very strongly-defended tradition of public reports. The same cannot be said of task forces, whose reports are made public on the whim of the government of the day. This potential for secrecy is defended by the argument that governments can expect more frankness on the part of the task forces because they will not pull their punches to avoid causing embarrassment to the government which established it. Alternatively, it may be argued that task forces can have their reports covered up by governments which find the recommendations to be offensive. Selecting a royal commission then suggests a commitment to openness which is less common in Canada than in many other democratic societies. By the same token, however, the choice of the task force approach does not preclude the publishing of a report, as in the case of the task Force on Conflict of Interest and its report issued in May 1984 and entitled *Ethical Conduct in the Public Sector*.[6]

The performance of this task force underlines, however both their weaknesses and advantages. The choice of the task to investigate and advise on matters on ethical conduct seems to have been made with the intentions of including members with government experience, wording a lengthy or costly inquiry and ensuring a greater sensitivity to the problems of application. On the other hand, it may be felt that the publication of the reoprt meant its contents were sufficiently appealing to the government to

6. For a general overview of task forces and royal commissions in Canada, see V. Seymour Wilson, The Role of Royal Commissions and Task Forces, in G. Bruce Doern and V.S. Wilson (eds), The Structures of Public Policy-Making in Canada. Toronto: Macmillan, 1971, pp. 113–129. Also see Audrey Doerr, The Machinery of Government in Canada. Toronto: Methuen, 1981, pp. 149–152.

54

dissuade it from using its power to withhold publication of a report which would prove to be too embarrassing politically. Moreover, the choice of Senators Mitchell Sharp and Michael Starr to head the Task Force would lead one to believe that scathing attacks on past government practices were not to be expected. Indeed, both co-chairmen of the Task Force were former cabinet ministers, thus the potential for a report which was relatively gentle in its approach to ethical conduct in the public sector was noteworthy and eventually realized.

One particular area in which the report seemed to lack sufficient censoriousness was in matters relating to post-employment practises, where the sensitivities of the co-chairmen to the problems of persons moving between the public and private sectors appeared much too flexible. Indeed, the fear of restricting the flow of personnel between the two sectors of Canada's mixed economy would seem to reflect an unstated business class bias which simply assumes, without providing reasonable and "objective" substantation, that, firstly, the government needs more personnel with private sector experience and, secondly, stronger provisions for post-employment restrictions would seriously alter the free flow of such personnel. The first assumption is particularly critical in that it proffers the vision of a vast sea of policy-makers who believe, to paraphrase an American cliché, what's good for General Motors is good for Canada. This predilection of the task Force seems to have been strengthened rather than challenged by the report's sources which were weighed heavily toward senior civil servants, former ministers, crown corporation executives, various officials from the provinces and some American states, and legal research staff.[7] While there were also submissions from the private sector and individual citizens, most of the witnesses and requests for information were drawn from the former group. Academic sources are mentioned as having been consulted but they were few in number and rarely cited it the report. The result is that, at least for those issues relative to post-employment practices, the report does not give an impression of disinterested analysis. It is hardly surprising, given the balance and weight of its sources, that the Task Force recommends relatively soft "cooling-off" periods of six months for ministers and one-year for non-elected officials. Furthermore, given the ministerial backgrounds of Sharp and Starr, some senior civil servants, especially deputy ministers dismissed or shunted sideways by incoming governments, might wonder at and even resent the suggestion that they – unlike ministers, parliamentary secretaries and ministers' exempt staff – "have better control over their futures than ministers", and therefore should be subjected to the longer period.[8]

7. Task Force, op. cit., Appendix A.
8. Ibid., p. 229.

There are two other aspects of the report that are troubling in their implications. First, in a general sense, the report promotes too great a degree of secrecy. While there are reasons for being cautious about the publicizing of certain kinds of information relating to ethical conduct these should not apply to suggestions such as the provision of meaningful annual reports which summarize, both in narrative and statistical form, patterns of ethical conduct violations in the public sector as a while. There seems to be a sense of government by ''gentlemen's agreement' in the report, which implies that cases of ethical misconduct are very rare in the public sector. Yet little is said about verifying that implicit assumption by providing a system of annual reporting that would indicate the numbers and types of violations, unresolved cases and so on. Second, there is little specific discussion of sanctions beyond mere disclosure. While disclosure is a useful element of any sanction system in this area, it does not go far enough. Though it is clearly not the intention of the Task Force to limit sanctions to disclosure, the absence of any detailed analysis of the sanctions question leaves a large gap that requires filling.

On the positive side, the report has value beyond its utility as a temporary ethics consciousness-raiser. Much more than scholarly texts it provides detailed discussions of the mechanics of compliance relating to the various trust arrangements which allow individuals to free themselves from conflicts of interest (Chapter 6) and the development of an Office of Public Sector Ethics (Chapter 13). The former is usually discussed in rather vague terms, if at all, and the latter is a new departure based partly on American experience. Both chapters would be very useful teaching and policy guides for students and practitioners. Also serving this same interest, but lacking novelty, are the syntheses of material on the history of conflict of interest policy in Canada (Chapter 7) and on the comparative examination of approaches to conflict of interest in the provinces, other English-speaking democracies, the professions and business. Somewhere between the novelty of the earlier examples and the syntheses of the latter are chapters on judges and quasi-judicial bodies (16) and on crown corporations (17) which are condemned as rare glimpses at areas which are not frequently found as separate entities in studies of ethics. Given the widespread use of crown corporations in Canada, it is to be regretted that Chapter 17 was so terse.

The final appendix in the volume (Appendix E) presents a ''tentative draft'' bill which summarizes the report's recommendations not only on conflict of interest, but also on partisan activity and public comment. The latter two elements are covered in separate sections of the bill. Once again, if educational value is to be considered important, a comparison of the Task Force draft with the Mulroney government's new guidelines would be an excellent learning experience. In any event, the report's major weaknesses on post-employment restrictions, secrecy and sanctions – are repeated in the

56

proposed 14-page bill.

If, however, there is a positive element in the report which goes beyond educational value it is the proposal for the development of the Office of Public Sector Ethics. In this recommendation there is particular policy merit which stems from the realization that such an office, whatever failings it might or might not have, will ultimately raise the public awareness of the ethics question and assist in maintaining ethics on a relatively higher agenda priority than is now the case. It has long been evident that issues of ethical conduct have a sporadic impact on policy-makers and the public. With the advent of such an office, there is the potential for a long-term approach not only to awareness but also to policy-making and a move away from the long established pattern of ad-hoc decisions. Furthermore it may also serve to reduce the ability of offenders to claim that opponents seek only political advantage by their accusations if cases could in the future be handled by an independent public body. The proposed functions of administering ethics policy, providing information and guidelines, educating the public service and the public, investigating cases, waiving and possibly modifying requirements regarding specific applications, and issuing reports, will provide the foundation for a longer-term, consciousness-raising effort. There are problems with the proposal for an Office of Public Sector Ethics, most importantly in terms of a restricted ability to investigate – the Office would not be permitted to initiate investigations[9] and in terms of the secrecy of the Office's reports.[10] However, it may be assumed that such an institution may well develop its own personality, its own dynamic, for not only generating greater public and policy-maker awareness of the ethics issue but also greater urgency for minimizing conflicts of interest and related ethical problems. Further, the process of centralizing ethical issues in one body will tend to reduce the variations in commitment to ethical behaviour that seem to be present in the public service today and will help to provide a sense of continuity and clarity ot ethics policy. Indeed, the provinces might also be persuaded to follow suit with similar arrangements.

In the final analysis, the Task Force should be congratulated for following, at least in a general sense, an existing American institutional arrangement and modifying it appropriately to fit the Canadian parliamentary practice. But, by the same token and given criticisms previously noted, it is hoped that the Task Force co-chairmen were not appointed as the first Ethics Counsellors.

9. Ibid., p. E-6.
10. Ibid., p. 216.

Part IV
Civil Service

PUBLIC ADMINISTRATION AND DEVELOPMENT, VOL. 17, 487–509 (1997)

Cleaning up and invigorating the civil service

ROBERT KLITGAARD*

RAND Graduate School

SUMMARY

Reliable quantitative estimates are not available of: (1) the quality of civil service performance and changes therein as the result of development projects, or (2) the importance of civil service performance for various development outcomes. Nonetheless, anecdotal evidence indicates that in some countries government performance has indeed collapsed, with calamitous effects on development. Although poor government performance is theoretically overdetermined—there are many possible causes, which we cannot disentangle in practice—a plausible story can be told based on institutional economics, using such concepts as information, incentives, and credible commitment. This version of both problems and solutions is supported by examples of successful reforms. The article argues that "institutional adjustment' deserves more consideration as a basis for reforms. Two practical examples are discussed in some detail: improving incentives in the public sector and strategies to combat corruption.

Public Admin. Dev. Vol. **17**, 487–509 (1997).
No. of Figures: 2. No. of Tables: 3. No. of Refs: 51.

THE CHALLENGES

On September 28, 1996, the African Governors of the World Bank presented President James D. Wolfensohn with an alarming report.

> If there is one, most obvious lesson that can be drawn from the experience of the generation after independence in Africa, it is the crucial importance of establishing good governance ... (p. 2).
>
> The picture that emerges is even more troubling than what is generally believed. There are severe capacity constraints in literally all sectors in almost all the countries, characterized by a shortage of skilled staff [and] weak institutional environments which undermine the proper utilization

*Correspondence to: Robert Klitgaard, Dean and Ford Distinguished Professor of International Development and Security, The RAND Graduate School, P.O. Box 2138, Santa Monica, CA 90407 USA.

The author is grateful for the support and comments of Gerardo Sicat and the study group on civil service reform of the Operations Evaluation Department of the World Bank, and for the help of Anil Bhandari, Stephen Butters, Martha De Melo, Shiranthi Gnanaselvam and the Institutional and Social Policy Unit in the Africa Region of the World Bank, Arturo Israel, Tony Land, Patricia Langan, Barbara Nunberg, Manuel Penalver, Christophe Schwyzer, Mary Shirley, David Steedman, Mike Stevens, Devi Tewari, Jacques Tollie, and Clay Wescott. Rosa Dias helped with the econometric analysis. The usual caveat protecting these courteous people from further responsibility is, of course, in order.

> of existing capacity ... Almost every African country has witnessed a systematic regression of capacity in the last thirty years; the majority had better capacity at independence than they now posses ... (p. 5).
>
> In practically every country, the civil service was found to be too large in nonessential areas and in critical need of personnel in others. The civil service is also too politicized and lacking in professionalism. Even where skills are available, they are underutilized because of poor deployment, a weak institutional environment, lack of morale, or political interference in administration and the assignment of responsibilities ... (p. 6).
>
> Civil service remuneration is extremely low, and employment benefits (such as pension schemes, health facilities, and loan schemes), which used to make the civil service attractive, are no longer attainable in many countries. This has led to 'institutionalized corruption', laxity and general lack of discipline in the civil service (p. 6).

This remarkable erosion has occurred despite numerous efforts in civil service reform and 'capacity building'. Nunberg and Nellis (1995) reviewed many of the 90 World Bank lending operations from 1981 and 1991 in which civil service reform was a 'prominent feature'. 'The record suggests that reforms to date have been insufficiently ambitious in scope to bring about the degree of change that is needed. Meaningful change is going to require more forceful reforms' (Nunberg and Nellis, 1995, p. 42).

The African Governors laid part of the blame on the World Bank's own strategies.

> Consensus is building around the idea of a different kind of government and civil service—smaller and less expensive in the aggregate, but staffed by a highly motivated, capable, and competitively paid corps of public servants. However, in the past, adjustment programs have tended to emphasize the first half of this agenda—fiscal restraint—while paying little attention to how best to reorient the civil service. This has contributed to a steady decline in real public sector wages, the undermining of capacity to deliver public services, and erosion in the credibility of public administration. Adjustment policy matrices, while specific in terms of wage bill limits and reductions in civil service employment, are usually vague, or even silent, on how to implement such restraints without further damage to morale and the effectiveness of the public service (pp. 25–26).

To the African Governors, a 'more of the same' approach is not acceptable.

> African governments must commit themselves to reforming and revitalizing their civil services, rebuilding them around the ideals of professionalism, meritocracy, accountability, and provision of quality services to citizens. Much has been said, written, and attempted in the past in this area, while results have been far from satisfactory. This suggests that governments must be willing to take bold and radical actions that require political courage. These may include drastic reductions in the size of the civil service so that governments can afford to pay competitive salaries to the civil servants who remain (p. 33).

These problems are especially severe in Africa, but variations of the same themes are found in many other developing and transitional countries (for example, Samad, 1993; Tantuico, 1994; Naím, 1995). '... [B]asic personnel management in many developing and transitional country administrations is in a state of collapse. Lacking suitable rewards and sanctions, civil servants are often unmotivated and demoralized ... Mechanisms of authority and often probity have broken down' (Nunberg, 1995, p. 1). But according to many evaluations, projects aimed at overcoming these weaknesses have not lived up to expectations. The World Bank's Operations Evaluation Department has made new efforts to gauge whether 'institutional development' objectives have been fulfilled. Among completed projects evaluated in 1994, 'only 44 per cent of the evaluated operations were expected to sustain their benefits throughout the operational phase that follows the completion of Bank loan disbursements. This proportion differed little from the average for 1989–94, though there was a noticeable drop in the share of operations judged clearly unlikely to sustain their benefits. Institutional development goals were substantially achieved in 39 per cent of the operations, better than the 30 per cent in the 1993 cohort and the average of 31 per cent for the last five years, but again a low figure' (World Bank, 1996).

What might explain these failures? How important are they for development? What new approaches might help?

WHAT ARE THE PROBLEMS WITH THE CIVIL SERVICE?

Different development activities emphasize different needs for civil service reform. In structural adjustment loans, civil service reforms are driven by macroeconomic concerns. The public sector wage bill is too large, given the country's macroeconomic situation. The solution is to reduce the wage bill, preferably through deep cuts in the number of civil servants, but when this proves politically impossible, through hiring freezes, modest retrenchments, and cuts in the real levels of already low salaries.

In sectoral projects, however, the problems of the civil service are differently envisaged. Evaluations of development projects ranging from infrastructure to education to agriculture cite the poor performance of the civil service as an impediment, yet as an issue beyond the sectoral project's purview. In particular, evaluations note that civil servants have poor incentives. The World Bank's Dunston M. Wai (1995, p. 25) summarizes:

> It is no secret that inadequate salaries direct public officials into unprofessional forms of behaviour. When senior jobs produce opportunities to collect bribes, to evade income-inhibiting restrictions on private trade, to win government contracts for one's family or associates, or to misappropriate public funds, incentives are created to do one's job in ways that are inconsistent with the public interest.
>
> Getting *incentives* 'correctly aligned' means employees must be persuaded that they actually will be able to do better for their families in the long run if they eschew nepotism, etc., and do their jobs effectively and in the public interest. This also means that setting salaries high

> enough to attract talented people is not enough; there must also be incentives to perform their jobs effectively and honestly.

'Without this added feature', namely better incentives, Wai concludes, 'capacity cannot be built ...'.

These problems are in tension. On the one hand, slashing the public sector wage bill does not tend to improve incentives. On the other hand, calling for stronger incentives seems unrealistic when the treasury is bare. 'The problem', notes Wescott (1993, p. 17), 'is that official receipts are insufficient to pay competitive salaries to government employees, and even so salary payments are major contributors to public deficits'. 'The civil services of many developing countries today are too large, too expensive, and too unproductive', concludes Lindauer (1994, p. 28). 'Governments in many developing countries', agrees Nunberg (1994, p. 120), 'are unable to manage and finance their civil services. These civil services are frequently too large, too expensive, and insufficiently productive; and civil servants, especially those in managerial positions, get few incentives and are poorly motivated'.

Another issue has recently gained salience, the formerly taboo subject of corruption. At the 1996 Annual Meetings of the International Monetary Fund and the World Bank, the leaders of both organizations made headlines by underscoring the need to fight corruption. The United Nations Development Programme, the InterAmerican Development Bank, the Asian Development Bank, and many bilateral donors have given 'good governance' a renewed emphasis. But it is not just international organizations that are pushing change. Leaders from Nicaragua to Pakistan successfully campaign on anti-corruption platforms. Around the world, citizens express disillusionment with government, with an emphasis on corruption and inefficiency (Nye, forthcoming). Issues of governance are assuming prominence on the development agenda.

HOW IMPORTANT IS CIVIL SERVICE PERFORMANCE?

But what are the links between such variables as the budget deficit, the size of the civil service, the real wages of civil servants, and the levels of corruption with the performance of government? And how much do various dimensions of government performance influence development outcomes, under what conditions?

Consider public sector wages. To assess their importance, ideally one would begin with a model of the size, structure, and remuneration in the public sector, and one would assess the contributions of various reforms after holding other variables constant. But existing models and data are insufficient. For example, no theoretical model exists to specify for a given country the appropriate number of public employees of various types and grades. In some countries it even proves difficult to estimate the number of public sector employees. Regarding pay levels, theory suggests a complicated problem indeed, including the steepness of the pay pyramid, the nature of the monitoring system, the nature of the private sector labour market, and other dimensions—to the extent that even for private companies experts admit that complete models of optimal personnel systems are far away (Lazear, 1995). In practice, it is hard to say what compensation levels are in many civil service systems, as there are many poorly documented changes in non-wage benefits, which can sometimes turn out to be worth more than the salary.

More broadly, it is notoriously difficult to estimate how well a government, or an agency, is functioning. One finds no studies with reliable figures, much less comparisons over time or across countries, on such indicators as:

- *Measures within public agencies.* Turnover rate. Vacancy rate. Salaries (conditioned on various things such as age, education, rank; relative to the private sector and to the cost of living in the capital city; over time). Benefits (housing, pensions, perks, travel, participation in seminars or task forces). Wages and benefits relative to foreign advisers (and perhaps weighted by the number or proportion of same).
- *Outcome measures.* Delivery of services (cost/unit, delays, quality). Corruption of various kinds. Client satisfaction. Health indicators, educational indicators, etc. Economic growth. Political stability. Economic volatility. Measures of rights.

Even if such information were available, an assessment of the impact of a civil service reform would have to take account of intervening variables that affect the functioning of public institutions and development outcomes. These variables often change over time. Without taking them into account, it would be perilous statistically to estimate how much reform efforts have improved performance or eroded it.

As an illustration, consider econometric studies of the effects of corruption. Brave souls have undertaken quantitative studies of corruption's importance to investment and economic growth, but estimation encounters grave statistical difficulties (data quality, inferences from small populations and atheoretical models, omitted variables). For what they are worth, the studies show that the level of corruption in a country, as estimated by international investment advisory services, has a strong negative impact on investment and growth, even after controlling statistically for a host of other variables (Mauro, 1995; Knack and Keefer, 1996; for a broader review of 'governance' for economic growth, see Fedderke and Klitgaard, forthcoming).

For this article new econometric investigations were undertaken on the relationships schematically summarized in Figure 1. The outcome variable was the economic rate of return (ERR) of World Bank projects, and the predictors included such variables as the size of the civil service, the pay level of the civil service relative

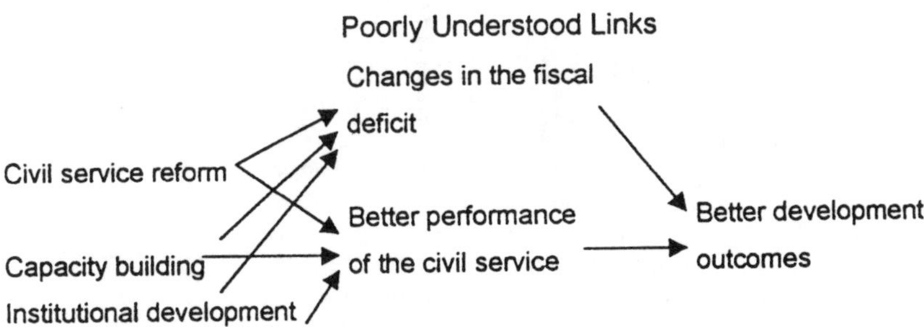

Figure 1. Relationships between variables and performance of government

to the private sector, the budget deficit, measures of macroeconomic distortions such as the black market premium on the exchange rate, estimates of 'corruption' and 'bureaucratic delay' and others. One lesson of these statistical explorations is how little of the variance in project performance (less than 10 per cent) can be explained with country-level predictors. Nonetheless, with many other variables held constant, countries with lower civil service wages have significantly and importantly worse performance on World Bank projects, although there are many exceptions. A typical result would have a one standard deviation increase in the ratio of manufacturing to central government wages lead to a 2 percentage point reduction in the ERR, other things equal. However, I am not happy with the assumption that the other supposedly independent variables (such as GDP growth) are exogenous, and for this and other statistical reasons I believe such results should be treated with great caution (see also Fedderke and Klitgaard, forthcoming).

Figure 2 shows the economic rate of return against the ratio of manufacturing wages to public sector wages. The simple correlation is $= -0.125$, significant at the 0.01 level ($N=407$ projects). The few projects with ERR >50 were omitted as outliers.

For a variety of reasons, then, cross-country statistical studies are limited in their ability to answer our questions. Theory provides some guidance. For example, regarding corruption, relatively simple economic models show that when government agencies suffer from systematic corruption and inefficiency, most citizens lose, even though corrupt politicians, businesses, and officials may gain (Rose-Ackerman, 1978; Klitgaard, 1988; Bardhan, 1996; Tirole, 1996). Regarding the collapse in pay scales in some countries, economists have developed models wherein 'rational' governments will pay civil servants' wages below their private sector alternative ('capitulation wages') and allow civil servants to make what they can through corruption (Besley and McLaren, 1993). Other lines of reasoning conclude that once societies develop corrupt equilibria, it is difficult even for willing

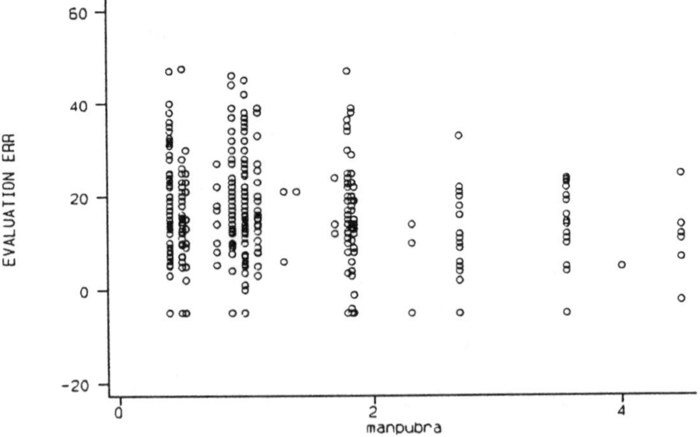

Figure 2. The economic rate of return on World Bank projects and the country's ratio of manufacturing wages to public sector wages

politicians to engineer change—see for example, Manion (1996) and Tirole (1996). These analyses underscore the importance of credible commitments to better monitoring and incentives. Yet case studies suggest that such credibility is precisely what many developing countries lack—see, for example, World Bank 1995 on the incredibility of promised incentive reforms in public enterprises, and Levy and Spiller 1996 on problems of commitment in government regulation.

These ideas are suggestive, but even enthusiasts would admit that available models capture only the coarsest features of real settings. Thus, for theoretical reasons, as well as because of the unavailability of reliable empirical estimates, it is difficult to say what kinds of corruption or inefficiencies in government are associated with what kinds and levels of development outcomes.

And yet. It is nonetheless remarkable the extent to which many project evaluations and synthetic studies, as well as judgments such as those by the African Governors, agree that bad goverance cripples development. For example, case studies describe devastating consequences when corruption undermines the justice system, undercuts property rights and contracts, and distorts the policies of governments (Klitgaard, 1988; Pope, 1996; Johnston, 1997). More broadly, evaluations of development projects show that 'institutional development' in the public sector is correlated with 'project success' (Israel, 1987; Rondinelli, 1989; Berg, 1993; World Bank, 1994; Schacter, 1995).

Unfortunately, such institutional development is not generally the outcome of civil service reforms or capacity-building projects. Why not?

WHY HAVE CIVIL SERVICE REFORMS DISAPPOINTED?

It is difficult to distinguish among the possible causes and to determine their appropriate weights. One view, not written down much but certainly heard in developing countries, is that low levels of human capital are responsible for organizational failure. (Many private-sector organizations in these countries are awful, too.) But why would governments be performing less well over time, despite increases in standard measures of human capital? Another view is that aspects of some cultures militate against Weberian bureaucracies—for example, hierarchy, kinship and tribal networks, the importance of leisure and celebration, an emphasis on consensus, or a preference for equality that cuts against effective incentives. A third idea is that civil servants work because they identify themselves with their countries, with revolutionary aims, with the *noblesse oblige* of a government elite. As these aims and identifications have broken down in many countries, so has performance.

Without passing judgment on these or other explanations, this article emphasizes institutional economics. This story emphasizes an informational environment that is constrained in many ways, a political environment that favours control over competition, a state that has taken on too many tasks and grown too large, and incentive systems that have failed to function. When information about government performance is constrained by monopoly restrictions and low capabilities for information transmission and processing, then feedback loops to government incentives at political and bureaucratic levels will not function well, with negative effects on performance. When governments expand their scope and exercise monopoly power and discretion over the allocation of goods and services, and when accountability is weak, corruption will grow. As incentives collapse, so will performance.

The argument is that most civil service reforms have adopted inappropriate strategies for such situations. International aid has emphasized the supply side of capacity building but overlooked demand. It has softened budget constraints, distorted local incentives through technical assistance, and not taken sufficient advantage of its ability to help governments commit to civil service reforms.

The importance of incentives

Consider the incentives facing civil servants in many poor countries. In Latin America real wages in the public sector have fallen 30–40 per cent since the early 1980s (three times more than wages in the private sector) (Naím, 1995). Even more dramatic numbers emerge from Africa and some of the former communist countries. In 1983 real wage rates for 'highly skilled' members of the civil service were 11 per cent of what they were in the mid-1970s in Ghana, 5 per cent in Uganda, 30 per cent in Nigeria, and 45 per cent in Zambia (Nunberg and Nellis, 1989). Another study found that in 1985 the base civil service salary rate at the 'highest grade' was 4 per cent of what it was in 1975 in Somalia, 16 per cent in Sierra Leone, 19 per cent in Tanzania, and 22 per cent in Nigeria (Robinson, 1990). All of the 15 countries surveyed by Robinson (1990) fell below 60 per cent of the figure a decade before. Another review found that government wage bills divided by the number of employees tended to show sharp reductions during the 1980s—40 per cent is not an uncommon rate of decline over the decade (Berg, 1993, p. 204). Using more recent data at the national level, Ul Haque and Sahay (1995) confirmed the plummeting salary levels in African countries. Further data are found in Lindauer's review (1994, p. 22) and in Klitgaard (1991, ch. 7). Although perks and non-wage benefits for government employees tended to rise to compensate partly for this decline, 'government salary levels at the beginning of the 1990s were so low that many civil servants reviewed them as inadequate to meet customary needs' (Berg, 1993, pp. 204, 207).

Under such conditions, it is not surprising that so many 'capacity building' projects discover that as soon as public servants are trained to higher skill levels, they depart to the private sector. Nor is it surprising that key technical posts go unfilled. With such poor incentives, many projects report underperformance due to an inability to get and motivate competent local staff.

The levels of salaries are only part of the story. Incentives are also weak in the sense that often good performance is not rewarded and bad performance is not punished. The 'tournaments' that reward achievement through promotions to higher rank become almost meaningless as salaries become more compressed (Lazear, 1995). For example, by the late 1980s in Ghana the average pay for 'highly responsible jobs at the upper levels of the civil service was only two to three times as high as average pay in the lower skill categories' (Berg, 1993, p. 207).

These problems have long been noted by the designers and evaluators of development projects, yet few reforms have adequately dealt with incentives for performance. Sometimes project papers posit that economic growth plus improved tax collection plus a public employment freeze will allow public sector wages to recover. Tanzania was one of the few countries actually to analyse this proposition. The result: 'it would take more than thirty-five years to restore public service pay to the real level enjoyed by the civil servants in the mid-1970s ... In short, when public employment has grown two to three times as fast as revenues for a decade or longer, government wage bills cannot be expected to grow back into balance by revenue growth alone' (Stevens, 1994, p. 76).

Civil service reforms have not been bold enough to improve incentives meaningfully, and they have usually been silent about corruption. This may explain their lack of success.

Supporting evidence for this explanation

This line of reasoning has been broadly applied to areas such as infrastructure projects (Ostrom *et al.* 1993), credit programmes, extension and the meagre results of efforts to build evaluative capacity. In each case, if one asks whether government officials have the incentives to carry forth the programmes as designed (and whether information is available to which incentives can be tied), the answer is usually no. And in some cases when incentive reforms have been tried, such as in some public enterprise reforms, a careful reading shows that the incentives were not credible to employees and were small in any case—no surprise, then, that they failed (World Bank, 1995).

Below we shall see that performance-based incentives are not appropriate for all situations. However, even in very poor countries there are cases where improved incentives and information have led to better performance. A few quick examples may dispel a tendency simply to dismiss the idea.

In Uganda 'it was agreed that two overriding objectives would inform the civil service reform process: the payment of a minimum living wage and the introduction of result-oriented management, both intended to lead to improved public service delivery' (Langseth, 1995, p. 4). Although the Ugandan reform effort is far from complete—in particular, the incentive objectives have not yet been met—there has been considerable progress. Tax collection, for example, has increased markedly. Part of the success stems from incentive payments to civil servants. Mookherjee (1997) describes other successful cases of performance inducements in revenue agencies.

The Gambian port authority apparently successfully implemented incentive pay. In the mid-1980s Ghana used food incentives for the attainment of agreed-upon performance targets in ports and railways, and performance improved significantly (Klitgaard, 1991).

In Equatorial Guinea in the late 1980s, my colleagues and I found that agricultural extension agents were poorly paid and frustrated by a lack of resources and knowledge. Working with them, we developed an experiment where the extension agents helped define measurable indicators of their performance, including the results farmers were obtaining. Incentives were linked to those indicators. The extension agents hit their targets and received bonuses, and indicators of agricultural production rose (Klitgaard, 1990).

In another difficult African country, a World Bank project providing agricultural technical assistance was successful in part because it provided 'performance bonuses' to 50 staff members. According to an independent evaluation, 'By the third year of project implementation, the Government assumed 100 per cent of the funding of the bonuses, which by then were applied to 260 staff.' The project evaluators noted that these bonuses were project-specific and therefore 'cannot serve as more than a temporary solution to the broader more generalized problems of inadequate remuneration of civil servants'. The project did not have the mandate to 'tackle the main problem of inadequate remuneration directly'. Nonetheless, tying bonuses to achievement galvanized staff of the Ministry of Agriculture and Rural Development. (This independent evaluation and the next cannot be referenced for reasons of confidentiality.)

In a World Bank-funded water supply and sanitation project in another African setting, performance incentives contributed to a successful project. 'Very low salaries in the civil service have contributed to a low working morale because of the need for individuals to earn additional income on the side ... The situation has improved markedly since project completion, as higher revenues have enabled NWSC to pay substantial performance allowances to its staff'.

Indonesia's successful rural credit programme shows that incentive reforms matter. By creating in effect local profit centres and rewarding bank officers based on how many loans they made and how many were repaid, local banks became profitable, and credit expanded rapidly (Snodgrass and Patten, 1989; Yaron, 1992).

In Bolivia when Ronald MacLean-Abaroa became mayor in 1985, he encountered an institution full of theft, bribery, extortion and nepotism. He engineered a series of reforms based on principles of institutional economics, which dramatically raised revenues, investment, and public satisfaction—and significantly cut corruption (Klitgaard *et al.* forthcoming).

These brief examples hardly make an airtight case. No one would suggest that non-economic factors are unimportant. But it is worth considering how more emphasis on incentives might be built into civil service reforms and institution-building efforts. The next two sections suggest new approaches to old problems. How can government incentive systems be improved? What can be done about corruption?

INCENTIVE EXPERIMENTS IN THE CIVIL SERVICE

Civil service reforms often work with assumptions that guarantee disappointment, given the conditions that prevail in many developing countries. Often reform is conceptualized as a system-wide assessment of each job and the reform of pay and perquisites in every compartment of the civil service. When civil service reforms and institutional development projects do address poor performance, they adopt a supply-side strategy, or a strategy of *more*: more training, computers, administrative records, controls, technical assistance, materials, jeeps and studies.

In short, these reforms do not redress the collapsed, distorted incentives facing public officials and politicians. What alternative approach might be tried? Table 1 provides an outline. Two key ideas are *experimentation with performance-based incentives* coupled with system-wide investments in better *information about outcomes*.

'Efficient organizational design', writes Paul Milgrom, 'seeks to do what the system of prices and property rights does in the neoclassical conception: to channel the self-interested behavior of individuals away from purely redistributive activities and into well-coordinated, socially productive ones' (Milgrom, 1988, pp. 58–9). Both structural adjustment and what might be called 'institutional adjustment' (Klitgaard, 1991, 1995) involve changes in the rules of the game, a new enabling environment, so that incentives can be improved. Both emphasize individual and team responsibility as opposed to command and control. Both focus on satisfying the legitimate demands of clients and citizens. Both emphasize information and incentives. But there are important differences, two of which should guide civil service reforms: experiments and process.

Experiments

The idea of designing an incentive master-plan for every part of the civil service at once is misguided. Performance measures are so problematic that we are well-advised to begin with experiments and then learn from experience. How might such experiments be designed? Some recent economics literature provides helpful insights. Milgrom and Roberts (1992) derive the optimal degree to which pay should be linked to performance (see also Lazear, 1995; Klitgaard, 1995, 1997). Table 2 summarizes four key dimensions. Notice that many agencies in developing countries would tend

Table 1. Two approaches to incentives in civil service reform

	Prevalent approach	Proposed approach
Objectives	Across-the-board pay increases; horizontal equity across jobs	Selective pay increases that eventually spread; incentives linked to performance targets
Means	Small cuts in personnel based on long-term studies carried out by foreign TA. Learning by planning. Supply-side strategies	Experiments where civil servants and clients help define measures of success. User charges. Learning by doing. Try to combine with deep cuts in personnel. Demand-side strategies
Constraints	Budgetary austerity; donor pressure to reduce wage bill	Overcome constraints by starting with revenue-raising and cost-saving experiments that can pay for themselves. Use aid to fund experiments
Facilitating conditions	Studies; technical assistance; political will to reduce the size of the public service	'Institutional adjustment', including better information, more client feedback, competition. Political will and bold help from donors

Table 2. Conditions favourable and unfavourable to incentives based on performance

Dimension	Favourable to incentives based on performance	Unfavourable to incentives based on performance
Marginal social benefits of more effort by agent	Additional efforts by public servants lead to big gains in effectiveness	Because of other constraints, additional efforts by public servants yield no gains in effectiveness
Agent's risk aversion	Employees are almost risk-neutral, perhaps because plentiful opportunities exist and they are already well-off	Employees are very risk averse, perhaps because poor
How accurately agent's effort can be measured	Effort and results are easy to measure	Effort and results are almost impossible to measure
Responsiveness of agent's effort to incentives	Effort is very responsive to incentives (for example, high discretion)	Effort is not responsive to incentives (for example, fixed-pace activity)

to fall in the right-hand column of the table, meaning that their environment is unfavourable to performance-based incentives.

There is a second discouraging observation. When performance pay is implemented, one can expect from both theory and experience that agents and principals may take dynamic steps that undermine incentives and information. consider agents first:

- Agents may shift their efforts toward those things easily measured at cost of those things not easily measured.
- Agents may engage in 'influence activities': distorting information, influencing those who evaluate the information, and not revealing useful private information.
- If relative rankings of agents are used, agents may avoid useful teamwork or even sabotage others.
- Agents may avoid job transfers or the learning of new skills, for fear of losing bonuses attached to existing arrangements and competencies.
- Agents may act collectively to transform performance bonuses into higher base pay.

Principals may also take steps that undermine the system:

- Ratchet effects: after instituting performance-based pay and generating greater results by agents, principals may try to move the goal posts, leaving agents worse off than before.
- Intermediate layers of the bureaucracy may themselves lack incentives to undertake performance appraisal.
- Intermediate layers of the hierarchy may collude with or extract rents from lower levels, undermining the system (and in extreme models leaving underlings no better off than before).

Such issues have been analysed in the literature, and the complexities of reality soon overwhelm available economic models. Without a host of special assumptions, even in theory we cannot pretend to 'compute' the optimal incentive scheme (Laffont and Tirole, 1993).

Performance-based incentives are not a panacea. Sometimes, the environment may be such that they will not by themselves lead to improvements. But it is also true that under the same conditions, bureaucracies exhibiting very low pay, weak links between careers and performance, and corruption are unlikely to be improved by the usual approaches to civil service reform. This suggests that the underlying conditions are what deserve systematic attention.

Here enter once more the analogy to structural adjustment. Price reforms by themselves will not liberalize an economy with thin, monopolistic markets, poor information, poor property rights and contract enforcement, and corruption. Under such conditions, the creation of fair and efficient markets requires 'adjusting' many of these underlying conditions.

So, too, for performance-linked incentives. The categories of Table 2 provide a starting point for considering how to improve the underlying conditions on which their success depends (Klitgaard, 1997). Reform efforts should consider ways to:

1. Strengthen the links between employees' efforts and agency's value-added—for example, by defining key tasks, inviting employee participation in the definition of objectives, training, and team-based analyses of performance.
2. Reduce the risk aversion of employees—for example, through experiments that can be reversed if they turn out badly, employee self-selection into performance-pay programmes, and credible commitments backed by international organizations.
3. Improve performance measures—for example, through systematic client surveys, peer reviews, benchmarking, detailed studies of performance samples, ratings by superiors, and other techniques. Statistically take into account intervening variables where possible.
4. Reduce the costs to employees of additional effort—for example, through training and better equipment.

It is unlikely that such reforms can take place simultaneously throughout the entire civil service. They should begin in ministries and activities with favourable underlying conditions. Experiments—working with civil servants and the public to design pilot efforts with performance-based incentives that are transparent and evaluated after a year or two—have many advantages. Risks are reduced and trust is enhanced. Civil servants together rediscover agency missions, define key tasks, work through alternative ways to measure results, and contemplate ways to raise funds to pay for incentives (documented cost savings, fees for service, and so forth).

Process

Compared with structural adjustment, institutional adjustment is slower, involves more participation by employees and clients, and varies more according to the conditions in different agencies and countries. It is wise to involve employees and clients in the design of performance measures and incentive schemes, and in the evaluation of performance-pay experiments. The dynamics and political economy considerations of incentive reforms—such as the danger of manipulation and influence activities, and the threat of ratchet effects later denying employees the benefits of their improved performance—can in many cases only be mitigated through a transparent process that builds trust, creates objective measures, and enables credible commitments. International agencies can help ensure transparency, objectivity, and the credibility of commitments.

'Systematic client surveys' have been used in parts of India, Nicaragua, Uganda, and Indonesia (among other places), with encouraging results. By involving citizens in the assessment of performance, one creates new information on results—thereby contributing to an environment more able to support incentive experiments.

Experiments with performance-based incentives promise a break with past civil service reforms that have underemphasized both performance measures and incentives. Experiments can pay for themselves through revenues generated (tax bureaux, customs agencies) or costs saved (public works, procurement). The experiments should begin in agencies where performance is relatively easy to measure. Once the principle is established that civil servants and civil society can be involved in a process of reform, further experimentation and spread may follow.

PREVENTING CORRUPTION

It has been unusual for civil service reforms to mention 'corruption'. Until recently, the subject was off-limits. As with many problems that are regretted but not discussed, analysis suffered, and it is fair to say that countries and donors have lacked a strategy for reducing corruption.

Corruption is a term of many meanings. At the broadest level, corruption is the misuse of office for unofficial ends. The catalogue of corrupt acts includes bribery, extortion, influence-peddling, nepotism, fraud, speed money, embezzlement, and more. Although we tend to think of corruption as a sin of government, of course it also exists in the private sector, NGOs, and international organizations. Indeed, the private sector is involved in most government corruption.

Different varieties of corruption are not equally harmful. Corruption that undercuts the rules of the game—for example, the justice system or property rights or banking and credit—devastates economic and political development. Corruption that allows polluters to foul rivers or hospitals to extort patients can be environmentally and socially corrosive. In comparison, some speed money for public services and mild corruption in campaign financing are less damaging.

Of course the extent of corruption matters, too. Most systems can stand some corruption, and it is possible that truly awful systems can be improved by it. Though every country has corruption, the varieties and extent differ. When corruption becomes systematic and undermines the rules of the game, it cripples institutional performance.

Experience teaches us that broad social changes, as well as specific anti-corruption efforts, can make a difference. In the long run, more democracy, a more limited state, and freer markets will help. Privatization may also reduce corruption, but it is often a scant improvement to reinstall another monopoly that happens to be private. Metaphorically, corruption follows a formula: $C = M + D - A$. Corruption equals monopoly plus discretion minus accountability. Whether the activity is public, private, or non-profit, whether one is in Britain, Brazil, or Brunei, one will tend to find corruption when someone has monopoly power over a good or service, has the discretion to decide whether or not you receive it and how much you get, and is not accountable.

Another point is crucial for designing anti-corruption strategies. Corruption is a crime of calculation, not passion. True, there are saints who resist all temptations, and honest officials who resist most. But when the size of the bribe is large, the chance of being caught small, and the penalty if caught meagre, many officials will succumb.

Solutions, therefore, begin with better systems. Monopolies must be reduced and carefully regulated. Official discretion must be clarified. Accountability must be enhanced. The probability of being caught must increase, and the penalities for corruption (for both givers and takers) must rise.

Each of these headings introduces a vast topic. But notice that none immediately refers to what most of us think of first when corruption is mentioned—new laws, more controls, a change in mentality, an ethical revolution. Laws and controls prove insufficient when systems are not there to implement them. Moral awakenings do occur, but seldom by the design of our public leaders. If we cannot engineer incorruptible officials and citizens, we can nonetheless foster competition, change incentives, enhance accountability: in short, fix the systems that breed corruption.

The first step is *assessment*. What kinds of corruption exist, in which functions and agencies, to what degree, who is helped, who is hurt, and what are the conditions that contribute to the corruption?

Then comes the development of a *strategy* against corruption. A strategy focuses on corrupt systems, not (just) corrupt individuals. Instead of thinking about corruption in terms of an immoral individual breaking the law and violating a trust, one thinks about systems that are more and less susceptible to various illicit activities.

The third step is *implementation*. Tactics here demand great sensitivity to the local situation. Nonetheless, rules of thumb do exist (see Klitgaard, 1988; Klitgaard *et al.*, forthcoming).

Political will

What about political will? If the people on top in the public and private sectors are benefiting, can reforms have a chance of taking hold? It is true that with regard to corruption many governments have not done what they are supposed to have done. But in the decade ahead the paradigmatic problem may not be inducing governments to do something about corruption but figuring out what to do and how. Because of democratic reforms, new leaders dedicated to improving public administration are entering power. Many of them seek to improve customs and tax agencies, clean up campaign financing and elections, reduce bribery and intimidation in legal systems and the police, and, in general, create systems of information and incentives in the public sector that foster efficiency and reduce corruption.

Many leaders appreciate and decry the costs of systematic corruption. But they also recognize that a lone actor has little chance to make a difference—even perhaps a President—and they may be cognizant of personal and party benefits from a corrupt system. To generate political will, several almost psychological steps are necessary.

First, leaders must see that improvements are possible without political suicide. Here it can be particularly helpful to have examples from other countries and an analytical framework for dealing with corruption. For example, the World Bank's Economic Development Institute, in partnership with Transparency International and the Ford Foundation, have sponsored the publication of an anti-corruption sourcebook (Pope, 1996) and useful workshops.

Second, leaders must develop a strategy that recognizes that not everything can be done at once. One should undertake a kind of benefit-cost analysis, assessing those forms of corruption where the economic costs are the greatest (for example, corruption that distorts policies as opposed to who gets a specific contract) but also taking into account where it is easiest to make a difference. A campaign against corruption must build momentum and support; it must have a political strategy. For example, a good rule of thumb is that to be credible an anti-corruption campaign must have some tangible successes within six months. And the campaign might give early emphasis to types of corruption which, even if not economically crucial, the public perceives acutely (for instance, corruption in the issuing of drivers' licences or in the distribution of medicines in state hospitals).

Third, leaders need political insulation. International collaboration may help provide it, for example if a group of countries together admit a common problem and move to address it. A leader can then convey the message, 'Corruption is not just our country's problem, or my party's, or my administration's'. (More below on international contributions to the fight against corruption.)

All these steps, from preventive measures to political tactics, are part of what it means to have a strategy against corruption. Many pieces of a civil service reform can in principle enhance accountability and improve efficiency and therefore are useful in fighting corruption. But in fact too often civil service reforms have lacked a strategy for fighting corruption, in the senses just described.

How international agencies might help

International agencies face ever greater pressures not to work with countries perceived as corrupt. At the same time, more countries are seeking help in controlling bribery, extortion, kickbacks, fraud, and other forms of illicit behaviour. International organizations can assist in a variety of ways, ranging from the indirect and subtle to the direct and forceful. In this spirit, consider two interrelated proposals.

Regional diagnostic studies

Purpose. Galvanize systematic action by both the private and public sectors to reduce corruption in a region (for example, Latin America or francophone Africa).

Basic idea. Each country invites the *private* sector to carry out confidential diagnostic surveys of three or four areas prone to corruption, such as procurement, government contracting, health care and revenue agencies. The surveys ask business people to diagnose anonymously how possibly corrupt systems work in practice—where the weaknesses and abuses reside. The idea is to analyse systems rather than identify particular individuals. The goal is not academic research but an action-oriented diagnostic; a small sample of 40 business people is sufficient. When each country's study is complete, an international conference shares the results and considers remedial measures, including possible international cooperation.

Political benefits. That such a study is international makes it clear that corruption is not just a problem of country X, but an international problem needing international solutions. It also makes it clear that corruption is not just a problem of the government (or 'this' government); the private sector is part of the problem and part of the solution. Political leaders can attack corruption without opening themselves to attack.

An international contest for anti-corruption strategies

Purpose. Capture the imagination of people around the world via an international contest. Communicate the message that a country can have a strategy against corruption. (For an illustration of the beginnings of such a strategy for one African country, see Appendix 1.)

Basic idea. International aid should be allocated to countries willing to undertake reforms to address systematic corruption. Suppose an international agency creates a programme that promises seven years of special support to the three developing countries that propose the best national strategies against corruption. To kindle interest in this 'contest' the agency funds international and local workshops. Then country studies involving both the private sector and the government examine key areas such as revenue raising, procurement and public works, and the justice system. The focus is on the vulnerability of systems to corruption, rather than on particular individuals. The measures included in an anti-corruption strategy will depend on the context, but they will often include experiments with incentive reforms; mechanisms to enhance accountability, especially through the involvement of business and citizens; enhancing capabilities in investigation, prosecution, and judging; legal reforms in campaign finance, illicit enrichment, and regulatory and administrative law; deregulation; and administrative reforms that designate an anti-corruption focal point and simultaneously facilitate inter-agency coordination.

Then, interested countries would prepare their national strategies against corruption. The three best strategies—perhaps one each from Africa, Asia, and Latin America—would be supported by special funds from the agency and perhaps other sponsors.

Political advantages. A competition would motivate countries to show they are serious about corruption. In preparing for the competition they would be assisted in learning (including from each other) what a strategy against corruption might contain.

Such an initiative could also be politically helpful to an international agency in its efforts to show that it is taking corruption seriously. It would give the agency a chance to fit various development initiatives, including civil service reform and institutional development, into a new framework with high political salience.

CONCLUSIONS

Civil service reform and, more generally, the improvement of the functioning of the public sector are especially important where institutions have grown 'sick'—where salaries have plummeted, where information about performance is scant and unreliable, where corruption has become widespread. One response is to cut back the size of the state and limit government's role. Some tasks can be allocated to the private sector or to NGOs. But inevitably there are important functions of government—management of the economy, some regulation of the private sector, most aspects of the justice system—which remain in government hands and indeed must be run even more competently when the state's role is circumscribed and more space is given to the private sector. In these domains, many governments perform poorly, and as a result economic growth and social justice are constrained. Better performance means more competent people in better working conditions with better information and management systems. But training, investments in working conditions and information technology, and reorganizations will only lead to brain drain or frustration if incentives and corruption are not addressed.

Past efforts have had a disappointing impact on the performance of the civil service, in part because they addressed a different problem or were constrained in their vision and means. The problem some reforms addressed was the budget deficit, in particular the size of the civil service payroll. As part of economic reform programmes, it was essential to reduce the deficit, and therefore to cut the payroll. This meant rethinking what the state did, but also reductions in force. Pay increases would only be possible in the long run, and they would be small. As part of civil service reforms, training and technical assistance would improve the state's functioning, but the main thrust was macroeconomic.

'Capacity building' and 'institutional development' have tended to focus on the supply side: training, equipment, studies, technical assistance, and so forth. Because they have not had much effect on incentives and have addressed corruption only indirectly, in difficult environments these efforts have tended to fail. Once trained, many key civil servants have left for the private sector. Projects providing new studies and systems and laws have seen them ignored or undermined by corruption.

These strategies, especially cutting the public payroll, may have been necessary in their time, and indeed may still be necessary. In many countries public employment was allowed to grow far beyond the means of citizens to afford it. For macroeconomic reasons, as well as the efficient allocation of tasks between state and market, there was a need to cut back on the civil service. But it is also fair to say that these efforts did not solve many of the problems that now appear on the front burner of public discussions, electoral campaigns, and international conferences: how to control corruption and more generally make the state a more effective and responsive partner in dealing with the public's problems. The reforms did not adequately address incentives, information, corruption and commitment.

If civil service reform can be given a different face—challenging civil servants to earn a good living if performance targets are reached, and simultaneously cracking down on corruption and abuse—it is plausible that both popular and civil service resistance to reform could be reduced. Moreover, such positive steps toward good governance may appeal to the international agencies' constituents, who increasingly demand symbolic and practical evidence that the agencies are 'doing something' about corruption and waste.

Today there are excellent opportunities to launch new strategies building on initiatives from the developing countries. For example, the recent entreaty by the African Governors of the World Bank (1996) could be used as an invitation for a number of bold cooperative endeavours, such as a worldwide competition for national anti-corruption strategies, regional diagnostics of corrupt systems, experiments that pit government agencies and NGOs against each other in the provision of some social services, and experiments with performance-based pay.

The development agenda is moving from policy reform to institutional reform. If the past fifteen years were notable for macroeconomic and macropolitical reforms, I believe that the next fifteen years will emphasize institutions:

- In the private sector, not just the declaration of 'competitive markets', but also the improvement of market institutions, especially vis-à-vis the poor.
- In public administration, not just less government and fewer employees, but also systems of information, incentives, and partnerships which encourage productivity, decentralization, and participation and which discourage rent-seeking and abuse.
- In democratic policies, not just multiparty elections, but also improvements in campaign financing, legislatures, and local governments.
- In legal systems, not just better laws and constitutions, but also systematic initiatives to improve the honesty and capacity of police, prosecutors, and judges.

To meet these challenges, the principles of institutional adjustment will:

- Enhance information and evaluation. Put it in the hands of clients, legislators, and those with official oversight (regulators, auditors, judges, etc.).
- Improve incentives. Link incentives to the attainment of objectives.
- Promote competition, partnerships, countervailing forces (including the institutions of civil society, the media, the legislature and the courts, and political parties), and procedures that allow different interests and voices to make a difference in policymaking and management.
- Systematically attack systematic corruption.
- Harden the budget constraint. One possibility is to reduce foreign assistance. Another is to make aid contingent on progress in institutional adjustment.

When it comes to civil service reform, institutional adjustment means going beyond supply-side strategies. When incentives break down as they have in many civil service systems in developing countries, the usual approaches to civil service reform and institutional development are likely not to work. We must go beyond the old capacity-building projects, the old supply-side strategies of more staff, more experts, more computers, more training, more rules and regulations. They are part of the answer, but they are incomplete.

Appendix 1. The beginnings of a strategy against corruption in an unnamed African country

Problem areas	Possible solutions
Lack of overall strategy and coordination	• Run workshops with participatory diagnosis, at the highest political level • Develop a strategy against corruption • Overcome the sense of impunity by 'frying a few big fish', especially those already identified; but don't get into a large-scale, retrospective witch hunt • Promulgate a simple code of conduct for public officials and private firms doing business with the State • Create an inter-agency committee to coordinate the anti-corruption effort, including following up individual cases but also prevention (perhaps committees at two levels, ministerial and technical) • Garner support and leverage by international donors • Invite Transparency International to set up a chapter and try to become one of TI's 'islands of integrity'
Reporting of evidence of corruption	• Create a public complaints commission • Resuscitate the Commission to Evaluate the Assets of Public Servants, based on existing law • Invite Transparency International to involve private sector in self-policing • Use systematic client surveys and other techniques • Involve the private sector in diagnostic studies of corrupt systems
Auditing and accounting	• Design experiments with performance targets and incentives • Selectively involve private auditors and accountants • No ability to undertake and implement preventive measures against corruption: need to broaden mandate and beef up capabilities • Run workshops with participatory diagnosis
Police investigation of corruption, fraud, and white-collar crime	• Design experiments with performance targets and incentives • Strengthen investigatory capabilities • Consider creating an anti-corruption unit that would be centred here
Prosecution	• A key problem is the perception of insufficient political support; 'frying a big fish' and otherwise attacking the sense of impunity will help • Run workshops with participatory diagnosis

Courts	• Implement the Commercial Court • Monitor speed and quality of performance and make information known to judges • Run workshops with participatory diagnosis
Revenue raising	• Create experiments with performance targets and incentives • Implement long-standing managerial recommendations in Customs and tax collection • Run workshops with participatory diagnosis (separately for Customs and Internal Revenue)

REFERENCES

African Governors of the World Bank (1996). *Partnership for Capacity Building in Africa: Strategy and Program of Action', a report to Mr James D. Wolfensohn, President of the World Bank Group*, September.

Bardhan, P. (1996). 'The economics of corruption in less developed countries: a review of issues', Working Paper No. C96-064, Berkeley: Center for International and Development Economics Research, University of California.

Berg, E. (1993). *Rethinking Technical Cooperation: Reforms for Capacity Building in Africa*, United Nations Development Programme, New York.

Besley, T. and McLaren, J. (1993). 'Taxes and bribery: the role of wage incentives', *The Economic Journal*, **103**, 416.

Fedderke, J. and Klitgaard, R. (forthcoming). 'Economic growth and social indicators: an exploratory analysis', *Economic Development and Cultural Change*.

Israel, A. (1987). *Institutional Development: Incentives to Performance*, The Johns Hopkins University Press, Baltimore.

Johnston, M. (1997). 'What can be done about entrenched corruption?', paper presented at the Annual Bank Conference on Development Economics, The World Bank, Washington, DC.

Klitgaard, R. (1988). *Controlling Corruption*, University of California Press, Berkeley and Los Angeles.

Klitgaard, R. (1990). *Tropical Gangsters*, Basic Books, New York.

Klitgaard, R. (1991). *Adjusting to Reality: Beyond 'State vs. Market' in Economic Development*, International Center for Economic Growth and ICS Press, San Francisco.

Klitgaard, R. (1995). 'Institutional adjustment and adjusting to institutions', Discussion Paper No. 303, The World Bank, Washington, DC.

Klitgaard, R. (1997). 'Information and incentives in institutional reform' in Clague, C. (ed), *Institutions and Economic Development*, Johns Hopkins University Press, Balitmore.

Klitgaard, R., *et al.* (forthcoming). *Corrupt Cities: A Practical Guide to Prevention and Reform.*

Knack, S. and Keefer, P. (1996). 'Institutions and economic performance: cross-country tests using alternative institutional measures', *Economics and Politics*, **7**, 207–227.

Laffont, J.-J. and Tirole, J. (1993). *A Theory of Incentives in Procurement and Regulation*, MIT Press, Cambridge.

Langseth, P. (1995). 'Civil service reform in Uganda: lessons learned', EDI Working Papers No. 95-05, Regulatory Reform and Private Enterprise Division. The World Bank, Washington, DC.

Lazear, Ed. (1995). *Personnel Economics* MIT Press, Cambridge.

Levy, B. and Spiller, P. T. (ed) (1996). *Regulations, Institutions, and Commitment: Comparative Studies of Telecommunications*, Cambridge University Press, Cambridge.

Lindauer, D. L. (1994). 'Government pay and employment policies and economic performance' in Lindauer D. L. and Nunberg, B.

Lindauer, D. L. and Nunberg, B. (1994). *Rehabilitating Government: Pay and Employment Reforms in Africa*, Regional and Sectoral Studies series, World Bank, Washington, DC.
Manion, M. (1996). 'Policy instruments and political context: transforming a culture of corruption in Hong Kong', paper presented at the 48th Annual Meeting of the Association for Asian Studies, Honolulu, Hawaii, April.
Mauro, P. (1995). 'Corruption and growth', *Quarterly Journal of Economics*, **109**, 681–711.
Milgrom, P. (1988). 'Efficient contracts, influence activities, and efficient organizational design', *Journal of Political Economy*, **6**, 1.
Milgrom, P. and Roberts, J. (1992). *Economics, Organization and Management*, Prentice-Hall, Englewood Cliffs.
Mookherjee, D. (1997). 'Incentive reforms in developing country bureaucracies: lessons from tax administration', paper presented at the Annual Bank Conference on Development Economics, World Bank, Washington, DC.
Naím, M. (1995). 'Latin America's journey to the market: from macroeconomic shocks to institutional therapy', occasional paper No. 62, International Center for Economic Growth and ICS Press, San Francisco.
Nunberg, B. (1994). 'Experience with civil service pay and employment reform: an overview', in Lindauer, D. L. and Nunberg, B.
Nunberg, B. (1995). 'Managing the civil service: reform lessons from advanced industrialized countries', Discussion Paper No. 204, World Bank, Washington, DC.
Nunberg, B. and Nellis, J. (1989). 'Civil service reform and the World Bank', World Bank, Washington, DC.
Nunberg, B. and Nellis, R. (1995). 'Civil service reform and the World Bank', Discussion Paper No. 161, World Bank, Washington, DC.
Nye, J. (ed) (forthcoming). *Why Americans Don't Trust Government*, Harvard University Press, Cambridge.
Ostrom, E., *et al.* (1993). *Institutional Incentives and Sustainable Development: Infrastructure Policies in Perspective*, Westview, Boulder.
Patten, R. H. and Rosengard, J. K. (1991). *Progress with Profits: The Development of Rural Banking in Indonesia*, a co-publication of the International Center for Economic Growth and Harvard Institute for International Development, ICS Press, San Francisco.
Pope, J. (ed) (1996). *National Integrity Systems. The TI Source Book*, Transparency International, Berlin.
Pritchett, L., *et al.* (1995). 'Governance and returns on investment', Policy Research Working Paper No. 1550, World Bank, Washington, DC.
Robinson, D. (1990). *Civil Service Pay in Africa*, International Labour Organisation, Geneva.
Rondinelli, D. (1989). *International Assistance for Institutional Development: Forty Years of Experience*, Research Triangle Institute, Research Triangle Park, NC.
Samad, A. (1993). *Governance, Economic Policy and Reform in Pakistan: Essays in Political Economy*, Vanguard Books, Lahore.
Schacter, M. (1995). 'Recent experience with institutional development lending in the Western Africa Department', The World Bank, Country Operations Division, Western Africa Department, Washington, DC.
Snodgrass, D. R. and Patten, R. H. (1989). 'Reform of rural credit in Indonesia: inducing bureaucracies to behave competitively', Development Discussion Paper No. 315, Harvard Institute for International Development, Cambridge, MA.
Stevens, M. (1994). 'Public expenditure and civil service reform in Tanzania' in Lindauer, D. L. and Nunberg, B.
Tantuico, F. S. Jr. (1994). *Performance and Accountability: Central Pillars of Democracy*, Fiscal Administration Foundation, Mandaluyong, The Phillipines.
Task Force on Evaluation Capacity Development (1994). 'Report of the Task Force on Evaluation Capacity Development', The World Bank, Washington, DC.
Tirole, J. (1996). 'A theory of collective reputations (with applications to the persistence of corruption and to firm quality)', *Review of Economic Studies*, **63**, 1.
Ul Haque, N. and Sahay, R. (1995). 'Do government wage cuts close budget deficits? A conceptual framework for developing countries and transition economies', International Monetary Fund, Washington, DC.

Wai, D. M. (1995). 'The essence of capacity building in Africa', James Smoot Coleman Memorial Papers Series, JSC African Studies Center, University of California, Los Angeles.
Wescott, C. (1993). 'Background paper: civil service reform in Africa', paper prepared for the Public Administration Working Group of the Special Programme for Africa, United Nations Development Programme, New York.
World Bank (1994). *Evaluation Results, 1992*, World Bank, Operations Evaluation Department, Washington, DC.
World Bank (1995). *Bureaucrats in Business: The Economics and Politics of Government Ownership*, Oxford University Press for the World Bank, New York.
World Bank (1996). *Annual Report* [From the Internet].
Yaron, J. (1992). 'Successful rural finance institutions', World Bank Discussion Paper No. 150, World Bank, Washington, DC.

[14]

The role of the public administration in fighting corruption

Frederick Stapenhurst and Petter Langseth
Economic Development Institute, The World Bank, Washington, DC, USA

Introduction

Structural adjustment focused attention on the need for more effective and efficient public service institutions and use of public resources. To date, public sector reform activities have largely focused on:

- capacity development where public institutions lack the requisite capacity and expertise to adjust to a market economy;
- introducing results-oriented management, emphasizing the importance of monitoring performance and measuring results; and
- public participation in the reform process, underscoring the need to tap into the valuable resources and creativity of civil society.

A significant issue, however, has been ignored until recently: the promotion of national integrity (see Figure 1). All of these issues – capacity development, results orientation, public participation, and the promotion of national integrity – need to be addressed holistically if the public sector, and hence the delivery of public services, is to be both efficient and effective. It is the thesis of this article that the promotion of national integrity is an integral part of this process since corruption inhibits the performance of public institutions and the optimal use of resources. As this paper explains, levels of national integrity need to be enhanced, and corruption reduced, if efforts to promote sustainable and equitable development are not to be undermined.

Corruption engenders wrong choices. It encourages competition in bribery, rather than in quality, and price of goods and services. Moreover, it distorts economic and social development, and nowhere with greater damage than in developing countries. Too often, corruption means that the world's poorest must pay for the corruption of their own officials and of companies from developed countries, although they are least able to afford its costs. Moreover, available evidence shows that, if corruption is not contained, it will grow. Once a pattern of successful bribes is institutionalized, corrupt officials have an

This paper develops some of the concepts in EDI's working paper "The Role of a National Integrity System in Fighting Corruption", The World Bank, 1997.

International Journal of Public Sector Management, Vol. 10 No. 5, 1997, pp. 311-330. © MCB University Press, 0951-3558

IJPSM
10,5

312

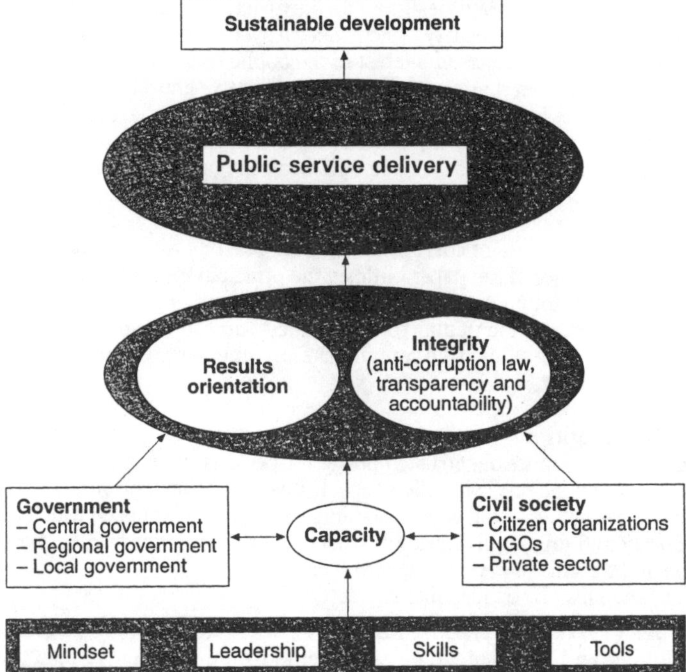

Figure 1.
Promotion of national integrity

incentive to demand larger bribes, engendering a culture of illegality that in turn breeds market inefficiency[1].

The argument is not simply a moral or cultural one. Forms of grand corruption need to be contained for practical reasons. Faced with the challenge of maintaining or improving standards of public service delivery, no country can afford the inefficiency that accompanies corruption. While apologists for corruption may argue that corruption can help grease the wheels of a slow-moving and over-regulated economy, evidence indicates that it increases the costs of goods and services, promotes unproductive investments and leads to a decline in the quality of public services[2,3].

Corruption depends on three factors: the overall level of resources at stake, the risk inherent in corrupt deals, and the relative bargaining power of the briber and the person being bribed[2]. As a single event, corruption takes place where there is a meeting of opportunity and inclination. The strategies to contain it, therefore, should address both elements. Opportunities can be minimized through systematic reform, and inclination reduced through effective enforcement and deterrent mechanisms.

Such mechanisms, when designed as part of a national effort to reduce corruption, comprise an integrity system. Such a system of checks and balances, designed to manage conflicts of interest in the public sector, limits situations in which conflicts of interest arise or which have a negative impact on the common good. This involves both prevention and penalty. An integrity system embodies a comprehensive view of reform, addressing corruption in the public sector through government processes (leadership codes, organizational change) and through civil society participation (the democratic process, private sector, media).

After offering some definitions and examining conceptual issues, this paper analyses the main costs of corruption, and the reasons for its existence and growth. The balance of the paper outlines the principal elements of a national integrity system founded on a holistic approach, bringing together various methods and actors. Particular focus is placed on the role of government processes and administrative reform; the involvement of civil society is considered elsewhere[4].

What is corruption?

Corruption is the abuse of entrusted power for personal gain or for the benefit of a group to which one owes allegiance. It involves behaviour on the part of officials in the public sector, whether politicians or civil servants, in which they improperly and unlawfully enrich themselves or those close to them by the misuse of the public power entrusted to them[5].

Corruption may be divided into two categories:

(1) *petty corruption* practised by public servants who may be grossly underpaid, and depend on small rents from the public to feed their families and pay school fees; and

(2) *grand corruption* of high public officials who make decisions involving large public contracts.

Corruption occurs in all countries, regardless of levels of social and economic development. It is most likely to occur where public and private sectors meet, and especially where public officials have a direct responsibility for the provision of a public service or the application of specific regulations or levees.

For corruption to take place, the following elements must be present: a public official, discretionary power, a misuse of that public power by the public official, and a benefit (whether in money or in kind) resulting to that official[6]. There are two general cases: the first where services or contracts are provided "according-to-rule"; the second where transactions are "against-the-rule". In the first situation, an official receives private gain illegally for doing something which he or she is ordinarily required to do by law. In the second situation, the bribe is paid to obtain services which the official is prohibited from providing (for example, granting contracts that would not otherwise be awarded)[7]. Each situation requires different solutions, as noted later in this article.

The significance and impact of corruption varies considerably across the world. In this regard, it is often suggested that corruption is part of the culture of many countries. Yet, the fact that people in a particular country may tolerate demands for small payments in return for official services (for example, the issuing of permits and licences) does not necessarily imply that they approve of it; it may simply be that they "perceive it as the most workable way of obtaining things they want or need ... [a] perception that may gradually be undermined by rising prices ... or dashed more abruptly if consumers come to believe that the underlying scarcities are artificially contrived or that more desirable alternative processes are really possible"[8].

In some cases, corruption may reflect practices introduced to a culture by external influences. Some Asian countries might be beset by corruption, yet certain historians have noted that this phenomenon originated, not with the locals, but with the colonizing Dutch East India company. The company's men "were underpaid and exposed to every temptation that was offered by the combination of a weak native organization, extraordinary opportunities in trade, and an almost complete absence of checks from home or in Java ... Officials became rich by stealing from the company"[9]. The same author writes, "Corruption was introduced into [the Philippines] during the Spanish colonial period". In Singapore after the Second World War, "the British Army officers in charge of local purchases had probably never before been exposed to the type of temptations ... whatever resistance there was in them melted away with mercurial speed"[9]. (See also[10].)

There are significant differences in perceptions and practices between various cultures. What some accept as reasonable and appropriate will differ widely. These differences, however, may have more to do with how business is conducted (through the giving of presents and of hospitality) than with attempts to buy favourable decisions. There is a clear distinction between reciprocity and reciprocities classified as bribes[11].

The costs of corruption

Surveys of business people indicate that the problem varies widely across countries and that, even within countries, some public agencies (for example, customs and tax collection) are more prone to corruption than others. Surveys also indicate that, where corruption is endemic, it imposes a disproportionately high cost on small businesses[2]. Most important, the heaviest cost is typically not in the bribes themselves but rather in the underlying economic distortions they trigger[2].

Once a pattern of successful pay-offs is institutionalized, corrupt officials have an incentive to raise the size of bribes demanded and to search for alternative ways to extract payments. Officials may refuse to serve clients unless a bribe is paid. They may design a major procurement project at too large a scale and with too much specialized equipment as a way of generating large bribes and keeping them hidden. They may accept payments to reveal secret information on tenders and privatization projects and to favour insiders. All of these examples risk imposing large costs on society.

Market misallocation and inefficiency

There are many costs associated with corruption. David Gould and Jose Amaro-Reyes[3] argue that corruption leads to economic inefficiency because of its impact on the allocation of funds, on production, and on consumption. Money illegally obtained is unlikely to be invested in the local economy since it is typically used in conspicuous consumption or is transferred to foreign bank accounts. Furthermore, bribery is an entry barrier, and firms that make pay-offs may expect not only to win the contract or the privatization auction, but to obtain future benefits in the form of subsidies, monopolize markets, and a laxness in enforcing regulatory procedures. Additionally, when payments are commonplace, privatized operations and concessions may not be allocated to the most efficient bidders. Projects may be too large and too numerous for bribe revenues to increase with the dollar volume of procurement. They may also be too technically complex, since corrupt payments are easier to hide in one-of-a-kind projects. Quality suffers if contractors bribe officials to allow them to ignore safety and procedural requirements.

The gains from corruption tend to draw labour away from productive, non-corrupt activities. Moreover, corruption affects recruitment and promotion patterns. The most efficient employees may not even be recruited and those receiving positions may be under-employed, or worse, incompetent. This situation is exacerbated if efficient potential employees are discouraged from competing for government positions. Employees' energies are directed towards less efficient corrupt activities and away from socially valuable ones. Consequently, corruption lowers the general welfare of the populace.

Recent econometric research suggests there is a negative association between high levels of corruption and economic growth[12]. Case study materials from around the world indicate that illegal pay-offs can increase the cost and lower the quality of public works projects, sometimes by as much as 30-50 per cent[13,14].

It is extremely difficult to calculate the economic damage produced by corruption owing to the secrecy surrounding illicit payments systems. Initial studies suggest that corruption-related costs to the world economy have reached significant levels, estimated at several billions of US dollars per year[15,16]. Other sources, however, suggest that these estimates are very conservative, and speculate that the "commissions" paid by arms dealers in one European country alone are at least US$2 billion a year[17].

In a corrupt environment, resources may be directed towards non-productive areas – the police, the armed forces and other organs of social control – as the élite move to protect themselves, their positions and their material wealth. Resources otherwise available for socio-economic development will be diverted into security expenditure. This, in turn, can cause the weakening of market institutions as rent-seeking, rather than investment, becomes the major objective of policy makers.

Why corruption flourishes

The sources of corruption are numerous and complex. Poverty, some say, is at the root of the problem; without poverty there would be no corruption. However, even if poverty is an underlying cause, it cannot be the only one. If poverty were the cause of corruption, then it would be hard to explain why industrialized countries are beset by scandals, very few of which involve anyone who might be categorized as poor.

Corrupt leaders unquestionably deepen the poverty of their people. Public expenditure decisions are fuelled by private gain and subsidized by bribes with scant regard for the good of the country or its people. Corruption can thus be seen as a cause of poverty, not only a result of it.

In the poorest countries – often those with corrupt élites – there is a manifest failure by government to pay a living wage to public servants. Frequently, the state is wholly unable to afford to do so. Thus, as is described in further detail below, inadequate remuneration for public officials is widely regarded as being a contributing cause of corruption, at least at the petty level, if not throughout the system[18].

Systemic bureaucratic corruption

Systemic corruption occurs where corruption has become an integral part of the system. Such corruption is the nemesis of anti-corruption reformers, and a new government may find itself impotent in reforming the very system it must rely on to govern.

This type of ingrained corruption tends to flourish in situations where public sector wages fall below a living wage. Several consequences can ensue:

(1) Public servants cease to place any value on the job they hold. Individuals may feel forced to augment their income from outside sources (second jobs, absenteeism, moonlighting).

(2) If the salary differentials from promotions are low, any salary increase would be unlikely to reflect adequately the work and responsibility that accompany such a promotion. This leads to low motivation for merit-based advancement.

(3) Unnecessary or extended foreign travel may be undertaken by government elites. Windfalls coming from foreign travel are seen as an unofficial (and tax-free) way of bringing income up to an acceptable level.

(4) "Ghosts" will appear on the state payroll. Persons who are deceased or retired will continue to be paid, and fictitious names will appear so that as much as a quarter of those on the public payroll are actually non-existent.

These four categories of behaviour can be regarded as petty corruption. No one is getting very rich; rather, it is a strategy for survival. These public servants are victims, as well as perpetuators, of a systemically corrupt government. The result of their behaviour, however, can be cumulative and costly.

Other activities typically classified under petty corruption include:

- revenue officials practising extortion by threatening to levy surcharges on tax payers or importers unless bribes are paid, in which case unjustifiably low tax assessments are made or goods are passed for importation without payment of any duty at all;
- law enforcement officials extorting money for their own benefit by threatening to impose penalties unless bribes are paid (which are frequently less than the penalty the offence would attract if it went to court);
- providers of public services (for example, drivers' licences, market stall permits, passport control) insisting on payments to speed up service or prevent delays; and
- superiors in the public service charging "rents" from their subordinates, requiring them to raise set sums each week or month and to pass these upwards.

More alarming are abuses of bureaucratic discretionary power, usually occurring in rigid systems with multiple sources of monopoly power. A planned economy, where many prices are below market-clearing levels, provides incentives for pay-offs as a way to allocate scarce goods and services. Transactions that would be legal trades in market economies are illegal pay-offs in these systems. In addition to selling goods and services to the highest bribe bidders, public servants can have incentives to create even more bottlenecks as a way of extracting higher pay-offs.

Officials, for example, might create delays or introduce costly conditions. The fundamental problem is not simply the existence of controlled prices set below the market-clearing level, but also the monopoly power of state officials who are not threatened with entry by more efficient and lower-priced competitors[19-21].

Other activities associated with bureaucratic discretionary power include:

- ministers "selling" their discretionary powers;
- officials taking percentages on government contracts, which are then often paid into foreign bank accounts[22];
- officials receiving excessive "hospitality" from government contractors and benefits in kind, such as scholarships for the education of children at foreign universities;
- officials contracting government business to themselves, either through front companies and "partners" or even openly to themselves as "consultants";
- political parties using the prospect of power, or its continuation, to levy large rents on, say, international businesses in return for government contracts (which may be dressed up as a "donation" to a designated "charity").

Private sector involvement

Private sector companies, be they domestic or international, feel the pressure to bribe. These firms provide two main justifications for their actions:

(1) In certain countries, it is often perceived to be very difficult for anyone to win a major government or parastatal contract without paying a large bribe.

(2) Although any form of bribery may be thought to be legally wrong, off-shore bribery is generally condoned "because everybody does it". Illegal payments made by companies in order to obtain foreign contracts are often tolerated, if not actively encouraged, in many industrialized countries because winning export orders creates employment opportunities.

Establishing a national integrity system

The ultimate goal of establishing a national integrity system is to make corruption a high-risk and low-return undertaking. As such, it is designed to prevent corruption from occurring in the first place and, because corruption tends to be a systemic problem, the primary emphasis is on changing systems, rather than blaming individuals.

An overview of some of the past successes and failures in combating corruption reveals the following problems:

- the limits of power at the top: an incoming administration may wish to tackle corruption effectively, but inherits a corrupt bureaucracy that impedes efforts for change;
- the absence of commitment at the top: without demonstrated commitment there is a lack of moral authority to enforce laws and to punish the corrupt, an absence of confidence among rule enforcers that enforcement actions against powerful people will be supported by the top leadership, and an absence of public belief that the leadership is serious[23];
- overly ambitious promises leading to unrealistic and unachievable expectations, and a loss of public confidence;
- reforms that are piecemeal and unco-ordinated: no one owns the reforms, and no one is committed to seeing that the reforms are implemented and kept up to date;
- reforms that rely too much on the law or too much on enforcement: this leads to repression, abuses of enforcement power and the emergence of further corruption;
- reforms that overlook those at the top and focus only on the "small fry": if the law is applied unfairly and unevenly, it soon ceases to have any legitimacy or deterrent effect;
- the failure to establish institutional mechanisms that will outlive the leaders of the reforms; and

- the failure of government to draw in the actors best able to assist it from civil society and the private sector.

Country strategies vary a great deal, but worldwide the policy responses to corruption typically involve one or more of the eight following "pillars"[24]:

(1) public sector anti-corruption strategies;

(2) "watchdog" agencies;

(3) public participation in democratic process;

(4) public awareness of the role of civil society;

(5) accountability of the judicial process;

(6) the media;

(7) the private sector and international business;

(8) international co-operation.

These pillars are interdependent. If one pillar weakens, an increased load is thrown on to the others. If several weaken, their load will tilt, so that the round ball of sustainable development rolls off. Establishing a national integrity system requires identifying gaps and opportunities for utilizing each of these pillars, as well as catalysing the work of the government, civil society and donors into a coherent framework of institutional strengthening. The remainder of this paper examines the first two of these pillars: public sector anti-corruption strategies and public watchdog agencies[4, 25] (see Figure 2).

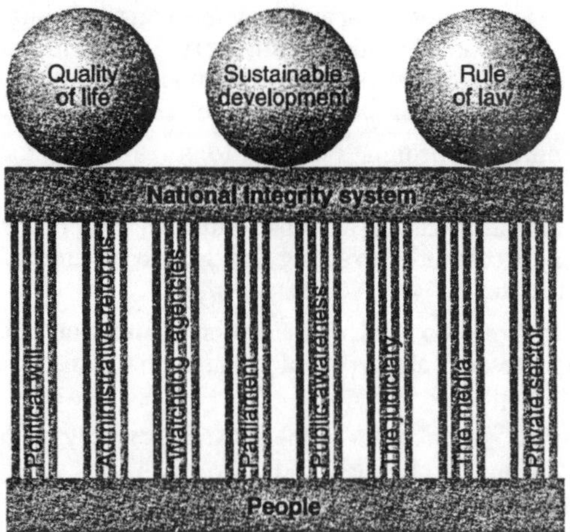

Note: *Anti-corruption agencies; Ombudsman; Auditor General

Figure 2. Eight pillars of a national integrity system

Public sector anti-corruption strategies

The responsibility for maintaining standards and minimizing corruption within the public service falls on the public service itself.

If properly conceived, regulations governing conflict of interest in the public service are directed towards erecting and maintaining an administrative and management system to protect the public decision-making process. Rather than detecting and punishing the wrongdoer after the fact, such a system reduces the risk of corruption occurring in the first place. In a well-managed administrative system, the incidence of corrupt practices would be minimized and, where they did occur, swift disciplinary action would be the norm[26]. Focus should be placed, therefore, on reforming public service procedures and systems to make them more accountable to the public interest.

In other words, in an environment of systemic corruption, significant public service reform will prove elusive if corruption is ignored. In fact, the result could be a reformed but more efficiently corrupt system. Corruption should be faced from the onset of the reform process and dealt with as an integral part of the process.

Ethical codes. Fighting corruption requires a clear ethical commitment by political leaders to combat corruption wherever it occurs. One promising extension of this principle is the establishment of a public sector ethical code in some countries. The code sets out the ethos which should guide those in managerial/leadership positions; it reminds them of their responsibilities to the public and requires declarations of assets and income. Yet, these codes have not met with great success, mainly because of lack of enforcement. An exception is Papua New Guinea, where the code is central to activities of, and enforced by, the ombudsman's office. Political figures at all levels have felt the weight of the ombudsman's authority and, in a number of cases, senior political careers have come to an abrupt end[27].

Establishing and maintaining ethical codes depends on a number of critical conditions:

- the ethical environment must be accepted by a broad segment of the public sector;
- deviations must be dealt with equally and consistently across the public sector;
- the ethical environment requires political commitment and leadership, as well as broad support by civil society.

Improved remuneration. The inadequacy of public sector salaries contributes greatly to corrupt activities at the level of need, of petty corruption. Ensuring living wages is crucial to public sector efficiency and effectiveness. Singapore has been conspicuously successful in this endeavour. An anti-corruption strategy was put into place in the country, along with gradual pay rises, fair salary structures, and strict penalties. Now, Singapore's public service salaries are among the highest in the world, and its productivity and effectiveness widely recognized. In common with other countries, there will be occasional Singaporean officials who succumb to the temptations of grand corruption, but the problem of corruption is fairly under control[28].

The Government of Uganda has undertaken the challenge of civil service reform with support from the World Bank and substantial bilateral assistance (for details, see [29]). In the course of this reform, all civil servants' benefits are being "monetarized". Public servants are now allowed to decide whether they wish to receive benefits or have them replaced with their monetary equivalent. It is hoped that this freedom to create discretionary spending with their benefits package will enhance the value they attach to their posts, decrease temptations to accept bribes, and lead to higher standards of service delivery to the public.

It is essential, of course, for public servants and the public at large to understand fully the rationale behind any major public sector pay rises, and for them to appreciate that, together with the benefit of higher pay, comes the responsibility of enhanced accountability. Raising pay with no increases in oversight could simply result in prospective job candidates paying for the privilege of obtaining a government job.

Administrative reform. Organizational change within the public service can help minimize the opportunities for corrupt practices. Such measures include:

- improving work methods and procedures to reduce delay;
- increasing the effectiveness of supervision to enable superior officers to check and control the work of their staff;
- carrying out surprise checks on the work of officers;
- instituting in-service training for civil servants at all levels, together with the formulation and dissemination of clearly-defined ethical guidelines and rules of conduct;
- developing internal financial management systems that ensure adequate and effective controls over the use of resources;
- providing channels for complaints to enable junior officials to complain about their superiors' corruption;
- rewarding achievement, recognizing good behaviour and acclaiming role models;
- making the necessary security arrangements to prevent unauthorized persons from having access to a department's premises; and
- reviewing the anti-corruption measures taken once in three to five years with the aim of introducing further improvements[28].

A discretionary element in decision making contains the potential for abuse. Eliminating discretionary decisions altogether, while resolving the dilemma, would be impossible and impractical. Instead, in those areas where discretion must be maintained, it would be more realistic to reduce the "monopoly power" of bureaucrats by providing rival sources of supply. For example, citizens may apply for a driver's licence at any motor vehicle office; businesses may obtain operating licenses from any of several officials or offices. Conversely, police forces could operate in overlapping jurisdictions so that no official can guarantee a lawbreaker he will not be arrested. Such reforms may not end unofficial charges, but they will at least drive the price down. If the level of bribes is low enough, even a modest effort at law enforcement may discourage corrupt officials[30].

In short, it is possible to limit the scope for abuse more systematically by keeping the areas for discretion narrowly defined and by providing clear, public guidelines for the exercise of this discretion.

Disclosure of income/assets/gifts. One of the key instruments for maintaining integrity in the public service is the periodic completion by all in positions of influence of forms stating their income, assets and liabilities. Disclosure of assets and income certainly will not be accurately completed by those taking bribes. However, it will force them to record their financial position and, in so doing, lay an important building block for any subsequent prosecution. However, today's evidence points to the inadequacy of any voluntary or informal system. Corruption can be reduced only if it is made a high-risk and a low-return undertaking[31].

To whom should disclosure be made? Disclosure may be made by politicians to the Speaker of Parliament or to the Ombudsman, or publicly to the people at large. The matters to be disclosed will differ from country to country. Clearly, this disclosure should cover all significant assets and liabilities, and a few countries insist that they include a copy of the latest income tax return. Some countries extend these requirements to close blood relations, but others will limit disclosure to the official and his or her spouse (although even this is contested, on the grounds that a spouse should be entitled to privacy from his/her partner). In any case, laws must embody what a society regards as fair and reasonable. If not, enforcement will be impossible, therefore serving to undermine the integrity system itself.

The problem does not end with disclosure. There is also the matter of gifts received by those in public office. Gifts can take many forms – a lunch, a ticket to a sports event, an expensive watch, shares in a company, a holiday abroad, perhaps school fees for a child. Some are acceptable; others are not. What is unacceptable is excessive hospitality, such as all-expenses paid holidays for a purchasing officer and spouse[32].

More difficult to classify are such things as lunches or festive presents; though, even here, the acceptance of seemingly trivial gifts and hospitality over time can lead to situations where an official has unwittingly become ensnared by the "donor". The dividing line usually rests at the point where the gift places the recipient under some obligation to the gift-giver. The acceptable limit will differ from one society to another, but it can be set in monetary terms so that gifts exceeding it must be declared.

Most governments have written rules clarifying what is and is not acceptable for a minister to accept as a personal benefit. For example, Malawi recently adopted the following guidelines:

> A "casual gift" means any conventional hospitality on a modest scale or an unsolicited gift of modest value offered to a person in recognition or appreciation of his services, or as a gesture of goodwill towards him, and includes any inexpensive seasonal gift offered to staff or associates by public and private bodies or private individuals on festive or other special occasions, which is not in any way connected with the performance of a person's official duty so as to constitute an offense under Part IV [which governs corrupt use of official powers][33].

Policy and programme rationalization. Public programmes riddled with corruption can sometimes be reformed through redesign and rationalization efforts[6,34]. The first option, however, is programme elimination. Many countries have rules and regulations that, even if honestly administered, serve no broad public purpose. They can and should be discontinued. Other programmes might serve a valid function, but are not effective where corruption is endemic.

Second, the programme's basic purpose could be retained, but redesigned to make it simpler and easier to monitor. For example, if economic efficiency is a programme goal, then reforms could introduce legal, market-based schemes, but simplification will not always reduce corruption if the rules are very rigid. Bureaucratic rigidity frequently breeds illicit behaviour on the part of both public servants and suppliers. Thus, simplicity will work only if it is not excessively arbitrary and if senior officials or independent enforcement officials aggressively pursue anti-corruption measures.

Finally, privatization of state-run enterprises and services can reduce the opportunities for corrupt practices, mainly because private sector accounting methods and competitive market pressures can reduce corruption and make corruption more difficult to hide. These benefits, however, must take into consideration the possible adverse effects of privatization (unemployment of public servants and risk of private sector monopolies).

Substantive policy reform, involving reform of the regulatory and tax systems, and the elimination of unnecessary programmes, is a difficult and time-consuming task. It is also an undertaking that must be geared to the needs and problems of a particular country. Attempts to identify sources of corruption in programmes and to reduce or eliminate them require detailed, country-specific knowledge.

Improved procurement procedures. Public service procurement procedures can be improved in the following ways:

- Procurement should be economical. It should result in the best quality of goods/services for the price paid, or the lowest price for the stipulated/ acceptable quality of goods/services; this does not necessarily mean procurement of the lowest priced or best quality goods available, but the best combination of these factors to meet the particular needs.
- Contract-award decisions should be fair and impartial. Public funds should not be used to provide favours; standards/specifications must be

non-discriminatory; suppliers/contractors should be selected on the basis of their qualifications and the merit of their offers; there should be equal treatment of all in terms of deadlines and confidentiality.

- The process should be transparent. Procurement requirements, rules and decision-making criteria should be readily accessible to all potential suppliers/contractors, preferably announced as part of the invitation to bid/make an offer; opening of bids should be public; and all decisions should be fully recorded.
- The procurement process should be efficient. The procurement rules should reflect the value and complexity of the items to be procured; procedures for small-value purchases should be simple and fast; as purchase values and complexity increase, more time and more complex rules are required to ensure that principles are observed; "decision making" for larger contracts may require committee and review process, but bureaucratic interventions should be kept to a minimum.
- Accountability is essential. Procedures should be systematic and dependable, and records should be maintained that can explain and justify all decisions and actions. Competence and integrity in procurement encourages suppliers and contractors to make their best offers, in turn leading to improved procurement performance. Purchasers that fail to meet high standards of accountability and fairness should be identified quickly as poor partners with which to do business.
- A sound and consistent framework is required to establish the basic principles and practices to be observed in public procurement. This can take many forms, but there is increasing awareness of the advantages of a unified Procurement Code setting out the fundamentals and supplemented by more detailed rules and regulations of the implementing agencies. A number of countries are consolidating existing laws that may have developed in haphazard fashion over many years, into such a code[35].

Watchdog agencies

A nation serious about fighting corruption may need to establish new public institutions to carry out anti-corruption functions. Anti-corruption agencies, the office of the ombudsman, and supreme audit institutions are reviewed below for the "watchdog" role they might assume.

Anti-corruption agencies. In recent years, governments have sought to bolster detection efforts by introducing independent anti-corruption agencies or commissions. Given that prevention is more efficient and effective than prosecution, a small investigative and monitoring unit with appropriate authority – perhaps reporting directly to the legislative body – may be much better placed to ensure that effective preventive steps are identified and taken. To operate successfully, an anti-corruption agency should possess the following:

- committed political backing at the highest levels of government;
- political and operational independence to investigate even the highest levels of government;
- adequate powers of access to documentation and to question witnesses; and
- leadership which is publicly perceived as being of the highest integrity[36].

From the outset, the shape and independence of a commission may well be determined by how the office holder is appointed or removed. If the appointing mechanism ensures consensus support for an appointee through parliament, rather than government, and an accountability mechanism exists outside government (for example, a parliamentary select committee on which all major parties are represented), the space for abuse for non-partisan activities can be minimized.

It is important that the agency has the power to freeze those assets it reasonably suspects may be held on behalf of people under investigation. It may be desirable for the agency to do so prior to getting a court order when speed is of the essence. Without this power, funds can simply be transferred electronically in a matter of minutes. This presupposes the need for a vital tool – a well thought-out and effective system for monitoring the assets, income, liabilities and lifestyles of decision makers and public service officials.

It is usual for an agency to have the power to seize and impound travel documents to prevent a person from fleeing the country, particularly as its power of arrest arises only when there is reasonable cause to believe that an offence has been committed. It is also customary for the agency to have the power to protect informers. In some cases, informers may be junior government officials who complain about the corrupt activities of their supervisors.

If an extravagant lifestyle is only corroborative evidence in support of a charge of actual corruption, it will not be of much use. Where a public servant in a position to profit personally is enjoying a lifestyle wholly out of line with his or her known income, it is thought in some countries not to be unreasonable for the individual to be required to provide an acceptable explanation for his or her wealth, as is the case, for example, in Hong Kong.

Ombudsman. The ombudsman constitutes an office that independently receives and investigates allegations of maladministration. The primary function of the ombudsman is to examine:

- a decision, process, recommendation, act of omission or commission which is contrary to law, rules or regulations, or is a departure from established practice or procedure; is perverse, arbitrary, unjust, biased, oppressive or discriminatory; or, involves the exercise of powers motivated by bribery, jobbery, favouritism, nepotism, and administrative excesses; and
- neglect, inattention, delay, incompetence, inefficiency and ineptitude in the administration or discharge of duties and responsibilities.

As a high-profile, constitutional institution, the office of ombudsman is potentially better able to resist improper pressure from the executive than are other bodies. It can perform an auditing function to stimulate information flows to reveal and contain the limits of corruption in government; the confidentiality of these procedures gives the office an added advantage in providing a shield against the possible intimidation of informants and complainants[37]. The office of the ombudsman also acts to prevent corruption and maladministration. It can recommend improvements to procedures and practices, and act as an incentive for public officials to keep their files in order at all times.

The office of the ombudsman should be responsible for its own budget and not be subordinate for funding to another, larger department. With a lack of resources to fulfil the mandate of the post, it is often only "the will of the ombudsman" that sustains the office-holder in the job. This undesirable situation should be addressed when reforming a country's integrity system.

Supreme audit institutions. Responsible internal financial management is crucial to national integrity, but supreme audit institutions are in many ways the linchpin of a country's integrity system. As the agency responsible for auditing government income and expenditure, the supreme audit institution acts as a watchdog over financial integrity and the credibility of reported information (as well as "performance" or "value-for-money" auditing). While supreme audit institutions can vary from country to country – for example, in Anglo-Saxon countries this institution is the auditor-general, while in many French-speaking countries it is the *cours de comptes* – the functions of the office are not dissimilar:

> The [Auditor General] audits the Appropriation Accounts on behalf of the House of Commons. He is the external auditor of Government, acting on behalf of the taxpayer, through Parliament, and it is on his investigations that Parliament has to rely for assurances about the accuracy and regularity of Government accounts[38].

The responsibilities of the office of the auditor-general also include ensuring the executive complies with the will of the legislature, as expressed through parliamentary appropriations; promotes efficiency and cost-effectiveness of government programmes; and prevents corruption through the development of financial and auditing procedures designed to reduce the incidence of corruption and increase the likelihood of its detection.

The supreme audit institution is of such significance that it warrants special provisions concerning appointment and removal procedures, and the protection of the office-holder's independence from the control of the governing party, politicians, and senior public servants. Ideally, the issues of selection, accountability and authority can be incorporated into a country's constitution.

To be effective, any external auditor must be devoid of accountability to, or susceptible to pressures from, the clients or institutions being audited. The office should not be a part of, or managed by, a government department it has to audit. To be so would create a systemic conflict of interest and to open the door to forms of "management". The supreme audit institution's clients are parliament (or comparable bodies) and its subjects are the public officials entrusted with public expenditure.

Unfortunately, this office can be particularly vulnerable to pressure from its clients and, in the majority of cases, the executive. To assure independence, the office should have relative freedom to manage the department's budget, and to hire and assign competent professional staff. The latter is important if it is to maintain its ability to match the capability of senior officials in government.

Conclusions: managing change for national integrity

The issue of corruption has come to centre stage. The economic consequences of pervasive corruption and recent trends towards democratization have increased the pressure on those in public office for accountability and transparency in the performance of their duties.

This article does not suggest there are easy solutions that can be applied in the fight against corruption; neither does it suggest any country has yet found an ideal model, or indeed that such a model exists. What this article does argue is that, while each country or region is unique in its own history and culture, its political system, and its stage of economic and social development, similarities in a national integrity system do exist and lessons learned are often transferable.

A national integrity system comprises a number of principle elements. Those reviewed in this article – public sector anti-corruption strategies and watchdog agencies – together with public awareness and participation, accountability of the courts, roles of the media and the private sector, and international co-operation can be taken as the pillars on which a national integrity system can be built and on which sustainable development depends.

Any one of these elements will have only limited impact in the fight against corruption. Ethical codes or new procurement rules, for example, will have little effect unless implemented and enforced by independent agencies; an ombudsman, supreme audit institutions, and anti-corruption agencies are examples of watchdog authorities that can perform these functions. (Similarly, anti-corruption strategies depend on the active support and vigilance of civil society and the media; a responsible media can be enlisted to raise public awareness of the harmful repercussions of corruption and of citizens' rights to expect ethical conduct from civil servants. The elements of a national integrity system are mutually reinforcing.)

While all of these elements do not need to be carried out or strengthened simultaneously, how a national integrity system is initiated and managed can determine the success or failure of reform efforts. It is vital for each country to define the most strategic elements for reform in order to maximize existing opportunities for positive change while providing critical support to weak areas that, left unattended, could undermine the reform programme. Moreover, a few successful and substantial measures will demonstrate to the public that government leaders and representatives are seriously fighting corruption.

The broader societal and political context within which reforms are undertaken will condition the effectiveness of a national integrity system. A democratic political framework creates different incentives for corruption than an authoritarian regime. Opportunities for bribery will vary in market and state-run economies.

In all countries, regardless of the stage of development, it is crucial that promotion of a national integrity system and the fight against corruption be as politically-inclusive and citizen-friendly as circumstances allow. This requires:

- a committed political leadership that shows its commitment by willingly submitting to a comprehensive monitoring of assets, incomes, liabilities and life-styles;
- participation by public service unions and other employees' groups;
- involvement of professional groups as well as community and religious leaders; and
- public involvement and participation in the reform process, with proposed changes debated widely to generate a sense of ownership among the public and reinforce the values embodied in reform.

Performance targets and monitoring systems are necessary to measure progress towards reduced corruption. To be effective, results-oriented public sector management must create incentive structures and an enabling environment to encourage achievement of public service reform targets and quality results. These results should be disseminated to the public at large; sharing information with civil society represents a significant step in ensuring transparency and accountability in government.

Notes and references

1. Rose-Ackerman, S., "Redesigning the State to fight corruption", *Viewpoint* (World Bank), No. 75, May 1996.
2. Rose-Ackerman, S., "The political economy of corruption: causes and consequences", *Viewpoint* (World Bank), No. 74, April 1996.
3. Gould, D.J. and Amaro-Reyes, J., "The effects of corruption on administrative performance: illustrations from developing countries", World Bank Working Paper No. 580, The World Bank, Washington, DC, 1983.
4. Stapenhurst, F., "Public participation in fighting corruption" (forthcoming).
5. Corruption in the private sector is outside the scope of this paper.
6. Klitgaard, R., "Adjusting to reality: beyond State versus market", in *Economic Development,* International Center for Economic Growth, San Francisco, CA, 1991.
7. Husted, B.W., "Honor among thieves", *BusinessEthics Quarterly*, Vol. 1 No. 1, 1994, pp. 17-27.
8. Johnston, M., "The political consequences of corruption: a reassessment", *Comparative Politics,* July 1986, pp. 467-8.
9. Quah, J.S.T., "Bureaucratic corruption in the ASEAN countries: a comparative analysis of their anti-corruption strategies", *Journal of Southeast Asian Studies,* Vol. 13 No. 1, 1982, pp. 153-77.
10. Siew-Wah, Y., "Some aspects of corruption", *National Youth Leadership Training Institute Journal,* January 1973, pp. 55-6.
11. Noonan, J.T., *Bribes,* University of California Press, Berkeley, CA, 1984. This study of bribes records that reciprocities classified as bribes were censured, among others, in the

ancient kingdoms of Egypt, Mesopotamia, and Palestine and, even more harshly, in Cicero's Rome.

12 Mauro, P., "Corruption and growth", *Quarterly Journal of Economics*, Vol. 109, 1995, pp. 681-712.

13. Wade, R., "The system of administrative and political corruption: canal irrigation in South India", *Journal of Development Studies*, Vol. 18, 1982, pp. 287-327.

14. Manzetti, L. and Drake, C., "Market reforms and corruption in Latin America: new means for old ways", *Review of International Political Economy* (forthcoming).

15. Rubin, S.J., "International aspects of the control of illicit payments", *Syracuse Journal of International Law and Governance*, Vol. 9, 1982, pp. 315-21.

16. See also the rough figures suggested by Rose-Ackerman, S. in "Proposal for research in the level and impact of corruption in international business", presented at the annual meeting of Transparency International in Milan, 27-28 March 1995.

17. *Le Monde*, 17 March 1995. In the same issue, *Le Monde* reported that revenue authorities do not question commissions of up to 15 per cent of the global total of a contract.

18. The conventional view – which virtually relates poverty to dishonesty – is attacked vehemently by a number of critics, who see this alleged linkage as being little short of a blanket defamation of the poor. "Can a person not be poor yet honest?", they ask. They point to the fact that many officials remain honest. General Obasanjo observes that: "Sharp practices have characterized the banking industry in Nigeria in recent years. Most bank officials were more than well paid, yet their fraudulent and corrupt practices have been outrageous. Contrast these with other officials, much less well paid, who have maintained their integrity and incorruptibility throughout". See "Letters to the Editor", *Financial Times*, 14 October 1994.

19. Computerization has generally and substantially decreased the numbers on the public service payroll – for example, in Uganda.

20. Shleifer, A. and Vishney, R., "Pervasive shortages under Socialism", *Rand Journal of Economics*, Vol. 23, 1992, pp. 237-46.

21. Montias, J.M., and Rose-Ackerman, S., "Corruption in a Soviet-type economy: theoretical considerations", in Rosenfielde, S. (Ed.), *Economic Welfare and the Economics of Soviet Socialism: Essays in Honor of Abram Bergson*, Cambridge University Press, Cambridge, 1981.

22. The various ways in which this is done, including public procurement rules laid down by international lending institutions, are described in Moody-Stuart, G., *Good Business Guide to Bribery*, Transparency International, Berlin, 1994.

23. The case of Tanzania, where President Mkapa has demonstrated a strong commitment to the fight against corruption, is illustrative.

24. This list reflects the consensus view of participants at World Bank (EDI)/Transparency International seminars and workshops designed to promote national integrity.

25. Langseth, P., Stapenhurst, F. and Pope, J., "The role of a national integrity system in fighting corruption", EDI Staff Working Paper, The World Bank, Washington, DC, 1997.

26. Botswana falls into this category. Although corruption has not been a serious problem, in Botswana, when it did occur, swift remedial action was taken against the culprits and institutional arrangements were tightened and repaired. See *TI Newsletter*, June 1995.

27. Pope, J. (Ed.), *The TI Source Book*, Transparency International, Berlin, 1996.

28. Quah, J., "Singapore's experience in curbing corruption", in Heidenheimer, A.J. (Ed.), *Public Corruption: A Source Book*, Transaction Publishers, New Brunswick, 1989.

29. Langseth, P., "Civil service reform: experience from Uganda", World Bank Discussion Paper, The World Bank, Washington, DC, 1995.

30. Rose-Ackerman, S., *Corruption: A Study in Political Economy*, New York Academic Press, New York, NY, 1978.

31. Atkinson, M. and Mancuso, M., "Edicts and etiquette: regulating conflict of interest in Congress and the House of Commons", *Corruption and Reform*, Vol. 7 No. 1, 1992, pp. 1-18.
32. Such holidays were provided, for example, to purchasing staff at Britain's Ministry of Defence in the early 1990s.
33. Corrupt Practices Act, Section 3.
34. Rose-Ackerman, S., "Reducing bribery in the public sector", in Trang, D.V. (Ed.), *Corruption and Democracy*, Institute for Constitutional and Legislative Policy, Budapest, 1994.
35. Several models are available as a starting point, including those of the GATT/World Trade Organization, the United Nations Committee on International Trade Law (UNCITRAL), the European Union, and a host of national codes.
36. Legislation can provide that the head of the agency be appointed either by the leaders of the governing and main opposition political parties, or in the same way as a superior court judge.
37. Hatchard, J., "The office of the Ombudsman", in *National Human Rights Institutions in the Commonwealth*, Commonwealth Secretariat, London, 1992.
38. House of Commons, "First Special Report from the Committee of Public Accounts, Session 1980-81", in *The Role of the Comptroller and Auditor-General, Vol. I, Report*, HMSO, London, 1981.

Part V
Agencies

[15]

PUBLIC ADMINISTRATION AND DEVELOPMENT, VOL. 15, 151–165 (1995)

Good government and sustainable anti-corruption strategies: a role for independent anti-corruption agencies?

ALAN DOIG

Liverpool John Moores University

SUMMARY

Aid donors are increasingly seeking to link assistance to sustainable reform, including the provision of a responsible and responsive political and legal framework, the improvement of recipient countries' social, health and educational prospects, and the promotion of economic development and liberalization. Much attention is given to the first of these because of the size and cost to the state and the perceived constraints it exercises on the longer-term changes to the economy and society; in general terms, *good government* is an essential precondition for *good governance* and economic development. Increasingly donors have focused on corruption, both as a core obstacle to the encouragement of good government, and on the steps taken to dealing with it as evidence of commitment and the will of recipient countries to their introduction. While the types of activity associated with corruption are readily identifiable, as are the means to attempt to deal with it, it is usually much more difficult to determine effective implementation, particularly with limited resources at a time when longer-term political and economic reforms are also being promoted. It is therefore especially important that, in relation to corruption and good government, a practicable, effective and sustainable means is available to deal with corruption from preventative, investigative and reform perspectives.

CORRUPTION, GOOD GOVERNMENT, GOOD GOVERNANCE AND ECONOMIC DEVELOPMENT: THE HYPOTHETICAL FRAMEWORK?

The prevalence of corruption, fraud, and other benefits extracted from their office and through their powers by politicians and public officials, and the exacerbation of such conduct in relation to the performance of the roles of the state or its dealings with the private sector, have been documented in the literature on politics, modernization and economic development (Huntington, 1968; Scott, 1972; Clapham, 1982; Clarke, 1983; Williams, 1987; Theobald, 1990). In December 1989 the Report of an Interregional Seminar on Corruption in Government ('Report'), organized by the United Nation's Department of Technical Cooperation for Development, noted that 'the problem of corruption in government has come to be recognized universally as a major concern in public management' (United Nations, 1989, p. 1).

Good government provides a responsive governmental and state administrative framework, facilitating good governance and, while good governance and economic development must be longer-term goals than good government, the former will not be achievable without attaining the latter. Good government in practice (British Council, 1993) would mean: political legitimacy for the government through democratic elections and transfer of power, political opposition and representative government;

Alan Doig is Professor of Public Services Management, Liverpool Business School, Liverpool John Moores University, 98 Mount Pleasant, Liverpool, L3 5UZ, UK.

CCC 0271–2075/95/020151–15

accountability through the provision of information, separation of powers, effective internal and external audit, low levels of corruption and nepotism; official competency such as having trained public servants, realistic policies and low defence expenditure; and human rights as indicated by freedom of religion and movement, impartial and accessible criminal justice systems, and the absence of arbitrary government power.

Defining corruption as 'the abuse of public power and authority for private and other group gains', the Report also makes it plain that, whatever the academic debates concerning the definition of corruption (Gardiner, 1993; Heidenheimer *et al.*, 1989), its manifestations are readily identifiable:

> 'as regards the various forms of corruption, it was noted that they range from acceptance of money or other rewards for awarding contracts, violations of procedures to advance personal interests, including kickbacks from development programmes or multinational corporations; pay-offs for legislative support; and the diversion of public resources for private use, to overlooking illegal activities or intervening in the justice process. Forms of corruption also include nepotism, common theft, overpricing, establishing non-existing projects, payroll padding, tax collection and tax assessment frauds.' (United Nations, 1989, p. 4)

Recognizing the 'strategic significance that good government plays in the development process', and that good government requires the 'highest standards of integrity, open-ness and transparency', the Report was also particularly concerned, not only with 'new forms and dimensions' of corruption, but also its pervasive effect on government performance, the use of public resources, the general morale in the public services and the legitimacy of the state and the law (United Nations, 1989, p. 1). Dealing with corruption is thus perceived as crucially important: 'corrupt activities of public officials can destroy the potential effectiveness of all types of governmental programmes, hinder development, and victimise individuals and groups' (United Nations, 1990, p. 4).

Such concern has been reflected more widely within the context of general societal development and the issue of good governance. Defined as the 'use of political authority and the exercise of control over society and the management of its resources for social and economic development', governance encompasses the 'nature of functioning of a state's institutional and structural arrangements, decision-making processes, policy formulation, implementation capacity, information flows, effectiveness of leadership, and the nature of the relationship between rules and the ruled' (Serageldin and Landell-Mills, 1991, p. 4). Governance, therefore, concerns not just the integrity, efficiency and economy of government but also its effectiveness in terms of the ends to which government organization and activity are directed.

No checklist of good government or good governance indicators would be either effective or workable with the pervasive and continuous use of money and influence to manipulate them; 'while corruption is manifest in every society, and in democratic as well as authoritarian regimes, systems corruption is a deadly sign that a society can no longer effectively manage its resources for public purposes ... Every resource is privatized—appropriated for private gain at the expense of those members of the public who are supposed to be served by governance' (Charlick, 1992–93, p. 177). The failure to sustain good government also has implications for the future of good governance. The World Bank argues that, 'for example, sophisticated systems of financial accounting and auditing may be established but the government may not absorb or use the results to good effect. A legal framework could be created, but arbitrariness or corruption in its implementation could undermine its value'. Furthermore, given 'the long-term nature of the task of developing appropriate institutions and the strengthening of budgetary decision-making and accountability, development management concerns must be integrated, where appropriate and relevant, into a long-term perspective of a country's development strategy and prospects' (World Bank, 1992, pp. 54–55).

Economic development is concerned with the fundamental restructuring of state activities and the promotion of macroeconomic policies that in turn would provide a favourable environment for private sector investment, initiative and growth. Pressure on governments to establish longer-term economic goals is reinforced by requirements for 'milestone' evidence of interim progress, with donor or lender pressure invariably focused on deregulation to allow trade liberalization and private sector investment, removing controls on inward investment and promoting capital market development, market-pricing of state-subsidised activities such as food prices, power, transport and rents, reducing state support of public sector employment or wages, reduction and reorganization of public sector enterprises, and privatization. Whatever the source or focus of external pressure for reform—and the European Union also supports the linking of aid to human rights, political pluralism and less corruption—there would appear to be a 'remarkable consensus' among aid donors and creditors 'on the need for democracy, less corruption, greater respect for human rights and "good governance" or "good government" ...' (Riley, 1992, p. 4). A synthesized hypothesis would recognize good government as the precondition for good governance and sustainable economic development. The building blocks of good government would include: freedom of information and association, political accountability, objective and efficient judiciary and bureaucratic accountability. Within the general approach to good government specific attention would be paid to corruption, and the circumstances in which it flourishes:

> 'in order to stimulate economic development, a stable legal environment and basic conditions of law and order must be present ... in order to monitor and promote good sound economic development, there must be a restructuring of ministries/departments, general management improvement, better pay, incentives and conditions of service, improved training, and higher professional standards. Along with administrative financial reforms with respect to procurement, tax and customs procedures, and auditing and expenditure control, corruption can be controlled.' (United Nations, 1989, p. 30)

A good government framework would develop into a good governance framework as the state's legitimacy with, and the participation of, the population became accepted as the former demonstrated: its responsiveness to the needs of the population and commitment to improving its welfare; its competence in providing law and order and delivering public service; its provision of an effective policy environment and its openhandedness in its conduct. Such a system of government would want to disengage itself from direct involvement in other areas, particularly economic production, to concentrate its efforts and abilities on societal priorities. Once the move to good governance is underway, the centrally controlled economy dismantled and the state domination of industrial activity wound down or privatized, so, the argument runs, liberal market principles can begin to promote general economic development, which, in turn, should encourage participation in the political processes—the establishment of good governance. The long-term economic and political objectives would thus complement each other to develop 'an educated population, with both political knowledge and the will to act, coupled with a modern industrial economy, a homogenous society, and a long-established set of democratic political values' (Riley, 1992, p. 18). Such conditions would produce an internally generated and sustainable tax base and a sizeable economic class outside the political system whose enthusiasm for participation and reform is less for self gain than for the promotion of the state to regulate and benefit society. Society's confidence in, and acceptance of, the legitimacy of the neutrality and responsiveness of the state would be confirmed by its efforts on behalf of the country as a whole, in turn reinforcing the state's political stability and financial viability (Theobald, 1993).

CORRUPTION AND GOOD GOVERNMENT: CONSTRAINTS ON CHANGE

Whatever the advantages and disadvantages of such a synthesized hypothesis, or the likelihood of effective donor agreement on coordination and strategy in relation to the various goals, the underlying themes are present in some form in the expression of donor intentions and expectations, particularly in terms of the increasing awareness of aid leverage and the history of wasted funds, failed opportunities and political opportunism on both sides. Moves to promote and encourage good government must, however, confront a number of issues where there is, on the one hand, no integrated donor approach and, on the other, sometimes conflict between and conflation of good government, good governance and economic development objectives. These may be further exacerbated by the existing political and economic conditions of countries to which they are directed: 'the generation of adjustment out of crisis and donor pressure means that changes in the role and performance of government have to be managed under difficult circumstances where there are political tensions, resistance from the losers in the population, demoralisation in the public sector and multiple changes occurring at the same time' (Batley, 1994, p. 492). Furthermore, with 'as yet little agreement among donors on the best means to achieve policy objectives', a lack of clarity and consensus 'may cause resentment and uncertainty among aid recipients ... may allow recipient governments to play donors off against one another ... efforts to promote participation and democratisation may also impede economic reform by generating unsustainable demands from newly mobilised interest groups' (Overseas Development Institute, 1992, p. 4). Seeking to encourage countries to undertake steps towards good government, therefore, may not be straightforward and will have to take account of the functions of the public sector, the complexities of economic development, and the roles of the existing political leaderships.

First, developing countries' state sectors are generally argued to be overstaffed and inefficient, weighed down by procedural and control functions, with senior levels penetrated by special interest economic groups and political influence, and employing large numbers of poorly paid and poorly trained officials with few opportunities for legitimate promotion and financial improvement. On the other hand, a large state sector has allowed governments to absorb manpower and give it 'a fundamental mechanism for gaining command of society. Broad groups in society had come to depend on the massive state enterprise ... The groups which were benefitting from the state enterprise became committed to the elite which was running it. In this sense the elite was creating the basis of its own indispensability' (Cooper, 1982, p. 23). Measures to tie politically significant parts of the population to the state by employment have also been part of many states' mistrust of market principles and an independent commercial sector as well as a preference for direction and control of the economy.

While state sectors' domination of GNP and the labour market is under donor pressure to reduce, rapid retrenchment of personnel and cuts in public expenditure may 'leave public enterprises short of funds for vital maintenance, equipment and supplies ... a balance must therefore be struck between improved efficiency and better management, on the one hand, and the requirements of proper maintenance and utilisation of existing capacity and enterprises, on the other' (Abbott, 1993, p. 23). Thus, while it may be generally accepted that

> 'governments have frequently and inappropriately overextended the public sector ... it would be counterproductive to push private sector expansion too fast and too far. Inefficiency in public monopolies does not necessarily create a case for private monopolies. The mix of state and private sector activity varies, and should vary, with the specifics of individual countries' economic, political and administrative structures. Indeed, many public sector enterprises were set up because the private sector offered inadequate services or no services at all. For external agencies to push national governments too far on this or other such issues, could risk the credibility of otherwise sound programmes.' (Commonwealth Secretariat, 1989, p. 59)

Furthermore, the assumption that economic development is hindered by the size and inefficiency of the state, as well as its existing prior claims on resources and funding, should be offset by weaknesses of the private sector infrastructure, as well as the private sector's relations with the state, and the time and means necessary to resolve both to a point where economic development is sustainable. For some countries 'the fact that both domestic and overseas private investment, especially in the poorer developing countries, have often fallen rather than risen in response to cuts in public development expenditure' has been compounded by 'a squeeze on public sector development spending'. In such circumstances, the demands of economic liberalization may be counterproductive: 'true structural adjustment requires the building up of the country's export sectors and associated infrastructure, which in the short term may require more rather than less state intervention' (Mosley *et al.*, 1991, pp. 303–4).

Second, the private sector may be in no position to take advantage of economic liberalization. Even if it is, it may not welcome the volatility of the export market, particularly in agricultural or extractive commodities, as much as it may not wish to take over state enterprises with their attendant problems of reducing workforces, reskilling those that remain and replacing old equipment. It may prefer instead to focus on high-value import or franchised brandname goods or services or exploit the existing regulatory, licence and quota systems to provide short-term gains and, in the longer term, create a commercial class with little interest in good government or economic liberalization. Such constraints and uncertainties will both discourage reinvestment and the accumulation of productive capital, as well as encourage corruption and other means of influence, to avoid or seek an accommodation with unreformed bureaucracies and the arbitrary use of political power.

In sub-Saharan Africa, overregulated and predatory state controls have encouraged entrepreneurial activities 'which bring quick and sizeable returns' intended to avoid penalization and provide the means to 'maximise the influence or the power position of the owners' (Dia, 1993, p. 23). In Latin America, the impact of fluctuations in the world prices of staple commodities 'discourages long-term planning and sound business practices' while 'changeability of laws and regulations, combined with prevalence of evasion, favour mushroom get-rich-quick firms, and handicap solid business. Absurdly high tariffs coupled with inability to prevent mass smuggling produce a situation in which practically every merchant is implicated in illegal deals while unrealistic social security laws compel most of the employers to evade them' (Andreski, 1970, pp. 112–13). In India, where urbanization and the decline of traditional values were 'replaced by those encouraging materialism, impersonalism, status seeking, greed for money, and an unwillingness to adhere to moral values', businessmen have long appreciated the role of bribery in capital accumulation to secure licences, avoid taxes and manipulate company accounts (Alatas, 1990, p. 71). In Kenya, economic uncertainty has prompted employers to invest profits in land and housing rather than expansion (Cockcroft, 1990, p. 160) while, in North Yemen, similar investments by Yemeni working abroad took place because of 'the scarcity of land for sale and the lack of opportunities for investment in the country's rural areas ...' (Sultan, 1993, pp. 381–2).

On the other hand, governmental policies that actively seek to promote economic development or a new economic class may themselves generate new problems. In Malaysia the New Economic Policy, designed to promote the role of indigenous Malays in the economy, was used by many for immediate personal gain, and underlined 'the limits to which private regarding behaviour can be tapped for the overall good of the system' as well as the political gamble between the creation of public 'goodwill' and loyalty and increased general propensity to rule breaking (Tharan, 1979, p. 62; Sivalingam, 1983, p. 429). In North Yemen, the government's measures to deal with its economic problems increased the opportunities for corruption, as officials and businessmen operated their own market mechanisms to circumvent import restrictions, price controls and the sale of food and other commodities by state companies to offset private sector exploitation (Sultan, 1993, p. 388). In Venezuela, 'government efforts to stimulate exports through tax incentives—rational in principle—foundered as a result of fraud' when 20 companies were discovered to have claimed back millions of dollars in tax credits on non-existent exports (Little, 1992, p. 55). More recently in China, the government's 'immediate concern over the stagnant economy and therefore the necessity of revitalizing society' as it 'relaxed its control over resource allocation, given great autonomy to local authorities to direct investment and decentralised its managerial power over enterprise' in the economic sector, led not only to the revival of old patron-client networks but also new patterns of corruption (Gong, 1993, pp. 317, 323–4).

Finally, political leaderships may be ambivalent toward reform and its sustainability. Anti-corruption rhetoric sentiments have been a routine feature of politics, invariably less as a means to longer-term reform than as a means to diffuse opposition to the incoming regime, placate external agencies and secure tenure on office (Gillespie and Okruhlik, 1991). The rhetoric in countries like Nigeria underlines their cosmetic nature: 'the preoccupation with panic measures and the creation of *ad hoc* panels and tribunals to replace non-functioning legal institutions for ensuring public accountability have not been particularly helpful' (Oluwu, 1987, p. 230) while 'political actors often talk of accountability and integrity but this by itself does not translate into a genuine commitment to detect and penalise unethical behaviour. Even when anti-corruption agencies are created, they are usually denied the resources needed to achieve their stated purpose ... in many cases the codes of ethics they are asked to enforce have no broad-based popular understanding or support' (Oluwu, 1992–93, p. 231). Mexican governments increasingly used anti-corruption rhetoric during the 1980s to deflect attention from its economic difficulties; 'indeed, many of the outcries and mobilisations against corruption of the 1980s were staged or triggered by the government in a well-orchestrated effort to use corruption symbolically to divert attention away from the economic difficulties and rejuvenate popular faith in the government' (Morris, 1991, p. 122). In Sierra Leone, new governments proposed commissions of inquiry, anti-corruption squads and tough legislation, but the legislation lacked any specific means to enforce it while the 'plans to establish an ongoing independent commission against corruption, to revise salaries, to provide incentives to public workers and to reorganise the civil service ... remain to be accomplished' (Kpundeh, 1992–93, p. 242). Repetitive rhetoric unmatched by sustainable reform will lead to indifference or cynicism within and outside the political system over the value and sustainability of reform: 'in too many cases, the problem is a non-problem in that far from attempting to improve the situation, governments, or at least major parts of them, are the problem. Anti-corruption campaigns then degenerate into political rhetoric designed more to appease foreign donors and international financial institutions than to address the major issues' (Williams, 1987, p. 125).

Where there is political reform—particularly in the short-term proliferation of the trappings of participation and decentralization to satisfy donor pressure—there is a danger that the widening of involvement, particularly among politicians and political activists, will lead to increased competition for patronage and party funding and thus extend and replicate the existing political environment: 'certain characteristics that are often thought of as increasing representativeness, such as multi-party systems that reflect a wide spectrum of interests and open list proportional representation, may paradoxically cause elected officials to be less responsive to the public interest' (Geddes, 1991, p. 389). Conversely, and equally likely, is an awareness among political leaderships and their client groups (and, on occasion, donors) that any expansion of political participation is to be resisted because of the implications for the stability of the state and the potential for social or political turbulence: 'the masses, once aroused, are unwilling to limit their demands to the reforms prescribed by the government. They will tend to broaden out their programme to include demands for far-reaching changes to domestic policies, such as greater political freedom, radical measures to reduce inequalities in income distribution and effective agrarian reform. In many Latin American countries ... the ruling elites seem well aware of the dangers they would face in the wake of wide-spread popular mobilisation. Indeed, almost all factions of Latin America's bourgeoisie appear to prefer to see their countries slip back into underdevelopment and dependency rather than run the risk of being forced into radical social and economic reforms' (Brandford and Kucinski, 1988, p. 134).

THE FOCUS OF GOOD GOVERNMENT: DEALING WITH CORRUPTION

Given the sensitivity of political conditionality, the rhetoric calling for the implementation of good government practices at the political or participatory level (and to a lesser extent at the legal and judicial levels) has tended to shift from an essential to a necessary to a preferable requirement, where its fulfilment may in any case only be realized in a very general or superficial form. Much less defensible by recipient countries and much more realizable as a basic building block of good government has been the focus on the public sector and administrative delivery:

> 'the public sector in many developing countries has been characterised by uneven revenue collection, poor expenditure control and management, a bloated and underpaid civil service, a large parastatal sector that provides poor return on the scarce public funds invested in it and weaknesses in the capacity of core economic agencies to design and implement policies that would address these problems. Not only does this state of affairs contribute to large fiscal deficits requiring adjustment measures, but it also progressively erodes the capacity of the state to provide economic and social services.' (World Bank, 1992, p. 12)

Donors routinely require the rationalization, realignment and reduction of public sector organizations, staffing levels and activities to make the public sector more responsive, effective and economical through the following: markets rather than governments allocating resources; involvement of end-users in implementing allocation of resources; fewer but better-paid public officials; reasonable and clear rules on conduct; more punishments for transgressions; better investment and budget programming; better personnel management; cost-containment measures; moves toward privatization and rationalization; decentralization; clarifying public enterprise-government relations; transparency of decision making; contract competition; removal of unnecessary controls and regulations; rationalization of employment levels in state enterprises; and transfer of resources toward health and primary education (World Bank, 1992; Dia, 1993).

Few, if any, of such reforms, however, would be effective without complementary preventative and investigative measures against corruption as part of the process, among which the Report included: public service training; staff rotation, particularly in the customs, revenue and contract-awarding agencies; suitable salary levels; codes of ethics and related disciplinary procedures; 'watchdog' units within departments but reporting to senior ministers; effective organization of decision-making and work distribution procedures; effective administrative procedures; task forces, including the use of lawyers, accountants and engineers, to carry out investigations; the use of publicity and educational programmes; and the establishment of anti-corruption agencies with extensive investigative powers, a high public profile, honest staff and governmental support. The 8th UN Congress also argued for: defining the type of offences that should be made illegal—including theft, abuse of office without personal gain, conflict of interest, and non-disclosure of financial interests; encouraging the reporting of corruption—including the means to receive and assess allegations of corruption as well as offer rewards to, and protect, informants; developing staff training and motivation—including the development of the role of departmental ethics officers; the development of an investigative strategy—including priorities on seriousness of cases to be investigated, intelligence gathering, and the independence of the investigating agency; and sanctions against wrongdoers—including the confiscation of assets.

These proposals, however, raise two crucial issues; investigation and prosecution can only be arbitrary and individualized in organizations where corruption may be pervasive, and 'however desirable punishment may be, it is merely a means of satisfying a social demand for retribution. It is not a deterrent and never has been' (Hope, 1987, p. 143). On the other hand, reliance on prevention, particularly through codes and other means of inculcating standards of conduct, may be ineffectual without complementary means to police them in operation and change the behaviour that the code, by its introduction, deems unacceptable (Findlay and Stewart, 1992). Increasingly governments with varying degrees of commitment to good government are considering a suitable and cost-effective means to pursue the two functions—prevention and investigation—that could also encompass wide cross sector responsibilities as well as providing an effective means to enforce reforms or sanctions, and also liaising with key departments to complement each other's efforts.

A MODEL FOR ALL REASONS? THE ROLE OF AN INDEPENDENT ANTI-CORRUPTION AGENCY

In such circumstances, Hong Kong's Independent Commission Against Corruption (ICAC) has been the focus of much attention, from countries as diverse as Australia and Botswana, not only because of its operational success, its relative freedom from internal corruption and outside interference, and its ability to attract widespread public support, but also because of its apparent capacity to fit into a heterogeneous society with several strong cultural imperatives as well as being able to work across both public and private sectors. Although organizationally weighted toward operational investigations, ICAC also comprises preventative and educational departments as well as having intelligence, complaints and advice capabilities. While ICAC was established at a time when the government wanted to retain the confidence of foreign investors, the main reason for its creation was political—'to persuade citizens that an agency independent of the police and the civil service was more likely to be effective than the existing system' (Clark, 1986, p. 61). ICAC also from the outset saw its role extending beyond the investigation of specific cases, to identifying major structural factors that gave rise to corrupt behaviour by evaluating how work should be done (formal procedures), how it is actually done (informal practices) and how it is tasked and controlled (management) (Allan, 1992). These factors include: policy weaknesses; inadequate departmental instructions, unnecessary procedures, inadequate supervision, excessive discretion, unnecessary administrative delays, unenforced laws and regulations, public ignorance of an official's powers, and misuse or abuse of position.

ICAC provides a report-back and assistance service on organizational and procedural reforms, an activity that has been further enhanced by its ability 'in persuading private sector managers to examine their own systems of internal accountability and has encouraged the modernisation of business practices' (Clark, 1986, p. 62). It has the power to freeze and request the forfeiture of unexplained assets and wealth, and the requirement that administrative departments consult it as appropriate on policies and legislation to assess potential vulnerability and risk. Its policy and investigative strategies are subject to external review while, internally, it has its own complaints, investigative and monitoring unit to provide a degree of quality control.

The emergence of ICAC as a model under consideration in a number of states does, however, raise questions about its transferability as an independent agency. ICAC is a particular product of a particular environment. It is very well resourced, its higher echelons have been staffed with seconded and expatriate officers and it has a very intensive selection and training programme. It operates within a relatively well-regulated administrative culture alongside a large and, again, well-resourced police force under a supportive political and legal framework. It has deliberately developed a highly successful public relations profile, exploiting both mass communications and a media-using population at a time of economic growth:

> 'one of the special features of the Hong Kong experience has been that the government introduced new legal standards at a time of, and under conditions of, rapid modernisation ... some of these changes might never have occurred were it not for the government's overall policy of promoting Hong Kong as an international business centre. In any event the authorities were singularly fortunate that opposition to the new laws were muted and that the shift to universalistic legal standards occurred when the society and the economy were moving in the same direction. This is not a case of a government presiding over a disintegrating economic and social system, or a society verging on collapse. The administrative machine was strong and efficient and able to secure idealistic and talented personnel. Hong Kong also enjoyed an advanced level of economic development that cumulatively permitted successful implementation of the policy.' (Clark, 1987, pp. 250–51)

For many developing countries, an ICAC may appear to offer not just another layer of expensive control but one whose efforts may be negated by corrupt or political influence unless it is established within the necessary climate of political and judicial support. Nevertheless, some countries have already introduced independent agencies, albeit for limited purposes or as a result of specific circumstances. In Zambia a special investigation agency has dealt with malpractice under exchange control and banking legislation while Zimbabwe established an investigation unit within the Ministry of Finance to deal with exchange control, banking, and import/export and trading offences. In Mexico, continuing public concern about corruption, after the government used the issue as a means of deflecting criticism from itself, (Morris, 1991, pp. 122–23), led to the government setting up a department that does the following: receives allegations about corrupt officials; adjudicates on allegations of corruption involving contracts; monitors the possibility of corruption in the National Solidarity Programme (designed to develop infrastructure, services and agriculture at community level) through locally elected 'Control and Vigilance Officers' on locally elected Solidarity Committees; and promotes improvements in public service with a complaints procedure and free telephone service (Vazguez Nava, 1992).

While the ICAC model may be too expensive and too politically threatening to many countries, and other examples of independent agencies too limited or too constrained by departmental control, an anti-corruption agency, whose agenda and focus are determined from the outset after internal and external consultation, may offer the opportunity, with donor support, to provide an immediate building block for good government where other administrative reforms may be more problematical. The comprehensive approach to public sector reform that takes in the redrafting and updating legislation and the judicial infrastructure, as well as the training, organization and accountability of a reduced number of public sector departments, is also costly, time consuming and prone to substantial slippage. On the other hand, the enclave approach of transferring activities into semi-autonomous, externally led and funded agencies is, unless long-term future government support is certain, a short-term solution that may well raise resentment among other departments, political interference and the possibility of the loss of experienced personnel to other organizations (Demongeot, 1994; Dia, 1993).

An anti-corruption agency offers the opportunity to take lead ownership of, and responsibility for, the activities and offences identified by the Report and the 8th UN Congress and, in seeking to resolve the structural factors that give rise to them across the public sector, offers a route to institutional strengthening and capacity building, subject to certain requirements on location and staffing, agenda and support.

Such an agency should be located centrally within the public sector, preferably close to the Treasury or the Director of Public Prosecutions, have clear guidelines on selection and tenure of senior personnel, as well as on operational responsibilities and reporting procedures, and with a dedicated budget. It would be usefully part of a limited 'establishment and maintenance of "cross-executive corps" of senior policy and programme managers', promoted on merit from within the civil service (Demongeot, 1994, p. 481), which would help create 'islands of competence within the bureaucracy and concentrates advocates of further reform strategically inside government. Though they lose many battles, they rarely disappear from the scene completely' (Geddes, 1991, p. 387). The agency should be linked into the process with either a posting to the agency as part of career progression of such personnel, or secondment from key government departments as a means of developing expertise inward and later transmitting expertise and the development of networks outward. Experienced personnel should be drawn from key departments such as the Treasury, the Central Bank, the Central Audit Office and the Foreign Office. Agency training should be underpinned both by cascade training from outside consultants and by the provision of senior management training on a regular regional or overseas-based arrangement, preferably with professional organizations to maintain both morale and professionalism. Additionally the agency should be provided with basic training and equipment in documentation, record keeping, inquiry management and case control to guard against turnover in staff and to encourage the development of an intelligence and analysis resource. It should also agree regular formal relations with other agencies, such as the police and prosecuting authorities, to be able to draw on competent staff on a needs basis and to reinforce its networking and information-gathering activities.

The choice and rotation of staff in this manner should have a strong influence on the agency's balance of activities, both in terms of having a flexible approach to staffing levels, and avoiding a tendency toward becoming overly committed to policing and investigative functions. Not only does this make the agency heavily dependent on the integrity of the judicial system for its results and the tolerance of the political leadership for its continued independence, but it can focus its resources and manpower in the costly pursuit of cases. With the inevitability of fraud and corruption, such a focus on investigation, while an essential capability of the agency in being able to demonstrate a competent and robust deterrence and potential prosecution capability, is of less long-term value than structural reform—focusing on procedures, control systems, accountability and the exercise of discretionary authority.

A more effective approach would, depending on country-specific issues, be to balance features of an ICAC with those of Inspector-Generals (IG) in the USA in state and federal governments. As internal rather than external agencies, and without the political or legal framework of an ICAC, IGs seek to bridge preventative-investigative capabilities within the departments whose activities they monitor. Their establishment was intended to combine and coordinate investigation, audit and sanctioning powers that do not replace established lines of operational authority, but allow for independent intervention and evaluation in a number of areas, including: audit; the promotion of economy, efficiency and effectiveness in reaching departmental goals; the enforcement of rules and laws; and the prevention of fraud and waste. They are usually required to report their findings formally to their department but also to external agencies at the same time. IGs have also tended toward the more interesting and quantifiable investigative work but their remit has included an evaluation and preventative function that could be much more effective in the long-term: 'instead of participating in programme reviews on a *post-hoc* basis, after the damage already has been done, capacity building would require a more active role for the IGs at the beginning of the legislative and regulatory process' with the emphasis on the anticipation and the prevention of the circumstances that gave rise to corruption and fraud (Light, 1993, p. 194).

If, from the outset, an anti-corruption agency drew on both the ICAC and IG perspectives, and established the primacy of an evaluations and inspections agenda as a move towards capacity building, then it could establish structured and pro-active programmes based on organized intelligence gathering and analysis. This would be achieved through an understanding of public sector organizations to assess potential risks and to highlight areas for in-depth inquiries by focusing on: selective investigations of signs of possible serious waste, extravagance, inefficiency, ineffectiveness or weaknesses in control; broad-based procedural and control investigations of a whole body, or of important activities, projects or programmes; and reviews of standard managerial operations ('good housekeeping' and 'good practice' examinations). Built into an annual information and inquiry programme, the agency will have the knowledge of activity as well as an inter-organizational perspective to make assessments and recommendations on vulnerability, risk and reform, and the basis for return monitoring, in a wide range of areas such as: the management of assets, improved information bases, better fraud awareness (particularly when dealing with the private sector), effective project management (including donor projects), better means for monitoring and controlling routine expenditure and the promotion of good housekeeping and good practice management and delivery. The intelligence and expertise built up by the agency would provide a framework for investigations that would be led, organized and controlled by the agency; both would provide achievement milestones to secure continued donor support.

CONCLUSION

Anti-corruption agencies will require both donor operation and coordination over a number of years to provide effective support, not only to establish the agency, but also its operations. Such support is necessary because corruption should not necessarily be 'associated with political modernisation. Neither is corruption doomed to destruction as a political system matures. Corruption alters its character in response to changing socio-economic cultural and political factors. As these factors affect corruption, so does corruption affect them. Significantly, because corruption is in equilibrium, the concept of entropy is not applicable. Simply put, corruption may be controlled through alterations of its character but, most importantly, not destroyed' (Werner, 1983, p. 638). Thus, while it may be difficult to perceive 'that public administration can even aspire to, let alone sustain, acceptable levels of honesty and efficiency against a background of punishing indebtedness, galloping inflation, chronic unemployment, dismal standards of living and the serious civic strains that such conditions inevitably produce ... to assert that corruption is simply a consequence of underdevelopment runs the risk of embracing a rude evolutionism which envisages a proportionate decline in the volume of abuse with each percentage improvement in GDP' (Theobald, 1990, p. 164).

Given the issues relating to political and economic change, corruption is unlikely to disappear or diminish. The establishment of properly focused independent anti-corruption agencies may provide an effective means of promoting probity in government and protection of state income and expenditure, building up a public service ethic and encouraging better administrative procedures, offering a means of public redress and promoting good practice across the public sector, and thus beginning to make the machinery of government work more productively and efficiently with a concomitant benefit of improving the reputation and performance of the public sector. Such goals will only be achieved on an incremental and gradual basis but the use of an anti-corruption agency may offer a catalyst and a building block with a number of complementary roles that, in the immediate future, may offer donors a sustainable anti-corruption strategy to help progress toward good government.

REFERENCES

Abbott, G. C. (1993). *Debt relief and Sustainable Development in Sub-Saharan Africa*, Edward Elgar, Aldershot.

Alatas, S. H. (1990). *Corruption: Its Nature, Causes and Functions*, Avebury, Aldershot.

Allan, P. (1992). 'Empirical knowledge on strategies for corruption control', *5th International Anti-Corruption Conference*, Amsterdam.

Andreski, S. (1970). *Parasitism and Subversion: The Case of Latin America*, Weidenfeld and Nicolson, London.

Batley, R. (1994). 'The consolidation of adjustment: implications for public administration', *Public Administration and Development*, **14**(5), 489–505.

Brandford, S. and Kucinski, B. (1988). *The Debt Squads*, Zed Books, London.

British Council (1993). *Development Priorities: Good Government*, British Council, London.

Charlick, R. B. (1992–93). 'Corruption in political transition: a governance perspective', *Corruption and Reform*, **7**(3), 177–187.

Clapham, C. (1982). *Private Patronage and Public Power: Political clientism in the Modern State*, Frances Pinter, London.

Clark, D. (1986). 'Corruption in Hong Kong—the ICAC story', *Corruption and Reform*, **1**(1).

Clark, D. (1987). 'A community relations approach to corruption: the case of Hong Kong', *Corruption and Reform*, **2**(3), 235–257.
Clarke, M. (ed) (1983). *Corruption Causes, Consequences and Control*, Frances Pinter, London.
Cockcroft, L. (1990). *Africa's Way*, I B Taurus, London.
Commonwealth Secretariat (1989). 'Reinforcing International Support for African Recovery and Development', *The IMF, the World Bank and the African Debt*, Zed Books, London.
Cooper, M. N. (1982). *The Transformation of Egypt*, Croom Helm, London.
Demongeot, P. (1994). 'Market-oriented approaches to capacity building in Africa', *Public Administration and Development*, **14**(5), 479–487.
Dia, M. (1993). *A Governance Approach to Civil Service Reform in Sub-Saharan Africa*, World Bank Technical Paper Number 225, World Bank, Washington, DC.
Findlay, M. and Stewart, A. (1992). 'Implementing corruption prevention strategies through codes of conduct', *Corruption and Reform*, **7**(1), 67–85.
Gardiner, J. (1993). 'Defining corruption' in Punch, M., Kolthoff, E., van der Vijer, K., and van Vliet, B. *Coping With Corruption in a Borderless World*, Deventer, Netherlands.
Geddes, B. (1991). 'A game-theoretical model of reform in Latin American democracies', *American Political Science Review*, **85**(2), 371–392.
Gillespie, K. and Okruhlik, G. (1991). 'The political dimensions of corruption cleanups: a framework for analysis', *Comparative Politics*, **24**(1), 77–95.
Gong, T. (1993). 'Corruption and reform in China: an analysis of unintended consequences', *Crime, Law and Social Change*, **19**(4), 311–327.
Heidenheimer, A. J., Johnston, M., and LeVine, V. T. (1989). *Political Corruption: A Handbook*, Transaction Books, New Jersey.
Hope, K. R. (1987). 'Administrative corruption and administrative reform in developing countries', *Corruption and Reform*, **2**(2), 127–147.
Huntington, S. (1968). *Political Order in Changing Societies*, Yale University Press, New Haven.
Kpundeh, S. J. (1992–93). 'Prospects in contemporary Sierra Leone', *Corruption and Reform*, **7**(3), 237–247.
Light, P. C. (1993). *Monitoring Government*, The Brookings Institution, Washington, DC. See also McKinney, J. B. and Johnston, M. (1986). *Fraud, Waste and Abuse in Government*, ISHI Publications, Philadelphia.
Little, W. (1992). 'Political corruption in Latin America', *Corruption and Reform*, **7**(1), 41–66.
Morris, S. D. (1991). *Corruption and Politics in Contemporary Mexico*, University of Alabama Press, Tuscaloosa.
Mosley, P., Harrigan, J., and Toye, J. (1991). *Aid and Power: The World Bank and Policy-Based Lending*, Volume 1, Routledge, London.
Oluwu, D. (1987). 'Bureaucratic delay and the prospects for regeneration in Nigeria', *Corruption and Reform*, **2**(3), 215–233.
Oluwu, D. (1992–93). 'Roots and remedies of governmental corruption in Africa', *Corruption and Reform*, **7**(3) 231.
Overseas Development Institute. (1992). *Briefing Paper: Aid and Political Reform*, Overseas Development Institute, London.
Riley, S. (1992). 'Political adjustment? Democratic politics and political choice in Africa', Centre for African Studies seminar, University of Liverpool.
Scott, J. C. (1972). *Comparative Political Corruption*, Prentice-Hall, Englewood Cliffs, NJ.
Serageldin, I. and Landell-Mills, P. (1991). 'Governance and the external factor', *Proceedings of the World Bank Annual Conference on Development Economics*, World Bank, Washington, DC.
Sivalingam, G. (1983). 'Bureaucratic corruption in Malaysia', *Phillipine Journal of Public Administration*, **27**(4), 418–435.
Sultan, N. A. (1993). 'Bureaucratic corruption as a consequence of the Gulf migration: the case of North Yemen', *Crime, Law and Social Change*, **19**(4), 379–393.
Tharan, S. (1979). 'Systems corruption and the new economic policy', *Phillipine Journal of Public Administration*, **23**(1), 39–60.
Theobald, R. (1990). *Corruption, Development and Underdevelopment*, Macmillan, London.
Theobald, R. (1993). 'Corruption in a changing world: comparisons, theories and controlling strategies', *The 3rd International Conference on Ethics in the Public Service*, Jerusalem.

United Nations Department of Technical Cooperation for Development and Centre for Social Development and Humanitarian Affairs (1989). *Corruption in Government*, report of an interregional seminar.
United Nations (1990). *Crime Prevention and Criminal Justice in the Context of Development: Realities and Perspectives of International Cooperation: Practical Measures Against Corruption*, 8th United Nations Congress on the Prevention of Crime and the Treatment of Offenders, Cuba.
Vazquez Nava, M. E. (1992). 'Controlling corruption as a social responsibility', *5th ICAC Conference*, Amsterdam.
Williams, R. (1987). *Political Corruption in Africa*, Gower, Aldershot.
World Bank (1992). *Governance and Development*, World Bank, Washington, DC.

[16]

Pillars of Integrity: The Importance of Supreme Audit Institutions in Curbing Corruption

Governance as defined by the United Nations Development Programme (UNDP) is the "exercise of economic, political and administrative authority to manage a country's affairs at all levels. It comprises the mechanisms, processes and institutions through which citizens and groups articulate their interests, exercise their legal rights, meet their obligations and mediate their differences...Governance encompasses the state, but transcends the state by including the private sector and civil society organizations." (UNDP, 1997).

Good governance is accountable, participatory and transparent (see Box 2). It ensures that political, social and economic priorities are based on broad consensus in society and that the voices of the poorest of the poor and the most vulnerable are heard in decision-making over the allocation of resources. One of the principal causes of "bad governance" is the existence of corruption. Conversely, one of the core foundations for good governance is accountability—the obligation to render an account for a responsibility conferred. (In government, accountability is a process that subjects a form of control over departments and agencies, causing them to give a general accounting for their actions, an essential concept in democratic public administration).

This paper discusses the role of supreme audit institutions (SAIs) in promoting accountability and transparency in government and thus, in curbing corruption. An effective SAI can be one of the key institutions charged with the responsibility of controlling corruption through preventative measures (Sahgal, 1996). However, the full potential of the SAI to address the issue has not been exploited, in part because of the lack of understanding of the SAI's potential for controlling corruption.

The purpose of this paper is to contribute to the review of how SAIs might help control corruption. The first section presents a short definition of corruption and summarizes some of the reasons why it is important to curb corruption. The second section summarizes the concept of "pillars of integrity"—those institutions that play a role in curbing corruption. Section three, the core of the paper, discusses the role of one of the pillars—supreme audit institutions—in promoting accountability and transparency and the linkages between the audit institutions and other pillars, notably the media and Parliament. The final section presents some conclusions and recent developments regarding the role of SAIs in curbing corruption.

I. Corruption

News media around the world are reporting on corruption on a daily basis; and clearly demonstrate that it is not something that is exclusively, or even primarily, a problem of developing countries. Recent events in Europe and North America have shown all too clearly that corruption is not something that is exclusively, or even primarily, a problem of developing countries.

Clearly, corruption is a complex issue. While its roots are grounded in a country's particular social and cultural history, political and economic development, bureaucratic traditions and policies, one can generalize to state that corruption tends to flourish when institutions are weak and economic policies distort the marketplace (World Bank, 1997b). It distorts economic and social development, by engendering wrong choices and by encouraging competition in bribery rather than in the quality and price of goods and services. Moreover, it is the poor countries—and the poor within poor countries—which can least afford the costs of corruption (Langseth, Stapenhurst and Pope, 1997). Moreover, evidence suggests that if corruption is not contained, it will grow and that once a pattern of successful bribes is institutionalized, corrupt officials have an incentive to demand larger bribes, engendering a "culture" of illegality that in turn breeds market inefficiency (Rose-Ackerman 1996).

Corruption has been described as a "cancer." It violates public confidence in the state and endangers social cohesion. Grand corruption—where millions of dollars change hands, is reported with increasing frequency in rich and poor countries alike. Petty corruption is less reported, but can be equally damaging; a small bribe to a public servant for a government service may only involve a minor payment, but when such bribes are multiplied a million times, their combined impact can be enormous. If left unchecked, the accumulation of seemingly petty bribes can erode legitimacy of public institutions to the extent that even noncorrupt officials and members of the public see little point in remaining honest (World Bank, 1997b).

Forms of corruption need to be contained for practical reasons. Faced with the challenge of at least maintaining, if not improving, standards of public service delivery, no country can afford the inefficiency that accompanies corruption. While some may argue that corruption can help grease the wheels of a slow-moving and over-regulated economy, evidence indicates that it increases the costs of goods and services, promotes unproductive investments, and leads to a decline in the quality of public services (Gould and Amaro-Reyes 1983). Indeed, recent evidence suggests that rather than expediting public service, corruption may be more like "sand in the wheels" : recent corruption surveys in Tanzania, Uganda, Ukraine and elsewhere show that people paying bribes to public officials actually received slower service than those who did not.

Simply defined, corruption is *the abuse of public power for personal gain or for the benefit of a group to which one owes allegiance*. It occurs at the intersection of public and private sectors, when public office is abused by an official accepting, soliciting, or extorting a bribe. Klitgaard (1996) has developed a simple model to explain the dynamics of corruption:

$$C \text{ (Corruption)} = M \text{ (Monopoly Power)} + D \text{ (Discretion)} - A \text{ (Accountability)}$$

In other words, the extent of corruption depends on the amount of monopoly power and discretionary power that an official exercises. Monopoly power can be large in highly regulated economies; discretionary power is often large in developing countries and transition economies where administrative rules and regulations are often poorly defined. And finally, accountability may also be weak, either as a result of poorly defined ethical standards of public service, weak administrative and financial systems and ineffective watchdog agencies.

Successful strategies to curb corruption will have to simultaneously seek to educe an official's monopoly power (e.g. by market-oriented reforms), discretionary power (e.g. by administrative reform) and enhance accountability (e.g. through watchdog agencies). Such mechanisms, when designed as part of a national effort to reduce corruption, comprise an integrity system. This system of checks and balances, designed to manage conflicts of interest in the public sector, limits situations in which conflicts of interest arise or have a negative impact on the common good. This involves both prevention and penalty. An integrity system embodies a comprehensive view of reform, addressing corruption in the public sector through government processes (leadership codes, organizational change) and through civil society participation (the democratic process, private sector, media). Thus, reform is initiated and supported not only by politicians and policy makers, but also by members of civil society.

II. The Concept of National Integrity Systems

Appropriate economic policies, which reduce the opportunity for corruption (or, in the above model, M—the monopoly power of officials), may be considered a prior condition for successfully curbing corruption. With regards to institutional strengthening, country strategies vary a great deal, but worldwide the policy responses to corruption typically involve one or more of the eight following institutions or "pillars":

- political will;
- administrative reforms
- "watchdog" agencies (anti-corruption com-

Box 1: The Pillars of Integrity

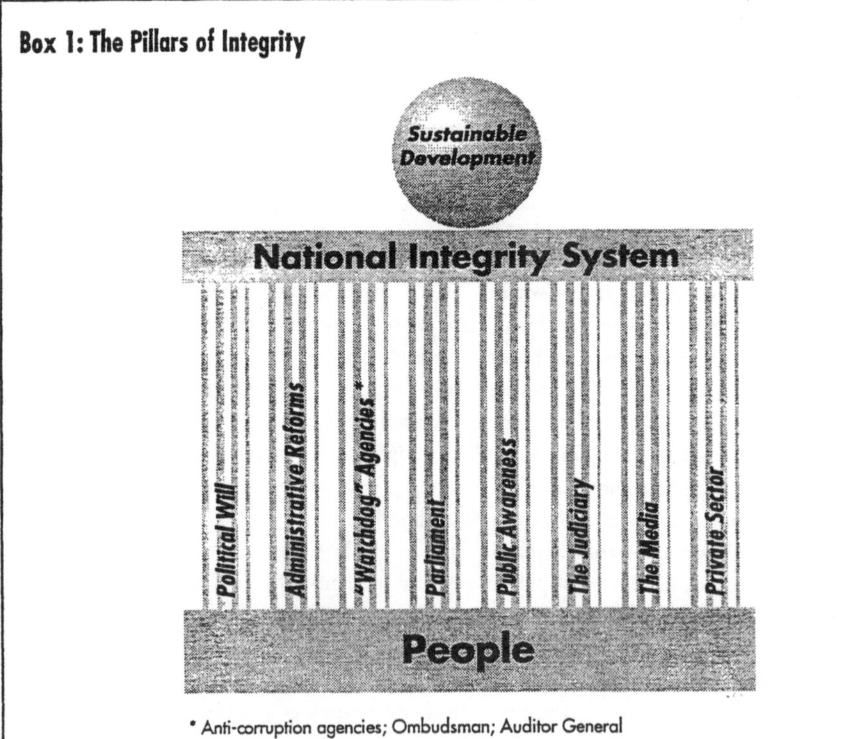

Source: Langseth, Pope, and Stapenhurst (1997).

missions; supreme audit institutions; ombuds offices)
- parliaments;
- public awareness/involvement;
- the judiciary;
- the media;
- the private sector.

The notion of a "national integrity system" was developed by Ibrahim Seushi, President of Transparency International-Tanzania. The concept is straight forward : the eight institutions identified above are interdependent and together support the notional of 'national integrity', much the same pillars might support the roof of a house (see Diagram 1). Pushing the analogy further, if any one of these "integrity pillars" weakens, an increased load is thrown on to the others. If several weaken, their load will tilt, so that the round ball of 'sustainable development' rolls off" (Langseth et al. 1997). The general equilibrium of the pillars is therefore important, and a government has an incentive to keep the eight pillars in balance.

III. Supreme Audit Institutions as a "Pillar of Integrity"

Responsible internal financial management is crucial to national integrity, but national audit offices, or supreme audit institutions (SAIs), are (or at least, should be) the linchpin of a country's integrity system. As the agency responsible for auditing government income and expenditure, the supreme audit institution acts as a watchdog over financial integrity and the credibility of reported information (as well as 'performance' or 'value-for-money' auditing: see Annex A).

Auditing is a function that serves accountability as it adds credibility to the assertions of the person or entity rendering account, and it provides valuable insights and information to the person or entity conferring the responsibility (see Annex B for a brief history of auditing). Audits are fundamental to accountability—a key component of Klitgaard's equation ($C = M + D - A$)—and are a necessary component of public sector performance. They can be a very cost-effective means of promoting transparency and openness in government operations, and can contribute to improved government performance. Also, the audit function contributes to public information about violations of accepted standards of ethics and deviations from principles of legality, accounting, economy, efficiency and effectiveness.

Audits can help curb corruption and act as a potent deterrent to waste and abuse of public funds by, for example, helping restrain any tendency to divert public resources for private gain. Audit can help reinforce the legal, financial and institutional framework which, when weak, allows corruption to flourish; it can help establish a predictable framework of government behavior and law conducive to development, it can reduce the arbitrariness in the applications of rules and law and it can help simplify administrative procedures, particularly where they hinder the smooth functioning of markets (Sahgal, 1996). It can also expose non-transparent decision making that is clearly not in the public interest (World Bank, 1991).

While a plethora of polls in industrial countries indicate that many citizens do not trust their governments to always act in the public interest, the SAIs are widely viewed as independent watchdogs of the public interest and are thus well situated to promote transparency and ethical behavior in their jurisdictions. If the currency of accountability If information, then transparency allows accountability to work effectively; it focuses on public reporting and availability of information, with the objective of making what governments do more visible (Sahgal, 1996). Thus, one can rewrite Klitgaard's equation as :

$$C = M + D - A(T)$$

to highlight that Accountability itself is a function of Transparency.

The aim of adding has evolved beyond an emphasis on minimizing waste, abuse and fraud and ensuring compliance with financial and administrative laws and regulations to value-for-money assessments (see Annex A). Thus, audit's potential for proactively promoting good governance is generally recognized as an important factor in public sector reforms. The responsibilities of the SAI's now include, in addition to ensuring that the executive complies with the will of Parliament (as expressed through parliamentary appropriations), the promotion of ethical behavior, efficiency and cost effectiveness and the encouragement of sound internal financial controls to reduce the opportunities for corruption and increase the likelihood of its detection (Sahgal, 1996).

Box 2: The European Court of Auditors

The European Court of Auditors, located in Luxembourg, is responsible for auditing all European Union budgetary expenditures. The court is composed of one member from each of the fifteen European Union countries. This diversity of members reflects the different audit approaches from their home countries. The court is divided into three Audit Development and Reports Group and a Statement of Assurance Group. The Statement of Assurance Group deals with new requirement under the Treaty on European Union to provide the European Parliament with an annual statement as to the reliability of the accounts and the legality of and regularity of the underlying transactions. Each Group is composed of between three and five Members of the Court.

As well as examining the legality and regularity of transactions, the Court also is required to examine the soundness of financial management, meaning of whether funds have been used with due regard for economy, efficiency and cost effectiveness. The Court also assesses the adequacy of internal systems of office administration, and the adequacy of safeguards against fraud. In addition, the Court relies on country SAIs and performs joint audits with national audit bodies.

Auditing Models

While the importance of SAI's may have increased, there is no common approach to legislative auditing. There are three basic auditing models: the Napoleonic model, the Westminster model and the Board system. The French have exported the Napoleonic system or *Cours des Comptes* model to the Latin countries of Europe and to some extent in South America and Africa. It is a compliance-oriented system that makes legal judgments on compliance with laws and regulations. The *Cours des Comptes* systems have a large number of magistrates who enjoy judicial independence. Most European-conducted performance audits are smaller and less expensive than those in North America, and many are directed at whole government programs. Yet, like SAIs in North America, the most sophisticated European SAIs give a significant role to social objectives in determining what to examine.

The Westminster system is designed to have an Auditor General (AG) make periodic reports to parliament using the professional audit staff of the Office of the Auditor General (OAG) (Box 3). While the AG is personally responsible for the operations of his office, the system is essentially collegial in nature. The AGs usually report annually to parliament although there are some exceptions such as in the United Kingdom and Canada where reporting is more frequent. The auditors report on financial statements and the operations of government entities; generally, there is less emphasis on compliance although compliance issues are not ignored if they are identified.

The Board model is similar in nature to the Westminster system and is prevalent in Asia. Indonesia, Japan and Korea use a Board system with a chair and a small committee. Like the Westminster model, these systems are essentially collegial and the chairman is de facto the Auditor General.

International Audit Standards

For many years the public sector financial auditing community did not observe international standards of audit reporting, although the International

Box 3: The National Audit Office (NAO) of the United Kingdom

The introduction of performance auditing in Britain was legislated in response to the demands of the Parliament (the Public Accounts Committee, or PAC) for audited information extending beyond mere financial audit opinions. Increasing parliamentary concerns about the influence that the executive body, particularly the Treasury, retained over the NAO created the political climate to pass the National Audit Act in 1983, which gave the Comptroller and Auditor General (C&AG), who reports to the House of Commons (Public Accounts Committee), express powers to carry out investigations of how departments use their resources (see Annex C). Thus, the C&AG is now able to provide assurance about performance and about whether public money has been spent properly and for the purposes intended by Parliament. However, the C&AG is not entitled to question the merits of policy objectives; examinations are focused on the means employed to achieve the policy objectives set by the government and approved by Parliament.

Selection of performance audit studies are made annually based on a variety of criteria which include the amount of money involved; prima facie evidence of poor value-for-money; the level of political, parliamentary; and political concern; and the likely added value to be derived from the NAO conducting a study. The choice of audits is solely that of the C&AG, but the views of the PAC are taken into account, and its response to the NAO report may be included in the final report to Parliament.

NAO is one of the leading SAIs and emphasizes rigorous audits, quality assurance, and objectivity. A well trained staff conducts a wide variety of performance and financial audits with the latter having become increasingly important in the face of government restructuring. During the past decade, NAO has offered a lot of training to its staff, hired a large number of accountants and social scientists, enabling integrated audit teams—supplemented by experts from the private sector and academia—to use multi-disciplinary approaches to performance auditing by combining diverse skills and background.

Similar to the US GAO contribution to government savings, the UK NAO performance auditing has identified savings of £270 million (US$425 million)—equivalent to £7 saved for £1 spent on audits. From an annual budget of US$66 million, about 38 percent of NAO resources are dedicated to performance auditing to produce over 50 reports annually. The cost of performance audits continues to decline as a result of better management and planning, with an emphasis on tighter, faster, and sharper examinations. Also, performance auditors have improved the quality and value of their reports by:

- identifying financial savings;
- adopting emerging trends such as market testing;
- using a thematic approach;
- applying rigorous methodologies that provide defensible findings and conclusions; and
- contracting with private sector experts when their expertise enhances a performance audit.

As in Canada and the United States, NAO undertakes internal quality reviews of ongoing and completed work, through contractual arrangements with independent quality panels. The panels provide advice on audit issues, evidence and report drafting.

Federation of Accountants (IFAC) has for many years published international audit standards which have direct application to commercial entities and state-owned enterprises.

In recent years, however, there has been more acceptance of public sector auditing standards. In the middle 1980s, IFAC established a Public Sector Committee (PSC) to focus on accounting and auditing standards applicable to public sector audits and accounts. Currently there are numerous pronouncements available from the IFAC PSC, which offer guidance to public sector auditors and many countries with institutes of professional accountants have established their own public sector committees, which provide useful guidance to auditors of public sector entities.

Box 4: INTOSAI

The International Association of Supreme Audit Institutions (INTOSAI), based in Vienna, Austria, is the worldwide association of national audit offices. INTOSAI has developed its own audit guidance for the SAIs of the world to conduct financial, compliance and performance audits. These auditing standards were accepted and adopted at the 1992 conference of INTOSAI. The INTOSAI Auditing Standards are compatible with the Government Auditing Standards produced by the United States General Accounting Office in a publication widely known as the Yellow Book. They can also be easily adapted to the needs of developing country SAIs until these countries are ready to develop their own standards. Developing country SAIs should make the intellectual investment needed to understand these standards as they apply to performance audits. An international auditing standards team should be part of the research and methodology group of a developing SAI.

3.1 Factors for SAI Success

Several factors have been identified to SAI success. Of these, the most important are: having a clear mandate; independence (both from the executive and to investigate issues at its sole discretion); adequate funding and staff; and the sharing of knowledge and experience.

CLEAR MANDATES

Auditing mandates should be rooted in a set of rules and boundaries agreed to by parliament. Audit acts that define parliament's objectives are the most effective way of communicating and authorizing an audit mandate (Box 5). Failure to set out auditing requirements in legislation leaves an SAI vulnerable to criticism that it is exceeding its mandate. Also, an audit act ensures that the SAI addresses all the issues that parliament wishes to be scrutinized by an independent body.

In developing audit mandates, developing country SAIs need to reconsider the role of sanctions and penalties. Although they are no longer common in the Western world, many developing country institutions regularly apply sanctions and penalties. This practice creates an environment where the auditor is feared and perhaps not respected as a professional advisor who adds value to the entity. The modern view is that learning lessons from mistakes is more constructive than penalizing bureaucrats.

SAIs wishing to create mandates should review the explicit performance auditing mandates of other audit institutions. Before legislation can be drafted, SAIs and governments must define auditing and determine the independence of auditors, the scope of audits, the entities to be audited, and the reporting responsibilities of auditors.

SAI INDEPENDENCE

Independence is a fundamental feature of all the industrialized country SAIs. Not only is the independence of the organization clearly enunciated, the personal independence of the AG (sometimes a Chair or President) or members of a Court of

Box 5: Common features of Audit Mandates

The purpose of setting out an audit mandate is to assure parliament that it will receive independent credible audit assurance and other useful information about the management of public funds. Audit legislation often contain these features:

- criteria for the selection of an Auditor General (Comptroller & Auditor General; President of the Court of Accounts; Chairman of the Board of Audit);
- term of service;
- provisions for retirement or dismissal;
- scope of audit, when and what to report upon, will be influenced by whether:
  - all information and explanations have been received,
  - accounts and essential records and systems are maintained properly,
  - financial statements meet international and country standards,
  - money has been expended as intended,
  - expenditures have proper authority,
  - there has been due regard for economy, efficiency and effectiveness,
  - there are appropriate systems in place to prevent fraud and waste,
  - the Auditor has recommendations to improve government operations, and
  - fraud exists.
- reasonable access to records;
- immunity from liability for the Auditor General;
- requirement to report regularly rather than annually;
- right to hire and fire SAI employees;
- right to contract out for professional services; and
- provision of adequate budget.

Audit is always carefully set out in legislation and acknowledged in tradition. This was and is true for financial and compliance auditing and is equally, if not more important, for performance auditors, because performance audit reports on government operations have more potential to embarrass a government and its ministers. If SAI independence in developing countries is not protected by legislation or strong tradition, the situation needs to be changed. The SAI leader should be able to report directly and frequently to the parliament without interference from the politics of the executive government. Such independence demands freedoms for the Auditor General to audit and report as deemed necessary, with adequate personnel and financial resources.

Independence of a SAI and its leader is a hallmark of an effective SAI. If the SAI is going to audit the government, it must have the authority to do its job without threat of retaliation and the power to proceed with its plans. It must not be dependent on those that it audits to determine how auditing will be conducted. The SAI leader also needs status to persuade very senior members of the government bureaucracy of the importance of his recommendations or requests for information. Independence can be strengthened by including the role of the AG in the constitution of the country, as has been done in Indonesia, India, Japan and Zambia.

In Japan, the Board of Audit is independent of the Cabinet. The Board has three Commissioners who are appointed by the Cabinet and attested to by the Emperor. The Commissioners, who hold the same status as State Ministers and Supreme Court Judges, hold office for a 7-year term and his/her status is assured during the term to secure the Board's independence from the Cabinet. In Indonesia, the Chairmen, Vice Chairman and Members of the Supreme Audit Board are appointed by the President on their nomination by Parliament. In India, the Comptroller and AG is appointed by the President and his oath of office requires him/her to uphold the Constitution of the country and the laws made thereunder. In Canada and India, it takes both houses of Parliament to terminate the AG before the normal retirement time. In Belgium, Members of the Court can only be removed by the Chamber of Representatives, and in the United Kingdom removal of the Comptroller and Auditor General is by the monarch on a resolution of both houses of Parliament. A similar requirement for approval by the legislature exists in Ireland, Luxembourg and in Austria, where a verdict of the Constitutional Court can also remove the President. In Portugal only the State President can remove the President of the Tribunal de Contas.

There is another dimension of SAI independence: freedom to determine what shall be audited. In all developed country SAIs, there is little or no interference by executive government on the choice of issues to be audited. Those being audited should have no influence on the choice of who or what gets audited. Likewise SAIs need the freedom to determine what shall be reported. The reporting of audit findings should be the sole decision of the SAI, not the auditee. There should be room for discussion and negotiation, but at the end of the day, it is the responsibility of the audit office to decide what will be reported.

Adequate Funding and Staff

SAIs are often short of funding, especially throughout the developing world. While it is probably true that some improved efficiencies could be obtained in these SAIs, it is unlikely that improved efficiency would generate sufficient savings to provide competitive salaries and modern technology for SAIs. Governments will have to consider the adequacy of resources for many developing country SAIs. Budgetary constraints often inhibit the upgrading and maintenance of staff skills. Few developing countries set annual targets for performance audit training or devise budgets that take the cost of courses and external training into account.

SAI staff must be adequately paid and trained. Effective SAIs subscribe to the principle of continuous development of their staff. To ensure high-quality work, they need to employ qualified staff, remunerate them adequately, emphasize continuous improvement and encourage subject-matter expertise. For example, there is a need for auditors to improve their skills in fraud detection and information technology through a combination of training, education and experience (Sahgal, 1996). In those circumstances where professional knowledge is required, calling on outside expertise may be desirable (INTOSAI, 1977).

Developing country SAIs seldom produce statistics on individual and project levels of effort.

Box 6: SAI Independence

To be effective, any external auditor must be devoid of accountability to, or susceptible to pressures from, the clients or institutions being audited. The office should not be a part of, or managed by, a government department it has to audit. To be so would create a systemic conflict of interest and to open the door to forms of "management." The supreme audit institution's clients are parliament (or comparable bodies) and its subjects are the public officials entrusted with public expenditure.

Unfortunately, this office can be particularly vulnerable to pressure from its clients, and in the majority of cases, the Executive. To assure independence, the office should have relative freedom to manage the department's budget and to hire and assign competent professional staff. The latter is important if it is to maintain its ability to match the capability of senior officials in government.

The responsibilities of the office of the Auditor General also include ensuring the Executive complies with the will of the Legislature, as expressed through parliamentary appropriations; promotes efficiency and cost effectiveness of government programs; and prevents corruption through the development of financial and auditing procedures designed to reduce the incidence of corruption and increase the likelihood of its detection.

Box 7: Puerto Rico's Comptroller General

In Puerto Rico, the Comptroller General embarked on an aggressive modernization program and the current Comptroller General, Ileana Colon Carlo, credits the fact that her office had, by the end of 1996, recovered $28 million in unlawfully disbursed funds. In 1987, for example, the large majority of employees of the Office operated with typewriters, manual ledgers and adding machines. A decade later, the Office had become the best-equipped and most updated of all government departments . Accountability, No. 14, June 1997.

Costs are not assigned to individuals or performance audit projects, and data are not used to gauge the progress of projects. In the absence of project budgets and management information systems, performance audits are likely to be inefficient and expensive, since no records are kept and there is no accountability for project management. In addition, a lot of SAIs are overstaffed, with undertrained auditors who add little value to the audit process. For SAIs to maintain credibility, they must manage themselves in an effective manner that would result in a favorable performance audit report if the SAI itself were subjected to a performance audit of its own operations.

Although SAIs are often responsible for commenting on the economy, efficiency, and effectiveness of government operations, few engage in cost management themselves. Most do not track the resources that are consumed by each audit or overall operating costs. Budgets are rarely produced for performance audit projects, audit administration, or training and methodology development. None of the developing country SAIs surveyed has a capital budget. Timesheets are rarely used, thus there is no database for determining the cost of performance audits, administration, or training. Developing country SAIs should develop annual training budgets and set targets for the resources to be committed to training. This target could be expressed as a percentage of the office budget or as a mandatory number of days of training for each auditor and administrator. In addition, requiring staff to use timesheets would simplify the management of audit costs.

Sharing of Knowledge and Experience

International exchange of ideas, knowledge and experience is an effective means of raising the quality of audit, harmonizing standards, sharing best practices and generally helping SAIs to fulfill their mandates. To this end, international congresses and training seminars, regional and inter-regional conferences and the publication of international journals have promoted the evolution and development of the auditing function (INTOSAI, 1977). Increasingly, too, SAIs need to liaise closely with enforcement officials in other government agencies to ensure that skills and insights are shared and that they become more adept at uncovering corruption (Sahgal, 1996).

IV. Increased Role of SAIs

A well performed and reported audit serves as an essential instrument for development, promoting good governance by improving public sector management. Any SAI that provides high quality audit services clearly has the potential to assist its legislature and other governing bodies in holding the government accountable for its stewardship of public resources. There are currently many innovations in public sector auditing. The Canadian OAG has been studying well performing organizations, and conducting studies on ethics, values and learning organizations. In Europe, the SAIs are focusing on audits of programs that directly affect the public's concerns. SAIs are collaborating on audits. Results-based audits and audits of the environment have recently gained popularity proving that auditing is not a static process.

In the developed world, SAIs have moved towards more proactive involvement in better accountability and more effective operations of government. The shift has been described as moving from a role of observer to a more pro active role as an improver. Executive government takes some risk in allowing an informed critic to make comments about its operations and financial statements. However, if the government is not willing to allow such exposure, the lack of commitment to audit will weaken the auditing process considerably. Governments must be willing to provide an appropriate strong mandate, and to provide the financial and human resources to fulfill the mandate. Likewise there needs to be unrestricted access to information.

Following decades of experimentation with audit strategies, a number of lessons emerge from industrialized countries that have shown an effectiveness in their work to promote governmental accountability. Although there are differences in methodology, common successful strategies can be borrowed and used to advance auditing in the developing world (see Box 8).

Box 8: Developing and Improving Audit Capacity

Countries that choose to develop and improve their audit capacity should adopt strategies that have proven successful after 30 years of experience by SAIs in some industrialized countries:

- free SAIs from government interference;
- establish clear auditing mandates in legislation;
- compensate auditors competitively to avoid costly brain drain;
- carefully recruit high quality auditors from a variety of disciplines, especially for performance auditing;
- provide each SAI with its own training facility and audit program;
- document audit methodology and support with training;
- publish reports upon audit completion, and not wait for annual report;
- produce audit reports that are clear and interesting;
- focus performance audit reports on a few significant topics;
- establish quality control and quality assurance mechanisms for performance auditing; and
- attract attention to audit reports by encouraging media interest.

Transparency is built on the free flow of information, i.e. enough information to determine responsibility for failure, incompetence or deceit. An auditor cannot come to a final conclusion if there is a limitation in the scope of an audit due to a restriction on information access. Auditors need to have complete and accurate evidence to conclude their opinions. Barriers such as a need to obtain permission to receive evidence should be eliminated in clear legislation that enables the auditor to obtain whatever information he or she deems essential.

In most advanced countries, the SAI is given complete access to information that it needs to do its audit work. Examples are found in the SAI legislation for the following countries: Japan, Canada, India, the United Kingdom, Sweden, Spain, the Netherlands, Germany, Moldova, Romania, Estonia, Zambia and the Slovak Republic. In certain countries, access is limited, for example, limitations exist in the United States, France and the Czech Republic. Unfettered access to information is an indication of the extent of independence conferred upon the SAI. In the most advanced countries, access is complete and unfettered.

SAIs can become key instruments for maintaining and enhancing the credibility of the state in the eyes of the public. In many countries, the AG enjoys high credibility in the eyes of the public. Sometimes it is the individual him or herself but more often it is the good reputation of the institution. Faith in SAIs is developed from good auditing over a long time where the public comes to understand that the auditor is not a political person and can be trusted to stick to the facts and be objective and fair. When the public places faith in an SAI, it is well positioned to report on government's progress in improving its operations. SAIs can contribute to reforms and monitor how changes are occurring. They can develop recommendations to make reform more effective and make the management of change as transparent as possible. Good auditing in many countries is seen as a major contributor to the evolution of public sector reform.

V. SAIs and Other Pillars of Integrity

The concept of an integrity system highlights the interlinkage between institutions, or pillars. The SAIs, if they ate to be effective, rely on an effective Parliament—to whom they report—and media, which can publicize wrongdoing discovered by the SAI.

The Media

The media plays a significant part in enhancing the role and public stature of an SAI. Effective SAIs have established a good working relationship with the media. All forms of media, i.e. television, print and radio are useful for getting the audit message across to parliamentarians and the public. Audit reports tend to be written in very cautious and stilted language, which is not easily read or understood. Sometimes important issues get lost in the careful phrasing of an audit report. However the media gives the SAI an opportunity to use plain language and in a short article or interview, convey succinctly the essential points of an audit finding. While the use of the media is not popular with bureaucrats because context is lacking, the clarity of the message is enhanced.

Politicians are particularly interested in media items. If audit findings are highlighted in a media presentation, parliamentarians are likely to pay close attention. Many auditors realize that their reports are not read directly, only the media messages are absorbed. So it is important for an SAI to have access to the media to convey essential audit findings and recommendations.

The media also play a large role in shaping the public's attitude towards the audit office. SAIs need public support to gain the confidence of parliamentarians. Good media relationships certainly enhance the SAI reputation for competence, independence and fairness.

SAIs and Parliament

The relationship between a Parliament and its SAI is at the core of the objectives and purpose of Parliament's oversight function (Stapenhurst and Miller). Effective Parliamentary oversight requires that Parliaments scrutinize public expenditures and revenues. Since few MPs have the skills to undertake this function, Parliaments typically rely on SAIs to audit the public accounts on their behalf, requiring the SAIs to report regularly on their findings.

In the Westminster Parliamentary system, the reports from the Auditor General's Office are usually referred automatically to the Public Accounts Committee (PAC) for review. In the United Kingdom hearings are held almost every week when Parliament is in session and the Auditor General personally attends hearings on their reports. Witnesses from government departments and agencies are called to these hearings and the Auditor General and his auditors attend and offer comment on their findings. The PAC considers the testimony of the witnesses and sends its reports to Parliament for comment and action. Frequently, there are recommendations requiring follow-up action by the Auditor General. Sometimes, too, the Auditor General is called as a witness before other Parliamentary committees, thereby allowing these committees to focus on financial and operational matters pertinent to their mandate.

Box 9: Comptroller's Office In Venezuela

Prior to 1938, Venezuela's General Accounting Office was a generally weak, powerless organization, located within the executive branch. With assistance from the United States, the Office of the Comptroller General was established and is now autonomous. Based on the Colombian model, it is only loosely affiliated to Congress. Like the Comptroller General in Puerto Rico, the GAO is undergoing a period of intensive modernization; it is moving away from ex-ante control of contracts and payments towards a system of comprehensive ex-post financial and performance audits. Accountability, December 1996.

In Parliamentary systems other than the Westminster-type, there are similar relationships between the Parliament and the SAI. An exception is the *Cours des Comptes*-style SAIs, where Parliaments do note automatically receive the SAI reports (although they may receive a report on the work of the court). Rather, audit issues under this system are dealt with by magistrates in a judicial fashion.

VI. Conclusions: SAIs and Recent Anti-Corruption Efforts

Experience indicates that no one institution, acting alone, can significantly reduce corruption. Indeed, the very concept of a "national integrity system" highlights the *linkages* between institutions. In the case of the SAIs, their reporting to Parliament and relationship to the media is important.

Corruption has been identified as a symptom of something gone wrong with the management of the state. The World Bank has defined corruption as " the abuse of public office for private gain". Such a definition would include bribery with government contracts, bribery influencing government benefits, bribery to reduce taxes owing, bribery in issuance of licenses, bribery with registrations and permits, bribery to change or not change laws. Benefits to those who bribe can be enormous and corruption associated with international business transactions could involve both politicians as well as bureaucrats. The most successful corrupt practices are those where the corruptor and the corruptee both gain sufficient advantage to be satisfied with the transaction. Other forms of corruption such as theft of state assets by those who are in charge of the assets is a huge problem. A recent form of corruption has emerged with the privatization of state-owned enterprises for the benefit of officials . Theft of government financial resources such as pocketing revenues, not repaying advances are all forms of corruption that auditors must be more vigilant in identifying.

Audit can be a powerful force to combat corruption. It also can be a potent deterrent to waste and abuse of public funds exposing non transparent decision-making that was not in the public interest. Curiously though, auditors in the private or public sector who have been trained to audit financial statements do not have

Box 10: The SAI and the Control of Corruption

Vinod Sahgal (1996) has identified the following steps that an SAI can take to improve its capacity to curb corruption:

- Clarify its mandate and mission statement regarding its role as a catalyst for combating corruption
- Proactively promote policies that encourage ethical behavior in the public service
- Actively promote improvements in the quality of the public service
- Strengthen their Reporting and communication strategies
- Raise the public's awareness about ethics and corruption
- Work with educators to enhance communications in schools and homes on the subject of corruption

a history of finding much fraud through their audits. Their main contribution to preventing corruption has been the strong psychological factor of deterrence. However the deterrence factor is not enough to prevent corruption in the public sector. Reporting on corruption and criminal activity is required of the General Accounting Office of the USA and of the SAIs of the Philippines, Bhutan, Indonesia, Malaysia, Spain, Romania, Moldova, China, Estonia, Lithuania, Germany, the Netherlands, Sweden, India, the United Kingdom, South Africa, the Czech Republic and the Slovak Republic. It is noteworthy that this list suggests that some *developing* country SAIs are ahead of their counterparts in the industrial world when it comes to detecting corruption.

Within the International Organization of Supreme Audit Institutions—the international organization of SAIs—there is an increasing interest in corruption and fraud. SAIs are going to study corruption and develop new audit methods to prevent it as much as possible. They need to examine whether the checks and controls devised by governments to deal with corruption are adequate and actually working. Two areas where auditors have been quite successful in identifying corrupt practices is detecting situations where managers are drawing pay for ghost workers, and identifying substandard construction through inspection. Auditors are developing better methodologies to detect corruption and bring to light corrupt practices. ❧

Annex A: Types of Audits

Audits can be classified into three basic types: attest or financial auditing, compliance auditing and performance auditing or value-for-money (VFM) auditing. In financial auditing, the auditor attests to, or verifies, the accuracy and fairness of presentation of financial statements. Attest audits result in opinions that indicate whether reliance can be placed on a government's financial statements. Auditors plan and perform attest audits using their knowledge of accounting and auditing, and of the government organizations being audited. As part of these audits, they gather evidence, on a test basis, to support the amounts and disclosures in the financial statements. Audit procedures might include comparing the results of operations with planned results, checking the reliability of an organization's financial control systems and checking samples of transactions and balances.

Ultimately the financial auditor adds credibility to financial statements prepared by an organization by providing an unqualified audit opinion on the financial statements. Where the auditor cannot express an unqualified opinion, he/she will provide additional useful information to the reader of the financial statements explaining his/her reservations. Auditors will qualify or deny opinions if financial statements are materially misstated, accounting principles are violated, the scope of the audit was compromised or if underlying systems are inadequate to produce reliable financial statements.

In compliance auditing, the auditor asks if the government collected or spent no more than the authorized amount of money and for the purposes intended by the government. The audit team reviews transactions to see if the government department or agency conformed to all laws and regulations that govern its operations. This includes checking the spending authority contained in the annual budget and relevant legislation.

In performance auditing or VFM auditing, the auditor asks whether or not taxpayers got value for their tax dollars. Often the audit team works closely with an advisory committee of experts who offer advice and review audit results. Performance auditing seeks to ensure that administrative procedures adhere to sound management policies, principles and practices. Also, it looks to see that the best use is made of human, financial and other resources including procedures, information systems and performance measures and monitoring arrangements used by audited organizations and that the organization's performance helps achieve its institutional objectives. Performance audits encourage governments to improve the way they manage public funds. They will focus on matters of due regard to the "3 E's" and will also address the protection of assets. This type of auditing has much more effect on democracy than any other approach to verification.

Financial, compliance and performance audits combine to form an audit framework ("comprehensive auditing") that, over time, provides a complete view of an organization. Audits that promote an honest, accountable and productive government can be described as constructive audits; they encourage government to manage for results and be concerned about managing revenues and expenditures in an effective manner. These audits ask the right questions about what was accomplished and whether there was success or failure, and if there was a concern for economy and efficiency. The most effective audits demonstrate the transparency of government programs and reveal important lessons to be learned. ❧

Annex B: Historical Background

Auditing has been an important part of public administration for a long time—going back to early centuries in Egypt, China and Korea. Early emperors and pharaohs wanted to know if their assets were being protected, so auditors were sent out to ensure that rice was stored as reported and that taxes were being collected properly. In 18th century Europe, audit systems were developed that focused very much on compliance with rules and regulations decreed by various rulers. In the Anglo Saxon tradition, the notion of compliance with laws was extended to auditing financial accounts and giving opinions on the fairness of account presentations. In the latter part of the 20th century, the notion of auditing performance and operations emerged and became an important part of the audit process.

In the 1960s and 1970s, parliamentarians were looking for reliable data to assure parliament that executive government was accountable for its programs and taxpayers were calling for a more efficient and less expensive government. As a result, industrialized country SAIs made considerable progress in developing and experimenting with performance auditing methods and techniques. Criteria for measuring government performance were established, methodological approaches were invented and applied and performance indicators were developed. Concepts of significance and indicators for economy, efficiency and effectiveness (sometimes referred to as the "3 E's") were explored and developed. These efforts improved the audit reporting about government operations, most notably in Canada, Sweden, the United Kingdom, and the United States. Now performance auditing is widespread in Europe, North America, Australia and New Zealand, and is emerging in Asia and South Africa. ❧

Annex C: SAIs and Performance Auditing

Traditionally, most SAIs have exercised their function through audits that concentrated on whether government expenditures and operations complied with various laws and regulations. However, in recent years a number of SAIs have been directing their audits to the economy and effectiveness of government operations, i.e. performance auditing or VFM auditing to provide information about the operations of an entity or of a program or project.

For auditing to be valued by bureaucrats in government, it is necessary for auditing to add value to their functions. Performance auditing seems to add more value to the stock of knowledge about government operations than do financial audit opinions which give assurance about the credibility of financial statements. Compliance audits, while useful for ensuring compliance with law or casting blame, do not add as much value as performance audits. For a modern SAI to fulfill its role, performance auditing should be an important mandate feature (and there should be sufficient budget and training to perform such audits as well). In tiny Bhutan, for example, the Royal Audit Authority is mandated to conduct comprehensive audit, financial and compliance audits, performance audits and/or any form of audit as it may deem proper.

Approaches to performance auditing have evolved in response to economic and political pressures. An early approach was to audit all the main systems used by a government organization. The theory behind this top-down, process-oriented approach was that if systems were complete and met good management standards, then it followed that processes and activities would inevitably lead to good performance. However, this approach was time-consuming and expensive, and such audits were often unwieldy to review and difficult to understand.

A more modern approach is to audit projects or groups of projects. Smaller audits have fewer criteria to meet, although they also can focus on processes. The reports are more useful because they focus on a few topics, and their finds and recommendations are understandable and practical. And, since the audits of projects are smaller and easier to manage, costs are lower and reports are shorter and more frequent. Another modern approach to performance auditing is to audit a function across a number of departments of government. Audits of personnel practices, cash management, travel, and procurement lend themselves to this cross-cutting approach.

Performance auditing has always emphasized the need to better define government and program objectives. As governments become more accustomed to and increase their use of performance auditing, program objectives and performance standards and targets will become more clearly stated, greatly improving the relevance and efficiency of auditing. Better definitions of expected financial performance, quality of service, efficiency, output, outcome and impact will significantly improve the base of auditable evidence, thereby vastly expanding the range of auditable activities. Performance auditing will also become more efficient as computerized audit procedures take hold.

While computers have been used for many years for administrative and word processing activities, SAIs have changed their methods of auditing computerized agencies by employing Computer-Assisted Auditing Techniques (CAATs). These computer systems allow the auditor to download information from government systems and audit off-line or audit in real time. The Canadian SAI invented Interactive Data Extraction and Analysis software (IDEA), which is used in many SAIs for auditing compliance, financial statements as well as performance.

Performance auditing will continue to evolve as SAIs gain more experience. However, most current mandates limit the scope of performance auditing by not allowing comment on government policy, only on the implementation of policy. SAIs of Germany and Vietnam are exceptions as they are allowed to comment on government budgets. Some countries may allow their audit institutions to expand their mandates and evaluate programs and policies, as in the United States.

A new approach to performance auditing, similar to that used in financial statement auditing, is being promoted by Canada's CCAF-FCVI, previously known as the Canadian Comprehensive Auditing Foundation. This new approach has been described as Management Assertions on Attributes of Effectiveness (see Box 7). In this model, management makes assertions on up to 12 fundamental effectiveness attributes thereby producing a self-assessment of the organization's performance. And the auditor assesses how complete and reasonable each assertion is, thereby producing a self-assessment of the organization's performance.

Box A: CCAF-FCVI Attributes of Effectiveness

- management direction,
- relevance,
- appropriateness,
- achievement of intended results,
- acceptance,
- secondary impacts,
- costs and productivity,
- responsiveness,
- financial results,
- working environment,
- protection of assets, and
- monitoring and reporting.

This approach has not yet gained widespread acceptance by many public institutions or private enterprises. The main obstacle is convincing managers that they can offer honest and realistic assertions without risking their careers or exposing their organization to legal liabilities. With some experimentation, this more efficient approach to performance auditing may prove its worth.

Another recent trend has been to shift the focus of audits from processes to results. As with audits oriented to examining processes, the audit criteria for auditing results are developed beforehand to ensure that audit findings concentrate on the three E's of operational outputs, usually at the project or program level. This approach abandons a long-held regard for processes and systems, and gets to the point of the exercise: *did the activity achieve the intended result?*

Results-oriented auditing has sharpened the focus of performance auditing, and reduced the need for field work and lengthy reporting procedures.

Choosing audit topics that affect the entire society or a broad cross section of society is yet another recent trend in some industrialized countries. With performance audit reports, politicians can respond quickly to current events and concerns. In Sweden, for example, priority is given to areas where an external, independent, and impartial audit is expected to help improve efficiency and effectiveness of government operations. Also, as health care costs rise around the world, governments may well use their SAIs for health care auditing. Similarly, environmental auditing may become more commonplace. ❧

References and Bibliography

Accountability, December 1996.

Accountability, June 1997.

Canada. Office of the Auditor General. September 30, 1994. *Response to the Study Group Survey Questions: Significance in Value-for-Money Auditing.*

———. June 1994. *Special Examinations of Crown Corporations—Audit Guide 23.*

———. August 1995. *VMF Auditing Practices—A synthesis.*

———. 1994. *Auditing of Efficiency —Audit Guide 1, Part I.*

———. 1994. *Choosing and Applying the Right Evidence Gathering Techniques in Value-for-Money Audits—Audit Guide 24 (Field-Testing Draft).*

Canadian Comprehensive Auditing Foundation (CCAF). 1996. *Accountability, Performance Reporting, Comprehensive Audit—An Integrated Perspective.*

———. 1994. *Comprehensive Auditing: An Introduction.*

———. 1988. *Accountability, Accounting and Audit—Responding to a Decade of Experience.*

———. 1991. *Comprehensive Audit Reporting—Concepts, Issues and Practices.*

———. 1991. *How Can You Influence a Comprehensive Audit—A Client's Guide.*

———. 1984. *Knowledge Requirements for Comprehensive Audit—A Practitioner's Guide.*

———. 1987. *Reporting and Auditing Effectiveness in the Public Sector (Full Report)*

———. 1987. *Reporting and Auditing Effectiveness in the Public Sector (Summary Report).*

———. *Reporting on Effectiveness* (12-minute videotape).

———. *Reporting on Effectiveness with an introduction and Summary Comments by Executive Decision-Makers* (65-minute videotape).

———. 1993. *Reporting and Auditing Effectiveness—Putting Theory into Practice.*

———. 1994. *In Search of Effective Governance* (videotape and written material).

———. 1988. *Accountability, Accounting and Audit-Responding to a Decade of Experience.*

———. 1987. *Canadian Hospitals: Accountability and Information for Cost-Effectiveness—An Agenda for Action.*

———. 1986. *A New Dimension to Reliance on Internal Auditing in Canada*

———. 1987. *Special Examinations, Internal Audit and Reliances: A Practitioner's Guide*

———. 1984. *Value for Money in Municipalities: A Practitioner's Guide to Municipal Comprehensive Auditing.*

Germany. Federal Court of Audit. *Audit Guide*, September 1993.

Gould, David J., and Jose Amaro-Reyes. 1983. "The Effects of Corruption on Administrative Performance: Illustrations from Developing Countries." World Bank Working Paper No. 580. Washington, D.C.: The World Bank.

Hoffman-Burchardi, Economy. January 1989. *Efficiency, and Effectiveness Audits.*

Hong Kong. Director of Audit. *A Report of the Director of Audit on the Results of Value for Money Audits*, Report No. 25, October 1995.

House of Commons. 1981 "First Special Report from the Committee of Public Accounts, Session 1980–81." In *The Role of Comptroller and Auditor General, Volume 1, Report.* London: HMSO.

India. Office of the Comptroller and Auditor General, Training Division. *Efficiency-Cum-Performance Audit.*

International Federal of Accountants (IFAC). *Performance Reporting by Government Business Enterprise.* January 1996.

International Organization of Supreme Audit Institutions (INTOSAI). *Training Program for National Audit Offices, International Journal of Government Auditing.* Washington, DC, 1995.

————. June 1992. *Auditing Standards Committee,* Auditing Standards.

————. October, 1977 *Lima Declaration of Guidelines on Auditing Precepts.*

The IX Congress of INTOSAI, Lima, Peru

Klitgaard, Robert. 1996. "Bolivia: Healing Sick Institutions in La Paz." In *Governance and the Economy in Africa: Tools for Analysis and Reform of Corruption.* Edited by Patrick Meagher. College Park, MD: Center for Institutional Reform and the Informal Sector.

Langseth, Petter Jeremy Pope and Rick Stapenhurst. 1997. "The Role of a National Integrity System in Fighting Corruption". Washington, D.C. : The World Bank,

Pakistan, Office of the Auditor General. 1993. *Performance Audit Guidelines—Book 2—Undertaking Performance Audit*

————. 1984. *Performance Audit Guidelines—Volume 1—Measuring Performance.*

Pope, Jeremy (ed.). 1997. *National Integrity Systems: The TI Source Book, 2nd Edition.* Washington, D.C.: The World Bank.

Radburn, William. F. and Maria Barrados. 1994. "Results-Based Auditing." World Bank Discussion paper No. 68.

Reuter, Dr. Hans-Henner. *Performance Audit - Summary.* November 1990. Seminar on Selected problems of Public Sector Auditing of High-Ranking Representatives of the Supreme Audit Institutions of Kenya, Uganda and Zimbabwe, Germany.

Rose-Ackerman, Susan. 1996. "The Political Economy of Corruption: Causes and Consequences" *Viewpoint* (World Bank) 74 (April).

Sahgal, Vinod 1996. "Strengthening Legislative Audit Institutions: A Catalyst to Enhance Governance and Combat Corruption" (unpublished manuscript).

Stapenhurst, Rick and Robert Miller, forthcoming. "The Role of Parliaments in Curbing Corruption". Washington, D.C.: The World Bank.

Sweden, National Audit Office. 1995. *Performance Auditing at the Swedish National Audit Office*

————. 1994:38, 1995. *A Strategy for Performance Auditing of Social Security Systems.*

————. 1995. *Management of Program Aid —Coordinated British, Dutch and Swedish Audits.*

Tanzania, The United Republic of. 1996. Presidential Commission of Inquiry Against Corruption, *Service Delivery Survey: Corruption in the Police, Judiciary, Revenue and Land Services.* Dar es Salaam.

United Kingdom National Audit Office. *Performance Measurement and Value for Money Audit,* April 1995.

————. August 1991. Snelling, J. and J. Towns, *Designing and Carrying Out a Survey,* Unit A, Investigative Techniques Guide No. 1.

———. Snelling, J., *Use of Sampling—Value for Money Studies.*

———. 1993. *Study Selection,* Unit A, Investigative Techniques Guide no. 5,

———. Towns, Julia, *Case Studies as a Method of Evidence Collection and Analysis,* Unit A, Investigative Techniques Guide No. 3.

United States General Accounting Office (GAO). 1994. *Government Auditing Standards—1994 Revisions,* GAO/OCG-94-4, Washington, DC

World Bank, 1991. *Managing Development: The Governance Dimension.* Washington, D.C.

World Bank, 1997a. *Helping Countries Control Corruption.* Washington, D.C.

World Bank, 1997b. *World Development Report.* Washington, D.C.:

Zavelberg, Dr. H. G., June 1995. *Legislatures and Performance Auditing,* Symposium of the OECD on Performance Auditing and Performance Improvement held in Paris.

[17]

INSTITUTIONAL ARRANGEMENT FOR CONTROLLING CORRUPTION IN PUBLIC LIFE: KARNATAKA EXPERIENCE

S.N. SANGITA

Following a broader look at the concept and quantum of corruption, and the anti-corruption structure at the Central level, the author discusses different anti-corruption agencies of Karnataka. He then, on the basis of relevant data gathered by him, attempts to analyse the phenomenon of corruption in the state's public administration departments covering its nature, modes and causes. While high-lighting five critical factors contributing to growth of corruption, he lays greater emphasis on lack of political will.

CORRUPTION HAS become a way of life in India. What is most depressing is that it is spreading like cancer. With increase in corruption, economic disparities are widening.[1] A large portion of our resources is siphoned off through corrupt practices in the form of pilferages, leakages, etc., and the common man is loosing faith in our political institutions. Some of these, alienated from the State, are resorting to violent means. It is alarming to note that a large section of youth is in the forefront of secessionist, radical and other violent movements.

Let us, therefore, analyse the effectiveness of existing anti-corruption institutions (laws and machinery) which are meant to control corruption in public life. To take a closer look, let us responed to the following questions: How effective are the anti-corruption institutions (ACI)? Whether a positive change has been notified over the years in the corrupt behaviour of departments and groups of officials with the intervention of anti-corruption machinery (ACM)? To what extent, this behaviour can be attributed to the design of ACIs as well as to political and administrative will? In other words, whether the existing ACIs are suitable and compatible with the nature, pattern and causes of corruption? Whether the existing judicial, political and administrative processes are conducive to controling corruption ?

---

[1]According to scholars (like Wade 1968, Szeftel, 1983, and Clark 1983.), corruption has more negative consequences, although functionalists (like Myrdal, 1968, Huntington 1966, Left 1964, and Nye 1967) do not agree with this view point. According to former scholars, corruption perpetuates economic inequalities and brings instability in the political system.

INTRODUCTION

The main assumption in this article is that the institutions developed for controlling corruption in developing countries are quite inadequate. Most of these are established with little understanding of the nature and causes of corruption specific to them. ACIs and laws evolved in the country are *ad hoc* and partial in nature. They are punitive rather than preventive. Besides, there is a lack of strong political and administrative will to tackle this menace effectively. Let us take up these issues for discussion in the context of Karnataka State, which has a unique history of adopting comprehensive ACIs and legislations.

The analysis is based on a study conducted in Karnataka State. Main sources of this study are: statistical data (number of complaints against the public servants, officials punished under corruption charges and trapped while accepting the bribes), interviews of senior officers of ACM and public men, and important cases of corruption (reported in the annual reports and newspapers). Cases relating to experiences of other states have been used to analyse the nature, pattern and causes of corruption. The period covered is 1956 to 1990.

Definition and Quantum of Corruption

It is not an easy task to define corruption, as it is not a unified phenomenon. Corruption has many forms with different types of participants, settings, stakes, techniques and cultures. The divergence of corruption becomes much apparent, if distinction is made according to formal, legal and cultural definitions of corruption. However, Heidenheimer identified three types of corrupt behaviour definitions --public-office centered, market-centered and public-interest centered.[2]

Public-office-centered definitions revolve around violation of public trust placed in the office. In other words, deviation from bureaucratic norms, like rationality, universalism and achievement orientation in meeting responsibilities. An important scholar to be mentioned in this regard is James S. Nye. According to him, "Corruption is the behaviour, which deviates from the normal duties of public role because of private regarding (personal, close, private clique), pecuniary or status, violates rules against exercise of certain types of private regarding influence. This includes such behaviour as bribery (use of reward to prevent the judgment of a person in position of trust), nepotism (bestowal of a patronage by reasons of ascriptive relationship rather than merit) and misappropriation (illegal appropriation of public resource for private regarding uses)".[3]

Market-centered corruption refers to the situation in which officials see their position as an authority to maximise personal gains by dispensing public benefits. Public-interest-centered definition stresses the violation of common interest that

[2] Heidenheimer, Nas Tevfik, Albert Price, and Charles Weber, "A Policy Oriented Theory of Cororuption", *American Political Science Review*, Vol. 80, No.1, March, 1986, p. 109.

[3] James S. Nye, "Corruption and Political Development: A Cost-Benefit Analysis", in Heidenheimer (ed.), *Political Corruption: Readings in Comparative Analysis*, New York, 1970 pp. 566-67.

provides direct or indirect benefits to the public officials. Here, priority is given to private interests rather than the public concern. In this article, public-office-centered definition refers to corruption. It broadly refers to abuse of public office for personal gain.

It is very difficult to estimate the magnitude or status of corruption in India in the absence of statistical data. The same has been expressed by the Santhanam Committee, which went into the problems of corruption in 1964. According to it, it is not possible to give even a rough estimate of number of government servants, or amount of money or value or percentage of illegal gratifications that may be involved.[4]

However, according to some studies, the black operations (black money* and criminal activities) which are closely associated with political and administrative corruption are in ascendancy.[+] The black money (unaccounted for money, generated through tax evasion, smuggling, encroachment and illegal acquisition of urban real estate and leakages from government expenditure) which constituted 41.71 per cent of GDP in 1980-81 rose to 45.81 per cent in 1983-84 and 51.7 per cent in 1987-88. The growth rate of black money was slightly higher than the GDP during 1980-88 (46.5 per cent for black money and 40 per cent for GDP).[5]

Black money, on account of tax evasion, is both wide-spread and large. According to the Wanchoo Committee estimates of income, on which tax was evaded, increased from 700 crore in 1961-62 to 10,000 crore in 1965-66 and Rs. 14,000 crore in 1968-69.[6] However, according to the latest guess estimates, the income-tax evasion (including income, state and corporate taxes, and customs and excise duties) had gone up to Rs. 68,324 crore in 1987-88 from Rs. 26,528 crore in 1980-81. [Among these, income-tax occupied the first place with Rs. 34,329 crore during 1987-88. It was followed by state taxes (Rs. 16,131 crore), excise duty (Rs. 10,951 crore), customs duty (Rs. 5,953 crore), and corporate tax (Rs. 1,030 crore].[7]

While black income from urban real estates, smuggling and government expenditure accounted for around a little less than half of the total black money. Black income, due to encroachment and acquisition of valuable urban property and so on, was estimated around Rs. 5,260 crore in 1980-81 and it was 18,847 in

[4]Government of India, Ministry of Home Affairs, *Report of the Committee on Prevention of Corruption.* (Chairman: K. Santhanam), 1964, p. 14.

*Black money as tainted money--money which is not clean or which has a stigma attached to it. It symbolised money which has been earned by violating the provisions of the law and even social conscience and which is kept secret and unaccounted for.

[+]For instance tax evasion and corruption are inseparable and mutually reinforcing. One causes the other. The tax evaders need protection against regress of law which is provided by the political leaders and administrators for their personal gains.

[5]Suraj Gupta, *Black Income in India*, New Delhi, Sage Publications, 1992, p. 146.

[6]Government of India, Ministry of Finance, *Report of the Direct Taxes Enquiry Committee, Final Report* (Chairman: K.N. Wanchoo), 1971.

[7]Gupta, *op. cit.*, p. 146.

1987-88. Smuggling money was estimated to be a few hundred crore in 1960s which rose to Rs. 1,200 crore in 1980-81 and Rs. 12,000 crore in 1987-88[8].

Leakages from government expenditure is yet another source for black money and corruption. It was believed that 10 to 20 per cent of illicit money was collected on government contracts/purchases. According to Robert Wade, illicit income to the engineers in canal maintenance in a South Indian State in late 1972 was estimated around 25 to 50 per cent.[9] It was 50 to 60 per cent, according to Pant, in Kosi Canal System in Bihar[10]. Talwar has estimated that 25 to 30 per cent of the recorded cost of public works in Delhi and neighbouring states was siphoned off illicitly by government functionaries, politicians and contractors, while it was as high as 80 per cent in land development, acquisition and other works.[11] Leakages are reported even in the implementation of development and welfare programmes. In 1989, Rajiv Gandhi, the then Prime Minister of India, used to say that only 15 per cent of the developmental benefits reach the targeted poor. A large portion of these benefits are taken away by the intermediaries.

Anti-corruption Institutional Arrangement

Anti-corruption institutions at the Central level mainly comprise: *(i)* major legislations/acts including: The Prevention of Corruption Act 1947, The Indian Penal Code, The Representation of People's Act 1950, and *(ii)* The Central Vigilance Commission (CVC), Public Grievances Redressal Machinery, Central Bureau of Investigation, and Administrative Vigilance Division (of Home Ministry). For grievances redressal, Administrative Reforms Commission (ARC) recommended setting up of ombudsman-like institution to be known as Lokpal at the Central level and Lokayukta and Uplokayukta at the State level. A Bill for Lokpal was introduced five times in Lok Sabha by successive governments of different political parties but it is yet to be endorsed by Lok Sabha.[12] However, several state governments have already introduced institutions of Lokayukta and Uplokayuktas. By the end of 1990, the institutions similar to Lokayuktas were operating in half of the India states, covering three-fourths of its population. These states are Orissa (1971); Maharashtra (1971); Bihar (1973); Rajasthan (1973), Uttar Pradesh (1975), Madhya Pradesh (1981), Andhra Pradesh (1983), Himachal Pradesh (1983), Kerala (1984), Karnataka (1985), Assam (1986), and Gujarat (1985).

---

[8]Gupta, *op. cit.*

[9]Robert Wade, "The System of Administrative and Political Corruption: Canal Irrigation in South India", *Journal of Development Studies*, Vol. 18, No. 3, 1982, pp. 287-328.

[10]N. Pant, *Some Aspects of Irrigation Administration (A Case Study of Kosi Project)*, Patna, ANS Institute of Social Studies (mimeo), 1979.

[11]T.R. Talwar, "Real Worth of Assets Created in Construction", paper presented at the Conferences of Indian Association for Research on National Income and Wealth, December 1984.

[12]R.K. Dhawan, *Public Grievances and the Lokpal*, New Delhi, Allied, 1981.

ANTI-CORRUPTION INSTITUTIONS IN KARNATAKA

Directorate of Anti-corruption and Efficiency Audit

Karnataka is the first state which appointed a committee on prevention of corruption in public life as early as 1945. On the basis of its recommendations, two separate sections (units), known as Efficiency Audit and Anti-Corruption, were established in 1946 under the charge of a special officer. These were treated as separate branches of the General and Revenue secretariat under the control of a Minister. Subsequently, they merged together and were placed under the Directorate of Anti-Corruption and Efficiency Audit. All matters related to corruption were taken away from various departments and assigned to it.

The Directorate mainly deals with cases of bribery and corruption among the public servants. On the basis of information, departmental inquiries are ordered against the officials. Even in some cases, prosecution is conducted in criminal courts. It also recommends severe action against the accused officials.

While the Efficiency Audit Cell conducts regular inspections of government offices to prevent delays in the dispatch of its business, it also examines existing government procedures and methods and suggests their simplification for efficiency reasons. The Directorate also ensures strict adherence of departments to office rules, standing orders and policies of government. It organises surprise inspections to detect and prevent losses and leakages of resources. On the request of government, it conducts investigations on irregularities in departments. It also helps to bring about proper coordination among various departments to ensure efficiency.

Vigilance Commission

The Directorate was, however, replaced in 1965 by a Vigilance Commission (VC) on the lines of the CVC. It is headed by the Vigilance Commissioner who is appointed by the Governor from amongest the sitting Judges of the High Court in consultation with the Chief Justice of Karnataka. He holds the office for a term of five years or until he attains the age of 65 years, whichever is earlier. He can be removed by the Governor only after a proper enquiry, conducted by a High Court Judge. He is not eligible for any appointment after his retirement. He provides direction and coordinates the activities connected with maintenance of integrity in state administration. The Vigilance Commissioner discharges his responsibilities through its three wings, *viz.*, Directorate of Vigilance, Bureau of Investigation, and Technical Cell.

The Commission mainly looks into allegations (including corruption and misconduct)against state government employees (including local bodies and public sector undertakings). It conducts detailed enquiries on the complaints received against public servants and recommends to the government or the concerned head of the department the action to be taken. The government reviews the recommendation and takes appropriate action in the matter. The VC also arranges traps, investigates cases of government servants amassing wealth beyond their sources of income. The commission is also vested with *suo motu* powers to initiate investigation against any public servants on its own. It has to present an annual report of its work to the government which, in turn, is placed before the state legislature.

Lokayukta and Up-lokayukta

In 1986, the Lokayukta institution was introduced in the place of VC. In many respects, it is similar to VC. In fact, the entire staff of VC and its functions have been transferred to the Lokayukta. However, the status and powers of the Lokayukta have been enhanced to control corruption at higher levels. Two persons of the status of justice of Supreme Court and High Court are appointed as Lokayukta and Up-Lokayukta respectively, in place of the Vigilance Commissioner. Both of them are from outside the state for reasons of greater objectivity.

They are appointed by the Governor in consultation with the Chief Justice of the High Court, Presiding Officers--Speaker and Chairman--of the state legislature as well as opposition party leaders of both the houses of the state legislature. Both of them hold office for a period of five years. They are not removable, except by a set procedure.

Perhaps Karnataka is the first state which has vested enormous powers with the Lokayukta institution to investigate actions and decisions of public servants, which include state government servants and functionaries of other organisations financed by the state government. Its scope has been further enlarged to cover former public servants, who held these positions at any point of time in the past. The Lokayukta investigates charges against the Chief Minister, ministers, legislators, and secretaries; and Up-Lokayukta covers other government servants, not covered by the Lokayukta.

However, certain categories of people are not under the jurisdiction of Lokayukta and Up-Lokayukta. They are: Speaker and Chairman of the Legislative Assembly and Council respectively, the Accountant General, the Chief Election Commissioner and his Commissioners, the Chairman and Members of the Karnataka Public Service Commission (KPSC), and officers or servants of civil and criminal courts.

As for the investigation, they cover both the allegations (corruption, nepotism, favouritism) and complaints (grievances) which arise out of maladministration. However, certain types of actions of public servants are excluded from the purview of Lokayukta and Up-Lokayukta.

They also perform the functions of the erstwhile VC. These include investigation of cases involving offences under prevention of corruption act and allied penal laws. They also deal with cases of demand and acceptance of bribe, amassing of wealth, misappropriation, disciplinary proceedings and so on. Besides, the government also can refer any set of allegations against public servant to Lokayukta and Up-Lokayukta for investigation. In addition , the Lokayukta has to receive and preserve the annual statements of assets and liabilities of Chief Minister, ministers, MLAs and MLCs.

Any citizen can make a complaint against a public servant in the prescribed form, supported by an affidavit. After holding a preliminary enquiry into the allegations made in the complaint, the Lokayukta has to furnish a copy of it to the concerned public servant to offer his comments. The investigation may then be conducted either in public or in camera at his discretion. However, the information obtained or evidence collected during investigation has to be kept confidential. The Lokayukta and Up-Lokayukta can refuse to investigate a complaint, if it fails to fulfil stipulated conditions.

While investigating complaints, they can invoke powers of civil court under the Civil Procedure Code Act of 1908. They can summon attendance of any person and examine him on oath. They can ask for any public record from any court or office. They can also appoint a commission for examination of witnesses. They are also empowered to issue a warrant to search any building, place or person for recovery of any article.

If the Lokayukta or Up-Lokayukta finds that the 'grievance' has been proved, he should communicate the same to the competent authority to redress the grievance in the manner suggested. The competent authority has to inform back to Lokayukta about the action taken in redressing the grievance within a month. Same is the case with the procedure adopted for allegation. However, in this case, the time given to competent authority to reply about the action taken or proposed to be taken is three months. The case will be closed, if Lokayukta or Up-Lokayukta are satisfied with the reply. Otherwise, he can refer the case to the Governor, who in turn could place it before the state legislature. The Act has provided for vacating of the office by the concerned public servant, if Lokayukta or Up-Lokayukta is satisfied that the allegation lodged against him is proved. Both Lokayukta and Up-Lokayukta are supported by four wings, *viz.*, Investigation (Police), Investigation (Technical) and Administration to discharge their responsibilities.[13]

Efficiency Audit and Vigilance Bureau

Besides Lokayukta institution, Efficiency Audit and Vigilance Bureau (EAVB) was established in 1990 to eradicate corruption and ensure efficiency and accountability in administration. Additional Chief Secretary of the state government is its chairman and officers of the rank of Inspector-General of Police (IGP) and Senior Group 'A' Officer from the finance are the other two members. It deals with cases of corruption, negligence, dereliction of duties, inefficiency and wasteful expenditure, and lack of accountability in government departments.

It investigates charges of corruption against government servants, maladministration and instances of misuse of funds. It also investigates public interest cases, like atrocities against SC/ST/women/minorities and other socio-economic problems to identify causes and suggest remedial measures.

---

[13]S.N. Sangita and Suvarchala, "The Lokayukta Institution in Karnataka: A Trend Setter for Three Tier Structure Ombudsman in India". *Indian Journal of Public Administration*, Vol. XXXV, No. 4, 1989.

The EAVB conducts surprise inspections periodically and suggests changes in the procedures, rules and regulations to achieve maximum efficiency. It also suggests re-deployment of underutilised personnel and conducts performance audit to identify bottlenecks in implementation of programmes and suggests improvements (for instance, the EAVB conducted a number of inspections in 1991 to verify implementation of programmes like JRY, IRDP and PDS).

Public Grievances Redressal Organisation

Prior to appointment of Lokayukta and Up-Lokayukta, public grievances organisations were operating to redress grievances that arose out of maladministration. It was established in 1983 in the Department of Personnel and Administrative Reforms of the state government under the overall supervision of the Chief Secretary. Grievances redressal officers were nominated at the secretariat and field level departments. Deputy Commissioner, Assistant Commissioner and Tahsildar were entrusted with the responsibilities of grievances redressal officers at their respective levels.

The complaints received from the public were communicated to the concerned departments for necessary action. The concerned department has then to intimate the action taken on these complaints to the grievance redressal officer and to the complainant within a stipulated time. Grievance redressal officers review periodically the progress of disposal of complaints.

Thus, evolution of institutional development in Karnataka State can be broadly classified into three phases. The first phase covers both preventive and punitive aspects of corruption. Efficiency and Audit Unit, which is a part of Anti-Corruption machinery, conducts regular inspections of various government offices to find out administrative bottlenecks and irregularities in government departments. It also examines existing administrative procedures and methods to suggest improvements for achieving efficiency. Besides, Anti-Corruption Bureau investigates allegations against private individuals, like black-marketeers and other offenders. However, this institution does not enjoy autonomous status, although a senior officer of proven integrity heads the institution.

In the second phase, the emphasis is more prevention of corruption and grievances arising out of maladministration. The institution is structured similar to Ombudsman of developed countries, as recommended by the Santhanam Committee on prevention of corruption. Since Anti-Corruption Bureau was merged with this institution, it carries its erstwhile functions. The prestige of the institution has been enhanced by making it autonomous and by appointing thereto sitting High Court Judges. Besides, its scope has been widened to include employees of public undertakings and local bodies. The Commission is even vested with *suo motu* powers to initiate action against government servants.

In the third phase, many steps have been initiated to enhance the status of the institution to control corruption at the higher levels. Highest judicial officials of the land from outside the state are appointed as Lokayukta and Up-lokayukta. In order to enjoy respect from all sections, they are appointed by the Governor after consultation with Chief Justice of High Court, presiding officers of the legislature and opposition leaders of the state legislature. However, the *suo motu* powers are not entrusted with the Lokayukta. Similar to Lokayukta institution, EAVB was established in 1990, but this institution, however, focuses more on prevention of corruption rather than the punitive aspect and suggests simplification of administrative regulations, procedures and methods to achieve efficiency.

ANALYSIS OF CORRUPTION IN KARNATAKA

To assess the change in the corrupt behaviour of the state government departments and officials as a result of anti-corruption measures, a number of complaints received by the ACM were examined along with people's perception about corruption. Ever since the State came into existence (1956), the ACM on an average receives 2,196 complaints per annum (see Table 1). However, their number was the highest under VC during 1966-85, *i.e.*, 3,553 complaints. The corresponding number under Lokayukta and ACB was 1,572 and 1,463 respectively. In 1975-76, the VC received the highest number of complaints (5,359). Although, there is no set trend regarding rise in number of complaints, it is a fact that complaints are growing over the years.

TABLE 1 DETAILS OF RECEIPTS AND DISPOSAL OF COMPLAINTS PER ANNUM BY ANTI-CORRUPTION MACHINERY DURING 1956-90

Sl. No.	*Particulars*	*Anti-Corruption Bureau 1956-65*	*Vigilance Commission 1965-80*	*Lokayukta 1985-90*	*Average*
(1)	(2)	(3)	(4)	(5)	(6)
1.	Opening balance	886	486	73	482
2.	No. of complaints received	1,464	3,554	1,572	2,196
	Total :	2,350	4,040	1,645	2,675
3.	Cases dropped	833 (35.45)	754 (18.66)	233 (14.14)	607
4.	Referred to Depts. for investigation	535 (22.76)	2,188 (54.15)	1244 (13.62)	1,322
5.	Referred to Depts. for action	89 (3.80)	185 (4.58)	16 (0.94)	97
6.	Pending	871 (37.07)	437 (10.82)	73 (4.40)	460

NOTE : Figures in parantheses are percentages.
SOURCE: Compiled from Annual Reports.

The average number of complaints received in Karnataka is quite high, when compared to other states. For instance, it was 4,365 in Andhra Pradesh; 2,728 in Bihar; 85 in Himachal Pradesh; 4,806 in Madhya Pradesh; 1,381 in Maharashtra; 505 in Rajasthan; and 102 in Uttar Pradesh. Table 2 gives a picture of performance of ACIs in Karnataka and a comparison of Lokayukta performance in Karnataka and Andhra Pradesh. Compared to the developed world, the number of complaints per one lakh population is far less. It does not mean that corruption is less in our states. In fact, many aggrieved persons avoid lodging of complaints as it involves risks, including retaliation from the officials with whom he has to interact very often. Complicated procedure involved in filing the complaint also prevents them from lodging complaints. This is more among the poor, living in the backward and rural areas. In fact, 60-80 per cent of complaints received by ACM were from urban areas.

It is evident from our data that the ACM is mainly dealing with administrative corruption. In spite of bringing elected representatives under the purview of Lokayukta institution in 1986, there is no major change in this regard. Only, 1.45 per cent of the total complaints were received against the elected representatives during 1985-90. None of them were punished.

Group-wise and Department-wise Corruption

During 1965-80, 119 gazetted officers (higher level officials) and 294 non-gazetted officers (lower level officials) were punished under corruption charges by ACM (see Table 3). More or less, the same trend is reflected in regard to trap cases by ACM-Vigilance Commission. Eighty seven gazetted officers and 263 non-gazetted officers were trapped during 1965-70. Similarly, larger quantum of complaints were against 'B' (higher middle) and 'C' (lower middle) group officials during 1985-90 (see Table 4). It accounted for 36 and 32 per cent respectively out of the 12,437 total complaints received by the Lokayukta and group 'A' (higher level officials) accounted for only 14.14 per cent. This was less than one per cent (0.88) for group 'D' (lower level officials). However, there were few complaints against officers of All India Services, like IAS, IPS and IFS: IAS and IPS officers accounted for 1.27 per cent each.

There are certain departments where corruption is very high (see Table 2). These include Revenue, Police, Health, Education and Public Works Departments, which account for around three-fourths of the corruption in all departments. During 1961-62, 75 per cent of the officials punished on charges of corruption by the Anti-corruption Bureau were from these departments. Same trend was reflected by both VC and Lokayukta institutions. The corruption cases related to grievances, traps and punishments under VC, during 1965-78, accounted for 65 per cent from these departments. Similarly, 52 per cent of the total complaints under Lokayukta institution during 1985-90 were directed against these departments.

There is another set of departments, where corruption remained consistent all these years. These are: Commercial Taxes, Road Transport, Excise, Registration, Treasury, Weights and Measures, Industry and Commerce. On the

TABLE 2 DISPOSAL OF DEPARTMENT-WISE CORRUPTION CASES BY ANTI-CORRUPTION BUREAU, VIGILANCE COMMISSION AND A COMPARISON OF PERFORMANCE OF LOKAYUKTA IN KARNATAKA AND ANDHRA PRADESH

(in percentage)

Department	Officers Punished by Anti-Corruption Bureau in 1961-62	Vigilance Commission				Karnataka Lokayukta 1985-90 Complaints Average	A.P. Lokayukta 1985-87 Complaints Average
		Grievances Cases in 1965-75	Trap Cases in 1965-78	Officers Involved in 1965-75	Average of ol.4, 5 and 6		
(1)	(2)	(3)	(4)	(5)	(6)	(7)	(8)
Revenue	13.91	12.79	29.32	28.71	23.60	10.11	11.53
Police	18.55	9.00	12.90	7.78	9.89	6.09	7.93
Education	5.67	31.75	4.98	8.51	15.08	17.36	10.13
Health	6.17	9.00	12.90	10.70	10.43	6.65	8.80
P.W.D.	30.94	9.00	0.58	1.27	3.61	11.84	11.72
Municipality	0.51	0.94	2.34	1.94	1.74	7.13	6.92
B.D.A.	-	-	-	0.24	0.24	3.68	-
Panchayati Raj	2.06	-	4.10	5.35	4.72	5.01	6.08
Cooperation	-	3.31	1.46	0.97	1.92	2.66	13.57
Commercial Tax	1.03	-	5.57	3.40	4.48	2.08	1.39
Excise	7.73	1.42	0.21	1.94	1.19	0.77	1.56
Forest	3.60	6.00	0.87	4.62	3.83	3.21	2.94
Land Reforms	-	-	3.51	0.24	1.87	0.61	-
Survey & Land Records	0.51	-	-	-	-	0.43	-
Registration	2.06	-	2.93	2.18	2.55	1.48	0.61
Labour	0.51	1.42	1.17	0.97	1.18	0.49	0.17

(Contd.)

(1)	(2)	(3)	(4)	(5)	(6)	(7)	(8)
Transport	2.57	-	1.75	2.67	2.21	2.03	1.55
Treasury	-	0.94	1.75	-	1.34	0.23	1.04
Agriculture	0.51	0.94	0.87	-	0.90	2.37	2.49
Animal Husbandry	-	1.89	1.17	-	1.53	0.35	0.56
Judiciary	1.54	-	2.63	0.97	1.80	0.46	-
Social Welfare	-	-	-	-	-	1.05	2.26
K.E.B.	1.03	0.47	2.34	-	1.40	2.90	-
Town Planning	-	0.94	-	-	-	-	-
Accounts	-	0.94	-	4.62	2.78	0.61	-
University	-	-	-	-	-	-	0.45
Industry & Commerce	0.51	0.94	1.74	2.18	1.62	1.19	-
Employment	-	-	-	-	-	-	1.26
Weights &	Measures	-	0.58	0.24	0.41	0.26	0.10
Food & Civil	Supplies	-	-	-	-	1.23	-
Mines & Zoology	-	-	0.87	0.48	0.67	0.54	-
Elected Representatives	-	-	-	-	-	1.42	4.25
Others	0.59	8.31	3.46	10.02	7.26	5.59	2.29
TOTAL	100.00	100.00	100.00	100.00	100.00	100.00	100.00

SOURCE : Compiled from Annual Reports.

TABLE 3 DETAILS OF OFFICERS PUNISHED BY KARNATAKA VIGILENCE COMMISSION DURING 1965-80

Sl. No.	Officers	Years										Total	Percentage
		1965-66	1966-67	1967-68	1968-69	1972-73	1974-75	1975-76	1977-78	1978-79	1979-80		
(1)	(2)	(3)	(4)	(5)	(6)	(7)	(8)	(9)	(10)	(11)	(12)	(13)	(14)
Gazetted													
1.	Deputy Commissioner/ Assistant Commissioner	-	1	1	3	1	-	-	-	-	-	6	5.04
2.	Tahsildar	-	1	2	1	2	1	5	2	-	-	14	11.76
3.	Mysore Administrative Service/Under Secretary/ Section Officer	-	-	-	1	-	-	1	-	-	-	2	1.68
4.	District Treasury Officer	1	-	1	0	-	-	1	4	-	-	7	5.88
5.	Executive Engineer/ Assistant Engineer	-	1	-	1	-	-	-	-	2	1	5	4.20
6.	Medical Officer/ Surgeon/Assistant Surgeon/Professor	-	-	9	4	-	3	11	9	2	3	41	34.45
7.	Commercial Tax Officer/ Assistant Commercial Tax Officer	1	-	-	-	-	-	1	6	-	-	8	6.72
8.	Joint/Deputy/Assistant Director	-	-	1	2	-	-	1	1	-	2	7	5.88
9.	Educational Officer/ Assistant Educational Officer	-	-	-	-	-	-	-	3	-	-	3	2.52
10.	Land Acquisition Officer	-	2	2	2	-	-	-	3	-	-	9	7.56
11.	Regional Transport Officer	-	-	-	2	1	-	2	-	-	-	5	4.20
12.	Block Development Officer	-	1	1	3	-	-	-	-	1	-	6	5.04
13.	Others	-	-	2	1	-	-	1	2	-	-	6	5.04
	TOTAL	2	6	19	20	4	4	23	30	5	6	119	

(Contd.)

(1)	(2)	(3)	(4)	(5)	(6)	(7)	(8)	(9)	(10)	(11)	(12)	(13)	(14)
Non-Gazetted													
1.	Sub Inspector	3	1	3	2	2	3	5	2	1	-	22	7.48
2.	Constable	-	1	-	-	-	1	6	2	-	-	10	3.40
3.	Inspector of Schools/Head Master/Lecturer/Instructor/ Teacher	-	2	3	12	1	-	1	2	1	2	24	8.16
4.	Deputy Tahsildar/Revenue Inspector	-	-	8	5	2	4	11	5	1	1	37	12.58
5.	Village Accountant	-	-	-	-	-	4	12	27	3	6	52	17.68
6.	Accounts Officer/Accountant/ Auditor	-	2	1	2	-	-	1	-	-	-	6	2.04
7.	Range Forest Officer/Forester/ Forest Guard	-	-	8	1	-	-	-	3	-	-	12	4.08
8.	Motor Vehicle Inspector/ Conductor/Driver	1	-	2	4	1	-	-	-	-	-	8	2.72
9.	Food Inspector	-	1	1	-	-	-	-	-	-	-	2	0.68
10.	Supervisor	-	1	3	5	-	-	1	-	-	-	10	3.40
11.	Social Welfare Inspector	-	2	1	1	-	-	-	-	-	-	4	1.36
12.	Surveyor	-	-	4	-	-	-	-	-	-	-	4	1.36
13.	Extension Officer	-	-	-	4	-	1	-	4	-	-	9	3.06
14.	Sub Registrar	-	-	-	-	1	-	1	1	-	-	3	1.02
15.	Assistant Medical Officer	-	-	1	-	-	-	-	-	-	-	1	0.34
16.	Sirstedhar	-	-	-	-	-	-	2	-	-	-	2	0.88
17.	Junior Engineer/Foreman	-	-	1	-	-	-	5	-	2	-	8	2.72
18.	Excise Inspector	-	1	2	1	-	-	-	-	-	-	4	1.36
19.	Commercial Tax Inspector	2	-	-	1	-	-	1	1	-	-	5	1.70
20.	Labour Inspector	-	-	1	-	-	1	-	1	1	-	4	1.36
21.	UDC/LDC	-	1	5	3	2	8	10	12	3	4	48	16.32
22.	Others	-	3	6	1	-	-	3	6	-	-	19	6.46
	TOTAL	6	15	50	42	9	22	59	66	12	13	294	

SOURCE : Compiled from Annual Reports.

TABLE 4 GROUP-WISE DATA OF COMPLAINTS RECEIVED, DISPOSED OF AND PENDING WITH KARNATAKA LOKAYUKTA OFFICE DURING 15.1.85 TO 31.3.90

Group	*No. of Complaints Received*	*Disposed of After Scrutiny*	*Disposed of After Enquiry*	*Disposed of After Investigation*	*Action Recommended After Investigation*	*Pending*
(1)	(2)	(3)	(4)	(5)	(6)	(7)
A	1,796	1,421	208	26	53	88
B	3,234	2,681	332	18	59	144
C	2,676	2,324	226	13	68	45
D	110	110	-	-	-	-
IAS/IPS/IFS	176	129	33	01	1	12
Elected Leaders	138	99	24	1	1	12
General	4,307	4,307	-	-	-	-
TOTAL	12,437	11,071 (89.03)	823 (6.60)	58 (0.46)	182 (1.46)	303 (2.43)

NOTE : Figures in the parantheses are percentages.
Source: Compiled from Annual Reports.

other hand, corruption among the local bodies (Municipality, Panchayati Raj and Cooperatives) is also significant. In fact, there is a steady increase of corruption in urban local bodies, like Municipal Corporation, Bangalore Development Authority, Housing Board and so on. On the other hand, corruption is less in departments, like Agriculture and Animal Husbandry, if their size is taken into consideration. However, in recent times, corruption in Animal Husbandry is on an increase.

Mode of Corruption

There is no set pattern of mode of corruption. It varies from department to department and even within the departments. Keeping this in view, let us analyse this aspect in this section. Corruption pertaining to issuance of certificates, licenses, and permits occupied first position (see Table 5). It accounted for around 14.9 per cent, if all the departments are put together; it is more than half in departments like Labour, Food and Civil Supplies, Weights and Measures, Mines, Excise, Forest, Industry and Animal Husbandry. While it was around 50.2 per cent in departments like Transport, Revenue, Registration, Municipality, Panchayats, and Education, it accounted for only 11 per cent in the department of Health and Family Welfare. The certificates mainly include caste and income certificates, vehicle registration and no objection certificates and so on. The licenses primarily include: driving license, license for liquor shops, rice mills, and so on.

On the other hand, permits pertained to: cutting and transportation of trees, collecting stones or undertaking mining activities, plying buses on unauthorised routes, and so on. In fact, licenses and permits, according to the Santhanam

TABLE 5 DETAILS OF NATURE OF CORRUPTION IN DIFFERENT DEPARTMENTS UNDER THE PREVIEW OF VIGILANCE COMMISSION DURING 1965-78

Sl. No.	Department	*Different Processes and Matters* *												*Total*
		1	2	3	4	5	6	7	8	9	10	11	12	
1.	Revenue	30 (31.57)	16 (16.85)	20 (21.05)	9 (09.47)	-	-	-	-	-	-	-	20 (21.05)	95
2.	Police	-	3 (10.34)	-	-	6 (20.68)	2 (6.89)	-	-	-	12 (41.37)	-	6 (20.68)	29
3.	Transport	-	2 (28.57)	3 (42.85)	-	-	-	-	-	2 (28.57)	-	-	-	7
4.	Commercial Tax	-	3 (17.64)	-	-	-	-	-	-	11 (64.70)	-	-	3 (17.64)	17
5.	Excise	-	-	3 (60.00)	-	-	-	-	-	-	2 (40.00)	-	-	5
6.	Weights & Measures	-	-	1 (50.00)	-	-	-	-	-	-	-	-	1 (50.00)	2
7.	Mines	-	-	1 (50.00)	-	-	-	-	-	-	-	-	1 (50.00)	2
8.	Food & Civil Supplies	-	-	1 (50.00)	1 (50.00)	-	-	-	-	-	-	-	-	2
9.	Labour	-	-	4 (100.00)	-	-	-	-	-	-	-	-	-	4
10.	Forest	-	-	2 (50.00)	1 (25.00)	-	-	-	-	-	-	-	1 (25.00)	4
11.	Industries	-	-	1 (50.00)	1 (50.00)	-	-	-	-	-	-	-	-	2
12.	Registration	-	4 (44.44)	3 (33.33)	-	-	-	-	-	-	-	-	2 (22.22)	9
13.	Employment	-	-	-	-	2 (100.00)	-	-	-	-	-	-	-	2
14.	Judiciary	-	-	-	-	-	3 (42.85)	-	-	-	-	-	4 (57.14)	7
15.	Treasury	-	-	-	-	3 (75.00)	-	-	-	-	-	-	1 (25.00)	4

16.	Municipality	-	-	2 (28.57)	2 (28.57)	-	-	-	-	3 (42.85)	-	-	-	7
17.	Panchayati Raj	-	-	4 (33.33)	3 (25.00)	2 (16.66)	-	-	-	-	-	-	3 (25.00)	12
18.	Co-operative	-	-	-	3 (60.00)	2 (40.00)	-	-	-	-	-	-	-	5
19.	Agriculture	-	-	-	1 (50.00)	-	-	-	-	-	-	-	1 (50.00)	2
20.	Animals Husbandry	-	-	2 (50.00)	-	2 (50.00)	-	-	-	-	-	-	-	4
21.	Education	-	-	4 (28.57)	-	6 (42.85)	-	-	-	-	-	-	4 (28.57)	14
22.	Health	-	-	11 (29.72)	-	20 (54.05)	-	-	-	-	-	-	6 (16.21)	37
23.	PWD	-	-	-	-	-	-	29 (21.96)	63 (47.72)	-	-	10 (7.57)	30 (22.72)	132
24.	Others	-	4 (13.33)	3 (10.00)	6 (19.99)	5 (16.66)	1 (3.33)	3 (10.00)	-	-	-	-	10 (33.33)	30
	TOTAL	30 (6.88)	32 (7.33)	65 (14.90)	27 (5.73)	48 (11.00)	8 (1.83)	32 (7.33)	63 (14.49)	16 (3.66)	14 (3.21)	10 (2.29)	93 (21.33)	434

*1 = Supply of Records, 2 = Changes in Record (Registration), 3 = Issue of Certificate/Licence/Permit, 4 = Allotment of Resources—Land/Quota/Loan/Grant, 5 = Providing Services/Facilities, 6 = Granting of Official Favour, 7 = Allowing Payment in Excess of the Due, 8 = Condoning Sub-standard Works, 9 = Reducing Tax/Penalty, 10 = Allowing Unlawful Action, 11 = Condoning Misappropriation, and 12 = Others.

NOTE : Figure in parantheses are percentages.

Committee, fetched 100 to 500 per cent of its face value, if it was sold. The import licenses worth of Rs 238.24 lakh were obtained by fraud and other types of malpractices.[14]

Another important and common mode of corruption is charging services and facilities provided by the government. Altogether corruption on this account accounted for around 11 per cent. It is the highest in departments like Health and Family Welfare, Education, Cooperation, Treasury and Police. Its quantium was 54.05 per cent in the department of Health and Family Welfare. These mainly include admitting patients into hospitals, providing treatment, giving injection and medicine, termination of pregnancy and so on. Similarly, appointments, confirmation, transfers, release of arrears and pensions, release of grants to the aided institutions, passing of bills in education department, filing of FIR, release of people on bail, return of stolen articles or goods kept in police custody, treating animals in Animal Husbandry, and registration of deeds can be mentioned in this category.

Another type of corruption which is common to some departments is distribution of government resources, like allotment of land/quota, sanction of loan/grant and award of contract. These accounted for around 5.13 per cent in all departments put together. However, it is around 50 per cent in departments, like food and civil supplies, industry, revenue, cooperative, and agriculture.

Yet another form of corruption common to some departments is to effect changes in the records, which included deletion or inclusion of some names. It accounted for around 7.33 per cent in all departments put together. This is very much prevalent in Revenue department, particularly at the grassroot level (17%). Village Accountant and RI normally charges Rs. 300-100 for Katha transfer, Similarly, registration of vehicles in transport department, registration of deeds in the registrar's office, and registration of dealership in commercial tax can be mentioned in this regard.

Supply of information or provision of records is another form of corruption. It accounted for 6.88 per cent of the total corruption. However, it was the highest in the revenue department. A little less than one-third of corruption in the revenue department accounted for this. The RI and Village Accountants normally collect Rs. 100-150 for issuing *phani* or other documents related to land.

Approving or purchasing of sub-standard works/goods is the mode prevalent in PWD and purchasing departments. A little less than half in PWD accounted for this. It is customary in these departments to offer certain percentages in respect of awards of contracts of construction, purchases and sales. Santhanam Committee estimated that around 7-11 per cent is paid on construction contracts. The Committee also noted prevalence of buyer's commission or kick-backs, ranging from 1.5 to three per cent, which is quite sizeable in absolute figures. The Committee estimated that such transactions constituted around five per cent of the

[14]Government of India, Ministry of Home Affairs, *Report of the Committee on Prevention of Corruption*, *op. cit.*

total investment on construction and purchases during the Second Five Year Plan.[15]

The over-payment for works executed by the contractor or goods supplied by the dealers is another form of corruption. This accounted for around 7.33 per cent. However, it was 22 per cent among all the departments. This type of corruption is also noticed by the Santhanam Committee. According to it, during 1957-62, nearly 1593 cases of over payment involving an amount of 43.66 lakh was noticed in the CPWD.[16]

Under assessment of tax or reduction of tax or penalty, leasing out and selling of government property for low price is yet another form of corruption. This accounted for 3.66 per cent of the total cases in all departments. It was the highest in commercial tax department (64.70 per cent) followed by Municipalities and Transport with 42.85 and 28.57 respectively. Santhanam Committee also found pervalence of under-assessment of taxes. According to it, the Comptroller and Auditor General noticed under-assessment of taxes, when they conducted test audit in 235 income wards out of 1,310 wards in the country and found a number of cases involving under-assessment to the tune of Rs. 120.77 lakh, which worked out to be about 16 per cent of the total number of cases audited (*i.e.*, 13,357).[17]

Corruption under unlawful activities accounted for around 3.21 per cent at the aggregate level. It was the highest in police department (41.37%), followed by Excise with 40 per cent. These departments were entrusted with the responsibility of checking unlawful activities, like smuggling, drug-trafficking, black marketing, illicit distillation of liquor and so on.

Another interesting feature was that corruption has been institutionalised in certain departments. Rates were fixed for different activities. In some departments, the money derived from these transactions was shared in an agreed proportion among concerned officials. The Kripalini Committee on Corruption confirmed similar practices in the Railways. The Railway contractors paid regularly to the officials 20 per cent of the total investment, which was distributed in the following manner; EE, AE, and Supervisor (5% each), Accounts Sections (2 %), Head Clerk and Mistry (1 % each), Pay Clerk (0.35 %) and miscellaneous (0.75 %). Similar practice was being followed in a number of departments, although PWD topped the list. For instance, certain percentage of JRY and NREP funds were shared between Village Sarpanch, Junior Engineer, Engineering Supervisor, dealing clerk and others in an agreed proportion.

FACTORS OF GROWTH OF CORRUPTION AND REMEDIES

Just like many forms/patterns of corruption, there are several contributory factors responsible for growth of corruption. With the main assumption that the existing ACIs were quite inadequate to address the problems of corruption, as these

[15]Government of India, Ministry of Home Affairs, *Report of the Committee on Prevention of Corruption*, *op. cit*

[16]*Ibid.*

[17]*Ibid.*

concentrate more on punitive rather than on preventive aspect, let us now identify these factors with the overall objective to help device the most appropriate strategies and instruments for controlling it.

Individual Factor

It is evident from the analysis in preceding paras that corruption is present almost everywhere although the pattern and scale differs. This can be attributed to lack or absence of ethics and moral standards in the conduct of public affairs. The ethics and values in the public life seem to have completely eroded. Pre-Independence period leaders sacrificed everything for the sake of nation, which is no longer the case with the present leadership which is prone to adopt any means to justify their ends. Same is the case with the ethics in civil service.

Moral values and ethics in public life can be best restored by adopting a code of conduct in public life. A beginning has to be made by the leadership at the higher levels. Similarly, professional standards and ethics should be maintained in the civil service. Our educational system should be reoriented to inculcate high values and standards among the younger generation. Similarly, political parties can play a significant role to build the national character by recruiting people with proven record of honesty and integrity and by reorienting the people to maintaining higher standards in public life. Mass media can also contribute in this regard.

Structural Factor

Electoral competition based on money and muscle power is the main source of political corruption. In the absence of well-knit organisation and cadre, political parties resort to money power and muscle power (criminal gangs come handy for this purpose) to mobilise people. This is evident from reports showing that a large percentage of members in Bihar and UP Assemblies were having criminal background. Democratisation of political parties and introduction of a code of conduct appears to be a viable method to arrest such trends. Electoral reforms, including funding of elections by the government, is also an essential requirement to control political corruption.

A major source for political corruption is appointments and transfers in the government. It is a fact that a certain percentage of postings and transfers are priced. As a result of this, a large section of unemployed youth appear to have lost faith in the impartial conduct of provincial public service commissions (irrespective of the state). The image of these commissions can be restored by allowing their activities for scrutiny by Lokayukta. Similarly, initiative has to be taken to control corruption in transfers through evolving unambiguous transfer policy to avoid frequent transfers. In fact, according to David Potter's study of 1985, the average stay of district level officers in Karnataka was less than a year.

Another contributory factor is existence of several bottlenecks in administration. In fact, many existing laws are obsolete and redundant. People bribe the officials to overcome these administrative hurdles. This is more so in departments, like education, revenue, Bangalore Development Authority, and other urban local bodies, which could be minimised by streamlining the administration with clear-cut set of procedures and effective communication. In this regard, certain recommendations of Andhra Pradesh Lokayukta were quite innovative. For instance, in some cases, where Lokayukta noticed prevalence of red-tapism and cumbersome procedures and formalities in fixing rent for buildings taken on rent by the government departments, certain reforms for cutting such delays were suggested.

Expanding role of state with more discretionary powers and controls was also contributing to greater corruption. According to some studies, corruption in developing countries has increased with the increase in number of socio-economic programmes. Excessive regulation, along with greater discretionary powers, provide opportunities for corruption since regulations can be used to frustrate the public and extort bribes. We found this trend in our findings as corruption due to regulatory controls accounted for the highest percentage.

Ineffective supervision and inspection also leads to more corruption. The sub-standard works and goods, and payment in excess could be controlled by effective supervision and monitoring. In this regard, the Efficiency Audit Unit under anti-corruption bureau has a remarkable role.

A major source for corruption is the absence of a vigilant public. It is a fact that departments like health and revenue are extorting money for providing facilities and services which these are supposed to provide gratis. Besides, there are many leakages in implementation of anti-poverty programmes. This type of corruption can be effectively controlled through vigilant committees constituted by people themselves or voluntary organisations or panchayati raj institutions (PRIs). For instance, according to Krishna Swamy Committee, there is improvement in the attendance of school teachers and doctors after the introduction of PRIs in Karnataka.[18] Similarly, according to some studies, leakages in the government sponsored anti-poverty programmes have been minimised with the involvement of many voluntary organisations. In the same way, village food committees could check to some extent irregularities in the public distribution system.

Lack of Political Will

Although political leadership, in general, favoured institutions like Lokayukta to control corruption, yet the genuineness of their feeling in this regard was hardly reflected in their behaviour. This is one of the reasons why similar institutions could not be established at the national level, in spite of several efforts in the last three decades. Similar trend is also evident at the state level, although the institution has been established in half of the states. The state leadership adopted negative attitude in extending support, whenever Lokayukta initiated action against them.

For instance, in Maharashtra, the Lokayukta was compelled to recommend placing of a special report in the legislature, when the Chief Minister failed to take action against two of his colleagues who were found guilty by the Lokayukta. Even

[18]Government of Karnataka, *Report of the Expert Committee on Panchayati Raj* (Chairman : K. S. Krishnaswamy), Bangalore, 1989.

repeated requests by the Lokayukta to make suitable recommendations in the Act to cover former ministers and civil servants were unheeded. Similarly, in Orissa, the Finance Minister filed writ petition in the High Court challenging Lokayukta's jurisdiction to investigate corruption charges against the minister. In some cases, political leadership not only questioned the bonafide of the Lokayukta but also challenged the appointment of Lokayukta, when notices were issued against them on the basis of the complaints. They even restrained the Lokayukta from proceeding further in making investigation against them.

Lack of Administrative Capacity and Support

In some states, extraordinary delay in sending requisitioned information by the state government departments constituted a major irritating factor in the conduct of investigations by the Lokayukta. For instance, in Rajasthan, the departments failed to send the requisitioned information even after repeated reminders. The average delay ranged from two to six years. Similarly, in one particular case in Bihar, the Lokayukta was forced to close a case after eight years, as he failed to get the report from the concerned department.

Similar conditions also prevail with respect to cases where senior officers are involved. For instance, in Rajasthan, the Lokayukta's investigation against a super-time scale IAS officer was withdrawn by the state government. In Madhya Pradesh, no action was taken within the stipulated time against the guilty officers, despite the recommendations of the Lokayukta. In some states, the recommendations sent by the Lokayukta were not even acknowledged.

Complexity of Judicial System

The complex system of justice hinders prosecution of officers found guilty. Many recommendations were questioned in the court of law, though we do not have details about number of such instances. Some of these cases were pending for years together. According to a press report, "Even after ten to eleven years, the officers, on whom the corruption charges were proved by the earlier Vigilance Commission in Karnataka, were yet to be punished. None of them were jailed. All of them were retired from the service. But they kept on appealing in one court after another. The cases are still pending in the High Court. Even if the High Court found them guilty, they will go to the Supreme Court. Same thing may happen to the cases recommended by the Lokayukta. Already Central Administrative Tribunal gave the stay in the case of two senior IAS and IFS officers who were suspended by the state government on the basis of Lokayukta recommendation."

Same is the situation in other states also. For instance, in Andhra Pradesh, there were many instances, where Lokayukta successfully completed investigations against many senior civil servants and former and serving ministers. But the High Court and Administrative Tribunal came in the way of awarding punishments to them. Most of the cases were admitted in the High Court and Administrative Tribunals and interim orders were passed, stopping further action in the matter till the disposal of the case. Many such cases are pending before the High Courts.

CONCLUSION

It is evident from our analysis that corruption in Karnataka, just like any other part of India, is a way of life in spite of evolving the most comprehensive institutional arrangement to control it. However, the degree and magnitude of corruption varies from time to time, depending on the state leadership. But it is a fact that corruption has been institutionalised. Secondly, corruption is not a unified phenomena. It assumes different forms and patterns in different contexts. It is just like a kaleidoscope, which exhibits different colours in different angles. Thirdly, multiple factors--political, administrative, economic, social and cultural--are responsible for corruption. Fourthly, the existing institutional arrangement is inadequate to control corruption as it is punitive rather than preventive. Fifthly, there is no political will and administrative capacity to tackle corruption. To this could be added the complex judicial system and laws.

Corruption can be contained within acceptable limits through a strong political will backed by administrative capacity, establishment of democratic ethics, and fragmented countervailing power centres (people's organisations and movements/voluntary organisations/and PRIs) evolving of legal rationale for administrative norms, inculcation of personal honesty and integrity, and effective enforcement of public ethics, though its complete elimination is still beyond human capability. Thus, in the words of Caiden, the strength of these countervailing factors makes the difference between corruption as a fact of life and corruption as a way of life, between isolated infrequent occurrences, and regularised, institutionalised, systematic corruption.

[18]

ANNALS, *AAPSS*, **547**, September 1996

Promise and Peril in Combating Corruption: Hong Kong's ICAC

By MAX J. SKIDMORE

ABSTRACT: Since its founding, Hong Kong had been troubled with corruption. Eventually, the corruption became so serious as to threaten some of the basic institutions of society. In response, the government attempted an approach different from its past efforts. It created an Independent Commission Against Corruption (ICAC), which immediately began to have considerable success. ICAC not only eliminated much of the corruption, but it succeeded in changing public attitudes. Although its powers are enormous, ICAC by and large has operated within the restraints set for it. Nevertheless, its existence is a potential danger. Its powers could be abused even in a society characterized by moderation and the rule of law. In a society whose leaders are less restrained, no legal changes would be required to operate ICAC as the enforcement agency of a police state. Its vast authority therefore becomes a direct, not merely an implied, threat.

Max J. Skidmore is professor of political science at the University of Missouri–Kansas City. He directed the American Studies Research Centre in India (Distinguished Fulbright Lecturer), and the American Studies Programme at the University of Hong Kong (Senior Fulbright Scholar, 1994-95). He is the author of numerous books and articles on political ideologies, American politics, and American political thought and has been appointed Honorary Fellow, Hong Kong–America Center, and Honorary Professor, Shanghai University.

HONG Kong's unique society presents a blend of Western and Asian traditions and institutions. Although often appearing Western, Hong Kong remains predominantly Chinese. The society has worked well in numerous ways but fallen short in others. The early British brought with them a highly commercial orientation, creating an atmosphere whose major attraction was largely economic. Thus both British and Chinese settlers tended to have narrow interests, and society as it developed in Hong Kong was not fully representative of either culture.

It is understandable that corruption, however defined, came to be a major component of that society. Asia has had its traditions of corruption as has the West. Definitions may differ; what appears on one side to be corrupt might not necessarily be so regarded by the other. Even within cultures, what is deemed corrupt or acceptable by one generation might be viewed in a different manner by another. Nevertheless, Western and Asian societies share a common desire to rid themselves of corruption, as the numerous anticorruption efforts in Asian countries demonstrate.[1]

One British historian of Hong Kong wrote that following World War II, corruption among the police

> settled into a generally accepted and comfortable pattern. Apart from the official hierarchy of the force, the organization of the police on the beat was in the hands of staff sergeants . . . and . . . the station sergeants working under them. With very few exceptions these Chinese officers were all profitably engaged in a highly organized system of corruption. They acted as "caterers," arranging liaisons between their subordinates and the criminals and collecting payment for their services. These considerable sums were then distributed in agreed proportions among their subordinates and superiors. In return the heads of criminal fraternities and gangs undertook to settle their own differences and to allow the ordinary citizen to go about his business.[2]

The view one takes of this depends upon many things. The system perhaps had its advantages. Some observers might also have concluded that it represented Asian values rather than corruption. Davies and Roberts present a perceptive discussion of this position. If a person uses an office to reward in return for a bribe, that is corrupt. Nevertheless, there are those who would argue that such a definition depends upon a specific notion of office and that where a different idea prevails, gifts to officials may be acceptable. There, "the giving and receiving of gifts by an official should not be construed as an inducement to act in certain ways, but rather as a recognition of that official's standing by both parties. If in fact the official then acts in ways which benefit the giver of the gift, this is not corrupt, but a cementing of the hierarchy to which both parties belong."[3] This argument would ap-

1. For cooperative efforts against corruption between Hong Kong and China, see, for example, Bertrand de Speville, *Annual Report on the Activities of the Independent Commission Against Corruption for 1993* (Hong Kong: Independent Commission Against Corruption [ICAC], 1994), p. 10.

2. Frank Welsh, *A History of Hong Kong* (London: HarperCollins, 1993), p. 489.

3. Stephen Davies with Elfed Roberts, *Political Dictionary for Hong Kong* (Hong Kong: Macmillan, 1990), p. 92.

peal to those in the West who wish to avoid the imposition of Western standards upon other cultures.

However commendable the motives of those who hold this view may be, their assumptions, Davies and Roberts point out, are erroneous. One might even conclude that their position thus is condescending. Their "view of the matter has never been part of colonial, or . . . Confucian, understanding. The idea that such a treatment of office is corrupt is common to both traditions. Equally, corruption as described above is common to both." Adam Lui's studies of corruption in early China verify this point.[4] Regardless of whether corrupt practices may be useful in avoiding legal and bureaucratic obstacles resulting from bureaucratic inertia and rapid social and economic change, "it is clear that beyond a certain point, widespread bribery of officials becomes counterproductive. It brings the impartiality of a governmental and legal system into question and thereby undermines both efficacy and legitimacy."[5] Virtually all writers on the subject agree that by the late 1960s, such a result was very close in Hong Kong, if indeed it had not already been reached.

To be sure, values attached to gifts in different cultures may vary, but no differences that exist between Confucian and Western cultures have been such as to justify, nor have they been demonstrated to be correlated with, modern corruption. On the contrary, such studies as exist suggest that corruption in the Hong Kong Police (later named the Royal Hong Kong Police), rather than being traditionally Chinese, was closely related to modern economic principles and functioned much like current business organizations.[6]

Ordinances against corruption were adopted in 1898 and 1948 but were largely ineffective. One reason was that the police were the enforcers, yet were part of the corruption.[7] Concern increased following riots that took place in 1966. There had been riots in 1956 also, but the authorities were able to cite a clash between rival Chinese Communist Party and Kuomintang activists as the cause of the earlier disturbances. In 1966, the riots followed the announcement of a proposed increase in fares on the Star Ferries, then the primary (and still a major) mode of transportation between Kowloon and Hong Kong Island.

In both cases, there had been considerable discontent resulting from social and economic inequities, widespread poor living conditions, and a perception of government as unresponsive. The lack of democratic mechanisms whereby the people could exert effective influence on government was surely a contributing factor, as was the clearly enormous extent of corruption in the Hong Kong Police. The government called

4. See, for example, Adam Y. C. Lui, *Corruption Under the Early Ch'ing, 1644-1661* (Hong Kong: University of Hong Kong, Centre of Asian Studies, 1979).

5. Davies with Roberts, *Political Dictionary for Hong Kong*, p. 92.

6. Peter N. S. Lee, "The Causes and Effects of Police Corruption: A Case of Political Modernization," in *Corruption and Its Control in Hong Kong*, ed. Rance P. L. Lee (Hong Kong: Chinese University of Hong Kong Press, 1981), pp. 182-83.

7. See Davies with Roberts, *Political Dictionary for Hong Kong*, pp. 209-10.

a committee of inquiry to look into the causes. The commissioner of police, Henry Heath, conceded that the police were corrupt but argued that they were no more so than other parts of the government. "In any case police were different, since detectives needed to take bribes if they were to be able to pay their informers."[8] Welsh wrote sardonically, "The colony managed to avoid its commission for a few years yet."[9]

The more serious riots of 1967 were connected with the Cultural Revolution. Because of this connection, there was no investigation, but poor social and economic conditions again were relevant. "The government took sufficient fright to put its house in order; the greater involvement of government in local affairs . . . can be traced back to these years."[10]

One of the toughest pieces of legislation in Hong Kong's history, the Prevention of Bribery Ordinance, became effective in 1971. The ordinance made it an offense for a crown servant to possess assets greater than income would justify, unless the excess could be explained. This reversed the traditional presumption of innocence until proven guilty. Departing from British tradition and looking to Asian precedents, much of the ordinance "was based on Singaporean and Ceylonese [Sri Lankan] legislation."[11] The Anti-Corruption Branch of the police received authority to enforce the ordinance.

The incident that changed everything came in 1973. Police Chief Superintendent Peter Fitzroy Godber was under investigation. On the fourth of June, he was served notice that he would have to explain how he could maintain foreign accounts containing six times the total earnings for his twenty years of service. Three days later he escaped and fled to Britain, assuming that he could not be extradited because having unexplained assets was not an offense under British law.

There was widespread outcry, based partly on the erroneous assumption that the police had deliberately permitted him to escape.[12] The entire episode was especially shocking because Godber had been "one of the most distinguished veterans of the riots."[13] He "had been prominent in the street battles against the 1967 rioters and was well respected within the force," said literature issued by the Independent Commission Against Corruption (ICAC). But he "used his skills and knowledge as a policeman to slip through the security barriers at Kai Tak International Airport and board a plane which jetted him away from trouble."[14]

The government appointed a commission of inquiry headed by Sir Alastair Blair-Kerr, a senior judge. Two reports followed. The first, in July, concluded that Godber had es-

8. Welsh, *History of Hong Kong*, p. 490.

9. Ibid., p. 491.

10. Davies with Roberts, *Political Dictionary for Hong Kong*, p. 114.

11. David Clark, "A Community Relations Approach to Corruption: The Case of Hong Kong," *Corruption and Reform*, 2:244 (1987).

12. Davies with Roberts, *Political Dictionary for Hong Kong*, p. 171.

13. Welsh, *History of Hong Kong*, p. 491.

14. *The ICAC: An Introduction to the Independent Commission Against Corruption*, 3d ed. (Hong Kong: ICAC, 1989), p. 5.

caped unaided. The second, in September, considered corruption and recommended the transfer of anticorruption authority away from the police. It further recommended that legislation regarding advantages be strengthened, that Hong Kong adopt restrictions on the traditional Anglo-American right to remain silent and on the right against self-incrimination, and that powers of search and seizure be widened extensively.[15]

The governor, Sir Murray MacLehose, moved with dispatch. He announced the creation of ICAC, which began operation in 1974. "Sir Alistair's [*sic*] report thus led, indirectly, to the arrest, extradition, trial, and imprisonment of Superintendent Godber. For it was the pugnacious new ICAC which explored the full possibilities of English extradition law and discovered a way of charging Godber with an offense under both Hong Kong and English laws."[16]

HONG KONG'S ICAC

Other jurisdictions, such as Singapore, Malaysia, and the Australian state of New South Wales, now utilize some form of anticorruption agency. The idea seems increasingly popular.[17] Nevertheless, the ICAC is unique. It does not confine its activities to enforcement, which perhaps explains a major reason for its successes. Rather, it devotes enormous resources to the changing of attitudes and practices, as reflected in its three departments: Operations (enforcement), Corruption Prevention, and Community Relations. The Corruption Prevention Department works with government agencies and private industry to suggest methods to avoid corrupt practices, and the Community Relations Department conducts a barrage of publicity, including professionally produced television spots and written materials, extensive educational packages for schools, and public activities of all kinds.[18]

A typical campaign broadcast numerous advertisements sharing a common theme over Hong Kong's two English-language television channels in June 1995. In one spot, the screen flashed black, while the voice-over said "white." Then it flashed white while the voice said "black." After a few repetitions, comments followed that corruption distorted the truth. Then came the theme, spoken in a pronounced British accent: "Hong Kong. Our advantage is the ICAC."

Such an approach flows directly from the enabling legislation. The ICAC Ordinance specifically mandates an emphasis on community re-

15. See Anoop Gulab Gidwani, "The Impact and Accountability Implications of the Bill of Rights in Relation to the Independent Commission Against Corruption" (MPA diss., University of Hong Kong, 1994), p. 25.

16. Davies with Roberts, *Political Dictionary for Hong Kong*, p. 31. Godber's trial took place in Hong Kong in 1975, and he received a four-year prison sentence.

17. Interview with Rosaline Cheung, Regional Officer of the Community Relations Department of the ICAC, 13 June 1995. See also Davies with Roberts, *Political Dictionary for Hong Kong*, p. 209.

18. For statistics and information on organization, see the ICAC commissioner's *Annual Report on the Activities of the Independent Commission Against Corruption* (various years).

lations. The commissioner is required to "educate the public against the evils of corruption" and to "enlist and foster public support."[19] Clark has compared Chicago's "throw the rascals out" movements with Hong Kong's efforts. He remarked accurately, if not profoundly, that if a

> moral climate can be created then so much greater will be the prospects for controlling corruption. Even where there is a measure of popular disapproval this will have little impact on actual behaviour if this disapproval is not given institutional expression and full support by top officials.[20]

By all accounts, the ICAC's effectiveness has exceeded expectations. Governor MacLehose appointed Sir Jack Cater as the first commissioner, and as Welsh put it, the ICAC "quickly proved embarrassingly successful. Cater, a quietly impressive and independent officer, was reinforced by Sir John Prendergast. . . . The team was, if anything, too effective. Policemen were arrested in veritable droves . . . as investigations revealed highly organized corruption on an enormous scale. This was too threatening, and the police took matters into their own hands, staging a mass meeting which resulted in the offices of ICAC being stormed and members of staff assaulted."[21]

This was in 1977, by which time ICAC had uncovered 18 syndicates operated by the police, and had placed hundreds of officers under arrest. The previous year, a superintendent had committed suicide because of ICAC investigations, and the entire middle management of the Wan Chai Division was either under investigation or had been arrested. In October of 1977, ICAC raided three Kowloon police divisions, arresting 140 officers and detaining 35 others. Following a meeting of several thousand police on 27 October, another meeting and march of 2000 the next day, and threats to march on the governor's residence, Governor MacLehose backed down and issued a partial amnesty. Unless prosecutions already were under way, or the offense was extraordinary, no further prosecutions would be undertaken for offenses committed prior to 1 July 1977. Prosecutions of police now have come to be a minor part of ICAC's activities, the majority of which in recent years have dealt with the private sector.[22]

DRACONIAN POWERS?

Under Hong Kong's colonial heritage, democratic institutions hardly exist. Perhaps as a result, concern for formal limits on governmental powers is likewise rudimentary. This is not to say that Hong Kong suffers from arbitrary rule. On the contrary, Hong Kong residents exercise a high degree of personal liberty, and the territory maintains a vigorous and independent judiciary that does not hesitate to issue rulings contrary to governmental preferences. The press is as free as any in Asia, despite in-

19. Clark, "Community Relations Approach," p. 244. See "Responsibilities of the Commissioner," *Annual Report on the Activities of the Independent Commission Against Corruption for 1993*, pp. 6-7.

20. David Clark, "Mobilizing Public Opinion Against Corruption: A Commentary," *Corruption and Reform*, 4:124-25 (1989).

21. Welsh, *History of Hong Kong*, p. 492.

22. See the relevant annual reports.

creasing tendencies toward self-censorship to avoid offending China. By world standards, Hong Kong's human rights record is good; by Asian standards, it is enormously good.

Nevertheless, Hong Kong's atmosphere of freedom is attributable more to traditions of restraint on the part of leaders than to a spirit of reverence for civil liberties. There was a flurry of excitement in the press in 1995 when tax investigators seized the records of 9000 patients from a physician—not merely financial records but medical records—and the courts upheld the seizure.[23] Some of Britain's most authoritarian laws and practices prevail with none of Britain's democratic institutions to moderate them. The Official Secrets Act forbids any person from divulging any governmental information that the government wishes to keep private. Hong Kong operates under a Film Censorship Ordinance, which includes political censorship of anything offensive to "neighboring countries"—that is, to China. It adopted a Public Order Ordinance following the 1966 riots, authorizing the police commissioner to prohibit any public gathering on any given day. The governor-in-council could ban public gatherings for up to three months; police officers of commissioned rank could halt and disperse public processions and could conduct warrantless searches of premises; and unlawful assembly could consist of as few as three persons.[24] Amendments in 1970 and 1980 curtailed search powers and lessened restrictions on public assembly.

The 1987 Public Order (Amendment) Ordinance, however, became known as the Press Gag Ordinance. It created a new offense, the publication of "false news," which applied only to newspapers. Reversing the presumption-of-innocence rule, it required a person charged to demonstrate that there had been "reasonable measures" taken "to verify the truth of the news." Legislative Council (LegCo) member Martin Lee Chu-ming worked diligently against the provision but failed. In November 1988, this ordinance became a topic of concern in the United Nations Human Rights Committee. On 10 January 1989, LegCo repealed the rules relating to the press.[25] Nevertheless, in May 1994, the International Press Freedom Day report charged that Hong Kong's press freedom was worse than it had been in the previous year and that the press in China was "one of the world's most repressed."[26]

Even some pro-democracy advocates favor extreme censorship. On 2 April 1995, a number of MTR (subway) stations became the scene of demonstrations by some members of

23. There were numerous press articles for several weeks. One that presents a good sense of the situation is Cliff Buddle and Mariana Wan, "Taxman's Right to See Patient Files Upheld: Ruling Angers Medical Bodies," *South China Morning Post*, 13 Apr. 1995.

24. Davies with Roberts, *Political Dictionary for Hong Kong*, p. 405.

25. Ibid., pp. 405-6. Martin Lee is the author of "Political Developments in Hong Kong: Implications for 1997," this issue of *The Annals* of the American Academy of Political and Social Science.

26. See Donald H. McMillen and Man Si-wai, eds., *The Other Hong Kong Report, 1994* (Hong Kong: Chinese University of Hong Kong Press, 1994), p. xxii.

the Democratic Party (not to be confused with the Democratic Alliance for the Betterment of Hong Kong, a pro-Chinese group). The demonstrators attacked the government for being "too soft on soft porn" and called for books to come under the same categorization scheme as films. They would require publishers to submit their works to the Obscene Articles Tribunal for approval. The effort, in short, was "to have all books censored by the Government," and it would have been prior censorship.[27]

Contrary to its image in the West, Hong Kong is essentially Victorian—at times to a ludicrous extent. In May 1995 the Obscene Articles Tribunal discovered that a nude male statue had stood for some months in a building open to the public. Immediately, the shocked officials ordered that it be moved to an art museum. Until the statue, which actually was reasonably discreet, could be moved, there had to be a cover placed over its genital area. Despite considerable ridicule, the ruling stood. The tribunal's presiding magistrate defended the action, arguing that artistic merit was irrelevant. "The Tribunal is not supposed to apply double standards for artists' and non-artists' freedom of expression," was his defense, and he cited a survey showing that "70 per cent of interviewed people found explicit nude photographs offensive."[28]

In such a climate, it could have been expected that the government, when it found corruption to be so pervasive, would grant extraordinary powers to its new ICAC or that the ICAC, behaving as law enforcement agencies do, would use those powers to the fullest. ICAC was made responsible only to the governor, whose authority in theory—although not in practice—borders upon the absolute. This places the personnel resources of the ICAC outside the authority of the Public Service Commission.[29] ICAC's powers to search, seize, and compel suspects and witnesses to divulge information are far in excess of what is customary in liberal democracies. Gidwani speaks of fears "that ICAC officers if they so wish can intrude vigorously into the private lives and affairs of practically every resident in Hongkong. For example ICAC officers are empowered to search premises by virtue of a warrant signed by their Commissioner and not necessarily by a Magistrate. For certain offences the onus rests on the defendant to prove his innocence. . . . Yet another example is that under common law, the right of silence applies to suspects and witnesses alike. However, certain provisions contained in the Prevention of Bribery Ordinance give the right to the ICAC to question people and demand answers."[30]

The ICAC Ordinance empowers its officers to arrest without warrant, "if they reasonably suspect that such

27. Tim Hamlett, "Comic Crusade Just Isn't Funny," *South China Morning Post*, 5 Apr. 1995.

28. Sam Mok, "Obscene Power Stays," *Eastern Express*, 21 June 1955.

29. Jeremiah K. H. Wong, "The ICAC and Its Anti-Corruption Measures," in *Corruption and Its Control in Hong Kong*, ed. Lee, p. 51.

30. Gidwani, "Impact and Accountability," pp. 29 and 76. The authorizations are in sec. 13 of the ICAC Ordinance, and secs. 13 and 14 of the Prevention of Bribery Ordinance.

a person is guilty of an offence in contravention of the ICAC Ordinance, the Prevention of Bribery Ordinance, or the Corrupt and Illegal Practices Ordinance; or an offence disclosed during an investigation into a Prevention of Bribery offence."[31] ICAC even has the authority to arrest for suspected offenses that are not its obligation to investigate.[32] The ICAC brochure outlines some of its other powers: "Powers are also given to the ICAC to seize passports with an order from a magistrate, to search bank accounts and to hold and examine business and private documents. These powers are essential if evidence against devious, cunning conspirators is to be obtained."[33] All persons are forbidden from identifying any subject under investigation, and the brochure discusses the secrecy of its investigations at length, saying that when questioned, "the suspect is often amazed how so much is known about his affairs without his having been aware of the enquiries."[34]

Any power that ICAC possesses is enhanced considerably by the lack of real definition of "corruption." The discussion of corruption, even in the legislation, is so loose as to permit ICAC tremendous leeway.

PROTECTIONS

The ICAC functions only according to law, and there are numerous structures that provide at least some scrutiny of its operations. "The ICAC is often likened to the watchdog of society," ICAC literature says. "But who watches the watchdog?"[35] There is a Complaints Committee; an Advisory Committee on Corruption, which looks into ICAC actions; and a separate committee to oversee the activities of each of the three divisions. These are the Operations Review Committee, the Corruption Prevention Advisory Committee, and the Citizens' Advisory Committee on Community Relations. The governor appoints the members of all these groups. Additionally, there is "an internal monitoring system" that is "so secretive that few in the Commission know how it works."[36]

The courts remain a major protection. The authority to prosecute is reserved to the attorney general, and only a court can determine guilt. Yet this protection is incomplete. ICAC literature boasts that many persons have been punished even when there has been inadequate evidence to prosecute. "What are the corrupt like in Hong Kong?" it asks. "Over the years the ICAC has uncovered thousands, with the majority of them eventually brought to justice in the courts. *Those who could not be prosecuted for reasons such as insufficient evidence* were quickly flushed out of the public service by disciplinary action to prevent them from doing more damage to society"[37] (emphasis added).

31. Gidwani, "Impact and Accountability," p. 60.
32. Ibid., p. 62.
33. *ICAC*, p. 7.
34. Ibid., p. 13.
35. Ibid., p. 39.
36. Ibid. On advisory committees, see ICAC's annual reports.
37. *ICAC*, p. 15.

THE BILL OF RIGHTS

Governor David Wilson suggested a Bill of Rights that was adopted on 8 June 1991. There appears to be wide public support, "with a majority perceiving it as a preventive measure designed mainly for use after 1997."[38] The support varies throughout the community. It is strongest among the district boards, academicians, and members of the news media. There appears to be weaker support from people in business and the professions and from educated members of the working class, but their concern is primarily with other issues. Among blue-collar groups and the lower white-collar levels—the so-called grassroots—the picture seems different. The Bill of Rights might "work more to the advantage of criminals, corrupt government officials and rich people who could afford expensive lawyers," they fear. Their concerns were "triads, drug pushers, and corrupt civil servants, as such activities would affect their daily lives directly."[39]

Gidwani has conducted an extensive study of the effects of the Bill of Rights on ICAC's powers. He catalogued the instances in which the courts have declared ICAC authority inconsistent with the new protections, and he outlined where they have reduced or eliminated those powers accordingly. He also examined the overall authority of the ICAC and identified which powers are likely to withstand further judicial review and which will possibly be restricted. On balance, he concedes some dangers, especially after 1997, but he praises ICAC's professionalism and its willingness to look critically at its own authority. "It must be appreciated," he wrote, "that the prompt response of the ICAC to look into its legislative authority and its compatibility with the Bill of Rights Ordinance is a clear sign that the ICAC is not unaware of the importance of its accountability to society."[40] One must note that it also is a reflection of ICAC's awareness of political reality and especially of the importance of its public image. To be sure, it has suffered some restrictions of its authority, but that authority remains enormous. Gidwani himself has asked what could happen if ICAC were to be headed by a corrupt commissioner.[41]

A PUBLIC EMBARRASSMENT

ICAC suffered considerable public embarrassment with the Alex Tsui case. Tsui was the highest-ranking Chinese official of the ICAC before Commissioner Bertrand de Speville sacked him in November 1993 with no explanation.[42] The only public statement for some time was this ICAC press release:

> Following an ICAC internal investigation, the Commissioner Against Corruption today terminated the employment of Mr. Alex Tsui Ka-kit, Senior Assistant Director holding the post of Deputy Director of Operations with immediate ef-

38. Gidwani, "Impact and Accountability," p. 49.

39. Ibid., p. 50.

40. Ibid., p. 116.

41. Ibid., p. 147.

42. Sonny S. H. Lo, "Independent Commission Against Corruption," in *Other Hong Kong Report*, ed. McMillen and Man, p. 27.

fect under the provisions of Section 8(2) of the ICAC Ordinance.[43]

The section cited empowers the commissioner to remove any ICAC employee without providing a reason.

Tsui embarked upon a public campaign to defend himself and appealed to LegCo. He also made a number of countercharges, which included sexual misconduct on the part of his expatriate superior, racism, and misuse of ICAC powers—including "political vetting," on behalf of the government.

Eventually, the commissioner agreed to testify. "The public hearings were politically significant. . . . For the first time in Hong Kong's history, LegCo members utilized the Legislative Council [Powers and Privileges] Ordinance to summon people to testify. These events represented an experiment with democratization, making the ICAC answerable to the legislature."[44]

Although investigations supported ICAC and called most of Tsui's allegations into question, public faith in the ICAC appeared to have suffered damage.[45] The commissioner denied any "political vetting," without defining it, and said that ICAC merely had conducted "integrity checks." The case publicized ICAC's powers—such as wiretapping and surveillance—and demonstrated that they could be used for political purposes. It also demonstrated that "the ICAC had not been adequately accountable to any watchdog body for its action. Specifically, the existing advisory committees . . . are relatively weak."[46]

The result of the episode was the appointment, in February 1994, of a nine-member committee to look into ICAC's powers. The chair is Helmut Sohmen, a former LegCo member. China's reaction, when it heard of allegations that ICAC might have engaged in political spying, was not to question the propriety of such action but to demand that the results be made available to China.[47]

CONCLUSION

The Bill of Rights was a significant advance for Hong Kong, but it does not have constitutional status. LegCo could, with the governor's approval, repeal it. The Basic Law that is to govern the Hong Kong Special Administrative Region provides that China will recognize legislative protections in effect at that time, providing that they are consistent with the Basic Law.[48] It probably is safe to say, however, that no one, including the Chinese, really know how the law will be interpreted.

ICAC has had significant successes, foremost among which is the changing of a political climate that previously accepted corruption and now largely rejects it. The pendulum

43. Cited in Gidwani, "Impact and Accountability," p. 125.

44. Lo, "Independent Commission Against Corruption," p. 28.

45. For details of the Tsui case, see Gidwani, "Impact and Accountability," pp. 122-35.

46. Lo, "Independent Commission Against Corruption," p. 43.

47. Ibid., p. 38.

48. See *The Basic Law of the Hong Kong Special Administrative Region of the People's Republic of China* (Hong Kong: One Country Two Systems Economic Research Institute, 1992), esp. chap. 1.

has swung so far that many people are nervous about the most trivial situations. An ICAC representative indicated that it would be unnecessary to report receipt of a cup of coffee; that was approved. A faculty member received a box of chocolates from a student, took none, and gave it to the entire department to share. If a question were raised, there would be no personal advantage.

Enforcement agencies can fall victim to a bureaucratic mentality that blinds itself to fundamentals. For example, obtaining a driver's license for a Hong Kong resident requires a yearlong wait even to take the test.[49] ICAC discovered corruption to issue licenses speedily, but fraudulently. The agency prosecuted offenders and recommended changes in procedures. Investigation also discovered that Hong Kong residents sometimes went abroad, obtained a foreign license, and then returned to obtain quick issuance of a Hong Kong license through reciprocity. ICAC recommended "legislation to restrict the automatic exchange of overseas driving licences for Hong Kong licences." ICAC proudly said that the legislation "also effectively blocked opportunities for corruption."[50]

There is no doubt that some were obtaining unfair advantage. Nonetheless, ICAC was unconcerned about a more fundamental issue: the cumbersome process that required a year to obtain a license in the first place. Surely corruption would have been combated at least as effectively if ICAC had devised a method to give greater convenience to all applicants, rather than reducing the convenience of a few.

The community seems to be highly supportive of ICAC, although admittedly much of the measurement comes from ICAC's own periodic surveys. A Chinese colleague, though, says that "they're afraid of ICAC—afraid not to be supportive." The agency's reputed tactics certainly contribute to any fear that exists. Those whom ICAC has taken in for questioning say that a usual practice is to knock on the door at 4 a.m., achieving maximum intimidation when people are unprepared. "They're tough boys," is a typical comment.[51] Nevertheless, strong support for ICAC certainly does exist, and it reflects consistency with the local culture and with the traditions that developed during long years of colonialism.

There have been criticisms, reminding one of the Federal Bureau of Investigation under J. Edgar Hoover, that ICAC propaganda is so extensive that it obscures some agency failings. "It is an open secret that some Mainland companies operating in Hong Kong are corrupt," remarks one observer, "Neither the central government in Beijing nor the local New China News Agency [the agency that currently exercises diplomatic powers in Hong Kong on China's behalf] seems to be able to control [them]."[52] ICAC has been criticized as unwilling to challenge these Chinese-owned companies.[53] Another critic alleges

49. See *ICAC*, p. 24.

50. Ibid., p. 25.

51. For obvious reasons, such persons wish not to be identified in any way.

52. Lo, "Independent Commission Against Corruption," p. 25.

53. Davies with Roberts, *Political Dictionary for Hong Kong*, p. 211.

that the very low incidents of drug charges demonstrates "either an increase of effectiveness unparalleled elsewhere in the world, or a degree of collusion with Triad dealers."[54] Such criticism may be unfair, but it indicates the existence of concern. When asked what could be cited as ICAC's greatest failure, one representative complained that the courts frequently are too lenient, thus reflecting a frustration often felt by law enforcement agencies throughout at least the Western world.

As ICAC has functioned, despite its climate of utmost secrecy, it seems to have reflected a relative restraint, based on adhering to the rules of the game. With Chinese control, the rules certainly—if not the game itself—will change. A new commissioner appointed by the Chinese will report to a chief executive who retains the governor's virtually absolute authority but reports to China. After 1997, even if the Chinese adhere rigidly to their agreements and even without violating the law as it currently exists, the ICAC could become the major enforcement authority of a police state.

54. Welsh, *History of Hong Kong*, p. 493.

Part VI
Prevention and Sanctions

[19]

Taxation, Corruption and Reform

JOHN TOYE and MICK MOORE

Corrupt tax officials often collude with taxpayers to understate tax liabilities. What can governments of poor countries do to reduce this collusion? This study argues that their incentive for anti-corruption reform of their tax systems increases with their dependence on revenues that are 'earned', in the sense that their collection requires substantial political and organisational inputs from the government. It further argues that the redesign of tax systems, and specifically their simplification, can reduce corrupt leakages. The Indonesian tax reform of the 1980s, including its adoption of a simple value added tax, is referred to for illustration of these arguments.

INTRODUCTION

What is the scope for governments of poor countries to reform taxation systems to reduce corruption? That is our central question. It can be divided into two somewhat more precise questions, that are treated in the first and second halves of this study respectively. In what circumstances will governments be likely to take effective action against corruption in tax collection? And how might the re-design of existing tax systems help the governments of poor countries to achieve that goal?

Our objective is to suggest useful ways of thinking about these questions from a political economy perspective. For the subject of tax reform has so far been treated mainly in technical terms. Yet it is primarily a political topic. We suggest that an understanding of the politics of government revenue and taxation systems can help us move towards a more practical appreciation of the circumstances in which reform might be achieved. Our main point here concerns the political and economic character of governments' revenue bases. These vary widely in respect of the amount of effort expended by the state to raise revenue. These variations – expressed in terms of relative dependence on 'earned' and 'unearned' income – affect both the scope for reform and the

---

John Toye and Mick Moore, Institute of Development Studies at the University of Sussex. The excellent research assistance of Francis Hutchinson and Garett Pratt is gratefully acknowledged. The authors have benefited from the extensive comments on an earlier draft by participants in a DFID-sponsored Workshop on Corruption and Development that was held at IDS in May 1997. Special thanks are owed, for their most helpful comments, to Ajay Chibber, Satya Mohanty, Mark Robinson and an anonymous referee. The usual disclaimer applies.

incentive for governments to embark on reform. Governments dependent on 'earned' income are likely to be best placed and best motivated to reduce corruption in tax collection.

How should they go about doing so? Can existing tax systems be re-designed in ways that squeeze out corruption, and particularly that most intractable form of it, collusion between officials and taxpayers wrongly to lower assessments? Our main point here, illustrated by the Indonesian case, is that progress can be made in this direction by reforms that give a greater revenue-raising role to a value-added tax. However, no purely technical re-design can wholly eliminate collusive corruption.

We recognise that the background against which we reach these conclusions is one where the published literature on corruption and taxation in poor countries is rather sparse. Academic writing on wrongdoing in the revenue collection business refers mainly to OECD countries, and official methods of combating tax evasion on the part of taxpayers. But tax evading behaviour on the part of citizens and companies may interact with corrupt behaviour on the part of tax bureaucrats: the two can cut deals at the cost of the public treasury. There is no necessary or tight connection: in some circumstances taxpayers can evade taxation despite the best efforts of honest tax collectors; in others they might dutifully hand over money that goes into the officials' private pockets. However, we have chosen to focus here on the interaction between corruption on the part of officials in poor countries' taxation systems, and tax evasion on the part of taxpayers. The 'deals' of collusive corruption are the most intractable of the problems that tax reformers in developing countries have to face.

Why do we know so little about corruption and taxation in poor countries? Part of the reason is that, if we are to define 'knowledge' as having detailed information about methods, channels, dynamics and quantities, we have little knowledge about corruption of any kind. Wade's [*1985*] explanation of the way in which official posts were allocated and re-allocated on a purchase basis within the Irrigation Department in a South Indian state is highly unusual in that it provides these kinds of detail. Another reason for our ignorance lies in the dominant role of the International Monetary Fund in framing debate about public revenue issues in poor countries. To a greater extent than the World Bank, the Fund avoids public engagement with 'political' issues. The literature and discussion on taxation that it generates and stimulates is predominantly technical in orientation. We refer to some of that literature here, but prefer to begin from a political economy perspective.

THE POLITICAL ECONOMY OF 'EARNED' AND 'UNEARNED' STATE INCOME

Do Fiscal Deficits Motivate Tax Reform?

In what circumstances are governments of poor countries likely to make the effort substantially to reduce corruption in tax collection? Would that an important component of the answer were: 'When taxpayers become incensed about the issue and become influential through electoral and pressure group activity.' Unfortunately, this happens all too rarely in poor countries. There are several reasons. First, direct taxpayers typically comprise only a very small proportion of the population. Second, they often benefit from collusion with tax officials in assessment and collection, at the expense of the public treasury. Third, tax bureaucracies can strike back at those who lead public campaigns against corruption: a special investigation of an individual's tax affairs is easy to justify and can be made very costly to the victim, even where there has been no wrongdoing.

The most likely factor motivating governments to tackle corruption and other leakages in revenue collection would seem to be a perceived fiscal deficit arising from some combination of a fall in revenues or an increase in expenditure commitments. The proposition that governments will reform when they need money most desperately is intuitively appealing, and no doubt contains some truth. Unfortunately, it is not a proposition with a very high predictive value. Some governments preside over long-term declines in revenue in much the same way that they continue to resist economic reform more generally, that is, long after the point at which it appeared to outsiders that they had no choice but to reform. For example, the Peruvian government took radical, effective action to increase tax collection in 1991 only when tax revenue had fallen steadily from 20-22 per cent of GDP in the 1960s to less than four per cent of GDP [*Thorp, 1996*]. Clearly, factors other than fiscal need affect the willingness of governments to tackle tax reform in general, and corruption in tax administration in particular, and many of the factors are specific to particular circumstances.

Defining Earned and Unearned State Income

We suggest that it is possible to develop some initial propositions on the propensity to fiscal anti-corruption reform by categorising states according to the different sources of state income. In this we take our cue from Rudolf Goldscheid, who sketched the outlines of a grand theory of societal development in which the sources of public finance played the same critical role in driving social change as social class and class struggle did in Marxist analysis. His theme was that:

> the pattern of public finance has at all times had a decisive influence on national and social evolution. Tax struggles were the oldest form of class struggle, and fiscal matters were an important contributory cause even in the mightiest spiritual movements of mankind [*Goldscheid, 1958: 202*].

Goldscheid's work is now unread, and largely deservedly so. Yet it does foreshadow recent developments in the political analysis of states and state development. Through a variety of channels, political scientists and historians are beginning to recognise that the politics and institutions of public finance play a significant but under-appreciated role in the formation and evolution of states.[1] The field as yet has no specific conceptual tools of its own. There is however a conceptual framework latent in some of the relevant literature. In particular the concept of 'rentier states' appears very useful for present purposes: the notion that state income can be categorised on a continuum between 'earned' and 'unearned'.

The term 'earned income' is not used normatively but as a positive description. It refers here to the notion of 'having to work for' something, that is, having to put purposive effort into attaining a goal.[2] The contrast is with income that is unearned, because it is received passively, without any work or effort. This idea of 'effort' must be clearly distinguished from the term 'tax effort' which has been much used in studies sponsored by the IMF. These studies measure the amounts of revenue raised in relation to the size of available tax bases (for example, customs duties in relation to the size of the foreign trade sector, excise duty in relation to luxury consumption) to give an overall indicator of aggregate 'tax effort'. In the conventional terminology, 'tax effort' refers to an output or result more than to an input. We use it here in a more political and organisational sense, to refer to the input made by government to raise revenue. The effort required to exploit some types of tax bases is much greater than the effort that is required to exploit others. It takes more effort to collect ten per cent of the value of imports as customs duties than it does to collect ten per cent of the value of oil production as a petroleum revenue tax. Tax bases can be graded according to the effort required to capture x per cent of each as revenue. Any measure that adds up the actual percentages of revenue collected into an aggregate measure of 'tax effort' will, therefore, be misleading, precisely because it fails to make any distinction between the different efforts involved.

The 'tax effort' that concerns us specifically is the effort made by the state in relation to the mass of its citizens or subjects (henceforth, citizens). There are two fiscal criteria that we can use to judge how far any state is engaging with the mass of its citizens. One is the extent to which state income is earned, and this in turn depends on:

(i) *Organisational effort*: How large, efficient and differentiated is the bureaucratic apparatus that the state deploys to collect its income? A state that has a number of distinct and effective services to assess and collect, for example, income, property, and turnover taxes, is working much harder for its income than is a state that receives a large annual cash subvention from an oil-rich neighbour and collects the remainder through a flat rate import duty.

(ii) *Reciprocity*: How far are citizens obtaining some reciprocal services in return for their tax contributions? This fiscal criterion of the degree of state engagement with the mass of its citizens concerns its expenditure priorities, and harks back to the voluntary exchange theory of taxation. 'Reciprocal services' range from (a) what we may term 'rudimentary' (a state apparatus that does not coercively and arbitrarily exploit citizens when collecting taxes or otherwise interacting with them); through (b) a 'minimal contractual relationship' (the provision of law, order, justice and security); to (c) 'extended reciprocity' (for example, the services associated with 'welfare' and 'developmental' states).

In this study, we do not further consider the expenditure side of the budget, or the reciprocity criterion. On the income side, however, criterion (i) – organisational effort – needs further elucidation. It is not a matter of the state deploying a large organisation as such. Size is not a criterion on its own, for the obvious reason that a large bureaucracy is quite capable of sitting in its offices, making little impact on the potential tax payers and raising a small amount of revenue at a very high administrative cost. But neither is efficiency of collection a criterion on its own, because it is clear that the most efficient forms of taxation, at least in terms of the smallness of the average cost of collection, are precisely those which require hardly any interaction with citizens. Differentiation is not a criterion on its own, because it may result in both extra inefficiency of collection and additional leakage of revenue through corruption. On the other hand, it is unlikely that any state would wish to earn all its revenue from only one or two types of taxes. Earning state income, therefore, requires the deployment of instruments which, taken together, are large, efficient and differentiated.

This multiplex criterion allows us, in principle, to rank different types of taxes on a scale of the degree of 'earnedness'. The deployment of a relatively elaborate bureaucratic apparatus to nurture, monitor and tax a concentrated, major income source (for example, a large phosphate deposit) would lead to a lower ranking on the 'earnedness' scale than would an equivalent revenue raising effort that was more widely dispersed (for example, collecting an urban property tax). Efforts to establish a good relationship with a major foreign aid donor would rank low on the scale for the same kinds of reasons. One indicator of the extent to which state income is earned is the proportion of potential income providers throughout the whole country who are brought into the revenue net.

Our earlier argument about the different effort required to raise a given percentage of any tax base as revenue can be extended to apply to different variants of the same type of tax. The extent to which one generic source of state income – say, property tax – is earned may vary from one situation to another depending on local factors: the concept of 'earnedness' refers to relations between state and citizens, and what appears to be the 'same' tax may have very different implications for state-society relations in different contexts. Differences between societies in the distribution of real property and in the nature of the classes and groups who own real property will mean that the 'earnedness' of a three per cent property tax is likely to vary from one country to another. For this and other reasons, the statistical information currently generated on state income sources, organised as it is by general descriptive categories, can provide us with only the crudest indications of the 'earnedness' of particular state income sources. Thus all that we can attempt here is to make some generalisations about where particular sources of government income are likely to be located on the 'earnedness' scale.

(1) *Sources of government income that are generally earned to a relatively high degree*: business turnover taxes; income taxes; property taxes; head taxes; contributory social security funds; profits from state ownership of productive enterprise, especially activities that are organisationally and technically demanding and non-monopolistic; and commercial borrowing.

(2) *Sources of government income that are generally earned to an intermediate degree*: commodity export taxes; control of location-specific physical infrastructure (canals, oil transmission lines, military facilities for other states, airports, harbours); and monopoly state activities which are relatively low technology but require active 'husbandry' (commercial forestry with protection and replanting; liquor sales monopolies).

(3) *Sources of government income that are generally unearned*: direct grants and the concessional element in soft loans; profits from maintaining fixed, overvalued exchange rates; royalties, fees and taxes from authorising the extraction of natural resources – oil, timber, minerals, etc.

Even these broad categories are not clearly distinguishable in standard public finance statistics. For example, income from oil or other natural resources appears in very different forms in the accounts of different governments. Any attempt to map the dependence of different categories of state on income classified on the 'earnedness' scale is necessarily done on a broad-brush basis. The results are however striking: the 'earnedness' of state income is positively and strongly related to levels of national income. Governments of poorer countries are highly dependent on unearned income, especially mineral revenues and foreign aid. Moore [*1998*] took 53 countries for which relevant data were available for 1988. The countries were classified in a four-by-four table: by income level and by degree of 'earnedness' of state income. The government of the average low income country obtained 43 per cent of its income from the least 'earned' income source (foreign aid), and only 14 per cent from the most 'earned' income source (taxes on income, profit and capital gains, and social security contributions). By contrast, the government of the high low income country obtained 58 per cent of its income from the most 'earned' income source.

This result is not wholly surprising, since one of the criteria for the allocation of foreign aid by country is a fiscal 'gap' that may be larger because of the difficulty of raising 'earned' income. The room for manoeuvre to do this may be very limited, because (in the case of sub-Saharan Africa, for example) shifting cultivation and pastoralism make rural direct taxes much harder to levy than in countries with permanently settled agricultural populations. But there may also be a moral hazard effect of foreign aid, that it relieves recipient governments of the need to seek out all possible sources of 'earned' income.

It is argued more fully elsewhere [*Moore, 1998*] that the 'earnedness' of state income is a significant political economy variable: that earned income is positively and causally associated with states that are (a) effective, in the sense of exercising sovereignty, and (b) responsive to citizens, partly to the extent of being more democratic. We argue here that the same conceptual framework can help us understand how states treat their taxation systems and bureaucracies, and, therefore, the ways in which they may respond to pressures or opportunities to reform those systems to reduce corruption.

How is Taxation-Corruption Organised?

The literature yields only sparse information about corruption and taxation in developing countries. We can however combine fragments of information on taxation with (a) the earned-unearned income framework set out above and (b) some knowledge about how corruption mechanisms operate (from, for example, Wade [*1985*]) to produce some hypotheses about how and how far taxation systems may be corrupt in particular circumstances. These ideas may at least serve to guide further research, and provide some ideas about which anti-corruption mechanisms might work.

For these purposes, it matters little whether we conceive of states as coherent organisations or simply as sets of powerful self-interested individuals. Where states depend heavily on 'earned' income, the taxation system receives considerable attention from the political leadership. First, it is considered important that the taxation apparatus is manned and led by competent bureaucrats. Honesty, in the citizens' sense of the term, may not be important. In so far as the taxation system is also used as a source of illicit revenue for political parties and elites, what matters is not that the tax bureaucracy should be honest, but that it should be dishonest in a predictable, controllable fashion, that is, that the understood percentages should be paid over to the right people at the right time.

Second, because political parties and elites are relatively dependent on the taxation apparatus for their illegal incomes, they tend to develop an interest in how it is managed. In these circumstances, the primary political function of the tax assessment and collection system is revenue collection. Most of that revenue goes to the public treasury. The revenue that is used illicitly is channelled in a relatively centralised fashion: it is first transferred up to high levels in the taxation apparatus, and then handed over to high level politicians (or bureaucrats in other agencies). Local and low-level politicians are not much involved directly, although they may share in redistribution effected by high level politicians. The corruption networks involved tend to be relatively wide-ranging, stable, homogenous and widely understood.

There is a considerable amount of knowledge about the 'value' of particular posts and activities: the post of Chief Tax Inspector at P is 'worth' about T thousand dollars a year, and one can expect to pay about U thousand dollars for a two-year transfer there; a front line Tax Inspector in a particular post may expect to pay about V thousand dollars to his boss each year simply to remain in post and free of trouble. The local Chief of Police may expect about W per cent of estimated 'revenues' each year to guarantee that there is no trouble. At the top, the Minister of Finance has a good idea of how much he should receive each month from each taxation agency. In this kind of system, there is no contradiction involved in one corrupt person accusing another of being a cheat. Given broad political stability, overall patterns of relationships in relation to taxation-corruption will remain relatively stable. There will however be instability in the laws, rules and procedures relating to assessment and collection: the state has both revenue motives to change the system (that is, there always seems scope for collecting a little more money) and corruption motives (that is, introducing changes in liabilities and collection procedures gives more scope to extract a surplus from tax payers).

Let us now look at the opposite situation, where governments depend heavily on unearned income. A few of these governments are also notoriously wealthy. The Saudi or Kuwaiti regimes may spend vast amounts of money on large, non-meritocratic, inefficient bureaucracies that reallocate state mineral wealth to large sections of the population [*Chaudhry, 1989*]. While it is often true that unearned state incomes are also large incomes, especially where oil is the source, it is helpful to separate source from size when assessing the consequences for corruption and tax reform.

Unearned sources of state income tend to be concentrated: a few mines or wells and the foreign companies which operate them; a canal; or a few foreign aid donors. Governments tend to concentrate their most effective public servants on tapping these sources. These are the main wellsprings of public revenue, political funds and private surplus for members of the political elite. Most areas of the taxation system are of little interest to state elites from a revenue perspective. They come instead to be treated largely as a source of political patronage: appointment to posts in the tax bureaucracy is a way of rewarding supporters (and potential opponents), and providing them with resources on a continuing basis. Several things follow.

The corruption networks – the number of people who share in any corrupt appropriation – tend to be relatively narrow, fragmented, heterogeneous and secret. Chief Tax Inspector X makes one set of arrangements with colleagues, friends, relatives and members of political or other bureaucratic networks in his locality; Chief Tax Inspector Y may make a very different set in his domain. As individual bureaucrats are moved around, the 'system' might change. There are continual processes of individual renegotiation, fuelled by the dearth of information about how the cake is being shared, and dearth of norms, based on 'common practice', about how it should be shared. No one has general oversight or insight into the system. The political elite has little direct interest in the revenue that is generated through routine taxation because it is feeding from elsewhere. As the elite and the state have neither a powerful corruption or revenue interest in tax assessment and collection, there is little incentive to amend legislation, ordinances or formal procedures.

Implications for Reform Initiatives

What does the previous discussion imply about the prospects for reducing corruption in tax collection in different public finance regimes? The scope for steady, incremental improvement is greater in situations where governments are dependent on earned incomes. There are two reasons for this. One is that the tax bureaucracies tend to be relatively meritocratic, competent and disciplined. The underlying structure of the tax collection system is relatively sound, and therefore amenable to gradual improvement. The other reason is that dependence of governments on earned income actively fosters interaction between state and society, and these interactions tend to promote demands for improved accountability of the state apparatus. Taxpayers are likely to exercise some voice, and that is likely to contribute to dampening down corruption in tax collection.

The dependence of states on earned income leads to the existence of effective accountability of the state to societal forces. One would expect to observe this effect over time in individual countries: regimes that become more dependent on earned income should become more accountable, possibly even democratic. We do not have the data needed to demonstrate this point conclusively.[3] There is however some striking supporting evidence from Indonesia, a country which has had much the same political system – and to a large extent the same political leaders – for the 30-year period since the mid-1960s, but has experienced major changes in the sources of public revenue. The 1970s was a period of booming oil revenues, when the regime became largely autonomous of other social and economic forces, including private capital [*Winters, 1996*].

Unlike many other regimes dependent on mineral wealth, the Indonesian government foresaw a future when it would have greater need of what we have here called earned income, and prepared for this through tax reforms in the 1980s. When oil revenues began to decline in the 1980s, taxpayers were obliged to substitute. Indonesia is far from a democracy, but has a growing democratisation movement, that has received considerable stimulus from the effectiveness of the new, broad-based tax system: democrats have explicitly linked their demands for political rights to the fact that the regime is now levying taxes on the population to a much greater extent than before [*Winters, 1996: 161*]. The old logic of 'no taxation without representation' seems to be at work here.

Indonesia is unusual in the extent to which the government prepared for the decline in unearned income and made a smooth transition to earning income from large numbers of its citizens. Regimes which are very dependent on unearned income are very vulnerable. On the one hand, the major unearned income sources – mineral revenues and aid – are unstable and prone to sudden declines. On the other hand, states which have lived from unearned income rarely have a tax bureaucracy of sufficient competence to switch quickly to earned income sources. For them the choice may lie between not replacing lost revenue or adopting the 'autonomous revenue agency' model that has become more popular in recent years. In collecting customs revenues, the autonomy stems from the employment of a foreign company to assess and/or collect duties on an incentive basis – the more the revenue collected, the greater the company's reward (Indonesia, Mozambique).

For 'internal' revenue, the preferred model is a new public agency, with highly paid staff, and considerable political and legal authority to collect taxes. This approach has resulted in considerable improvements in revenue collection in Ghana, Peru and Uganda. To some extent this may result from reducing levels of corruption in tax collection. But, after some period of time, the autonomy enjoyed by these agencies begins to lead their staff into corrupt practices. Autonomous, authoritative revenue agencies may be an essential first step in a crisis situation, but the long term problems of corruption and non-accountability in tax collection remain. There are various options open to policy-makers to address these problems by improving the structure of incentives that tax officials face, such as making bonus payments to them that are related to the amount of tax that they collect or legislating a more effective combination of penalties for corrupt collusion between them and the evading taxpayers. We do not examine these policy options which are well discussed by Bardhan [*1997: 1320–46*]. Instead we ask the question whether one particular more radical approach, that of re-designing the whole system of taxation to make it less corruption-friendly, would be likely to succeed.

CORRUPTION AND THE DESIGN OF TAX SYSTEMS

Political and Administrative Biases in Tax Design

We have argued that a collapse of unearned income that forces the state to substitute 'earned' tax revenues for the lost unearned income reduces the degree of insulation of the government from the governed. It creates a possibility for taxpayers to call the government to better account for its spending. To the extent that the government decides to respond to these demands, the basis exists for the growth of government accountability, and therewith the growth of government legitimacy. Indeed, such demands and responses have historically led on towards the emergence of more democratic types of government.

However attractive such an evolution may seem, and however much one would wish to encourage it, it is also true that democracies have drawbacks of their own in the matter of revenue raising. Politicians in a democracy tend to think that they have to be concerned more with what the taxation system looks like to the median voter than with how it actually performs in terms of criteria of net revenue raised, horizontal and vertical equity and its distorting effects on the economy.[4] They will, therefore, be inclined to prefer taxation that is as invisible to the general public's eye as possible, and when visible as equitable-looking as possible. Thus politicians will favour indirect taxation over direct, since the former tends to become consolidated into the purchase price of the taxed goods and services. They will also favour cascading indirect taxes to VAT, because the headline rate per unit of revenue is lower [*Due, 1976: 86*]. In direct taxes, steep progression of rates with numerous detailed exemptions will be preferred to mild progression or proportionality with no exemptions, because the former appears to be less harsh on the median voter.

Thus we caution against exaggerated expectations of rational taxation in new democracies. But whether the over-arching political constraints are set by an autocrat or by democratic politicians, it is important to be aware that, within those constraints, the detailed design of particular taxes can be shaped to fit the preferences of the tax officials themselves. Is this such a bad thing? The answer depends on what assumptions one makes about what the preferences of the tax officials themselves are likely to be. We assume the existence of corrupt tax officials, as well as dishonest taxpayers [*Besley and McLaren, 1993: 120 n.2*].

If tax officials are corrupt, or would seriously like to become so, a discreetly manipulative approach to tax design is an important lever to advance their purposes. Corrupt officials will have their own favoured methods for collecting any tax. Essentially, their collection methods should be complicated enough for them to be able, without undue difficulty, to make the life of the honest taxpayer miserable. If they can do that, then they will be able to turn some honest taxpayers into dishonest taxpayers who will collude in a secret agreement that, if their tax assessments are wrongly reduced, part of the revenue that the state loses thereby will be paid to the tax officials themselves. Both dishonest parties can secure private benefits at the expense of the state.

In order to structure incentives in a way that will promote such dishonest bargains, corrupt tax officials will prefer particular methods of tax collection. Four of these preferred methods are:

(a) multiple, overlapping tax jurisdictions (not unified jurisdictions);
(b) complex eligibility criteria (not simple ones);
(c) discretionary procedures (not automatic ones);
(d) full investigation of cases (not summary disposals).

These features can readily be legislated into any tax system, whatever the balance between direct and indirect taxes and whatever the nature of the separate tax bases [*Toye, 1989: 811*]. Moreover, either singly or in combination, they effectively set up a situation in which the typical encounter between tax officer and citizen has the following characteristics: (1) relevant information will be grossly asymmetric, in favour of the tax officer; (2) more than one type of tax officer can be involved in settling an individual case; (3) one or more face-to-face meetings may take place before the assessment is confirmed; (4) the severity of the assessment can vary widely without any breach of the tax rules. Such an encounter will contain ample scope for oppressive behaviour intended to induce collusion, the actual offer of bribes in return for a reduced assessment, and punitive sanctions on those honest taxpayers who still refuse to bribe.

To lend some verisimilitude to this account, below are some instances of this kind of collusion, taken from Nigeria, Taiwan and Indonesia. We may note at this point that each of these three countries falls in the bottom half of the Transparency International Corruption Perception Index, Taiwan being ranked 29th, Indonesia 45th and Nigeria 54th out of the 54 countries represented. The Index is a composite one based on various measures of corruption, as perceived by private sector business people.

The first example is taken from an anthropological narrative, referring to a village in south-east Nigeria.

> When the tax man came the following day, the (village council) had not met to decide how to welcome him; the food, drinks and money usually offered to mitigate the harsh tax assessment were not ready. When the tax man left, the elders and teenagers who had been exempted from the tax the previous year were now enroled to be taxed [*Iyam, 1995: 170–71*].

Since no gifts were available for him at the meeting, the tax man was able to punish the villagers by exercising his legal discretion on the question of which persons were liable to head tax in the way least favourable to their interests.

Another description of the same problem, this time from Taiwan, is as follows:

> It is this unintentional 'flexibility' of the tax laws that has yielded discretion to individual tax officials in interpreting the law. From the taxpayer's point of view, this arbitrariness means that the tax officials can raise hell with anyone they pick, and that 'anyone' could very well be the one that fails to buy them out. Unless the taxpayers receive extremely unfair treatment, they are usually reluctant to bring their cases to court [*Chu, 1990: 394*].

The situation was similar in Indonesia in the early 1980s.

> We had a dense forest of overlapping regulations that no one really understood. It could take years to figure out which laws were in effect and which ones had been superseded. This put businessmen and individual taxpayers at the mercy of tax officials ... The result was that businessmen needed to develop personal links with individual officials to ensure that all went well ... Of course, you had to pay a lot to this person to be certain he'd take good care of you [*Winters, 1996: 165-6*].

The exercise of discretionary power as a method of extracting bribes from taxpayers seems to be quite widespread in Africa and Asia.

The Strategy of Tax Simplification

It is in order to prevent this sort of outcome that the strategy of simplifying the structure of the tax system has been widely adopted in the current wave of tax reform in developing countries. Needless to say, the tax simplification strategy has more than this one objective. Other objectives include increasing total tax revenue by broadening the tax base, improving horizontal (if not vertical) equity and minimising tax-induced distortions of the economy. But in addition to these aims, tax simplification was expected to pay dividends in terms of the reduction of corruption. According to the head of the HIID tax reform mission to Indonesia in the mid-1980s, 'it was expected that simplification would reduce the scope for corruption, since the complexities and ambiguities in tax law were used by tax collectors and taxpayers alike to cloak their transgressions' [*Gillis, 1989: 93*].

One of the benefits of a less complex tax structure and a less ambiguous tax law is that it should reduce the frequency of face-to-face interactions between tax officials and taxpayers. There is much support in the tax literature for such a reduction, on the grounds that it reduces the temptation and the practical scope for tax officials to solicit bribes or to accept those offered. The introduction of withholding systems (like pay-as-you-earn) and presumptive assessments (where liability is assessed by reference to publicly monitorable factors) are effective ways of reducing the need for face-to-face interactions. Another benefit of tax simplification should be that the number of separate but overlapping tax jurisdictions are reduced, and that this reduces the degree of discretion that individual tax officials are allowed to exercise. This decreases the area of uncertainty about true liability, and thus the taxpayer's incentive to offer a bribe for a wrongly reduced settlement. 'Public officials who are in direct contact with their clients and those who can exercise discretion tend to figure more prominently' in the corrupt practices of revenue-raising agencies, according to one study of seven Asian countries [*Alfiler, 1986: 39*].

Is there a conflict between the two anti-corruption tactics of reducing face-to-face interactions between tax officers and taxpayers and reducing official discretion over liability assessments? Does not the resort to presumptive methods of assessment widen the tax officer's discretion? The answer is that it does not, provided that the presumptive rule is well defined and is based on available and transparent data. Consider the example of a tax which is intended to fall on incomes in the agricultural sector. Given that households' annual crop yields and the costs of producing them vary from year to year, it might be decided that regular on-farm inspections were needed to determine liability, and that tax inspectors should be allowed discretion to estimate the off-farm income of the farmer. Suppose that this method gave rise to corruption. A presumptive assessment method is then substituted for regular site inspections. Henceforth liability is determined by the size of the farm household's land holding, after allowance is made for the fertility of the soil. If there are accurate numbers from a recent cadastre of the size of all farm holdings, plus a transparent official classification of agro-climatic zones, presumptive tax liabilities can be calculated at once with no inspections and no scope for official discretion. What suffers in such a change is horizontal equity. Less discretion may cause more arbitrariness, for example, as between farmers who are able to cultivate their holding fully and those who are not. The reduction of corruption may have to be traded off against the degree of horizontal equity in a tax-simplifying reform, if extensive resort is had to presumptive methods.

Value-Added Tax and the Costs of Tax Simplification

Another trade-off exists between tax simplification and collection costs. The simplification of the tax system does not necessarily make it less costly to administer: it may make it more so. The proposition that tax simplification can raise the cost of revenue collection may be illustrated by reference to a policy of transition from assorted indirect taxes to a value-added tax (VAT). In the first place, it is clear that the introduction of a VAT does typically involve a great simplification of the structure of indirect taxation, in that it normally replaces a number of different existing indirect taxes. These are export taxes, excises (both specific and *ad valorem*), sales taxes (at manufacturing and/or wholesale and/or retail levels), selective taxes on services (usually those defined as luxuries) or, indeed any indirect tax that the government has thought fit to impose. Each of these different existing taxes will typically have its own structure of rates, its own list of exemptions, its own set of compliance requirements and so on. Many rate structures will be excessively differentiated. There will be many examples of overlapping incidence, leading to an irrational and inefficient distribution of the tax burden as well as the wide scope for official discretion that is conducive to corruption. Compared with all this, a VAT of the tax credit type is an immense simplification.

But this does not necessarily imply that adoption of a tax credit type of VAT will lower the costs of collecting the previous amount of revenue. All VATs which use tax credits, and therefore incorporate the potential anti-evasion advantage of the ability to cross-audit, i.e. to check the declarations of one taxpayer by reference to the declarations of others, are likely to require:

(1) a more extensive taxpayer registration than pre-existing taxes, as efficiency benefits depend on comprehensiveness of coverage (as well as simplicity of rate structure). In addition, the work of registration is heavier, for both parties, than registration for other types of taxes.

(2) the establishment of a refund or credit facility, partly for those taxpayers whose purchases and sales volumes are 'lumpy', that is, discontinuous and variable in size, but particularly for those whose sales are wholly or mainly for export, and therefore zero-rated.

(3) a significant upgrading of tax officers' skills to operate this more sophisticated method of indirect taxation. This will involve high training costs, particularly in countries that previously relied more heavily on revenue from excises than from sales taxes.

Thus simplification by means of transition to a VAT is likely to generate additional recurring costs. This has some interesting implications.

In principle, such costs can be traded off against the efficiency gains that tax simplification brings by reducing economic distortions, and this sets a limit to how much simplification is worthwhile. Also, the acceptable level of the costs of simplification will be affected by the size of the government's revenue target. If the government wants to raise more revenue than it did before, the distortion costs of persisting with the previous system of assorted taxes will rise at the margin, and this will make the additional costs of moving to a broad-based tax system like VAT more acceptable [*Gemmell, 1991*]. Tax reform inevitably requires achieving a balance between progress towards a number of different objectives, of which minimising collection costs is only one.

Will a Credit-type VAT Reduce Corruption?

We have already referred to the fact that the tax credit form of VAT makes cross-auditing a possibility. Cross-auditing means the ability to use information from one taxpayer's returns to check on the accuracy of the information supplied in another taxpayer's returns. This possibility arises because every transaction involves both a buyer and a seller, and under a comprehensive VAT both buyer and seller will have to file returns, each recording one side of an identical transaction. Also, the incentive to mis-declare the amount of tax paid works in opposing directions. A buyer may want to over-state the amount of VAT in her purchases of inputs, because that amount may be deducted from her own VAT liability. But a seller will not be willing to collude in this, because she can only do so by raising her own tax liability.

How in principle a cross-audit can be done is illustrated by the following table. In Table 1, the rows represent the stages of production, starting at the top and working down. To make this less abstract, one can visualise a farm growing wheat, a mill milling the wheat into flour, a bakery using the flour to make bread and a sandwich shop using the bread to make sandwiches to retail to the public. The columns represent the build up of gross costs of production, including VAT, at each of these stages of the production of retail sandwiches. In the fifth column, it can be seen that the seller's tax payment at any stage should be equal to the claim for tax credit of her buyer, who is also the seller of another product with additional value-added at the subsequent stage of production. If there are four stages of production from a to d, if VAT a = 1, then VAT credit b = 1; if VAT b = 10, then VAT credit c = 10; and if VAT c = 13, then VAT credit d = 13. Observed inequality of any of these three required equalities indicates error or, more likely, malfeasance. So much is well known and has been much discussed. But how far is this cross-audit feature of VAT likely to reduce corruption in practice, when corruption takes the form of collusion between dishonest tax officials with dishonest taxpayers? There are two major considerations which derive from two characteristic features of a credit-type VAT: the desirability of comprehensive coverage and the need for a refund facility.

TABLE 1
ILLUSTRATIVE VAT CALCULATION, SHOWING POTENTIAL FOR CROSS-AUDIT

Stage of Production	(a) Raw Material	(b) Manufacturing	(c) Wholesale	(d) Retail
Value of purchases	0	11	110	143
VA added by stage	10	90	30	70
Cumulative VA	10	100	130	200
Tax due at stage (10%)	**1** – 0 = 1	*10* – **1** = 9	**13** – *10* = 3	20 – **13** = 7
Cumulative VAT	1	10	13	20
Sale price to next stage	10 + 1 = 11	100 + 10 = 110	130 + 13 = 143	200 + 20 = 220

Source: Authors.

As emphasised earlier, the VAT has many advantages that make it a good form of taxation, whether it reduces corruption or not. It is income elastic, very productive of revenue with much reduced distortion of economic incentives, and neutral with respect to vertical equity. But these benefits are realised in full only if coverage is made as comprehensive and uniform as possible. There are good reasons, then, apart from a government's desire to raise the portion of its income that it 'earns', for the desire to register and tax as many small businesses as possible. The question is how far to go in this direction. To exclude entirely the retail stage, as was initially done in some francophone African versions of VAT, is probably to be too pessimistic about what can be done.

The difficulty of their inclusion, however, arises from the illiteracy and poor record-keeping of many retailers and owners of small businesses in developing countries. Their inclusion by use of the *forfait* (or negotiated assessment) procedure, while increasing the efficiency benefits of the tax and augmenting its revenue, can easily lead to bribery and corruption. It introduces into the new system the face-to-face meeting and the wide permitted discretion that opened the door to corruption in the old. It is particularly vital that, if resort is had to the *forfait*, it should be confined to sales, and not applied to purchases. Tax credits should be permitted against actual invoices only [*Due, 1976: 179*]. The collection of the latter is not onerous, even in a world of tropical rainstorms and hungry rats, and it provides an important reality check on the negotiated assessment of sales volumes. But the best solution is probably to steer clear of *forfait* altogether, and instead grant outright exemption to some small firms and farms with less than a stated threshold value of sales.

With the exception of the *forfait*, when used, the VAT operates by taxpayer self-assessment, based on records of sales and purchases. For every transaction, therefore, two independent records should be available to the VAT administration. In an ideal world taxpayer returns could be extensively, but not completely, cross-checked by computer, as a means of identifying discrepancies and possible delinquencies. In most developing countries, that time is still distant. In practice, the much-heralded cross-audit is so onerous as to be, with rare exceptions, useless as a means of policing self-assessment. There are still too many cash transactions without invoices or receipts [*Chu, 1990: 404*]. Moreover, a market in forged invoices can quickly develop. Bear in mind also that the cross-audit does not, in any event, detect every possible form of VAT evasion. Therefore, much of the success in reducing corruption still depends on more low-tech, and thus more fallible forms of audit and inspection.

It is usually impossible to audit every taxpayer every year, so a selection has to be made. Although the choice of who to audit, and who to ignore should be made on rational and impersonal criteria, this does not always happen. It is clear that discretion about who to audit will be a residual source of corruption. There have certainly been cases of policy failure in the auditing of VAT returns. The ratio of inspectors to taxpayers may be acceptable, and numerous audits and inspections may take place. Yet these may be quite ineffective where clear audit priorities are not established, a system for reporting findings does not exist and the regular reviewing of audit work by senior officials is absent, as is all too often the case. This kind of laxity will act as a breeding ground for corruption even when a VAT is in place.

But much more damaging is the fact that, without a workable cross-audit facility, there is nothing in the pure mechanics of a VAT that would stop the tax inspector and the tax payer meeting in advance to agree the level of the assessment, and then hiring corrupt accountants to prepare false paperwork which appeared to validate the wrongly reduced assessment. It is, after all, still in the interest of both the taxpayer and the tax official to agree on a wrongly reduced assessment and a bribe smaller than the amount of the reduction. Where corruption is already endemic, as in Indonesia, some collusion is likely to survive the introduction of VAT. In Taiwan, apparently, the existing system of regular pay-offs to the local tax office can be relied upon to secure at the very least an under-statement of the amount of evaded tax, if evasion is detected and reported from an audit [*Chu, 1990: 397*].

Do Corrupt Tax Officials Rationally Resist the Tax Simplification Strategy?

A final difficulty of implementing a tax simplification strategy is that, alongside the various pressures on government to move forward on tax reform, which have already been noted, other pressures exist that deter them from moving very vigorously and wholeheartedly [*Bird and Casanegra de Jantscher, 1992: 100*]. One of the reasons for this may be the existence of corruption in the tax administration. It is a matter of great interest, therefore, to enquire whether corrupt tax officials try to resist policy-makers' efforts to bring in reforms that restrict their meetings with taxpayers and the scope of their discretion, and if so whether they can succeed.

The focus here is on the Indonesian tax reform of the 1980s. The original aim of the technocratic economics ministers who conceived the tax reform was to modernise a tax system which had become over-complex, income-inelastic and administratively lax through years of high-level neglect. But as the oil price declined from its 1979–80 peak, the motivation for the reform came to include the enhancement of 'earned' government income, as well as squeezing out corruption within the tax administration. Both of these objectives were to be served by a drastic tax structure simplification centred on the introduction of a VAT.

> The second part of the Indonesian tax reform was the replacement of its complex sales tax structure with a more general credit-type VAT. The drastic simplification of the rate structure (to only one basic rate) and the elimination of many exemptions and other forms of special treatment reduced much of the discretionary authority of the tax officers ... Equally important in this regard was the built-in incentive under the credit-type system for taxpayers to engage in self-monitoring of tax collections [*Flatters and Macleod, 1995: 409*].

Flatters and Macleod testify to the active opposition of the tax officials:

> The Indonesian customs service and the sales tax office strongly resisted both of these aspects of the tax reform. Similar stories could be told about resistance of tax collectors, in Indonesia and elsewhere, to simplifications in property tax administration, income tax laws and tariff structures [*Flatters and Macleod, 1995: 409*].

Flatters and Macleod's story of bureaucratic resistance is corroborated by one of the key Indonesian tax reformers, as follows:

> The strongest resistance to tax reform, as it turns out, came from the tax officials themselves. They had the most to lose from the depersonalisation and simplification of the system. It was the same with customs. Before we could go ahead with tax deregulation, we had to replace the director general of taxes. Without this move, we could achieve nothing [*Winters, 1996: 166, n.62*].

Despite this clear documentation of the tax reformers' view that the resistance of the tax officials to tax simplification in Indonesia was strong, it has been argued that the resistance was more apparent than real, and that the tax officials were content with mere shadow-boxing. The tax reformers' view could, after all, be criticised as complacent, on the grounds that, if the tax officials had not resisted, this would show that the design of their reforms were in fact inadequate to prevent corruption, and seen by insiders to be toothless. By the same token, the tax officials would have been obliged to do some shadow-boxing, if they were not in effect to admit publicly that they saw the reforms as toothless against corruption, and thus push the reformers into trying more effective measures. We should be wary of accepting the tax reformers' view without considering some of the subtleties of political signalling that might be involved. How can we check the likelihood that the resistance of the Indonesian tax officials was rationally motivated by fear of the anti-corruption impact of the tax reform?

The weight of the evidence is on the side of the view that Indonesian tax officials did see the reforms as a threat, and that fear was a rational one given that they did indeed have a corruption-reducing effect within the tax system. We would not go so far as to claim that corruption in Indonesia has declined in the last decade: corruption may have decreased in the tax system and increased elsewhere in the economy. But a decline within the tax system does seem probable, for the following reasons. The Indonesian VAT was designed to be as simple a VAT as existed anywhere in the world. It did not extend below the importer and manufacturer levels, not even to wholesalers. There are very few exemptions, and there is only one rate of levy, ten per cent. Perhaps most important of all

> nearly two-thirds of the base of the tax passes through three bottlenecks that are easily accessible to the government, and therefore the tax administration: the customs house, sales of refined petroleum products by Pertamina ... and sales of the 200-odd government-owned enterprises ... Given these bottlenecks, the tax administration is in a position to collect more than half the potential VAT revenues with minimal expenditure of administrative resources, thereby allowing enforcement efforts to be focused on the remaining, less accessible portions of the tax base [*Gillis, 1989: 99*].

In these circumstances, and given also that the task of certificating the value of all Indonesian imports has been contracted out to a European firm, it is hard to argue that the same or a larger percentage of potential indirect tax revenue would be lost through corruption than was previously the case. Second, the VAT revenue figures are too high to be consistent with a constant or increasing level of leakage. This can be shown by a simple calculation. The nominal proceeds of a single-rate VAT with completely comprehensive coverage have to increase at the same rate as the total of value added at current prices, i.e. the nominal rate of economic growth. Between 1985 and 1995, the real rate of growth of GDP in Indonesia was approximately seven per cent per annum, while the GDP deflator was approximately eight per cent per annum. If nominal GDP was growing at 15 per cent per annum, the tax base for a comprehensive single-rate VAT would be growing at 15 per cent also.

According to the IMF *Government Finance Statistics Yearbook 1996* (p.192) the revenue from 'general sales tax, turnover or VAT' amounted to 2,327 billion rupiahs in 1985, and had grown to 18,335 billion rupiahs in 1994. This is a rate of growth of approximately 22 per cent per annum. It follows from this that the degree of exploitation of the VAT tax base was growing rapidly and significantly in the period 1985–94, at a rate of around seven per cent a year. Although in an initial transitional phase, this rate of growth could theoretically occur while the degree of revenue leakage was rising, growth of the exploitation of the tax base *plus* increasing revenue leakage could not persist over the longer term. There must come a point of inflection in both growth functions after which both decelerate as the limits of the VAT tax base are reached. Under the collection conditions described, it seems likely to us that the revenue leakage already has been, and will continue to be, squeezed.

Third, the obvious success of the VAT in revenue enhancement, deriving from the inherent income elasticity of the tax base as well as the increase in the degree of exploitation of that base, created a virtuous circle. Once the government had succeeded in putting in place a 'cash machine' of this degree of productivity, short term revenue pressures were reduced. The temptation to set revenue targets for other types of taxes, and allow discretion as to the means by which they are met, becomes less urgent and easier to resist.

CONCLUSIONS

One very frequent practical obstacle to the successful implementation of a strategy of tax simplification is that the tax authorities are rarely left alone to develop simpler and more productive revenue-gathering systems. They are often the victims of a policy-activism that is dictated by considerations of visibility rather than effectiveness. Governments often make sudden highly visible changes in tax policy, which look dramatic but are undertaken primarily to demonstrate that 'the government is doing something about it', whatever 'it' may happen to be at the time. The real impact in solving the chosen short-run problem may be small, but the side effects on the task of simplifying the tax system may be large. A good example of this is the proliferation of different rates and exemptions within a VAT in response to the agitation of particular socio-economic groups. Another example is the existence of short term pressures for extra revenue which lead to the retention or introduction of taxes that are productive of revenue but quite undesirable from the viewpoint of the other goals of taxation [*Gray, 1989: 2*]. It is worth noting, with reference to the Indonesian reform, that neither of these things happened.

In the 1980s, there has been a particular kind of policy activism, which goes under the name of structural adjustment. The reform of the budget or tax system was a condition in over two-thirds of the World Bank's structural or sectoral adjustment loans in the period 1980–86 [*Mosley, Harrigan and Toye, 1995: 44*]. Inevitably in the circumstances, in some countries schemes of tax simplification themselves came to be regarded as a quick fix for a burgeoning fiscal deficit. Guatemala's 1983 tax reform may be cited as an example of this. Under the guidance of the IMF, the government decided to increase revenue by replacing the existing turnover sales tax and a stamp duty with a tax credit method VAT. The VAT became operational one month after it was announced, leaving no time to organise and train the tax administrators or to educate the taxpayers. Far from being 'self-enforcing', as the authorities seemed naively to believe, the VAT got into immediate difficulties because the administration received a flood of refund requests, most of which were believed to be fraudulent, but which there was no capacity to audit. The refunding was suspended, re-introducing cascade effects, public confidence was lost, the VAT rate was drastically lowered and the stamp duty brought back to fill the consequent revenue gap [*Bird and Casanegra de Jantscher, 1992: 79–83*]. This was *not* the way to simplify the Guatemalan tax system!

Much ground would be gained in the war of attrition against corruption if politicians could be weaned away from their habit of pursuing the politics of visibility in taxation decisions. There is an obvious link between the adoption of tax policies that look good to the median voter and the maintenance of extensive bureaucratic discretion. This is because tax policies that look good to the median voter would be unworkable if their regulations were to be enforced as written. This is true of income taxes with an extremely steep rate of progression, for example. Such taxes would be very difficult to collect without allowing enough bureaucratic discretion to ensure that the effective progression of the tax incidence is much milder than the nominal rate schedule would lead one to expect. Thus the pursuit of visibility politics in taxation is not merely compatible with bureaucratic tax discretion, it is symbiotic with it. The symbiosis is, needless to say, strengthened when the proceeds of bureaucratic tax corruption are partly siphoned off by politicians. However, what looks good to the median voter (assuming here the success of the democratisation agenda) need not remain fixed and unchanging. Electorates may learn eventually that all that glistens is not gold, and that democratic politicians, like conjurors, win the applause of their parties by the extravagant practice of mis-direction. As Abraham Lincoln memorably put it: 'you can fool some of the people all of the time and you can fool all of the people some of the time, but you cannot fool all of the people all of the time'.

The Indonesian case shows that tax reform does not always fail, and that the tax simplification strategy can bring some anti-corruption dividends. However, the Indonesian case, in tax reform as in structural adjustment policy more generally, has unusual features which mean that it is not easy to draw easily applicable policy lessons for other developing countries. For one thing, Indonesia since 1966 has benefited from an economic leadership that is far-sighted and technocratically skilful. The lesson of Indonesia is not that there are technical fixes for cultural dispositions that hinder development, but that what is required is a long-lasting political drive from a very high level to a particular vision of development, and that vision must be technically well informed.

Where such political pre-conditions are lacking, however, second best and n-th best solutions have to be considered. These involve some toleration of corruption, but also an attempt to limit the damage that it can do to a government's efforts to 'earn' more of its income. Under this scenario, corruption will never disappear, and anti-corruption policy will always be a matter of containment, a little more or a little less.

Flatters and Macleod [*1995*] analyse this problem using a model of collusion between tax collectors and taxpayers to reduce the latter's liability, the difference between this and the true liability being divided between them. They argue the case for limited toleration of this corruption, when four conditions apply. They are that:

(1) the government cannot pay tax collectors more than the normal civil service rate;
(2) the tax collectors have better knowledge of the true tax liability than is available to the Finance Minister;
(3) for the collectors, bribes are a perfect substitute for wages;
(4) collectors exert more effort to establish true liability when they are paid higher wages-plus-bribes.

In these conditions, if the Finance Ministry tolerates limited corruption, it can overcome the handicap imposed by poor knowledge of individual tax liabilities. It can collect more revenue compared with a situation in which the tax collectors are uncorrupted, but also unmotivated to exploit their superior knowledge to increase the Finance Ministry's revenue total. Corruption of tax officials may be one problem, this model is telling us, but personal integrity when it is combined with a minimal incentive to work is another.

This is a good warning against the practical consequences of taking an excessively moralistic approach to policy-making, and in that sense it follows a familiar tradition in political economy. The four assumed conditions are not wholly implausible individually, and there may indeed be countries where all hold good at the same time. The Indonesian case certainly shows that they are not universally true, and that the strategy of tax simplification ought to reduce the need to tolerate corruption because it reduces the asymmetry of information between the Finance Ministry and the tax officials.

Even where the conditions of the Flatters and Macleod model do hold, and limited corruption does augment government revenues, the government remains vulnerable to the evaporation of its revenues, unless it is able to enforce its chosen limits to corruption. It must at all times be able to exercise powers of dismissal and financial penalty over both excessively lazy and excessively greedy tax collectors. If it cannot do these two things, the revenue benefit of its Faustian bargain will disappear. Maybe the disciplining of the excessively greedy tax collectors will prove easier than it seems. In this connection, one is much heartened by the true story of the developing country government that introduced a system of self-assessment for import duties, stood down all its customs officers and found that its customs revenue sharply increased.

NOTES

1. For sources, see Moore [*1998*].
2. The use of the concept of 'earned income' is indeed a logical extension of the term 'rentier': rentier income is 'unearned' in the language of classical political economy.
3. It would be a major undertaking, because many other factors are involved.
4. Horizontal equity refers to the equal tax treatment of equally placed individuals, or companies: it requires the like treatment of like. Vertical equity requires that differently situated individuals (or companies) are treated differently and in a manner appropriate to their differences. What is appropriate is controversial. Some argue for proportionate taxation, that is tax payments proportionate to income, while others argue for progressive taxation, where the tax rate rises as income increases, on the grounds of the declining marginal utility of income. The distorting effects of taxation on the economy arise if the tax element in the prices of goods and services is not strictly proportional to the non-tax element. In this case, the relative prices of goods and services will be changed by the taxation, and people's economic behaviour will be distorted away from the pattern that they would freely choose in the absence of taxation, and which ipso facto they regard as preferable. The neutral impact of VAT, as shown later in Table 1, is therefore a highly desirable feature of any tax, but which very few other taxes have in the same degree as VAT.

REFERENCES

Alfiler, C.P., 1986, 'The Process of Bureaucratic Corruption in Asia: Emerging Patterns', in L.V. Carino, *Bureaucratic Corruption in Asia: Causes, Consequences and Controls*, Quezon City: JMC Press.

Bardhan, P., 1997, 'Corruption and Development: A Review of Issues', *Journal of Economic Literature*, Vol.XXXV, Sept., pp.1320–46.

Besley, T. and J. McLaren, 1993, 'Taxes and Bribery: the Role of Wage Incentives', *Economic Journal*, Vol.103, No.416, pp.119–41.

Bird, R.M. and M. Casanegra de Jantscher (eds.), 1992, *Improving Tax Administration in Developing Countries*, Washington, DC: International Monetary Fund.

Chaudhry, K.A., 1989, 'The Price of Wealth: Business and State in Labor Remittance and Oil Economies', *International Organization*, Vol.43, No.1, pp.101–45.

Chu, C.Y.C., 1990, 'A Model of Income Tax Evasion with Venal Tax Officials: the Case of Taiwan', *Public Finance/Finances Publiques*, Vol.XXXXV, No.3, pp.392–407.

Due, J.F., 1976, 'Value-added Taxation in Developing Countries', in N.T. Wang (ed.), *Taxation and Development*, New York: Praeger.

Flatters, F. and W.B. Macleod, 1995, 'Administrative Corruption and Taxation', *International Tax and Public Finance*, Vol.2, pp.397–417.

Gemmell, N., 1991, 'Tax Collection Costs and the Choice of Tax Base in Less Developed Countries: A Geometric Note', University of Nottingham, Credit Research Paper No.91/3.

Gillis, M., 1989, 'Comprehensive Tax Reform: The Indonesian Experience, 1981–1988', in M. Gillis (ed.), *Tax Reform in Developing Countries*, Durham NC: Duke University Press.

Goldscheid, R., 1958 (1925), 'A Sociological Approach to Problems of Public Finance', in R.A. Musgrave and A.T. Peacock (eds.), *Classics in the Theory of Public Finance*, London and New York: Macmillan.

Gray, C.W., 1989, *Issues in Income Tax Reform in Developing Countries*, World Bank, Working Paper Series No.267.

Iyam, D.U., 1995, *The Broken Hoe: Cultural Reconfiguration in Biase Southeast Nigeria*, Chicago, IL: Chicago University Press.

Moore, M.P., 1998, 'Death without Taxes: Democracy, State Capacity, and Aid Dependence in the Fourth World', in M. Robinson and G. White (eds.), *Towards a Democratic Developmental State*, Oxford: Oxford University Press.

Mosley, P., Harrigan, J. and J. Toye, 1995, *Aid and Power: The World Bank and Policy-based Lending*, second edition, Vol.1, London: Routledge.

Thorp, R., 1996, 'The Reform of Tax Administration in Peru', in A. Silva (ed.), *Implementing Policy Innovations in Latin America: Politics, Economics and Techniques*, Social Agenda Policy Group, Inter-American Development Bank, Washington DC.

Toye, J., 1989, 'Tax Reform in South Asia: Yesterday and Today', *Modern Asian Studies*, Vol.23, Part 4, Oct., pp.797–813.

Wade, R., 1985, 'The Market for Public Office: Why the Indian State is not Better at Development', *World Development*, Vol.13, No.4, pp.467–98.

Winters, J.A., 1996, *Power in Motion: Capital Mobility and the Indonesian State*, Ithaca, NY: Cornell University Press.

[20]

ARTICLES

Blacklisting Public Contractors as an Anti-Corruption and Racketeering Strategy

JAMES B. JACOBS & FRANK ANECHIARICO

In New York City, the struggle against organized crime and the most recent round of corruption scandals have prompted a series of "reforms" aimed at denying public contracts to individuals and firms that are "mob-connected" or otherwise corrupt. While the motivation behind these initiatives is understandable, the initiatives themselves raise complex and difficult issues of governmental ethics, fairness, and efficiency. For example: (1) Should government operating agencies attempt to punish corrupt individuals and organizations by denying them public contracts? (2) Does government have an ethical responsibility to avoid doing business with corrupt contractors? (3) Can blacklisting be implemented fairly and systematically so as not to jeopardize the efficient operation of government?

Background

In August, 1991, the New York City School Construction Authority (SCA)[1] announced that it was blacklisting for up to five years more than fifty construction firms. The policy was shaped by SCA's inspector general, Thomas D. Thacher II, formerly director of the joint Manhattan D.A. and NYS Organized Crime Task Force's strike force on corruption and racketeering in the New York City construction industry. Nearly half the disqualifications were based on purported mob ties or criminality—such as bribery of a union official or inspector, tax fraud, minority business enterprise fraud, and money laundering—not on poor performance on previous government contracts or inability to perform future contracts.[2] The SCA's move is the farthest in a progression of steps by City agencies to sanitize the multi-billion-dollar contracting process of any taint of corruption. It attests to the political strength of anti-corruption reforms following the 1980s City corruption scandals,[3] and the growing influence of law enforcement agencies and personnel in all facets of public administration and public policy.

The SCA prequalification procedure for would-be contractors includes a 30-page prequalification questionnaire which, among other things, asks:

> In the past ten years has the applicant firm, or any of its current or past key people or affiliate firms
>
> . . . taken the Fifth Amendment in testimony regarding a business related crime?
>
> . . . given or offered to give money or any other benefit to a

James B. Jacobs, author of, Drunk Driving: An American Dilemma (1989), *is Professor of Law and Director, Center for Research in Crime and Justice, New York University School of Law. Frank Anechiarico is Professor of Government, Hamilton College, Clinton, NY.*

labor official or public servant with intent to influence that labor official or public servant with respect to any of his or her official acts, duties or decisions as a labor official [*sic*]?

. . . agreed with another to bid below the market rate?[4]

An applicant can be prosecuted as well as blacklisted for a false answer. Given the pervasiveness of payoffs to labor officials and building inspectors in the New York City construction industry, a large percentage of firms that answer these questions in the negative are making themselves vulnerable to administrative and criminal sanctions.

Agencies subject to the New York City Charter operate under a similar, but somewhat less stringent, regimen. Under new contract procurement rules, each agency's contracting officer and chief administrator must determine whether a contractor or vendor is financially, operationally, and *morally* responsible. If the agency believes the would-be contractor to be "corrupt," the contract must be denied. Even if the agency finds the contractor to be morally responsible, the City Comptroller has authority to review the agency's judgment and to object to the registration of a contract if it may reasonably be supposed that the contractor or the agency is "corrupt."[5] However, the Charter does not define "moral" or "corrupt," nor does it specify the grounds for the agency's or the Comptroller's objections.

Under new contract procurement rules, each agency's contracting officer and chief administrator must determine whether a contractor is financially, operationally, and morally responsible.

In the last few years, law enforcement agencies and anti-corruption units within city government have been exhorting government agencies to refuse to do business with criminals and racketeers and their companies. For instance, in late October, 1991, City Comptroller Elizabeth Holtzman (former Brooklyn District Attorney) urged Mayor David Dinkins to overrule his Chief Procurement Officer's decision to enter into a contract with a construction firm which had failed to report that it had once been investigated by the Occupational Safety and Health Administration for a workplace safety issue.[6] The Chief Procurement Officer argued that an OSHA investigation is not the kind of (corruption-type) investigation that must be reported. The Mayor ultimately agreed, but not without criticism for being soft on corruption.

During the summer and fall of 1991, the Comptroller sparred with the Department of Correction (DOC) with respect to an emergency jail construction contract that DOC intended to sign with the DeMatteis Construction Company. DOC asserted that the contract did not need to be let by competitive bidding because of the emergency caused by dangerous overcrowding on Rikers Island.[7] The Comptroller disagreed and raised questions about contracting with a company that was under investigation in another jurisdiction and whose officers allegedly had business dealings with the relatives of organized crime figures. DOC counter-charged that the Comptroller was risking a public safety crisis. In January, 1992, Mayor Dinkins canceled the contract and initiated proceedings to debar the company from all City work.[8]

In another example of the stringent integrity tests for government contractors, the City suspended a contract to remove abandoned cars from Brooklyn streets held by a carting company run by Carmine Agnello, John Gotti's son-in-law. According to Comptroller Holtzman, the C & M Agnello Company and its owner "had been implicated in a 'chop shop' operation in Queens and [Carmine Agnello] was under investigation for possible jury tampering in an organized crime trial in Brooklyn involving Mr. Gotti's brother Gene."[9] Agnello employees, in protests widely covered by the media, argued that they were engaged in legitimate business, that Mr. Agnello was on the job every day, and that the company's employees were, in effect, being convicted and punished without trial and for alleged offenses unrelated to the public contract they had been performing.[10]

These cases and many others raise fascinating and important questions about governmental ethics, fairness, and efficiency. Everyone can agree that firms which are unqualified to carry out government jobs can and should be denied contracts and, if possible, the right even to bid on such contracts. Likewise, firms which have performed unsatisfactorily on past contracts ought to be "debarred" from future City business unless there is some satisfactory explanation for the past behavior or some convincing reason why future performance is almost certain to be satisfactory. Thus, a strong justification for blacklisting public contractors is protection of the City and its taxpayers from being victimized by firms with a demonstrated record of fraud, shoddy workmanship, and incompetence.

Four different questions are: (1) whether the City and public authorities ought to attempt to deny contracts to "morally irresponsible" companies on the ground that government ought not to do business with "corrupt" individuals and firms; (2) whether government agencies and public authorities ought to support law enforcement's war on organized crime and other forms of racketeering and corruption by blacklisting companies controlled or influenced by, or associated with, Cosa Nostra, regardless of whether these companies perform their contracts adequately; (3) whether such a policy is capable of fair implementation; and (4) whether its costs in terms of administrative delay and reduced competition would be worth the advantage of keeping government free of whatever taint comes from a contractual relationship with a morally irresponsible firm.

Is Blacklisting A Sound Crime Control Strategy?

The New York State Organized Crime Task Force's *Final Report on Corruption and Racketeering in the New York City Construction Industry* (1991) documents the pervasiveness of organized crime in New York City's construction industry since the early 20th century. The City's five organized crime families operate, control, or influence a large number of construction and supply firms; they also dominate a number of important unions. The *Final Report* applauds the City's efforts to build an information base about the mob ties of construction companies and recommends that debarment be used more liberally to eliminate undesirable companies.[11] The *Final Report* does not recommend that government agencies deny contracts to contractors who hire workers belonging to mobbed-up unions, perhaps because adoption of that policy would shut down public works altogether.

On its face, the recommendation that government agencies refuse to deal with companies run by racketeers looks uncontroversial. There would seem to be something perverse about government investigators and prosecutors spending millions of dollars to destroy organized crime syndicates and the companies they control while City operating agencies pay millions of dollars to these same companies.

But will blacklisting "work"? Implicit in OCTF's recommendations is the belief that denying public contracts to "mobbed-up" or "mob-influenced" firms will weaken the financial base of organized crime and ultimately its power. Moreover, implicit in the policy of mobilizing government contracting to aid law enforcement is the belief that threatening to deny contractors a significant portion of their business will deter them from dealing with racketeers. However, the assumptions, logic, and practicality of this policy should be carefully examined. It is not easy to eliminate mobbed-up or otherwise immoral companies from government contracting. A blacklisted company may continue to do business with the government under a different corporate identity and through different officers (fronts without criminal records). It is extremely difficult to prove that a new firm is the alter ego of one previously blacklisted. One recent case dealing with fraud that was not mob related involved a chameleon-like vendor of metal working tools, Diversified Products. Rather than blacklist the company, the New York City Comptroller and Corporation Counsel have decided to seek debarment of the individual most closely associated with several contract defaults and bid rigging charges against predecessor companies; the matter has been pending since the summer of 1990.[12] This strategy could also be thwarted if the blacklisted person shifts his or her authority to a "clean" friend or relative. For blacklisting to have any hope of success in the case of a powerful organized crime figure, it would require extensive and expensive investigation and monitoring.[13] Even then, we cannot assume that such a policy will "work."

The argument that legitimate businessmen will be deterred from getting involved with racketeers if their public contracts are at risk assumes that contractors have control over these relationships and that, if properly motivated, they have the capacity to resist the pressures of racketeers. In many case—and the New York City construction market is a good example—contractors have had no real option to refuse to deal with mobsters and racketeers. Failure to cooperate with Cosa Nostra has meant being put out of business by labor unrest or no labor at all as well as by sabotage and violence.[14]

Even if the mob could be purged from certain industries, like construction and waste hauling, does it follow that it would be substantially weakened as an organization or institution? On reflection, the issues are more complex. For example, suppose that, purged from the legitimate economy, Cosa Nostra expanded its operations in drugs, extortion, and other rackets: would society be better off? The answer depends upon whether racketeers perform their construction contracts satisfactorily, the extent and cost of any corruption perpetrated in that performance, and whether the denial of public contracts would significantly weaken organized crime syndicates.

Is Blacklisting Ethically Required or Justifiable?

Is it unethical for a government agency to enter into contracts with "known" or suspected members of organized crime syndicates or with other racketeers? One might argue that government agencies, as repositories not only of the public's trust but of the public's money, must maintain "clean hands" and therefore never knowingly bargain or cooperate with "mobsters," "racketeers," or "criminals." Otherwise, the public's trust in and support for government might be undermined. But this would be an enormous moral and administrative burden for government to shoulder. There are tens of thousands of City contractors, each owned by and employing various numbers of individuals. On what basis could a fiscally strapped City government judge the moral character of all these contractors, and at what cost? Furthermore, what would be the practical implications of limiting contracting only to a subset of all contractors? Fewer services? Higher costs? Less competition? More delay?

It can be argued that in contracting for services or supplies, a government agency is not vouching for the integrity or good character of the consultant, contractor, or vendor. A further argument is that an operating agency's foremost duty is to get satisfactory performance for the best price, no mean feat in itself. In this view, government operating agencies are not responsible for law enforcement or for policing the moral character of the individuals and firms that provide pencils, concrete, painting, or computer systems. Even if government agencies had the time and expertise to investigate and pronounce on the moral character of their contractors, there is the question of what standard should be set for disqualification. It is hardly obvious that the government ought to exclude ex-convicts (much less suspected or acquitted "criminals") from the legitimate economy. But even if it is, in principle, sound ethics not to deal knowingly in any way with morally questionable individuals and firms, is a government operating agency in a good position to investigate the character of the principals, managers, and employees of the tens of thousands of firms with which it does business, much less the suppliers and subcontractors with whom those firms do business? An entire system of norms, rules, and procedures and a larger bureaucracy would be necessary to implement a fair and comprehensive system to judge the moral eligibility of government contractors. Isn't that the kind of exaggerated ambition that will ultimately come back to haunt government agencies as journalists and other observers and critics confront officials with contracts that have been let to all sorts of morally questionable individuals who inevitably will slip through the net?

Whose Influence or Control Disqualifies A Firm From Government Contracting?

Assuming that either for crime control or ethical reasons, government agencies are justified in refusing (indeed, have an affirmative duty to refuse) to deal with morally "tainted" firms, how are such firms to be identified? What relationship between a morally irresponsible individual and a firm serves to so taint that firm that it would be justifiable to blacklist it as a government contractor? The paradigmatic case is one in which a company is operated by a mafia don. In fact, this possibility is hypothetical since crime syndicates specialize in selling connections and protection to criminals and non-criminals, not in managing companies.[15] "Mobbed-up" companies are typically operated by organized crime associates who are themselves not "made members" of organized crime.[16] It is not uncommon, of course, for organized crime figures to establish themselves as partners (silent or of record) or investors in a firm. Whatever the legal arrangement, they exercise little control over day-to-day operations but take a percentage of the profits.

It would be no easy matter to specify the point at which organized crime's connection with or investment in a firm so taints it as to require or justify disqualifying it from public contracting. For instance, in the controversy over the emergency jail construction contract with DeMatteis Construction, the Comptroller (opposing the contract) argued that federal and New Jersey officials had evidence that the company's president owned a majority interest in a concrete company that was operated by the son-in-law of former Gambino Crime Family boss Paul Castellano. If this kind of association is enough to blacklist a firm, it means that the relatives and in-laws of reputed organized crime figures have become pariahs, barred from fully participating in the legitimate economy. The suspension of the carting and towing contracts of John Gotti's son-in-law, Carmine Agnello, is a recent example.

If only mid- or lower-level employees of a firm are linked to organized crime, would that justify blacklisting the firm? How many (or what percent of) Cosa Nostra members, associates, relatives, or friends are enough to justify blacklisting? The only public agency in New York City that has developed written criteria to deal with these questions is the School Construction Authority. Its rules provide for disqualification of contractors on the following grounds:

1. For a criminal conviction within the past five years of the applicant, or its current or past officers or principals, indicating unfair or unethical business practices or moral turpitude, the applicant will be barred from doing work for the Authority for a period of five years from the date of conviction.

2. In case of a pending criminal investigation of an applicant or its officer(s) or principal(s) or its affiliated companies, the applicant will be precluded from doing work for the Authority during the pendency of the investigation.

3. In the event that the applicant, or any of its officer(s) or principal(s) or its affiliated companies, are under indictment, the applicant will be precluded from doing work for the Authority.

4. A material false statement or omission made in response to any question in the prequalification application will result in debarment of the applicant for a period of three years from the date of filing of the application.

5. If the applicant's lack of integrity and ethics arises from circumstances other than the ones noted [above], the Authority will evaluate the facts and circumstances on a case-by-case basis and debar an applicant up to five years.[17]

These criteria are broad enough (especially #5) to give SCA officials authority to blacklist practically any company that they believe to be criminal, immoral, unethical, or tainted by organized crime connections.[18]

Interestingly enough, the rationale for these blacklisting criteria is not stated. Perhaps #1 (previous conviction) is predicated on the belief that a company convicted of unfair or unethical business practices poses a significant risk of future wrongdoing on government contracts. Ought there to be such a strong presumption of future wrongdoing? Major American corporations like Westinghouse and General Electric have been convicted of crimes involving unethical business practices and are still allowed to bid on government contracts.[19] Should Stanford University's misuse of government grants or MIT's price fixing on financial aid disqualify them from all government contracting? Perhaps the circumstances in the New York City construction industry are different, and its wayward firms less likely to rehabilitate themselves. We are not arguing that SCA's policy is wrong, merely that it raises many and complex questions that ought not to go unexamined, especially inasmuch as similar (albeit less well-formulated) policies are seemingly being adopted all around City government.

What Counts As "Organized Crime"?

Is it only Cosa Nostra tainted firms that should be disqualified from government contracts? What about firms whose officers are members of other crime groups or are simply corrupt individuals, unaffiliated with a syndicate, group, or gang? Devotees of scholarship on organized crime will recognize that we have bumped up against the intractable problem of defining organized crime. Lawmakers and law enforcement officials have long been uncomfortable defining organized crime by reference to Italian-American crime syndicates.[20]

Principled blacklisting policy would have to apply to firms whose principals are members or associates of any crime syndicate or crime group, and perhaps to non-syndicate criminals or racketeers as well.

What Constitutes Proof of Being a Mobster?

One possibility is to say that anyone who has been convicted in an organized crime case is a member or associate of organized crime, and that his relationship to a firm disqualifies it from public contracting. This would first require agreement on what is an "organized crime case." In any event, only a small number of organized crime figures are convicted, and they typically get long prison terms that separate them from the companies they tainted. Should the firms with which they were previously associated be blacklisted?

In many cases involving blacklisting issues, the criminal associations of certain individuals will be alleged, reputed, or suspected. Putting aside the question of some sort of statute of limitations (for example, a ten-year-old conviction), what inferences should be drawn from an indictment, "pending investigation," or agency belief or suspicion?

We also need to ask whether all criminality justifies blacklisting. Only "organized crimes"? Crimes related to bid rigging and contract fraud? Given pervasive labor racketeering in the New York City construction industry, should conviction for making payoffs to corrupt labor officials disqualify a construction company from future government contracts?

The recent dispute over the letting of a City jail construction contract to DeMatteis Construction is again illustrative. Comptroller Elizabeth Holtzman based her oppostition to the contract on the grounds that

> [T]he chief executive of this company is or was also the owner of another company which is currently the target of a civil anti-trust action that alleges involvement in a bid rigging scheme for concrete supply [and that] a recently issued federal appellate court opinion contains information suggesting that federal prosecutors believe that the executive may have perjured himself when he appeared before a grand jury investigating allegations against the alleged Genovese crime family.[21]

In other words, blacklisting of company A was predicated on (1) company A's CEO's ownership of company B, a defendant in a civil anti-trust case, and (2) a prosecutor's *belief* that company A's CEO *may* have committed perjury before a grand jury investigating an organized crime family. None of the parties—the Department of Corrections, the Department of General Services, the Mayor's Office, or the Comptroller—contended that DeMatteis was incapable of completing the job on time and to specifications; nor did the dispute involve an allegation that DeMatteis's president was a member of an organized crime family.

Casting the net still wider, government agencies might seek to blacklist firms run by or employing organized crime "associates." Classifying someone as an organized crime "associate" is sensible for law enforcement investigators whose job is to sniff out criminal cabals, but it is a rather vague status on which to ground public contracting policy. Who counts as an "organized crime associate" (even assuming a satisfactory definition of organized crime)? A relative of a "known" organized crime figure? How close a relative? A friend? How close a friend? A person who, in other contexts, has business dealings with an organized crime figure? A person who pays off (extortion? bribery? tribute? fees for services?) organized crime figures? Law enforcement agencies do not have to worry about these problems, but a public contracting blacklisting *policy* will have to struggle with them to avoid becoming hopelessly arbitrary and capricious.

How Much Mob Control Does It Take To Taint a Firm?

Obviously, a construction company whose chief executive officer is a Mafia don could properly be defined as mob-controlled, although it is a closer question whether the firm should necessarily continue to be defined as mob-controlled after the don has been sent to prison for life. In the real world, Mafia dons do not function as CEOs. More likely, law enforcement agencies point to organized crime members and associates who hold (often no-show) jobs with particular companies. For example, reputed Gambino Crime Family boss John Gotti was allegedly employed by ARC Plumbing as a salesman.[22] Should employing a member or associate of organized crime as a salesman or consultant disqualify a firm from public contracting? This would be a harsh policy in light of Cosa Nostra's ability to coerce firms to put them and their members and friends on construction company payrolls.

The problem becomes even more complex when we consider labor racketeering. The Organized Crime Task Force identified fifteen New York City construction unions as controlled or strongly influenced by organized crime; these unions include Local 282 of the International Brotherhood of Teamsters, Local 6A of the Cement and Concrete Workers, Local 95 of the Housewreckers Union, and the New York City and Vicinity District Council of the Carpenters Union.[23] In effect, these powerful unions determine whether a contracting firm can do business at all in New York City because they can shut down a project by withholding labor, causing labor strife or blocking the delivery of supplies. The result is that construction firms have no choice but to pay off mob-connected labor officials in cash, no-show jobs, or other creative ways. Thus, all major construction projects in New York City might be labelled "tainted" by the fact that the companies performing them are engaged in collective bargaining arrangements with Cosa Nostra-controlled or influenced unions or make payoffs to organized crime members or associates who are officers of these unions. Should all companies employing workers who are members of "mobbed up" unions therefore be disqualified from public contracting? Should City agencies and public authorities themselves shun collective bargaining agreements with mobbed-up unions and sever the agreements with unions whose officials have been convicted of racketeering?[24] The principle that government must not deal with racketeers and corrupt individuals will turn out to be very difficult to contain.

How to Decide: The VENDEX Data Base

If government operating agencies have to operate under the injunction not to deal with "mobbed-up" firms, how will they determine whether a firm falls into this category? Ironically, law enforcement agencies which are pressing to enlist and mobilize the support of all public sector agencies in the war on organized crime have been notoriously unwilling to share information, especially on pending investigations. Moreover, they are legally barred from divulging information obtained from grand jury testimony.

Several years ago the City set out to create a data base, called VENDEX, into which all public record information on corrupt and racketeer-dominated firms would be entered and to which all agencies would have access. While VENDEX is now up and running, it is not nearly as comprehensive as its architects envisioned.[25] The original idea was to include data bearing on the future performance and integrity of contractors (for example, those contractors who had defaulted on a previous public contract.). As it now operates, the only information consistently entered into the system is whether a company has been either debarred from all City contracts or found "not responsible" by one or more agencies for fraud (in bidding, performance, or certification as a minority business enterprise) or declared a poor performer; however, very few companies have either been formally debarred or found not responsible. Thus, up until recently, VENDEX has not been much help in assessing the integrity of contractors.

The Mayor's Office of Contracts has centralized the determination of VENDEX "cautions"; that is, the Office decides whether a contractor's prior behavior merits a warning to City contracting agencies. However, Local Law 5 specifies additional sources of cautions, including findings and debarments by "other governments" and "information from public reports of . . . the New York State Organized Crime Task Force which indicates [contractor] involvement in criminal activity." Beginning in January, 1992, the Comptroller and the Mayor's Office of Contracts became co-administrators of VENDEX. The Comptroller's staff is committed to expanding the criteria for entering cautions. This means that a wider variety of allegations, investigations, and "suspicious" business relationships will be entered into the data base.

VENDEX is only as reliable as the information in its data base, and there is reason to believe that erroneous integrity cautions have been entered in the past. In several cases that we are aware of, names of companies have been entered into VENDEX by clerical personnel simply because they appeared in an investigation file. Such entries are made without any analysis of context much less any application of formal criteria defining "morally irresponsible" or "corrupt." Once a caution is entered into VENDEX, a contractor is suspect and may be declared irresponsible without any agency explanation. At the very least, a VENDEX caution will delay the letting of a contract to a low bidder pending further investigation.

In addition to scanning VENDEX for indications of criminality and moral irresponsibility, agency contracting personnel routinely seek information from the Department of Investigation (DOI) and the agency's inspector general, who also works for DOI. The inspector general checks the target company's VENDEX questionnaire responses and DOI files for any prior convictions, investigations, or statements that might be false.[26]

Ultimately, agency officials must decide whether there are too many doubts about integrity. But such decisions are made in a political environment. If the agency head gives the contractor the benefit of the doubt, she risks being blasted by the media, Comptroller, law enforcement officials, and politicians for dealing with crooks, mobsters, and corrupt businessmen. One can understand risk-averse agency officials deciding that the safer course is to disqualify a would-be contractor if there is *any entry* in VENDEX or anything negative in the DOI files. This could lead to more delay and to fewer contracts being let.

Should the Disqualification Decision Be Made on an Agency-by-Agency Basis or by a City-Wide Integrity Board?

If government agencies are justified, or have an affirmative duty, not to contract with criminally tainted firms, should a decision by one City agency that a firm is criminally tainted be dispositive for all other agencies? On the one hand, why should one agency's determination that company X is morally irresponsible even presumptively bind every other agency? On the other hand, wouldn't it be wasteful, expensive, and time-consuming for every agency to carry out its own independent inquiry and evaluation of company X's moral responsibility? Moreover, what commissioner would want to take the political risk of letting a contract to a company that another agency had blacklisted for being morally irresponsible?[27]

Ultimately, if the current drive to blacklist corrupt contractors continues, it seems inevitable that the City will assign a single mega-agency responsibility for a City-wide determination of moral responsibility. Given tens of thousands of City contractors, that agency will face a daunting challenge which could threaten to delay further the City's tortuously slow contracting system. And we have not yet considered the status of subcontractors. All the effort to keep the government from contracting with corrupt and immoral firms could be defeated or at least severely undermined if "clean" firms are free to subcontract their jobs to morally irresponsible firms. A truly comprehensive effort to keep City agencies from doing business with crooks would require scrutiny of subcontractors!

What Process is Due a Disqualified Firm?

When an agency makes a determination that a firm is not moral enough to be a public contractor, should that firm be entitled to challenge the agency's determination at a hearing? Even though it has long been held that there is no right to public contracts,[28] New York City has provided due process in responsibility and debarment determinations.[29] Basic fairness would seem to require that where the City seeks to blacklist a firm on grounds of moral irresponsibility, there should be an opportunity to confront and rebut the charges before the agency or an independent administrative board. Currently, a blacklisted firm has no such opportunity.

Administrative appeal of non-responsibility findings, first to the agency head and then to the Mayor, and judicial appeals that may follow are weighted against the contractor in several ways. While the appeal is pending, the agency can award the contract to the next lowest bidder because of a "substantial city interest" in getting public contracts let and projects completed. Should administrative appeals fail, a contractor can take the City to court. However, there is little economic incentive to do so because damages in such cases do not include profits foregone, but only expenses incurred in preparing the bid. One contractor who had been debarred from all City business for five years did win his appeal, but it took the courts four-and-a-half years to decide that his company had been wrongly debarred. There are good reasons for not holding up City contracts while legal disputes over disqualification or debarment are being decided, but this also means that decisions to disqualify and debar should be made cautiously on the basis of clear agency substantive and procedural guidelines that are subject to examination and comment.

The Costs of Good Intentions

Preventing government agencies from entering into contracts with morally irresponsible persons and firms entails considerable costs. Direct costs include conducting investigations, maintaining data bases, and implementing due process procedures. Indirect costs include delay in bidding and executing public contracts and the higher prices that result from reducing the number of eligible bidders on public works.

There are no systematic cost figures on the blacklisting process, but the SCA has generated some rough estimates. SCA has an inspectional staff of fifty (plus fifteen personnel from the DA's office) and a budget of $3 million per year. Investigating a typical applicant costs approximately $2,000; a complex case can reach $10,000.[30]

One example of the kind of indirect costs that may be generated by a strict policy of refusing to do business with morally irresponsible companies is illustrated by New York City's experience with road surfacing in the Bronx and Queens in 1987. The low bidders on each of the contracts had affiliations with Lizza Industries, which had previously been convicted on state racketeering charges and bid rigging. The City Department of Transportation sought a Board of Responsibility hearing to have the contractors declared not responsible for reasons of integrity. Both low bidders withdrew before the hearings were held. The second lowest bidder for the Queens contract had also recently been convicted of bid rigging. The third lowest bidder also withdrew in advance of a hearing. A similar situation eliminated the next lowest bidder for the Bronx contract. After another round of bids, the contracts were awarded to a company that turned around and purchased much of the asphalt for the job from the two original low bidders, thus making a mockery of the whole effort while adding many costs resulting from a year's delay.[31]

Another example of how difficult it is to implement blacklisting of morally irresponsible contractors is the New York State Department of Transportation's (DOT) refusal in 1984 to do business with any of the major asphalt supply firms on Long Island after DOT officials found that bids for jobs on Long Island were consistently 30 percent or more above the DOT engineer's estimates because of payments to labor racketeers, intimidation of competitors, and bid rigging. Because of DOT's position, there was little road building or road reconstruction on Long Island for several years. After several attempts to attract more bidders produced only one bid, and that from a Cosa Nostra-connected New York City firm, the State caved in and accepted bids from the original bidders! The ultimate price tag on the job was significantly higher than the original price, and motorists had endured pot holes for several years.

These examples do not mean that it is wrong to refuse to deal with companies that have a track record of defrauding the City by bid rigging, overcharging, and underperforming. On the contrary, we believe this is a justifiable rationale for blacklisting. However, these examples illustrate a more controversial policy: refusing to do business with corrupt firms and individuals.

Alternative Anti-Corruption Strategies

Our purpose has been to expose to public scrutiny and debate the emergence of a policy of blacklisting public contractors to further law enforcement goals or to ensure that New York City will contract only with morally responsible persons and companies. Yet thorny problems concerning rationale, implementation, feasibility, fairness and costs remain. It might be wise to stop here. However, we wish to go one step further, suggesting that blacklisting is not the only anti-corruption strategy that can protect the city from being victimized by bid rigging and performance frauds. A comprehensive assessment of blacklisting ought to take into consideration the availability of alternative strategies towards the same end.

Obviously, if government is committed to keeping morally pure in its contractual relationships, there is no alternative to disqualifying contractors who flunk an integrity test. Although blacklisting is not essential to law enforcement's anti-mob attack, it does significantly enhance the law enforcement arsenal, and there is no real substitute for it.

We have argued that the only justifiable rationale for blacklisting is to protect the government from fraud and other victimizations perpetrated by contractors. There are other means to this end. A substantial and impressive body of research and commentary on public contracting advocates "professionalized procurement management" as an anti-corruption strategy. The argument made by procurement professionals and by two recent commissions is that contract and payment supervision and auditing can be made thorough enough to ensure honest contract compliance no matter what the moral proclivities of contractors and vendors.[32] Contrariwise, an incompetent and shoddy system of contract supervision invites fraud, waste, and abuse even from contractors who are basically honest. One way to begin would be to upgrade the status and training of agency chief contract officers (ACCOs). The findings of the New York State Commission on Government Integrity and an earlier study of contracting by the Institute of Public Administration (IPA) link professionalism and corruption prevention.

> The City must devote serious attention and resources to training its contracting staff. Over and over again, witnesses at our October 1989 hearings testified that there is an urgent need to upgrade the skills of City contracting personnel who, compared with their peers in other major cities, lack exposure to modern government contracting practices. Although professionalism "is the key to both *improving the quality of [the City's contracting] performance and minimizing opportunities for corruption,*" the IPA found that the City suffers from a "crisis-level" shortage of technically skilled contracting officers" and that "professionalism in contract management is inadequate at *all* levels of government."... Indeed, the lack of competition for city business can be partly attributed to the inexperience of some city contracting staff, who are often ill-equipped to attract new vendors to the City [emphasis added].[33]

Currently, none of the dozens of ACCOs in New York City government has professional procurement certification. Arguably, competent and sophisticated contract supervision from bid through performance to final payment could protect the City and taxpayers from being defrauded.

Admittedly, it is hard to be optimistic about the adoption of professional procurement practices. It would require at least the "development of formal training programs by (and for) the ACCO, and professional procurement organization certifications and affiliation."[34] While these improvements are being considered by the City Council, they require a substantial investment in personnel in a time of fiscal crisis. Moreover, scandals that are likely to occur while such reform is being undertaken will push politicians toward promising quick and dramatic "fixes." Revelations that mobsters, crooks, and their relatives hold City contracts will likely convince more public officials that the imperatives of anti-corruption politics in the 1990s require supporting the "toughest" anti-corruption positions. In an environment charged with anxiety about corruption charges, it is good politics to declare "NO PUBLIC MONEY FOR CORRUPT BUSINESSES."[35] The problem is that this "hard-line" may not significantly reduce corruption and may add significant costs and delays to an already over-burdened and muscle-bound contracting system.

Conclusion

The three reasons for contractor blacklisting—crime control, clean government, and efficient contracting—are not easily balanced. The goal of using blacklisting to protect the government from being victimized in the future is sensible and ought to be pursued. Companies that have in the past defrauded the City or that have grossly failed to carry through on their contracts ought not to be awarded new contracts.

Even if crime control arguably is the responsibility of all government agencies, public agencies and their administrators, having neither the resources nor the training of law enforcement professionals, are ill-suited to fighting Cosa Nostra efficiently or effectively. Cosa Nostra has enormous power and resources to resist blacklisting. Moreover, there are many conceptual and practical difficulties in determining the degree and significance of racketeer connections to legitimate businesses.

The requirement that governmental ethics extend even to the government's choice of contractors is even more ambitious. If it means that the government should not engage in any business dealings with individuals or firms that have ever been convicted, indicted, or suspected of criminality, carrying out public works and various other services will be very difficult. Our analysis suggests that character concerns *per se*, unrelated to fraud or failure on previous contracts, ought not to disqualify an individual or firm from doing business with the public sector.

The drive to rid contracting of corrupt influences is similar to other contemporary morality movements such as the war on drugs. The overreach of various drug war strategies is said to be the price that must be paid for a drug-free society. Likewise, the goal of a corruption-free City, which avoids every appearance of corruption, even being involved in business relationships with morally irresponsible persons, would require a war on corruption, the costly investigation and monitoring of thousands of contractors and vendors, and the blacklisting of an indeterminable number, depending upon the breadth of the blacklisting criteria and the vigor of the government's investigative effort. The whole enterprise bristles with questions of fairness and practicality. Perhaps even more importantly, if the drive to prevent corruption, and even the appearance of corruption, in public contracting is not carefully thought through, it could actually make the implementation of public works more difficult and more costly.

NOTES

The authors are grateful to Graham Hughes for suggestions and to Stacey Kinnamon for research assistance. They are also grateful to the NYU School of Law for support that made possible the research upon which the article is based.

1 The New York City School Construction Authority was created by the New York State Legislature in 1989 in response to decades of corruption and paralysis in the New York City Board of Education's building program. The Authority is funded by the City and State of New York but is governed by independent trustees appointed by the Mayor and the Governor. *See* Thacher, *Institutional Innovation in Controlling Organized Crime,* in ORGANIZED CRIME AND ITS CONTAINMENT: A TRANSATLANTIC INITIATIVE 169-82 (C. Fijnaut & J. Jacobs eds.1991).

2 In response, Francis K. McArdle, Managing Director of the New York City General Contractors Association, warned against arbitrary action by contracting agencies and called for the creation of an appeals board to protect contractors from the use of "subjective reasons" in the exclusion of bidders. Raab, *52 Companies Banned from School Construction Bids,* N. Y. Times, Aug. 27, 1991, at B-1.

3 J. NEWFIELD & W. BARRETT, CITY FOR SALE: ED KOCH AND THE BETRAYAL OF NEW YORK (1988).

4 N.Y. STATE SCHOOL CONSTRUCTION AUTHORITY, PREQUALIFICATION APPLICATION: CONSTRUCTION CONTRACTORS 26, 29 (Nov. 1990).

5 N.Y.C. CHARTER §328(c): "The comptroller may, within thirty days of the date of filing of [a] contract with the comptroller's office, object in writing to the registration of the contract, if in the comptroller's judgment there is sufficient reason to believe that there is possible corruption in the letting of the contract or that the proposed contractor is involved in corrupt activity." For a comprehensive view of the Comptroller's policies, see CITY OF NEW YORK, OFFICE OF THE COMPTROLLER, NO MORE BUSINESS AS USUAL: KEEPING CITY CONTRACTS OUT OF THE HANDS OF DISHONEST CONTRACTORS (Sept. 1992).

6 Letter from Comptroller Elizabeth Holtzman to Mayor David Dinkins, "Re: Contract Nos. 9121992 and 9122457 between EMD Construction Corporation and HPD," (Oct. 28, 1991).

7 The controversy over the emergency jail construction contract is documented in an internal Comptroller's Office Memorandum from David Eichenthal, Counsel for Special Projects and Elizabeth Lang, Special Counsel for Investigations to Comptroller Elizabeth Holtzman, "Re: Contract Award to Leon DeMatteis Construction," (Aug. 23, 1991).

8 Raab, *New York Cancels Builder's Contract, Citing Reports on Mob Ties,* N. Y.Times, Dec. 26, 1991, at B11. In October, 1992, DeMatteis Construction won a judgment against the City "to the extent of declaring the Mayor's upholding of the Comptroller's objections arbitrary and capricious and vacating that decision as well as the direction that debarment proceedings be commenced." DeMatteis v. Dinkins, Index No.7500/92 (N.Y. Sup. Ct. Oct. 7, 1992).

9 Raab, *New York Halts Contract With Gotti Son-in-Law,* N. Y. Times, Nov. 19, 1991, at. B1.

10 Another contractor, Hi-Tech Mechanical, allegedly funneled profits from city work to a mob associate. The New

York City Housing Authority has announced that it will seek to recover all $9.6 million that Hi-Tech received as payment for completed construction work over a period of years. *See Housing Agency Contractor Named in Fraud Indictment*, N. Y. Times, Feb. 28, 1992, at B3.

11 N.Y. State Organized Crime Task Force, Corruption and Racketeering in the New York City Construction Industry 259 (1991)[hereinafter cited as Corruption and Racketeering].

12 Letter from Comptroller Elizabeth Holtzman to Mayor David Dinkins, August 31, 1990, recommending consideration of "whether the corporation, its named principals, and its apparent real parties in interest....should be barred from doing business with the City of New York."

13 Recognizing the problem of using debarment in many cases, an alternate approach has been suggested by the Organized Crime Task Force and implemented by the SCA. A "problem" contractor agrees to hire an independent investigating firm: (1) to design a code of ethics for the contractor; (2) to implement a corruption prevention program; and (3) to audit the contractor's compliance with the code and program. *See* Office of Inspector General, N.Y.C School Construction Authority, Press Release, July 29, 1991. Although paid by the firm he or she is to oversee, the independent auditor is responsible for detecting and reporting to public authorities any waste, fraud, or abuse within or perpetrated by the firm.

14 Meyer S. Frucher, former President of the Battery Park City Authority, was able to save several million dollars in construction costs by using a labor consultant who persuaded the teamsters on the job to forego their usual gateway charges on non-union haulers. It turned out later that the labor consultant had been implicated in, but cleared of, charges related to a gangland murder. Frucher's achievement in completing the project and raising money through the Authority for low-income housing elsewhere was impugned by a report of the State Investigation Commission because of his use of the labor consultant. The effect of such criticism may be to deter public entrepreneurship like Frucher's. *See* State of New York Commission of Investigation, Investigation of the Building and Construction Industry: Report of Conclusions and Recommendations 27-38 (1986).

15 *See* Gambetta, *Fragments of an Economic Theory of the Mafia*, 29 Archives Europeenes de Sociologie 127-45 (1988); Schelling, *Appendix D—Economic Analysis and Organized Crime*, Task Force Report on Organized Crime, President's Commission on Crime and the Administration of Justice (1967).

16 For example, Corruption and Racketeering, *supra* note 11, found that several concrete and dry wall contractors fell into this associate category.

17 New York City School Construction Authority, Contract Administration: Procedure No. CA-1(1991).

18 Another agency conducting thorough review of the moral character of private parties is the New Jersey Casino Control Commission, which is empowered to require Casino license applicants to provide

> . . . such information, documentation and assurances as may be required to establish by clear and convincing evidence that applicant's good character, honesty and integrity. Such information shall include, without limitation, information pertaining to family, habits, character, reputation, criminal and arrest record, business activities, financial affairs, and business, professional and personal associates, covering at least the 10-year period immediately preceding the filing of the applications. N. J. Stat. Ann. § 5:12-84.

19 *See* Schmitt, *Guilty Plea by Unisys Is Expected: Military Contractor Would Admit Fraud and Pay $190 Million*, N. Y. Times, Sept. 6, 1991, C-1; and Duffy and Glastris, *The Enemy Within*, U.S. News & World Report, July 4, 1988, at 16.

20 Letter from Comptroller Elizabeth Holtzman to Correction Commissioner Allyn R. Sielaff, July 9, 1991.

21 *See* National Advisory Committee on Criminal Justice Standards and Goals, Report of the Task Force on Organized Crime 10 (1976):

> Law enforcement officers stress that organized crime is not limited to La Cosa Nostra or Italian-surnamed individuals, although they say that in some areas where La Cosa Nostra does function, it creates a more complex problem than do other criminal organizations. . . . The issue of ethnic succession is one that needs immediate study in order to understand the implications for future crime prevention and control work.

22 Corruption and Racketeering, *supra* note 11, at 85.

23 *Id.* at 79-82.

24 For example, more than a thousand city employees are members of locals that are part of the New York City and Vicinity District Council of the Carpenters Union. The Council is cited by the New York State Organized Crime Task Force as a union with ties to organized crime. *Id.* at 80.

25 A description of vendex (Vendor Information Exchange System) is set out in City of New York, Mayor's Office of Contracts, Vendex: Policies and Procedure, March 1990.

26 *Id.* at 30. Vendex embodies the tension in regulating public contracting. On the one hand, it is intended to make contracting more efficient and effective by identifying poor performers and expanding information on contractors and vendors who may be asked to bid on subsequent jobs. On the other hand, it is intended to override effectiveness and efficiency considerations when doubts ("cautions") about integrity arise.

27 *See* Raab, *Contractor, Barred by One Agency, Works for Another*, N.Y. Times, Sept. 7, 1991, at 25. In the DeMatteis case, for example, the SCA found no basis for excluding DeMatteis Construction from school construction contracts.

28 "The mere fact that a party who has made proposals for public work in the city of New York is the lowest bidder and knows that fact, does not necessarily entitle him to the contract and does not constitute an award to him of such contract within the meaning of the law regulating the letting of work upon competitive bids . . . . The commissioner may reject all the bids and readvertise the work, if in his judgement and discretion such course is for the best interest of the

municipality." Erving v. Mayor of N.Y., 131 N.Y. 133, 29 N.E. 1101.

29 *See* New York City Charter § 335 (b) (1) (1990). "Upon the petition of the head of an agency, after reasonable notice and reasonable opportunity for the person or firm to respond at a hearing to be held on a record, the office of administrative trials and hearings shall determine whether a person or firm should be debarred for cause from consideration for award of any city contract for a period not to exceed five years."

30 Interviews with Joseph DeLuca, Assistant Inspector General, New York City School Construction Authority (September 25, 1991, and November 18, 1991). Investigation costs are adapted from private sector estimates.

31 *See* Raab, *Asphalt Inquiry Delays Queens and Bronx Road Work*, N. Y. Times, April 18, 1987, at 21, 24. "[City officials] said the contracts have not been awarded because investigators uncovered possible financial ties between the two companies and a construction company that has been convicted of bid rigging. . .

"'A number of questions have arisen about the backgrounds of these companies, and we are not sure they are responsible bidders,' Mr. [Hadley] Gold, the General Services Commissioner, said, referring to Jet and Mt. Hope. 'The questions,' he added, 'concern the corporate entities or relationships with other companies.'"

32 For example, in place of the seldom used "poor performer" label, effectiveness and efficiency might be emphasized by a gradated rating of contractors on a number of performance measures that would be entered in VENDEX. However, such ratings are only useful if done by trained professional inspectors and procurement officers.

33 New York State Commission on Government Integrity, *A Ship Without a Captain: The Contracting Process in New York City*, in Government Ethics Reform for the 1990s: The Collected Reports of the New York State Commission on Government Integrity 487 (B. Green ed. 1991). *See also*: Institute of Public Administration, Contracting in New York City Government, Final Report and Recommendations (Nov. 1987).

34 City of New York, Office of the Comptroller, Bureau of Audit, Survey of the Qualifications of New York City Agency Chief Contracting Officers (Jan. 17, 1992).

35 *See*: Manning *The Purity Potlach: An Essay on Conflicts of Interest, American Government, and Moral Escalation*, 24 Federal Bar Journal 239-56 (1964).

[21]

The Inter-American Convention Against Corruption: A Comparison With the United States Foreign Corrupt Practices Act

LUCINDA A. LOW*
ANDREA K. BJORKLUND**
KATHRYN CAMERON ATKINSON***

TABLE OF CONTENTS

---

* Member, Miller & Chevalier, Washington, D.C.
** Former Associate, Miller & Chevalier. Law clerk to the Hon. Sam J. Ervin III, U.S. Court of Appeals for the Fourth Circuit.
*** Associate, Miller & Chevalier.

An earlier version of this article was presented as a paper to the XXXIIId Conference of the Inter-American Bar Association in Rio de Janeiro on May 20, 1997.

I. INTRODUCTION

On March 29, 1996, a Specialized Conference of the thirty-four-member Organization of American States (OAS) approved the Inter-American Convention Against Corruption (Convention or IACAC), which establishes the first international legal framework aimed at eliminating bribery and corruption of government officials.[1] Twenty-one of the thirty-four OAS member states signed the Convention at the March 29 meeting in Caracas, Venezuela.[2] On June 2, 1996, the United States became the twenty-second nation to sign the Convention, and Canada signed later that year. The OAS Convention took effect March 6, 1997, following the deposit of notices of ratification by Paraguay and Bolivia.[3]

As of the signing of the OAS Convention, the only binding national criminal law that sought to combat foreign official bribery was the U.S. Foreign Corrupt Practices Act (FCPA), enacted in 1977 to criminalize the bribery of foreign officials by U.S. companies seeking to obtain business.[4] From 1977 until March 1996, the FCPA stood alone in the world as a legal barrier to transnational bribery.[5] As the first such instrument, the FCPA was a natural point of reference for the OAS in drafting its Convention. But as a unilateral statute that was designed in accordance with the legal principles of a single country and that targeted principally the activities of U.S. nationals overseas, the FCPA could not be the sole basis for a multilateral anticorruption convention that would be implemented in numerous jurisdictions with different legal systems, and would also serve as the basis for international cooperation. Thus, although the Convention bears the mark of the

1. Inter-American Convention Against Corruption, Mar. 29, 1996, 35 I.L.M. 724 (1996) [hereinafter Convention]. Member states of the Organization for Economic Cooperation and Development (OECD), along with several other states participating in its Working Group on Bribery in International Business Transactions, agreed on November 20, 1997 on the terms of a Convention on Combating Bribery of Foreign Public Officials in International Business Transactions (OECD Convention). *See* Convention on Combating Bribery of Foreign Public Officials in International Business Transactions (visited Jan. 21, 1998) <http://www.oecd.org/daf/cmis/bribery/20nov1e.htm>. This Convention was signed on December 17, 1997. It had yet to enter into force as of the writing of this Article. Among OAS member states, Argentina, Brazil, Chile, and the United States participated in the OECD Convention negotiations.

2. The countries signing the Convention on March 29 were: Argentina, Bolivia, Brazil, Chile, Colombia, Costa Rica, Ecuador, El Salvador, Guyana, Haiti, Honduras, Jamaica, Mexico, Nicaragua, Panama, Paraguay, Peru, the Dominican Republic, Suriname, Uruguay, and Venezuela. Convention, *supra* note 1, at 724.

3. The other countries that have deposited notices of ratification with the OAS include Argentina, Bolivia, Costa Rica, Ecuador, El Salvador, Mexico, Paraguay, Peru, and Venezuela. The Convention is open to ratification by any country, not just OAS member states. Convention, *supra* note 1, art. XXIII.

4. 15 U.S.C. §§ 78m, 78dd-1, 78dd-2, 78ff (1994). *See infra* Part III for a detailed discussion of the FCPA.

5. Virtually every country in the world has domestic antibribery laws, but only the United States has a foreign antibribery law.

FCPA's influence, it departs from the FCPA's principles in certain respects and goes well beyond its scope in others.

This Article compares key aspects of these two legal weapons against corruption. Part II of this Article provides an overview of the Convention. Part III summarizes the provisions of the FCPA. Part IV compares the Convention to U.S. law, focusing on three areas: First, it compares the Convention to U.S. measures to combat bribery of foreign officials, principally, but not limited to, the FCPA, and examines allocation of jurisdictional competence; second, it examines the Convention's illicit enrichment and ethics-in-government provisions from a U.S. law perspective; and, finally, it seeks to show how the Convention's enforcement regime fits with existing U.S. law and treaties and addresses issues of extradition and double jeopardy. Part V concludes.

II. SUMMARY OF THE OAS INTER-AMERICAN CONVENTION AGAINST CORRUPTION

The OAS Convention seeks to promote the development and strengthening of legal mechanisms in signatory countries to "prevent, detect, punish and eradicate" official corruption and to facilitate cooperation among the signatories to combat official corruption.[6] The Convention consists of twenty-eight articles. The first twenty contain the substantive provisions of the Convention; the final eight address signature, ratification, reservations, and similar matters. Articles I through V contain general provisions, including definitions of key terms used in the Convention, and important provisions regarding scope (art. IV) and jurisdiction (art. V). Articles VI through XII set forth the obligations of states with respect to their domestic laws, while articles XIII through XX deal with international corruption, enforcement, and other agreements between states parties.

The Convention can thus be divided roughly into two spheres—domestic and multilateral. Certain articles in the Convention concentrate on the domestic measures states parties need to institute to fight corruption. Other articles, in recognition of the difficulty of enforcement in an area where activities are often cloaked in secrecy and cross national borders, target multilateral cooperation to aid in enforcement. In both the domestic and multilateral spheres of the OAS Convention, states parties incur different levels of ob-

6. Convention, *supra* note 1, art. II. The Convention does not address private commercial bribery or corruption.

ligation. Certain articles are binding on states parties, others are conditional, still others are subject to progressive development, and a fourth category are aspirational. Some of the binding commitments are self-executing, while others require the member states to pass new laws, in particular criminal laws.

Subsections A and B of this Part will review first, the mandatory domestic measures of the Convention, next, the aspirational domestic measures, and finally, the multilateral measures. Subsection C will then review jurisdictional issues.

A. *Mandatory Domestic Measures*

The mandatory domestic provisions of the Convention are a thorough assault on bribery and are remarkable in their scope. The Convention *requires* states parties to criminalize both domestic and foreign bribery and to enact measures to combat the illicit enrichment of government officials. The provisions on domestic bribery are aimed at both the person offering a bribe and the recipient; the foreign bribery provisions, appropriately, focus on the offeror alone. The recipient is the focus of the illicit enrichment provision.

1. *Criminalization of Certain "Acts of Corruption"*

In article VI, the Convention identifies a number of activities that it categorizes as "acts of corruption" and, therefore, fall within the scope of the Convention.[7] Article VII of the Convention requires, without qualification, states parties "that have not yet done so" to criminalize the specific acts of corruption listed in article VI(1). Those acts of corruption include: solicitation or acceptance of a bribe; offering or granting of a bribe; improper acts or omissions by public officials; fraudulent use or concealment of property; and conspiracy.[8]

7. Article XII provides that for the Convention to apply, no harm to State property need be caused by these acts.

8. Convention, *supra* note 1, art. VI(1)(a)-(e). The Convention defines these acts as:

> a. The solicitation or acceptance, directly or indirectly, by a government official or a person who performs public functions, of any article of monetary value, or other benefit, such as a gift, favor, promise, or advantage for himself or for another person or entity, in exchange for any act or omission in the performance of his public functions.
>
> b. The offering or granting, directly or indirectly, to a government official or a person who performs public functions, of any article of monetary value, or other benefit, such as a gift, favor, promise, or advantage for himself or for another

2. *Foreign Bribery*

A separate article of the Convention, article VIII, then focuses on foreign (transnational) bribery. Under this article, a state party agrees to prohibit and punish:

- the offering or granting, directly or indirectly, by its nationals, [residents], and businesses domiciled there,
- to a government official of another State,
- of any article of monetary value, or other benefit, such as a gift, favor, promise, or advantage,
- in connection with any economic or commercial transaction,
- in exchange for any act or omission in the performance of that official's public functions.[9]

The obligation the Convention imposes on states to criminalize foreign bribery is limited by a potentially significant condition, however: a state party's obligation to enact foreign bribery measures is "[s]ubject to its Constitution and the fundamental principles of its legal system."[10] Thus, states may use this "escape

---

> person or entity, in exchange for any act or omission in the performance of his public functions;
>
> c. Any act or omission in the discharge by a government official or a person who performs public functions for the purpose of illicitly obtaining benefits for himself or for a third party.
>
> d. The fraudulent use or concealment of property derived from any of the acts referred to in this article; and
>
> e. Participation . . . in the commission or attempted commission of, or any collaboration or conspiracy to commit, any of the acts referred to in this article.

Id. The terms "government" or "public" official and "public function" are defined in article I of the Convention. A "public official" is "any official or employee of the State or its [agencies/entities], including those who have been selected, appointed, or elected to perform activities or functions in the name of the State or in the service of the State, at any level of its hierarchy." Convention, *supra* note 1, art. I. (As discussed below, there is some confusion between the English and Spanish versions as to whether the narrower word "agencies" or the broader word "entities," which could include state-owned enterprises, is used.) "Public function" means "any temporary or permanent, paid or honorary activity, performed by a natural person in the name of the State or in the service of the State or its institutions, at any level of its hierarchy." *Id.* For a comparison of these terms with their FCPA counterparts, *see infra* Part IV.

9. Convention, *supra* note 1, art. VIII.

10. *Id.* This limitation is primarily directed to those countries that do not exercise jurisdiction over their nationals residing or acting outside their territory. *See* Organización de los Estados Americanos, Comité Jurídico Interamericano, Informe Anual Del Comité Jurídico Interamericano a la Asamblea General (Elementos para la preparación de legis-

clause" to avoid implementing article VIII without having to take a reservation to the Convention. Among those states parties that do make foreign bribery an offense, it will be considered an "act of corruption" for purposes of the Convention, thus triggering the treaty obligations of states parties.[11] States that have not criminalized foreign bribery are nonetheless required, "insofar as [their] laws permit," to cooperate with other states parties in the enforcement of other states' foreign bribery laws.[12]

3. *Illicit Enrichment*

The third principal tool of the Convention focuses on illicit enrichment of public officials. Under article IX, states parties agree to establish as an offense "a significant increase in the assets of a government official that he [or she] cannot reasonably explain in relation to his [or her] lawful earnings during the performance of his functions."[13] Like the foreign bribery offense contemplated in article VIII, the obligation of states to do so is subject to their Constitutions and fundamental legal principles.[14] Also like article VIII, illicit enrichment under article IX will be considered an "act of corruption" for purposes of the Convention among those states parties that do make it an offense, which means the international obligations imposed by the Convention will be applicable. Those states that have not criminalized illicit enrichment are required, "insofar as [their] laws permit," to cooperate with other states parties in the enforcement of other states' laws.

When states parties adopt legislation criminalizing foreign bribery and illicit enrichment, they must notify the Secretary General of the Organization of American States, which will in turn notify the other states parties.[15] Those crimes will be considered acts of corruption for purposes of the Convention thirty days after that notification.[16]

---

lación modelo con respecto al enriquecimiento ilítico y el soborno transnacional (CJI/RES.I-1/97)), section III(e) (Apr. 17, 1997) [hereinafter Juridical Committee Report].

11. It is not clear whether the ancillary acts of corruption identified in article VI in connection with domestic bribery, such as conspiracy, aiding and abetting, and fraudulent use or concealment of property, will also apply in the transnational bribery context.

12. Convention, *supra* note 1, art. VIII.

13. *Id.* art. IX.

14. *Id.* This reservation was included at the insistence of the United States because of constitutional problems posed by the criminalization of unjust enrichment. *See infra* Part IV.B.

15. Convention, *supra* note 1, art. X.

16. *Id.*

C. *Aspirational Domestic Measures*

In addition to the binding commitments in articles VII through IX, states parties agree in other provisions of the Convention to consider other measures of good governance and other anti-corruption provisions, including the establishment of additional offenses.

1. Additional "Acts of Corruption"

Article XI of the Convention enumerates four additional "acts of corruption" that states parties agree to consider criminalizing under domestic law in order to promote uniformity among the Member states and to further the purposes of the Convention. These acts, which are subject to progressive development, are: the improper use of information by government officials; the improper use of property by a government official; the attempt by any person to obtain illicit benefits; and the diversion of state property.[17]

Once a state party establishes any of these acts as a criminal offense, it will be considered an act of corruption for purposes of the Convention and will trigger the international obligations of the states parties under the Convention.[18] States parties that do not enact such laws are required, consistent with their domestic laws, to assist other states parties with respect to those offenses.[19]

---

17. Convention, *supra* note 1, art. XI(1)(a)-(d). The Convention defines these additional acts as follows:

> a. the improper use by a government official or person performing public functions, for his own benefit or for that of a third party, of any kind of classified or confidential information . . . obtained because of, or in the performance of, his functions;
>
> b. the improper use by a government official or person performing public functions of, for his own benefit or for that of a third party, any kind of property belonging to the State or any firm or institution in which the State has a proprietary interest, to which the official or person has access because of, or in the performance of, his functions;
>
> c. any act or omission by any person who, personally or through a third party, or acting as an intermediary, seeks to obtain a decision from a public authority whereby he illicitly obtains for himself or another person any benefit or gain, whether or not such act or omission harms State property; and
>
> d. the diversion by a government official, for purposes unrelated to those for which they were intended, for his own benefit or that of a third party, of any movable or immovable property, monies or securities belonging to the State, to an independent agency, or to an individual, that such official has received by virtue of his position for purposes of administration, custody, or for other reasons.

Id.

18. *Id.* art. XI(2).

19. *Id.* art. XI(3).

2. *Broader Anti-Corruption Initiatives*

Under article III, which contains the "softest" measures in the hierarchy of the Convention, states parties agree to consider preventive measures to "create, maintain, and strengthen" their domestic laws. These measures, which go beyond criminalizing certain conduct as offenses, fall into three primary areas: transparency and accountability in government; ethical standards for government officials; and measures applicable to private concerns.

a. Transparency and Accountability in Government, Especially Procurement

First, states parties agree to consider measures relating to transparency and accountability in government functions, including procurement. In particular, states parties agree to consider measures relating to the government procurement and government hiring processes to ensure their "openness, equity, and efficiency," and similar measures relating to the government revenue collection and control systems that "deter corruption."[20] States parties also agree to consider systems for registering the income, assets, and liabilities of certain public officials and, where appropriate, to make that information public.[21]

b. Ethical Standards for Government Officials

Second, states parties agree to consider measures to create, maintain, and strengthen ethics rules applicable to public officials. In particular, these include: standards of conduct for the "correct, honorable, and proper fulfillment of public functions"; standards to prevent conflicts of interest; standards to "mandate the proper conservation and use of resources entrusted to government officials"; and standards to require government officials to report acts of corruption to the appropriate authorities.[22]

c. Measures Applicable to Private Concerns, Including the Tax Deductibility of Bribery and Accounting Standards

Third, states parties agree to consider measures to create, maintain, and strengthen prophylactic safeguards against corrupt activities by private concerns. In particular, states parties agree to con-

20. *Id.* art. III(5), (6).
21. *Id.* art. III(4).
22. *Id.* art. III (1)-(3).

sider laws that deny favorable tax treatment for expenditures made in violation of the states parties' anticorruption laws.[23] They also agree to consider mechanisms to ensure that publicly-held companies and similar organizations "maintain books and records which, in reasonable detail, accurately reflect the acquisition and disposition of assets, and have sufficient internal accounting controls to enable their officers to detect corrupt acts."[24] Also, states parties agree to consider measures to protect public servants and private citizens who report acts of corruption (whistleblowers), including protection of their identities, in accordance with the basic principles of states parties' domestic legal systems.[25]

Finally, states parties agree to consider measures to advance the anticorruption effort, including anticorruption oversight bodies, programs to encourage broader involvement in the effort, and further measures that account for the correlation between "equitable compensation and probity [honesty] in public service."[26]

D. *Jurisdiction*

A delineation of the activities to be criminalized is one critical part of the Convention. The jurisdictional provisions also affect its scope. Here, the Convention aspires to be inclusive and accommodating of the differing principles of personal jurisdiction applicable in member states, while giving primacy to territoriality. The Convention requires that parties adopt measures to establish their jurisdiction (a) over Convention offenses committed in their territory, and (b) when the alleged criminal is present in their territory, but not extradited to another state due to nationality.[27] In addition, states parties may adopt measures to establish jurisdiction over those offenses committed by their nationals or residents, whether or not those crimes were committed inside their territory. The Convention also explicitly preserves the established rules of criminal jurisdiction of states parties under their domestic laws.[28]

23. *Id.* art. III(7).
24. *Id.* art. III(10).
25. *Id.* art. III(8).
26. *Id.* art. III(9), (11), (12).
27. *Id.* art. V(1), (3).
28. *Id.* art. V(4).

E. *Penalties*

In requiring criminalization of the array of acts just reviewed, the Convention does not specify the penalties that states must impose for their violation.

We now turn to the multilateral provisions of the Convention, a key element, especially in the case of transnational bribery, to the effective investigation and prosecution of offenses.

F. *Multilateral Obligations*

The Convention's multilateral framework consists primarily of mandatory obligations to cooperate and assist other states parties in the prosecution of foreign and domestic corruption. Some of the recommended actions are general; for example, article XIV states that parties shall "foster exchanges of experiences by way of agreements and meetings."[29] Others, such as the extradition provisions, are specific and quite important to effective enforcement.

1. Extradition

The extradition provisions are set out in article XIII. They apply only to the "acts of corruption" established by the states parties as offenses in accordance with the Convention.[30] Under article XIII, the Convention extends existing extradition treaties among states parties to include the offenses established under the Convention. States parties further undertake to include these offenses in any future extradition treaties.[31] The Convention can also serve as a self-executing extradition treaty among the states parties that have not concluded extradition treaties with one another, or which do not condition extradition on the existence of such treaties.[32]

2. Assistance and Cooperation

The Convention emphasizes cooperation among states parties in the pursuit of the Convention's anticorruption goals. In addition to the specific requirements of cooperation already mentioned under articles VIII and IX, under article XIV states parties agree to "afford one another the widest measure of mutual assistance" in preventative, investigative and enforcement efforts of other states parties, "in accordance with their domestic laws and applicable

29. *Id.* art. XIV(2).
30. Thus, they would include any of the acts specified in articles VI, VIII, IX, or XI.
31. Convention, *supra* note 1, art. XIII(2).
32. *Id.* art. XIII(3)-(4).

treaties."[33] The mutual assistance article thus looks to existing treaties and domestic laws to define the content of the states parties' obligations, rather than enlarging them, as the extradition provision does. In two potentially very important provisions, the Convention prohibits the use of bank secrecy laws or the allegedly political nature of an act of corruption as a basis for refusing to cooperate with other states parties.[34]

This mutual assistance and cooperation also extends to the "exchanges of experiences" by states in their anticorruption efforts.[35]

3. *Measures Regarding Property*

The Convention specifically provides for cooperation among the states parties in the seizure and forfeiture of assets connected with "acts of corruption," both domestic and foreign. Under article XV, states parties agree to provide each other "the broadest possible measure of assistance in the identification, tracing, freezing, seizure and forfeiture of property or proceeds obtained, derived from or used in the commission of offenses" established in accordance with the Convention.[36] Article XV suggests that states parties may want to transfer all or part of properties or proceeds to other states parties if doing so would assist in an underlying investigation or proceedings.

G. *Entry Into Force, Reservations and Implementation*

Under the Convention, the ratification of only two countries is necessary for the Convention to enter into force.[37] The Convention permits countries to take reservations when ratifying it, provided such reservations are not incompatible with the "object and purpose of the Convention."[38] Using the article VIII and IX "escape clauses," however, states may avoid enacting the transnational bribery and illicit enrichment provisions of the Convention without taking a reservation. The Convention contains no timetable within which states must implement its provisions, and no provision for declarations when the escape clauses are invoked. Nor

33. *Id.* art. XIV.
34. *Id.* arts. XVI, XVII.
35. *Id.* art. XIV(2).
36. *Id.* art. XV.
37. *Id.* art. XXV.
38. *Id.* art. XXIV.

does the Convention provide for any oversight or monitoring mechanism by the OAS.

Accordingly, implementation appears to be left largely to the discretion of each state. Of the eight states ratifying to date, none appear to have taken reservations. Several have made declarations identifying their competent central authority for cooperation purposes.[39] The Inter-American Juridical Committee of the OAS has been tasked with the development of model clauses or legislation to which states could refer in developing national laws.

The implementation of the Convention is critical in at least two respects. First, it is important that implementation take place promptly, and that it reflect fully the Convention's provisions. The escape clauses should be used sparingly, and their invocation should be reported and subject to review by the OAS. Second, a high degree of uniformity among states parties is desirable in the definition of offenses (acts of corruption). This will lessen the compliance burdens placed on international businesses, and will increase the prospects of successful cooperation among states parties in investigation and enforcement.

It is with those concerns and objectives in mind that we turn to a comparative analysis of the Convention and U.S. law. To do so, we first review the relevant U.S. legal provisions.

III. OVERVIEW OF THE FOREIGN CORRUPT PRACTICES ACT

The principal U.S. foreign antibribery law is the Foreign Corrupt Practices Act. For many years prior to the FCPA's enactment, the United States had legislation prohibiting domestic bribery.[40] The United States first attempted to address the issue of foreign bribery in 1958, when the government amended federal income tax laws to deny any tax deduction for bribes paid to foreign officials.[41] The revelations in the early to mid-1970s, under a voluntary disclosure program of the U.S. Securities and Exchange Commission (SEC), that many major U.S. companies had secured foreign contracts through the payment of bribes, often using slush

39. Paraguay reported to the OAS Secretariat that it had designated the Office of the Attorney General as the central authority. Asuncion, Mar. 20, 1997, Note 46/97, received on Apr. 21, 1997. Ecuador also designated its Attorney General as the central authority. Washington, D.C., Aug. 14, 1997, Note 134/97 MPE/OEA.

40. 18 U.S.C. § 201 (1994). This legislation dates back to 1948, but was overhauled in 1962. Section 201(b), as enacted in 1962, served as a model for the FCPA. H.R. CONF. REP. NO. 95-640, at 8 (1977); S. REP. NO. 94-1031, at 7 (1977).

41. Internal Revenue Code, 26 U.S.C. § 162(c) (1994).

funds and off-book accounts to disguise their practices, led to a public outcry. Congress responded with the passage of the FCPA in 1977. The law has been amended only once in its twenty-year life span, as part of the Omnibus Trade and Competitiveness Act of 1988.[42]

The FCPA consists of two distinct sets of provisions: the antibribery provisions and the accounting standards and internal control provisions.

A. *The Antibribery Provisions*

1. *Basic Prohibitions*

In general terms, the antibribery provisions of the FCPA prohibit U.S. companies and individuals from paying bribes to foreign officials for the purpose of obtaining a business benefit. Specifically, the FCPA prohibits U.S. "issuers" and "domestic concerns"[43] from:

- making use of the mails or any means or instrumentality of interstate commerce in furtherance of
- a payment, offer, promise to pay, or authorization of a payment, promise, or offer
- of money or anything of value
- to any foreign official, to any foreign political party or party official, or to any candidate for foreign political office
- corruptly
- for the purpose of (i) influencing any act or decision of that person in his official capacity; (ii) inducing that person to do or omit to do any act in violation of his or her lawful duty; or (iii) inducing that person to influence any government act or decision
- for the purpose of obtaining or retaining business, or directing business to any person.[44]

---

42. Pub. L. No. 100-418, 102 Stat. 1107 (1988).

43. Issuers are essentially public companies required to register with the SEC, while domestic concerns are U.S. nationals, residents, or business enterprises. *See infra* Part V.

44. 15 U.S.C. §§ 78dd-1(a), 78dd-2(a)(1994).

The FCPA defines "foreign official" to include "any officer or employee of a foreign government or any department, agency, or instrumentality thereof, or any person acting in an official capacity for or on behalf of any such" entities.[45]

2. *Third-Party Liability*

In addition to liability for direct payments, enterprises and individuals subject to the Act may also be held liable for indirect payments to foreign officials, that is, payments, promises or offers made to a foreign agent or other third party while "knowing" that the third party will make improper payments, promises, or offers of the type described above to a foreign official. "Knowing" is a defined term which sweeps more broadly than actual knowledge. Even if the first party did not specifically authorize the payment, under certain circumstances, it may be deemed to have knowledge of the third party's action.[46]

3. *Exceptions and Affirmative Defenses*

There is one statutory exception to the FCPA's antibribery provisions—for gratuities given to government officials performing "routine governmental action." These so-called "facilitating" or "grease" payments, used to expedite the processing, typically by a low-level official, of non-discretionary permits or licenses or other routine documentation, are not prohibited by the Act.[47]

---

45. *Id.* § 78dd-1(f)(1).

46. Under the Act as amended in 1988, a person's state of mind is "'knowing' with respect to conduct, a circumstance, or a result" if the person has actual knowledge of the conduct, circumstance, or result, or "has a firm belief" that the conduct, circumstance, or result exists or is "substantially certain to occur." 15 U.S.C. § 78dd-2(h)(3)(A). The statute explains further that when knowledge of a circumstance is a required element of the offense, that knowledge is established "if a person is aware of a high probability of the existence of such circumstance, unless the person actually believes that such circumstance does not exist." *Id.* § 78dd-2(h)(3)(B).

Prior to the 1988 Amendments, the FCPA imposed a "reason to know" standard, which many were concerned set a simple negligence standard of liability. Although the 1988 Amendments eliminated that standard as an inappropriate basis for criminal liability, they made clear that the definition of "knowledge" continues to extend beyond actual knowledge to include a "conscious disregard" of the truth. *See* H.R. CONF. REP. NO. 100-576, at 920 (1988).

47. 15 U.S.C. §§ 78dd-1(b), 78dd-2(b). This exception was added in the 1988 Amendments. A similar exception existed in the original Act by virtue of the original definition of "foreign official." Prior to the 1988 Amendments, government employees whose duties were primarily "ministerial or clerical" were excluded from the definition of "foreign official." *See* H.R. CONF. REP. NO. 95-831, at 12 (1977); S. REP. NO. 100-85, at 52 (1987). Thus, payments to those employees were not payments to "foreign officials" and, accordingly, fell outside the scope of the Act's prohibitions. The original exception hinged on

In addition to the exception for facilitating payments, the FCPA, since 1988, has featured two affirmative defenses for certain types of payments. First, an affirmative defense exists where the payment at issue "was lawful under the *written* laws and regulations of the foreign official's . . . country."[48] The "written laws" requirement was chosen to ensure that only the law in a country, not its customary practices, could be the basis for this defense.

Second, an affirmative defense may be asserted where a payment was a "reasonable and bona fide expenditure, such as travel and lodging expenses," incurred by or on behalf of a foreign official and "directly related" to the "promotion, demonstration, or explanation of products or services" or "the execution or performance of a contract with a foreign government or government agency."[49]

The Act contains no express exceptions or defenses for payments of small monetary value, or for gifts and entertainment.

4. *Persons Covered*

There are two separate but parallel antibribery provisions—one for "issuers" and the second for "domestic concerns." "Issuers" are essentially public companies and include any entity that has a class of securities registered pursuant to section 12 of the Securities and Exchange Act of 1934 (15 U.S.C. § 78l) or that is required to file reports under section 15(d) of the 1934 Act (15 U.S.C. § 78o(d)). "Domestic concerns" include any U.S. citizen, national, or resident, as well as any corporation, partnership, association, joint-stock company, business trust, unincorporated organization, or sole proprietorship that has its principal place of business in the United States, or that is organized under the laws of a state of the

cial." *See* H.R. CONF. REP. NO. 95-831, at 12 (1977); S. REP. NO. 100-85, at 52 (1987). Thus, payments to those employees were not payments to "foreign officials" and, accordingly, fell outside the scope of the Act's prohibitions. The original exception hinged on the duties of the recipient, rather than the purpose of the payment. As a practical matter, however, it was often difficult to determine whether an employee's duties were ministerial or discretionary. S. REP. NO. 100-85, at 52-53; H.R. REP. NO. 100-40, Part 2, at 77 (1987). Therefore, the 1988 Amendments changed the exception to focus on the purpose of the payment, to allow only those payments that secure or expedite performance of duties that an official is required to perform in the normal course of business and that do not involve the exercise of the official's discretion. S. REP. NO. 100-85, at 52-53; H.R. REP. NO. 100-40, Part 2, at 77.

48. 15 U.S.C. §§ 78dd-1(c)(1), 78dd-2(c)(1)(emphasis added).

49. *Id.* §§ 78dd-1(c)(2), 78dd-2(c)(2).

United States, or a territory, possession, or commonwealth of the United States.[50]

Foreign subsidiaries of U.S. companies, companies that are incorporated under the laws of foreign countries and have their principal place of business outside the United States, do not fall within the definition of "domestic concerns."[51] Foreign enterprises that qualify as "issuers," however, are subject to the Act.[52] The exclusion from the Act of foreign-incorporated companies that are not issuers, and foreign citizens, nationals, and residents who are not officers, directors or shareholders of domestic concerns or issuers, [53] coupled with the territoriality nexus as an element of a violation, means that the FCPA applies primarily to those doing business in the United States. Thus, the FCPA, although by its nature dealing with transnational activity, is not as aggressive in its extra-territorial reach as some U.S. laws. For example, the Iran and Libya Sanctions Act of 1996 penalizes those persons engaging in certain prohibited transactions with Iran and Libya, regardless of whether those persons are U.S. nationals or whether the transactions have connections with U.S. commerce.[54] Title III of the controversial Cuban Liberty and Democratic Solidarity (LIBERTAD) Act of 1996 (popularly known as the Helms-Burton Act) authorizes U.S. nationals claiming an interest in Cuban property confiscated by the Castro regime to sue foreign nationals who are currently "trafficking" in such property.[55] In addition, the Cuban Assets Control Regulations, which predate the Helms-Burton Act and which codify the U.S. embargo against Cuba, subject "any person within the United States" to U.S. jurisdiction, but do not require the person to be a U.S. resident, national, or citizen.[56]

50. 15 U.S.C. §§ 78dd-2(h)(1).

51. The legislative history of the Act makes clear that Congress considered and rejected the inclusion of foreign subsidiaries in the definition of "domestic concern." H.R. CONF. REP. NO. 95-831, at 13-14 (1977). U.S. courts have recognized this limitation on the Act's application. *See, e.g.*, Dooley v. United Technologies Corp., 803 F. Supp. 428, 439 (D.D.C. 1992).

52. This would include, for example, foreign companies that list American Depository Receipts (ADRs) on a U.S. stock exchange.

53. The penalty provisions of the Act effectively expand the FCPA's application to non-U.S. persons by making any officer, director, employee or agent of a domestic concern subject to penalties. 15 U.S.C. § 78dd-2(g).

54. Iran and Libya Sanctions Act of 1996, Pub. L. No. 104-72, §§ 5(a), 5(b), 14(14), 110 Stat. 1541, 1543 (1996).

55. The Cuban Liberty and Democratic Solidarity (LIBERTAD) Act of 1996, Pub. L. No. 104-114, Title III, 110 Stat. 785, 814-822 (1996). The President, however, has suspended enforcement of Title III in response to strong diplomatic pressure from U.S. allies.

56. 31 C.F.R. §§ 515.329, 515.330 (1997).

5. *Penalties and Enforcement*

The FCPA's antibribery provisions are enforced by two federal government agencies—the Department of Justice and the SEC. U.S. courts have held that private companies cannot sue each other under the law.[57] The SEC's enforcement authority only extends to "issuers." The Department of Justice has enforcement authority under both antibribery provisions. To date, there have been approximately forty criminal prosecutions under the antibribery provisions. The Department of Justice has also established an Opinion Procedure pursuant to which it advises of its present enforcement intentions with respect to a proposed transaction or conduct.[58] Thirty-three opinions have been publicly announced under this Procedure since the law became effective.

A criminal violation of the antibribery provisions by enterprises may result in fines of up to $2 million per violation.[59] Officers, directors, employees, stockholders acting on behalf of an enterprise, or agents may also face fines of up to $100,000 and/or five years of imprisonment per violation.[60] Those fines may not be reimbursed by their employers.[61] Furthermore, if the criminal offense causes a pecuniary gain or loss, U.S. law authorizes alternative maximum fines against enterprises equal to the greater of twice the gross gain or twice the gross loss.[62] The amount of the fines and/or prison terms will be determined according to the Federal Sentencing Guidelines, which take into account factors such as the size of the bribe, the number of counts, and prior convictions, as well as any mitigating factors such as corporate compliance programs and cooperation in the government's investigation.[63] In the recent *Lockheed* case, the application of these provisions resulted in a

57. *See, e.g.*, Lamb v. Philip Morris, Inc., 915 F.2d 1024, 1024 (6th Cir. 1990), *cert. denied*, 498 U.S. 1086 (1991); McLean v. International Harvester Co., 817 F.2d 1214, 1219 (5th Cir. 1987).

58. 28 C.F.R. § 80 (1997).

59. 15 U.S.C. §§ 78dd-2(g)(1)(A), 78ff(c)(1)(A).

60. *Id.* §§ 78dd-2(g)(2)(A), 78ff(c)(2)(A).

61. *Id.* §§ 78dd-2(g)(3), 78ff(c)(3).

62. 18 U.S.C. § 3571(d) (1994). Section 3571, part of the Crimes and Criminal Procedure Title, defers to the substantive statute, in this case the FCPA, in determining the maximum fine and prison term if that statute specifies a lower fine. *See id.* § 3571(b), (c), (e). However, it allows a court to choose the gain/loss formula as an alternative to the substantive statute's penalties where appropriate. *Id.* § 3571(d). Individuals may be fined on this basis, or in the alternative up to $250,000. *Id.* § 3571(b)(3).

63. *See* U.S. SENTENCING GUIDELINES MANUAL § 2B4.1 (1997). The sentencing guidelines apply to any violations by individuals committed after November 1, 1987, and to violations by enterprises committed after November 1, 1991.

settlement in which Lockheed agreed to pay a combined civil and criminal fine totaling $24.8 million.[64] To date, this is the largest fine ever imposed under this law, and the first case involving prison terms for company officials.

The FCPA penalty provisions also arguably extend to foreign nationals in certain situations. One section of the Act imposes penalties against "[a]ny officer or director of an issuer, or stockholder acting on behalf of such issuer" for willful violations of the Act.[65] A second section of the Act, in contrast, imposes penalties against "[a]ny employee or agent of an issuer who is a United States citizen, national, or resident or is otherwise subject to the jurisdiction of the United States (other than an officer, director, or stockholder acting on behalf of such issuer)."[66] The statute's separate penalty provisions for these two groups of individuals suggest that the Act purports to create subject matter jurisdiction over officers and directors of issuers and stockholders acting on behalf of issuers, regardless of whether they are U.S. nationals or residents or otherwise subject to U.S. jurisdiction.

In addition to criminal penalties, the FCPA authorizes civil penalties of up to $10,000 against enterprises and individuals for violations of the antibribery provisions. The SEC or the Department of Justice (depending on whether the violation is committed by an issuer) may also seek injunctive relief to enjoin any act of an enterprise or individuals acting on behalf of an enterprise which violates or may violate the FCPA.

Finally, FCPA violations may trigger costly collateral sanctions. For example, the mere indictment of a company for violation of the FCPA may trigger debarment from U.S. government contracting, ineligibility for government benefits (such as financing), and/or suspension of export licensing for defense goods and services. Many U.S. states also impose procurement and other sanctions in such circumstances. For many companies, these "collateral" consequences are at least as serious as the penalties for a violation of the FCPA itself.

64. *See* Plea Agreement at 2, United States v. Lockheed, No. 1:94-CR-226-01 (filed Jan. 30, 1995)(on file with authors).

65. 15 U.S.C. § 78ff(c)(2)(A).

66. *Id.* § 78ff(c)(2)(B).

B. *Accounting Standards and Internal Control Provisions*

The second part of the FCPA is the accounting standards and internal control requirements found in 15 U.S.C. § 78m.

1. Requirements in General

In general terms, the accounting standards and internal control provisions of the FCPA require "issuers" to keep accurate books and records and to establish and maintain a system of internal controls adequate to ensure accountability for assets. These provisions were designed to ensure the integrity of the financial information presented by "issuers" to shareholders and potential investors, and to prevent the use of "slush funds" and off-book accounts to finance improper activities, including, but not limited to, foreign bribery.[67]

The accounting provisions require issuers to reflect accurately all transactions and dispositions of assets "in reasonable detail."[68] This requirement applies to all expenditures, rather than just those that would qualify as "material" in an accounting or disclosure context. Although the provisions thus require reporting in greater detail than a "materiality" standard, the FCPA requires "reasonable" rather than absolute assurance that accounting controls are adequate.[69] The records must be kept in "such level of detail and degree of assurance as would satisfy prudent officials in the conduct of their own affairs."[70] The Senate Report accompanying the original Act recognizes that "standards of reasonableness must apply" and that "management must necessarily estimate

67. In particular, the accounting provisions require "issuers" to:

A. make and keep books, records, and accounts which, in reasonable detail, accurately reflect the transactions and dispositions of the assets of the issuer; and

B. devise and maintain a system of internal accounting controls sufficient to provide reasonable assurances that—

i. transactions are executed in accordance with management's general or specific authorization;

ii. transactions are recorded as necessary (I) to permit preparation of financial statements in conformity with generally accepted accounting principles . . . and (II) to maintain accountability for assets;

iii. access to assets is permitted only in accordance with management's general or specific authorization; and

iv. the recorded accountability for assets is compared with the existing assets at reasonable intervals and appropriate action is taken with respect to any differences.

15 U.S.C. § 78m(b)(2).

68. *Id.* § 78m(b)(2)(A).

69. *See* 46 Fed. Reg. 11,544, 11,546 (1981)(SEC Chairman's discussion of the FCPA).

70. 15 U.S.C. § 78m(b)(7).

and evaluate the cost/benefit relationships" in establishing a system of controls.[71]

2. *Covered Persons*

Unlike the antibribery provisions, the accounting provisions apply only to "issuers."[72] "Issuers" in this context has the same definition as the antibribery context. Thus, not only U.S. public companies but foreign companies with publicly-traded stock in the U.S. may be "issuers."[73]

The accounting rules apply to *all* operations of issuers, domestic and overseas. Moreover, issuers are required to ensure that their majority-owned domestic and foreign subsidiaries comply with the accounting requirements of the FCPA. Where an issuer holds fifty percent or less of the voting power of a foreign subsidiary, however, a 1988 amendment to the accounting provisions requires only that the issuer make a "good faith attempt" to cause the affiliated company to maintain the internal accounting controls.[74]

Thus, the application of the accounting provisions to foreign subsidiaries turns strictly on equity ownership and not on a broader concept of control. Although issuers with minority status in foreign affiliates still need to take steps to satisfy the "good faith attempt" requirement, having satisfied that, the affiliates themselves will not be subject to the law.

3. *Penalties*

Like the antibribery provisions, the accounting and internal control requirements of the FCPA are enforced by the Department of Justice and the SEC. Generally, the SEC polices inadvertent or negligent violations, and refers willful violations to the Department of Justice for prosecution.

---

71. S. REP. NO. 95-114, at 8 (1977), *reprinted in* 1977 U.S.C.C.A.N. 4106.

72. 15 U.S.C. § 78m(b).

73. Thus, under these provisions foreign issuers will be held to the same standards of financial reporting and fair dealing as domestic issuers. This policy has most recently been exhibited in the ongoing SEC enforcement action against Montedison, S.p.A., an Italian company that traded American Depositary Receipts (ADRs) on the New York Stock Exchange and for several years falsified its reports to disguise an estimated $400 million in bribes. *See* Complaint for the Securities & Exchange Commission at 5-7, Securities & Exch. Comm'n v. Montedison, S.p.A., No. 1:96CV02631 (D.D.C. Nov. 21, 1996)(on file with authors).

74. *See* 15 U.S.C. § 78m(b)(6).

The SEC may impose civil penalties under its general enforcement authority over all reporting companies.[75] Under this authority, the SEC may impose civil fines, bring an injunctive action or enter a cease-and-desist order against a person who violates, or is about to violate, the antibribery provisions, and/or order disgorgement of ill-gotten gains.

The Department of Justice has enforcement authority over criminal violations of the accounting rules. Under the 1988 amendments to the FCPA, persons may be criminally liable under the accounting rules only if they "knowingly circumvent or knowingly fail to implement a system of internal accounting controls or knowingly falsify any book, record, or account" required to be maintained under the FCPA.[76]

The penalties for such violations are not set out in the FCPA, but are the same penalties applicable to other criminal violations of the securities laws, set out in the general criminal penalties provision of the Exchange Act of 1934. Under that provision, individuals found to have committed a "willful" violation may be fined up to $1 million and/or imprisoned up to ten years; enterprises found to have "willfully" violated the accounting requirements may be fined up to $2.5 million.[77]

IV. COMPARISON OF THE OAS CONVENTION TO U.S. LAW

The FCPA's antibribery provisions and accounting controls, in conjunction with portions of the U.S. tax laws, are designed to prohibit and penalize foreign official bribery by U.S. companies and promote transparency in the transactions of public companies. In contrast, the Convention, as we have seen, covers a much broader array of public corruption issues. In addition to foreign official bribery, the Convention addresses additional domestic public sector anticorruption efforts and multilateral enforcement of the anticorruption laws it covers, as well as ethics-in-government rules. Although virtually all aspects of the Conven-

75. *Id.* § 78u-1(d)(3).

76. *Id.* § 78m(b)(5). "Knowledge" in this context parallels the general U.S. criminal law definition and is thus narrower than that used in the third-party provisions of the antibribery prohibitions. *See supra* note 46. The "knowledge" standard in the accounting rules is merely intended to align the FCPA's standard for liability with the SEC's general enforcement policy that inadvertent conduct not be subject to criminal penalties. The legislative history explains that this standard is meant to criminalize the "deliberate falsification of books and records and other conduct calculated to evade the internal accounting controls requirements." S. REP. NO. 100-85, at 50 (1987).

77. 15 U.S.C. § 78ff(a).

tion have counterparts in U.S. law, it would not be practical to attempt to compare each aspect of the Convention with U.S. law in this Article. Thus, the comparative analysis below focuses on three primary areas of the Convention and their U.S. law counterparts (or lack thereof). First, the Article compares the Convention with U.S. efforts to combat foreign official bribery, namely the FCPA's antibribery provisions and accounting and internal control requirements, and section 162(c) of the Internal Revenue Code, which denies tax deductibility for foreign bribes and other improper payments. Second, the Article examines the Convention's illicit enrichment provision and its U.S. constitutional ramifications. Third, the Article examines the Convention's framework for multilateral enforcement efforts from a U.S. legal perspective.

A. *Comparison of the Convention to U.S. Efforts to Combat Foreign Bribery*

A comparison of the OAS Convention with U.S. laws to combat foreign bribery reveals that they share much common ground, with several potentially significant differences in scope and emphasis.

1. *Scope of the Prohibition Against Foreign Bribery*

The basic prohibition of transnational bribery described in article VIII of the Convention parallels the FCPA's antibribery provisions in many respects. A detailed analysis reveals, however, that the Convention is in some respects broader and in other respects narrower than the FCPA.

a. Subject of the Prohibition

Like the FCPA, article VIII addresses only the "supply" side of a bribe; it prohibits only the "offering or granting" of a bribe, rather than the solicitation or receipt of one. In the terminology of some countries' legal systems, it thus focuses on "active" rather than "passive" bribery. In this sense, both the FCPA and the Convention recognize the limits of domestic legislation to address activity within another sovereign's territory. Nevertheless, as set out below, the states parties could have overlapping jurisdiction in some instances.

b. Prohibited Acts

Both the Convention and the FCPA proscribe acts beyond the actual payment of money. Both, for example, apply to offers as well as to payments. As a result, an enterprise could potentially be liable under both regimes not only for making improper payments, but also without actually paying any money. An offer to pay could be sufficient to constitute a violation. Unlike the FCPA, however, the IACAC does not expressly cover a "promise" to pay or the "authorization" by one party of another party's (such as a foreign agent's or intermediary's) payment of a bribe. The significance of the omission of promises remains to be seen, particularly since "offering" something of value to a foreign official in exchange for a benefit is an act of corruption, and the Convention attempts to cover all parties to an illegal bribe, including "instigators."[78] The omission of authorization, on the other hand, could be significant. Authorization liability can be a significant basis of control over the parent company in a multinational enterprise located in a country whose subsidiary is beyond the jurisdictional reach of national law. Since the Convention does not preclude countries from establishing liability for promises or authorizations, countries implementing article VIII should consider including these elements in their domestic legislation.

c. Benefits Considered Improper

Although the FCPA is broad in the types of benefits that may not be given to officials, the Convention may go beyond it. The FCPA prohibits the giving of "money, or . . . anything of value."[79] Thus, contract rights, waivers, and even entertainment and gifts can run afoul of U.S. law under certain circumstances. No effort has been made by enforcement authorities, however, to extend the FCPA to benefits having no specific pecuniary value. Thus, for example, general reputational benefits and goodwill are commonly believed to fall outside the scope of the FCPA's antibribery prohibitions.

The Convention also prohibits the transfer of "any article of monetary value."[80] The Convention goes further, however, to prohibit the giving of any "other benefit, such as a gift, favor, promise, or advantage" to a government official.[81] Thus, the Convention appears to cover a broader scope of benefits, possibly including non-financial benefits.

78. Convention, *supra* note 1, art. VI(1)(b). *See also infra* note 85.
79. 15 U.S.C. §§ 78dd-1(a), 78dd-2(a).
80. Convention, *supra* note 1, art. VI.
81. *Id.*

The Convention's more expansive language could be significant in state party implementation, since it allows the states parties to choose among a range of prohibited benefits. If the states parties enact significantly different provisions, companies competing in several jurisdictions will confront varying standards of conduct. In response, they will either need to conform their conduct to the standards set by the strictest jurisdiction with the broadest scope, or attempt to keep track of what is or is not permitted in each country.

Similarly, variations among jurisdictions with regard to the basic prohibitions may affect states parties' willingness to assist one another in enforcement efforts. While the principle of dual criminality, which is contained in most extradition treaties, requires an offense to be illegal in both the requesting and the requested countries before extradition will be permitted, small variances in the definition of an offense will not defeat extradition under the principle of dual criminality, so long as the statutory provisions are "substantially analogous" or are directed at "functionally identical conduct."[82] Nevertheless, a country that has chosen to prohibit a narrow range of activities may be loathe to assist in the prosecution of one of its nationals under a foreign law that criminalizes a far broader range of conduct.

d. Direct and Indirect Payments Prohibited

Both instruments cover not only direct but also indirect payments to officials. Indeed, both instruments first explicitly prohibit the payments of bribes "directly or indirectly." In separate provisions, both instruments establish principles of vicarious liability, although the Convention's vicarious liability provision falls under the progressive development article. Under the FCPA, vicarious liability for the acts of third parties may attach to a covered person even if that person did not specifically authorize the payment, if it can be shown that the covered person "knew" that the intermediary would make an improper payment.[83] A similar concept appears in article XI of the Convention, which suggests that states parties criminalize as an act of corruption "any act or omission by any person who, personally or through a third party, or acting as an intermediary, seeks to obtain a decision from a public authority

82. 4 MICHAEL ABELL & BRUNO A. RISTAU, INTERNATIONAL JUDICIAL ASSISTANCE § 13-3-3(4) (1995)(citing Peters v. Egnor, 888 F.2d 713, 719 (10th Cir. 1989)).
83. *See supra* note 46 (providing the definition of "knowledge").

whereby he illicitly obtains for himself or for another person any benefit or gain."[84] Unlike the FCPA, however, the Convention's provision appears to make the intermediary, as well as the main actor, liable, regardless of whether the intermediary can be considered the main actor's "agent."[85] Thus, the Convention targets the middleman as well as the primary payor in a broader range of factual situations than contemplated under the FCPA. In addition, the Convention does not address what level of awareness the main actor must have in order to be held responsible for an intermediary's payment. As noted earlier, the FCPA's standard goes beyond actual knowledge to willful ignorance.[86] If special standards (like the FCPA's knowledge standard) were to be established under the Convention, this would presumably be done under the domestic laws of the states parties in their implementing legislation,[87] again raising an issue of uniformity.

Although the FCPA's knowledge standard has been a source of great concern for U.S. companies seeking to comply with the FCPA, the extension of indirect liability to willful blindness is a defensible policy decision. The murky nature of bribery and corruption means that companies will rarely know with certainty what their agents or partners are doing. The more sophisticated the agent or partner, in fact, the less likely the U.S. company will have actual knowledge. Although criminal liability should not be predicated on merely negligent behavior, sanctioning a willful "head in the sand" attitude towards the activities of one's representatives may be the best way for a country to leverage its enforcement resources. Such an approach effectively places policing responsibility on the party entering into the relationship with an agent or consultant. Although a "willful blindness" standard is thus defensible, countries taking this approach need to ensure that the scope of that responsibility is clearly defined, so that companies will be able to determine what they need to do to comply.

84. Convention, *supra* note 1, art. XI(1)(e).

85. In addition to the quoted language of article XI, a mandatory provision of the Convention calls for criminalization of the "[p]articipation as a principal, coprincipal, instigator, accomplice or accessory after the fact, or in any other manner, in the commission or attempted commission of, or in any collaboration or conspiracy to commit, any of the acts referred to in this article." Convention, *supra* note 1, art. VI(1)(e).

86. *See supra* Part III.A.2.

87. If no special standard were set, we assume general criminal law awareness (*scienter*) standards would apply.

e. Business Context and Quid Pro Quo Requirement

Although article VIII of the Convention does not adopt the FCPA's "business purpose" test, it includes a similar requirement that the payments be made "in connection with any economic or commercial transaction." Furthermore, just as the FCPA implies that the payment or other value is given in return for some official action (a quid pro quo requirement), so the IACAC specifies that payments must be made "in exchange for" the government official's act or omission in the performance of his "public functions." As a practical matter, it is likely that payments in connection with a commercial transaction and in exchange for an official act or omission would almost always be payments made for the purpose of "obtaining, retaining, or directing business to any person." Thus, depending on its implementation by states parties, this difference in language may not hold practical significance, though it could result in the IACAC extending to a broader array of transactions, including, as the following section discusses, facilitating payments.

f. Facilitating Payments

A key textual difference between the Convention and the FCPA relates to gratuities paid, typically to low-level government employees, to secure or expedite their performance of routine duties. Under the FCPA, such "facilitating" or "grease" payments are explicitly excepted from the prohibitions against bribery of foreign officials. The original legislative history from 1977 makes clear that the FCPA was never intended to cover such payments, because in Congress's view those payments are not made "for the purpose of obtaining business" and, indeed, may merely seek "the proper performance of duties."[88] The exception does not by its terms apply to payments made to affect discretionary decisions of government officials.[89] In many cases, however, such payments nonetheless violate the host country's laws against bribery and corruption.[90] Thus, in effect, the FCPA allows U.S. companies to make payments to government officials that may violate the laws of the host country, and thereby contribute to low-level corruption.

---

88. S. REP. NO. 95-114, at 11 (1977).

89. *See* 15 U.S.C. §§ 78dd-1(f)(3), 78dd-2(h)(4) (1994).

90. *See, e.g.*, Georges Charles Fischer, *Facilitating Payments*, LATIN AM. L. & BUS. REP., Apr. 30, 1995 (discussing the illegality of facilitating payments under Brazilian law).

Unlike the FCPA, the Convention does not explicitly provide an exception for facilitating payments. Facilitating payments clearly are payments made to an official "in exchange for [an] act . . . in the performance of his public functions,"[91] which means they may be considered acts of corruption under the Convention.

The report of the Inter-American Juridical Committee on model elements for inclusion in domestic implementing legislation at least implicitly recognizes that states parties may be able to exclude facilitating payments from their legislation implementing article VIII. The Juridical Committee Report emphasizes that only bribery in relation to activities of an economic or commercial nature is meant to be covered by the Convention.[92] This qualification could be viewed as similar to the FCPA's focus on payments made to "obtain or retain business," and excluding those designed to expedite routine governmental activity. The Juridical Committee Report also notes that states should consider how to distinguish the concept of bribery from other acts, such as small gifts or favors to expedite the transmission of documents, though it does not elaborate on the term "small."[93]

The Juridical Committee Report also emphasizes the importance of considering the practical application of the Convention and the need for effective judicial cooperation and assistance, which requires especially that the legislation reach all officials at a certain level of importance.[94] In the context of illicit enrichment, however, it notes that although the definition of public official appears to include even the most insignificant government employees, states parties should consider sanctioning more senior public officials more severely than their juniors.[95] Taken together, these provisions suggest that the emphasis of the Convention, with an eye towards realistic enforcement capabilities, is on preventing corruption of senior government officials, though the definition of public official extends to officials at any level of hierarchy.[96]

States parties could thus have legitimate policy reasons for excluding facilitating payments from the acts of corruption criminalized in their domestic legislation without undercutting the larger objectives of the treaty. In order to ensure a uniform interpreta-

91. Convention, *supra* note 1, art. VI.
92. Juridical Committee Report, *supra* note 10, § III(a)(ii).
93. *Id.* § III(a)(viii).
94. *Id.* § III.2.c.
95. *Id.* § IV.2.c.
96. Convention, *supra* note 1, art. I (broadly defining government official).

tion of the treaty, it would be preferable for the states parties to address the issue multilaterally. If that is not possible, and facilitating payments are indeed prohibited by the treaty, states parties could take a reservation on that issue when they ratify the Convention; alternatively, states parties could declare their understanding that such payments are not prohibited. Either course would make the enforcement position of a state clear; however, the existence of alternatives obviously increases the risk of lack of uniformity and could undermine the effectiveness of the Convention.

If the Convention is widely implemented to prohibit facilitating payments, there will be a continued conflict between U.S. law and the laws of other countries. The ratification of the OAS Convention will give the United States the opportunity to amend the FCPA, should it choose to do so, to eliminate the facilitating payments exception. The distinction between facilitating payments and payments made to obtain or retain business is often difficult to make in practice; by amending the FCPA to bar facilitating payments the United States could close one loophole through which U.S. businesses may try to channel payments in order to remain at least facially in compliance with the FCPA. On the other hand, enforcement of the law with respect to such payments would be difficult and arguably a misallocation of priorities at this time, given the prevalence of higher-level corruption. In our view, the most important concern at present is for the position of states parties regarding the permissibility of facilitating payments to be clear and for there to be as much uniformity as possible in interpretation and implementation of the Convention.

g. Definition of Public Official

(i) Applicability to Employees of State-Owned Enterprises

Another interesting area of comparison between the OAS Convention and the FCPA is in the definitions of key terms. For example, "public official" is defined in article I of the Convention to include "any official or employee of the State or its agencies, including those who have been selected, appointed, or elected to perform activities or functions in the name of the State or service of the State, at any level of its hierarchy." Under the FCPA, a foreign official means "any officer or employee of a foreign government or any department, agency, or instrumentality thereof, or any person acting in an official capacity for or on behalf of any such" entities.[97] Thus, both instruments consider officers and employees of the government and its agencies to be officials. But where the FCPA makes clear that employees of state instrumentalities are covered, the absence of a reference to "instrumentalities" of a state in the Convention suggests such individuals are not "public officials" for purposes of the Convention. This is another issue worthy of attention in a multilateral context to ensure uniform interpretation. The Spanish version of the Convention, however, refers to *entidades*, which could be read to include instrumentalities.[98]

The state parties should clarify whether their implementation of the Convention includes employees of state-owned enterprises (in U.S. law, instrumentalities). In our view, it is critical that they be covered; a failure to do so would create an important gap in the Convention's scope and an asymmetry with the FCPA. States parties should also consider defining the term "instrumentality," perhaps by establishing a standard requiring a majority of government ownership, or government control, before a company is treated as an instrumentality.[99]

If this were to occur, it would be desirable for the United States to amend the FCPA, which does not define the term "instrumentality," to bring it in line with the Convention. Such amendment, by excluding from the definition of government instrumentality those companies with only a minority percentage of government ownership or lacking government control, and would exclude from the definition of foreign official employees of those companies that are not instrumentalities. This change would give added clarity and predictability to U.S. law.

97. 15 U.S.C. §§ 78dd-1(f)(1), 78dd-2(h)(2) (1994).

98. Convención Interamericana Contra la Corrupcíon, Mar. 29, 1996, articúlo 1 (visited Jan. 21, 1998) <http://www.oas.org/SP/PINFO/CONVEN/corrupts.htm>. *See* 1981 COLLINS SPANISH-ENGLISH, ENGLISH-SPANISH DICTIONARY at 232 (defining *entidad* as an "(a) entity; (*Pol etc*) body, organization . . ."). The English and Spanish versions of the Convention are equally authentic. Convention, *supra* note 1, art. XXVIII.

99. The OECD Convention Commentary indicates that, under that agreement, majority government ownership or control would make an entity an instrumentality. It also suggests that private companies that enjoy subsidies or other government benefits that allow them to operate on a non-commercial basis would also be treated as instrumentalities. OECD Negotiating Conference, *Commentaries on the Convention on Combating Bribery of Officials in International Business Transactions*, Nov. 21, 1997, art. 1 (visited Jan. 21, 1998) <http://www.oecd.org/daf/cmis/bribery>. In our view, the latter concept would introduce into compliance efforts an element that is impractical. Although alignment with the OECD Convention is desirable in general terms, the OAS member states should retain the discretion not to incorporate suggested elements that they believe would be unwieldy or impractical.

(ii) Political Parties, Party Officials and Candidates

In addition to payments to officials, the FCPA expressly covers payments to political parties, party officials, and candidates for political office.[100] The Convention is silent on this point. This difference in scope is potentially quite significant. Although the ongoing campaign finance debate in the United States illustrates the complexities of attempting to define the boundary between legitimate and corrupt campaign contributions in the domestic context,[101] the argument for covering such payments in the transnational bribery context is very strong.

(iii) Other Differences

On the other hand, the Convention offers better guidance than the FCPA in stating that persons "selected" or "appointed" to perform functions for the state are considered public officials, and that the level of hierarchy that the official occupies is not relevant.[102]

Similarly, only the Convention defines "public functions," whereas the FCPA leaves the question of when someone is "acting in an official capacity" open to interpretation. The Convention and the FCPA each target the same type of payments to a government official, that is, payments made to affect the official's "performance of his [or her] public functions" (in the Convention)[103] or "any act or decision of such foreign official in his [or her] official capacity" (in the FCPA).[104] Whether a person is "acting in an official capacity" also can determine whether that person is a "foreign official" under the FCPA.

The Convention explains that a public function may include any activity "performed by a natural person in the name of the State or in the service of the State," whether the activity is temporary or permanent, paid or honorary, and regardless of where the function falls in the state's hierarchy.[105] The FCPA, in contrast, does not explain when a person is "acting in an official capacity."[106] This

100. 15 U.S.C. §§ 78dd-1(a)(2), 78dd-2(a)(2).

101. *See* Robert Suro, *Reno Decides Against Independent Counsel to Probe Clinton, Gore*, WASH. POST, Dec. 3, 1997, at A1; *In GOP, Two Sides of the Debate*, WASH. POST, Sept. 27, 1997, at A4.

102. *See supra* note 8; *supra* Part III.A.1.

103. Convention, *supra* note 1, art. VI.

104. 15 U.S.C. §§ 78dd-1(a)(3)(A)(i), 78dd-2(a)(1)(A)(i).

105. Convention, *supra* note 1, art. I.

106. *See* 15 U.S.C. §§ 78dd-1(a)(3)(A)(i), 78dd-2(a)(1)(A)(i).

means that companies must do their own analysis of a person's status first, to determine whether the person is a "foreign official" covered by the FCPA and second, to determine whether the act they seek the official to perform is one performed "in his [or her] official capacity" and therefore prohibited.[107] The Convention arguably offers clearer guidance to companies and individuals seeking to determine whether an individual is likely to be considered a public official for purposes of the antibribery prohibitions. The United States should consider adopting this definition to serve the dual purpose of bringing its legislation into conformity with the Convention and to provide better, clearer guidance to U.S. companies seeking to do business abroad.

2. Jurisdictional Changes and Challenges

Having compared the Convention and U.S. law with respect to the scope of the transnational bribery offense, we turn next to the jurisdictional scope of the Convention. Here we see potentially important differences between the FCPA and the Convention. As noted earlier, the Convention requires states parties to adopt measures to establish their jurisdiction (1) over Convention offenses committed within their territory and (2) when the alleged criminal is present in their territory, but not extradited to another state due to nationality.[108] In addition, states parties may, but are not obligated to, take measures to establish their jurisdiction over the offenses established in accordance with the Convention when the offense is committed by one of their nationals or by a person who habitually resides in their territory.[109] These jurisdictional provisions must be considered alongside the provisions of article IV of the Convention, which require that the offense either be committed in, or have effects in, the state's territory to be a covered act of corruption.

In contrast, the FCPA at present only applies to U.S. nationals or those foreign companies that have publicly traded securities in the United States, but only if some activity "in furtherance" of the improper conduct has a nexus to U.S. commerce. Thus, jurisdic-

107. Our experience counseling many U.S. companies in the interpretation of U.S. law on this point indicates that this can be difficult to do.

108. Convention, *supra* note 1, art. V(1), (3).

109. *Id.* art. V(2). The Convention preserves established rules of criminal jurisdiction of state parties under their domestic laws. *Id.* art. V(4). These may offer other jurisdictional bases as well.

tion under the FCPA is principally on the basis of nationality, but with a territorial nexus requirement.[110]

a. Territoriality

It is axiomatic under international law that states parties have the right to criminalize and enforce offenses committed within their territories.[111] In reality, however, many offenses are not committed wholly within one state's territory. Recognition of this fact has led some nations to adopt the subjective territorial principle, which permits a nation to punish offenses planned within its territory but carried out in another nation's territory, and the objective territorial principle, by which nations punish offenses (1) started in another nation's territory but consummated or completed within their territory or (2) "producing gravely harmful consequences to the social or economic order inside their territory."[112] Conspiracies, or other crimes, like transnational bribery, that may involve several people and/or communications across national boundaries might be subject to the territorial jurisdiction of more than one country.

Objective territoriality has also been referred to as "effects" jurisdiction.[113] Although the jurisdictional provision of the Convention does not address "effects" jurisdiction, the scope of the Convention, as noted earlier, extends to acts of corruption committed in or having effects in a state party.[114] It is thus almost certain that some states parties will enact legislation prescribing activities that have effects in their territories—and that other states parties will have criminalized the same activities due to some portion of the activity that occurred, or had effects, within their territories. This

110. This may change as the result of the OECD Convention. The jurisdictional provisions of the OECD Convention are similar to those of the OAS Convention. If the OECD Convention is ratified by the United States without a reservation, an amendment to the FCPA to cover "any person" acting with the requisite territorial nexus will be required. *See* OECD Convention, *supra* note 1, arts. 1, 4.

111. IAN BROWNLIE, PRINCIPLES OF PUBLIC INTERNATIONAL LAW at 300 (3d ed. 1979).

112. J. Starke, *Introduction to International Law*, *in* Barry E. Carter & Phillip R. Trimble, INTERNATIONAL LAW 704-05 (1991).

113. The allowable scope of "effects" jurisdiction has been widely debated by courts and legal scholars. *See id.* at 704-07; Asahi Metal Indus. Co. v. Superior Court of California, 480 U.S. 102, 113 (1987) (discussing rule of reason, among other considerations, in deciding whether to exercise jurisdiction in context of a civil suit); RESTATEMENT (THIRD) OF THE FOREIGN RELATIONS LAW OF THE UNITED STATES § 403 & nn.1-3 [hereinafter RESTATEMENT 3D].

114. Convention, *supra* note 1, art. IV.

is especially true if the required effects are small. The Convention does not define the term "effects," and therefore states will be free, consistent with international law, to define the term in the implementing legislation. However, because the assertion of jurisdiction over non-nationals based on effects in the territory is controversial, states should be hesitant to adopt too aggressive a standard in this area. In the antitrust area, perhaps the most prominent example, both the United States and the European Union have effects tests. Since 1982, the United States has required that the effects be "direct, substantial and foreseeable."[115]

b. Nationality

Many nations assert authority over their nationals (and sometimes over residents) regardless of where their nationals are located.[116] This practice is more common in civil law countries;[117] the United States has only sparingly used nationality alone as the basis for asserting jurisdiction,[118] though it has used nationality in concert with other bases for exerting jurisdiction.[119] The FCPA, for example, applies to U.S. entities doing business overseas, but also requires a nexus to U.S. commerce. To satisfy the terms of the Convention, the United States would not have to retain the nexus to U.S. commerce provision of the FCPA for its nationals; however, constitutional restraints may require some connection to the United States beyond mere nationality for U.S. courts to exercise jurisdiction.[120]

The Convention also requires that states parties establish jurisdiction over alleged criminals present in their territory, but whom they refuse to extradite on the basis of nationality. This "extradite

115. RESTATEMENT 3D, *supra* note 113, § 403(2)(a).

116. BROWNLIE, *supra* note 111, at 303.

117. *Extraterritorial Application of Criminal Law*, 85 AM. SOC'Y INT'L L. PROC. 383, 387 (1991) (remarks of Christopher L. Blakesley).

118. RESTATEMENT 3D, *supra* note 113, § 402 n.1.

119. The United States is often regarded by other nations as asserting jurisdiction too broadly over foreign corporations through their U.S. subsidiaries or through their activities within the United States. *See generally* BROWNLIE, *supra* note 111, at 300-04; Carter & Trimble, *supra* note 112, at 748-60 (excerpting various authors).

120. The constitutional due process concerns that generally arise whenever U.S. courts seek to assert jurisdiction are beyond the scope of this article. *See generally* RESTATEMENT 3D, *supra* note 113, § 402 n.1; MYRES MCDOUGAL & W. MICHAEL REISMAN, INTERNATIONAL LAW IN CONTEMPORARY PERSPECTIVE 1370-85 (1981); *Extraterritorial Application of Criminal Law*, 85 AM. SOC'Y INT'L L. PROC. 383, 388-91 (1991) (remarks of Andreas F. Lowenfeld); Geoffrey R. Watson, *Offenders Abroad: The Case for Nationality-Based Criminal Jurisdiction*, 17 YALE J. INT'L L. 41 (1992).

or prosecute" approach is not unique to the Convention, and is important to ensure enforcement against offenders.

c. Implications of the Convention's Jurisdictional Provisions

On their face, the Convention's jurisdictional provisions are non-controversial—territoriality and nationality are the two most widely accepted principles in international law on which nations base their jurisdiction to prescribe laws.[121] International jurisdiction is, however, generally divided into three categories—jurisdiction to prescribe, jurisdiction to adjudicate, and jurisdiction to enforce.[122] The Convention concentrates on jurisdiction to prescribe, which does not in itself necessarily lead to conflict among states parties. The Convention's discussion of adjudication and enforcement refers primarily to existing extradition treaties and multilateral assistance treaties, but does not establish which state party's interests should predominate in the event of a conflict. In practice, therefore, each state party's interpretation of these provisions could lead to conflict among the states parties as to who should have primary responsibility for adjudication and enforcement of the offense conduct.

The Convention itself does not devise a hierarchy as to who should have primary responsibility for enforcement and adjudication, but general international law principles and notions of comity provide some guidance. Territorial locus, for example, is one such principal: States parties should have the primary right to enforce their own criminal laws within their own territories.[123] Under this principle, for example, Peru should have primary responsibility for prosecuting the bribery of a Peruvian official in Peru, even if the

121. RESTATEMENT 3D, *supra* note 113, § 402. The other generally recognized, though differentially accepted, bases for establishing jurisdiction, not at issue here, are the passive personality principle, by which a state may punish aliens for acts abroad harmful to nationals of the state; the protective or security principle, by which states assert jurisdiction over aliens for acts abroad that threaten the national security of the state; and the universality principle, which permits states to exercise jurisdiction over anyone committing acts, such as piracy, hijacking, and genocide, that are of universal concern to the international community. RESTATEMENT 3D, *supra* note 113, § 404; BROWNLIE, *supra* note 111, at 300-05.

122. RESTATEMENT 3D, *supra* note 113, § 401; European Committee on Crime Problems, Council of Europe, *Extraterritorial Criminal Jurisdiction*, 3 CRIM. L. F. 441, 456 (1990) [hereinafter Council of Europe].

123. This accords with the fundamental principle that a state has primary responsibility for prescribing criminal conduct within its territory. *See* BROWNLIE, *supra* note 111, at 300.

offense was planned outside Peru and the offender was an American.

In many cases, however, the territorial principle may not provide such an easy assignment of responsibility, or intervening considerations may complicate the matter. If all of the evidence was in the United States, as was the offender, the United States might choose to exercise jurisdiction, feeling itself justified on grounds of the nationality of the offender and the convenience of the forum. Peru, on the other hand, might not agree. In such instances, diplomatic negotiations and comity will come into play.

Comity, famously defined by Justice Gray as "the recognition which one nation allows within its territory to the legislative, executive or judicial acts of another nation, having due regard both to international duty and convenience, and to the rights of its own citizens or of other persons who are under the protection of its laws," is not a binding legal obligation.[124] Nevertheless, it underpins international law and generally instructs that nations exercise restraint in exerting jurisdiction that intrudes on the territory of another sovereign.[125] The goal of eradicating corruption, mutually shared by all states parties, may facilitate the sharing and allocation of adjudication and enforcement under the Convention, and may help resign some states parties to the exercise of extraterritorial jurisdiction by another state party that they would ordinarily deplore.[126]

3. *Penalties*

While the FCPA prescribes substantial civil and criminal penalties,[127] the Convention is silent on the question of penalties for acts of corruption, including transnational bribery. As noted by the Agreed Common Elements of Criminal Legislation and Related Action approved by the Working Group on Bribery in International Business Transactions of the Organization for Economic Cooperation and Development (OECD) on May 23, 1997, "the offense of bribery of foreign officials should be sanctioned/punished by effective, proportionate and dissuasive penalties, sufficient to secure effective mutual legal assistance and extradition, compara-

124. Hilton v. Guyot, 159 U.S. 113, 164 (1895).

125. *See generally* Brian Pearce, Note, *The Comity Doctrine as a Barrier to Judicial Jurisdiction: A U.S.-E.U. Comparison*, 30 STAN. J. INT'L L. 525 (1994).

126. Council of Europe, *supra* note 122, at 463-65 (discussing international solidarity as a basis for the assertion of extraterritorial jurisdiction).

127. *See supra* text accompanying notes 54-62.

ble to those applicable to the bribers in cases of corruption of domestic public officials."[128] Countries that lack sufficiently strong penalties to dissuade transnational bribery, especially as other countries besides the United States prescribe strong penalties, will increasingly have to be seen as encouraging corruption.

The OAS Juridical Committee Report notes that more senior government officials should be punished more severely than more junior officials, but does not elaborate on that statement.[129] The Report also recommends that penalties be of sufficient gravity to have a deterrent effect and be proportional to the crime committed.[130] For individuals, the Report recommends that states parties contemplate jail sentences, while for both individuals and corporations states parties should consider fines, forfeiture, or restitution of the benefits resulting from the bribe.[131] To protect the integrity and efficacy of the Convention, states parties must enact significant penalties to emphasize their commitment to the Convention and its prohibitions.

4. *Accounting and Recordkeeping Requirements*

The second major component of the FCPA, the accounting standards and internal control requirements, also has parallels in the Convention, but parallels that do not create immediate obligations on states parties. Indeed, they represent the lowest of the four levels of state obligations under the Convention. Under article III(10), the states parties "agree to consider" measures to require "publicly held companies" to maintain books and records which "in reasonable detail, accurately reflect the acquisition and disposition of assets," and have "sufficient internal accounting controls to enable their officers to detect corrupt acts." These requirements are at present aspirational, with no attached timetable. States parties, having only an obligation to consider them, may thus choose to impose them or reject them.

---

128. *Organisation for Economic Co-operation and Development: Revised Recommendation C(97)123/FINAL on Combating Bribery in International Business Transactions*, May 23, 1997, 36 I.L.M. 1016, 1024 (1997) (reproduced from OECD Doc. C(97)123/FINAL, May 29, 1997).

129. Juridical Committee Report, *supra* note 10, at IV.2.c. This recommendation is made in the context of the discussion on illicit enrichment, though the same consideration would seem to apply to the transnational bribery provisions.

130. *Id.* at III.d. This recommendation is made in the context of the transnational bribery recommendations.

131. *Id.*

The Convention language includes the key elements of the FCPA requirements regarding accounting and recordkeeping. First, its scope embraces only publicly-held companies.[132] Second, it envisions a "reasonable detail" standard to be applied in recordkeeping.[133] Third, it indicates that the records should accurately reflect the "acquisition and disposition" of assets.[134] By addressing the acquisition of assets, and not just their disposition, the Convention arguably goes further than the FCPA toward policing all participants in corrupt activities, and not just payors. Finally, it calls for internal accounting controls sufficient to enable officials to police the companies' financial activities.[135]

In the United States, the books and records provisions have been vigorously enforced by the SEC, and have done much to support shareholder confidence in public companies and therefore in securities markets generally. Though these provisions are not mandatory under the Convention, countries in Latin America wishing to strengthen these markets in their own countries and to enhance their abilities to combat corruption will want to give a high priority to implementation of these provisions.

5. *Tax Treatment of Bribes*

The third major prong of U.S. law targeting foreign bribery exists in the tax laws. Under section 162(a)of the Internal Revenue Code, U.S. taxpayers may deduct all "ordinary and necessary" expenses paid or incurred in carrying on a trade or business. In 1958, Congress amended the Internal Revenue Code to add section 162(c), which denies tax deductibility under section 162(a) for any payment that is an illegal kickback or a bribe.[136] Section 162(c) also precludes deducting any payment that is unlawful under the Foreign Corrupt Practices Act.[137] These tax measures predated the FCPA and have been an important step in affecting corporate behavior in the United States.[138]

Article III of the Convention contains a similar tax provision, with a status equivalent to that of the books and records provision

132. Convention, *supra* note 1, art. III(10).

133. *Id.*

134. *Id.*

135. *Id.*

136. 26 U.S.C. § 162(c) (1994).

137. *Id.*

138. *See* Morgan Chu & Daniel Magraw, *The Deductibility of Questionable Foreign Payments*, 87 YALE L.J. 1091 (1978).

just discussed. States parties "agree to consider" laws to deny favorable tax treatment for any "expenditures made in violation of the anticorruption laws of the states parties."[139] Thus, like section 162(c), it appears to address domestic as well as foreign bribery. Denying the tax deductibility of bribes sends a message that corruption is not "business as usual" and can be a powerful tool for governments. This provision should, therefore, be a high priority for implementation. Such a provision is also consistent with the efforts of many countries in the hemisphere to reform their tax systems.

B. *Illicit Enrichment and Related Ethics-in-Government Provisions of the Convention*

Article IX requires states parties to make illegal significant increases in a government official's assets that the official "cannot reasonably explain in relation to his [or her] lawful earnings."[140] Closely to tied that provision is greater enforcement of ethics-in-government rules, which can help police government officials.

1. *Illicit Enrichment*

The illicit enrichment provision was controversial for the United States during the drafting of the Convention because, as written in the Convention, it appears to create a presumption of guilt on the part of the accused. That structure almost certainly violates the presumption of innocence guaranteed by the Fifth Amendment of the U.S. Constitution to any criminal defendant. The United States therefore secured the inclusion of a qualifying provision that criminalization of such action would not be required if to do so would violate a state's constitution or its fundamental legal principles.[141] Nevertheless, illicit enrichment could be a significant weapon in the fight against transnational bribery.

For the United States, the most significant problem with article IX is that, on its face, it appears to place the burden of proof on the foreign official to refute the illegal acquisition of the funds, rather than to place the burden of proof on the prosecutor to show the illegality of the funds. Fundamental due process rights derived

139. Convention, *supra* note 1, art. III(7).

140. *Id.* art. IX.

141. *Id.* The United States had attempted to eliminate the provision altogether. According to informal conversations with State Department officials, the United States agreed to include the qualified illicit enrichment provision in return for the Latin American countries' agreement to adopt an expansive jurisdictional provision.

from the Fifth Amendment to the U.S. Constitution require that an accused person be presumed innocent until proven guilty.[142] A fundamental corollary to that proposition is that the prosecutor has the burden of proving each material element of an offense beyond a reasonable doubt.[143] That burden cannot constitutionally be shifted to the defendant, although a defendant can bear the burden of proving an affirmative defense.[144]

Article IX risks being held unconstitutional in the United States if implemented as written. As the offense is described, its material elements involve the possession, by a government official, of an amount of money in excess of the amount the official could earn by his salary or through other legitimate sources of income. The other element is that the money was obtained by corrupt means, which implicitly places the burden on the defendant to prove the money was legally acquired.

Article IX would also apparently violate the Fifth Amendment's privilege against self-incrimination by requiring a criminal defendant to testify or face an automatic determination of guilt.[145] U.S. courts have refused to permit conviction of a defendant based solely on the illegal possession of a controlled substance when the defendant refused to demonstrate a legal source for his drugs.[146] The U.S. government cannot be relieved of its obligation to prove its case by placing the burden on the criminal defendant, even if the defendant is in a better position to have knowledge of the source of the funds.[147]

The United States could, however, attempt to remedy this problem through legislation that would place the burden of proof upon the prosecutor to show that the unexplained funds derived from an unlawful source or by unlawful means. In order to stay closer to the intent of the Convention, Congress could try to provide that a government official's possession of sums of money disproportionate to the official's legitimate sources of income could

142. *See, e.g.*, *In re* Winship, 397 U.S. 358, 363 (1970). For the purposes of this Article we address only federal laws; the constitutional requirements described herein would also apply to state laws by virtue of the Fourteenth Amendment.

143. *Id.* at 364; Patterson v. New York, 432 U.S. 197, 210 (1977); Mullaney v. Wilbur, 421 U.S. 684 (1975).

144. *Patterson*, 432 U.S. at 210.

145. *See* U.S. CONST. amend. V.

146. *See* Leary v. United States, 395 U.S. 6, 34-36 (1969); Tot v. United States, 319 U.S. 463, 469-70 (1943).

147. *Leary*, 395 U.S. at 34.

be presumptive evidence of its corrupt acquisition. Properly structured, such a presumption might pass constitutional muster.

While certain statutory presumptions are unconstitutional, U.S. law does permit some, even in criminal cases.[148] Statutory presumptions in criminal statutes are described as either "permissive" or "mandatory."[149] A permissive presumption is the more common device, allowing, but not requiring, a trier of fact to infer the elemental fact based on other evidence adduced by the prosecutor.[150] A mandatory presumption *requires* a trier of fact to accept the existence of an element of a crime from one or more evidentiary or basic facts even if the presumption is the sole evidence of the element in question.[151]

A permissive presumption is constitutional under U.S. law so long as there is a rational connection between the basic facts that the prosecution proved and the ultimate fact presumed, and the latter is "more likely than not to flow from" the former.[152] The application of this standard can vary greatly depending on the facts of a specific case.[153]

The constitutionality of a permissive presumption permitting a factfinder to assume corruptness based on an official's possession of funds disproportionate to the official's salary would not be guaranteed. The possession of such funds would have to be "more likely than not" a result of corrupt behavior.[154] Meeting that stan-

148. County Court of Ulster County, New York v. Allen, 442 U.S. 140, 164-67 (1979) (upholding New York law that the presence of a firearm in a vehicle is presumptive evidence of its illegal possession by all persons then occupying the vehicle); *see generally* JACK B. WEINSTEIN & MARGARET A. BERGER, WEINSTEIN'S FEDERAL EVIDENCE § 303.05 (2d ed. 1997) [hereinafter WEINSTEIN].

149. *Allen*, 442 U.S. at 157-60.

150. *Id.* at 157.

151. *Id.* at 157-58.

152. *Leary*, 395 U.S. at 36; *see also Allen*, 442 U.S. at 157.

153. *See, e.g.*, Turner v. United States, 396 U.S. 398, 418-19 (1969) (finding that illegal importation of heroin could be presumed from mere possession because no heroin is produced in the United States, whereas illegal importation of cocaine could not be presumed because cocaine is produced in the United States); United States v. Romano, 382 U.S. 136, 141, 144 (1965) (Court struck down law providing that presence at a still is sufficient to authorize conviction for possession of a still); *cf.* United States v. Gainey, 380 U.S. 63, 70-71 (1965) (interpreting same law as *Romano*, the Court held that presence at a still was sufficient to authorize conviction for distilling without a license because anyone present at the site was likely involved in the activity though the presence did not establish ownership).

154. If the factfinder were to rely solely on the presumption to find guilt, he or she would apparently have to apply the more rigorous "beyond a reasonable doubt" standard used for mandatory presumptions. WEINSTEIN, *supra* note 148, § 303.05[2][a] (citing *Allen*, 442 U.S. at 167).

dard would not be easy in this case. Money, unlike narcotics or unlicensed whiskey stills, is not a contraband item. The official could have acquired the funds from legal sources, or from illegal sources having no relation to domestic or foreign bribery.

Mandatory presumptions, on the other hand, have to satisfy a more stringent "reasonable doubt" standard because they leave no discretion to the factfinder.[155] A factfinder must find the elemental fact to exist if the prosecutor proves the existence of the basic or evidentiary fact. There could be no reasonable doubt that the elemental fact did not flow from the basic or evidentiary fact. It is unlikely that the court would find the possession of money disproportionate to one's salary and other legal sources of income to lead "beyond a reasonable doubt" to the conclusion that the money was corruptly obtained.

The United States could possibly avoid the constitutional problems arising from article IX by providing that only civil liability would attach to any violations of the illicit enrichment provision. Civil penalties do not trigger the same constitutional protections that criminal penalties do. Congress can, and does, create statutory presumptions that shift the burden of production (and arguably the burden of persuasion) from the plaintiff to the defendant.[156] These shifts have been upheld by the courts.[157]

While the penalties would be less severe, civil prosecution would give the United States leverage to prosecute suspected corruption without violating the Constitution. The "net worth" method of proof, used by the IRS to prosecute fraudulent tax evasion under the Internal Revenue Code's Crimes subchapter is one way U.S. law prosecutes the unjust enrichment of government officials without violating constitutional rights.[158] In addition, other U.S. ethics-in-government rules, described below, combat illicit enrichment without making it an actionable offense.

155. *Allen*, 442 U.S. at 157-60.

156. WEINSTEIN, *supra* note 148, § 301.02[2].

157. *See, e.g.*, United States v. Banco Cafetero Panama, 797 F.2d 1154, 1160 (2d Cir. 1986) (Congress permissibly placed burden on defendant to show proceeds from bank accounts were not traceable to drug transactions once government showed suspicion that property was drug related); Texas Dep't of Community Affairs v. Burdine, 450 U.S. 248, 254 (1981) (establishing a prima facie case of discrimination pursuant to Title VII creates a presumption-shifting burden of production to defendant).

158. *See* 26 U.S.C. § 7201 (1994).

2. *Ethics in Government*

Article III of the Convention creates only a "soft" commitment for states parties to institute standards for the "correct, honorable, and proper fulfillment of public functions," including requirements for government officials to report acts of corruption.[159] The United States already has comprehensive measures requiring government officials to adhere to certain ethical standards.

The most well-known, and perhaps most effective, weapon against corruption on the part of U.S. government officials is the financial disclosure statements required of all senior government executive branch employees. Each year, these individuals must report property interests greater than $1,000 (with a few exceptions); all income, from whatever source; and most purchases, sales, and exchanges in excess of $1,000 (again, with a few exceptions).[160]

Article III also provides for states parties to agree to consider establishing "systems of government hiring and procurement of goods and services that assure the openness, equity and efficiency of such systems." The U.S. Government has a highly regulated system of government procurement to ensure the fairness of the process to government vendors and to the American taxpayer. The Federal Acquisition Regulations are over 3,000 pages long.[161] The United States also regulates sales by U.S. companies to foreign governments. A special set of regulations relates only to defense items.[162]

These types of regulations can be an efficient tool in preventing bribery. One of the requirements, which limits the amount of commissions payable to foreign agents to $50,000 and requires that all commissions be disclosed, justified, and supported,[163] enabled the Department of Justice to prosecute a case against Lockheed, which allegedly paid a commission of $1 million to a foreign official.[164]

159. Convention, *supra* note 1, art. III(1).

160. 5 C.F.R. §§ 2634.301 - 2634.305 (1997).

161. Federal Acquisition Regulation (FAR), 48 C.F.R. §§ 1-51 (1997).

162. Department of Defense FAR Supp., 48 C.F.R. §§ 201-51 (1997).

163. 48 C.F.R. § 225.703-4 (1997). That provision is generally enforced through the certification requirements set out in 48 C.F.R. § 252.243-7027 (1997).

164. United States v. Lockheed Corp., No. 1:94-CR-226-01 (N.D. Ga. Jan. 27, 1995), 3 FCPA Rep. 699.176, 699.179.

C. *Comparison of the Convention's Enforcement Provisions and U.S. Law*

The Convention's provisions on extradition and multilateral judicial assistance will enhance the efforts of the United States and other OAS member states to investigate and prosecute corruption in the Americas, assuming ratification not only by the United States but by a large number of the other OAS member states.

1. *Extradition*

The Convention provides for mandatory extradition based on acts of corruption under the Convention in most cases. States parties are required to include the offenses provided for in the Convention among the extraditable offenses contained in the extradition treaties to which they are party.[165] Parties also undertake to include those offenses in any future extradition treaties into which they enter.[166] States parties that do not make extradition conditional on the existence of a treaty are required to recognize the offenses criminalized in the Convention as extraditable offenses between themselves.[167]

The only "soft" commitment in these provisions relates to those states parties that require extradition to be based on a treaty, but which are not party to a treaty with a particular country requesting extradition. In that case, states parties may, but are not required to, consider the IACAC itself to be an extradition treaty with respect to any offense criminalized under the Convention.[168]

In all cases, the Convention provides that extradition is subject to the requirements of the law of the requested state.[169]

U.S. law confers on the executive and judicial branches of the government the authority to extradite only if the requesting country and the United States have a binding treaty agreement.[170] The United States already has extradition treaties with all of the countries that have signed the IACAC,[171] although one of those treaties

165. Convention, *supra* note 1, art. XIII(2).

166. *Id.*

167. *Id.* art. XIII(4).

168. *Id.* art. XIII(3).

169. *Id.* art. XIII(5).

170. 18 U.S.C. § 3181 (1994). The U.S. Constitution would permit Congress to confer extradition authority on the executive branch by means of statute rather than by treaty, Grin v. Shine, 187 U.S. 181, 191 (1902), but Congress has not enacted such a law.

171. *See supra* note 2 (listing IACAC signatories).

is not currently in force.[172] Many of them are older treaties, however, and their efficacy is limited because extradition is restricted to offenses specifically listed in the treaty.[173]

The IACAC is not the first case of states using multilateral treaties to extend the number of offenses for which extradition is permitted under existing treaties. Both the Protocol Amending the Single Convention on Narcotic Drugs, 1961[174] and the United Nations Convention Against the Illicit Traffic in Narcotic Drugs and

---

172. Extradition Treaty, June 14, 1983, U.S.-Jam., SEN. TREATY DOC. 98-18 (entered into force July 7, 1991); Extradition Treaty, Dec. 4, 1982, U.S.-Costa Rica, SEN. TREATY DOC. 98-17 (entered into force Oct. 11, 1991); Extradition Treaty, May 4, 1978, U.S.-Mex., 31 U.S.T. 5059 (entered into force Jan. 25, 1980); Treaty on Extradition, May 24, 1973, U.S.-Para., 25 U.S.T. 967 (entered into force May 7, 1974); Treaty on Extradition, Apr. 6, 1973, U.S.-Uru., 35 U.S.T. 3197 (entered into force Apr. 11, 1984); Treaty on Extradition, Jan. 21, 1972, U.S.-Arg., TIAS No. 7,523 U.S.T. 3501 (entered into force Sept. 15, 1972); Treaty on Extradition, Dec. 3, 1971, *amended* June 28 and July 9, 1974, U.S.-Can., 27 U.S.T. 983 (entered into force March 22, 1976); Protocol Amending the Treaty on Extradition, Jan. 11, 1988, U.S.-Can., SEN. TREATY DOC. 101-17 (entered into force Nov. 26, 1991); Treaty of Extradition, Jan. 13, 1961, U.S.-Braz., 15 U.S.T. 2093 (entered into force Dec. 17, 1964); Additional Protocol to the Treaty of Extradition of January 13, 1961, June 18, 1962, U.S.-Braz., 15 U.S.T. 2112 (entered into force Dec. 17, 1964); Treaty with United Kingdom (Guyana), Dec. 22, 1931, 47 Stat. 2122 (entered into force June 24, 1935); Treaty on Extradition, Jan. 19 & 21, 1922, U.S.-Venez., 53 Stat. 1698 (entered into force Apr. 14, 1923); Treaty of Extradition, Apr. 18, 1911, U.S.-El Sal., 37 Stat. 1516 (entered into force July 10, 1911); Treaty on Extradition, June 19, 1909, U.S.-Dom. Rep., 36 Stat. 2468 (entered into force Aug. 2, 1910); Extradition Convention, Jan. 15, 1909, U.S.-Hond., 37 Stat. 1616 (entered into force July 10, 1912); Supplementary Extradition Convention, Feb. 21, 1927, U.S.-Hond., 45 Stat. 2489 (entered into force June 5, 1928); Convention Providing for the Mutual Extradition of Fugitives from Justice, Mar. 1, 1905, U.S.-Nic., 35 Stat. 1869 (entered into force July 14, 1907); Treaty for the Mutual Extradition of Criminals, U.S.-Haiti, Aug. 9, 1904, 34 Stat. 2858 (entered into force June 28, 1905); Treaty Providing for the Mutual Extradition of Fugitives from Justice, May 25, 1904, U.S.-Pan., 34 Stat. 2851 (entered into force May 8, 1905); Treaty on Extradition, Apr. 21, 1900, U.S.-Bol., 32 Stat. 1857 (entered into force Jan. 22, 1902); Treaty Providing for the Extradition of Criminals, Apr. 17, 1900, U.S.-Chile, 32 Stat. 1850 (entered into force June 26, 1902); Treaty Providing for the Extradition of Criminals, Nov. 28, 1899, U.S.-Peru, 31 Stat. 1921 (entered into force Feb. 22, 1901); Convention for the Extradition of Criminals, U.S.-Neth., June 2, 1887, 26 Stat. 1481 (entered into force July 11, 1889); Supplementary Treaty on Extradition (extending extradition treaty to Colonies, including Suriname), Jan. 18, 1904, U.S.-Neth., 33 Stat. 2257 (entered into force Aug. 28, 1904); Extradition Treaty, June 28, 1872, U.S.-Ecuador, 19 Stat. 199 (entered into force Nov. 12, 1873), Supplementary Extradition Treaty, Sept. 22, 1939, U.S.-Ecuador, 55 Stat. 1196 (entered into force May 29, 1941).

The United States has an extradition treaty with Colombia, Extradition Treaty Between the United States of America and the Republic of Colombia, Sep. 14, 1979, SEN. TREATY DOC. 97-8 (entered into force Mar. 4, 1982), but the Colombian Supreme Court declared it without effect because Colombia had not ratified it in compliance with required procedures. *See* 4 ABELL &RISTAU, *supra* note 82, at A-289.

173. 4 ABELL & RISTAU, *supra* note 82, at 14.

174. Amendment of the Single Convention on Narcotic Drugs, 1961, Mar. 15, 1972, TIAS No. 8,118 at 1,439 (entered into force Aug. 8, 1975).

Psychotropic Substances[175] were used to extend extradition capability for all significant drug offenses to those countries sharing bilateral extradition treaties that ratified the UN conventions.

2. *Double Jeopardy*

One important issue the Convention does not address in its article on extradition is double jeopardy. The principle that persons should not be tried twice for the same acts or offenses is firmly grounded in both the common law and civil law, where it is termed *non bis in idem*. For the United States, the omission does not raise constitutional issues because the Fifth Amendment's prohibition against double jeopardy does not prohibit the punishment of the same acts or offenses by different sovereigns.[176] Though there is no constitutional prohibition, most extradition treaties to which the United States is party contain double jeopardy clauses and thus preclude extradition when a person has already been convicted or acquitted of the same offense.[177] Some treaties, particularly those with civil law countries, preclude extradition for the same "acts." Interpreting what constitutes the same "acts" or "offenses" for double jeopardy purposes is often difficult.[178]

This issue is thrown into sharp relief by the Convention's transnational bribery provisions. The Juridical Committee Report recommends that the states parties consider whether a person who has been convicted of bribery by the country of the government official in question can then be tried by the country of his nationality, or whether the principle of *non bis in idem* applies.[179] Multilateral consensus on this issue would facilitate uniform application and enforcement of the Convention. Though the states parties

175. United Nations Convention Against Illicit Traffic in Narcotic Drugs and Psychotropic Substances, opened for signature Dec. 20, 1988, SEN. TREATY DOC. 101-4 (entered into force Nov. 11, 1990).

176. United States v. Abbate, 359 U.S. 187 (double jeopardy clause no bar to federal and state prosecution of the same acts). The same principle has been extended to prosecutions by other sovereign nations. *See, e.g.*, Chukwurah v. United States, 813 F. Supp. 161, 167 (E.D.N.Y 1993).

177. 4 ABELL & RISTAU, *supra* note 82, at 100-01. The Restatement suggests that the principle of *non bis in idem* may have become customary international law by virtue of the International Covenant on Civil and Political Rights. RESTATEMENT 3D, *supra* note 113, § 476 cmt. c.

178. Sindona v. Grant, 619 F.2d 167, 176-79 (2d Cir. 1980) (noting broad range of possible interpretations for "same offense" and "same conduct"); United States v. Jurado-Rodriguez, 907 F. Supp. 568, 577-78 (E.D.N.Y 1995) (indicating that *non bis in idem* may provide broader protection for defendants in extradition cases than the Fifth Amendment to the U.S. Constitution in U.S. domestic prosecutions).

179. Juridical Committee Report, *supra* note 10, § III.2.a.vii.

could agree that *non bis in idem* does not apply (so long as it is not customary international law), considerations of efficiency and fairness suggest that only one country prosecute the alleged offender, with full assistance and cooperation provided by the other country(ies) involved, at least once there is substantial equivalence in the legal regimes of member states and in the capacity of countries to enforce their laws effectively. Until then, countries with strong enforcement capabilities will be reluctant to defer to countries that may not, for example, impose adequate penalties.

Once the states parties have enacted domestic laws criminalizing foreign and domestic bribery, the United States will be able to extradite on the basis of the acts of corruption delineated in the Convention, subject to a showing of sufficient evidence warranting extradition.[180]

3. *Assistance and Cooperation*

OAS Convention article XIV, on international assistance and cooperation, is not as far-reaching as the extradition provision. While establishing an obligation on states parties to afford each other the "widest measure of mutual assistance," the scope of the obligation appears to be defined by existing national laws and treaties. Thus, the Convention itself does not expand the nature or scope of mutual assistance, nor does it require states parties to enact any other laws. Rather, it exhorts states parties to cooperate to facilitate the investigation and prosecution of acts of corruption.

In the United States, international assistance in criminal matters is not limited solely to judicial acts—prosecutors and the police also play active roles in enforcement.[181] When there is no need to follow judicial formalities in the means of procuring documents, the U.S. enforcement officers will often help their foreign counterparts by obtaining information, serving process, and providing general investigative cooperation and assistance.[182]

---

180. The United States will be able to extradite to a requesting state for alleged violations of the Convention's illicit enrichment provisions, even if the United States does not make illicit enrichment an act of corruption, unless the underlying treaty contains a dual criminality provision. These provisions provide for extradition so long as the offense is punishable under the laws of the United States and of the treaty partners. *See, e.g.*, Extradition Treaty, Dec. 4, 1982, U.S.-Costa Rica, SEN. TREATY DOC. 98-17, art. II (entered into force Dec. 4, 1982). Dual criminality is not constitutionally required before the United States can extradite. *See* Factor v. Laubenheimer, 290 U.S. 276, 290 (1933).

181. *See* 3 ABELL & RISTAU, *supra* note 82, at 17-18.

182. *Id.* at 18. For example, the United States has several agreements regarding the exchange of information in securities matters. *Id.* at 102.

When more formal cooperation is required, the United States can assist foreign counterparts when authorized by treaty or by statute. The United States is party to several bilateral treaties on mutual assistance in criminal matters, several of which are with OAS countries that have signed the Convention.[183] The treaties generally provide for assistance in locating persons, serving documents, producing and authenticating government documents, and producing and authenticating some business records and other non-government documents, conducting searches and seizures (only if the request would warrant such action under the laws of the requested country), and obtaining testimony of witnesses. All of these functions are subject to U.S. constitutional limitations, and most permit governments to refuse to render assistance on a variety of grounds.

In addition to these treaties, U.S. law contains statutory authorization for international judicial assistance on criminal matters in several areas. U.S. law permits the transmission of letters rogatory issued by foreign courts through either official or unofficial means.[184] U.S. law permits district courts to order service of foreign judicial documents on persons resident in their district.[185] Service is also permitted without a court order, although many civil law jurisdictions will request court assistance because unofficial service is not deemed proper under their laws.[186] In practice, service is usually made through the use of letters rogatory.[187] U.S. courts may also, but are not required to, order the production of documents or testimony of witness in connection with foreign criminal proceedings.[188]

183. Treaty on Mutual Assistance in Criminal Matters, Apr. 11, 1991, U.S.-Pan., SEN. TREATY DOC. 102-15 (entered into force Sept. 6, 1995); Treaty on Mutual Legal Assistance in Criminal Matters, Dec. 4, 1990, U.S.-Arg., SEN. TREATY DOC. 102-18 (entered into force Feb. 9, 1993); Mutual Legal Assistance Cooperation Treaty, Dec. 9, 1987, U.S.-Mex., SEN. TREATY DOC. 100-13 (entered into force May 3, 1991); Mutual Assistance in Law Enforcement Matters Treaty, Aug. 15, 1986, U.S.-Haiti, T.I.A.S. No. 11,389 (entered into force Aug. 15, 1986); Treaty on Mutual Legal Assistance in Criminal Matters, May 6, 1991, U.S.-Uru., SEN. TREATY DOC. 102-19 (entered into force Apr. 15, 1994).

Certain multilateral conventions, like the United Nations Convention Against Illicit Traffic in Narcotic Drugs and Psychotropic Substances, *supra* note 175, art. VII, also contain mutual judicial assistance provisions.

184. 28 U.S.C. § 1781 (1994). Letters rogatory are a much more cumbersome method of providing and obtaining international judicial assistance than are multilateral assistance treaties.

185. 28 U.S.C. § 1696(a) (1994).

186. 3 ABELL & RISTAU, *supra* note 82, at 200-01.

187. *Id.*

188. 28 U.S.C. § 1782 (1994).

The Convention should make these cooperation mechanisms more effective. Particularly important for Latin American countries is the requirement of cooperation through administrative, and not just judicial, channels. The designations by at least two states parties to date of central authorities suggests that the extra-judicial channel permitted by the Convention will be a viable one.

4. *Measures Regarding Property*

Article XV calls upon states parties to provide each other with the "broadest possible" means of assistance in the "identification, tracing, freezing, seizure and forfeiture of property or proceeds obtain abroad." It also suggests that, where possible, states parties should transfer all or part of such money or proceeds if doing so would assist in the investigation of the underlying proceeding.

Most of the mutual assistance treaties contain provisions relating to the freezing of assets and/or forfeiture of property acquired through illegal activity.[189] U.S. law permits the Attorney General to share with a foreign country forfeited or seized property or proceeds when the foreign country participated in the seizure or forfeiture of the property.[190] This is a device used by the United States to encourage other states to participate in the investigation and prosecution of international crimes.

These property measures should, again, enhance the ability of states parties to investigate and prosecute cases of corruption.

V. CONCLUSION

The Convention is a pathbreaking effort to combat official corruption in the Americas. If ratified by a large number of member states and fully and consistently implemented, it could be a dramatic step in promoting ethics in government, and in deterring official corruption for commercial gain. The Convention takes into account and in some respects clarifies U.S. foreign antibribery laws. In the area of illicit enrichment, it takes a different legal approach to the "demand side" of corruption than the United States—one that cannot be adopted by the United States consistent with the U.S. Constitution. There may, however, be ways to

189. 3 ABELL & RISTAU, *supra* note 82, at 145-46.
190. 18 U.S.C. § 981(i)(1) (1994).

modify this Convention provision so as to cure those constitutional defects; this Article raises two possibilities in that regard.

The Convention also attempts to deal with the key issue of enforcement in the transnational sphere through its cooperative provisions. Particularly important are the extradition provisions, the denial of bank secrecy laws, the bar on political offense claims as shields for refusing to cooperate, and the mutual legal assistance obligations.

Although the Convention's rapid entry into force and attraction of a number of states to ratification are encouraging signs, much more needs to be done for the Convention to achieve its potential. Those states that have not yet ratified it should do so promptly, and with minimal reservations. Though the "escape clauses" expressly permit countries to avoid passing legislation on the issues of transnational bribery and illicit enrichment if they are constitutionally or legally unable to do so without taking a reservation to the Convention, states parties should justify their actions under those provisions to prevent eroding the Convention's integrity. Model legislation or clauses should be developed quickly, so that the momentum for implementation will not be lost and uniformity will be promoted. States will also need to cooperate and negotiate in those instances, which are sure to arise, where states parties have overlapping jurisdiction. The Convention, pathbreaking as it is, is just the first step on a long and assuredly difficult road. Having seized leadership on the issue of corruption, OAS member states should focus on staying the course.

[22]

Crime, Law & Social Change **29:** 225–249, 1998.

Internal strategies against corruption: Guidelines for preventing and combating corruption in police authorities

PETER POERTING & WERNER VAHLENKAMP
Bundeskriminalamt, Criminological Research Unit, Wiesbaden, Germany

Abstract. While corruption is not an entirely new phenomenon in Germany, the number of cases suggests that proactive measures should be taken to strengthen prevention and detection. This article proposes a number of measures which, used separately and in combination, aid prevention and detection. It then proposes a wider management approach to dealing with corruption which ranges from general to specific strategies and actions that are intended to prevent corruption, to design out the circumstances in which it may occur and to provide means of detecting areas of risk and vulnerability. The article particularly focuses on police organisations but has applied relevance to all public sector organisations.

Introduction

Corruption is not really a new criminal phenomenon in Germany; it has always been around. The rising number of registered corruption offenses in recent years allows the assumption that – in contrast to the past – light is being cast on a larger percentage of undetected crimes, either through intensified activities on the part of the law enforcement authorities or as a consequence of an increased sensitivity on the part of the public and the media. On the other hand serious experts assume that the number of corruption cases is continously increasing. Table 1 shows the number of registered corruption offenses in the Federal Republic of Germany for the last four years.[1].

While the number of offenses committed by bribers (the 'payers') fluctuates at about 2000 per year the number of offenses by the 'paid' (employees in all branches of public administration taking bribes) is rather continously increasing. The relation between payers and paid has fundamentally changed in these few years: while the number of bribers' offenses in 1994 nearly doubled those of the receiving public employees, offenses of the latter were considerably higher than those committed by payers in 1997. Compared to corruption in the public sector only few corruption offenses in the private sector are reported to police authorities.

In 1994 a Police Corruption Survey was started in Germany. It provides additional information from police criminal intelligence for all corruption proceedings handled by police. Most data are gathered by local or regional

Table 1. Registered offenses.

Year Offense	1994	1995	1996	1997
Taking bribes in the public sector	*1142*	*1039*	*1902*	*2307*
– *Vorteilsannahme,* Sect. 331 Penal Code	291	241	621	1068
– *Bestechlichkeit,* Sect. 332 Penal Code	851	818	1281	1239
Offering bribes to the public sector	*2100*	*1816*	*2391*	*1899*
– *Vorteilsgewährung,* Sect. 333 Penal Code	194	150	474	406
– *Bestechung,* Sect. 334 Penal Code	1906	1666	1917	1493
Corruption in the private sector				
– *Angestelltenbestechung*	not available	161	149	198

Table 2. Proceedings and offenses.

	1994	1995	1996
Number of police proceedings	258	291	410
Number of registered offenses	11241	15969	9505

offices of the police forces of the German federal states (in Germany most police tasks come under the jurisdiction of the 16 federal states). The Police Corruption Survey is based on an evaluation of current police investigations, while in the Police Crime Statistics only completed investigations are registered, so that the figures of both cannot be compared to each other. The Survey data are aggregated at a federal level by Bundeskriminalamt, the federal criminal police office. A second survey was carried out for the years 1995 and 1996.[2] Some figures are only available for the years 1995 and 1996.

The number of proceedings has increased though the number of registered offenses was decreasing (Table 2). The increased number of investigations can – among other reasons – be explained by the fact that investigations often produce new information and additional suspects which gives rise to new investigations.

As the Police Crime Statistics already illustrated most reported corruption offenses are targeted against the different branches of public administration (Table 3). In addition Table 4 shows that the predominance of public construction authorities regarded in former years seems to decrease.

During the reported periods public procurement was the main focus of corruption. A considerable risk of corruptive influence also exists in branches

Table 3. Targets of corruption.

(number of respective proccedings)	1995	1996
Public administration	203	279
Police and the Judicial	80	113
Private sector enterprises	15	23

Table 4. Branches of public administration.

(by percentage of suspects)	1994	1995	1996
Construction authorities	38,8%	25,2%	21,8%
Police	15,9%	13,0%	4,4%
Other	29,8%	54,2%	68,6%

of civil administration where permits and licenses (work permits, residence permits, driver's licenses, construction permits etc.) are issued.

While the number of suspected payers is decreasing, the number of suspects having been paid tends to increase (Table 5). That corresponds to the results from Police Crime Statistics (Table 1). Employees and responsibles of enterprises obtain a rising predominance among the suspected payers (Table 5a).

More than 50% of the suspected public employees continued to perform their respective duties for more than five years, the vast majority of them for more than 10 years. In most of the surveyed cases the corruptive relationship between payers and paid persisted for a minimum of three years. That leads to the distinction of two patterns of corruption: situational corruption and planned corruption. While the first develops spontaneously at a given moment

Table 5. Suspects.

	1994	1995	1996
'Payers'	1080	920	807
'Paid'	477	410	832
Total	1557	1330	1639

Table 5a. Background of suspected 'payers'.

	1994	1995	1996
Citizens	52,1%	47,3%	27,6%
Business	40,0%	50,0%	66,5%
Criminals	7,9%	2,3%	5,8%

Table 5b. Function of suspected recipients.

	1995	1996
Clerical function	55,6%	51,5%
Managerial function	31,2%	32,3%
Unknown	13,2%	16,2%

without preparation, the latter is regularly prepared and the resulting relationship tends to persist over a long period. Table 6 shows that the percentage of proceedings concerning situational corruption increased continously during the reported years 1994 to 1996.

In 1997 the German Penal Code was modified with respect to corruption-related crime:

- some statutory offenses were modified in order to facilitate their application,
- threats of punishment were stiffened,
- new statutory offenses were created.

Figures concerning these new or modified offenses are only available from the reported year 1998 on.

Table 6. Situational vs. planned corruption.

	1994	1995	1996
Number of proceedings concerning situational corruption	55	79	128
Percentage of all proceedings	21,3%	27,1%	31,2%

Preventing corruption

All branches of public administration are susceptible to corruption – as the cases that have become known illustrate. Police officers and judicial authorities must accept the fact that they are going to be measured against particularly strict criteria because, as the keepers of law and order, an above-average degree of integrity and resistance to corruption are demanded of them. Therefore, a successful fight against corruption must begin internally. Instead of waiting for individual cases to become known, systematic preventive measures are required. The continuous implementation of measures that have already been discussed and recommended in the federal, state and local administrations clearly suffer from the lack of coordination and the preference for insular solutions, in the form of the realization of only isolated measures. One of the causes for this is the lack of model solutions.

However, corruption is a system and corruption has a system. Therefore, it can only be combated with a system. Anti-corruption measures on the government-agency level must, therefore, be bundled together into a systematic concept of prevention. In view of the large number of requisite measures that need to be harmonized, centralized coordination of these should be undertaken by an authorized (anti-) corruption commissioner, who also acts as an internal and external point of contact and performs corruption-risk analyses. Under certain circumstances, this function can be linked with the establishment of an internal auditing system.

The aforementioned framework concept, which can be described as being 'state of the art', is to be understood as an aid to orientation and as an aid to formulate tailor-made anti-corruption strategies in police authorities. It is a way to prevent and combat corruption in government agencies and namely police authorities in a systematic way.

Defining corruption

Bundeskriminalamt's criminological research unit has already intensively dealt with the phenomenon of 'corruption' and with adequate means of prevention.[3] The following definition of the term was assumed:

Corruption is:

- the misuse of any public office, a political mandate or function in trade and industry;
- to the advantage of another person;
- committed upon the inducement of such other person or at the officials own initiative;
- with the intent to procure some benefit for himself or for another person;

- resulting in or expected to result in (pecuniary) damage or other detriment to the public (in the case of a public or political function) or for a company (in the case of an business function).

This definition of the term is the basis for the following anti-corruption concept. It also comprises cases of so-called 'step-by-step corruption', namely preparatory acts or acts aimed at creating a climate in which corruption is acceptable, aimed at the later misuse of office (e.g. the mere granting of benefits with the goal of 'cultivating a good working climate').

Identifying corruption: indicators of corruption

Indicators are not evidence. Therefore, they mostly do not have any or only very little meaning, when considered alone. Only if they occur repeatedly, frequently or in certain constellations they are suitable for contributing towards the growth of a suspicion.

The handling of corruption-indicator grids assumes a particular sensitivity on the part of the user. If used excessively or thoughtlessly, they can lead to unjustified suspicions and inadmissible conclusions, instead of making a positive contribution towards the fight against corruption. Under no circumstances should such a grid of indicators be used with the goal of initiating a 'witch-hunt'.

1. Neutral indicators

Neutral indicators are to be seen, as a rule, in connection with personal manners and behavior. Not infrequently, they are socially accepted or even favorably interpreted by the viewer. Nevertheless, these are indicators which are found relatively frequently in corruption structures.

Examples:

- Lavish lifestyle that can not be explained by a person's income; presentation of status symbols;
- Suddenly changing lifestyle;
- Social and personal problems (dependency, addiction, indebtedness, bragging, etc.);
- Outside employment that is critically close to one's official duties;
- Acceptance of invitations (e.g. on the occasion of visits to trade shows or companies or local inspections); paying for food and beverages for others in restaurants, bars, etc.;

- Frequent private meetings with public contractors or bidders; participation in private or business events;
- Granting unusual special terms for purchases (e.g. purchase price / discounts / financing / reduction in the usual waiting periods);
- Delivery of lavish 'advertising' gifts (including to one's home address); unusual generosity on the part of contractors; offers to sponsor activities;
- Presuming oneself to be indispensable: giving up one's free time, coming to work despite being ill (to avoid insight by others into one's work);
- Additional work assumed on one's own initiative (e.g. going to allegedly important meetings outside the office on days off);
- Taking work (cases) home;
- Inexplicable isolation; taciturnity towards colleagues and superiors;
- Sudden, inexplicable changes of opinion (e.g. advocating a project which was previously rejected);
- Inexplicable refusal to accept reassignments or promotions (in particular, if this means an improvement);
- Unusually casual tone between employees and contractors or applicants;
- Absence of complaints or conflicts where they are customary or to be expected; impeccable processing of difficult cases where the employee does not have sufficient specialized knowledge / or expertise.

2. Specific indicators

In contrast to the indicators that are neutral with respect to corruption, corruption-specific indicators are to be assessed as warning signals or signs, which – in particular in cases of repeated or simultaneous occurrence – should lead to the suspicion of existing irregularities.

Examples:

- Inexplicable decisions which should not have been made in this fashion;
- Different assessment or processing of cases having the same or very similar facts;
- Abuse, unilateral interpretation or overuse of one's discretionary powers;
- Waiver of controls or audits, even though there is reasonable cause;
- Manipulating the handling of a case by other departments or employees within an agency or police authority;
- Deliberately bypassing decision-makers or superiors in critical cases;
- Repeated exercise of outside appointments without any plausible explanation of their relation to work;
- Inadmissible expansion of the powers delegated;

- Entering into an agreement with unfavorable terms which bind an agency for a long time;
- Repeated preference for or support of certain bidders or contractors during the procedure for awarding contracts ('purveyors to the court');
- Noticeable indulgence during contract negotiations;
- Missing receipt or clock stamp on correspondence with bidders and contractors;
- Guideline made by a superior that a critical case be processed 'favorably' without any additional reviews;
- Inexplicable acceleration of a case;
- Neglecting doubts as to the lawfulness of an act, bypassing regulations (e.g. waiving the imposition of special conditions or duties, ignoring the principle of thrift);
- Sealing off individual departments or employees or allowing them to become independent, supposed uncontrollability;
- Bypassing public tenders; lack of variety in offers;
- Splitting/reducing the volume of an order in order to enable a discretionary award;
- Procurement of unnecessary or technologically obsolete logistics systems;
- Purchases at excessive prices that are not in line with market conditions;
- Splitting or duplicating remittances of invoice amounts;
- Frequent subsequent amendments to and supposed arithmetic errors in bidding documents;
- Noticeable discrepancy between invoice and offer amounts;
- Missing or superficial records of decisions, meetings, local inspections, etc.;
- Disappearance of important bidding or contract documents;
- Superficial processing of work; missing or deficient records;
- Playing out of assumed positions of power by contractors;
- Constant visits by contractors to certain employees or visits only when certain employees are present;
- Repeated official trips to certain companies without any plausible work reason (in particular, when not really necessary overnight stays occur);
- Complaints by contractors or administrative customers who were bypassed in competitions or disadvantaged when their applications were reviewed;
- Unambiguous statements / references by employees to incorrect procedures, rumors within a certain environment.

Moreover, there are certain indicators which occur, preferably in conjunction with the performance of jurisdictional police duties in the operative sector or environment, such as:

- Media publications about internal police or investigatory matters;
- Disappearance of criminal files or parts thereof;
- Private possession of internal police documents by unauthorized parties;
- Prior knowledge of crime-fighting procedural measures (i.e. searches, arrests);
- Inexplicable revelation of the identity of undercover agents or confidential informants;
- Supposed 'investigatory successes' on the part of a (law) enforcement official or any 'investigatory successes' which can not be explained;
- Preferential treatment of / aiding perpetrators (e.g. taking detainees out of prison without a plausible reason);
- Being unable to locate a definitely expected piece of evidence during a search;
- Contacts made with the press or representatives of certain branches of business (e.g. security firms, detective agencies) while on duty and intensified off-duty;
- Noticeable close, and even private contacts between an investigator and criminals or with the criminal milieu (scene);
- Offer made by a victim to take goods from a scene of crime;
- Outside employment, in particular, in detective agencies, (credit) information bureaus or security firms, in the criminal scene or in other critical branches /departments (e.g. with a view to exploiting police knowledge);
- Offer of services by suspects provided for free or at favorable rates (e.g. expensive rental cars at special rates, offers with a sexual background);
- Inexplicable waiver of the taking of evidence;
- Explicit waiver of accompaniment by another official or bypassing the four-eyes principle when going out to work;
- Attempts to protract the investigation;
- Playing down or ignoring possibly important indications or suspicious circumstances during pending criminal cases;
- Absence of official reactions to events that might be relevant to the prosecution of crime.

Preventing and combating corruption: guideline for police authorities

This guideline to prevent and combat corruption consists of a general part with recommendations aimed at abstract corruption-related threats and risks arising from police tasks and its personnel, and a specific part oriented to a particular department or task, which is aimed primarily at certain target groups or areas within a police authority (organizational units, functions and tasks) facing a concrete risk of corruptibility. The recommendations of the general part may be adopted by any police or other government agency in this or in a similar form. The recommendations of the special part correspond to a 'set of building blocks', from which every department can compile a suitable bundle of measures. Due to the dynamics of official and task structures within a police authority, the concept needs to be constantly reviewed and updated. When implementing recommended anti-corruption measures there can be target conflicts with other guidelines or attempts to reform administrations ('lean state'). Such target conflicts require a thorough consideration of the diverging interests and a corresponding prioritization. The structure and wording of these conceptual ideas are characterized by the following guidelines:

- Preventing corruption is an urgent matter in politics and in public administrations. The willingness to act should not depend on the question of whether the act of corruption has already become public knowledge or not.
- Preventing corruption does not mean a distrust of individuals, but corresponds to the requirement to keep the organizational structures clean. This is both a legal and an ethical standard.
- Corruption has a broad range. Not all practices are basically illegal. Prevention considerations must also incorporate legally unobjectionable, but ethically or morally reprehensible acts (i.e. 'cultivating good relationships', 'services rendered out of friendship').
- The requisite acceptance for effective counter-measures begins with the widespread ostracism of this form of crime. Preventing corruption thus begins with sensitization and clarification measures. This is most effective in the form of personal discussions.
- Preventing corruption should not lead to the stigmatization of certain organizational units or employees, even if the degree of susceptibility to corruption is seen as being high.

Preventing corruption basically requires the acceptance and the understanding of all of the members of the organization. To this extent, the existence of a comprehensible model, to which employees can orient themselves (corporate identity), will essentially support the efforts to successfully prevent corruption within an agency. Such a model should contribute towards allowing every employee to identify with his or her agency and employer and to develop a high degree of loyalty. It also serves to reinforce the feeling of community among employees.

General anti-corruption measures

General measures and recommendations to prevent corruption are independent of any particular task or department. They are directed towards the abstract threats and risks to which the entire organization or the staff in general are exposed. They are aimed at the heads of the government agency, or the organization as a whole, and at employees. During their implementation, managers have a special responsibility, due to their duties of administrative and work supervision as well as to their function as a role model.

1. Formulation of a code of conduct

The code of conduct or code of ethics for public servants recommended by the United Nations essentially comprises standards which police employees should also adopt.

Police employees . . .

. . . must recognize without any reservations that their official function is a position of trust which obliges them to act in the interests of the general public.

. . . must exercise their office with integrity and loyalty to their employer and perform the tasks assigned to them lawfully and conscientiously.

. . . must perform their tasks with fairness and impartiality. They may not unjustly favor or prejudice anyone or misuse the official powers transferred to them in any way.

. . . may not use their public office or official powers to promote their own interests. They may not undertake actions, or aim for positions or offices or pursue financial, economic or other comparable interests, which are or could be incompatible with their official functions.

. . . must ensure that they lead settled lives whose economic and social circumstances are orderly and they must ensure that their private lives do not give rise to any impairment of their official duties.

. . . may not directly or indirectly demand, accept promises for or accept any gifts or other benefits related to their official function or to the fulfillment of their official duties or which could affect their judgments.

. . . must report all (part time) employment outside the agency to their employers. Such outside employment may not adversely affect the public's trust in the impartial performance of their official duties.

. . . are obliged to preserve official secrets and to treat all of the information acquired in connection with their duties confidentially, unless they are explicitly released from this obligation.

Police employees must also comply with this code of conduct even after quitting the service.

Action: The code of conduct will be issued to all employees, who will acknowledge receipt in writing, and will be explained by superiors.

2. Communication of recommendations for conduct

Every police employee can make a personal contribution towards combating corruption. In addition to accepting and supporting the measures taken to prevent corruption, this contribution lies especially in the critical review of one's own official and private conduct as well as in a certain alertness at work. To this extent, individual recommendations of conduct are based on the code of conduct. The following is recommended for all police employees:

- Ostracize corruption and make a contribution towards increasing the willingness to ostracize corruption in your environment.
- Help to develop and promote a positive community spirit. A sense of community contributes towards preventing corruption.
- Accept anti-corruption measures, even if the freedom to act or make decisions is thus restricted.
- Perform your duties correctly and conscientiously. You do not need any rewards or presents for this.
- Send clear signals during your contacts with people outside the agency that you can not be bribed and that your power to make decisions can not be influenced by gifts or promises.
- Take a particularly critical view of official files and decisions which affect individual interests and bring favors or disadvantages to individuals.
- Keep your official and private interests and projects strictly apart and do not use your official function or position to pursue private interests.
- Speak with your superior or with the (anti-)corruption commissioner if an attempt has been made to bribe you. Do not get involved in attempts to cover such acts up!
- Do not pass on any official internal data or information not intended for the recipient or the public at work or privately, not even if good friends or acquaintances ask you to do so.
- Do not carry your private problems over to your duties and do not offer third parties any opportunity to use their knowledge of such problems to influence official acts or your official judgment.

– Promote the reputation of your agency through your own exemplary conduct both inwardly and outwardly.

Your exemplary resistance to corruption will communicate itself to others.

Action: The recommendations of conduct will be conveyed to all employees as part of other educational measures (e.g. training and advanced training, official meetings, personnel discussions, leaflet).

3. Appointment of a corruption commissioner

The corruption commissioner is the direct point of contact in all questions relating to the prevention and combating of corruption within the agency. He or she advises, receives information, assesses suspicious circumstances and recommends suitable solutions and counter-measures. He or she is responsible for making the decision to inform the head of the department if the suspicions appear to be warranted. The corruption commissioner is given the opportunity to receive further training in the areas of 'corruption and preventing corruption' and to exchange experiences with the corruption commissioners in other agencies.

Depending on the need, 'ombudsmen'[4] can be designated in staff councils, who will be directly accessible to all employees as additional points of contact for persons seeking advice and for providers of information. The ombudsmen will be advised by the corruption commissioner and if involved, will maintain a constant dialogue with the corruption commissioner. Ombudsmen have a purely advisory and care-taking function. If necessary, they will act as intermediaries between petitioners and the corruption commissioner, his or her direct superiors and other control instances, but do not make any decisions on reactions or counter-measures. The corruption commissioner will have an indicator grid at his or her disposal to assess information received and possibly corrupted behavior.

Action: The head of the agency will appoint a corruption commissioner.
If necessary, the staff council will designate one or more ombudsmen.

4. Sensitization of police employees

The prevention of corruption demands a careful procedure and assumes a high degree of trust among the (potentially) affected parties. Corruption prevention measures that are systematically enforced and have a long-term orientation begin, therefore, with the sensitization and education of all police employees. This is the constant task of the corruption commissioner, who starts and maintains the awareness process as both the initiator and the driving force behind the process. Managers are required to support this project.

During the initial phase, managers will be the focus of the sensitization activities, in terms of 'training the trainers', as they will subsequently train their employees. Over the course of the successive development, there can be a focus on especially susceptible areas of work (e.g. activities with outside contacts). However, a stigmatization of the respective organizational units is to be avoided at all costs.

The corruption commissioner can be consulted by individual organizational units or other target groups for educational or advisory discussions.

Action:

- Offering internal training events (the phenomenology of corruption, recognizing manipulations, approaches to prevention, etc.);
- Publishing an educational brochure with the most important information on the subject of corruption;
- Publications in internal bulletins on certain subjects and problems related to corruption;
- Providing occurence-related, individual education, advice and assistance through the corruption commissioner.

5. Establishment of an internal auditing unit

Internal auditing is an instrument of management. It supports the duties of administrative and work supervision and the monitoring of the organizational structure and the processing of operations in the form of the implementation of auditing activities. Another focal task of internal auditing may be the internal prevention of corruption. Internal auditing conducts risks analyses, initiates general and specific anti-corruption measures within the agency and supports their implementation.

Action: Every (larger) police authority will establish an Internal Auditing Unit. In addition to the actual auditing assignment the task of preventing corruption within the police force will be transferred to the Internal Auditing Unit.

6. Performance of risk analyses

As a constant task, the Internal Auditing Unit (or the Corruption Commissioner) will examine the organizational structure and the operating processes of the police authority for areas of risk as well as susceptibilities and weak spots, which can induce or favor corruption. Increased susceptibility can exist, in particular, wherever there are outside contacts (e.g. police presence in the public, conduct of investigations, exercise of local inspections) and/or decisions are made or prepared, which could favor or disadvantage third parties (e.g. awards of public orders). Even dealings with sensitive data (e.g.

search data) are to be designated as such an area of risk. On the basis of the risk analysis, target-group-oriented concepts to prevent corruption can be developed and adequate counter-measures or other preventive measures and control mechanisms can be installed as needed.

Action: The Internal Auditing Unit (or the Corruption Commissioner) will perform risk analyses for the police organizational structure and operating processes as a regular task. This task can also be linked to specific monitoring activities.

7. Monitoring outside employment

Outside employment can not only have a negative impact on the deployability and motivation of police employees, but also can represent possible 'docking areas' and gateways to corruption. In police work, this applies particularly to such sidelines which could be closely related to police work or police interests (e.g. security services, detective agencies or public contractors of all kinds). Here the need for information by businesses or by the media (e.g. prospects for access to data) can play a significant role. Due to their basic importance in the prevention of corruption, taking stock of and auditing sidelines is a major prerequisite for a realistic assessment of the potential for risk. This measure is thus an important component of risk analysis.

At the order of the Human Resources Department, Internal Auditing Unit the Corruption Commissioner will review applications for the approval of sidelines and will indicate any possible risks (compatibility with duties, possible conflicts of interest, susceptibility to corruption). This also applies to already approved and reported outside employment. Examples of possible questions:

Could the employer of this outside employment see an advantage in the applicant being a member of the police force (e.g. accesss to data, police know-how on security issues)? Could the employer derive a benefit from knowledge about the planning and activities of the police? Does the applicant have to rely on up-to-date work know-how to perform this job? Is the pay for this job comparatively generous?

Actions: All officers are required to provide a statement about any sidelines that they might have. A statement of the effect that they do not have any such outside employment is required. The issue of outside employment should be addressed in the code of conduct and be included in the sensitization process.

8. Accepting rewards and gifts
Regulations pertaining to the acceptance of rewards and gifts – as provided in Germany for all public employees – are a major orientation aid with respect to preventing corruption when delineating the permitted scope of action from actions with a criminal intent. These regulations must be emphatically communicated to all employees.

Actions: The corruption commissioner will handle this subject as part of educational measures to prevent corruption.

Annual reference to the regulation in the internal bulletin or in another form.

Inclusion of a recommendation in the code of conduct. Managers, especially superiors in areas that have a higher susceptibility to corruption, will ensure that these regulations are complied with.

9. Regulating sponsorship
Strict regulation is also necessary when third parties are prepared to support the task of the government agency. In the public security sector private initiatives to contribute to the accomplishment of public functions by the means of financial, factual or personal support have to be evaluated in another way as for instance in the field of arts. Any appearance has to be avoided, that the independence and impartiality of police authorities could be influenced. Financial or material support to the police should be generally refused. The sponsorship policy should be clearly regulated.

Action: A regulation is put into operation which generally prohibits the acceptance of sponsorship and provides strict conditions for any exception.

10. Reviewing service regulations
Service regulations frequently contain regulations which collide with the interests of preventing corruption, or even counteract them in specific cases (e.g. recommendations on the subject of 'lean government', standards on simplifying and accelerating procedures, expansion discretionary powers for individual judgments, delegation of decision-making powers, etc.).

Action: Reviewing new and already existing service regulations for possible conflicts of interest; assessment of their 'compatibility' with the prevention of corruption, setting priorities.

Task-specific or department-specific anti-corruption measures

Special anti-corruption measures are to be individually tailored to different departments, units, areas of tasks and functions for which increased susceptibility may be supposed due to their respective jurisdiction or the description of the tasks to be performed and related contacts with outsiders. With reference to a police authority, there can be an increased risk in approximately the following areas:

- The award of public contracts of all kinds (including the determination of the need for such contracts);
- Issuance of licenses, permits or concessions and checks on the compliance with the conditions imposed by the agency;
- Implementation of cost-intensive individual projects (e.g. research and development projects);
- Preparation of expert opinions and other technical reports or provision of consultancy services;
- Performance of sovereign or national duties (e.g. prosecution of offenses/misdemeanors, measures to avert risks, conduct of investigatory proceedings, searches);
- Performance of service duties (e.g. inputting and maintaining data, logistics administration);
- Staff billing procedures for ancillary costs (e.g. travel expenses, moving expenses) and other use of budgeted funds (e.g. search costs);
- Lecture activities and presentations in business.

Special anti-corruption measures do not stand alone but are always understood to be in combination with or as a supplement to general measures (see general anti-corruption measures above). Thus there are recommendations which are equally implementable in several target areas and also those which are very specific and thus can only be applied in restricted areas. In all areas which have proved to be particularly at risk as a result of a risk analysis, special measures suitable for reducing the risk of corruption are to be reviewed and implemented. For reasons of practicality and the diversity of police fields of action, only a few sample approaches can be indicated in the following. The wording of fine-tuned, task-specific recommendations requiring a detailed knowledge of the respective procedures and tasks should be undertaken, as a matter of principle, by means of a dialogue with the respective departments. This is an important creative task of the person or persons responsible for prevention in police authorities.

Actions:

- Regular sensitization of the employees assigned to areas susceptible to corruption;
- Strict selection of personnel (technical, social and moral suitability of candidates);
- Deployment of selected executives (raising the issue of susceptibility to corruption as part of the selection discussions; high standards for the performance of monitoring and welfare obligations);
- Standards to intensify duties of administration and work supervision, e.g. checks on the files, reports at fixed 'milestone' intervals (up-to-date follow-up of cases);
- Express obligation to perform a minimum number of selective checks in particular problem areas, including keeping records;
- Staff rotations; roll over of susceptible employees at intervals suitable for the tasks to be performed; if necessary repeated changes (shuttles) between two organizational units;
- Avoidance of single rooms for employees with contacts with outsiders; fluctuations while performing the same tasks (e.g. changing rooms and responsibilities of the employees in charge);
- Separation of functions: splitting complex task areas and processes or decision making processes; avoidance of the concentration of competencies in one person;
- Standardization of recurring work or case processes (e.g. checklists, use of EDP);
- Maintenance of the four- or more-eye-principle in contacts with outsiders (justification for waiving this principle must be provided), formation of teams;
- Explicit prohibition against the acceptance of gifts, which exceed what would be considered 'low-value items' (e.g. simple calendar or pen); in cases of doubt: reference to a conversation with a superior (principle of transparency);
- Exploration of the problems related to certain categories of outside employment with the parties concerned/applicants;
- Thorough examination of all information and suspicious circumstances as they occur;
- Duty to document all work contacts with businesses, which go beyond the usual police activities (work at a scene of crime, interrogations, etc.); monthly report; input into a database;
- Internal and external checks of files and invoices (superiors, Internal Auditing, General Accounting Office);

- Assisting in the recognition of corrupton; elaboration of a grid, which provides information about function-specific indicators.

It must be kept in mind that not all of the recommendations listed can actually be implemented in all of the organizational units and work areas susceptible to corruption. Some proposals, such as staff rotation, can not be implemented at all or only with great difficulty in some areas, due to the special circumstances and possible consequences (risk of the loss of expert knowledge). Waivers of the implementation of important recommendations make increased alertness during the performance of the duties of administrative and work supervision, and in some instances, special control mechanisms, necessary. To this extent, the necessity and feasibility of specific actions must be checked ahead of time, as a matter of principle, by the person responsible for preventing corruption and by the respective managers.

1. Additional measures with respect to the awarding of public orders

Public orders are issued by police authorities, for example, with respect to procurements; construction and services; research and development projects; and preparation of expert opinions, but also in the form of smaller orders in connection with police assignments (e.g. the removal of a disturbance, the use of interpreters) as well as part of long-term contracts in individual cases (e.g. the operation of canteens) or as open-ended service agreements.

Basically it must be kept in mind that larger orders requiring a public tender should not be split up, in order to enable the discretionary award of such orders due to the reduction of the order amount. Attributes given contractors such as 'reliable' or 'reasonably priced' should not lead to competitors being ruled out or for preferring individual contractors over a long period of time without any plausible reason. This applies in particular to open-ended service agreements.

When awarding public orders of all kinds, the following preventive measures are to be considered, in addition to the previously cited recommendations:

- Instructing employees about bidding regulations and procedures, in particular, compliance with the requirement to make a public bid (if waived, written record of the reasons); strict check if award is not fully open to the public or made without a bidding process;
- Review of contracts with manufacturers, suppliers or service providers (e.g. inadmissable oral agreements, unfavorable contract terms with a long-term commitment, unusual clauses which unduly favor the contractor);

- Listing the consequences for the contractor for corruptly attempts to influence decisions (e.g. claim to damages, exclusion from bidding processes, etc.), adoption of an anticorruption clause in the contracts;
- Comparison of the planning and the implementation of cost intensive projects and plans (deviations from the planning, expansions of the order, etc.);
- Consistent refusal of possible offers by potential contractors, which could influence objectivity (e.g.invitations to dinner, assumption of hotel bills or other measures of 'looking after one's customers');
- Requirement to strictly separate official and private interests (e.g. no linking of public order with a private interest);
- Restrictive standards for visits to firms and trade shows or product demonstrations, e.g. visits of firms according of the principle to 'as seldom as possible, as often as necessary';
- Preserving the four-eye -principle (e.g. never working alone);
- Discussions with suppliers or bidders at work, if at all possible;
- Prohibition against leaving home addresses with (potential) bidders or contractors;
- Assessment of the bidder or the contractor prior to awarding the order (reliability, technical competency, economy);
- Preparation of an overview of all public awards of orders and contractors (e.g. determination of the relative frequency of awards to certain contractors).

Additional specific measures can be listed for the areas of procurement, services or construction orders, as well as research and development.

2. Additional measures with respect to the preparation of expert opinions
Police authorities may be involved in the preparation of expert opinions and expert reports in different ways. These include:

- Crime lab expertises of all kinds (technology, chemistry, physics, biology, etc.);
- Security expertise and reports (protection of persons and property);
- Expert opinions on real estate to be procured and on the use of new technologies; taking samples;
- Other expert opinions (e.g. scene of crime reports, psychological and dactyloscopic expertises, etc.).

Due to the economic goals (profit interests of potential contractors), expert opinions related to security issues (e.g. pertaining to the protection of buildings or other property) and procurement opinions (e.g. technology to be deployed) are highly susceptible to corruption. However, crime lab reports and other expert opinions can be exposed to increased risks (e.g. preparation of 'accommodating expert opinions' after being promised a lucrative job preparing expert opinions as a secondary occupation; a client's interest in influencing criminal or civil proceedings).

In addition to the general recommendations made above, the following specific actions can be considered:

- Treatment of the problem of the attempts made to influence experts as part of staff discussions;
- Assessment of the client, the purpose and the effects or consequences, respectively, of an expert opinion (e.g. unilateral interests of the beneficiary);
- Increased control with regard to the preparation of 'accommodating expert opinions' (i.e. those prepared as a favor to one party);
- Rejection of possible offers or promises by clients or lobbyists, which could influence the objectivity and neutrality of the expert witness (e.g. promise of lucrative expert opinions prepared in a non-official capacity, functions, publications or lectures);
- Restrictive practice regarding the approval of sidelines with respect to the preparation of private expert opinions, in particular in cases where official knowledge or official machinery and equipment is (to be) used.

3. Additional measures with respect to the issuance of licenses or permits and checking compliance

Police authorities which deal directly or indirectly with the issuance of government permits and licenses have to cope with applications having different interests and nationalities. Risky situations can also arise whenever the applicant is willing to push his interests and goals through with all of the means, even illegal means, at his disposal (e.g. while building up 'legal facades' by organized crime), or when foreign nationals, who due to their experience in dealing with public administrations in their native countries, show a certain familiarity with regard offering rewards and gifts, and who consciously or unconsciously transfer their behavioral patterns to Germany (or other countries). Moreover, it must be kept in mind that police authorities or employees can exert considerable influence on the issuance or withdrawal of licenses and permits within the areas of public administration (e.g. withdrawal of a driver's license, reliability check pertaining to the issuance of arms possession cards and withdrawal of such after the commission of a crime, revocation of a trade concession for noncompliance with duties or obligations).

The frequently strong position that a potential 'exerter of influence' thinks that he has makes police employees especially interesting as possible allies in the preservation of their interests for certain 'administrative customers' and criminals. To this extent, such employees are exposed to a relatively large risk of becoming the target of corruption measures. In addition to the general recommendations, the following specific actions can be considered:

- Clear definition and delineation of discretionary limits and decision-making powers;
- Enactment and posting of house rules (in several languages) which refer to the problem and consequences of corruption, in particular to the prohibition of the acceptance of rewards and/or gifts;
- Staff rotation at shorter intervals; flexibility in the processing of cases (avoidance of processing according to the letters of the alphabet);
- Consistent maintenance of the multiple-eye principle (no visitors to rooms with only one employee; team work);
- Intensive supervision of work in reports on the reliability of an applicant or when checking compliance with duties or obligations imposed by the authority (e.g. checks of reporting requirements while on probation);
- Increased alertness on the part of superiors with regard to possible opportunities for the acceptance of benefits/advantages (even in private life), in particular, performance of their obligation to look after the welfare of their employees.

4. Additional measures with respect to police work

There are groups of interested parties who have a particular need for information about the planning, activities and knowledge of the police authorities. This applies to suspects, media representatives (interest in reporting on topics of an explosive nature) or certain businessmen (e.g. early offer of interpreting services for upcoming interrogations). Susceptibility to corruption can also result from the aims of organized criminals to exert influence on pending investigations in the form of promises or gifts in general or on crime-prosecution measures in particular (goals: e.g. suppression of evidence, influencing witnesses). Taking the topicality and significance of police work into account, the powers to intervene and make decisions that law enforcement officials have, and the existence of numerous sensitive data, susceptibility to corruption is to expected in the following areas in particular:

- Outside contacts (e.g. with the media, criminals, lawyers or citizens) while performing police tasks (e.g. supervising traffic, prosecuting mis-

demeanors, public and undercover investigations, implementing measures to prosecute crimes);
- Handling of sensitive data (e.g. input and maintenance of personal data and up-to-date search data);
- Award of (smaller) public orders, for example, to avert risks (e.g. removal of an obstacle to traffic), the prosecution of misdemeanors (e.g. towing services), or the conduct of measures to prosecute crimes (e.g. using locksmiths, interpretation assignments).

Basically all employees who perform police-jurisdiction tasks and/or directly or indirectly have access to police EDP systems must be sensitized, in particular with regard to their possible susceptibility to corruption. Moreover, other actions are to be reviewed and introduced, if necessary.

Actions:
- Strict selection of staff for sensitive investigations or duties; limitation of the circle of those 'in the know';
- Sampling checks of investigation and search activities, exploration of omissions and superficialities;
- Monitoring of sealed-off organizational units; regular review of the necessity for internal sealing-off measures;
- Basic review of information and suspicious circumstances with regard to possible erroneous conduct (e.g. accusations made during trials, complaints by criminal lawyers, anonymous information, rumors from within the organization);
- Keeping records of inquiries into police databases (sampling); plausibility checks;
- Consistent reaction to the suspicion of aiding perpetrators after the fact (by preventing their prosecution), disclosure of official secrets or other service-related offenses (e.g. media reports about internal information from criminal proceedings, see above concerning – indicators in activities related to police-work);
- Signs of possible risks or influences via private-life contacts.

Concluding remarks

The task of the corruption commissioners, the persons in charge of combating corruption in police authorities, consists of reviewing the recommended measures – in dialogue with the respective organizational units, if possible – and then deciding on their implementation. Moreover, they must consider whether additional task-specific actions are to be implemented, which due to their specific uses were unable to be discussed as part of this concept. The recommended list of actions to be taken has a dynamic character in this respect. Creativity is possible and necessary, both during the planning and during the implementation phases.

The authors are well aware of the fact that some of the measures cited here have already been implemented in certain areas, or that they are being complied with, or that they are considered to be matter of course, even if this is not always primarily done with a view to preventing corruption. Preventive measures should not be introduced only after concrete situations making their introduction necessary have occurred. The prevention of corruption is comparable to preventing fires, in terms of approach. Just as fire prevention regulations and alarm systems or fire-extinguishing equipment exist for public buildings, so regulations to prevent corruption, preventive measures and monitoring facilities must be matter of course in public offices and police authorities.

Notes

We thank Dieter Steinbach for his contributions and support. Translation by Barbara M. Müller-Grant.

1. Source is the Police Crime Statistics for the Federal Republic of Germany: Polizeiliche Kriminalstatistik – Bundesrepublik Deutschland, Wiesbaden 1995, 1996, 1997, 1998.
2. The next Survey for the years 1997 and 1998 will only be available in 1999.
3. Werner Vahlenkamp, Ina Knauß: Korruption – hinnehmen oder handeln, Wiesbaden 1995, 2nd ed. Wiesbaden 1997; English summary: Werner Vahlenkamp, Ina Knauß: Korruption: ein unscharfes Phänomen als Gegenstand zielgerichteter Prävention (Corruption: Taking Precise Aim at an Amorphous Phenomenon), in: Trends in Organized Crime, Vol. 2, No. 4 (1997), p. 21–25.
4. Ombudsmen, as members of the Staff Council, are frequently persons whom the employees know personally and trust. As an additional point of contact, they can be suitable for reducing the inhibition of persons seeking advice and potential informants. This aspect is especially significant if the central point of contact for corruption issues and internal auditing are one and the same person or organizational unit.

Peter Poerting, Doctorate in Business Administration and Economics, 1979–1989 Research Officer at Bundeskriminalamt's Criminological Research Unit, specialized in Economic Crime, 1989–1996 Head of a Staff Unit, since 1997 Head of the Internal Auditing Unit and Corruption Commissioner.

Werner Vahlenkamp, Police Officer at Bundeskriminalamt since 1970, 1973–1983 investigator in the Weapons and Explosives Offences Section, 1983–1996 at Bundeskriminalamt's Criminological Research Unit, specialized in General Crime Forecast, Organized Crime and Corruption Prevention, since 1997 at the Internal Auditing Unit.

Part VII
People and Reform

[23]

Crime, Law & Social Change **23:** 315–343, 1995.

Layers of decision: Linking social definitions of corruption and willingness to take action *

ANGELA GORTA AND SUZIE FORELL
Independent Commission Against Corruption, GPO Box 500, Sydney, Australia 2001

Abstract. The literature available about social definitions of corruption is surprisingly discrete from that which addresses the issue of "whistleblowing" or the reporting of crime and corruption. The current study, however, empirically links the two. A survey of more than 1300 public sector employees was undertaken to explore: i) how and why public sector employees define some behaviours as corrupt; ii) factors which may hinder public sector employees taking action about corruption which they may observe at work; and iii) the link between i) and ii). The study found that within the New South Wales (NSW) public sector, views about what constitutes corruption are diverse and that this has a significant, though not exclusive, impact upon the action respondents said they would take in response to workplace corruption. The study discusses other factors which also impact upon the stated decision not to take action about corruption and suggests some possible courses of action for addressing these factors.

How do people decide whether an activity they witness is corrupt, and how does this relate to their willingness to take action about that conduct? There is very little published material which addresses these questions and examines the relationship between how people define corruption and how they respond to it. In order to explore this link, literature about defining corruption, workplace crime, public opinion definitions of corruption and possible responses to corruption including whistleblowing, need to be considered collectively.

Defining corruption

Corruption is a difficult concept to define. There is little consensus about its definition or boundaries: whole papers have been devoted to this subject alone (Peters & Welch 1978; Johnston 1986; Gibbons 1990; Heidenheimer, Johnston & LeVine 1990; Gardiner 1993). Writers analysing the different definitions of corruption (e.g. Scott 1972; Peters & Welch 1978; Malec & Gardiner 1987; Dolan, McKeown & Carlson 1988) have tended to categorise definitions into three types:

* The research upon which this paper is based formed part of the research program of the Independent Commission Against Corruption.

- *Legal definitions* – which assume behaviour is corrupt when it violates some standard or rule of behaviour set down by a political system (Peters & Welch 1978, p. 974);
- *Public interest definitions* – a belief that corruption exists if the public trust or good is betrayed, whether or not a violation of legal codes occurs (Dolan et al. 1988, p. 5);
- *Public opinion definitions* – which are based on socially-defined corrupt conduct, the seriousness of which may be influenced by mitigating factors not necessarily recognised in law (e.g. Johnston 1986).

Both Scott (1972) and Peters and Welch (1978) have emphasised that these types of definitions are overlapping rather than mutually exclusive.

It has been argued that public opinion or social definitions are more salient in governing behaviour than are legal or "formal" definitions. As has been repeatedly observed (see Hollinger & Clark 1983; Werner 1983; Johnston 1986; Greenberger, Miceli & Cohen 1987), the influence of the attitudes of co-workers on the behaviour of employees is significant. Hollinger and Clark (1983), for example, have stated:

> . . . these empirical results confirm . . . that employee deviance is more constrained by informal social controls present in primary work-group relationships than by the more-formal reactions to deviance by those in positions of authority within the formal organization (p. 126).

What do workers consider to be acceptable?

Some of the literature about workplace crime suggests that people may rationalise or excuse activities otherwise defined as corrupt. In a self-report study of workplace theft, Horning (1970) found that all property in an industrial workplace was categorised by the workers into three types: "personal property", "corporate property" and "property of uncertain ownership". He found that the theft of goods of "uncertain ownership" was regarded as acceptable if it remained within "a tolerable limit" (which was not clearly defined by the workgroup). Outside these boundaries theft was not supported.

Mancuso (1993) provided some additional examples of how the way people view their work can affect what they consider to be acceptable. Mancuso divided her sample of British Members of Parliament into subgroups, who, amongst other differences, used distinct types of rationalisations. One group, which she named the "Muddlers", justified the acceptance of retainers and outside employment by referring to their low salaries and poor facilities which, they argued, necessitated their securing additional income. Mancuso added that the Muddlers had no incentive to follow their consciences, believing "if I don't do it, somebody else will". Another group, which she labelled the "Entrepreneurs", rejected the traditional view that being a Member of Parliament is a reward in itself. Instead they "opted for tangible, bankable rewards . . . and . . . overwhelmingly favoured a legalistic interpretation of ethical rules: 'what is not legally forbidden is acceptable'" (p. 185).

In some environments, behaviour which might be labelled as corrupt is simply "taken for granted" by the "populace" (Malec & Gardiner 1987, p. 277). For example, Gronbeck (1990) described behaviours such as "graft, kickbacks, overzealous promotion through meritocracy, slush funds which have public effects without public accountability [and] favors which bypass normal channels" as "behaviours which many people take as part of the everyday cost of government" (p. 174).

Mars (1982), in his book about "the normal crimes of normal people in the normal circumstance of their work . . . activities that are an accepted part of everyday jobs" (p. 1), which he describes as "fiddles", defines "fiddling" as:

> the movement of resources to individual private use that do not appear in official accounts – or that appear in official accounts under different headings and which are acquired by individuals through their relationship to a job. These resources may derive directly from the job itself or be allocated from an outside source that relates to the job (p. 10).

He observed that the behaviour involved in "fiddles" is open to multiple definitions from different perspectives:

> If we fiddle in our own jobs we tend to view this as an entitlement – as a "perk"; whereas if we are victims of the fiddles of others we become morally indignant. In these circumstances the suspension of moral judgement is far from easy (p. 3).

Chibnall and Saunders (1977) have argued that it is possible for multiple definitions (or alternative moralities) to be held by members of the one group or even by the same individual at different times; that what makes a behaviour corrupt is not something which is intrinsic to the behaviour, but rather that corruption is an interpretation which one chooses to impose on the behaviour. They conclude:

> that in the final analysis, his choice of definition is likely to be highly dependent on both his practical purposes at the time, and his assumptions about the social world and his place within it (p. 144).

The existence of multiple definitions has consequences. Cressey (1986) has argued that it is the existence of such multiple definitions which enables an individual to rationalise their conduct and, in turn, facilitates the committing of crimes:

> . . . when multiple moralities abound, people disobey the law because they have learned that, from many points of view, one can be moral and criminal at the same time. . . . in the long run, the incidence of management fraud (and of street crime as well) will decline only as the neutralizing verbalizations supporting these crimes are themselves neutralized (p. 208).

The importance of public sector employees' attitudes

Although most definitions of corruption discuss private roles conflicting with public duties and hence are focussed on the public sector, very little is known about public sector employees' understanding of, or attitudes to, corruption. Relevant studies generally discuss the views of elected officials (e.g. Peters & Welch 1978; Atkinson & Mancuso 1985; Jackson & Smith 1993; Mancuso 1993) or of the public at large (e.g. Johnston 1986; Grabosky et al. 1987; Hauber, Toornvliet & Willemsee 1988) rather than the views of public sector employees.

The importance of public officials in combating corruption has been widely recognised, with comments such as that in the report of the Fitzgerald Inquiry (into possible illegal activities and associated police misconduct in Queensland):[1]

> Honest public officials are the major potential source of information needed to reduce public maladministration and misconduct (Fitzgerald 1989, quoted in Mason, undated, p. 3).

The current study focuses on the attitudes of public sector employees because:

- public sector employees are in the best position to observe and respond to potentially corrupt conduct; and
- it is recognised that employee or workplace attitudes to and social definitions of corruption may be more salient in governing behaviour than formally imposed definitions.

Empirical studies exploring public opinion definitions

Several studies have been conducted which explore public opinion definitions of corruption by determining what types of activities are considered to be corrupt by select samples. One of the earliest studies, (Peters & Welch 1978), has been used as a model by other researchers who have attempted to empirically examine definitions of corruption. Peters and Welch mailed questionnaires to 978 state senators in 24 US states. The major focus of their questionnaire was a set of ten scenarios. The senators were asked to rate each of these scenarios on a series of 5 point scales in terms of: whether they believed the scenario to be corrupt; whether they believed most public officials would condemn this act; and whether they believed that most members of the public would condemn this act. Peters and Welch presented their results in terms of the proportion of their sample who agreed that each scenario was corrupt or very corrupt.

Some researchers have adapted Peters and Welch's scenarios and applied the same methodology to different samples of politicians, for example: Canadian backbench Members of Parliament (Atkinson & Mancuso 1985); British Members of Parliament (Mancuso 1993); NSW[2] Members of Parliament (Jackson & Smith 1993). In some cases, the adapted scenarios do not conform as well to the different political structures as they did in their original American context, for example, one of Peters and Welch's scenarios was that which they named the AMBASSADOR scenario:

> A presidential candidate who promises an ambassadorship in exchange for campaign contributions (AMBASSADOR).

Jackson and Smith's adaptation of this scenario for NSW subjects is:

> A Prime Ministerial candidate promises an Ambassadorship in exchange for campaign contributions (AMBASSADOR).

While the concept of a presidential candidate is well understood in the US, given the different electoral process, the notions of a prime ministerial candidate or of campaign contributions for a prime ministerial candidate are not as common within Australia.

Other researchers have either evolved their methodologies from that of Peters and Welch or have taken a totally different approach. Gibbons (1985) asked his sample of university students to rate his nine scenarios on 12 semantic differentials (e.g. "common-rare", "necessary-unnecessary", etc.) in addition to rating them in terms how "corrupt-not corrupt" they thought the scenarios were. He described the inclusion of the 13 semantic differentials as a "new technique for investigating the concept of corruption" (p. 765). Johnston

(1986) used a slightly different methodology. He had students conduct telephone interviews with 241 residents of Pittsburgh. Respondents were asked to judge whether each of 20 scenarios were "extremely corrupt", "somewhat corrupt", "slightly corrupt" or "not at all corrupt".

The studies which have been conducted to date suggest that people are more likely to judge a scenario as corrupt when it involves:

- illegal actions (e.g. Peters & Welch 1978; Atkinson & Mancuso 1985; Mancuso 1993); though Gibbons (1985) appeared less certain of the effects of the illegality of the behaviour on judgements when he said that "they may define some activities as corrupt which are not treated as such by law or academic literature, but they may also do the reverse";
- a larger payoff (e.g. Peters & Welch 1978; Johnston 1986; Johnston 1989);
- a more direct payoff (e.g. Welch & Peters 1977; Peters & Welch 1978; Johnston 1986; Johnston 1989);
- a more immediate (short-range) payoff (e.g. Peters & Welch 1978);
- someone asking for money rather than simply accepting it (Johnston 1989). (This, however, was not the case with Johnston's (1986) American sample who made virtually no distinction between those who asked for money and those who received it);
- an offender who is a public official rather than a private citizen (Johnston 1986; Johnston 1989), who is a prominent person rather than an ordinary citizen (Johnston 1986) or who is a judge, in a non-political role, is held to higher standards than are legislators (Peters & Welch 1978);
- where there are no mitigating motives or circumstances to reduce the severity (Johnston 1986).

Less consensus has been found in what Mancuso (1993) termed "the problematic grey areas of constituency service and conflict of interest".

While it may be that members of some subgroups of the population (e.g. based on age, gender, education, etc.) share a common understanding of corruption which differs from the understanding shared by other subgroups, the existing literature has not revealed clear cut distinctions (cf. Gardiner 1970; Welch & Peters 1977; Atkinson & Mancuso 1985; Johnston 1986; Grabosky et al. 1987; Jackson & Smith 1993). Some of the differences in findings may reflect the studies being conducted in different decades with different groups of subjects, often from different countries. Alternatively, given the lack of clear cut distinctions, Gibbons (1985) has suggested that there may be "few great differences to be found, and views of corruption may transcend such social-economic-political distinctions" (p. 777).

Factors hindering reporting

Self-report surveys, victim surveys (e.g. Walker, Dagger & Collins 1989) and field experiments (e.g. Bickman 1975; Bickman & Rosenbaum 1977; Dertke, Penner & Ulrich 1974; and Gelfand, Hartmann, Walder & Page 1973 cited by Dozier & Miceli 1985) suggest that crime in general is significantly under-reported. The figures are exacerbated in relation to victimless crimes and white collar offences, both of which could describe corruption. For instance, a 1980 study in the United States found that 70% of federal employees claiming personal knowledge of corruption did not report it (Truelson 1987).

Factors contributing to the discrepancy between the actual incidence of criminal and corrupt activity and that which is reported have been a focus of victim surveys such as the International Crime Survey (Walker et al. 1989), self-report studies and studies concerning whistleblowing (including Near & Jensen 1983; Miceli & Near 1984, 1985; Dozier & Miceli 1985; Near & Miceli 1986; Greenberger, Miceli & Cohen 1987; Truelson 1987). Reasons offered for non-reporting by these studies include:

- fear of retribution for reporting crime or corruption;
- a belief that no efficacious action will result from reporting the incident or conduct;
- a belief that it is only worth reporting the conduct if it is considered to be serious enough;
- a belief that there is insufficient evidence to prove the misconduct; and
- the fact that the incident had little personal impact upon the observer.

Dozier and Miceli (1985) undertook a review of the "potential predictors of whistleblowing". As part of this work they proposed a "decision framework", summarising the process which they believed that members of organisations used in deciding whether or not to "blow the whistle", or report misconduct in their organisations. The process described is that before an individual "blows the whistle", he or she must decide whether:

- the activity in question is wrong;
- the situation is deserving of action;
- he or she feels responsibility for taking action;
- efficacious actions are available to be taken;
- these actions are appropriate; and
- the expected benefits of taking action outweigh the expected costs.

They proposed that if the answer is "no" to any of these steps, then the individual will not blow the whistle (Greenberger, Miceli & Cohen 1987, p. 529).

While the literature available about reporting crime or corruption and that about defining corruption appear to be mutually exclusive, Dozier and Miceli's

(1985) work provides a link between the two. The first step of the decision tree suggests that people have to recognise a behaviour as wrong before they will consider taking action about it. This article takes this step further by exploring the link between how and why people define different types of behaviour as *corrupt* and the type of action they take about that conduct. More specifically, we explore:

1. how and why public sector employees define some behaviours as corrupt;
2. factors which may hinder public sector employees taking action about corruption which they may observe at work; and
3. the link between 1 and 2.

Methodology

Questionnaires were distributed to a random sample of 1,978 NSW public sector employees between May and August 1993. The sample was selected in such a way that *all* NSW public sector employees, from the highest to the lowest paid, had an equal chance of inclusion. The resulting sample encompassed a broad range of public sector employees drawn from over 50 sites with a number of separate divisions at most of these sites: some worked in large agencies, while others worked in small; some worked in centralised agencies, while others worked in regionalised agencies; some worked in the city, while others worked in country areas; some were office workers while others delivered services directly to the public. The public sector employees in the sample were engaged in a wide range of occupations.

A total of 1,313 of these questionnaires were completed and returned (giving a response rate of 66.4%). The questionnaire used in this survey was designed to preserve the anonymity of respondents and their organisations.

Questionnaire design

Like other studies (e.g. Peters & Welch 1978; Atkinson & Mancuso 1985; Gibbons 1985; and Mancuso 1993), brief descriptions of scenarios were used in the questionnaire. The use of scenarios enabled all respondents to "observe" the same conduct and make decisions about those behaviours and their likely responses to them. In an actual workplace, not all public sector employees would be in a position to observe the same conduct and therefore make comparable judgements. Twelve scenarios were chosen to depict different types of potentially corrupt conduct which could occur in *any* public sector organisation. (The scenarios and the abbreviations by which they are referred to in the remainder of this paper are listed in Table 1.) For each scenario respondents were asked the same questions. They were requested to rate, on a

Table 1. Scenarios used and their abbreviations.

Scenario	Abbreviation
A government employee is offered $ 300 from a company to accept a tender which is before him. He takes the money to put towards a new stereo system.	(STEREO)
A government employee occasionally takes a box of note pads and pens from the office stores cupboard, to donate to the local community centre.	(TAKE NOTE PADS)
To avoid the hassle of advertising, a government employee appoints a colleague to a vacant position. She has the reputation of being the best person for the job.	(JOB FOR COLLEAGUE)
Each year, a government employee accepts a leather bound executive diary, from a firm of consultants whom she occasionally engages for use by her section.	(LEATHER DIARY)
A government employee, responsible for buying office equipment, takes a second job selling stationery to his own department.	(2ND JOB)
To hasten the process, a government employee bypasses tendering procedures and selects a company known for its excellence, to provide a $ 75,000 computer training package.	(COMPUTER TENDER)
A government employee uses her position to get a friend a public sector job.	(JOB FOR FRIEND)
A government employee threatens to dismiss another staff member, if he "blows the whistle" on fraud within their section.	(WHISTLEBLOWER)
A government employee often gives confidential information about department clients to a friend who works in a private insurance company.	(CONFIDENTIAL INFORMATION)
A government employee is offered $ 300 from a company to accept a tender which is before him. He only takes the money to cover his child's hospital bills.	(HOSPITAL BILLS)
A government employee regularly spends part of the day using office facilities, to organise his private catering business.	(CATERING BUSINESS)
A government employee regularly adds extra days onto her business trips to visit friends. She claims the extra days as part of her travel expenses.	(BUSINESS TRIPS)

six point scale, how *desirable* they believed the behaviour to be, how *harmful*, and how *justified* they considered it to be, where a rating of "1" was least desirable, most harmful and least justified. Respondents were also asked to judge whether the conduct was corrupt or not corrupt. They were then asked what they would do about it.

Selection of scenarios

Descriptions of scenarios can differ in a number of ways. Some studies have varied the perpetrators in their scenarios. Johnston (1986), for example, used 14 different perpetrators within his 20 scenarios. His perpetrators included individuals in public positions such as "a police officer" and "a city council member"; as well as other individuals such as "a homeowner", "a motorist", "your neighbour"; and one perpetrator, "a supermarket", which did not refer to an individual. Peters and Welch (1978) used eight different perpetrators in their ten scenarios. When a number of variable factors such as the nature of the perpetrator, the type of behaviour, the size of any amount of money involved and the directness of the benefits received are each varied, it is not possible to isolate one feature or to confirm which combination of features, has determined the respondent's assessment of the scenario. For this reason, in this study the basic description of the perpetrator ("a government employee") was kept constant so that attention could be focussed on the behaviours and the circumstances surrounding the behaviours which were described.

Scenarios were designed around activities which are common to public sector agencies: recruitment, purchasing, tendering, use of consultants, use of office resources and provision of information. Each of the scenarios contained one or more potentially undesirable elements. The scenarios described varied in the frequency of the activity: some were "once off" while others were ongoing. They also varied in the presence or absence of mitigating circumstances. Of the twelve scenarios, four had some type of mitigating circumstance: need (HOSPITAL BILLS), altruism (TAKE NOTE PADS) and the idea that the ends justify the means (COMPUTER TENDER and JOB FOR COLLEAGUE).

While ideally it may have been preferable to examine perceptions of a larger number of scenarios, the pragmatics of administering such a survey dictate that the number of scenarios be limited. Hence the conclusions drawn are restricted to the nature of the specific 12 scenarios we supplied. If we had used other scenarios describing other types of behaviour or where other aspects such as the amounts of money had differed our results may well have been different.

Measuring whether the behaviours were perceived as corrupt

Some previous studies have required their respondents to rate "how corrupt" they perceive the behaviour to be on, say, a scale from 1 (not corrupt) to 5 (very corrupt) (e.g. Peters & Welch 1978) or a 7 point scale (e.g. Atkinson & Mancuso 1985; and Mancuso 1993). This leads to a problem when the researcher wishes to dichotomise responses into "corrupt" versus "not corrupt". Atkinson and Mancuso (1985), for example, have stated that they counted the respondent as considering "an act corrupt if they selected scores of 1, 2, or 3 on the 7-point Likert scale, where low scores denoted the 'more corrupt' option" (p. 468). It might be that respondents who rated acts as a 4, 5 and/or 6 on this scale may also have considered the acts to be corrupt. Peters and Welch also appeared only to count two of the points on their five point scale as "corrupt".

In order to avoid the problem of misunderstanding how respondents were using such a scale to rate whether they saw acts as corrupt, we simplified the procedure by requesting that for each scenario respondents answer the question "*Do you think this behaviour is corrupt?*" with the possible responses being "yes" or "no".

Selection of additional scales

Some previous research (e.g. Peters & Welch 1978; Johnston 1986; Jackson & Smith 1993) has focussed simply on judgements of whether or not scenarios are corrupt. However, given that we were trying to explore under what circumstances the label "corrupt" is applied, such approaches are inadequate. To *only* ask respondents whether they believe a scenario is "corrupt" is potentially confusing the respondent's desire to express a generalised positive or negative feeling about the scenario and a real belief that the adjective "corrupt", rather than some other descriptor, is appropriate. For this reason, we asked respondents to judge how desirable they considered the behaviour to be on a scale of "very undesirable" (1) to "very desirable" (6), before asking whether or not the scenario was corrupt.

A scale of *very harmful – not harmful* was included to assist in ascertaining if people attend to the perceived consequences of the activity when forming judgements about the scenario's corruptness or undesirability. This is consistent with one of Hoffman and Hardyman's (1986) dimensions of offence seriousness and with comments by Gardiner (1993, p. 117) and by Malec and Gardiner (1987, p. 268).

A scale of *not justified – well justified* was included to allow exploration of a frequently advanced idea that people may rationalise corrupt conduct.

Recording willingness to take action

To simply ask respondents to choose whether or not they would report a behaviour is to deny that a range of alternatives is available in response to corrupt conduct. Accordingly, for each scenario respondents were asked to choose one of four responses to the question "what would you do about it?" Possible responses were "nothing"; "talk to the employee"; "talk to employee's supervisor or another appropriate person within the organisation" (discussed here as "report internally"); and "report it outside my organisation (e.g. Police, ICAC)".

Recognising that it is likely that more people would say they would "take action" about corruption than those who would actually respond if faced with this behaviour, the analysis focused on the factors which differentiated those who said they would do nothing from all others, rather than on the percentages who said they would take each type of action. Accordingly some valuable insight can be gained into some of the factors which hinder willingness to respond to corruption.

Background characteristics and attitude statements

In addition to perceptions of the scenarios, the questionnaire also included:

- questions about details of the respondent's position in the public sector (length of service, salary, supervisory status) as well as educational qualifications and gender; and
- twelve attitude statements: including three concerning definitions of corruption, three concerning the range of behaviours which may be considered acceptable and six concerning reporting corruption. Respondents were asked whether they strongly disagreed, disagreed, agreed or strongly agreed with each of the statements. These twelve statements were included so that more general attitudes to corruption, which would not be able to be measured by responses to the twelve scenarios, could be explored.

Considerations

When considering the findings it is necessary to bear in mind that the questionnaire came from the Independent Commission Against Corruption (ICAC).[3] Recognising that this could have potentially affected the results (possibly inflating both the percentage of respondents who considered each of the scenarios to be corrupt as well as the percentages who said that they would take some form of action about the scenarios), a number of steps to counter these effects were taken. These included designing the survey in such a way that people could express their condemnation of the behaviour without having to apply the label "corrupt"; stressing the study's focus exploring the range of *personal* views held about corruption (hence there being no right or wrong answers); assuring respondents that neither they nor their organisations could be identified at any stage; and enabling responses to be returned directly to the researchers rather than through senior officers of their own organisations. The potential impact of ICAC involvement in the study was also considered in the analysis of these results. While every effort was made to reduce the impact of this factor, we are unable to quantify the size or nature of the effect, if any, of having the study conducted by the ICAC.

Results

Which scenarios were considered corrupt?

The percentages of the respondents who considered each of the scenarios to be corrupt are depicted in Figure 1 (see Table 1 for scenario descriptions).

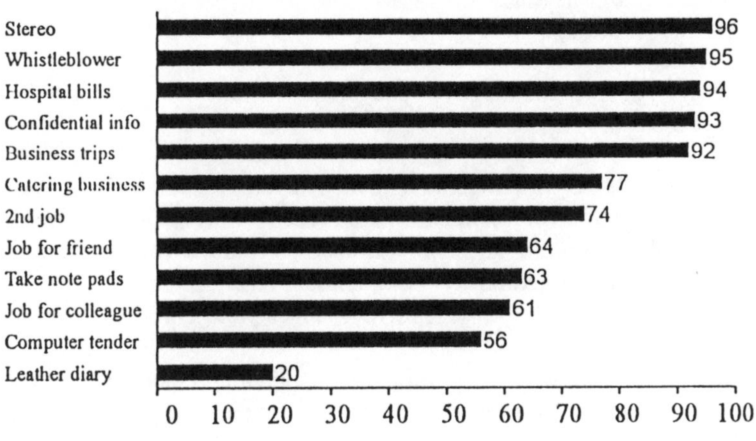

Figure 1. Percentage who considered each scenario corrupt.

From Figure 1 it is clear that the level of agreement among respondents' perceptions of corruption differed amongst the scenarios.

From the information collected in the study, we cannot know what led to these variations in level of consensus. However, by looking at differences between the scenarios where there is a high level of consensus and those where there is not, it is possible to hypothesise about the nature of the situations considered to be corrupt. It is of interest, for example, that:

- the three scenarios which involved a direct financial gain and where the behaviour would be illegal were considered corrupt by most respondents (STEREO (96.4%), HOSPITAL BILLS (93.6%) and BUSINESS TRIPS (92.2%));
- there was relatively less, though still substantial, consensus for those scenarios which involved a financial gain which was less direct (CATERING BUSINESS (76.7%) and 2ND JOB (73.7%));
- there was high consensus (94.8%) in the scenario describing threats to a potential whistleblower (WHISTLEBLOWER) and in the CONFIDENTIAL INFORMATION scenario, describing the provision of confidential information to a friend (92.9%). The latter is interesting given there was no direct personal gain received by the person supplying the information;
- opinion was divided for the scenarios in which rules were not followed yet where what may be considered as "reasonable" outcome for the

organisation was reached (JOB FOR COLLEAGUE (60.8%) and COMPUTER TENDER (56.2%).

Is there agreement in the range *of behaviours which are considered to be "corrupt"?*

While nearly all our respondents agreed that individual scenarios such as STEREO, WHISTLEBLOWER and HOSPITAL BILLS were corrupt, there was a lot of individual variation in the *combinations* of scenarios which were considered corrupt. The most common combinations were:

- all of the scenarios except LEATHER DIARY were corrupt (153 respondents);
- all of the scenarios were corrupt (141 respondents); and
- all of the scenarios except TAKE NOTE PADS and LEATHER DIARY were corrupt (43 respondents).

A total of 254 different combinations of the twelve scenarios were considered to be corrupt by the respondents. Such individual variation is obscured when one merely counts the proportion of respondents who consider each individual scenario to be corrupt. The large number of combinations also refutes any notion of there being a common understanding of what is meant by "corrupt conduct" which is shared by different public sector employees.

How do public sector employees decide which behaviours are corrupt?

Some insight into how public sector employees decide which behaviours are corrupt was gleaned from spontaneous comments made by respondents on the questionnaires. One general observation was that the criteria used for determining which behaviours are corrupt appear to differ both among individuals and among scenarios. More specific observations about the ways some public sector employees decide what is corrupt and what is not, include:

- some comments suggested that some respondents equate corruption with breaking the rules: as long as procedures are followed, behaviour cannot be corrupt;
- some people appeared to categorise their perceptions of undesirable behaviour into non-overlapping categories such that if it falls into another negative category then it cannot also be corrupt (e.g. "not corrupt, theft" (TAKE NOTE PADS, BUSINESS TRIPS), "not corrupt, just lazy" (CATERING BUSINESS), "not corrupt, just stupid" (STEREO, COMPUTER TENDER, CONFIDENTIAL INFORMATION));
- some considered that whether the behaviour, as stated in the scenarios, is corrupt or not is subject to a range of further qualifications about the behaviour (e.g. was it a temporary or permanent position? (JOB FOR

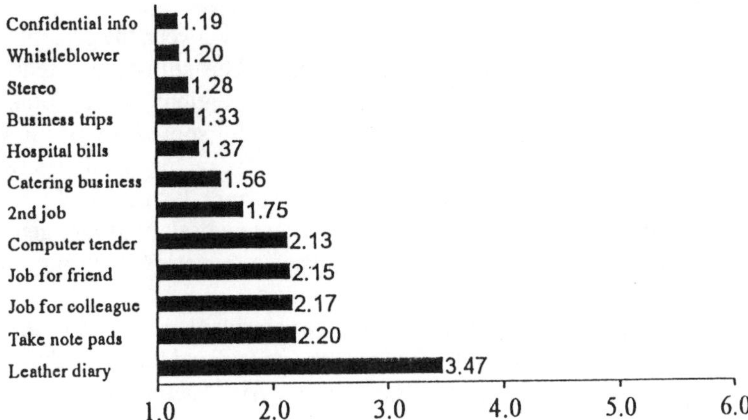

Figure 2. Average perceived desirability.

COLLEAGUE, JOB FOR FRIEND); depends on how often it happens (TAKE NOTE PADS); depends on quality and price of goods (2ND JOB));

- some indicated that TAKE NOTE PADS was not corrupt because it is an *appropriate* use of public resources, e.g.:

Given the under funding of community centres by the government and the importance of the community centres to their communities this is a robin hood situation (respondent number 0333).

How desirable, harmful or justified were the scenarios considered to be?

It is important to be aware that just because some public sector employees did not label a behaviour as corrupt, does not mean that they believed the activity to be desirable. On average, all of the scenarios, except LEATHER DIARY, were rated by our respondents, at the "very undesirable", "very harmful" and "not justified" ends of the scales. LEATHER DIARY was rated towards the middle of each of the scales.

For each of the twelve scenarios, those who considered the behaviour to be corrupt also considered it, on average, to be *more undesirable, more harmful* and *less justified* than did those who considered that the behaviour was *not* corrupt.

Can we predict who *consider the scenarios to be corrupt and who do not?*

Previous studies have not found clear cut distinctions between the perceptions of people from different demographic subgroups. This study found that the relationship between background variables and perceptions of the scenarios depended upon the specific scenario: for example, for some scenarios it was those on higher salaries, while for others it was those on lower salaries, who were more likely to consider the behaviour to be corrupt. It was, therefore, not possible to simplify the results by saying that any one salary group, gender, education group, etc., was more likely to perceive scenarios as corrupt than any other group.

In order to further explore differences between respondents who considered that the behaviour was corrupt from those who considered that the behaviour was not corrupt, we used a logistic regression analysis.[4] Factors included in the analysis were the background characteristics of the respondents, perceptions of the scenarios as harmful, justified and desirable, and responses to the attitude statements about defining corruption. The major findings were:

- characteristics which distinguished those who considered the scenarios to be corrupt from those who thought that they were not corrupt differed between scenarios;
- perceptions of the behaviours (e.g. perceived harmfulness, perceived desirability and perceived justifiability) were better predictors of who would consider particular behaviours to be corrupt and who would consider them not to be corrupt than were the background characteristics of the individuals;
- perceived harmfulness of the behaviour is the predictor which most frequently distinguished between those who consider the behaviour to be corrupt and those who do not.

These findings have implications for those involved in educational or corruption prevention strategies: first they warn against generalising that any group or subgroup – as defined by background characteristics – share a common perception of behaviour; second, they suggest that corruption, as an abstract term, is understood when translated into the more tangible contexts of behaviour and its effects.

What are respondents' attitudes to reporting corruption?

Respondents were asked whether they strongly agreed, agreed, disagreed or strongly disagreed with six statements about reporting corruption (see Table 2).

For each of the twelve scenarios, respondents were asked to state what they would do about the behaviour. For every scenario at least some respondents

Table 2. Attitudes about reporting corruption.

Question number	Statement	% who agreed or strongly agreed	% who disagreed or strongly disagreed
Q72	There is no point in reporting corruption as nothing useful *will* be done about it.	26.4	73.6
Q73	There is no point in reporting corruption as nothing useful *can* be done about it.	14.2	85.8
Q74	People who report corruption are likely to suffer for it.	74.1	25.9
Q75	Most corruption is too trivial to be worth reporting.	26.3	73.7
Q76	I would not know where to go to report corruption.	27.6	72.4
Q77	People who report corruption are just troublemakers.	4.4	95.6

said they would take each of the four actions put to them (do nothing, talk to the employee, report internally or report externally), though in most cases the majority indicated that they would report the behaviour internally (see Table 4). However, many also indicated that they might take more than one action: i.e., they would talk to the employee and then, if that were not effective, report internally. People tended to say that they would take increasingly serious action if nothing happened in response to their initial action.

Those who said they would do nothing

One aim of the study was to identify factors which may hinder people taking action about potentially corrupt behaviour they witness at work. For this reason respondents were compared as two groups; those who said they would do nothing and those who said they would take any action at all (talk to the employee, report internally or report externally), using a logistic regression analysis. Variables included in the analysis were the background characteristics of the respondents, perceptions of the scenarios as corrupt, desirable, harmful and justified, and the attitude statements listed in Table 2. Of these, the following five factors were found to be the most closely related to the choice to do nothing about the scenarios. (Refer to Table 3 which provides a summary of the variables which were found to be useful in differentiating those who said that they would do nothing from those who said that they would take any of the three actions in each of the scenarios.)

1. A belief by the public sector employee that the behaviour was justified in the circumstances. The study found that the belief that the behaviour was

Table 3. Variables which differentiate those who say they would do nothing from those who say they would take any action.

Scenario	Step[1]	Variable Entered[2]	Probability[3]	Correct classification %[4]
1. Stereo	–	–	–	89.33%
	1	Q72[5]	$p < 0.0001$	89.33%
	2	Justifiability	$p < 0.0001$	89.85%
	3	Supervisory status	$p < 0.0001$	90.02%
	4	Harmfulness	$p < 0.0027$	89.93%
	5	Q74[5]	$p < 0.0156$	89.59%
	6	Corrupt	$p < 0.0309$	90.10%
2. Take note pads	–	–	–	73.33%
	1	*Harmfulness*[6]	$p < 0.0001$	77.69%
	2	Q72	$p < 0.0001$	77.52%
	3	Supervisory status	$p < 0.0001$	79.57%
	4	Justifiability	$p < 0.0001$	79.57%
	5	Q75[5]	$p < 0.0029$	80.68%
	6	Gender	$p < 0.0072$	79.32%
	7	Q76[5]	$p < 0.0239$	79.83%
	8	Education	$p < 0.0172$	80.26%
	9	Q73[5]	$p < 0.0390$	80.60%
	10	Q74	$p < 0.0445$	81.03%
3. Job for colleague	–	–	–	69.86%
	1	*Justifiability*	$p < 0.0001$	82.02%
	2	Harmfulness	$p < 0.0001$	82.71%
	3	Q72	$p < 0.0001$	82.88%
	4	Corrupt	$p < 0.0001$	83.13%
	5	Gender	$p < 0.0016$	82.79%
	6	Supervisory status	$p < 0.0039$	83.05%
	7	Q73	$p < 0.0185$	82.96%
	8	Q74	$p < 0.0479$	83.30%
4. Leather diary	–	–	–	72.60%
	1	*Justifiability*	$p < 0.0001$	81.76%
	2	Corrupt	$p < 0.0001$	82.97%
	3	Q72	$p < 0.0001$	83.84%
	4	Q75	$p < 0.0001$	84.01%
	5	Supervisory status	$p < 0.0001$	83.75%
	6	Harmfulness	$p < 0.0001$	83.92%
	7	Gender	$p < 0.0442$	84.53%

Table 3. Continued.

Scenario	Step[1]	Variable Entered[2]	Probability[3]	Correct classification %[4]
5. 2nd job	–	–	–	80.81%
	1	*Justifiability*	$p < 0.0001$	85.65%
	2	Q72	$p < 0.0001$	84.96%
	3	Corrupt	$p < 0.0001$	87.04%
	4	Supervisory status	$p < 0.0001$	86.78%
	5	Harmfulness	$p < 0.0063$	86.95%
	6	Gender	$p < 0.0100$	87.64%
6. Computer tender	–	–	–	72.07%
	1	*Justifiability*	$p < 0.0001$	83.19%
	2	Q72	$p < 0.0001$	83.45%
	3	Harmfulness	$p < 0.0001$	83.88%
	4	Corrupt	$p < 0.0001$	84.74%
	5	Salary	$p < 0.0001$	84.74%
	6	Gender	$p < 0.0131$	84.91%
	7	Q74	$p < 0.0169$	84.66%
7. Job for friend	–	–	–	67.67%
	1	*Justifiability*	$p < 0.0001$	78.42%
	2	*Corrupt*	$p < 0.0001$	80.40%
	3	Q72	$p < 0.0001$	80.31%
	4	Q75	$p < 0.0004$	80.48%
	5	Supervisory status	$p < 0.0070$	80.22%
	6	Harmfulness	$p < 0.0080$	80.65%
	7	No. corrupt	$p < 0.0240$	80.91%
8. Whistleblower	–	–	–	94.06%
	1	Q72	$p < 0.0001$	94.06%
	2	Harmfulness	$p < 0.0001$	93.81%
	3	Supervisory status	$p < 0.0170$	93.72%
	4	Q77[5]	$p < 0.0431$	93.89%
9. Confidential information	–	–	–	93.61%
	1	Desirability	$p < 0.0001$	93.61%
	2	Q72	$p < 0.0001$	94.12%
	3	Corrupt	$p < 0.0020$	94.29%
	4	Supervisory status	$p < 0.0092$	94.29%
10. Hospital bills	–	–	–	87.42%
	1	Q72	$p < 0.0001$	87.42%
	2	Justifiability	$p < 0.0001$	88.51%
	3	Corrupt	$p < 0.0001$	88.93%
	4	Supervisory status	$p < 0.0001$	89.18%
	5	Harmfulness	$p < 0.0067$	89.35%
	6	Q77	$p < 0.0477$	89.18%

Table 3. Continued

11. Catering business	–	–	–	86.34%
	1	Harmfulness	$p < 0.0001$	87.19%
	2	Q72	$p < 0.0001$	87.19%
	3	Supervisory status	$p < 0.0001$	87.28%
	4	Justifiability	$p < 0.0255$	87.53%
	5	Q77	$p < 0.0525$	87.53%
12. Business trips	–	–	–	88.20%
	1	Q72	$p < 0.0001$	88.20%
	2	Harmfulness	$p < 0.0001$	87.95%
	3	Supervisory status	$p < 0.0001$	88.12%
	4	Corrupt	$p < 0.0060$	88.54%
	5	Q74	$p < 0.0080$	88.54%
	6	Q76	$p < 0.0452$	88.79%

[1] Variables are entered into the model in a stepwise manner: at each step the variable which is most strongly related to those remaining to be entered into the model (as measured by the smallest probability of no difference) is added to the model, provided that the probability is less than the cut-off level ($p \leq 0.05$).
[2] Variables which are not listed in the 3rd column of the Table were not found to make a statistically significant contribution to the predictive model.
[3] This is the probability of the observed X^2 (improvement) value if the null hypothesis (that the coefficient for the additional variable added in the last step is zero) is true. Small probabilities are associated with rejection of the null hypothesis and hence a decision that the additional variable does significantly contribute to the model.
[4] One way to assess the model is to compare the predicted values which would result from the model with the observed data. Of particular interest is by what percentage the percentage of correctly classified observations is an improvement on the percentage which could be correctly classified by chance. The initial percentage in each row represents the percentage which could be correctly classified by chance.
[5] See Table 2.
[6] Individual variables which increased, by more than 4%, the percentage which could be correctly classified by chance are italicised to distinguish them from other variables which had less effect on the percentage which could be correctly classified by chance.

justified was related to the choice to do nothing in nine scenarios (making a relatively large increase in percentage correctly classified in five of these). In two of these latter scenarios (JOB FOR COLLEAGUE and COMPUTER TENDER) mitigating circumstances were included in the descriptions of the scenarios. It is interesting that in both these scenarios the potentially corrupt behaviour involved furthering organisational rather than personal goals.

2. The attiude that "there is no point in reporting corruption as nothing useful will be done about it". The attitude that "there is no point in reporting corruption as nothing useful *will* be done about it" was related to the choice to do nothing in *every* scenario, and the most strongly related factor in four. This suggests that if people do not believe that effective action will result from reporting corruption they will be less inclined to take action about the conduct.

3. The belief that the scenario was not corrupt. A belief that the scenario was not corrupt was related to the choice to do nothing in nine of the scenarios. However, Table 4 reveals that, firstly, a number of those who *did* consider the scenarios to be corrupt said they would do nothing about the conduct. Secondly, a number of those who said the scenarios were *not* corrupt said that they *would* take some form of action about the conduct.

4. Supervisory status of the respondent. Of the background and workplace characteristics included in the study, supervisory status was the most closely related to the choice to do nothing about the scenarios (related to the choice to do nothing in 11 scenarios): in short, non-supervisors were more likely to say they would do nothing than were supervisors.

5. Concern about retaliation. Nearly three-quarters of our sample agreed or strongly agreed that "People who report corruption are likely to suffer for it" (see Table 2). The logistic regression found that this statement was *not* as closely related to the choice to do nothing about potential misconduct as were the factors listed above (it was related to the choice to do nothing in only five scenarios).

The types of concerns voiced by respondents who made spontaneous comments on the questionnaires, were not just about their becoming unpopular if they reported misconduct, but that they would be actively jeopardising their careers by taking such action. For example, one respondent stated:

> There is no protection for people who find corruption offensive. I would be a fool to put my career, peace of mind and safety on the line under these conditions. (0694)

The respondent's perception of his/her relationships with the perpetrator and the supervisor

A factor which was *not* tested in the logistic regression analysis but became apparent when examining the qualitative data collected concerned the idiosyncratic nature of the decision to report misconduct. Comments made by respondents suggested that some quite personal factors influenced their choice as

Table 4. Action respondents said they would take about the scenario: by whether the scenario is considered corrupt or not.

Scenarios		Action to be taken			
		do nothing	talk to employee	report internally	report outside
Stereo	not corrupt (n = 46)	47.8%	17.4%	30.4%	4.3%
	corrupt (n = 1232)	9.3%	19.8%	60.6%	10.2%
Take note pads	not corrupt (n = 473)	42.7%	48.8%	8.2%	0.2%
	corrupt (n = 794)	17.8%	49.1%	31.4%	1.8%
Job for colleague	not corrupt (n = 497)	57.1%	18.9%	23.3%	0.6%
	corrupt (n = 769)	13.2%	11.9%	67.5%	7.3%
Leather diary	not corrupt (n = 1004)	85.0%	12.6%	2.2%	0.2%
	corrupt (n = 255)	25.4%	37.1%	34.0%	3.5%
2nd job	not corrupt (n = 331)	49.8%	24.2%	25.4%	0.6%
	corrupt (n = 926)	8.6%	13.8%	70.3%	7.2%
Computer tender	not corrupt (n = 548)	49.3%	21.4%	27.9%	1.5%
	corrupt (n = 707)	11.4%	9.7%	66.8%	12.0%
Job for friend	not corrupt (n = 447)	63.3%	17.7%	18.6%	0.4%
	corrupt (n = 811)	15.6%	12.6%	64.2%	7.3%
Whistleblower	not corrupt (n = 66)	19.7%	12.1%	57.6%	10.6%
	corrupt (n = 1210)	5.0%	4.1%	50.2%	40.6%
Confidential info	not corrupt (n = 92)	23.9%	32.6%	37.0%	6.5%
	corrupt (n = 1193)	5.2%	9.3%	59.5%	26.0%
Hospital bills	not corrupt (n = 83)	44.6%	33.7%	21.7%	0.0%
	corrupt (n = 1205)	10.4%	24.5%	55.4%	9.8%
Catering business	not corrupt (n = 297)	24.6%	38.7%	36.7%	0.0%
	corrupt (n = 978)	10.2%	24.5%	61.5%	3.8%
Business trips	not corrupt (n = 98)	30.6%	30.6%	38.8%	0.0%
	corrupt (n = 1178)	10.3%	18.4%	64.6%	6.7%

to whether or not to take action about the scenarios. For example, a few respondents stated that they would only report the matter internally if they were on "chatting terms" with the relevant supervisor. Similarly, some people indicated that they would not report the potentially corrupt behaviour of a friend. Such considerations are not easily managed using a formal policy. What they do stress, however, is the impact of peers on employee views about matters which are as unclear and contentious as is corruption and in dictating behaviour in response to these matters.

Discussion

How do people decide what is corrupt?

The primary focus of the study was to explore *types of behaviour* people define as corrupt and how they respond to this behaviour. We were also interested in the *way* people decide what is corrupt or not. One feature of the decision making was the diversity of considerations which were taken into account by different respondents. Primarily, people attended to the consequences or harmfulness of the behaviour. However, numerous other factors including consideration of the value of the benefit received, who received the benefit, whether rules were being followed and how often the activity was happening appeared to impact upon whether the respondents defined particular scenarios as corrupt. These factors, in turn, can have an effect upon how people respond to corrupt conduct.

The link between identifying an activity as corrupt and taking action: layers of decisions

Corruption, as a form of "victimless" white-collar crime, is said to be significantly under-reported. This article has explored factors which may influence a person's decision not to respond to potentially corrupt conduct which he or she witnesses in the workplace. The results suggest that while identifying a behaviour as corrupt is often a precondition to willingness to take action about the conduct, this is just one of a number of influential factors. In some cases, it is not a factor at all.

Dozier and Miceli's (1985) "decision tree" provides a useful framework for discussing the survey results in general, though it is the first step, *a) identifying the behaviour as wrong*, which is the most relevant to the focus of this article.

a) identifying the behaviour as wrong. Dozier and Miceli (1985) suggest that a behaviour must be identified as wrongful before people will "blow the whistle" about that conduct. The results of the current study suggest, however, that even this first step must be subdivided. Identifying a behaviour as wrong implies that the behaviour must simply be identified as something which should not be happening. However, even when behaviour is identified as wrongful – characterised as "undesirable" in the current paper – we would add that for action to be taken in response to the conduct, there is still a definitional hurdle to be leapt. To explain by example: if an organisation demands that a particular course of action be taken when "corrupt" conduct is identified, then the observer must not only identify the conduct as wrongful to be motivated to take that course of action – but he or she also must identify the behaviour as "corrupt" (or at least potentially corrupt).

This definitional hurdle can be an obstacle in relation to the reporting requirements placed on numerous types of misconduct. However, the issue is very pertinent in relation to corruption because, as we have shown, there is such disparity between the ways that different individuals define and understand this class of behaviour. It is not difficult for behaviour to fall between the gaps of the differing perceptions about what is corrupt. Given the salience of informal or social definitions of corruption compared to legal definitions (Hollinger & Clark 1983; Werner 1983; Johnston 1986; Greenberger, Miceli & Cohen 1987) this lack of common understanding can have a significant impact upon the amount and type of conduct identified in the workplace and responded to as corrupt.

Furthermore, we find that a number of respondents place behaviour in mutually exclusive categories such that if a behaviour is characterised as "dishonest", "inefficient" or as "theft" then it might not also be characterised as "corrupt". Taken together, these results suggest that building strategies and policies which concern "corruption", without detailing what falls within this definition, will not be effective: it leaves open the opportunity for the response "I agree corruption is wrong and should be reported – but this activity I am engaged in is not corrupt".

In the case where people are reticent to report corrupt conduct (for reasons including concern about retaliation, the belief that nothing will be done about it anyway or their involvement in the conduct, etc.), there may be a clear temptation to define the behaviour out of the category which requires action. Studies by Horning (1970), Mars (1982) and Mancuso (1993) colourfully illustrate the ability of people to pragmatically redefine misconduct. One way to counter this is, as part of an education strategy, to highlight specific examples of corruption and to use these to foster debate about what it is that makes such behaviours "corrupt".

b) judgement that the situation is deserving of action. The relationship between the view that a behaviour was corrupt, harmful, undesirable or unjustified and whether or not people said they would take action about that conduct was explored. We found that, of these, it was how *justified* the behaviour was perceived to be which was most strongly related to the choice to take action about the conduct. We earlier made the point that employees may justify behaviour by referring to organisational as well as personal goals (e.g. "I had to get it done quickly"). This raises the need for organisations to be aware of conflicting demands placed upon employees (e.g. unrealistic financial or time constraints) which may be used to excuse corrupt activities. In addition, challenging likely rationalisations, for example, in corporate documents, such as codes of conduct, may be another valuable way of communicating that particular behaviours are unacceptable.

c) the person feels responsible for taking action. Miceli and Near (1984) discussed the notion of "role-proscribed" reporting. They suggested that people who see that reporting misconduct is part of their job, for example auditors or inspectors, are more likely to take action about misconduct they witness or find out about. Similarly, we find that supervisors were more likely to say they would take action than non-supervisors. These findings suggest that there is value in clearly communicating to staff that they have a responsibility to take action about corruption they witness at work (e.g. in their statements of duty, or the organisation's corporate plan, etc.). However, these measures require an equivalent commitment on the part of the organisation to support staff when they take such action about corruption. A first step is establishing a safe and effective system for receiving and responding to the information offered.

d) efficacious actions are available to be taken, e) these actions are appropriate and f) the expected benefit of taking action outweighs the expected costs. Several factors discussed in this paper support the notion that a cost-benefit analysis (albeit informal) forms part of the decision as to whether or not to "blow the whistle". Firstly the attitude that "there is no point in reporting corruption as nothing useful will be done about it" was particularly salient in the analysis. Secondly, there was the concern voiced about retaliation for reporting corruption.

Concern about the damaging implications to whistleblowers has been consistently raised in academic literature (e.g. Miceli & Near 1984; Truelson 1987; Mason undated). Publicity about the plight of various whistleblowers has also raised the prominence of this issue in NSW. In fact, 75% of the respondents in this survey agreed that "people who report corruption are likely to suffer for it". Accordingly, when undertaking our analysis we expected that concern about these implications would feature as a major disincentive to taking action about corruption. Contrary to expectation, however, most respondents – irrespective of whether they said they would do nothing *or* whether they said they would take action about the conduct – agreed that whistleblowers are likely to suffer for their actions. Furthermore, the most salient attitude of the group who said they would do nothing was the concern that nothing useful would be done in response to their actions. As one of these respondents commented:

> Nobody damn well cares any way. Waste of breath. Been there, done that, and believe me no one cares (0234).

In a sense the question of whether there is any value in reporting corruption (i.e. change will result) is a prior step to the consideration of whether you might suffer as a result of whistleblowing – if you know nothing will happen as a result of your action then why would you invite the potential trouble?

Thus, if people are to be encouraged to take action about corruption then they must feel that their contribution *will* make a difference to the situation. Safe and effective reporting channels will be of little value if people do not believe that there is any point in using them. Miceli and Near (1984), who analysed survey results from a very large sample of US federal public sector employees, also commented that:

> . . . policy changes to protect whistle-blowers against reprisal short of guaranteeing anonymity are unlikely to affect the behaviour of [observers of wrongdoing who do not whistleblow]; however, providing convincing evidence that corrective action would be taken appears to be important to nearly all potential whistle-blowers (p. 703).

As the NSW parliament moves to formalise whistleblower protection in legislation, public sector organisations need to focus not only on the safety of the reporting mechanisms which are created, but also on constructive ways to respond to the information that they receive. For instance, organisational responses to allegations of corruption need not only be that individuals are punished. It may be that there are also systemic or policy issues which the allegations reveal as in need of review. Furthermore, the presence of reporting channels and the possible outcomes which may be achieved by using them must be clearly communicated to staff (see Audit Office of NSW et al. 1995).

Differences between individuals

The Dozier and Miceli (1985) model was used to attempt to illustrate the hierarchy of decisions made when deciding whether or not to take action about potentially corrupt conduct to which public sector employees may be privy. However, such a model tends to underplay the fact that people respond to corruption in very idiosyncratic ways. In this study we found that how the behaviour is defined, the level of harm it is perceived to cause, how justified it is perceived to be in the circumstances, the perceived relationship between the witness and the perpetrator and the witness's view of the effectiveness of the organisation's reporting mechanism, all varied from person to person. In short, respondents with similar demographic or background characteristics did not necessarily respond in the same way to corruption or to dealing with corruption.

Conclusion

In summary, we cannot assume either that there is consistency among groups of employees about what constitutes corrupt conduct or that, once behaviour is identified as corrupt, people will take action about it. There are, however, a number of positive strategies which can be taken to encourage people to respond to corruption they witness in their workplaces. These include:

- fostering a common understanding of what behaviour is corrupt;
- recognising the influence of peer attitudes on how people identify behaviour as corrupt;
- emphasising the harmfulness of corrupt conduct;
- challenging the rationalisations used to excuse or ignore corrupt behaviour;
- including a responsibility to respond to corruption in the duties of employees;
- putting effective and safe reporting mechanisms in place within organisations; and
- considering and communicating what effective action can be taken by the organisation in responses to reports of corruption from employees (including systemic change).

Applied together, a combination of the above strategies may enhance the ability of organisations to respond constructively to corrupt conduct which may be taking place in their workplaces.

Notes

1. The Fitzgerald Inquiry (1989) arose from the allegations of police whistleblowers, which were broadcast as part of a television documentary program. The inquiry prompted major reforms to policing and to the investigation of police corruption in the state of Queensland, Australia.

2. New South Wales (NSW), with a population of approximately 6 million residents, is the most populous state in Australia.
3. The Independent Commission Against Corruption (ICAC) was established in March 1989 under an act of the NSW Parliament. The Commission's role is to expose and minimise corruption in the NSW public sector.
4. A logistic regression analysis is a statistical technique used to determine which of a set of variables can be used to predict an outcome which has two possibilities (e.g. consider scenario corrupt versus not corrupt).

References

Audit Office of NSW, Independent Commission Against Corruption and NSW Ombudsman (1995) *Internal Reporting Systems*. Sydney, ICAC.

Atkinson, M.M. and Mancuso, M. (1985) Do we need a code of conduct for politicians? The search for an elite political culture of corruption in Canada. *Canadian Journal of Political Science, XVIII (3)*, 459–480.

Chibnall, S. and Saunders, P. (1977) Worlds apart: notes on the social reality of corruption. *British Journal of Sociology, 28(2)*, 138–154.

Cressey, D.R. (1986) Why managers commit fraud. *Australian & New Zealand Journal of Criminology, 19*, 195–209.

Dolan, K., McKeown, B. and Carlson, J.M. (1988) Popular conceptions of political corruption: implications for the empirical study of political ethics. *Corruption and Reform, 3*, 3–24.

Dozier, J.B. and Miceli, M.P. (1985) Potential predictors of whistle-blowing: a prosocial behavior perspective. *Academy of Management Review, 10(4)*, 823–836.

Gardiner, J.A. (1970) *The politics of corruption: organized crime in an American city*. New York: Russell Sage Foundation.

Gardiner, J.A. (1993) Defining corruption. *Corruption and Reform, 7*, 111–124.

Gibbons, K.M. (1985) Towards an attitudinal definition of corruption: Evidence from a survey of Canadian university students. Paper given at the 1985 International Political Science Congress, Paris. Reprinted as "Variations in attitudes toward corruption in Canada". In Heidenheimer, A.J., Johnston, M. and Le Vine, V.T. (1990) (Eds). *Political corruption: a handbook*. New Brunswick, New Jersey; Transaction Publishers, pp. 763–780.

Gibbons, K.M. (1990) Toward an attitudinal definition of corruption. In Heidenheimer, A.J., Johnston, M. and Le Vine, V.T. (1990) (Eds). *Political corruption: a handbook*. New Brunswick, New Jersey: Transaction Publishers, pp. 165–171.

Grabosky, P.N., Braithwaite, J.B. and Wilson, P.R. (1987) The myth of community tolerance toward white-collar crime. *Australian and New Zealand Journal of Criminology, 20*, 33–44.

Greenberger, D.B., Miceli, M.P. and Cohen, D.J. (1987) Oppositionists and group norms: the reciprocal influence of whistle-blowers and co-workers. *Journal of Business Ethics, 6*, 527–542.

Gronbeck, B.E. (1990) The rhetoric of political corruption. In Heidenheimer, A.J., Johnston, M. and Le Vine, V.T. (1990) (Eds). *Political corruption: a handbook*. New Brunswick, New Jersey: Transaction Publishers, pp. 173–189.

Hauber, A.R., Toornvliet, L.G. and Willemsee, H.M. (1988) The perceived seriousness of white collar crime and conventional crime. *Corruption and Reform, 3*, 41–63.

Heidenheimer, A.J., Johnston, M. and Le Vine, V.T. Terms, concepts and definitions: an introduction. In Heidenheimer, A.J., Johnston, M. and Le Vine V.T. (1990) (Eds) *Political corruption: a handbook*. New Brunswick, New Jersey: Transaction Publishers, pp. 3–14.

Hoffman, P.B. and Hardyman, P.L.(1986) Crime seriousness scales: public perception and feedback to criminal justice policymakers. *Journal of Criminal Justice, 14*, 413–431.

Hollinger, R.C. and Clark, J.P. (1983) *Theft by employees*. Lexington, Massachusetts: Lexington Books, D.C. Heath and Company.

Horning, D. (1970) Blue collar theft: conceptions of property, attitudes towards pilfering, and work group norms in a modern industrial plant. In Smigel, E. and Ross, H. (1970) (Eds) *Crimes Against Bureaucracy*. NY: Van Nostrand Reinhold, pp. 47–64.

Jackson, M. and Smith, R. (1993) Everyone's doing it! Codes of ethics and New South Wales legislators' perceptions of corruption. Unpublished paper.

Johnston, M. (1986) Right & wrong in American politics: Popular conceptions of corruption. *Polity, XVIII (3)*, 367–391.

Johnston, M. (1989) Corruption and political culture in Britain and the United States. *Innovation, 2(4)*, 417–436.

Malec, K.L. and Gardiner, J.A. (1987) Measurement issues in the study of official corruption: a Chicago example. *Corruption & Reform, 3*, 267–278.

Mancuso, M. (1993) The ethical attitudes of British MP's: a typology. *Parliamentary Affairs, 46(2)*, 179–191.

Mars, G. (1982) *Cheats at work: an anthropology of workplace crime*. London: George Allen & Unwin (publishers) Ltd.

Mason, B. (undated) Blowing the whistle on government wrongdoing: a call for statutory protection of whistleblowers in the Australian public service. University of Cambridge. (unpublished).

Miceli, M.P. and Near, J.P. (1984) The relationships among beliefs, organisational position, and whistle-blowing status: a discriminant analysis. *Academy of Management Journal, 27*, 687–705.

Near, J.P. and Jensen, T.C. (1983) The whistle-blowing process: retaliation and perceived effectiveness. *Work and Occupations, 10*, 3–28.

Near, J.P. and Miceli, M.P. (1986) Retaliation against whistle-blowers: predictors and effects. *Journal of Applied Psychology, 71*, 137–145.

Peters, J.G. and Welch, S. (1978) Political corruption in America: a search for definitions and a theory, or if political corruption is in the mainstream of American politics why is it not in the mainstream of American politics research? *The American Political Science Review, 72(3)*, 974–984.

Scott, J.C. (1972) *Corporate Political Corruption*. USA: Prentice-Hall Inc. publishers.

Truelson, J. (1987) Blowing the whistle on systematic corruption: on maximising reform and minimising retaliation. *Corruption and Reform, 2*, 55–74.

Walker, J., Dagger, D. and Collins, M. (1989) *Crime in Australia: as measured by the Australian component of the International Crime Victim Survey 1989*. Canberra: Australian Institute of Criminology.

Welch, S. and Peters, J.G. (1977) Attitudes of US state legislators toward political corruption: some preliminary findings. *Legislative Studies Quarterly, 2*, 445–463.

Werner, S.B. (1983) New directions in the study of administrative corruption. *Public Administration Review, 2*, 146–154.

Corruption and Reform 5: 125–151, 1990

Citizen co-production and corruption control

PETER N. GRABOSKY
Australian Institute of Criminology, GPO Box 2944, Canberra, A.C.T. 2601, Australia

Abstract. This article introduces the concept of co-production, and emphasizes the importance of citizen assistance to complement public sector activities to control corruption in an era of fiscal restraint. Some examples of co-production from other areas of law enforcement are reviewed briefly. Citizen participation in corruption control activity is an important means of chilling the climate of apathy within which corruption flourishes, and citizen vigilance can be a deterrent to illicit transactions.

Some existing precedents for citizen co-production in corruption control are then noted. It is suggested that monetary incentives might supplement pure moral incentives for citizen assistance. Recognizing that the availability of monetary incentives might invite abuses and other adverse effects, the discussion then turns to appropriate safeguards. Citizen participation in corruption control is desirable, but only up to a point. There is an optimal level of citizen involvement, beyond which the climate of trust necessary for a free and open society may be subject to erosion.

The article concludes with a review of some of the political conditions which are conducive to an optimal amount of citizen co-production in corruption control, and suggests what directions citizen anti-corruption activities might take as we approach the 21st century.

1. The concept of co-production and the importance of citizen assistance in an era of fiscal restraint

The task which confronts governments genuinely concerned about corruption is not simply how their own corruption control efforts can be made more efficient and effective, but how they can enlist the support of the general public to combat corruption.

The concept considered here is that of citizen co-production. To complement the various anti-corruption initiatives which governments around the world have mobilized, members of the general public may themselves contribute to the fight against corruption by producing anti-corruption services. In their purest form, these services are what is termed 'off-budget' – that is, they entail no cost to the public treasury. Other variations may entail the provision of services on a commission basis, for a percentage of funds recovered. There is a point, however, at which citizen involvement occurs on a fee for service, retainer, or salaried basis, or which is otherwise contingent upon some kind of public expenditure, and therefore lies beyond the boundary of citizen co-production. Examples drawn from this latter category will nevertheless be used to illustrate the potential risks which co-production may entail, absent appropriate safeguards and accountability mechanisms.

The utility and the legitimacy of citizen co-production can be illustrated with a number of examples from political systems around the world. Many of these examples are hardly novel. Indeed, one dates back 125 years, with roots half a millenium older than that.

But first, it might be useful to review some contemporary examples of citizen co-production which exist in other domains of law enforcement. Each entails a significant increase in the pool of law enforcers at little or no public expense. The first, and perhaps the most familiar, is the ubiquitous Neighbourhood Watch, a common feature in many North American communities. Simply stated, Neighbourhood Watch entails residents organizing to be alert for and to report suspicious activity in their neighbourhoods. When it is operating successfully, the eyes and ears of Neighbourhood Watch participants provide surveillance services which would cost thousands of dollars if delivered by police or private security agents. These and other community crime prevention activities are reviewed by Skogan (1988).

Another example of citizen co-production can be drawn from occupational health and safety regulation in the Australian state of Victoria. There, the institution of elected worker safety representatives complements the government inspectorate (Braithwaite, Grabosky and Fisse 1986). Safety representatives may demand access to inspect any part of the workplace or to inspect company records relating to health and safety. They are empowered to issue provisional improvement notices when they discover a workplace hazard. These notices have the force of law, pending abatement of the hazard in question or authoritative determination by a government inspector. Breach of such a notice renders one liable to prosecution. Safety representatives now number in the thousands in Victoria. Regulatory vigilance in the Victorian workplace is thus enhanced far beyond the degree which could otherwise be provided by a government inspector.

Other examples of citizen involvement in the Australian regulatory process include the use of volunteers to monitor beach erosion and to submit regular reports to the Queensland Beach Protection Authority; the use of voluntary wardens to watch over historic shipwrecks in South Australia, and the use by the New South Wales Department of Consumer Affairs of a network of volunteers from the consumer movement to discover hazardous products on the market (Grabosky and Braithwaite 1986). In August, 1989, the Australian Customs Service announced that it would seek the assistance of workers in the airline industry, and service personnel at Sydney airport, in identifying illegal drug imports.

Australia is by no means unique in its provision for citizen involvement in the regulatory process. Indeed, worker safety representatives are a feature of many European occupational health and safety regimes.

In the United States, regulations under the Surface Mining Control and Regulation Act 1977 allow citizens to request an inspection by federal regulatory authorities. The citizen must submit a signed written statement which would give regulatory authorities reason to believe that a violation exists. The citizen may accompany the inspector in the course of the inspection, and is entitled to receive a copy of the inspector's report. In the event that no inspection is conducted, the citizen is entitled to a written explanation for the decision in question (Shover, Clelland and Lynxwiler 1986: 168). Most federal environmental legislation in the United States contains provisions permitting private parties to sue others for non-compliance, regardless of whether or not they have suffered injury (Greve 1989).

2. Citizen participation as a means of overcoming the culture of apathy within which corruption flourishes

There are very good reasons, beyond those of fiscal constraint in the public sector, to enlist the resources of the general public in the cause of corruption control.

It is almost tautologous to suggest that where corruption is accepted as a way of life, public officials, honest or otherwise, and members of the general public become resigned to the practice. In such a culture of public apathy, there are few disincentives to participating in corrupt transactions.

The reform movement in United States municipal politics, which dates back a century, sought to mobilize citizen indignation against corrupt political machines. The tradition of the 'muckraking' essayist and the emergence of concerned citizen groups established an important trend in American political culture (Noonan 1984: Ch. 17; Gardiner and Olson 1974). In recent years, Etzioni (1984: 281) has called for the energizing of the populace, to demand a new standard of public civility.

3. Citizen vigilance as a deterrent to illicit transactions

In a society where the citizenry has been mobilized against corruption, the risk of detection and disrepute looms larger. Perhaps even more important, in such an active society, a prevailing anti-corruption ethos may facilitate the development of moral inhibitions in otherwise corruptible individuals.

A citizenry mobilized against corruption may not be sufficient to deter all corrupt practices, and indeed, may drive the more determined partners in corruption to more artful concealment of their practices. But it should serve to inhibit a good deal of opportunistic or peripheral corrupt activity. The importance of this should not be minimized, for limited enforcement resources can then be concentrated on priority targets. This will have a wider beneficial effect as well, for the progression of a career in corruption often begins with small scale graft.

4. Public participation as enhancing participatory democracy

Public contribution to any civic enterprise can be healthy for its own sake. A successful democracy requires that citizens be involved and active in politics. A passive citizenry will inhibit the maturation of democratic institutions. When an individual sees him or herself as a citizen, and not merely as a subject, support for the political system, and ultimately the stability of that system, is enhanced. Active citizen involvement in the process of government may instill in members of the public a sense of belonging and cohesion and feelings of efficacy. To enhance one's estimation of one's competence as a citizen may in turn facilitate the development of higher moral and ethical standards. Civic engagement thus serves to improve both the government and the citizen (Barber 1984).

There is already ample precedent around the world for an active citizen role in the prevention and control of corruption. Governments actively seek information from the general public on matters relating to corrupt practices. Many actively encourage individual or group vigilance. But other governments have been less receptive to public involvement, prompting some citizens to resort to direct action in response to corrupt practices.

Direct action

The student protests in Beijing in May, 1989 were inspired in part by perceived corruption on the part of senior government and party officials. Some of the earliest activities of the Polish free trade union Solidarity involved public complaints over high level corruption (Los 1988: 151–160). The demise of Philippines dictator Ferdinand Marcos in the face of 'People's Power' is yet another example, as was the abdication of the Shah of Iran. At a greater extreme, countless *coups d'etat* have brought about the overthrow of corrupt leaders around the world.

On a smaller scale, individuals may engage in dramatic acts of protest in order to call attention to corruption and abuse of power. To cite but one example, in the United States, two Tuscarora Indians brandishing sawn-off shotguns took over a newspaper office and held hostages for ten hours in February, 1988. Claiming that their actions were a protest against corruption in local government, the two surrendered after having been told that the Governor of North Carolina agreed to appoint a task force to investigate allegations of official corruption in the area. The two were subsequently acquitted of all charges arising from the protest (*New York Times* 1988).

Our concern here is less with insurgency than with the more conventional political and judicial processes. One essential requisite of citizen vigilance is knowledge. Members of the public may be unaware of the deleterious consequences of corrupt practices and of the importance of integrity in the public sector. In most democratic societies, a free press and an energetic political opposition should suffice to perform the educational functions appropriate to these ends. But they need not be left to chance.

Community consultation

The Hong Kong Independent Commission Against Corruption has a well-developed public relations function. It has an entire department devoted to community relations. In addition, it is supported by a number of citizens' advisory committees, including one which advises on overall policy, another which advises on investigative procedures, a committee which provides guidance on publicity campaigns and educational programs, one concerned with corruption prevention strategies, and one which receives complaints from the public about Commission activities (Klitgaard 1988: 109).

In furtherance of its goals to educate and persuade the public to develop less tolerant attitudes towards corruption, the Hong Kong ICAC has produced a television drama series, has established store front offices, and has sought out the public in factories, offices and even on boats. The ICAC is even represented on the Education Department's curriculum development committee (Clark 1987).

Citizen involvement in corruption control is by no means unique to capitalist society. The Soviet Union encourages citizen participation in law enforcement, and invites individual citizens to expose corrupt practices. Those provisions of the Constitution of the USSR which encourage citizens to petition and to criticize pre-date Glasnost.

A major oversight role in the Soviet Union is performed by People's Control Committees, a network of agencies which serve to "conduct systematic checkups on the implementation of Party directives, Soviet laws and government decisions, to resolutely oppose everything that harms the state's interests..." including "all attempts to deceive the state, and to encroach on socialist property" (Lampert 1985: 40). The monitoring work of People's

Control Committees is supplemented by volunteer inspectors, and other 'citizen controllers' in the Party, the trade unions and the media. A 1977 study estimated the number of voluntary inspectors in the Soviet Union at $9^{1}/_{2}$ million, with an additional 13 million activists engaged in occasional monitoring activity. This amounts to approximately one in every five adult citizens (Adams 1977: 138).

People's Control Committees have certain powers of inspection, and even punishment. They may warn officials about violations, and may apply to authorities to have illegal decisions rescinded. They may impose reprimands, order an officer's dismissal, and recover damages arising from official misfeasance (Lampert 1985: 41). While they may exercise these powers on occasion, they provide an important source of information for traditional law enforcement agencies, and are an important vehicle of public involvement in corruption control.

The energies of Soviet trade unionists have also been mobilized. A 1962 decree entitled 'On Developing to the Fullest Public Participation in the Work of the Trade Unions' urged unions to encourage voluntary efforts of factory workers and office personnel to check on the expenditure of public funds, in addition to assisting state and union inspectorates in occupational health and safety inspections. Exemplary inspections are accorded detailed media coverage, in order to encourage readers to participate in similar undertakings. All major newspapers contain a 'People's Control' page (Adams 1977: 135–136).

In the People's Republic of China, hotel staff assist authorities by keeping a watchful eye on the movements of foreign businesspeople. According to Silk (1988: 26):

> Friendly elevator operators and floorboys normally report any seemingly deviant behavior to the authorities. One tax official wrote in an authoritative journal that hotel personnel are expected to cooperate with tax and other relevant authorities to report the number of days foreigners on extended visits stay in China, so as to effectively monitor which foreigners approach or exceed the number of days attaching tax liability, and thus detect tax evasion. Outside the hotels, the formidable informal network of control includes extra judicial grassroots organizations like street offices, residents' committees, residents' groups, and security defense committees.

Citizens' lobbying organizations

Perhaps the best example from a western democratic polity of a citizens' organization to oversee public sector ethical standards is Common Cause.

Common Cause is a non-partisan non-profit citizens' organization which monitors and lobbies U.S. federal and state governments with a view to improving the integrity of their operations. It is supported by dues and contributions from 275,000 members throughout the United States.

Founded in 1970, Common Cause bases its operations on democratic principles. A 60-member national governing board is elected by members. To decide priorities and policies, the board conducts an annual issues poll of the entire membership, supplemented by occasional in-depth surveys of random samples of members and conferences of active members. In its two decades of existence, the organization has contributed to significant reforms in the areas of election financing, public disclosure of lobbying activity and public officials' conflicts of interest, and other related reforms in public administration.

Its general oversight of the public sector, and vocal identification of unethical conduct on the part of public officials, have had considerable effect. Common Cause repeatedly called attention to questionable ethical conduct on the part of a former Attorney General of the United States (Common Cause 1984; Baldwin 1988); its efforts contributed to considerable delay in the confirmation of his initial appointment, and to his eventual resignation from office. In the life of the most recent U.S. Congress, Common Cause called for investigations into the activities of eight Members of Congress. One investigation led to the resignation of the Speaker of the U.S. House of Representatives (*Congressional Quarterly* 1989).

Prestigious organizations such as Common Cause can add considerable legitimacy to debate on corruption. Whereas allegations of corrupt practices emanating from political adversaries are too easily dismissed as 'partisan' attacks, the statements of a respected non-partisan body can carry considerable credibility and moral force. In the international human rights arena, such a role is played by Amnesty International.

A body modeled after Common Cause, and bearing the same name, has been established in India. Among its concerns is corruption in government telephone companies and diversion of tax overcharges to political campaign funds (Crosette 1989).

The Better Government Association, a citizens' group in Chicago, Illinois, has served as an independent monitor of government since the 1920s. One imaginative project to document electoral fraud entailed an Association investigator disguised as a derelict who from time to time checked into a number of skid row hotels under assumed names which included T.S. Eliot, James Joyce, and William Faulkner. The investigator made no attempt to register to vote, but the celebrated names later appeared on the city's voter registration list. Indeed, votes were cast in these names on election day.

Another Better Government Association project, undertaken in collaboration with a Chicago newspaper and a national television network, entailed the purchase and operation of a neighbourhood tavern, and the systematic documentation and recording of extortion against tavern proprietors by a variety of city inspectors (Manikas and Protess 1979: 16, 117–129; Smith and Zekman 1979).

Solidarity and support for whistle blowers

Private citizens, either as individuals or through organizations, may also contribute to corruption control by providing support to whistle-blowers (Glazer and Glazer 1989: 253–257). Blowing the whistle can be stressful at the best of times, but individuals who disclose organizational misconduct are often targets for harassment, persecution, or other forms of victimization by the organization in question or by other powerful interests. The whistle-blower's own personal safety or financial security and that of his or her family may well be at risk. Emotional and other support to ethical resisters is not only of immediate benefit to the individual under stress, but it can contribute to long term vindication of the public interest, and ultimately, through the heightened consciousness of individuals in organizational settings, to the integrity of public agencies and private corporations alike.

Public interest litigation

The use of the law by private individuals to combat corruption can be impeded by financial and procedural barriers. But some impressive achievements have nevertheless been recorded. In India, there has emerged what is termed an epistolary jurisdiction, through which citizens' groups may petition the courts on behalf of disadvantaged individuals who may have suffered as the result of maladministration or the abuse of power.

To cite one brief example of this 'social action litigation', Professors Upendra Baxi and Lotika Sarkar clipped a letter to the editor of The Indian Express which described horrendous abuses of female prisoners in a particular institution, and forwarded it to a justice of the Supreme Court of India. The accompanying letter asserted that fundamental rights were being jeopardised, and that duty required the two professors to bring this to the attention of the court. They suggested that their letter be deemed a writ petition on behalf of the abused prisoners. The petition was indeed entertained by the court, which ordered improvements in living conditions of prisoners, as well as complete medical examinations.

This expansion of the law of standing by the Supreme Court of India allowed public spirited individuals to seek redress on behalf of those who may lack awareness of their legal rights, who may feel politically powerless, and who may be too poor to afford legal assistance (Sturgess and Chubb 1988: 46–53).

5. Moral and monetary incentives for citizen assistance

Governments may explicitly invite citizens to come forward with information relating to corrupt practices. To this end, media advertisements are not uncommon. Indeed, governments often benefit from information relating to fraudulent practices which citizens volunteer. An estimated 30% of prosecutions for social security fraud in Australia result from anonymous advice given to the Department of Social Security by friends, neighbours, and workmates of the accused (Kirkwood 1986: 190). In Singapore, the business community has been specifically invited to report requests from members of the Customs and Excise Department for illicit payments (Klitgaard 1988: 129).

Legal obligations

In some individuals, the sense of civic obligation is sufficient to enlist one's co-operation in corruption control efforts. But this is not always the case. In many democratic societies, the perceived effort entailed in so simple an act as casting a ballot in general elections may be such as to outweigh the perceived benefits of so doing. In matters relating to corruption, the risk of retaliation and victimization may be substantial disincentives for becoming involved.

In some instances, citizens are obliged by law to disclose corrupt practices to government authorities. A number of jurisdictions, including Australia, require financial institutions to report significant cash transactions to a specified agency. The purpose of such provisions is to impede the 'laundering' of ill-gotten gains.

The efforts entailed in reporting corrupt practices may be considerable. Involvement in subsequent investigation and litigation may be more so. The question is, when should governments offer monetary incentives for citizen co-production in corruption control, and what form might these incentives take?

Administrative rewards

Rewards and bounties are old institutions indeed. While the two terms are sometimes used interchangeably, the term reward is more properly applied to a premium or compensation paid by private persons or by the government for a special or extraordinary service, whereas bounties are offered by governments to all persons engaging in particular industries or performing specified services for the public benefit.

Over the course of history, bounties have been paid to citizens for enlistment in military service, destruction of enemy vessels or noxious animals, production of sugar and salt, promotion of certain industries, engaging in certain types of fishing, planting trees and hedges, and the sinking of artesian wells.

The use of rewards for information leading to the identification and arrest of an alleged offender is a time honoured practice in some societies. Offered on an ad hoc basis in cases of serious crimes of violence, they also exist on an ongoing basis for assistance in other areas of law enforcement. In some cases, they may entail payment in the form of a commission for services rendered. An Alabama statute provides that individuals who confer information leading to the prosecution of drug offenders may receive a percentage of the value of any property condemned in the event the prosecution succeeds (Act Ab 81-6788 Ala. Acts 1109). Rewards are commonly, albeit discreetly, offered by private sector organizations, particularly banks and insurance companies.

Cash rewards can in principle be offered to citizens who assist in the identification of corrupt practices and in the recovery of illicitly gained public monies.

The justification for offering monetary incentives to citizens who assist in the control of corruption rests in the recognition that these citizens are providing a valuable public service – one which could entail considerable expenditure if performed by public employees. Moreover, the retaliatory power of the corrupt public official may be formidable, its very existence serving as a deterrent to citizen involvement. A reward can help neutralise the disincentive posed by this threat.

There exist, moreover, numerous disincentives to citizen co-operation which the availability of financial incentives may help offset. The time and effort which co-operation in a corruption investigation may entail can be a burden in its own right for many persons.

For obvious reasons, the fruits of corruption are rarely declared as income to taxation authorities. In the United States, section 7623 of the Internal Revenue Code and subordinate regulations permit the Internal Revenue Service (IRS) to pay a reward to citizens providing information leading to the detection and punishment of anyone violating the internal revenue laws. Special provisions are made to ensure the security and to preserve the confidentiality of informers' communications. Other provisions prevent the payment of rewards to informers who themselves participated in tax evasion schemes or who prepared returns for taxpayers with the knowledge that they were evading taxes. Reward payments are regarded by the IRS as taxable income.

The reward system, while more than merely symbolic, is hardly an essential element of revenue operations. Less than ten percent of all claims are judged worthy of a reward. In 1984, a total of $853,698 in rewards was paid on 350 claims; $34.1 million was recovered by the government as a result (*Wall Street Journal* 23 January, 1985: 1).

More recently, pursuant to the Insider Trading and Securities Fraud Enforcement Act of 1988, the United States Securities and Exchange Commission (SEC) has explicitly authorized the payment of bounties to persons providing information leading to the recovery of a civil penalty from an insider trader, from a person who 'tipped' information to an insider trader, or from a person who directly or indirectly controlled an insider trader. Civil penalties may be up to three times the illegal gains (or losses avoided); the bounty payable may be up to ten percent of the civil penalty assessed.

Both the IRS and SEC reward programs are general in their focus, but could easily embrace the activities of corrupt officials. The failure of a bribe taker to disclose his or her ill-gotten gains is an obvious infringement of revenue laws; similarly liable is the government officer who, in the course of his or her employment, acquires price-sensitive information which is then exploited for personal gain.

Private prosecutions

The institution of private prosecutions pre-dates the rise of the modern state. In those days, criminal prosecutions were brought by private citizens. Today, that function is almost exclusively the province of public officials. There nevertheless remains a vestige of the private right of prosecution in Australia and elsewhere in the common law world (Australian Law Reform Commission 1985: 182–209).

In theory, it would appear that private prosecutions possess great potential for corruption control. Indeed, if corruption extends to agents of the criminal justice system, to those whose very responsibility it is to mobilize the criminal process, the threat of prosecution by public authorities may be empty.

But private prosecutions are hardly a panacea. They may require considerable financial resources, and these may not always be available, even in those jurisdictions which offer legal assistance to the indigent for purposes of private prosecution. Moreover, where it exists, the right of private prosecution tends not to be untrammeled. An action may require the consent of the Attorney General or Director of Public Prosecutions. The Attorney General may take over a prosecution, or may terminate an action by entering a *nolle prosequi*.

Private prosecutions have been used in Australia in response to alleged abuses by police and prison officers, but without success (Grabosky 1989: 88; Australian Law Reform Commission 1985: 200). Similarly unsuccessful was a private prosecution to challenge unauthorized financial transactions on the part of a former Prime Minister of Australia and a number of his senior ministers (Sankey v. Whitlam (1976) NSWLR 570; (1978) 142 CLR 1). Although they are so constrained by safeguards against abuse that their utility against corruption is limited, they at least symbolize the right of the ordinary citizen to act where the government fails to do so.

In fourteenth century England, there emerged a means of private redress to supplement what were at the time modest efforts at public enforcement (Fisse and Braithwaite 1986). The term employed for these causes of action was *qui tam* (Latin for 'who as well'; that is, who sues for the state as well as for him or herself).

Qui tam litigation fell into disuse in the English speaking world, to be revived 125 years ago during the United States Civil War. At that time, the U.S. federal bureaucracy bore no resemblance to its counterpart today. There was no Federal Bureau of Investigation, and little in the way of fraud control apparatus. At the same time, support for the war was not uniformly enthusiastic. While many fought and died bravely to preserve the Union, others were able to avoid conscription by purchasing the services of a stand-in. Others still rioted. Purveyors of provisions and equipment to the Grand Army of the Republic were also inclined to cut corners from time to time. Cases purporting to contain gunpowder were opened on the battlefield, and found to contain only sawdust. Useless muskets were sold to the government at eight times their value. In 1861 one thousand mules were purchased by the U.S. Army at $119 each. Some were diseased, others were blind, almost all were useless. In the face of such abuses, and mindful of the lack of investigative resources within the government, the United States Congress enacted the False Claims Act of 1863. The legislation was noteworthy in two respects. First, it was a civil and not a criminal statute, intended to be remedial rather than punitive. It provided for double damages, that is, twice the amount falsely claimed, plus a civil fine of $2,000. The standard of proof required was civil, on the balance of probabilities, rather than the more formidable criminal standard of proof beyond reasonable doubt.

Second, the statute included *qui tam* provisions, authorizing private citizens to sue on behalf of the government, and to share in any recovery of up to 50 percent of defrauded funds eventually recovered by the government.

The False Claims Act fell into disuse for the best part of a century. Then, during the Second World War, a case brought under the Act resulted in a decision of the United States Supreme Court (U.S. ex rel Marcus v. Hess 317 U.S. 537 (1943)) which invited widespread abuse of the statute. In that case, the court held that a person could sue under the False Claims Act on behalf of the government even though the action was based solely on information acquired from the government itself. The decision thus invited citizens to ride piggyback on any government fraud investigation. The United States Congress promptly amended the Act to prevent any suits based on information the government had when the action was brought, and limited the damages available to a private plaintiff in cases joined by the government to 10 per cent of monies recovered–with no guarantee of any recovery. Thus emasculated, the False Claims Act lay all but forgotten until the Reagan Administration.

Among the events of the 1980s which precipitated a revival of the False Claims Act were numerous egregious abuses by U.S. defense contractors. Tales of $300 toilet seats, $5,000 coffee urns, and kennel fees for the family dog of one executive being added to the account for a nuclear submarine contract engendered media ridicule and not inconsiderable public indignation. The problem was by no means limited to defense procurement (Eagleton and Shapiro 1983). Given the Reagan Administration's pontifications about the necessity for fiscal restraint, the U.S. Congress decided to revitalize the False Claims Act.

As amended in 1986, the legislation (PL 99-562) incorporated the following:

1. Allowance for a private citizen who discovers fraud against the government to sue for damages.
2. Provision for an award of triple the damages sustained by the government.
3. Provision for a maximum civil fine of $10,000.
4. Guarantees that the private citizen who initiates the suit receives a proportion of the damage award–between 15 percent and 25 percent if the government enters the case; if the government does not enter the suit, the successful private plaintiff can receive between 25 percent and 30 percent of damages. (Awards are at the discretion of the presiding judge, based on his or her assessment of the citizen's contribution to the litigation.)
5. A requirement that the defendant pay the legal expenses of a successful private plaintiff.
6. Protection for private plaintiffs from harassment, dismissal, demotion or suspension by their employer.

Between October, 1986 and July, 1989, some 168 *qui tam* suits were filed under the False Claims Act. All were filed against companies or individuals who had allegedly defrauded the U.S. Government (Phillips 1989). Its potential for use against corrupt public officials would be significant, were it not for provisions which bar suits against specified senior federal officials.

Shareholders derivative suits

In the event that the resources of a public company are used for corrupt purposes, a cause of action may be available to its shareholders. This may be based on a jurisdiction's securities laws, such as those in the United States which require corporate disclosure of illicit payments. Shareholders have a right to know if the funds which they have entrusted to a company's management are being managed properly. They have a further right to know if the performance of their company may be dependent on illegal activity, which, if terminated, may have an adverse effect on performance. Shareholders suits may be brought in order to recover funds illegally or wastefully spent; shareholders are entitled to restitution for losses suffered as a result of investment in an offending corporation. They may also seek ancillary relief mechanisms to deter or control future illicit payments.

For example, two shareholders of Phillips Petroleum Company sued the company and certain directors alleging breach of fiduciary duty and violations of the Federal Election Campaign Act. The case was settled before trial, and included an agreement providing for a majority of independent, outside members on the company's board of directors, and for scrutiny by an independent public accountant of corporate and directors' records (Gelbar v. Keeler civil No. 75-611-EAC (C.D. Colo. Feb 24, 1975)).

Other shareholder actions

Shareholders, whether individual or institutional, may capitalize on their formal links with a corporation, and also use the occasion of annual meetings as an opportunity to raise issues of corrupt practices. In the late 1970s the United Church of Christ wrote to a number of U.S.-based trans-national corporations, in which the church held stock, requesting a statement of company policy on payments to public officials overseas. Subsequently, the church filed stockholder resolutions with a number of corporations requesting the disclosure of information relating to questionable payments made over the previous decade. Additional resolutions requested the establishment of a corporate anti-bribery policy and implementation plan (Adams and Rosenthal 1976: 12–13).

Even though concerned shareholders may not be sufficiently numerous for a proxy resolution to prevail, the ability to confront corporate officials in a public forum and in the presence of the news media can be a powerful deterrent to corporate misconduct.

Citizen suits against bribetakers

A number of jurisdictions allow citizen suits against public officials who take bribes. In the United States, New Jersey upholds the right of citizens to take action against the wrongful conduct of public officials without having to show any personal interest or injury (Levine 1981: 363). Any resident of Iowa 18 years of age or older may enforce the state statute which forbids the acceptance by officials of gifts with a value greater than $25 (Iowa Code Ann. s. 68B.9). The law of Alaska permits any qualified Alaskan voter to sue for enforcement of the statute which forbids the use of public office "for the primary purpose of obtaining financial gain" (Alaska Statutes s. 39.50.100 (1980)).

Of course, where a citizen has sustained direct financial loss as a result of corrupt practices, a cause of action may lie against the public official. One can, for example, envisage a case involving the corrupt rejection of a licence application, where the plaintiff's loss of profit arises from the corrupt granting of a license to a competitor. The harm inflicted on the plaintiff need not be intentional; it suffices that the injury be an inevitable consequence of the misfeasance in question (Aronson and Whitmore 1982: 131).

Civil RICO actions

Another avenue for citizen action in corruption control in the United States can involve the imaginative use of the civil provisions of the Racketeer Influenced and Corrupt Organizations Act (RICO). Originally enacted by the U.S. Congress as part of the Organized Crime Control Act of 1970, RICO was designed to enhance the resources of the federal government against criminal syndicates, and to prevent the infiltration of legitimate businesses by organized crime.

It prohibits the use of income derived from the commission of two or more of a range of specified (termed 'predicate') offences, including bribery, extortion, embezzlement, and obstruction of justice, to invest in, control, or operate an 'enterprise'. When these statutory conditions are met, an offender is liable for severe criminal penalties (in addition to those arising from the substantive offences) including a fine of up to $25,000, imprisonment for up to twenty years, and forfeiture of any interest acquired or maintained in violation of RICO.

The act also provided for private remedies for victims of RICO offences. Section 1964 (c) permits any person injured in his business or property as a result of the substantive provisions of RICO to sue and recover treble damages, plus costs and reasonable attorneys' fees.

The evolution of RICO has surprised many. By no means is it limited to so-called Mafiosi. The enterprise concept in RICO has been expanded well beyond the expectations which prevailed in 1970. Over thirty reported cases have held that governmental entities may be deemed to be enterprises for purposes of RICO. Among the agencies held to be 'enterprises' are police and sheriffs' departments, the warden of a prison, offices of state legislators, governors, and county prosecutors, courts, and a tax bureau (Smith and Reed 1988: 3.03; U.S. Department of Justice 1985: 27–29).

Commentators have argued that governmental use of civil RICO actions may be a preferable alternative to criminal prosecution of corrupt public officials because of the lower burden of proof and compensatory advantages (Vinegrad 1983). But civil RICO can be available to private plaintiffs as well.

An example of the private use of civil RICO (although one which appears to have been unsuccessful) may be drawn from the sordid events known colloquially as the Iran-Contra Affair. This involved the encouragement by White House staff of private entrepreneurs to circumvent prohibitions imposed by the United States Congress on military assistance to insurgents seeking to overthrow the government of Nicaragua.

The Christic Institute, a public interest law firm in Washington, alleged that the defendants, among them a leader of the insurgents, a former Deputy Director, Operations, for the Central Intelligence Agency, and other retired U.S. military personnel engaged in a number of illegal acts, including bombings and sale of drugs, in furtherance of their enterprise. The suit, which sought US$ 24 million in damages on behalf of a journalist injured in one bombing, was filed some months prior to the dramatic disclosures and Iran-Contra hearings of 1987.

In June 1988, the Chief Judge of the Federal District Court in Miami held that the plaintiffs had failed to prove their case, and dismissed the suit. Two of the defendants, retired Air Force general Richard Secord, and Iranian-American businessman Albert Hakim, later faced criminal charges arising from their activities in the Iran-Contra Affair.

Informers

Among the more unpalatable forms of citizen co-production is the use of informers. A citizen may be recruited by law enforcement agents to infiltrate a criminal enterprise. Alternatively, he or she may be recruited by virtue of already being in place as a member of that enterprise. A citizen may also offer his or her services to law enforcement agents for either of these strategic purposes. Although the use of informers usually entails some form of remuneration, there are some circumstances when it may be 'off-budget'.

Persons who serve as informers tend not to be ordinary citizens; indeed, for obvious reasons they tend to be drawn from the seamier side of social life. This type of citizen assistance in criminal investigations is rarely if ever grounded in altruism. Citizens who offer their services, whether unilaterally or by invitation of law enforcement authorities, usually have a personal agenda. They may seek personal enrichment, to wreak vengeance on enemies, or they may seek to avoid criminal charges. They may be in dire financial straits, drug dependent, or otherwise exceptionally manipulable by investigatory authorities.

Selective use of prosecutorial discretion can also serve to encourage individuals to come forward to disclose corrupt practices. The promise of indemnity against prosecution may encourage those private citizens who might be involved as parties to corrupt behaviour to testify for the state. The strategy is a familiar one in Italy (Walston 1987) as well as in the United States (Robinson 1988). Guidelines for the use of indemnity are incorporated in the prosecution policy of the Commonwealth of Australia (Australia 1986).

One of the best known law enforcement operations directed against corrupt public officials was the ABSCAM operation conducted by the U.S. Federal Bureau of Investigation. While this form of activity can be very useful to law enforcement authorities, it can be fraught with risk (Donnelly 1951). The 1990 prosecution of Washington D.C. Mayor Marion Barry, who had been lured to a hotel room and provided with cocaine by an ex-girlfriend, then in the service of the FBI, was a very controversial exercise of state power. By far the best overview of police undercover operations, including those involving citizen informers, is that of Gary Marx (1988). A useful colloquium on the merits and pitfalls of covert facilitation of crime is based on the work of Braithwaite, Fisse and Geis (1987).

In other circumstances, those recruited to assist law enforcement officers in their work may be weak or vulnerable. Consider the following example of the offer of rewards for citizen assistance which was arguably inappropriate. The case is that of little Reggie Penn, to whom a policeman offered five dollars if he would indicate where, in the family home, his mother had concealed a quantity of heroin. Reggie at the time was all of five years old. Little Reggie fulfilled his part of the agreement, and duly informed on his mother. (At the end of the day, he was not paid!)

This action was condoned by the United States Court of Appeals for the Ninth Circuit (U.S. v. Penn 647 F.2d 876 (1980)) Despite the fact that little Reggie, in addition to having been turned against his mother, did not get his five dollars, the behaviour of police officers was not found to be 'shocking to the conscience' or 'sufficiently violative of the decencies of civilized conduct' to constitute what is termed in the American language of jurisprudence a deprivation of due process.

The risk that citizens assisting law enforcement, like law enforcement officers themselves, may engage in illegal conduct, is pervasive. Indeed, this may be inspired or directed by officers for purposes of maintaining a 'cover'–credibility with the target of an investigation.

Alternatively, the government may be the unwitting beneficiary of an informer's wrongful acts. Consider the following: two accountants took corporate records and delivered them to the Intelligence Division of the Internal Revenue Service. The accountants then filed claims for reward. For this, the government could not be faulted. As the court held, "The Government is not bound at its peril to know that the offer of a reward for information will induce a violation of the law" (U.S. v. Goldberg 206 F. Supp 304 (1962) at 401).

Governments can also encourage illegality by citizens. In another case, an FBI agent persuaded an informer to engage in the illegal seizure of a briefcase belonging to the vice president of a bank, and to assist in the photographing of contents which led to the prosecution of a client of the bank on charges of falsifying income tax returns (U.S. v Payner 447 U.S. 727 1980).

In a third case, the accused acted as a lookout while three accomplices committed a burglary. Unbeknown to the accused, one of his accomplices was a police officer and the others were paid informers, earning weekly non-contingent salaries, and 'working-off' criminal charges which they would otherwise be facing (State vs. Hohensee 650 S.W. 2d 268, Missouri Court of Appeals 1982). The court regarded this as an impermissible violation of due process.

Governments may also tolerate conduct of questionable propriety by an informer which may fall short of criminality. In another case, the FBI continued to employ the services of an informer even after learning of her sexual involvement with a suspect whom she subsequently lured into selling heroin to undercover FBI agents (U.S. v Simpson 813 F. 2d 1462 (1987)).

6. Safeguards against potentially adverse concomitants of citizen action

What must be avoided is the incentive to manufacture crime in order to reap the rewards of assistance. Such a caveat is hardly a modern concern. One need only look to the infamous 'Thief-taker General' Jonathan Wild, to see that such a lesson was learned during the eighteenth century (Howson 1970). Before the advent of a public police force, Wild provided the service of recovering stolen goods for a fee. In order to ensure that the demand for his services remained robust, he doubled as a receiver of stolen goods.

Although malice and greed as motives for citizen co-production cannot be legislated away, one can design certain safeguards against citizen abuse of corruption control machinery, short of exempting certain officials entirely, as is the case with the False Claims Act. Those who would knowingly make a false complaint could be liable in tort for defamation. A more intrusive remedy would subject such a complainant to penalty, as is the case in Hong Kong (Klitgaard 1988: 117).

The concept of citizen suits has escaped neither scrutiny nor criticism (Yale Law Journal 1982; Greve 1989). Perhaps the most commonly voiced objections to the right of citizen action contend that:

- it is an invitation to frivolous or vexatious litigation, false allegations, politically motivated action, or retaliation by disgruntled employees or former intimates;
- it appeals to the base motives of the public by inviting 'bounty hunting';
- it invites parasitical behaviours such as joining a suit that has already been or would otherwise be brought by the government;
- it has the potential of prejudicing a concurrent criminal investigation, or otherwise interfering with steps taken by the government to recover the ill gotten gains;
- it is both economically and penologically inefficient, in that it is redundant to criminal action, and that the ultimate disposition may not occur until long after the conclusion of the criminal process, thus diluting the deterrent and the denunciatory effects of the legal process.

Closer inspection, however, reveals these objections to be ill-founded. In most legal systems which provide at least a modicum of access to justice by individual citizens, there exist ample safeguards to protect against frivolous or vexatious litigation. The allocation of those limited funds set aside by some governments for representation of the indigent is subject to strict accountability. Those lawyers acting on a contingency fee basis (if they lose, they get nothing; if they win, they get a proportion of the damages – usually one-third) would be disinclined to waste their time on a lost cause. Courts have ample powers to dismiss frivolous complaints; a vexatious plaintiff with both the inclination and the means to bankroll a frivolous lawsuit runs the risk of being thrown out of court (figuratively speaking). Courts may award costs against the plaintiff, and may also impose severe sanctions against plaintiff's counsel for abuse of process. Indeed, in the aftermath of the unsuccessful civil RICO suit brought by the Christic Institute, the plaintiffs were ordered to pay US$ 955,000 in attorney fees and US$ 79,500 in court costs.

The 'bounty hunting' objection would not apply to the individual who has sustained direct, tangible losses as a result of corrupt practices. Few would deny this person a right to compensation. Rather, the 'bounty hunting' objection is more applicable to the false claims litigation. This may be countered by the argument that citizens who provide valuable, indeed, often crucial investigative assistance to the government are entitled to modest compensation for their efforts. Many will have expended considerable time and energy in developing their case. For some, the experience will be emotionally costly if it entails a conflict of loyalties to one's employer and to one's nation. Moreover, in the case of false claims litigation, the citizen's reward is but a fraction of the total damages. At least 70 percent of all monies eventually recovered under the False Claims Act are returned to the U.S. Treasury.

The risk of parasitical litigation is neutralized by the ability of the courts to dismiss a *qui tam* complaint if the plaintiff's allegations were previously the subject of hearings, investigations, or media coverage.

The risk of prejudicing parallel criminal proceedings can be minimized by statutory provision, such as that under the False Claims Act which requires that the citizen-plaintiff's action be filed initially under seal in court, and only served on the Attorney General in Washington. It remains under seal for at least sixty days (subject for extension for good cause) before being served on the defendant. The purpose of this provision is to permit the government to conduct its own investigation without indicating to the defendant that such an investigation is underway. In the event that the government chooses to proceed with criminal charges, it may request that civil proceedings be stayed, so as not to prejudice the criminal case. The risk of disruptive, repetitious, or harassing behaviour on the part of the citizen-plaintiff is minimized by the power of the court to make specific findings to that effect, and thereby limit the private plaintiff's participation in the suit. The Christic Institute case did not appear to impede the criminal charges arising from the Iran-Contra affair.

The inefficiency arguments are weakened by their reliance upon the assumption that governmental response to corruption will always be swift and sure. Indeed, governments are often more of a problem than a solution. The disinclination of governments to delve too deeply into allegations of corrupt practices is hardly novel. A vigilant citizenry can goad a government otherwise inclined to inertia. When the decision to engage in a corrupt transaction is often based on the careful calculation of risks and benefits, knowledge of a more vigilant public with monetary incentives for maintaining that vigilance cannot be dismissed lightly.

In the Soviet Union, the Constitution of 1977 and enabling legislation enacted a decade later permit citizens to sue public officials who exceed their powers or who violate the law. The legislation provides that improper official decisions which are successfully challenged may be overturned. These too contain safeguards against abuse. Complaints related to national security are exempt, and frivolous actions may result in liability for court costs and possible slander suits (Keller 1987).

One of the most common criticisms of any proposal to involve private citizens in law enforcement is the potential for adverse effect on individual values and on the climate of interpersonal trust. Private citizens are not always motivated by a sense of public service or civic virtue. Indeed, they may be driven by base motives. The insight is hardly unique to the 1990s: Sir Edward Coke referred to common informers as 'viperous vermin'(1809). And the frank and uninhibited exchange which characterises normal discourse in a free society can be chilled by the suspicion that anyone may be a spy.

According to one report, there are some nine million 'neighborhood minders' in the People's Republic whose vigilance extends to the enforcement of China's one child family planning policy and to surveillance of political dissidents (*International Herald Tribune* 1990). If anything, these criticisms are even more apposite to matters of corruption control, which targets behaviour almost invariably intended to be private.

When monetary incentives are offered for citizen participation in corruption control activities, problems may be compounded. A nation of informers is bad enough; one would hardly wish to create a nation of bounty hunters and soldiers of fortune. An overzealous citizenry could conceivably create corrupt practices through entrapment, interfere with conventional law enforcement activity through officious meddling, or disrupt the formal process by means of spurious or vexatious complaints.

There is arguably a middle ground between a culture of *omerta*, where citizens are inhibited from disclosing illegality, and the informing society, the statist model of social control, where every citizen is an agent of the state. To be sure, the extreme limits of citizen co-production evoke images of the society envisaged by George Orwell, and implemented to a significant extent by Stalin and Hitler. As vexing a social and political problem as corruption may be, few would advocate such extreme remedies. Society has an interest in the propriety of countermeasures regardless of the evils which they are intended to prevent.

The incentives for co-operation may be so great that, in the absence of very strict controls, the informer may be tempted to go beyond the bounds of propriety to obtain incriminating evidence (Marx 1988: 152–158). The potential for entrapment and for the fabrication of evidence is substantial. Indeed, the use of informers may serve not to prevent, but rather to create, crime. The structure of incentives, for example offering a reward contingent upon the conviction of a particular target, carries great potential for abuse (Hirsch 1984).

The many risks which attend the use of informers require very strict precautions. In some instances, particularly cases involving testimony in court, these precautions are reinforced by prevailing social values. Any informer who may be called upon to testify in criminal proceedings, for example, will be subjected to aggressive challenge by the defence in an effort to impeach his or her credibility. Jurors are generally suspicious of those whom they perceive to have sold out. They will be particularly suspicious of those witnesses who have been granted immunity or who benefit financially from their testimony.

Other safeguards against abuses by informers, whether for private purposes or in furtherance of state interests, might include strict guidelines to define permissible conduct, and regular supervision to ensure adherence to those guidelines. These could be augmented by regular polygraph testing of informers, and by the use of multiple informers. Ultimately, in those cases where an informer has been promised immunity against prosecution, the terms of the agreement may contain conditions providing for withdrawal of the immunity in the event of unauthorized conduct on the part of the informer.

Beyond this, one might envisage a degree of judicial oversight of the use of paid informers, not unlike the means by which electronic surveillance is supposed to be conducted. Activities involving undercover informers could be conducted subject to a judicial warrant, based on probable cause that an offence has been or is about to be committed. Such warrants could, in precise detail, specify the target and the duration of the operation, and the general procedures by which it is to be conducted (see Braithwaite, Fisse and Geis 1987).

7. Conditions conducive to citizen co-production

Despite its attractiveness in principle, citizen co-production cannot be expected to flourish everywhere. Certain conditions are conducive to effective citizen co-production. One of these entails the simplification of laws and regulations, and the maximum feasible provision of information to clients of various government agencies. Clients who are unaware of their rights or of the rules by which a government body operates are especially vulnerable to official corruption (Klitgaard 1988: 86).

Notwithstanding the fact that some societies not renowned for their openness have structures in place to facilitate citizen anti-corruption activity, there can be little doubt that the liberal democratic state is most conducive to participatory corruption control. Only in these places is the tradition of participatory democracy strong, and the open and robust discussion of public issues encouraged. In the absence of an organized political opposition, a free press, and independent interest groups, corruption flourishes so much more easily. Public business must be conducted publicly. Public scrutiny is essential so that citizens of a democracy are able to judge public servants and their work fairly.

In the words of recent report on corruption in one Australian jurisdiction:

> The ultimate check on public maladministration is public opinion, which can only be truly effective if there are structures and systems designed to ensure that it is properly informed. (Fitzgerald 1989: 126)

This requires a free and aggressive press, unconstrained by laws of defamation which protect only the powerful, and often the corrupt.

Governments are also in a position to facilitate citizen involvement. The United States Government, for example, actually published a handbook on establishing a citizen's watchdog group (Manikas and Protess 1979). According to Adams (1977), the Government of the Soviet Union published nine booklets in a series entitled 'Library of the People's Inspector' to provide practical guidance to citizen inspectors in their control work.

8. Directions for the future

Gary Marx (1987) has cited examples of private detectives undertaking investigations in cases where public police may lack the resources or the will. He refers also to the emergence of new quasi-public or quasi-private organizations which may entail the establishment of a 'front' for a government agency. Marx notes that such an organization was involved in screening government employees working in sensitive areas. As the Iran-Contra Affair demonstrated, the lack of accountability surrounding such ventures would suggest that they are not part of the solution to corruption, but rather part of the problem. In addition to refinements of existing opportunities for legitimate public involvement, and the development of safeguards against their abuse, what is the potential for further avenues of citizen co-production in corruption control?

The risk of capture or corruption of regulatory agencies has prompted Ayres and Braithwaite (1989) to propose a tripartite model of regulation. They advocate that public interest groups be given explicit power to participate in regulatory activity, and be given standing to enforce agency regulations when capture or corruption impedes normal agency enforcement activity. To fulfil this responsibility, public interest groups would enjoy full access to information available to the regulatory agency, and would be party to interactions between the agency and the regulated company. The public visibility of the regulatory process, and the threat of outside intervention in the event of regulatory breakdown, can be a powerful deterrent to corrupt practices. The great strength of citizen involvement in corruption control lies less in equipping the general public with the machinery of enforcement than it does in fostering a climate of opinion which condemns the exploitation of public office for private gain as intolerable. A community thus mobilized against corruption will inhibit venality. These inhibitions will be reinforced by the stigmatization which will be brought to bear in the event that a corrupt official is exposed.

In conclusion, although citizen co-production is a necessary condition for efficient and effective corruption control, it is not by itself sufficient. The measures discussed above are just part of the arsenal of corruption countermeasures. A variety of administrative and managerial considerations, such as the recruitment, training and supervision of public servants, the structure of organizational disincentives to corrupt practices, and organizational incentives to report such activity, cannot be overlooked. Nor can we ignore the mechanisms by which corrupt practices are investigated, prosecuted and punished by state authorities.

To be sure, involvement of the ordinary citizen in corruption control carries with it some risk of abuse. An excess of public participation can lead to the deprivation of human rights. Some of the extreme examples described above have no place in a free and decent society. It would nevertheless be foolish to discard citizen co-production outright, simply because some extreme variations are unacceptable or pose a downside risk. There is, then, what might be termed an optimal level of participatory corruption control. Safeguards can be designed and incorporated in those institutions which exist for citizen involvement. And in the current fiscal climate, just as conventional law enforcement is strengthened by community policing, an optimal level of citizen co-production is one area of corruption control which governments can ill afford to neglect.

Acknowledgements

The author wishes to thank John Braithwaite, John Gardiner, Richard Harding, Kathryn Malec, Joachim Sevelsberg, Wesley Skogan, Bruce Swanton and Grant Wardlaw for comments on earlier drafts. Views expressed in this paper are those of the author, and not necessarily those of the Australian Government.

References

Adams, Gordon and Sherri Rosenthal, *The Invisible Hand: Questionable Corporate Payments Overseas* (New York: Council on Economic Priorities, 1976).

Adams, Jan, *Citizen Inspectors in the Soviet Union: The People's Control Committee* (New York: Praeger, 1977).

Aronson, Mark and Harry Whitmore, *Public Torts and Contracts* (Sydney: Law Book Company, 1982).

Australia, "Prosecution Policy of the Commonwealth: Guidelines for the Making of Decisions in the Prosecution Process" (Canberra: Australian Government Publishing Service, 1986).

Australian Law Reform Commission, "Standing in Public Interest Litigation", Report No. 27 (Canberra: Australian Government Publishing Service, 1985).

Ayres, Ian and John Braithwaite, "Tripartism, Empowerment and Game-Theoretic Notions of Regulatory Capture", Paper presented at the Annual Meeting of the Law and Society Association, Madison, Wisconsin, 9 June, 1989.

Baldwin, Deborah, "Friends in Need", *Common Cause Magazine* 14 (1988): 19–22.

Barber, Benjamin, *Strong Democracy: Participatory Politics for a New Age* (Berkeley: University of California Press, 1984).

Bersten, Michael, "ICAC: A Critique", *Criminology Australia* 1 (1989): 8–10.

Braithwaite, John, Brent Fisse, Gilbert Geis, "Covert Facilitation of Crime: Restoring Balance to the Entrapment Debate", *Journal of Social Issues* 43 (1987): 5–42.

Braithwaite, John, Peter Grabosky, Brent Fisse, *Occupational Health and Safety Enforcement Guidelines: A Report to the Victorian Department of Labor* (Melbourne: Department of Labor, 1986).

Clark, David, "A Community Relations Approach to Corruption: The Case of Hong Kong", *Corruption and Reform*, 2 (1987): 235–257.

Coke, Edward, *The Third Part of the Institutes of the Laws of England* (London: Clarke, 1809).

Common Cause, *The Case Against Edwin Meese III for Attorney General* (Washington: Common Cause, 1984).

Congressional Quarterly, "Chronology of an Investigation", *Congressional Quarterly* 15 April (1989): 795.

Crosette, Barbara "Now, At Least, The Customer is Sometimes Right", The New York Times, 26 January, 1989.

Donnelly, Richard, "Judicial Control of Informants, Spies, Stool Pigeons and Agent Provocateurs", *Yale Law Journal* 60 (1951): 1091.

Eagleton, Thomas and Ira Shapiro, "Federal Fraud, Waste and Abuse: Causes and Responses", *Government Accountants Journal* (Summer 1983): 1–8.

Etzioni, Amitai, *Capital Corruption: The New Attack on American Democracy* (New York: Harcourt Brace Jovanovich, 1984).

150

Fisse, Brent and John Braithwaite, *The Impact of Publicity on Corporate Offenders* (Albany: State University of New York Press, 1983).

Gardiner, John and David Olson, *Theft of the City* (Bloomington: University of Indiana Press, 1974).

Glazer, Myron and Penina Glazer, *Whistle Blowers: Exposing Corruption in Government and Industry* (New York: Basic Books, 1989).

Grabosky, P.N., *Wayward Governance: Illegality and its Control in the Public Sector* (Canberra: Australian Institute of Criminology, 1989).

Grabosky, Peter and John Braithwaite, *Of Manners Gentle: Enforcement Strategies of Australian Business Regulatory Agencies* (Melbourne: Oxford University Press, 1986).

Greve, Michael, "Environmentalism and Bounty Hunting", *The Public Interest* 97 (1989): 15–29.

Hirsch, Milton, "Confidential Informants: When Crime Pays", *University of Miami Law Review*, 39 (1984): 131-155.

Howson, Gerald, *Thief-Taker General: The Rise and Fall of Jonathan Wild* (New York: St Martin's Press, 1970).

International Herald Tribune, "China's 'Minders' are 9 Million Strong", 27 April 1990, p. 8.

Keller, Bill, "Soviet Gives Citizens Power to Challenge Abuses", *The New York Times* , 1 July 1987, p. 4.

Kirkwood, John, *Social Security Law and Policy* (Sydney, Law Book Company, 1986).

Klitgaard, Robert, *Controlling Corruption* (Berkeley: University of California Press, 1988).

Lampert, Nicholas, *Whistleblowing in the Soviet Union: Complaints and Abuses Under State Socialism* (London: Macmillan, 1985).

Levine, Beth A., "Defending the Public Interest: Citizen Suits for Restitution Against Bribed Officials", *Tennessee Law Review*, 48 (1981): 347-369.

Los, Maria, *Communist Ideology, Law and Crime: A Comparative View of the USSR and Poland* (London: Macmillan, 1988).

Manikas, Peter and David Protess, "Establishing a Citizen's Watchdog Group", Washington, U.S. Department of Justice, Law Enforcement Assistance Administration, 1979.

Marx, Gary, "The Interweaving of Public and Private Police in Undercover Work", in Clifford Shearing and Philip Stenning, eds., *Private Policing* (Beverly Hills: Sage Publications, 1987), 172–193.

Marx, Gary, *Undercover: Police Surveillance in America* (Berkeley: University of California Press, 1988).

New York Times, "2 Carolina Indians Acquitted in Hostage Taking", 15 October, 1988, p. 9.

Noonan, John, *Bribes* (New York: Macmillan, 1984).

Phillips, John, Personal communication, 20 July, 1989.

Robinson, Mark, "How to Obtain Cooperation in a Public Corruption Investigation", in U.S. Department of Justice, *Prosecution of Public Corruption Cases* (Washington: Corporate Crime Reporter, 1988), 157–173.

Shover, Neal, Donald Clelland and John Lynxwiler, *Enforcement or Negotiation: Constructing a Regulatory Bureaucracy* (Albany: State University of New York Press, 1986).

Silk, Michael, "Economic Crime in China", *China Business Review* 15 (1988): 25–29.

Skogan, Wesley, "Community Organizations and Crime", in Tonry and Morris, eds., *Crime and Justice: A Review of Research* Vol. 10 (Chicago: University of Chicago Press, 1988).

Smith, David and Terrance Reed, *Civil RICO* (New York: Matthew Bender, 1988).

Smith, Zay and Pamela Zeckman, *The Mirage* (New York: Random House, 1979).

Sturgess, Gary and Philip Chubb, *Judging the World: Law and Poitics in the World's Leading Courts* (Sydney: Butterworths, 1988).

Trott, Stephen, "The Successful Use of Informants and Criminals as Witnesses for the Prosecution in a Criminal Case", in United States Department of Justice, ed., *Prosecution of Public Corruption Cases* (Washington, D.C.: Corporate Crime Reporter, 1988), 115–133.

U.S. Department of Justice, Criminal Division, *Racketeer Influenced and Corrupt Organizations (RICO): A Manual for Federal Prosecutors* (Washington: U.S. Department of Justice, 1985).
Vinegrad, Alan, "Government Corruption and Civil Rico: Providing Compensation for Intangible Losses", *New York University Law Review* 58 (1983): 1530–1587.
Walston, James, "The Law and Proposed Reform of Political Corruption in Italy", *Corruption and Reform* 2 (1987) 175–183.
Yale Law Journal "Comment: Garnishing Graft: A Strategy for Recovering the Proceeds of Bribery", 92 (1982): 128–143.

[25]

Crime, Law & Social Change **29:** 197–208, 1998.

Are bribe payments in Tanzania "grease" or "grit"?

PETTER LANGSETH & BRYANE MICHAEL
Economic Development Institute of the World Bank, Washington, DC20433, USA

Abstract. This article uses empirical evidence from Tanzania to show that bribes there are not "greasing" but instead encumber economic transactions. The evidence suggests that bribe payments promote contacts with service providers, result in lower satisfaction with public service delivery, and result in less efficient public services. Further evidence against bribes as 'facilitators' is presented in the form of opinion polls and actions taken to reduce bribe payments.

Introduction

Corruption has been perceived as the 'grease' that speeds up economic transactions occurring in an overly regulated and controlled environment, an argument given credence by Leff (1964).[1] The implication of this idea is that spending a small amount of money on a 'corrupt' transaction – which is socially and individually welfare enhancing (either for investment or consumption purposes) – overcomes stifling regulations and raises the gross income of poorly paid civil servants. However, more empirical and anecdotal evidence is being accumulated to suggest that corruption acts as 'grit' in the economic mechanism. Myrdal (1968) noted this effect in India where government officials created bureaucratic obstacles to elicit bribes. In an environment where income is barely sufficient for survival, the motivation to extract rents becomes obvious. Other evidence suggests that since corruption usually arises from some form of market imperfection or market power, inefficiency results in the provision of services via slower and lower quality service. One respondent during focus group discussions in Tanzania summed up this inefficiency quite elequently; "if you have no money, then you cannot get service" (Cockcroft & Galt, 1996: p. 14). This article focuses on the results of household surveys conducted in Tanzania from which the above quote was taken, which supports the conception of corruption as 'grit' in economic transactions.

Service delivery surveys

The household surveys, which were in fact Service Delivery Surveys (SDS) conduced by CIETinternational, were the first large effort at obtaining a comprehensive view about services to representative communities across the country.[2] Specifically, the SDS collects data on the impact, coverage, and costs of services which are later used for planning and analysis purposes. Four services – police, judiciary, revenue service, and lands – were chosen because they are generally considered as the most corruption ridden services. Using a modified cluster sampling technique, data was collected from 10 districts, seven of which were urban. The ten districts were Babati, Mwanza, Musoma, Kahama, Singida, Korogwe, Dar es Salaam, Morogoro, Iringa, and Mbeya. At each district, 4 sites were chosen and 120 households were surveyed in each site. Site selection was based upon multiple stratification and purposive selection to reflect conditions in each district for a total of 4561 households representing the opinions of 24,676 individuals. In addition, a total of 153 service providers were polled from the Tanzanian police, judiciary, revenue, and lands services. Instruments included a household questionnaire, a focus group guide, a key informant interview, and questionnaires for service providers. Seven percent of households surveyed had contact with police, 5% with courts, 4% with revenue service officials, and 1% with lands officials.

Four stylized facts seem to emerge from these surveys which mitigate against the hypothesis that corruption in Tanzania is of the 'greasing' variety. First, one can not reject the claim no 'rent farming' behavior is present in the data. Second, bribe payers are less likely to be satisfied with the speed, quality, and spirit of the service delivered. Third, households perceive corruption as a harm and service providers see it as a necessity. Fourth, government has found it in its interest to address the problem.

Is there 'rent farming' in Tanzania?

Rent farming can occur in two ways – either service providers can promote contacts to extort more bribes or can increase the bribe payment per contact. Looking at the first case, Figure 1 shows that there seems to be a positive relationship between the percentage of households using a particular public service who pay 'extra payments' (where the phrase 'extra payment' used in the questionnaire is taken to mean bribe payment) and percentage of households having contact with service providers. Stated more simply, more contacts with services occur in districts which have a higher proportion of households who pay bribes. If this is true, bribes might be seen as 'grit'

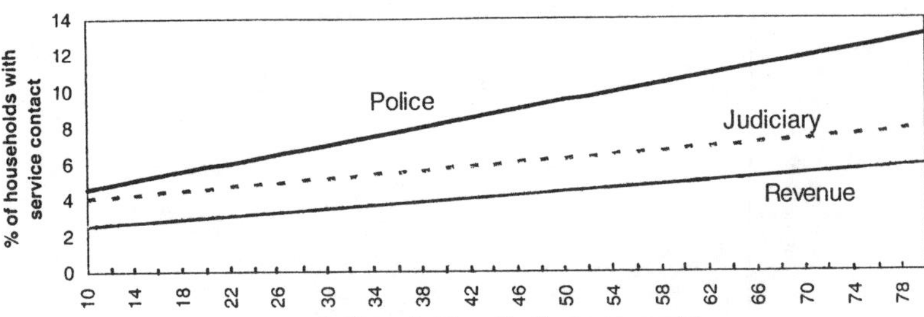

Figure 1. Comparison between contacts and payments for selected services.*

by promoting more contacts and raising the number of inefficient economic transactions.

Is this true? The answer is – not necessarily. It would be incorrect to think of these as regressions *per se* due to the small sample size (ten observations each representing a district). Instead, they should be seen as graphical illustrations of some trends in the data. Further, as for the issue of causality, it is not possible to say for certain that in the case of Tanzania that higher proportions of households paying bribes leads to more households having contact. Indeed, more households having contact may cause more households to pay bribes. The true answer, anecdotal evidence tells us, lies somewhere between the two cases. It should be noted however that the regression lines fit much worse as measured by the variation explained by the regression line (R^2 measure) when they were run with contacts as the independent variable and payments are the dependent variable. Once more data is collected, a Granger Causality Test can be run and causality can be determined. Until then, this illustration must only be seen as a graphical representation of a weak statistical relationship.

One other point to touch upon before leaving Figure 1 is the relationship between various service providers. It should be noted that a small change in the number of households making 'extra' payments bring incrementally more police, then judiciary, and lastly revenue workers. (In the language of mathematics, the slope – or derivative – of households making payments with respect to households making contacts is higher for police than for the other service providers). Further, some services have globally higher percentages of households contacted than others with police leading the list and lands scoring last place. Figure 2 shows the comparison of the percentage of households with service contacts and percentage of households making "extra payments". Looking at the trends across different services, one can see that the general trend is also that services which have contact with larger amounts of households have larger numbers of households paying bribes.

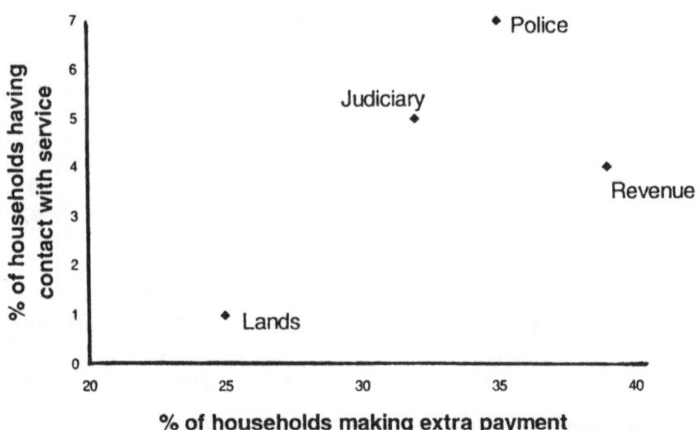

Figure 2. Comparison of contacts and frequency of payments.

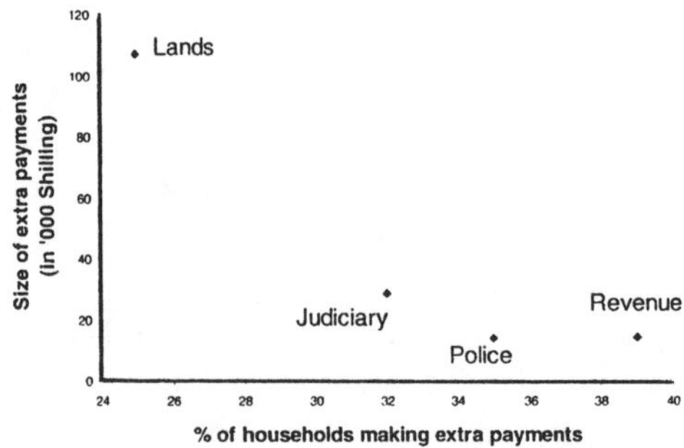

Figure 3. Comparison of size of payments vs. frequency of payments.

What are the two implications of the data? First, if bribes were 'grease payments', one would expect to see a zero or negative relationship between the number of households paying bribes and the number of households having contact with a service. Second, one reform solution might indicate that if the number of households paying bribes can be reduced, the level of contacts can be reduced (or visa-versa depending on the causality). No matter how the causality runs, *ceterus paribus*, fewer households having contact and paying bribes does not necessarily imply globally lower bribe levels.

Turning now to the second way service providers can farm rents, Figure 3 shows the relationship between the average *size* of these payments (by service provider) and the percentage of households making 'extra payments'. The data are plotted for the four services covered and shows that those services where average bribe size was the greatest in general saw fewer households paying bribes. Comparing Figures 2 and 3 roughly service providers which had contact with fewer households had larger average bribe payments. What is the cause of this relationship? It is not possible to say with these data and with a comparison of only four services. However, the possiblity exists that

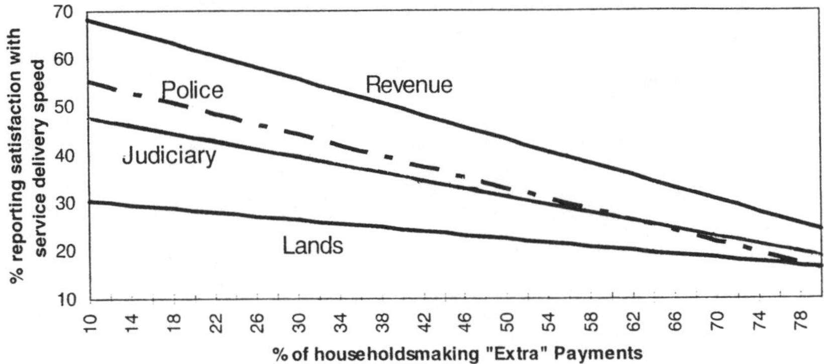

Figure 4. Comparison of satisfaction with speed of service delivery and "extra" payments.

services which have contact with fewer households (and consequently fewer householders paying bribes) might increase the average bribe amount.

Pay more, get less?

Having looked at the data and seen that the possibility of rent farming in the provision of Tanzanian public services can not be excluded, the question of whether bribes facilitate public service delivery can be addressed. In the original survey, the respondents were asked a number of questions, some of them including:

- were you satisfied with the speed of the service,
- did you see more than two staff,
- were you attended to within one day,
- did you complete your dealings within one week, and
- were you satisfied with staff behavior.

Taking the example of the first question (satisfaction with service speed), Figure 4 shows a more disaggregated relationship which holds true (though much less clearly) for the other variables. Again, the percentage of households making extra payments was regressed (using the methodolgy of simple Ordinary Least Squares) against the percentage of households satisfied with service delivery speed. For all the different service providers, districts which had lower incidences of bribe paying had higher satisfaction. Again, the preliminary statistical evidence suggests the causality does not go the other way – higher satisfaction as causing lower bribe payments. Furthermore, the slope of the regression line (or how much satisfaction is reduced by increasing marginally the percentage of households paying bribes) is different for the

Table 1. Correlation analyses comparing number of staff seen with bribes paid

Service	Number of staff seen	Paid bribe?	
		yes	*no*
Police	One or Two	16%	**42%**
	Three or More	20%	22%
Judiciary	One or Two	14%	**37%**
	Three or More	19%	30%
Revenue	One or Two	21%	**43%**
	Three or More	23%	13%
Lands	One or Two	11%	**48%**
	Three or More	15%	26%

Source: Cockcroft and Galt (1996).

different service providers. Further research needs to be done about why this might be true.

A clearer and more disaggregated approach to this question is to use correlation analysis. For example, in Table 1, a correlation analysis was done comparing the number of staff seen with bribes paid. In this chart, one can see that those who did not pay a bribe saw fewer staff. Taking the example of those who had contact with the police, the highest proportion (42%) of all respondents had not paid a bribe and saw one or two staff. On the other hand, the lowest proportion (16%) had paid a bribe and saw one to two staff. The trend is similar for all services, the highest proportion achieving the "good" outcome, namely seeing one or two staff, lies with those who did not pay bribes.

These statistics say nothing about whether the service was rendered more satisfactorially when less staff were seen. However the same correlation analysis indicates that service users who saw no more than two staff were more than twice as likely to report satisfaction with the speed of the service and more than twice as likely to report satisfaction with the behavior of the staff (Cockcroft and Galt, 1996, p.18). The same relationship roughly holds true with regards to the other questions, so aggregating these responses is not a problem.

Table 2 is the aggregated average of the five correlation tables corresponding to the questions mentioned above.[3] The basic finding from the survey data is that survey participants who did not pay a bribe were 2.9 times as likely to find a higher level of service provided. On the other hand, those who paid were 1.7 times more likely to receive poor service than good service. In fact,

Table 2. Service performance average and bribes (in % of total responses)

	Make bribe to staff	
Performance	*Yes*	*No*
Good overall	13%	**38%**
Bad overall	23%	26%

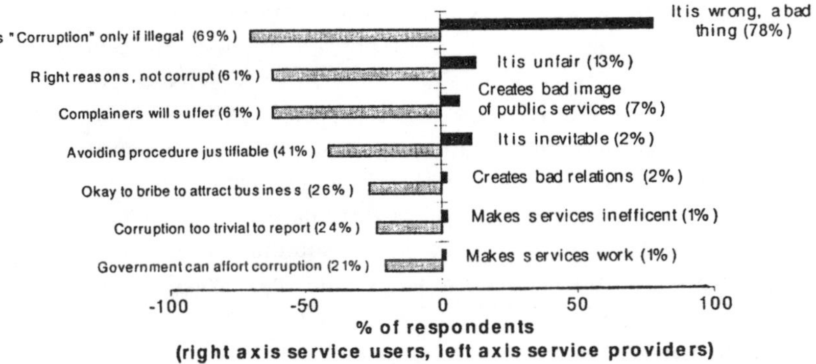

Figure 5. Comparison of service user and provider opinions.

only 13% of the participants paid the bribe and received good service. Again, the same relationships holds in all the individual correlation matrices. The statistical evidence clearly suggests that larger proportions of repondents experience better outcomes when they do not pay bribes. The other conclusion is that there is a significant proportion of respondents who, even after paying bribes, obtain less favorable outcomes.

Is corruption bad?

These opinion surveys of service users clearly and unambiguously indicate that bribes are not always 'greasing' in the sense that they promote service speed or quality. Further, sometimes better outcomes result from not paying bribes. Both households and service providers agree strongly with the fact that corruption is rampant (around 60% of both groups responded that corruption is high). However, the next question remains: is corruption generally good and useful in Tanzania? Opinions about this question are summarized in Figure 5.

One immediately notices a relatively different perception about the causes and consequences of corruption between service users and providers. The top response by households was that, "It [corruption] is wrong, it is a bad thing" (78%). However, the service providers' majority opinion rested with the belief that "conduct must be illegal for it to be called corrupt" (69%). The second majority opinion by service users was that "corruption is unfair" (13%), while service users stated that "if something is done for the right reasons, it can not be called corrupt" (61%). Notice that 0.7% of households respondents stated that "it makes services work".

This difference in the opinions of corruption between service users and providers also manifests itself with regard to solutions. When asked for measures for solving corruption, the households suggested: Prosecute Corrupt People (31%), Government to Take Action (21%), Discipline Corrupt Staff (13%), Educate Public (8%), and Better Supervision (6%). In focus group discussions, service providers did accept that corruption is prevalent. However, several service workers interviewed stressed that public perceptions are exaggerated or distorted. They felt that low salaries and inadequate resouces contributed to the corruption problem. They further stressed that the public needs to have realistic expectations and should be educated about how to use public services (Cockcroft & Galt, 1996: p. 29). If corruption were greasing economic transactions, one might expect households to see it more favorably. Indeed, one would expect that suggestions such as "Increase Civil Service Pay" (which did score 13%) would score higher than punishment.

Actions to date?

If bribe payments were a facilitating mechanism for promoting transactions in a low income, overly regulated economy, one would expect to not see the discouragement of these practices. The basic argument would be that 'grease' payments would be welfare improving (or at least not welfare decreasing) and government and civil society would not try to dismantle a facilitating mechanism which adds economic value.

However, the recent programs engaged by the Tanzanian government and civil society are a stylized fact which shows that these bribe payments do not facilitate the economic process. In general, a number of programs have been sponsored by the Economic Development Institute of the World Bank in collaboration with Transparency International. The first workshop in Tanzania, which took place in Arusha in August 1995, drew upon the broad participation of civil society, including parliamentarians, civil servants, media, judiciary, ombudsmen, religious organizations, the business community, NGOs, and provided an open forum to discuss the increase of corruption and ways to combat it. The workshop resulted in the Arusha Integrity Pledge as well as an 'Action Plan' which spelled out a comprehensive plan on fighting corruption and which sought to change deep underlying behaviors by encouraging leaders to pledge to fight corruption (see Table 3). The service delivery survey (the same one from which this article is drawn) which followed this workshop was the fulfilment of several of the proposed actions in the Action Plan.

Recognising the need for leadership, President Mkapa began his first term by promptly and publicly declaring his assets and those of his spouse. He then appointed the Warioba Commission to report against a tight time-scale. Another workshop (Arusha II) was held in December 1996 which discussed the findings of the Presidental Commission of Inquiry Against Corruption under the Honorable Joseph Warioba.

Since Warioba reported at the end of 1996, and throughout 1997, a number of actions have been proposed and taken. The report makes specific recommendations to the President to request, "reports on all leaders who are accused of corruption with a view to taking action against them" (Presidential Commission of Inquiry Against Corruption, 1996). Specific causes of weaknesses in police service delivery were identified (paragraphs 43–48 of the Warioba Report): "ineptitute" on the part of leadership, weakness in control and administration, poor recruitment procedures, lack of working tools, and poor compensation packages. In the judiciary (paragraphs 53–60), measures include improved supervision, expeditious hearings, better record management, more frequent review of injunctions by higher courts, bail set in accordance with the law, better recruitment and adequate compensation. As for revenue collection services (discussed in paragrahs 69–79), some recommendations included a careful screening of current and future employees, reduction in the 16 step procedure to import goods, and strengthening tax payer identification procedures and business recording requirements. In lands services (paragraphs 80–87), recommendations include strengthening surveying capacity, revising any conflicting legislation between local government and the Ministry of Lands, enforcing the procedures used by the Plot Allocation Committees, and simplifying procedures for obtaining or revocing a property title. Another event was the assessment of the progress made on the National Integrity Action Plan.

Evaluation of the Plan by counting the number of actions suggested versus the number of actions implemented shows that more than 60% of the proposed actions had been implemented. Some of the other actions taken have been the dismissal of 123 policemen due to allegations of corruption. A Minister of Finance has lost his cabinet post and 800 revenue collection officials have been dismissed for suspicion of corruption. Three magistrates

Table 3. Tanzanian national integrity action plan

General
1. Development of detailed integrity blueprint
2. Plan introduction of appropriate civil servant salaries and wages
3. Eliminate all unnecessary & inefficient procedures and install service orientation

Civil society
1. Formal launch of Transparency International-Tanzania Chapter
2. Follow-up on Arusha integrity pledge and action plan
3. Coordinate civil society around integrity issue

Parliament
1. Pre-election selection of candidates with integrity
2. Post-elections civil society meeting with elected leaders
3. Strengthen parliamentary committees
4. Promote discussion on improving accountability of MPs to electorate
5. Promote code of ethics

Media
1. Set and raise standards of professionalism through introduction of codes of ethics and training
2. Conduct public awareness campaign
3. Enact freedom of information laws, reform defamation laws

Judiciary
1. Improve accountability through strengthening monitoring systems
2. Revise code of conduct for judiciary, including disclosure of assets, etc.
3. Revise court procedures to opportunities for corruption
4. Conduct survey of civil society on present state of delivery of judicial services to the public

Police
1. Ascertain views of civil society on effectiveness of police

Prevention of corruption bureau (PCB)
1. Conduct survey of civil society on present state of prevention of corruption
2. Restructure and professionalize PCB and equip it
3. Remove political interference by making it responsible to parliament

Ombudsman
1. Ascertain views of civil society on effectiveness of present institution in redressing grievances
2. Remove political interference and enhance independence by making responsible to parliament

Customs
1. Ascertain views of private sector on honesty and effectiveness of customs

Tender boards
1. Remove political interference by making boards responsible to parliament
2. Revise procedures to ensure disclosure of commissions and rights to sue successful, corrupt tenderers

have been removed and another 43 'retired' in the sake of the public interest. Five court brokers have had their licences revoked. In addition, 20,000 'ghost' civil servants have been removed from the payroll, the Prevention of Corruption Bureau has had its powers expanded and an additional 77 investigators have been appointed.

So the questions remains, if bribes did not facilitate transactions and promote the efficiency of the fractionalized economic structure, why was nothing done to reduce the level of bribe payments earlier? Coordination failure? Lack of political will? Irrationality? The incentives facing economic agents has changed? Anedotal evidence suggests that 'grand corruption' (a problem which is politically more difficult to remove) is a problem in Tanzania. Whatever the reason may be, it is certain that presently agents understand and accept that bribe payments are bad and efforts are being made to reduce them. Looking at the suggested causes and solutions proposed by the Warioba Commission, it seems that salaries figure as only part of the problem. The problems and solutions underlying the Presidential Commission's Report do not seem like the same ones which would be suggested if corruption were facilitating economic transactions.

Looking at very narrow and specific data, this paper has sought to show that: i) one can not reject the claim no 'rent farming' behavior is present in the data, ii) bribe payers are less likely to be satisfied with the speed, quality, and spirit of the service delivered, iii) households perceive corruption as a harm and service providers see it as a necessity, and iv) government has found it in its interest to address the problem. As more empirical evidence is collected, some of these observations would rest on more solid ground. However, if these observations are true, the implication for policy makers is simply that increasing civil servant salaries is possibly a necessary but not sufficient condition for reducing the use of public power for private benefit. These observations would suggest a 'regime change' might be an important way of reorienting institutions and incentives. As the Tanzania experience evolves, the results offered by SDS data collected yearly might offer some very valuable observations.

Notes

1. Other ways corruption can add 'grease' to the economic system include reducing the costs of collecting information and providing insurance in a highly adverse environment.
2. CIETinternational is an international group of non-profit, non-governmental organizations working in 43 countries and dedicated to building community voice into in government through information gathering and feedback to communities.
3. The procedure used to obtain Table 2 is first to aggregate the number of respondents across service types (i.e. police, judiciary, revenue, and lands) yielding an aggregate matrix with

four quandrants. This aggregate matrix represents the average responses for a particular question across service type. The same procedure is used on the correlation charts corresponding to the other 4 questions listed in the text. Next, the corresponding quandrants on each of these 5 aggregate matrices are summed to obtain a composite matrix. For example, the category shown as "good overall" is the composite of seen two or less staff, seen in one day, one week or less to complete transaction, satisfied with speed of service, and satisfied with behavior. Aggregation in this instance is valid because the same relation exists between quadrants in all 5 correlation matrices. Each quandrant represents a proportion of the total responses, and these proportions are reported in Table 2.

References

P. Bardhan (1995) *The Economics of Corruption in Less Developed Countries: A Review of Issues*. Mimeo.

A. Cockcroft and K. Galt (eds.) (1996) *Service Delivery Survey: Corruption in the Police, Judiciary, Revenue, and Lands Services in Tanzania.* Published by EDI.

B. Cooksey, P. Langseth and F. Simpkins (eds.) (1996) *The National Integrity System in Tanzania: Parliamentarians Workshop*. Published by EDI.

J.G. Jabbra (1976) "Bureaucratic Corruption in the Third World: Causes and Remedy." *Indian Journal of Public Administration*, Vol. 22, (October-December), pp. 673–691.

S. Kpundeh and B. Heilman (1996) "Rushwa: An Examination of Corruption in Tanzania." (Submitted for publication to *Review of African Political Economy*).

N.H. Leff (1964) "Economic Development through Bureaucratic Corruption." *The American Behavioural Scientist.*

P. Langan and B. Cooksey (eds.) (1995) *The National Integrity System in Tanzania (Arusha I).*

P. Langseth, R. Stapenhurst and J. Pope (1997) "The Role of a National Integrity System in Fighting Corruption." *EDI Staff Working Papers.*

G. Myrdal (1968) *Asian Drama*. Random House, New York.

J. Pope (ed.) (1996) *National Integrity Systems: The TI Source Book.*

Presidential Commission of Inquiry Against Corruption. 1996. *Report on the Commission on Corruption.* Published by EDI.

S. Rose-Ackerman (1978) *Corruption: A Study In Political Economy*. New York: Academic Press.

S. Rose-Ackerman (1996) "The Political Economy of Corruption – Causes and Consequences." *Viewpoints*, Note No. 74, The World Bank.

Tanzania Chamber of Commerce, Industry and Agriculture. 1995. *Corruption and Drug Trafficking in Tanzania.* Popular Publications Limited. Dar es Salaam.

Petter Langsweth is a Senior Public Sector Management Specialist at the World Bank and **Bryane Michael** is a Consultant for the World Bank.

[26]

The decline of public trust in government in the United States is well documented. We know comparatively little, however, about how to maintain or restore the public's trust. This article attempts to advance our understanding of trust in government by addressing a relatively narrow question: How can we create, maintain, or restore public trust in government agencies and their employees? The article reviews several conceptions of trust and lays out a series of hypotheses regarding means for building and maintaining public trust. Although the hypotheses have not been empirically tested, they are grounded in well-established social science theories and suggest several avenues for future research.

MAINTAINING AND RESTORING PUBLIC TRUST IN GOVERNMENT AGENCIES AND THEIR EMPLOYEES

CRAIG W. THOMAS
University of Massachusetts, Amherst

Public trust in government has declined in the United States since the 1960s (Lipset & Schneider, 1983; Miller, 1974). The causes of this decline are still debated. Some believe that trust in government depends on the performance of elected officials (Citrin, 1974; Citrin & Green, 1986) or administrative leaders (Mitchell & Scott, 1987). In this view, we simply have had poor leaders, or at least the public perceives them as such. Others argue that the decline in trust is due to the public's general dissatisfaction with governmental institutions (Miller, 1974; Williams, 1987). In this

AUTHOR'S NOTE: *An earlier version of this article was prepared for the Secretary of Energy Advisory Board Task Force on Radioactive Waste Management and appears in a compilation of reports prepared for the Task Force (U.S. Department of Energy, 1993b). Between 1991 and 1993, the task force considered alternative organizational arrangements for enhancing public trust and confidence in both the civilian and defense radioactive waste programs. This article does not necessarily reflect the views of the Department of Energy, the advisory board, or the task force. For their helpful comments, I gratefully acknowledge Chris Ansell, Gene Bardach, Bruce Cain, Paula Consolini, Judy Gruber, Don Kettl, Todd La Porte, Aneil Mishra, Dan Tuden, Mayer Zald, and the referees.*

ADMINISTRATION & SOCIETY, Vol. 30 No. 2, May 1998 166-193

view, it will be much more difficult to restore public trust in government and thereby buttress the legitimacy of the political system.

Much of this debate centers on the Trust in Government Index, a series of survey questions in the biennial National Election Study that are used to construct measures of political trust.[1] Unfortunately, these survey questions speak to a limited conception of trust, in which trust in government is contrasted with cynicism or an individual's feeling of alienation from, or hostility toward, government. Yet, trust is a complex, multifaceted concept. It has cognitive, emotional, and behavioral components that operate at both the interpersonal and institutional levels. Accordingly, this article takes a more broad look at the multiple components of trust to address a narrowly tailored question regarding trust in government. That is, what can we do to maintain, restore, or create public trust in government agencies and their employees?

Recently, a panel of public and nonprofit managers, academics, and individuals from the private sector attempted to answer this question. In 1991, U.S. Secretary of Energy James D. Watkins established the Task Force on Radioactive Waste Management and asked the group to make recommendations as to how the Department of Energy (DOE) could strengthen public trust and confidence in its civilian and defense radioactive waste programs.[2] This was a daunting task because the DOE's radioactive waste management programs suffered from a great deal of public distrust. To aid them in their work, the task force asked me to prepare a background paper that summarized current knowledge on the means through which public and private organizations can build trust in their environments. At the time, I thought this would be a relatively easy task: I would simply cull hypotheses from journals and texts in organization theory, public administration, and related disciplines. Surprisingly, this strategy netted very little.

Organization theory, for example, despite its breadth, is relatively devoid of references to specific means through which organizations can build trust in their environments. Only recently has research emerged that speaks directly to the issue of maintaining or building interorganizational trust in the private sector (Husted, 1989; Mishra, 1995; Ring & Van de Ven, 1992, 1994). Concepts other than trust—such as dependence (Pfeffer & Salancik, 1978), transaction (Williamson, 1985), and legitimacy (Powell & DiMaggio, 1991)—have instead served as analytic linchpins at the interorganizational level. At the *intra*organizational level, the literature on trust is extensive and well established, but it focuses on the links between employer-employee relations, job satisfaction, and organizational productivity (Deluga, 1994; Fairholm, 1994; Frey, 1993; Miller, 1992; Ouchi, 1981). It thus tells us little about trust outside the organization. The same pattern is largely repeated in the literature on public organizations. Several authors address the links between employer-employee relations, job satisfaction, and the productivity of public agencies (Carnevale & Wechsler, 1992; Culbert & McDonough, 1986; Daley, 1991). Yet, only recently have authors given serious attention to the production, maintenance, and restoration of public trust in government agencies (La Porte & Metlay, 1996; Ruscio, 1996).

The word *trust* does not even appear in the indexes of most books on public administration, management, or policy. There are some notable exceptions, of course. Yates (1982) argues that street-level bureaucrats depend on public trust in delivering services: "Once the trust relationship has broken down, public employees find it more difficult to perform their tasks" (p. 124). Chisholm (1989, p. 118) reports that informal coordination among public employees in different agencies depends on mutual trust. Political appointees, according to Heclo (1977, pp. 158-159), cultivate relationships based on trust with civil servants to be effective within agencies. Conversely, a lack of trust in bureaucrats, according to Kelman (1990, pp. 14, 27), leads political principals to develop elaborate rules to constrain agency discretion, which, in turn, stifle performance in jobs requiring creativity.[3] Together, these books leave the reader with the impression that trust is an important variable in the environment of public agencies but with no clear sense of what trust means or how it can be produced, maintained, or restored.

In sum, our instrumental knowledge about building, maintaining, or recovering public trust is quite limited—despite routine laments about the loss of trust in government. In light of the limited research on public trust in government agencies and their employees, this article reviews the broad literature on trust in the social sciences to generate a model that can help us think about how public officials (and their academic educators) can produce, maintain, and perhaps even restore public trust. Although the restoration of trust in government is a daunting task, public officials should take heart in at least two respects. First, citizens generally perceive their concrete experiences with individual agencies in a favorable light (Goodsell, 1994, pp. 25-29). Second, the general public knows relatively little about most agencies; therefore, survey responses to questions about trust in specific agencies probably suffer from a halo effect from prior questions about general trust in government (Citrin, 1993, p. 6). Together, these observations suggest that public trust in government agencies and their employees can be produced and maintained on the margin.

THREE CONCEPTIONS OF TRUST

Trust has been a topic of moral and social philosophy for hundreds of years. Numerous conceptions of trust have been advanced and refined, the most prominent of which are outlined below. Despite the breadth and depth of this literature and the relatively recent efforts of Baier (1986), Blau (1964), Luhmann (1979), Williamson (1993), and Zucker (1986) to grapple with and define the concept in theoretically productive ways, it is surprising that trust has made so little headway into the literature on public organizations and their environments. Some authors even neglect to define trust when using the concept as a theoretically important variable.[4] Because of such oversights and because researchers differ in their approaches to trust, I devote considerable effort below to fleshing out various conceptions of trust prior to discussing trust production and maintenance.

Definitions of trust generally include some reference to expectations or beliefs that others will behave in a predictable manner (Luhmann, 1979), a manner not devoted entirely to self-interest (Williamson, 1993, p. 482; Zucker, 1986, p. 57). Rather than trusting others to be self-interested, we trust them to take our interests into account, even in situations in which we are unable to recognize, evaluate, or thwart potentially negative courses of action on their part (La Porte & Metlay, 1996, p. 342). Violating these expectations disrupts trust, but does not necessarily generate distrust. As Zucker (1986) argues, "Distrust only emerges when the suspicion arises that the disruption of expectations in one exchange is likely to generalize to other transactions" (p. 59).

In its purest form, trust is based on beliefs rather than expectations. Expectations imply that we are calculating the probabilities individuals will pursue particular courses of action. This is a weaker form of trust than simply believing that others will do good by us, without necessarily knowing what "doing good" entails. As March and Olsen (1989) argue, "the core idea of trust is that it is not based on an expectation of its justification" (p. 27). I, nevertheless, use the term *expectation* because it captures a more broad range of meanings. Without being precise, suffice it to say that trust exists along a continuum: The more we calculate the intentions of others, expect something specific in return, and subsequently monitor their performance, the less we are exhibiting trust. Similarly, the more others take our interests into account, putting their own interests aside in the process, the more they are worthy of our trust.

The three conceptions of trust outlined below generally include these characteristics. These conceptions are (a) fiduciary trust, which is notable for asymmetric relationships and attendant opportunities for malfeasance; (b) mutual trust, which develops between individuals who repeatedly interact with one another; and (c) social trust, which is embedded within institutions we know in common and take for granted.

FIDUCIARY TRUST

One long-standing conception of public trust in government arises from the notion of fiduciary relationships, in which an individual places trust in another to act in his or her capacity. Fiduciary trust emerges in principal-agent relationships when principals are unable to monitor or control the performance of their agents and are therefore vulnerable to both malfeasance and misfeasance. In such cases, the asymmetric relationship is supported by the unilateral obligation of the trustee to act in the other's interest. The principal trusts the agent, but the agent need not trust the principal.

Trust in professionals is one example of fiduciary trust. Because knowledge is distributed asymmetrically, patients and clients place their trust in doctors and lawyers because they are unable to monitor performance. As Barber (1983) writes,

> Technically competent performance can be monitored insofar as it is based on shared knowledge and expertise. But when some parties to a social relationship or some members of a social system cannot comprehend that expertise, performance can be controlled by trust. A fiduciary obligation is placed on the holder and user of the special knowledge and skill with regard to the other members of his social system. (p. 15)

In fiduciary relationships, individuals are trusted to carry out their duties in regards to others while not taking excessive personal advantage of their privileged position. The greater the asymmetry, the more the relationship depends on this moral obligation. It is therefore crucial that professional schools instill this sense of obligation—particularly because professional associations sometimes become self-serving, losing sight of the interests of their clients as they protect their organizational prerogatives. Yates (1982) labels this behavior *guild professionalism*.

Fiduciary trust is an important component of public trust in government (Barber, 1983; Kass, 1994). The relationship is highly asymmetric because it is difficult for citizens to know what their agents in government are doing and to monitor and control their performance. Elected officials can be voted out of office, but civil servants are relatively immune from such control. Therefore, citizens must place their trust in government agencies and their employees to act in their interest. In this regard, Kass (1990) argues that the appropriate role for public officials is stewardship, or "the administrator's willingness and ability to earn the public trust by being an effective and ethical agent in carrying out the republic's business" (p. 113). Stewardship implies more than simply being an efficient and professional technocrat. Public officials should also be "informed by, and subordinated to, the ethical norms of justice and beneficence" (Kass, 1990, p. 114).

But just what are these norms? Beneficence—the act of doing good—requires an ethical standard. There are at least three standards we might consider. Public officials can follow uniform rules and standard operating procedures that (attempt to) treat everyone equally. They can also heed the golden rule, treating each citizen as they would have other public officials treat them under similar circumstances. Notably, both of these ethical standards ignore the specific, individualistic concerns of citizens themselves. For this reason, we should also consider care as an appropriate ethical standard (Baier, 1986; Noddings, 1984). Rather than following uniform procedures or doing what we believe is best for others, caring requires taking the specific interest of each citizen into account as a basis for action. As Noddings (1984) argues, "When we care, we consider the other's point of view, his objective needs, and what he expects of us" (p. 24).

Rule-bound behavior presents a gauze of neutrality, the appearance of fairness, but it stifles the ability of public officials to care for the individual citizens with whom they interact. Examining fiduciary trust from the standpoint of care therefore entails giving agency employees greater discretion to consider and respond to the needs of each citizen with whom they interact. It also means inculcating the norms of care within agencies and professional schools. Unfortunately, ethics courses are not currently part of the core curriculum in most graduate schools of public policy and administration. Averch and Dluhy (1992) did not find ethics courses required at any of the 16 Association for Public Policy Analysis and Management (APPAM) and 35 National Association of Schools of Affairs and Administration (NASPAA) schools they reviewed. Microeconomic courses, which aim to increase the efficiency of government programs, are standard, as are management courses, which strive to improve organizational effectiveness. Without denying the importance of these courses, why is ethics not given similar consideration? If ethics were added to this stew, we would have an opportunity to heighten public officials' sense of fiduciary obligation, and thereby give citizens reasons to place their trust in government. Moreover, rather than continuing to instill a paternalistic, technocratic, rule-bound orientation in students, professional schools should give serious attention to care as an appropriate ethical standard by which public officials can fulfill their fiduciary obligation.

The content of ethics courses (whether required or optional) is certainly open to debate; but the following discussion of mutual trust will demonstrate why microeconomic analysis cannot provide an adequate alternative to ethics, at least not with regard to understanding or restoring public trust in government.

MUTUAL TRUST

Mutual trust is more symmetric than fiduciary trust. Mutual trust also differs from fiduciary trust in that it is always interpersonal. Whereas a public agency can be the recipient of fiduciary trust, individuals develop interpersonal relationships based on mutual trust. Accordingly, a student and a public school teacher can develop mutual trust, and the student's feelings toward the teacher may extend to expectations the student has with regard to other teachers in the public school, but the student cannot develop a relationship of mutual trust with the school. Nevertheless, it makes sense to say that the student's trust in this public organization increases because of the mutual trust she has developed with her teacher. Because street-level bureaucrats are the primary point of contact between citizens and public organizations, it is important to understand how mutual trust develops, in what ways mutual trust buttresses fiduciary trust, and whether mutual trust is itself desirable in public-private relationships.

Because mutual trust is often confused with cooperative behavior, it is important to begin by distinguishing trust from cooperation. Trust increases the propensity for individuals to cooperate, but the existence of cooperation does not imply that individuals necessarily trust one another. As Oliver Williamson (1993) argues, formal theorists often use the word trust to describe cooperative behavior that is calculated and self-serving rather than trusting. "Prisoners' dilemma" experiments (Axelrod, 1984;

Deutsch, 1973), for example, merely identify the antecedents to cooperative behavior, such as the ability to communicate and repeated trials, but they do not establish whether the decision to cooperate is based on trust. Axelrod (1984) was careful to observe this distinction when analyzing the stability of cooperation in his tournament of computer programs:

> The foundation of cooperation is not really trust, but the durability of the relationship. . . . Whether the players trust each other or not is less important in the long run than whether the conditions are ripe for them to build a stable pattern of cooperation with each other. (p. 182)

Moreover, experiments with human subjects are structured differently than social interaction. Not only are they time bound, the decision by research subjects to be "in the game" allows them to suspend social presuppositions and responsibilities as well as to "leave the game" whenever they choose (Garfinkel, 1963, p. 207). Trust includes cognitive, emotional, and behavioral components, but such experiments do not distinguish the degree to which these components are present at various stages of iterated games or how they are interrelated. Given that game theory does not consider how beliefs are acquired, formal theorists end up finding more equilibria—"usually more uncooperative ones"—than, in fact, exist in the real world (Gambetta, 1988, p. 217).

Blau (1964) addressed such concerns by drawing a distinction between economic and social exchange. Economic exchange rests on formalized contracts that stipulate the exact quantities of a good to be exchanged, whereas social exchange involves the reciprocity of favors, in which the exact nature and timing of some future return is "definitely *not* stipulated in advance" (p. 93). An individual's failure to discharge social-exchange obligations at some later date subjects him to group sanctions but not legal sanctions. According to Blau,

> An individual is obligated to the banker who gives him a mortgage on his house merely in the technical sense of owing him money, but he does not feel personally obligated in the sense of experiencing a debt of gratitude to the banker, because all the banker's services, all costs and risks, are duly taken into account in and fully repaid by the interest on the loan he receives. A banker who grants a loan without adequate collateral, however, does make the recipient personally obligated for this favorable treatment, precisely because this act of trust entails a social exchange that is superimposed upon the strictly economic transaction. (p. 94)

Although the "impersonal economic market is designed to strip specific commodities of these entangling alliances," many supposedly economic exchanges nevertheless contain social obligations (Blau, 1964, p. 96).

Yet, Blau's exchange theory does not clearly distinguish transactions based on reciprocity, obligation, and trust from transactions based on calculated self-interest. Williamson (1993), by contrast, attempts to establish a clear delineation between these forms of exchange and thereby demarcate the boundary between economics and sociology. Williamson begins by noting that economics is "decidedly more calculative" (p. 453) than the other social sciences, whereas trust is "nearly noncalculative" (p. 479). Because calculated behavior forms the basis of most economic transactions, Williamson argues that using the term trust only confuses analyses. Indeed, many writers, particularly rational-choice theorists, use *trust* and *risk* synonymously, such that "trust is warranted when the expected gain from placing oneself at risk to another is positive, but not otherwise" (p. 463). If rational actors are simply calculating expected payoffs based on perceived risks, as in a prisoners' dilemma game, then trust is not present, and risk is a more precise term.

Williamson (1993, pp. 469-475) takes this further, however, arguing that if observed behavior can be explained in calculative terms, then trust should not be part of the explanation. This parsimonious model leads us to believe that any behavior that looks calculated is calculated. Based on this logical distinction, Williamson seeks to sweep trust out of economic analysis as well as economic relationships. Although convenient for economists, trust cannot and should not be swept out of government, where moral obligations buttress asymmetrical relationships. Transaction cost economics, based as it is on the explicit assumption that individuals are not merely self-interested but seek their own self-interest "with guile" (Williamson, 1993, p. 458), leads to excessively cynical interpretations of interpersonal relationships. Indeed, Williamson only grudgingly concedes that "trust, if it obtains at all, is reserved for very special relations between family, friends, and lovers" (p. 484).

Maintaining a distinction between mutual trust and calculated behavior is nevertheless useful because individuals indeed calculate whether to interact with others based on perceived risks. They also trust, often without knowing what the risks may be. Trust sometimes occurs in the extreme form of blind faith, as with those who believe in papal infallibility. Yet, trust is not simply a dichotomous variable; it varies widely between the extremes of blind faith and complete distrust. Trust is typically accompanied by some form of calculation, whether risks are to some extent understood. As Lewis and Weigert (1985) argue, "trust is based on a cognitive process which discriminates among persons" (p. 970) who are trustworthy, distrusted, and unknown. Trust has a rational, experiential basis. We may not calculate risks and probabilities, but we do make decisions in deciding whom to trust and with what we entrust them (Baier, 1986). Because our ability to calculate and predict the future is limited, trust may simply begin where prediction ends (Lewis & Weigert, 1985, p. 976). Put another way, prediction is based on evidence; trust is based on the lack of contrary evidence (Gambetta, 1988, p. 234).

We know trust exists because of the emotional sense of betrayal that is aroused when it is breached (Baier, 1986, p. 235; Lewis & Weigert, 1985, p. 971; Williamson, 1993, p. 482). When we calculate expected payoffs, we are disappointed if we make the wrong choice, but we do not feel betrayed. Betrayal is an indicator of the presence of trust, including fiduciary trust. Watergate evoked feelings of betrayal, not simply regret over a poorly calculated electoral choice.

Mutual trust is a component of public trust in government. Although some might fear that public-private relationships built on mutual trust will lead to capture or cooptation, these outcomes tend to arise when decisions are made by a few individuals behind closed doors rather than in an open public forum. It is certainly possible for public servants to fulfill their fiduciary obligations and develop open relationships of mutual trust with individual citizens. If we nurture both fiduciary and mutual trust, particularly through an ethic of care, then we can increasingly avoid quid pro quo relationships based on guile and the mind-numbing rules and procedures used to control such relationships. Relying solely on fiduciary trust as a means for producing and maintaining public trust denies street-level bureaucrats the opportunity to develop relationships of mutual trust with their clients.

SOCIAL TRUST

Even if economic transactions are solely calculative, it is nevertheless true that they occur within social systems, which themselves may be based on trust. Indeed, Williamson (1993, pp. 475-476) concedes this point, arguing that social factors are exogenous to his analysis—culture, regulations, and professional norms simply constrain the set of choices available to calculating individuals. Yet, social factors do more than constrain the set of choices available to otherwise self-interested individuals; they shape motives and beliefs as well. Socialization leads individuals to be more or less self-interested and more or less calculating. Business schools, for example, presumably enhance the self-interested motivations of a self-selected sample of students, whereas schools of public policy, management, and administration imbue students with a sense of fiduciary obligation.

Mark Granovetter (1985) argues further that interpersonal relationships shape social factors. Granovetter critiques contemporary economists for gradually replacing an "undersocialized" view of individuals as atomized actors subject only to the use pursuit of self-interest with an "oversocialized" view, in which equally atomized individuals simply internalize social norms and are guided by them (pp. 484-485). The oversocialized perspective recognizes the existence and influence of social norms but discounts the influence of individual relations on the development of norms. As Granovetter argues, "culture is not a once-for-all influence but an ongoing process, continuously constructed and reconstructed during interaction" (p. 486). The existence and interaction of mutually trusting individuals, in other words, enhance a culture of trust or social trust.

Social trust is a form of "social capital," which a society gradually accumulates through the microlevel interactions of individuals and which then becomes a public good on which others draw (Putnam, 1993, p. 170). Once it exists, social trust makes transactions more efficient (Arrow, 1974, p. 23). Unfortunately, economic theory can only assume that trust is present or absent; it cannot predict the conditions that create or erode trust, nor can it tell us the degree to which trust is present. The assumptions underlying the model of perfect competition, for example, do not include or require trust because economic exchange theoretically occurs under conditions of perfect information and numerous suppliers and demanders. In this imaginary world, individuals can completely specify a contract, and if one party breaks the contract, numerous others exist with whom contracts can be made. In this repeated-game environment, individuals are driven to live up to their contracts because their reputation is a capital asset.

No market is perfect, however, and in less than perfect markets some amount of trust must exist prior to contracting (Neu, 1991b, p. 245). Because it is prohibitively costly, if not cognitively impossible, for contracts to include specifications of all possible contingencies, most exchanges rest on background assumptions (Garfinkel, 1964), in which the parties to a contract trust that each will act according to expectations that are not covered in the contract itself (Dasgupta, 1988, pp. 52-53; Macneil, 1978). This is reflected in Macaulay's (1963, p. 61) observation that businessmen avoid calling out their lawyers whenever discrepancies between contracts and outcomes arise. Businessmen also "welcome a measure of vagueness in the obligations they assume so that they may negotiate matters in light of the actual circumstances" (pp. 63-64) and thus maintain long-term business relationships. Even competitive relationships depend on social trust, because competing in a mutually nondestructive way requires trusting competitors to comply with at least some basic rules. As Adam Smith once noted, "if there is any society among robbers and murderers, they must at least . . . abstain from robbing and murdering one another" (cited in Gambetta, 1988, p. 214).

Although social trust is not something we think about in our daily lives, it nevertheless permeates and eases our day-to-day existence. Luhmann (1979), for example, argues that humans need to trust to reduce the complexity of even the most routine decisions. In his oft-cited opening passage, Luhmann writes the following:

> Trust, in the broadest sense of confidence in one's expectations, is a basic fact of social life. In many situations, of course, man can choose in certain respects whether or not to bestow trust. But a complete absence of trust would prevent him even from getting up in the morning. He would be prey to a vague sense of dread, to paralysing fears. He would not even be capable of formulating definite *dis*trust and making that a basis for precautionary measures, since this would presuppose trust in other directions. Anything and everything would be possible. Such abrupt confrontation with the complexity of the world at its most extreme is beyond human endurance. (p. 4)

Garfinkel's (1963, 1964) breaching experiments demonstrated the degree to which stable interactions are based on things known in common and taken for granted, and which thereby reduce the complexity of social life. In one experiment, Garfinkel (1964) instructed his students to engage unsuspecting friends or strangers in conversation and to act on the assumption that the other's motivations were hidden and thus that everything the person said was not to be trusted:

> One student spoke for several when she said she was unable to get any results because so much of her effort was directed to maintaining an attitude of distrust that she was unable to follow the conversation. She said she was unable to imagine how her fellow conversationalists might be deceiving her because they were talking about such inconsequential matters. (p. 234)

A world of distrust is essentially senseless because events appear "atypical, causally indeterminate, and arbitrary in occurrence, without a relevant history or future . . . or moral necessity" (Garfinkel, 1963, p. 189). Because all possible contingencies would have to be accounted for at every step, and because human rationality is bounded, pure distrust is impossible outside of a hermit's existence, even for routine social interactions. Therefore, people come to "trust in trust"—the idea that trust is indispensable and that we can assume it is so regarded by others (Gambetta, 1988; Luhmann, 1979, p. 67).

Although social trust occurs in the aggregate, it cannot be clearly delineated from either mutual trust or fiduciary trust. They are interwoven and mutually supportive. Mutual trust, generated through microlevel interpersonal relationships, gives rise to and shapes the character of social trust. In turn, social trust enhances the ability of individuals to develop mutual trust. Social trust also buttresses the sense of moral obligation that sustains fiduciary trust. Because social trust provides a requisite basis for stable, concerted interaction in a society, we can assume that some degree of trust always exists. Accordingly, the relevant question is not, How can we produce trust? but rather, How can we produce more trust and maintain the trust we already have?

THE PRODUCTION OF TRUST

Lynne Zucker (1986) identified three modes of trust production. Characteristic-based trust is tied to personal characteristics, such as family background and ethnicity; process-based trust is produced through repeated exchanges; and institutional-based trust is produced through formal institutional processes, such as professional certification and government regulation. By focusing on trust production, Zucker's relatively simple typology provides insight into the cognitive, emotional, and behavioral levels at which trust operates, as well as the respective problems associated with the production of trust. The typology is evolutionary rather than based on mutually exclusive categories; institutional-based trust gradually supplants characteristic-based trust and process-based trust as a society becomes increasingly complex and differentiated.

CHARACTERISTIC-BASED TRUST

Characteristic-based trust is produced through personal characteristics, such as race, gender, and family background, that "serve as indicators of membership in a common cultural system" (Zucker, 1986, p. 63). Given that humans need to trust to interact, personal characteristics are a simple heuristic for deciding whether other individuals share similar background expectations. Characteristic-based trust is most prevalent in small communities that seldom interact with outsiders. It is also present in complex modern societies as evidenced by individuals who cross the street to avoid strangers who appear different.

Because it is relatively difficult to change personal characteristics, the most viable means for building characteristic-based trust is to socialize with persons possessing similar characteristics. Accordingly, agency managers could strategically place employees in specific positions, such that employee characteristics match those of targeted communities. For example, a White geophysicist from an Ivy League university, employed by the U.S. Department of Energy to study potential sites for a radioactive waste repository in the American West, would be an unlikely recipient of characteristic-based trust from individuals in a Native American community. Conversely, Michael Jordan, sitting on an advisory committee or task force, could be a valuable spokesperson for the Department of Housing and Urban Development.

Pursuing only a characteristic-based strategy for building public trust would be rather shallow, of course, because individuals in complex societies do not invest much energy in a trusting relationship based solely on ascribed characteristics. Moreover, agency employees and spokespersons would eventually become tainted by agency pathologies and the conflictual nature of the political environment. By itself, characteristic-based trust is not a viable means for producing public trust in government agencies and their employees.

PROCESS-BASED TRUST

Process-based trust is produced through repeated exchanges rather than through ascribed characteristics and, thus, emerges over time. Whereas process-based trust may be facilitated by characteristic-based trust, initial exchanges may also be motivated by self-interest, with no trust already present. Once an economic-exchange relationship is initiated, however, subsequent exchanges increasingly "become overlaid with social content that carries strong expectations of trust and abstention from opportunism" (Granovetter, 1985, p. 490). Repeated exchanges also become increasingly governed by norms geared to the preservation of the relationship itself (Macaulay, 1963; Macneil, 1978).

The value of goods exchanged also affects the production of process-based trust.[5] Haas and Deseran (1981, p. 3), expanding on Blau's theory of exchange relationships, introduced the concept of symbolic exchange, a type of social exchange that captures the economic value of goods changing hands in a trust-producing relationship:

> The goods are symbolic in the sense that their principal utility lies in their capacity to symbolize the nature of the relationship between the receiver and the giver of the gifts. They are also symbolic in the sense that their high cost to the giver serves as a token of the giver's good faith.

Although some exchanges, such as a wave or a handshake, have little or no utilitarian value, other exchanges, such as an invitation to a dinner party, lie somewhere between social and economic exchange because they have both symbolic and utilitarian value. The utilitarian dimension of the exchange represents its intrinsic or economic value, whereas the symbolic or communicative dimension conveys information about the desire of the giver to enter into a trust-building relationship. In addition to offers of food, drink, and gifts, symbolic exchange includes attendance at formal ceremonies. Because the utilitarian importance of ceremonial attendance is measured in the time it requires, "an important person whose time is known to be valuable can express a considerable commitment to a person or a group merely by attending" (Haas & Deseran, 1981, p. 8).

Refusing symbolic or social exchanges is a gesture indicating distaste for entering into a trust-building relationship and could be interpreted as a sign of distrust toward the giver (Blau, 1964, pp. 107-108; Haas & Deseran, 1981, pp. 8-9). Even if a symbolic or social exchange is accepted, paying off debts quickly may be interpreted as a refusal to enter into a long-term relationship or even as a sign of mistrust (Luhmann, 1979, p. 44). As Blau (1964) argues, "social bonds are fortified by remaining obligated to others as well as by trusting them to discharge their obligations for considerable periods" (p. 99). Therefore, unlike economic exchange, in which rapid repayment of debts is usually expected, eagerness to discharge a social obligation may be interpreted as ingratitude.

Public officials are in a bind when attempting to build process-based trust with individuals outside of government through symbolic or social exchange. Many types of public-private exchanges are frowned upon in the United States because of the fear they will cement quid pro quo relationships with special interests. Yet, if a public employee refuses such exchanges, she risks producing distrust because refusals might be interpreted by individuals in the agency's environment as an indication that the employee—and, by implication, the agency—does not want to enter into reciprocal obligations and is therefore not worthy of trust. Ceremonial attendance, however, provides a good opportunity for public officials to build process-based trust, depending on the rank of the official. High-level political appointees, whose time is greatly valued, can instill a great deal of public trust with a single exchange, whereas individuals at lower levels of the hierarchy would have to rely on repeated attendance to build a similar amount of trust.

Tenure longevity is thus an important requisite for midlevel line managers, program managers, and street-level bureaucrats to produce process-based trust. Employee rotation systems impede trust production by limiting the number of times public officials can interact with specific individuals in an agency's environment. Moving employees from one place to another, like other organizational decisions, has both costs and benefits. Herbert Kaufman (1960) once extolled the U.S. Forest Service for maintaining a cohesive sense of mission despite its far-flung organizational structure. In part, the Forest Service achieved cohesiveness by rotating forest rangers every few years to new locations before they could develop personal relationships with, and become captured by, local residents (Kaufman, 1960, p. 217). Yet, the existence of close working relationships does not necessarily imply capture. Behind closed doors, repeated interactions among few individuals take on the appearance, if not the substance, of capture. Conversely, if agency employees interact with multiple interests simultaneously in public forums, then capture is less likely to occur.

Indeed, as Daniel Kemmis (1990) suggests, public officials can play the role of facilitators and consensus-builders among multiple interests in society, particularly at the local level. Rather than taking sides on policy issues, or mediating between interest groups although following organizational procedures, agency employees can serve as facilitators, bringing citizens together in search of collaborative solutions.[6] In the short run, each consensus-building group generates mutual trust, and in the long run, adds to the collective pool of social trust from which the entire society benefits (Putnam, 1993). Although multi-interest collaboration is a relatively new phenomenon in the United States, it offers an important opportunity for agency employees to produce process-based trust in their environment. If practiced routinely, the collaborative process itself might some day become institutionalized or taken for granted.

INSTITUTIONAL-BASED TRUST

Institutional-based trust is produced through institutions that have become accepted as social facts and are therefore seldom questioned.

Zucker (1986) argues that institutional-based trust became increasingly important after the 19th century as immigration and internal migration pulled apart the insular communities within which characteristic-based trust predominated. The increasingly complex and volatile economy also limited process-based trust as exchanges were made at ever greater geographic distances and as firms formed, merged, and folded with increasing frequency. In this context, institutional-based trust expanded to provide alternative guarantees for exchanges. Professional credentials served as an alternative to personal reputation; financial intermediaries (e.g., banks, brokers, and independent accountants) bridged distant exchange partners; and government regulations and laws provided a common framework for exchange, including general expectations and specific rules governing transactions.

Zucker (1986) identifies two types of institutional-based trust. The first type is specific to persons or organizations because it "rests on membership in a subculture within which carefully delineated specific expectations are expected to hold, at least in some cases based on detailed prior socialization" (p. 63). Professionals, for example, evoke fiduciary trust through the integrity of the social process through which the knowledge base of the profession is itself derived and applied, rather than through personal integrity or claims to expertise (Bella, 1987). Rigorous education and peer reviews, as well as constant conformance to codes of ethics, are signals to the public that professionals do not define their responsibilities solely through self-interest or organizational assignments. Accordingly, individuals and firms join professional associations and acquire credentials and licenses in part to signal to others that they intend to abide by certain rules and codes of conduct (Neu, 1991a, p. 188). Private organizations voluntarily adopt standard practices to signal the organization's willingness to conform to expectations in its environment (Dowling & Pfeffer, 1975; Zucker, 1986, pp. 90-94). Public agencies similarly signal conformance with social expectations, and thereby produce institutional-based trust, by adopting the latest administrative fad—be it zero-base budgeting, total quality management, or reengineering.

A second type of institutional-based trust is produced through intermediary mechanisms such as laws, regulation, and insurance. Zucker (1986) provides a pithy illustration of the social transition from interpersonal trust to this form of institutional trust:

> If you do not trust your neighbor to participate in a "barn-raising" after your house burns, you have to buy insurance; if you do not trust immigrants to

> behave according to common understandings . . . , then you have to "reform" city governments to give them less power by formalizing personnel procedures; if you do not trust corporations to behave "fairly" and ethically, then you have to formalize interorganizational relations by enacting antitrust rules (p. 69)

Principal-agent relationships also serve as intermediary mechanisms for producing institutional-based trust. Because fiduciary relationships have become increasingly prevalent in modern society, numerous guardians (or trustees) of trust now oversee these impersonal relationships, which have become increasingly layered to assure individual actors that their affairs are being well managed (Shapiro, 1987, p. 649). Although such redundancy can strengthen institutional-based trust, this outcome cannot be assured. Neu's (1991a) study of the Canadian securities market, for example, found regulators developing tacit agreements amongst themselves regarding regulatory responsibilities, but not routinely informing one another of changes in operating practices. Although gaps in institutional rules had not yet occurred, Neu (1991a, p. 194) believed these two factors, in conjunction, increased the probability of opportunistic violations of trust.

The research on institutional-based trust suggests several ways in which public organizations can produce trust in their environment. For example, because impersonal trust is signaled through the possession of academic and professional credentials, agency personnel can acquire credentials similar to or respected by members of the attentive public. These credentials will serve as a signal that the agency adheres to the same standards and codes of conduct as others in the targeted community. There is an organizational cost to this method of trust production, however, because professional associations usually have goals that differ somewhat from those of the agency; and these goals may also differ with some segments of the agency's clientele. Thus, agency managers must weigh potential gains in public trust among some segments of the public against increased conflict of interest within the agency, and possibly even a loss of trust among some of the agency's clientele.

Another means for producing institutional-based trust is regulation. Public agencies can call for increased regulation of their activities, thereby providing additional fiduciary layers. This strategy assumes of course that the public trusts the (new) regulator to carry out its duties. Agency managers can also call for additional legislative oversight, as well as new laws mandating that other agencies conduct external reviews or set performance standards. Interagency regulation is not unusual (e.g., the

Tennessee Valley Authority must comply with the Environmental Protection Agency's air pollution requirements), but interagency compliance is difficult to achieve at the national level because lines of accountability are unclear (Wilson & Rachal, 1977). At the intergovernmental level, public trust in federal agencies might be bolstered if they are monitored (or even regulated) by local or state agencies, because surveys suggest that local and state agencies are generally trusted more than federal agencies on issues with local origins (Muste, 1992).

Attempts to achieve public trust through institutionalized procedural constraints may, however, limit otherwise desirable agency behavior. Although this article focuses on public trust in government, trust also has important effects on productivity *within* agencies (Carnevale & Wechsler, 1992; Culbert & McDonough, 1986; Daley, 1991). Because trust permeates intraorganizational authority relationships (Bradach & Eccles, 1989), hierarchical control systems that overemphasize rules (Kelman, 1990) or monitoring (Frey, 1993) may have the unintended effect of stifling performance. Moreover, as previously noted in the section on fiduciary trust, strict adherence to rules and procedures impedes the ability of public officials to take the interests of individual citizens into account, and thereby fulfill their fiduciary obligation in terms of an ethic based on care. Even institutions established for the purpose of caretaking can lose sight of their purpose in the face of rational proceduralism. As Noddings (1984) suggests, "Those entrusted with caring may focus on satisfying the formulated requirements for caretaking and fail to be present in their interactions with the cared-for. Thus caring disappears and only its illusion remains" (p. 26).

MAINTAINING TRUST—OR, HOW TRUST IS LOST

Given that some degree of trust underlies all social interactions, trust can always be lost as well as gained. Yet, trust is not necessarily produced and lost in similar—but opposite—fashions. Therefore, separate consideration is given in this section to methods for maintaining public trust.

One way in which trust can be lost is through the extensive use of contracts detailing the precise responsibilities of each party in the event of remote or unlikely contingencies (Macaulay, 1963, p. 64). Not only is complete planning cognitively impossible and prohibitively costly, extensively detailed contracts imply a lack of trust because their purpose is to specify obligations and future returns—and thus to align expectations—when trust is low. The more contracts are used as a substitute for trust, the greater the signal of distrust or lack of trust. Neu (1991b, p. 247) refers to this as the "irony of contracting" because the use of contracts leads to a downward spiral characterized by the increasing use of contracts as imperfect alternatives for increasingly less trust. Unfortunately, detailed contracts may be necessary when exchanges involve complex performances to be performed over long periods of time, especially if the degree of injury in case of default is thought to be great (Macaulay, 1963, p. 65). Agencies managing high-risk, high-hazard technologies might have no choice but to rely on contractual relationships.

Trust can also be lost when role expectations are in flux. Reichman's (1989) analysis of insider trading in the stock market found that organizational changes increase the probability of trust violations because cultural norms and role behaviors also change. According to Reichman (1989),

> Role ambiguity helps free incumbents to believe that rules are bad or that they don't apply. When "anything goes," it is not so hard to justify deviant behavior as legitimate, "above," or "within the law." (p. 188)

This suggests that an agency can maintain trust through organizational stability. If role changes create opportunities for trust violation by increasing ambiguity in role performance, then reorganizations are likely to generate distrust. Not only might reorganizations increase opportunities for actual violations of trust (and thus public expectations of future malfeasance), but organizational changes also may not conform with existing expectations in the organization's environment, giving rise to bewilderment and unease, and thereby decreasing current levels of trust. Because reorganization is a clumsy and relatively ineffective tool for achieving desired ends (Thomas, 1993), it would not be surprising to find that one of its unintended side effects is the reduction of public trust.

Trust can also be lost through lying and the misuse of power. In her moral treatise on lying, Bok (1978) argues that individual lies not only erode trust between the liar and the recipient of the lie, each lie also wears away at the social system of trust that supports the institutions on which society is constructed. Her analysis is thus similar to the externalities argument in microeconomics, in that the full social cost of a lie is not borne completely by the liar. As an example, she notes that government officials often lie to the public to protect the secrecy of their programs, justifying these lies to themselves by arguing that program benefits outweigh the cost of the lie. In doing so, however, they fail to calculate the long-term, aggregate effect on the loss of public trust in government (Bok, 1978, pp. 27, 142). Similarly, Kass (1990) argues that the misuse of power by a public official for personal, professional, or organizational ends erodes the trust on which the legitimacy of government depends:

> Consistent violations by individual public agents, even if done in the name of the republic's welfare, ultimately raise the average individual's sense of vulnerability to the great power he or she has placed in this entity and adversely affects the legitimacy of both the agents involved and the republican association. (pp. 126-127)

Finally, trust in professions can be lost through individual incompetence, as well as through complacency in the social process through which professional trust is sustained. Public trust in professions depends on self-criticism within the profession. Constant peer review is a necessary means for preventing trustworthy communities from being "transformed into associations of self-serving functionaries" (Bella, 1987, p. 123). In particular, Bella (1987, p. 124) warns professionals to avoid being captured by the needs and demands of the organization within which they work because organizational biases would then enter the self-regulatory process of the profession. Public managers seeking to nurture public trust should therefore encourage employees to participate actively in professional communities, and should refrain from using professions to produce or justify public policies in contentious policy arenas. The scientific-based professions, for example, lose their credibility when their processes become attached to conflicting policy positions (Wynne, 1987). Self-serving professionals can also reduce public trust if they come to see the role of the professional not as someone giving advice but as someone with influence over policy. As March and Olsen (1989) argue, "The changed frame of reference tends to compromise the quality of expert information in the political process and to undermine trust not only in the individual expert but in the institution of expertise" (p. 32). Professionals are a source of public trust for government agencies because professional credentials signal the willingness of public employees (and, by extension, agencies) to conform to certain expectations; but this trust can only be maintained if these individuals remain grounded in the social processes of their respective professions and fulfill their fiduciary obligations.

SUMMARY

The means presented in this article for producing and maintaining public trust are hypothetical and inconclusive. Theories of trust constitute a rich and burgeoning literature, but this research is not currently geared to public trust in government. Although the hypotheses derived in this exploratory article provide a basis for discussing the production and maintenance of trust in government agencies and their employees, they have not been rigorously tested, and their relative effectiveness is therefore unknown. With these caveats in mind, the following means for producing and maintaining public trust are plausible.

First, reorganization should not be considered a panacea for agencies in which the relative absence of public trust is perceived to be hampering effective operations. In the short run, reorganizations are more likely to produce distrust by increasing opportunities for malfeasance due to role fluctuations, or by simply bewildering individuals in the agency's environment who have come to expect certain organizational behaviors. Measures short of wholesale reorganization are more likely to produce public trust. For example, because individuals are limited in their abilities to process information, they often rely on relatively simple heuristics, such as personal characteristics and professional affiliation, to make judgments about organizational trustworthiness. Therefore, agency managers might try matching the personal and professional characteristics of employees with targeted groups outside the agency, or appointing individuals outside the agency to sit on advisory boards. Managers can also encourage subordinates and peers to participate actively in professional communities as a means for signaling the agency's willingness to conform to institutionalized norms. In doing so, managers should refrain from using these professional processes and worldviews to justify contentious policy positions, and they should be wary of the self-serving tendencies of professions as well as the shallow nature of characteristic-based trust.

Regulations, oversight, and standard practices provide additional signals of institutional trustworthiness. Public employees should cooperate with government regulators, perhaps even publicly requesting increased oversight of agency operations to increase fiduciary redundancy. Lying and secrecy, of course, should be avoided. Professional schools of public policy, management, and administration also play an important role in these regards by providing an ethical—rather than simply a technocratic—foundation for public employees to aid them in defining and carrying out their fiduciary responsibilities. Because ethics is not currently part of the core curriculum at most of these schools, we should seriously consider raising the profile of ethics courses and adopting care as an ethical standard for producing public trust.

The literature on contracts is relatively ambiguous regarding the production and maintenance of trust. Detailed contracts align expectations when trust is weak, but such contracts also signal the absence of trust by one or more parties to the contract. Given that detailed contracts may be necessary when exchanges involve complex or hazardous activities performed over long periods of time, agency officials might have no option but to accept the necessity of detailed contracts under these circumstances. They can counteract some of the negative consequences of contracts by shoring up trust through other means, including symbolic or social exchanges. Although public officials are limited in their ability to participate in gift exchanges, ceremonial attendance at various social functions is feasible and is a productive means for building trust with specific groups in the agency's environment, depending on the rank of the official. In this regard, tenure longevity for street-level bureaucrats and midlevel managers is particularly important for building process-based trust. Public officials can also generate process-based trust by participating in consensus-building groups composed of multiple interests.

In closing, it should be noted that the existing literature on trust focuses primarily on private exchanges between individuals and market-based exchanges between firms. Because political exchanges are different from private exchanges, extrapolating from the private sector to the public sector may be a suspect exercise. March and Olsen (1989), for example, note that building a culture of trust in political organizations is "severely strained by exploitative political leaders, and may indeed be impossible to sustain in many heterogeneous societies with deep, persistent social cleavages and traditions of minimal regulation of conflict" (p. 34). Although pessimistic, their analysis is illuminating in the context of this article. Producing trust in government at a macrolevel may indeed be extraordinarily difficult in a heterogeneous society such as the United States, but public officials can nevertheless produce trust within their agency's environment. The means presented in this article are general and relatively modest, but they suggest that trust can be produced and maintained on the margin if agency officials adhere persistently to them.

NOTES

1. These questions include (but are not limited to) the following: "How much of the time do you think you can trust the government in Washington to do what is right?"; "Would you say that the government is pretty much run by a few big interests looking out for themselves or that it is run for the benefit of all people?"; and "Do you think that people in the government waste a lot of money we pay in taxes, waste some of it, or don't waste very much of it?" (Citrin & Green, 1986, p. 434).

2. For background, see the reports of the Task Force on Radioactive Waste Management (U.S. Department of Energy, 1993a, 1993b), which was one of several task forces of the Secretary of Energy Advisory Board. The board and its task forces provided independent advice to the Secretary of Energy on long-range strategic planning issues affecting the Department of Energy. For additional discussion of public trust with respect to radioactive waste management, see Bella, Mosher, and Calvo (1988); Kunreuther, Easterling, Desvousges, and Slovic (1990); La Porte and Metlay (1996); and the proceedings of a workshop sponsored by the National Academy of Public Administration (1991). Those seeking more specific guidelines for maintaining, producing, or restoring public trust than provided in this article should review the recommendations of the Task Force on Radioactive Waste Management (U.S. Department of Energy, 1993a) or the synopsis in La Porte and Metlay (1996).

3. Also see Behn (1995) on the role of trust in the "micromanagement cycle."

4. Reiss (1984), for example, argues that governments select regulatory enforcement models based either on trust or surveillance, without defining trust. Similarly, Bok (1978, p. 31), in her acclaimed book on the moral dilemmas of lying, argues that lies erode trust, although she never defines trust, and refers only briefly to some possible conceptions of trust in a footnote. Although the reader can infer from Bok's discussion that trust has something to do with expectations regarding the future behavior of others (pp. 18-19), she is never explicit on this point, and one is thus left to wonder about her conclusions. If lies indeed erode the general system of trust on which institutions and society are founded, how would we recognize the erosion of trust and thus prevent institutional collapse?

5. This is not to suggest that it is possible to buy trust from those in whom it is sought. As Arrow (1974) noted, "If you have to buy it, you already have some doubts about what you've bought" (p. 23).

6. Ruscio (1996) refers to a similar process he calls "civic discovery" (pp. 473-474).

REFERENCES

Arrow, K. J. (1974). *The limits of organization.* New York: Norton.

Averch, H., & Dluhy, M. (1992). Teaching public administration, public management, and policy analysis: Convergence or divergence in the masters core. *Journal of Policy Analysis and Management, 11*, 541-551.

Axelrod, R. (1984). *The evolution of cooperation.* New York: Basic Books.

Baier, A. (1986). Trust and antitrust. *Ethics, 96*, 231-260.

Barber, B. (1983). *The logic and limits of trust.* New Brunswick, NJ: Rutgers University Press.

Behn, R. D. (1995). The big questions of public management. *Public Administration Review, 55*, 313-324.

Bella, D. A. (1987). Engineering and erosion of trust. *Journal of Professional Issues in Engineering, 113*, 117-129.

Bella, D. A., Mosher, C. D., & Calvo, S. N. (1988). Technocracy and trust: Nuclear waste controversy. *Journal of Professional Issues in Engineering, 114*, 27-39.

Blau, P. (1964). *Exchange and power in social life*. New York: John Wiley.

Bok, S. (1978). *Lying: Moral choice in public and private life*. New York: Pantheon.

Bradach, J. L., & Eccles, R. G. (1989). Price, authority, and trust: From ideal types to plural forms. *Annual Review of Sociology, 15*, 97-118.

Carnevale, D. G., & Wechsler, B. (1992). Trust in the public sector: Individual and organizational determinants. *Administration & Society, 23*, 471-494.

Chisholm, D. (1989). *Coordination without hierarchy: Informal structures in multiorganizational systems*. Berkeley: University of California Press.

Citrin, J. (1974). Comment: The political relevance of trust in government. *American Political Science Review, 68*, 973-988.

Citrin, J. (1993). Political trust and risky policy. In *Compilation of reports prepared for the Secretary of Energy Advisory Board Task Force on Radioactive Waste Management*. Washington, DC: Secretary of Energy Advisory Board, U.S. Department of Energy.

Citrin, J., & Green, D. P. (1986). Presidential leadership and the resurgence of trust in government. *British Journal of Political Science, 16*, 431-453.

Culbert, S. A., & McDonough, J. J. (1986). The politics of trust and organization empowerment. *Public Administration Quarterly, 10*, 171-188.

Daley, D. M. (1991). Management practices and the uninvolved manager: The effect of supervisory attitudes on perceptions of organizational trust and change orientation. *Public Personnel Management, 20*, 101-112.

Dasgupta, P. (1988). Trust as a commodity. In D. Gambetta (Ed.), *Trust: Making and breaking cooperative relations* (pp. 49-72). New York: Blackwell.

Deluga, R. J. (1994). Supervisor trust building, leader-member exchange and organizational citizenship behavior. *Journal of Occupational and Organizational Psychology, 67*, 315-326.

Deutsch, M. (1973). *The resolution of conflict: Constructive and destructive processes*. New Haven, CT: Yale University Press.

Dowling, J., & Pfeffer, J. (1975). Organizational legitimacy: Social values and organizational behavior. *Pacific Sociological Review, 18*, 122-136.

Fairholm, G. W. (1994). *Leadership and the culture of trust*. Westport, CT: Praeger.

Frey, B. S. (1993). Does monitoring increase work effort? The rivalry with trust and loyalty. *Economic Inquiry, 31*, 663-670.

Gambetta, D. (1988). Can we trust trust? In D. Gambetta (Ed.), *Trust: Making and Breaking Cooperative Relations* (pp. 213-237). New York: Blackwell.

Garfinkel, H. (1963). A conception of, and experiments with, 'trust' as a condition of stable concerted actions. In O. J. Harvey (Ed.), *Motivation and social interaction* (pp. 187-238). New York: Ronald Press.

Garfinkel, H. (1964). Studies of the routine grounds of everyday activities. *Social Problems, 11*, 225-250.

Goodsell, C. T. (1994). *The case for bureaucracy: A public administration polemic* (3rd ed.). Chatham, NJ: Chatham House.

Granovetter, M. (1985). Economic action and social structure: The problem of embeddedness. *American Journal of Sociology, 91*, 481-510.
Haas, D. F., & Deseran, F. A. (1981). Trust and symbolic exchange. *Social Psychology Quarterly, 44*, 3-13.
Heclo, H. (1977). *A government of strangers: Executive politics in Washington*. Washington, DC: Brookings Institution.
Husted, B. W. (1989). Trust in business relations: Directions for empirical research. *Business and Professional Ethics Journal, 8*, 23-40.
Kass, H. D. (1990). Stewardship as a fundamental element in images of public administration. In H. D. Kass & B. L. Catron (Eds.), *Images and identities in public administration* (pp. 113-131). Newbury Park, CA: Sage.
Kass, H. D. (1994). Trust, agency and institution building in contemporary American democracy. *Administrative Theory and Praxis, 16*, 15-30.
Kaufman, H. (1960). *The forest ranger.* Washington, DC: Resources for the Future.
Kelman, S. (1990). *Procurement and public management: The fear of discretion and the quality of government performance.* Washington, DC: AEI Press.
Kemmis, D. (1990). *Community and the politics of place.* Norman: University of Oklahoma Press.
Kunreuther, H., Easterling, D., Desvousges, W., & Slovic, P. (1990). Public attitudes toward siting a high-level nuclear waste repository in Nevada. *Risk Analysis, 10*, 469-484.
La Porte, T. R., & Metlay, D. S. (1996). Hazards and institutional trustworthiness: Facing a deficit of trust. *Public Administration Review, 56*, 341-347.
Lewis, J. D., & Weigert, A. J. (1985). Trust as a social reality. *Social Forces, 63*, 967-985.
Lipset, S. M., & Schneider, W. (1983). *The confidence gap: Business, labor, and government in the public mind.* New York: Free Press.
Luhmann, N. (1979). *Trust and power.* New York: John Wiley.
Macaulay, S. (1963). Non-contractual relations in business: A preliminary study. *American Sociological Review, 28*, 55-67.
Macneil, I. R. (1978). Contracts: Adjustment of long-term economic relations under classical, neoclassical, and relational contract law. *Northwestern University Law Review, 72*, 854-905.
March, J. G., & Olsen, J. P. (1989). *Rediscovering institutions: The organizational basis of politics.* New York: Free Press.
Miller, A. H. (1974). Political issues and trust in government: 1964-1970. *American Political Science Review, 68*, 951-972.
Miller, G. J. (1992). *Managerial dilemmas: The political economy of hierarchy.* Cambridge, UK: Cambridge University Press.
Mishra, A. K. (1995). Organizational responses to crisis: The centrality of trust. In R. Kramer & T. Tyler (Eds.), *Trust in organizations.* Thousand Oaks, CA: Sage.
Mitchell, T. R., & Scott, W. G. (1987). Leadership failures, the distrusting public, and prospects of the administrative state. *Public Administration Review, 47*, 445-452.
Muste, C. (1992). *Public opinion and democratic governance in the U.S. federal system: The dimensions of public attitudes toward state and local government.* Paper prepared for the National Commission on State and Local Public Service.
National Academy of Public Administration. (1991). *Recovering public trust and confidence in managing radioactive waste.* Washington, DC: Author.

Neu, D. (1991a). New stock issues and the institutional production of trust. *Accounting, Organizations and Society, 16*, 185-200.

Neu, D. (1991b). Trust, contracting and the prospectus process. *Accounting, Organizations and Society, 16*, 243-256.

Noddings, N. (1984). *Caring: A feminine approach to ethics and moral education*. Berkeley: University of California Press.

Ouchi, W. G. (1981). *Theory Z: How American business can meet the Japanese challenge*. Reading, MA: Addison-Wesley.

Pfeffer, J., & Salancik, G. R. (1978). *The external control of organizations: A resource dependence perspective*. New York: Harper & Row.

Powell, W. W., & DiMaggio, P. J. (1991). *The new institutionalism in organizational analysis*. Chicago: University of Chicago Press.

Putnam, R. D. (1993). *Making democracy work: Civic traditions in modern Italy*. Princeton, NJ: Princeton University Press.

Reichman, N. (1989). Breaking confidences: Organizational influences on insider trading. *Sociological Quarterly, 30*, 185-204.

Reiss, A. J. (1984). Selecting strategies of social control over organizational life. In K. Hawkins & J. M. Thomas (Eds.), *Enforcing Regulation*. Boston: Kluwer-Nijhoff.

Ring, P. S., & Van de Ven, A. H. (1992). Structuring cooperative relationships between organizations. *Strategic Management Journal, 13*, 483-498.

Ring, P. S., & Van de Ven, A. H. (1994). Developmental processes of cooperative interorganizational relationships. *Academy of Management Review, 19*, 90-118.

Ruscio, K. P. (1996). Trust, democracy, and public management: A theoretical argument. *Journal of Public Administration Research and Theory, 6*, 461-477.

Shapiro, S. P. (1987). The social control of impersonal trust. *American Journal of Sociology, 93*, 623-658.

Thomas, C. W. (1993). Reorganizing public organizations: Alternatives, objectives, and evidence. *Journal of Public Administration Research and Theory, 3*, 457-486.

U.S. Department of Energy. (1993a). *Earning public trust and confidence: Requisites for managing radioactive waste*. Washington, DC: Secretary of Energy Advisory Board, U.S. Department of Energy.

U.S. Department of Energy. (1993b). *Compilation of reports prepared for the Secretary of Energy Advisory Board Task Force on Radioactive Waste Management*. Washington, DC: Secretary of Energy Advisory Board, U.S. Department of Energy.

Williams, J. T. (1987). Systemic influences on political trust: The importance of perceived institutional performance. *Political Methodology, 7*, 125-142.

Williamson, O. E. (1985). *The economic institutions of capitalism*. New York: Free Press.

Williamson, O. E. (1993). Calculativeness, trust, and economic organization. *Journal of Law and Economics, 36*, 453-486.

Wilson, J. Q., & Rachal, P. (1977). Can the government regulate itself? *Public Interest, 46*, 3-14.

Wynne, B. (1987). *Risk management and hazardous waste: Implementation and the dialectics of credibility*. Berlin, Germany: Springer-Verlag.

Yates, D. (1982). *Bureaucratic democracy: The search for democracy and efficiency in American government*. Cambridge, MA: Harvard University Press.

Zucker, L. G. (1986). Production of trust: Institutional sources of economic structure, 1840-1920. *Research in Organizational Behavior, 8*, 53-111.

Craig W. Thomas is an assistant professor of political science at the University of Massachusetts, Amherst. He received a master's degree in public policy and a doctorate in political science from the University of California, Berkeley. His articles on interagency cooperation, regulatory compliance, and reorganization have appeared in the Journal of Public Administration Research and Theory.

[27]

The System of Administrative and Political Corruption: Canal Irrigation in South India

*by Robert Wade**

The paper describes how some irrigation engineers raise vast amounts of illicit revenue from the distribution of water and contracts, and redistribute part to superior officers and politicians. It argues that the corruption 'system', which is centred on control of personnel transfers, is an important supply-side reason for poor performance of canal-irrigated agriculture. Insofar as the same system operates in other government departments, it may be more important for understanding Indian politics and the political influences on economic development than has previously been realised.

> Just as fish moving under water cannot possibly be found out either as drinking or not drinking water, so government servants employed in the government work cannot be found out while taking money for themselves [Kautilya, the Indian statecraft scholar, in about 300 BC, transl. *Shamasastry, 1967 (1915): 71*].

> The tendency to subvert integrity in the public services instead of being isolated and aberrative is growing into an organised, well-planned racket .... It was reported to us that corruption has increased to such an extent that people have started losing faith in the integrity of public administration [*India, Government of, Ministry of Home Affairs, 1964: 12*].

Canal irrigation can be looked at in at least two ways: as a system for delivering a particular agricultural input; and as a specific context of government action in the countryside.[1] One can study canal irrigation in India either to contribute to knowledge of canal irrigation systems in general; or to illuminate more general features of Indian society and government. This paper approaches the topic from both of these angles.

Economic planners and farmers have recurrently been dismayed—not only in India—to find that canal systems operate substantially below the expected level of performance [*Wade, 1975; Wade and Chambers, 1980*]. The causes of canal underperformance are many, including technical as well as

---

* Institute of Development Studies, University of Sussex. I have benefited from comments by Freddy Bailey, David Booth, Ronald Dore, John Harriss, Susan Joekes, and Michael Lipton, and from discussions in seminars at Harvard, Cornell, and (especially) Sussex universities, and at the World Bank. I am grateful to Professor J. D. Montgomery, of Harvard, and to the Lincoln Institute of Land Policy for providing the first occasion to present the paper. The several people in India who cooperated in a spirit of scientific enquiry should be thanked by name, but prudence says otherwise.

institutional factors. But one consideration which is likely to be an important part of the explanation of the underperformance of many government programmes—a lack of correspondence with the interests of the dominant class in the countryside—is *not* likely to be directly relevant to irrigation. Since the effective functioning of a canal system increases the profitability of private agricultural capital and is not redistributive between classes, and since canals (of the sort of size we are considering here) could not be operated and maintained privately, the collective interests of big farmers would seem to correspond rather closely with good performance by the canal bureaucracy.

Canal officials, on the other hand, have great discretionary power: they allocate big money for maintenance contracts; they are responsible for rationing a valuable input between competing users, who have (officially) to pay much less than they would be prepared to pay for it rather than go without; and the officials make decisions which impinge heavily on the political prospects of politicians and on the economic well-being of local communities. This paper argues that if instead of taking for granted that canals are everywhere operated and maintained primarily in the interests of farmers, one assumes as an initial hypothesis that in some regions and countries they might be operated and maintained so as to raise large amounts of illicit revenue for their staff and for politicians, one is led to examine a set of causes of underperformance which is normally left unexamined. One has to look at the responses of officials to opportunities for capturing for themselves a portion of the value of what they allocate, and at the responses of politicians to the fact that officials have these opportunities.

Much of this behaviour will be, of course, 'corrupt' by the standards of modern bureaucratic and legislative codes. To keep the analysis in perspective, one should recall that behaviour somewhat akin to that to be described here was familiar in the public bureaucracies of seventeenth- and eighteenth-century Europe [*Swart, 1949; Anderson and Anderson, 1967*]; and that, as periodic corruption scandals in Europe and North America suggest, the conception of public office as a public trust is still slow to take hold. India's bureaucratic and legislative codes, like their British counterparts, define a sharp separation between the public and private interests of public office-holders, and between the civil service and the legislature. But given such conditions as acute scarcity of resources, the inherited traditions of a patrimonial-bureaucratic state [*Weber, 1968, Vol. 3*] and a wide educational and status gulf between officials and the mass of the population, it is hardly surprising if a sizeable gap between legality and practice persists.

More surprising, however, is that the resulting 'corruption'—a phenomenon which affects administration, politics, business, education, health and a host of other crucial areas of social life—has been so little studied [*Bayley, 1970 (1966); Wertheim, 1970 (1963); Andreski, 1970 (1968); cf. Scott, 1972*]. It is surprising, too, that those studies which have been made (in India and elsewhere) tend to treat 'administrative' and 'political', 'high' and 'low' level corruption as distinct and unconnected forms.[2] The intention of this paper is to show how, in the specific context of irrigation in one south Indian state, they are systematically interconnected. If, as is likely, the same mechanism is found more widely and in other fields of government activity, it may be a more fundamental influence on Indian administration and politics than has hitherto been realised. Perhaps it is important in other poor, 'soft state' countries also.

SETTING

In our south Indian state, paddy (unhusked rice) is the main irrigated crop, followed by groundnut, hybrid sorghum and cotton. Roughly four million net acres are under gravity flow canal systems. Almost all of the canal-irrigated area is fed from systems constructed, operated and maintained by the state Irrigation Department. The Department also constructs and maintains small local reservoirs ('tanks').

Figure 1 shows a conventional picture of the Irrigation Department's structure. The principal unit of administration is the Circle, headed by a Superintending Engineer (SE); the unit of execution is the Division, headed by an Executive Engineer (EE). There are normally about four or five Divisions in a Circle. Both units have a geographical *and* a functional reference; in a given area, there might be a Circle for the 'regular' work—operation and maintenance (O & M) of existing structures, and construction of small structures—and another Circle for 'special' work—such as construction of medium and major projects, investigations of new projects, crop zoning under new projects, etc. Each Division will normally be specialised by function; so that in the same town one may find the headquarters of several Divisions belonging to either the same or different Circles, with partly overlapping geographical jurisdictions: a Division for construction of minor irrigation projects, another for O & M of a big canal system, and another for investigation of a proposed new project, for example.

Our concern here is mostly with Divisions for O & M of large canal systems. There are about 45 such Divisions, out of a total of about 350 Divisions in the Department as a whole.[3] Each O & M Division may have an irrigated area of anything between about 80,000 and 400,000 (gross) acres (the smaller Divisions may have more 'tank' maintenance responsibilities, by way of compensation).

Each O & M Division normally has a staff of about 300 to 350 people.[4] Ninety per cent or more of the staff are field workers (bankers and foremen). They have at most a high school education. Supervisors, responsible for an average area of 7,000 to 20,000 gross irrigated acres (a Section), have a two-year post high school diploma in civil engineering. Assistant Engineers (AEs), in charge of Sub-divisions of 30,000 to 100,000 acres, normally have a university degree in civil engineering. Field staff cannot be promoted. Supervisors are promoted (to AE) towards the ends of their careers, if at all. AEs in O & M posts are normally over 40 years old; they usually come to O & M only after quite a few years elsewhere in the department. EEs in O & M posts are normally fifty or more. In the following discussion the term 'officer' is used to refer to Supervisors and above—though it will be clear that initiative and control is in the hands of AEs and above, the Supervisor being the agent of the higher ranks.

FIGURE 1

CONVENTIONAL ORGANISATION CHART OF IRRIGATION DEPARTMENT

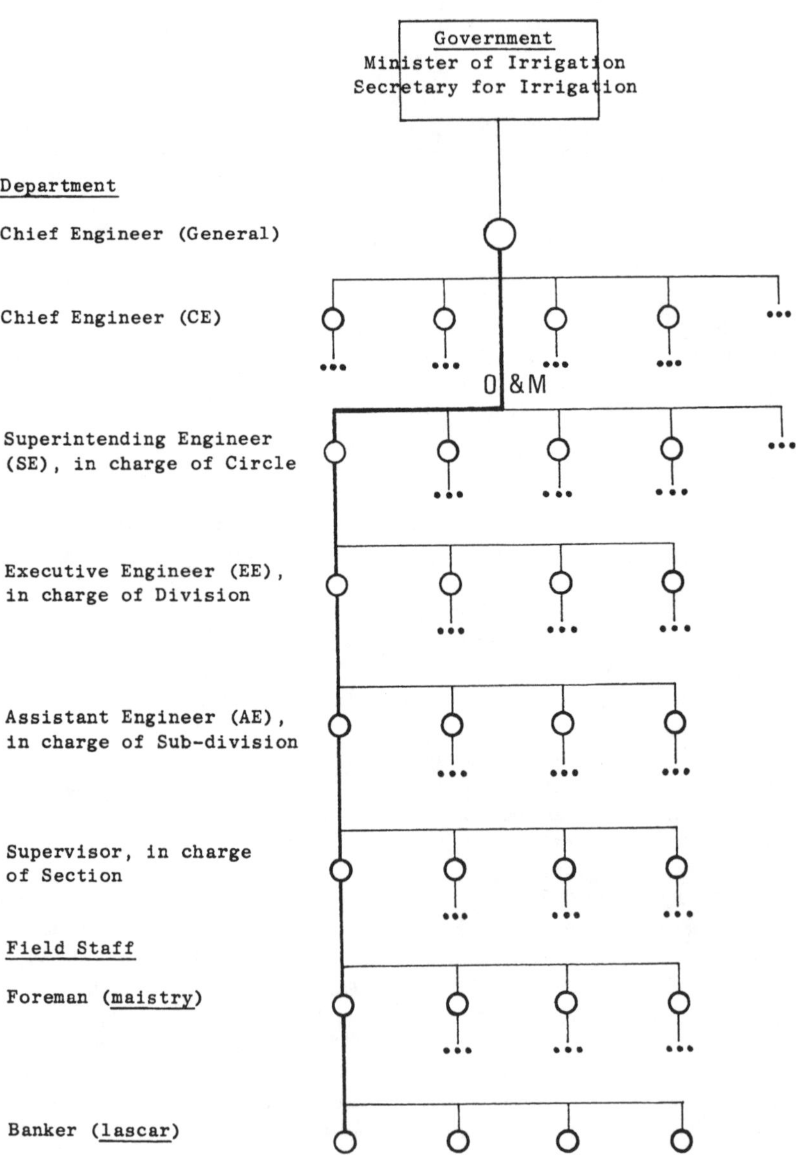

Note: The Chief Engineer (General) is responsible for O & M work. Other Chief Engineers have responsibilities for individual big projects, investigations, designs, drainage, etc. ... means pattern repeated.

Two other points of detail should be borne in mind. The year has two irrigation seasons: the rainy season (also called the first season), from June to December, and the dry (or second) season, from December to May, when crops are wholly dependent on irrigation. Official water rates are Rs.41 per acre per season for paddy, and Rs.28 for non-paddy crops (since 1978).

THE BASIS IN EVIDENCE

Given the extreme sensitivities at stake, it is necessary for the reader to be clear about the empirical basis of the discussion. Obviously one cannot work towards an understanding of the phenomena discussed here by the familiar methods of the random sample, the formal interview and structured questionnaire. One has to use, rather, more informal, more 'anthropological' means. The material on which the paper is based was collected in the course of six periods of fieldwork in the same small area of south India between 1976 and 1981, each of between one and four months' duration. The fieldwork has been directed towards understanding the way canal systems—two in particular, with some attention to a third (constituting three of the abovementioned 45 canal O & M Divisions)—are actually operated and maintained, in the hope of contributing to a more informed discussion of how the performance of canal-irrigated agriculture might be improved from the supply side. As part of the wider study, a detailed investigation was made of local irrigation organisation in some 30 canal-irrigated villages, involving residence for several months in one of them.

It was certainly not part of the original intention to study the phenomena discussed here. Only gradually, from conversations with dozens of engineers, government officials from other departments and farmers did it become apparent that a 'system' was at work, which probably had an important impact on how canals are operated and maintained. In particular, once some degree of trust was established, farmers often volunteered information about how much they had to pay the Irrigation Department; and while one would discount their figures in one, two or three instances, the regularity in farmers' statements across many villages did suggest that something more than wild exaggeration or generalisation was involved. Yet if one accepted their magnitudes as approximately correct or even as 100 per cent exaggerations, the amounts of money being aggregated upwards were clearly large indeed.

This led to cautious, always informal enquiries of officers in other departments and of irrigation staff themselves, as part of wider conversations about the sorts of difficulties they saw themselves facing in doing their jobs well. These conversations, it should be noted, were with irrigation staff from outside the area of detailed fieldwork as well as with many serving within it; and covered the way 'the department' and 'the government' worked in the state as a whole, as well as in the specific district. Some of the engineers were thoroughly disgruntled at the situation they were caught in, and since disgruntled people tend to exaggerate the reasons for their discontent, one had to be cautious about accepting details from any one person at face value. Again, as with farmers, it is the regularities in the individual comments and incidents, and the consistency in the orders of magnitude (as between, for example, what a district Collector told me a Superintending Engineer had told him he had had to pay to get a one-year extension, and what an Assistant Engineer in one Division—in another district from the first case—said in strictest confidence his Executive Engineer had had to pay to get the transfer) that gives confidence in the correctness of the broad picture.

This method undoubtedly leads one to look for the common elements in what people say, and therefore perhaps to give an impression of greater regularity and less variation than is in fact the case. There is no way to deal with this problem except by more research which attempts to probe variations more systematically than was possible in an exploratory study. On the other hand it should be emphasised that the present essay is based on prolonged residence and repeated enquiry, on *both* sides of the farmer-official transaction.[5] And a few other studies, to be referred to later, have provided evidence which, even though fragmentary, is consistent with the argument to be made here.

IRRIGATION OFFICERS' SUPPLY OF REVENUE

Officers can use their office to raise large amounts of illicit revenue—some offices (or posts) being much more profitable than others. We begin by describing in some detail how the revenue is raised. Later we consider how it is redistributed, especially via the sale of transfers to particular posts. The emphasis is on the general features and procedures of the corrupt system; but it must be noted at the beginning that not all engineers participate in it, and discussion of what happens to those who do not take part is deferred till later. It will suffice to say here that they are unlikely to spend much time in O & M posts.

Officers have two main sources of revenue, from the works budget ('from works', as the officers say), and from irrigators directly ('from the *ayacut*', the irrigated area). We take each in turn.

From the works budget

Each canal Division gets a regular grant for annual maintenance work, calculated at so much per irrigated acre[6] plus a lump sum for each major structure (like a weir). The grant has to cover the cost of the field staff's salaries as well. The Division may also get grants at irregular intervals for 'special works'. The overall works grant is split into Sub-division budgets. The Supervisors of each Section prepare the estimates of annual maintenance works; their estimates are inspected and coordinated by each AE, and then approved (or not) by the EE. The works are put out to tender, to be done by private contractors following the department's plans and estimates.

Kickbacks: By long-established convention $8\frac{1}{2}$ per cent of each contract is kicked back to the officers and clerical staff of the Division—$2\frac{1}{2}$ per cent to the EE (as tender-accepting authority; for contracts of more than Rs.100,000 the SE is the accepting authority, so maintenance contracts are generally shaped to be less than this amount); one per cent to the clerical staff and draughtsmen; and five per cent to the Supervisor and AE to be split between them.

This however is the minimum kickback, on the assumption that the work is actually done according to specification. Then there are 'savings on the ground', as distinct from the earlier 'savings on the estimates'. If, for instance, the estimates call for six inches of gravel to be laid but the contractor lays only three, or if four inches of silt are to be removed but the contractor removes only one, the balance is split between contractor and officers, perhaps half and half, or one third to the contractor and two thirds to the officers.[7] Using less cement than called for in the estimates can be very profitable indeed, but is dangerous beyond a certain point—if the structure falls down in the next monsoon, samples can be sent for testing. In contrast, fiddling on 'earthworks'—removing or adding less than the stipulated amount of earth—is both profitable and safe.[8] (Since the contractor has an interest in removing even less earth or silt than was agreed informally with the AE, the art of desilting from the contractor's point of view is to judge how far to go from a cross-over road before removing virtually no silt; and also to judge the rhythm of the work so that it is completed and ready for inspection just before the water has to be released into the channel, to make inspection less likely.) If what are called 'supplementary works' have to be done to repair work done inadequately the first time round, by convention the contractor keeps the whole rake-off.

'Savings on the ground' is the part that is haggled over—both the percentage taken, and how it is divided. The officers want to increase the share going to themselves but also to ensure a minimum level of quality. The contractor wants to increase *his* share, not least because of the increasing cost of labour and also because on top of what he pays the officers he may have to pay something to the local Member of the (state) Legislative Assembly (MLA), especially near election times and especially if the MLA uses his influence to help secure him contracts. But 'savings on the ground' are normally sufficient to bring the total rake-off to the officers (including the $8\frac{1}{2}$ per cent) to at least 25 per cent of the value of what is meant to be put on the ground, and sometimes to as much as 50 per cent.[9]

In the late 1970s the annual maintenance grant (for all canals in the state) was Rs.10 per irrigated acre, plus an amount for each major structure which varied according to size. In an upland Division this might total Rs.4,000,000. Between about one-third and a half of the total,[10] say 40 per cent, goes as salaries to the field staff, leaving (in this example) some Rs.2,400,000 for works.

From savings on the estimates the EE gets $2\frac{1}{2}$ per cent of the value of works contracts, or in this example about Rs.60,000 a year. By prior agreement with the AEs, the EE gets normally five per cent of each Sub-division's total works budget (including what has to be paid as field staff salaries), or in our example, another Rs.200,000 a year. Therefore the EE can expect roughly Rs.260,000 in additional income a year, *at least*.[11] The average EE official salary, including allowances, is Rs.28,500 a year (Rs.8 = US$1 approximately, at the exchange rate of the late 1970s).[12]

Subversion of tendering: We consider shortly how the AE manoeuvres to raise the EE's five per cent of the works budget plus his own profit. In the meantime let us pursue the question of how the public rules for protecting the impartiality of tender-awarding and preventing kickbacks are subverted. The tenders have to be opened simultaneously and in public, and the EE would have to show good cause for not accepting the lowest.

Preparation of the estimates is the job of the Supervisor in whose Section the work will be done. As he prepares each estimate he also fixes the contractor who will do the work, in consultation with the AE (who will himself be following the EE's guidelines as to which contractors are to be favoured). The estimate will include the payments to go to the officers and clerks. The Supervisor then gives the estimate to the contractor, who will henceforth spend much time at what is called 'travelling with the estimate'. (Hence one is always likely to find contractors hanging about a Division or Sub-division office, ready to pick up the bill when the officer orders coffee for a visitor.) The contractor takes the estimate to the AE, who passes it on to the EE with his recommendation. If the EE sanctions it, the contractor sits with the draughtsman while it is properly drawn up.

Tenders must be notified publicly. But while several contractors might apply, the designated one will normally get it (though he may have to tip the others in recompense). The reason is that no contractor of the small size interested in maintenance contracts can long survive without the approval of the EE. The EE is the only man in the Division authorised to sanction estimates and pay bills.[13] An uncooperative contractor simply finds that his bills are not paid—part of the art of the EE is to decide which bills should be paid and when, in order to keep his contractors in hand. And the EE may make some extra income from the contractors in return for speeding up, or not delaying, payment of the bills.[14]

The EE can also control the contractors through loans. Contractors need credit, and the EE may be prepared to lend at cheap rates of interest. He lends not primarily to get the interest, but to have the very large amount of money he collects each year held not in his own hands (where it might be discovered), and not all in a bank (where it might leave traces for the possible attention of the Anti-Corruption Bureau), but in the hands of people over whom he has tight control. Often the contractors are little more than the EE's dummies (to use the word of an engineer informant); he lends them money to do the works, they present him with their bills, he (legitimately) encashes the bills at the bank and pays them—and then directs the contractors what to do with 'his' portion of the funds.

In practice, there are far too many contracts held by separate contractors for the EE to deal with each individually. He works mostly through his AEs, and also through a number of intermediary contractors, a few big ones and a sprinkling of medium-sized ones covering different parts of the command area. Some of them may hold sizeable amounts of 'his' money. A small contractor may borrow directly from one of these banker-contractors, with the EE's approval. When—as explained below—the Minister calls for money, the EE may tell one of his banker-contractors to pay the Minister's agent (the Minister too never touches the money; ministerial tours of the districts are useful occasions for these transactions to be made). When the EE wants to give a senior officer a gift he never carries the cash from his own headquarters; he tells one of his banker-contractors to meet him and hand over the money just before he meets an agent at the officer's headquarters or the man himself at his residence (he will have booked a 'personal call').

Furthermore, the EE may be in a legal business partnership with some contractors—a so-called *benami* partnership, in which his interest is registered in the name of someone over whom he has close control. He can use his privileged (if often still difficult) access to cement, a rationed commodity, to get supplies for his partners at discount rates. In these ways the EE can exercise control over very large amounts of money without having the incriminating evidence on his hands.

This description has shown the contractors as highly dependent on the EE. But when big (and therefore 'special', not 'regular') contracts are involved, class A or B contractors have to be used, and such men are often able to exert much independent influence over Ministers and MLAs. They obtain their influence by paying the Ministers and MLAs large amounts of money (or by being their kinsmen). As the engineers say, 'He (a big contractor) has X and Y (names of Ministers), they are his men'. The EE has to be careful of such contractors (unless he is a *benami* partner); they can get him transferred out if he refuses to alter accounts or is uncooperative in other ways.[15] Furthermore, the local MLAs depend not only on big contractors but also on the myriad small contractors for funds and help at election time, and may use their influence over the EE and AE to put contracts with the right ones. Yet while these points qualify the earlier picture of the EE and AE determining the allocation of contracts, it remains true that the EE can normally exert great independent influence; especially because the great bulk of the work is done in very small contracts, by small local contractors.

Let us now take up the question of how the AE goes about raising the money he has to pay the EE, plus his own profit. The EE, as noted, gets most of his income from the $2\frac{1}{2}$ per cent savings on the estimates, plus the conventional five per cent of the total works budget of each Sub-division. When the Minister demands more money the EE divides the amount to be raised between his AEs. It is very unlikely that an AE will be able to meet his obligations to the EE *and* raise enough for his own uses (which include, as we shall see, the 'cost' of his next posting) from his works budget alone. He makes up the deficit 'from the *ayacut*' (irrigated area)—by selling water or promises of water. While the EE may take an active part in his AEs' efforts on the works budget, he generally leaves them to raise money from water as they will, limiting his role to broad oversight.[16]

From the irrigators

Organisation: The canals are 'continuous flow' (water normally flows through each outlet continuously, not in rotation), but it may often happen that land towards the end of a distributory is not getting enough water, either because too little water is reaching the lower part of the distributory or because particular sluices are not sufficiently opened. In some cases it is possible for farmers (against the rules) to open the sluices themselves, or obstruct the flow immediately downstream of their outlet to increase the discharge through it, or break the channel bank. But they run risks if they persistently interfere with the structures; the irrigation staff may refuse to help them subsequently, or may even cut off their water by way of punishment. If insufficient water is reaching the lower part of the distributory these options are in any case not open to farmers of lower-down villages. They may have no alternative but to approach the irrigation staff with a request for more water.

A second reason why irrigators may approach the irrigation staff has to do with the zoning of land for irrigation [*India, Government of, Ministry of Irrigation and Power, 1972, Vol. 1: Chapter 6*]. Very large areas of land under most south Indian canals—often running into tens of thousands of acres per canal—are being irrigated unauthorisedly, in the sense that they are not entitled by the crop zoning to any irrigation at all, or are zoned for non-paddy but are growing (water-intensive) paddy, or are taking water in the wrong season. Farmers taking water for out-of-zone irrigation may want an assurance from the AE or Supervisor that they will continue to get water. In many cases they will have to pay for that assurance. Since the stiff financial penalties which are meant to be collected for out-of-zone irrigation are not in fact being collected anywhere in the state, the out-of-zone irrigators have only this extra (and illicit) charge to bear on top of the official water rate. And in any case they are often not too worried about paying something for a water assurance. While the first reason applies more to farmers towards the tail-ends of distributories than to farmers higher up, the second applies wherever unauthorised irrigation is taking place, provided that the irrigation staff might be able to cut off the water.

The interaction between farmers and officers commonly goes something like this: a few farmers representing one village, or perhaps (less commonly) several nearby villages, will approach the AE in charge of the Sub-division in which their land is located, and put to him a request. The AE tells them, as they expect, 'No, I cannot agree. You please see Supervisor and see what he can do'. The AE, now informed, tells the Supervisor his price for giving them what they want. The Supervisor in turn tells the farmers how much it will cost them, perhaps with an initial show of reluctance. If the farmers do not agree some bargaining may follow, with the Supervisor sending them away with a coded refusal meaning that they should see him again after he has consulted the AE. If the AE does not agree to come down, he may even order the Supervisor to reduce the water flow through the sluice or into the distributory until they meet his demand. (Note that the AE takes care never to be seen asking money of farmers.) Not uncommonly however the farmers' representative is himself a local contractor for the Irrigation Department. Between the AE or Supervisor and some of these contractors develop relations of special intimacy, in which the bargaining will be more direct and more surreptitious. The AE can use the promise of works to induce the contractor to get his co-villagers to pay up.

Of course, with the AE often under pressure to raise revenue for the EE and for his own purposes, he does not always wait for the farmers to approach him. The distinction between a bribe, offered by farmers to get the officer to do something he might not otherwise do, and extortion money, demanded by the officer in return for not inflicting a penalty, is often difficult to draw in practice. The officer need not extort directly; he may simply ensure the farmers know they might suffer if they do not 'offer' a bribe.

The farmers organise the collection of the money amongst themselves.[17] The amount from each requesting (or extorted) village may run into several thousands of rupees. The AE may tell the Supervisor to ask the farmers to pay the money directly to a named contractor, or the Supervisor may take the money and immediately pass it to the contractor. The only person with any money (evidence) on his hands is thus the contractor. If by chance he should be investigated by the police and large sums of money found in his possession he can say he has taken out loans for his works.[18]

At the time of meeting the farmers' request the Supervisor will strike his own bargain with the farmers. This will always be much less than the AE's amount. Though the Supervisor is the man on the spot, he has no power independently of the AE and EE, and if his demand is in the farmers' opinion excessive they may complain to the AE or EE about him and they, ever watchful to maintain the hierarchy, may discipline him.

Price: Price in these water transactions seems to be related to the following:

(1) Season: In the second, dry season the crop is completely dependent on canal water (in most of the state conjunctive use of surface and groundwater is not common); and yields are higher and more secure than in the first season *if* canal water arrives. Hence more money is normally raised on the second season crop than on the first.

(2) Drought in the first season: Since the first (wet) season rainfall normally provides roughly one-third to a half of the paddy crop water requirement (under upland canals), and since canal supplies can be increased only a little (if only because of carrying capacity constraints), some areas must go short of water, and/or management inputs must be increased substantially during a drought [*Levine, 1977; Wade 1980*]. If the drought comes after the transplantation, farmers by then have a sizeable investment to protect. They will rush to protect their crops by offering money, either in response to an actual shortfall in their supplies (perhaps because irrigation staff are favouring other villages) or in anticipation of one. Even a short period without rain at the time of ear-head formation may induce farmers to approach the Irrigation Department, for at that time in the growth cycle water stress will cut yields sharply.

(3) Whether the water favour is for zoned or out-of-zone land: Other things being equal, out-of-zone irrigation has to pay more than zoned (authorised) irrigation. Recall the point made earlier, that tens of thousands of acres under each canal are typically unauthorised.

(4) Crop: Paddy normally pays more than other crops, because it needs more water. Groundnut (which is grown mainly in the dry season) is also

expensive, because it needs water at the time of harvesting in late April and May, when canal supplies are normally short.

(5) Locational difficulty of meeting a request for more water: Tail-end villages will normally have to pay more for water than upper villages on the same distributory, because it is more difficult for staff to get them water (more work will have to go into patrolling the upper section of the distributory).

(6) Locational ease of cutting off water: Some villages, even if in upstream, good water supply locations, may be placed in such a way that it is easy for irrigation staff wholly or partly to cut off their water supply. Such villages will have to pay more than villages whose water supply is less easy to disrupt without disrupting that of many other villages.

(7) Whether the village is known as politically powerful: In the extreme case, no engineer would insist on money from the native village of an MLA.[19]

Types of payment: One can distinguish two kinds of transaction (in addition to 'gifts' of grain which we come to later). One is a flat rate, normally in cash but sometimes in grain, for an assurance of water for the whole season; it is collected especially from areas of unzoned paddy, and the rate will be higher in the second (dry) season than in the first. More exactly, it is an assurance that the Irrigation Department will not try to cut off water supply to the area; how much it also entails an obligation on the part of the Supervisor and AE to intervene actively if water runs short varies from case to case, depending partly on the personality and revenue needs of the staff, and partly on the influence of the villagers. The whole amount is paid over at the start of the season, and there is no rebate if the crop fails because of lack of water.

The second type of transaction involves payment in return for more active intervention by irrigation staff to improve an area's water supply, and is more contingent on the immediate state of crop water need and overall water supply. For example, during a first season drought, and most years towards the end of the second season, many tail-end areas, zoned and unzoned, will run short of water. Villages will then try and negotiate with the Irrigation Department wetting-by-wetting (or for, say, three wettings at x day intervals). Farmers call these emergency irrigations 'life irrigations'.

Water distribution as a market: In this second type of transaction, how is discrimination in favour of payers exercised? It is true that the physical control structures and communication facilities of south Indian canals are not good enough for discrimination to be possible on a *wide* scale without much more intensive management inputs than normal, and that compliance methods within the bureaucracy are not strong enough for these higher management inputs to be provided from the field staff alone. However, when the officers are on the canal it is often not difficult for them to discriminate in favour of a *minority* of villages or distributories. Note that the unit of discrimination and payment is the village or the distributory, not individual irrigators; only very exceptionally could discrimination be exercised in favour of particular people below the sluice outlet as against others below the same outlet. It is mainly at times of water shortage that officers come onto the canal to patrol, to ensure that sluices are not interfered with by farmers or by field staff acting on farmers' orders. It is then that they can most easily run a kind of water market. They themselves can stand guard by a sluice and see that farmers from lower down do not lower the gate to its proper level or remove the cross-bund;[20] or more likely they will place one or two field staff there and return frequently to make sure their orders are being followed. Vice versa for lower sluices: the officers can make sure the upstream sluices are not opened, so that more is available for lower down (whereas the field staff on their own might find it difficult to keep the upstream sluices lowered).

The use of a rotational delivery rule can provide a pretext for highly discretionary, predatory behaviour by irrigation staff towards farmers, and this point is worth elaborating because the introduction of rotational delivery is often regarded in the literature as a step forward in canal management [*Levine, 1977; Levine et al., 1976*]. While the normal water delivery rule in south Indian canals is 'continuous flow' (all outlets in the system are open simultaneously), in recent years some attention has been given to the use of rotational delivery during the dry season, such that parts of the canal command area receive water in turn rather than simultaneously [*Wade, 1975, 1980*]. There has also been slowly growing pressure from economic policy-makers and some politicians to reduce the area under water-consumptive paddy in the dry season, so that the available supply may irrigate a larger area of less water-consumptive crops. The irrigation engineers have been encouraged to set long rotational periods, such that the interval between irrigations in any one block is too long for paddy to be grown.

In practice, what may happen is that the Irrigation Department keeps farmers uninformed about the likely water supply in the dry season; farmers go ahead and plant paddy over large areas; the EE announces a 'turn system' which has intervals too long for paddy; the farmers with paddy rush to pay the AE in return for assurance of adequate and frequent supplies; and in implementation the irrigation staff make the supposedly rigid turn system highly flexible, depending partly on price. The uncertainty created by the flexibility may prompt irrigators of non-paddy crops, too, to try to get privileged supplies. Or even where the official rotational interval is short enough for paddy (as in a rotation during a wet season drought, for example) the engineers may inform farmers in certain villages that they must pay to have their full entitlement; if the rotation is eight days on and eight days off, the Supervisor may tell a village that (to take an actual but extreme case)[21] unless it pays Rs.50 per acre it will get only four days on and 12 days off. Where the unit of discrimination is the distributory (which may serve several villages or more) one should be able to check to what extent this happens by looking at the gauge reading records for the gauge at the distributory offtake (though for small distributories serving only 3–4,000 acres or less, there will probably be no gauge, even if the distributory takes off directly from the main canal). However, the gauge registers are commonly left with gaps during periods of acute water shortage, on grounds of 'pressure of work'; even if entries are there, falsification of gauge readings is so easy and common (at least for small gauges) that one cannot have much confidence in their accuracy [*Wade, 1981*]. A flexible rotation is thus a lucrative and fairly safe source of revenue.

The above account suggests that water distribution can be understood in terms of a simple market model—price is related to the scarcity of water, the certainty of yield, the ability of the irrigation staff to discriminate against non-payers, and so on. But one must note that the 'market' is highly imperfect, because the farmers cannot be sure in advance that they will get what they paid for, or that when they get it, it will be worth what they expect (if heavy rains fall in the meantime, the value of additional irrigation water may be small). If the AE takes money for assuring a village of sufficient water for, say, unzoned second season paddy, he may then not be able to supply it with enough—perhaps because he is responding to bribes from other villages; perhaps because the upstream AE is not releasing as much water to his Sub-division as he should be (the upstream AE may falsify the gauge readings); perhaps because with a certain degree of shortage he simply cannot exert enough control over the upstream sluices of a long (say 15-mile) distributory to get enough water down to a paying tail-end village; or perhaps because there is an overall shortage in the reservoir (which may be not only for natural reasons, but also because other canals fed from the same reservoir take more than expected). Whatever the real reason, the AE can nonetheless tell the farmers of the paying villages that there is a general shortage, that he is helpless, that they are getting more than they would have got had they not paid.

Hence one understands a senior engineer's comment that 'rumour mongering' is one of the tricks of canal operation: merely by rumouring a shortage money can be raised.[22] If farmers scramble to increase their supplies, the rumour can be self-confirming. More generally, the point is that a good deal of revenue can be raised from farmers with little work on the part of irrigation staff, by rumours, threats (especially to cut off water for unzoned crops), and occasional appearances by officers in their jeeps along the canal.[23]

This last point needs particular emphasis if the impression is not to be given that the large amount of revenue raised from irrigators indicates that the irrigation bureaucracy has the system much more under control—albeit for purposes of revenue collection—than is commonly supposed. To raise large quantities of revenue does not require tight control over a wide area (raising money by agreeing *not* to cut off water supplies to unzoned crops *may* mean less rather than more work for the irrigation staff, and looser rather than tighter control, at least in upstream Sub-divisions). When tighter control *is* required to raise money, that control can be exerted in quite specific locations, not across-the-board. A general improvement in water control over a whole canal system, in the interests of improving the performance of its agriculture, would require bigger changes in the management *system* and in physical structures than are needed to make these temporally and spatially more limited interventions.

Politicians: A further qualification to the simple market model concerns the role of politicians. One might suppose that the AE would discourage farmers from approaching politicians, for in so doing they might shortcircuit the flow of bribes. In fact, however, the AE may sometimes encourage farmers to approach the MLA, perhaps to gain protection against complaints from other farmers who see themselves disadvantaged by favours done for the first group, or perhaps to build up the politician's obligation to the AE himself, to be called upon at the time of his next transfer ('I have obliged you then, you please help me now').[24] Further, a favourite way for an MLA or Minister to enhance his support—or prevent its erosion—is to order the AE to be very strict on water releases (in particular, to release none to out-of-zone land), wait till the farmers start clamouring, accept their and the AE's invitation to come and 'solve problem', be seen to order the AE to give them what they want, and take the credit.

Grain gifts: 'Gifts' of grain constitute a third type of water payment (in addition to the assurance payment, and the wetting-by-wetting payment). Grain gifts are made *after* the harvest, usually in paddy; they occur mainly after the *wet* season harvest, and (in this case) are more regularised than the money payments, less subject to bargaining, less dependent on the degree of water scarcity; and go mostly to the field staff. They are seen by villagers as a tip rather than a price; and are likened by them to *jajmani* payments [*Bailey, 1957; Epstein, 1962*]. In some villages, village servants collect the grain from farmers on a per acre basis, and give it to the field staff who cover that village; in others, the field staff themselves have to collect from each household. Some grain is also given to Supervisor and AE. For field staff these payments are their main source of extra income. Under one upland canal, field staff are able to get the equivalent of another one to three months' salary out of these payments, which is an important supplement but nothing like the monetary revenue of the officers. Hence the complete absence of rags-to-riches stories amongst field staff. For Supervisors and AEs, too, the total grain gifts might come to something like one or two months' salary.[25] What is surplus to household requirements they can sell to friendly traders.

Total revenue: It is hard to make even a rough estimate of how much is typically raised 'from the *ayacut*'. The amounts from each village and Sub-division depend on how favourable are all the factors listed earlier as determinants of price; and also on such matters as how big is the works budget of the Sub-division (a function not only of irrigated area but also of number of big structures)—the bigger the works budget the less needs to be raised from irrigators.

However some modest points can be made. Payment of money (the following discussion excludes grain gifts, which are made in most villages) is a practice well known to all irrigators. But in the study area not all villages have to pay all the time—some almost never do (perhaps because of features of their location in relation to water supply), others have to pay only in an occasional severe drought in the first season and for one to three 'life irrigations' towards the end of the second season, while others have to pay for assurances in both seasons and for additional wettings as the need arises. The most common payment is for an assurance for the second season paddy area, plus payment for additional wettings in either the first or second season for paddy and non-paddy as the need arises. In this case costs to irrigators would commonly amount to Rs.10–25 per acre per year. If it is a matter of giving an assurance to, say, an out-of-zone block of second season groundnut, the cost may rise to as much as Rs.50 per acre. But bribe/extortion payments of more than Rs.50 per acre are rare in the study area; this can be taken as the upper limit of the per acre price. With Sub-divisions normally having over 50,000 gross irrigated acres, one can be confident that a figure of Rs.50,000 per year from the irrigators in each Sub-division would be a rather conservative estimate. (Payments for changes in crop zoning are not included in this figure; see note 19.)

Following through the earlier illustration, we have the AE and his Supervisors getting five per cent of the works contracts by way of 'savings on the estimates'; if they split it half and half, each AE will end up with Rs.15,000.[26] He will probably be able to at least double that with 'savings on the ground'. If he gets Rs.50,000 from irrigators, his additional income for the year will be around Rs.80,000, a total based on even more conservative assumptions than the EE total given earlier. The average official AE income is Rs.23,000 a year.[27]

THE RELATIVE DESIRABILITY OF POSTS

It is safe to say that engineers can, and many do, earn many times their annual official income in these various ways. Our illustrative figures given above are from an upland area, and there is reason to think that on the more fertile, intensively irrigated coastal deltas the profitability of O & M posts is commonly considerably higher. One can, indeed, think of a rank ordering of posts in terms of their profitability, including not only O & M posts but also those in construction, investigations, design, etc. Investigations and design posts are at the relatively unprofitable end; while construction posts also *tend*, at AE and EE level, to be less profitable than O & M posts (in Construction units, initiative and control is normally higher in the hierarchy, at SE, CE and Ministerial levels). But profitability is only one factor in desirability. Looked at more comprehensively, the main determinants of desirability seem to be the following:

(1) How much money can be raised, which is a function of how much money is being spent through the post, and how much can be raised from outside the budget (mainly from farmers). O & M posts differ from one part of the state to another in how willing the farmers are to pay for water. Generally, O & M posts are less lucrative than construction posts in terms of money from the works budget (as distinct from farmers' payments)—unless the O & M post is in a badly drought-prone area where a drought can plausibly be declared often, thus making available a generous flow of Food for Work and other relief funds.

(2) How safely the money can be raised. O & M posts generally have an advantage over construction posts in this respect, since quality control is

minimal. O & M contractors will also usually have no reputation to protect, unlike some of the big contractors for canal construction. On the other hand, *if* an O & M engineer is caught raking off the works budget, his contractors are too small to be able to help in the ways canal construction contractors might.

(3) Living conditions. O & M posts generally do better in this respect too, since the posts are usually in well-established towns where, in contrast to many construction, and even more, investigation posts, clean drinking water is not a problem and one's children can be given a headstart in the qualifications race by attending English language schools.

(4) Prestige of the project. A construction post on a big dam site carries prestige for an engineer which no O & M post can confer.

(5) Nearness to native place. This is obviously idiosyncratic. Its weight depends on such things as whether a man has land to administer in his native place or brothers who might administer it in his absence. But in general, engineers at AE and EE level do value strongly being within half a day's journey of their native place. It is worth noting, conversely, that postings to the state capital are *not* widely sought after.

By rule officers must be transferred within three years, and can be transferred to any post in the Irrigation Department—there is no functional specialisation. No-one can expect to spend most of his career in O & M, for the number of such posts in relation to demand is too small. (Many senior engineers have no more than a few years' experience of O & M.)

Averaging out the above (and other) factors, most engineers will have distinct preferences about what type of work they wish to do, and where. They naturally want to influence their transfers in line with their preferences. There is enough overlap between individuals' preference rankings, for reasons to do with potential gain, schools, comfortable living, relatives, and the like, to ensure that for most O & M posts several people are likely to be interested at any one time. So as a man comes towards the end of the second year in a post he will study the vacancy listings with care. He knows he will be moved within three years, and he wants time in hand to allow himself some manoeuvre. If he wants to stay near a certain place, he may accept a temporary move away, thus satisfying the transfer rule; and then press hard to be transferred back to the first place after a year. But others may also be pressing hard for the same posts . . . .

THE SALE OF POSTS AND THE OFFICERS' DEMAND FOR REVENUE

It has not escaped the notice of politicians that irrigation engineers can earn large amounts of additional income in some posts. While it is difficult for them (or others) to manipulate who is *promoted* from one rank to another, it is not difficult to manipulate who is *transferred* into which post. Likewise, it is not difficult for senior officers to manipulate the same decision. Politicians and senior officers are able to obtain for themselves part of engineers' additional income by auctioning the transfer, and imposing additional demands as a condition of the successful bidder's not himself being transferred out before the normal term.

The normal term in practice is about two years. During an officer's tenure of a particular post (referring now to AEs and EEs—Supervisors are discussed separately) he will want to recoup what he paid out to get it, plus whatever extra he has to pay to senior officers and politicians during the tenure, plus his own profit—which has to include some of what he is to bid for his next post. This sets the amount of revenue he will try to raise.

Notice that the officer does not try to recoup a fee for entry to the irrigation service; for in most years since the mid-1950s there has been a shortage of engineering graduates and diploma holders, and no (illicit) payment for entry into the Irrigation Department has been needed.[28] Promotions are also not generally paid for, because for reasons we come to, a precise and public order of promotion is in fact generally followed, so discrimination between payers and non-payers is not possible. Let us consider the amounts involved in securing a transfer to a particular O & M post, and an aspirant's strategy for doing so.[29] The procedures differ for EEs and AEs.

Transfers and Politicians

(i) *Executive Engineers*: For transfers at EE level the sanctioning authority is the 'government'—the (elected) Minister of Irrigation, and the Secretary of Irrigation (the senior-most civil servant in the Irrigation Ministry, an IAS officer).[30]

The contenders for a particular EE's post normally deal with the Minister through a go-between, perhaps the Minister's Personal Assistant (PA). The applicant may wait in the ante-chamber to the Minister's office while the PA shuttles between him and the Minister inside, a meeting taking place only once price and other conditions are agreed. The Minister then issues transfer orders, the old incumbent is moved elsewhere (he may have been going through the same procedure over his next move), and the new EE takes charge.[31]

News of who is in the running for a particular post and the price paid travels fast within the relevant Division. Posts acquire price reputations—'X is a one *lakh* post, Y is a five *lakh* post', the engineers say (one *lakh* equals Rs.100,000). This refers to the amount it costs to get the transfer orders. On top of this the EE has to promise to meet the Minister's demands for more money (or for 'gifts' in kind—'you give my brother-in-law a fridge') from time to time during his tenure; and to respect the Minister's wishes on who is to get major contracts (though the latter condition is less important on O & M posts, where contracts tend to be small, than on construction posts). While most or all of the transfer price goes to the Minister for his personal purse, this second, more contingent component tends to be more for party funds,[32] and its size varies with the electoral cycle.

Normally the EE does not have to pay the local MLAs, but he will most likely visit the more powerful of them[33] before taking charge to obtain their approval, a condition of which is that he respect their wishes on choice of contractors. But if an EE is noticeably 'without influence' he may have to pay more, not only to the Minister but also to the MLAs and senior officers, in order to get the post. A Low Caste engineer, or an out-of-state Brahmin (recruited in the 1950s when the state's irrigation service was taking applicants from wherever it could find them) may well be without influence. In the mid-1970s, for example, one particular EE 'without influence' found that he had to pay a total of $1\frac{1}{2}$ *lakhs* to get a certain post, for which his predecessor and successor both paid one *lakh*; in his case, one *lakh* went to the Minister, and another half *lakh* had to go to local MLAs and senior officers to get their support.

On the fertile coastal deltas, where canal irrigation has been practised extensively for over a hundred years, an EE's (O & M) post may cost up to 3 to 4 *lakhs*.[34] On the uplands O & M posts cost considerably less, agriculture being less productive, canal irrigation more recent, and farmers more resistant to paying irrigation bribes. In the middle to late 1970s, some posts on the uplands could be had for as little as Rs.50,000, others for Rs.100,000.

So on the deltas an EE may pay up to 14 times his annual salary (about Rs.28,500) for the two-year tenure of certain O & M posts; on the uplands, three times or less. Nevertheless, in terms of our earlier example, the EE who pays Rs.100,000 for an O & M post and another Rs.50,000 over the course of the period to meet supplementary demands and gifts can expect an additional income of some Rs.260,000 a year from the post: a most pleasing profit.

(ii) *Assistant Engineers*: For AEs the transfer strategy is different, because the sanctioning authority is their own CE and the SE too has more of a role.[35] Further, the local MLAs will be at least as concerned about who their AE is as about the EE, since the AE is more influential in allocating water to their actual or potential supporters.

An AE wanting a certain post may begin with the local MLAs and the relevant EE. He visits the EE to obtain his consent, and confirms his willingness to pay over to the EE an agreed proportion (traditionally five per cent) of the Sub-division's works budget *and* to pay over additional amounts during his tenure depending on the EE's demands. He also visits the concerned MLAs (normally only one or two will have major parts of their constituencies in his Sub-division).[36] Unless he is a man of unusual influence he will pay them for help with the CE and SE, perhaps Rs.10,000 each.[37] As well, he may have to go direct to the CE's office and pay the agent there to secure the transfer orders. Notice the neat division of revenue opportunities from transfers: at Ministerial level for EEs, at Departmental and MLA level for AEs.

In a typical O & M post on the uplands, if the prospective AE cannot raise at least Rs.25,000 before he takes charge he should not waste time trying for it; but the amounts required are often considerably more.[38] If AEs or EEs want an extension beyond two years they may have to bid for it against other contenders. Even before the two years are up they can be removed at any time on the Minister's orders (the Minister can easily mobilise some petitions or letters against them to justify his action). They have no effective appeal[39]—and of course lose what they paid for the post. In one case in the late 1970s an AE paid a very senior politician Rs.40,000 (payments by AEs to very senior politicians are unusual) to secure transfer orders to a certain post, only to be transferred out less than a week after taking charge to make way for a man known to have paid Rs.50,000 (to the same politician). This sort of instant transfer swindle is, however, not common.

Though AEs and EEs in fact normally stay in place for two years they are preoccupied with being removed before time. If a new Irrigation Minister comes to power (on average only once in two or three years) the EE may rush him a payment to ensure that the Minister does not put his own man in his stead. And if a big public works programme (Food For Work, for example)[40] comes under his charge the EE may, even without being asked, pay out large amounts to the Ministers and senior officers throughout his tenure to ensure he stays in the post. Normally the supplementary demands on the EE from the Minister and senior officers might total roughly half a *lakh* in cash and kind over the two years, in a one *lakh* post; but in the run-up to an election the demands are commonly much higher.

(iii) *Supervisors and field staff*: Supervisors normally have to pay nothing for transfers within an O & M Circle, unless the EE of the Division they want to move to particularly does not want to have them. 'Crow catching' is enough—to 'yes sir whatever you say sir' the EE and the SE at every opportunity. But transfer into an O & M Circle may cost, on the uplands in the late 1970s, about Rs.5,000—though some SEs (who are the sanctioning authority at Supervisor level) are reputed not to take money for this sort of thing from Supervisors.

Foremen (*maistries*) and bankers (*lascars*), the field staff, normally do not pay anything; rather they have to promise the AE into whose Sub-division they wish to move always to be obedient. Perhaps the reason why they do not have to pay relates to the fact that they normally benefit rather little from the revenue-raising system. As the earlier discussion showed, the system is not one in which collections are made by the lowest level staff, then aggregated upwards, each rank taking its cut, but rather one in which the revenue transactions are made at the middle levels (especially Supervisor and AE), from where the upward re-channelling begins. On the other hand, it is often said by officers that their field staff are 'corrupt fellows'.

Inflation in the cost of posts

The prices of posts have gone up sharply in several periods, for reasons relating either to departmental or to wider political events, or to a combination of both. The first period of rapid increase, around 1966–68, was linked to a struggle for power within the old Public Works Department between two CEs, which led to its bifurcation into the Irrigation Department (now with Power added on) and the Roads and Buildings Department. This was accompanied by a sharp increase in the involvement of politicians in transfer matters. At about the same time, changes in national political leadership were linked by several informants to tougher demands on state level politicians for revenue for national politicians. The price increase of

1973 was attributed by these informants to another major, if informal, change in national political leadership.

Towards the end of the 1970s prices (and supplemental demands) rose again. A certain *AE*'s post on the uplands which cost Rs.30,000 at the end of 1977, two years later cost the same for a *one* year extension; and the man who succeeded to it in 1981 (beating three other contenders) reputedly paid one *lakh*. In the same area, inter-Circle (O & M) transfers for Supervisors have jumped from about Rs.5,000 to about Rs.10,000 in 1981,[41] divided between senior officers. The rises in the late 1970s may be related to the fact that this state was one of the few to retain a Congress government during the period of Janata Party rule at the centre, so its bureaucracy became an important means of raising money for the Congress Party nationally and in states where the party had lost office. Departments such as Irrigation and Forestry had an important financial role in the party's re-emergence in national power. The sharp increase in 1981 may be related to the sudden closure of a number of Construction Circles and the consequent increase in demand for O & M posts.[42]

The steady decline in the real value of engineers' salaries—by about half since 1965, the same as for all state civil servants of these ranks—may also be a factor in the upward movement of transfer prices, as engineers seek to compensate for the fall in real salaries by moving to more lucrative posts. But as one retired Chief Engineer observed when this argument was put to him, the engineer's salary is, even in the relatively less profitable posts, rather small in relation to what can be earned illicitly, so it is doubtful that the decline in real salary has been a *major* factor.

CONTROL FROM WITHIN THE IRRIGATION HIERARCHY

It is very important for the careers and comfort of many engineers that the process of revenue-raising should go smoothly and without undue interruption by uncooperative or inefficient subordinates. The Supervisor, as the front man in the AE's water negotiations, is extremely vulnerable. The AE can always deny he issued orders to release more water to sub-distributory X or cut off water to Y and have the Supervisor punished for disobeying orders—nothing is written down. The AE has no sanctioning power over works (with an exception to be mentioned later), and is therefore dependent on the EE; if relations break down, the EE can make his life difficult by refusing to sanction some of his works, or (in some locations) by withdrawing water from his Sub-division without informing him. The EE can in turn be transferred out on the Minister's say-so. If he resists the Minister's demands for extra revenue he is likely to be transferred within the two-year term, to make way for someone who has promised to be more obliging. A man who refuses to bend to the farmers' or MLA's or superior officer's illegal request—say, to release water down a distributory when it is supposed to be closed—can easily be charged with trying to extort money, with holding back until paid. As Bayley says, writing of the Indian bureaucracy more generally, 'Even the honest official may be blackmailed by the threat that unless he act unfairly he may be charged publicly with being corrupt' [*1970 (1966): 528*].

There are, moreover, normative justifications, heard within the community of engineers (though never voiced in public), for taking money from farmers. A man who has qualms can be appealed to by his fellows and superiors in terms of how hard they, the engineers, have to work to supply farmers with water, how difficult and prejudicial to their children the living conditions are, and how inequitable the discrepancy between the incomes of uneducated contractors and their own. If the farmers or contractors want to give them something by way of gratitude, who are they to refuse? In this way the line between 'taking gifts' and 'corruption' is blurred—especially because part of the maintenance budget rake-off is well institutionalised and an engineer would have to go out of his way to avoid receiving the money. Hence one can understand why, from the point of view of farmers and contractors, an 'honest' engineer is not one who does not take money, but one who takes no more than the normal rate, who does not haggle, and who having taken your money at least tries to help you in return.

Recalcitrants may find themselves transferred to one of several well-known dumping grounds—such as the Investigation Circles, concerned with preliminary design of new projects (the extent to which their work finalises the location of canals is neither firm nor fine enough for them to provide revenue by discretionary conferring of enhanced land values); or even worse, 'leave vacant postings', replacing individuals who have gone on leave, a situation in which one has neither power nor respect. (Husbanding the 30 days' annual paid leave allowance is part of the art of post hunting; if you don't like your transfer orders you go on leave and mobilise your forces to get them changed.) Even construction posts can be a punishment, when they provide less or more risky revenue than O & M postings at AE and EE level, and are in disagreeable locations.

There are also instruments of control over the EE which fall short of transfer. In particular, CEs have come to make use of what is called the Letter of Credit (LOC) technique. Every three months each Division has to submit a budget showing its expected expenditure in the next period, and the CE writes a LOC on which the EE is authorised to draw. If an EE is failing to satisfy the extra revenue demands, the CE can (perhaps at the request of the Minister) cut back his credit, thereby slowing down and greatly complicating the work of the Division.

However, it would be wrong to portray the irrigation hierarchy as a tightly organised, internally disciplined apparatus for collecting revenue. The cross-pressures on any Supervisor, AE or EE are often complex. Local MLAs may push hard on behalf of particular contractors or particular locations. The MLA may have disagreed with the CE's choice of AE, or may fall out with him subsequently, perhaps because the AE is not being responsive enough to his wishes; he may then harrass the AE by mobilising letters of complaint about the AE's work and then making representations to the CE or the Minister . He may even induce the contractors to do very poor work, under the promise of his protection, in order to provide the evidence that the AE is inefficient. It is said that contractors are becoming more closely identified with politicians than in the past, and less obedient to the engineers. The AE may be more beholden to the MLA than to the EE; if the MLA in the head-reach Sub-division is very powerful, he may be able to protect the AE who lets down less water to the remaining Sub-divisions than he is meant to (the AE may cover himself by falsifying the gauge readings or even the gauge itself). This makes the job of the EE and the other AEs more difficult. If the EE tried to rectify the situation or get the AE transferred, he might find himself transferred. It is this complex field of forces that engineers have in mind when they say, in the words of an EE, 'Water management is all human relations, adjusting to the various pressures'; or in the words of another, 'Water management is 25 per cent water and 75 per cent people, you have to soothe people and you have not to displease the politicians also'. They make such remarks apologetically, because 'human relations' seems the antithesis of hard-nosed, rational engineering.

It is clear, then, that the pressures on any one individual to behave in a 'corrupt' manner, whether in response to demands from superiors in the irrigation hierarchy or to satisfy the expectations of politicians and farmers, are very strong. Many engineers find the pressures to which they are exposed from all sides (especially on O & M jobs) very trying, and find the behaviour needed to stay in the post in varying degrees distasteful. Morale in the Irrigation Department is certainly low. Why do not some of these individuals express their resentment at the way they are being treated by taking action against those who harrass them, perhaps by complaining to the Secretary of Irrigation, or to the Anti-Corruption Bureau? In the words of an EE, 'I would be crushed, I have my family to support, so I just keep quiet'.

When this particular EE first took charge of a certain O & M Division he discovered that the sluice openings in the stretch of the canal which passed through the constituency of a powerful MLA had been enlarged, with the result that this part of the canal took far more water than intended, squeezing the areas lower down; he ordered them to be put right in the next maintenance period. As soon as the work started the MLA got on the 'phone to the CE saying 'my people will suffer'; the CE ordered the EE to stop, and within a week the EE received transfer orders, having arrived only a few months before. The EE acted quickly to mobilise the MLAs of lower down constituencies (whose irrigators would have benefited from the sluice-narrowing programme); the transfer orders were withdrawn, but the sluice-narrowing programme was stopped. And the EE was still transferred three months before the normal term ended (dilatoriness in meeting the Minister's supplementary revenue demands contributed)—transferred to the worst possible posting, outside the Irrigation Department. The pressures on any one individual to conform are all the stronger because few alternative civil engineering jobs are available. The outflow of engineers from the Irrigation Department is very small.

CHECKS

Official procedures

What stops irrigation engineers from taking more than they do? There are, first, a number of bodies to exercise continuing scrutiny of government departments. One is the Accountant-General's Office, which routinely scrutinises all financial accounts from each Division—sufficiently effectively to make correct charging for bad structures, rather than over-charging for good structures, the most promising strategy, since neither this office nor any other independent body makes checks on *physical* quantities. Another institution for continuing scrutiny is the Legislative Assembly. But the sort of information it gets on each canal is quite inadequate to allow it to perform a public interest monitoring function. The lack of routine public monitoring of the performance of canal systems is, indeed, one of the main problems.

Then there are means of conducting special investigations and disciplining offenders. The superior officer has to fill in 'Confidential Reports' on his subordinates each year, one column of which is titled 'Integrity'. Remarks in this column (or other communications) can bring into action the department's own investigative machinery—its Vigilance Cell—or the state Anti-Corruption Bureau (ACB) and Vigilance Commission.

However, in India as in many other countries, the gap between scandalous administrative and political conduct and specifically indictable offences is large. Disciplinary cases can drag on for years, and since the relevant provisions of the Indian Constitution place overwhelming stress on protection of the individual officer, the cases are not infrequently declared void. Even to put an adverse remark on an individual's annual confidential report is hazardous. The elaborate series of safeguards in the Anti-Corruption Bureau-Vigilance Commission mechanism tends to break down at the 'government' stage—the Minister or Secretary can easily intervene if he has a mind to, to ensure that a case does not go forward. If the Minister sold an EE his tenure and subsequently put the screws on him for more money, he may be a bit ambivalent about allowing an ACB investigation to proceed.

Nevertheless the possibility of investigation, even if remote, probably does act as a check on the proclivities of officials to exploit their powers to the full. Even if an engineer has powerful allies he can never be sure he will not be investigated if he behaves too flagrantly. Often investigations are triggered as part of a struggle for power and spoils. A senior officer may, for example, fall out with the Minister; then the Minister, previously his colluder, may order the ACB to investigate. Or the Minister may change, and especially if the new man and the old man are rivals, the new man may approve investigations which the other was squashing.

Since engineers are normally very careful to conceal their receipt and passing on of illicit funds, investigative bodies are likely to look for indirect signs, particularly for evidence of living far beyond official income. Engineers are well aware of the need to conceal extra income and its uses, and have many ways of doing so. Savings may be placed in a bank account under the name of a woman over whom the engineer has close control (police investigation of women's bank accounts is said to be less likely than of men's). Daughters can be given lavish dowries. Children can be provided for generously in private schools. A *benami* partnership can be formed to operate private buses in the next district, or to sell fertilisers and pesticides. A shop may be opened in the name of a family member back in the engineer's native place; the shop may in fact stay closed most of the time but can provide an excuse for living beyond official means. Donations to temples are a most attractive use, being both safe and productive of incalculable spiritual returns, as well as a natural form of thanksgiving for God's help in a successful venture. Finally, money needs to be accumulated for the special and limited purpose of buying the next post. In these and other ways, it is possible for some engineers to have incomes many times their official salary, yet not appear in daily life to be living extravagantly.

Farmers and politicians

But in the normal course of events, the main check on the engineers comes from the farmers whom they are meant to serve. It is true that the farmers themselves are often willing partners to bribery; as we have seen, they will rush to pay if their crops are at risk, and they will, in some locations at least, be willing enough to pay for water for unauthorised irrigation. However, if an engineer comes into a post and starts demanding significantly *more* from farmers and contractors than was usual previously, then they may try to take action to check or avoid his demands. They may in some locations break the channel banks or sluice gates to by-pass his control (which not only directly checks his power, but may also attract attention to their situation from higher officers), and/or visit their MLA, and/or write letters of complaint about him. The letters, probably anonymous (hence called generically 'anonymous petitions'), will go to the CE, to the Minister, to the MLA, to the ACB, to anyone the authors think might be able to harm the man—perhaps with a copy to the man himself. The local MLA may encourage constituents to do this, and armed with copies will make representations to the Minister 'on behalf of public'. If a man really is behaving extortionately to many people, especially if he is also patently living beyond his means, the flow of such letters and their level of detail, and the interest of the MLA in placating his constituents, may be such that the normal excuse for such complaints—that the officer is being made the object of a vendetta—cannot be used.

But this mechanism is limited to the extent that farmers fear that the engineer and local staff will strike back at them, perhaps by cutting off their water supply, if they complain.[43] It is also limited by differential willingness of MLAs to act. A village which has some wealthy, influential farmers can expect to have its complaints receive more attention than a village of poor, low caste farmers. Or, in the complacently-spoken words of an AE, 'Villages of small farmers just have to suffer, they won't dare approach Ministers or MLAs. Only the middle classes will have easy access to meet Ministers'.

Transfer

If a sizeable volume of complaints starts coming to MLAs or the Minister or the CE about a particular engineer, the easiest way to 'keep the peace', to use the engineers' phrase, is not to mount an investigation, with the possibility of disciplinary proceedings at the end, but simply to transfer him out at the first opportunity. No reasons need be given; no messy business of finding hard evidence need be contemplated.

The usual way to punish an officer is thus to transfer him before the usual two-year term is up, and /or to transfer him to an undesirable post and place.

So transfer is used both to punish someone who is taking 'too much', and to punish someone taking too little; it checks both the excessively corrupt and the insufficiently corrupt—both types 'threaten the peace'. Of course the transfer weapon is not always effective, in the sense that a corrupt man might have powerful allies who can ensure that the transfer orders are overturned. (And an MLA has to restrict his use of the transfer weapon; he will use up too much influence if he uses it frequently.) But it is clear that fear of transfer does check the extortion of engineers who buy themselves into lucrative posts; not only because of where they might end up, but also because the balance of their receipts over outlay to get the post will be smaller the sooner they are transferred.

Morality

These various points relating to punishment help to explain why the engineers take such care to conceal what they do. How much they are also checked by a feeling that what they are doing is wrong, morally reprehensible, is difficult to say, partly because an engineer talking about it with a stranger will always say it is wholly wrong, and also because even within the same person, remorse, shame and compunction are subject to alteration and ambivalence. However, it is clear that revenue-raising is *not* a matter for boasting—even AEs chatting amongst themselves in private would be very wary of discussing their revenue-raising exploits.

Second, in the irrigation context it seems likely that engineers discriminate between situations according to *how far* they are acting contrary to the law (as the farmers certainly do). For example, they would probably feel less of a sense of wrongdoing for taking money to supply an unauthorised crop, especially if the crop is paddy, than for demanding money to supply a village its full official turn during a rotational schedule. And in the case of unauthorised paddy and groundnut, one may have some sympathy with the engineers:[44] they know that large areas under these crops in the dry season mean they will have to work hard towards the end of the season to supply them with enough water; on the other hand, they know the farmers will not be made to pay the tough financial penalties which unauthorised irrigation is meant to incur. One can understand why they say, in effect, 'All right, if you want to grow paddy where it is not supposed to be grown, you will cause a lot of extra work, so you pay us something for our trouble'. This is distinct from active manipulation of the water supplies such that farmers have to pay for what they are fully entitled to. It would be wrong to suppose that all O & M engineers are actively engaged in the latter: some (a minority) try to limit their revenue collections to 'obliging', perhaps occasionally making smash-and-grab raids when a daughter's dowry has to be raised, then returning to principled or timid correctitude.

Promotions

The fact that promotions are insulated from money power or particularistic pressures helps to explain why the principled or timid *can* nevertheless rise to the top ranks, and sometimes do. The order of promotions is assigned at the start of a man's career by the Public Service Commission and is very rarely altered, either to move a man up or to hold one down. Lists showing promotion order are published in the annual departmental diaries the engineers carry around with them, and each batch of promotions is avidly studied to see if anyone has been passed over (the case of advanced promotion virtually never arises). A man who finds himself passed over will go to court, where he has a good chance of getting the decision reversed. The fact that promotion order is protected in law (while transfer procedures are not) and that the judicial process is not determined by particularistic demands is the short answer to the difference in 'rule-boundedness' between promotions and transfers. The only familiar manipulation of promotion is for the Minister to keep, say, 10 EEs' positions vacant until the 10 AEs next in line pay up. But there is a limit to how many positions can be kept vacant, and what the Minister cannot do is to promote number 11 or 12, say, in place of one of the first 10 AEs who refuses to pay.

This means that a man who gets a good position in the initial ranking, perhaps because of excellent examination results, can be fairly confident of rising to SE rank, even if he incurs the wrath of superior officers and politicians on the way. This can cut both ways, of course; but it undoubtedly does help some men to be less responsive than others to the pressures and opportunities to be corrupt. These people simply accept, more or less, that they will probably spend much of their careers in investigations and designs, or in difficult and out-of-the-way construction projects. At the same time, the highly bureaucratised procedures for promotions are a source of considerable frustration, because the engineers know that even if they consistently do very good work they will not be advanced in the promotion queue.[45]

Yet the normative checks are weaker than they might otherwise be because of the absence of any training for engineers in the principles of canal operation and maintenance. Their training is in the design and construction of hydraulic and other structures, and they simply have to learn operation and maintenance on the job. The explicit principles of operation and maintenance which they learn are few and rudimentary, and give no precise guides to decisions in many actual situations. Not knowing clearly how they *should* be deciding (when, for example, water is too limited to supply all their area at once, how to devise sensible rotational schedules?) they are more likely to give way to the pull of money or influence.

It bears repeating that the general public interest checks on the Irrigation Department are rather weak. The legislative scrutiny of canal performance is poorly developed, and the Accountant-General's Office confines itself to scrutiny of finances. The district Collector is too remote and too ignorant of the local situation to intervene.[46] In addition, the practice of investigative journalism is too rare for the press to provide a general check. In practice, how much an engineer is checked beyond his own conscience depends heavily on particular local circumstances.

EFFECTS ON IRRIGATION PERFORMANCE

It is clear that the demand-side effects of irrigation corruption are not significant, in the sense that farmers' production incentives are *not* much affected by illicit water payments. Net profits (including hired labour costs) are of the order of Rs.900 per acre (late 1970s) for paddy, and much more for groundnut; pre-harvest costs of cultivation are about Rs.900 per acre for paddy, and somewhat more for groundnut. Corruption costs of the order of magnitude indicated earlier—not more than Rs.50 per acre per crop, commonly Rs.10–25 per acre over two seasons, and sometimes much less (especially in villages with ample water supply)—form too small a part of cost of production to have much effect on production decisions: on which crops are grown, and how much they are irrigated. The gains to farmers from their elimination would be tiny in relation to potential gains from the elimination of Betterment Levy[47] and increases in paddy procurement prices (issues on which widespread farmers' agitations in 1980 were based). The worries, rather, are on the supply side.

A large part of the problem is that canal managers have no incentive to manage and maintain systems well when this would conflict with the generation of illicit income, which may be many times the official salary. On the water supply side, maximum surplus is extractable when water supply is insecure (in the short term); yet the ostensible function of the irrigation staff is to make it more secure. On the maintenance side, maximum surplus is extractable (in the short term) when the quality of maintenance is poor; yet the ostensible function of the irrigation staff is to ensure that the system is well maintained. If in some contexts the view that 'corruption oils the wheels' has some validity, canal irrigation does not seem to be one of them. The engineers' and politicians' pursuit of illicit income not only alters the discretionary allocation of individual (or village) benefit, but actually subverts the pursuit of public purposes. More specifically:

(1) Productivity and equity: If farmers know they will be provided with reliable supplies, the possibilities for engineers to earn bribes are reduced. Bribes are high where uncertainty is high. To get money, engineers may *create* scarcity and uncertainty, by cutting off supplies to a vulnerable village until they are paid, or as a by-product of diverting water from one area to another to respond to bribe-backed requests. Greater uncertainty of water supplies reduces the productivity of water. In particular, engineers persist with flexible, *ad hoc* and unannounced rotational delivery schedules partly because these practices facilitate revenue-raising (during a first season drought, for example). This is not to say that such behaviour is to be understood entirely as predatory. The engineers do face very real difficulties in meeting the demands upon them, and, as noted, are given no training in how to do so on a 'scientific' basis.

The point about the revenue-raising potential of rotational irrigation is worth re-emphasising; as was indicated, the introduction of rotational irrigation both above and below the outlet is normally seen in the literature as a step forward in canal management. Indeed, the key point of the World Bank's new thinking on canal irrigation over the next two or three decades in South Asia is that canals have to be built to ensure 'flexibility' of operation—to ensure that varying quantities of water can be delivered through each outlet over the crop season in line with changing crop water requirement below that outlet. If this is to be done, then the question of how the much enhanced discretionary power in the hands of the engineers is to be disciplined needs careful thought [*Wade, 1982a*].

However, it is certainly possible that tail-end villages can offset to some extent their locational disadvantage by offering bribes, and that this makes for a spatial re-allocation from upstream areas where the marginal productivity of water is lower, to where it is higher—a re-allocation which would not be made in the absence of an (illicit) incentive to irrigation staff to patrol upstream sluices more vigorously than they would otherwise. In this sense the corrupt system *could* promote efficiency and equity. One *can* identify tail-end villages or distributories which almost certainly would not have received water during a shortage had the irrigation staff not worked much harder than usual to bring water down—because they were being paid to do so. If—and there do seem to be cases—upstream villages did not suffer corresponding losses of yield because of the sending of more water downstream, this would be a gain for efficiency as well as equity.

However, my strong impression is that this pulling in of water to tail-end villages by means of bribes does not happen on a *big* scale, sufficient to offset the adverse effects of the *general increase in uncertainty* which it is in the engineers' interest to promote.[48] It must be remembered that the prospect of additional income from working hard to push water to tail-end villages is not a *sufficient* condition for such extra effort by irrigation staff, because they can make plenty of money 'from works' with little effort and plenty more 'from the *ayacut*' merely by cutting off or threatening to cut off supplies to vulnerable areas (upstream as well as downstream), or even just by rumouring a shortage.

(2) Interest in scientific principles and operational reform: The preoccupation of the EE and AEs with running a vast financial enterprise would seem likely to blunt their interest in canal operation as a serious and demanding professional and intellectual activity. They can make plenty of money without running the system well. For the same reason they can be expected to oppose any reform which might weaken their hold over O & M decisions [*Ali, 1980*]. For example, the Irrigation Department has shown no interest in involving farmers more systematically in major O & M matters; and has often been lax to the point of negligence in informing farmers about changes or expected changes in water supply. Relatedly, in one southern state where a new department of Command Area Development was set up (at World Bank prompting) to concern itself with ways of improving the performance of existing canal systems, the Irrigation Department has opposed it tooth and nail, even in its activities below the outlet and still more so in its attempts to influence how the main systems are being run.

(3) Credibility of Irrigation Department: In the eyes of farmers, the Irrigation Department's announcements on matters such as when the canal will be opened at the start of the first irrigation season, when it is to be closed, and how much water is available, are not to be trusted. Farmers are liable to take the EE's warnings that water will be short in the second season as a signal to start coming forward with bribes. Thus the *workable* authority of the

Irrigation Department is undermined, with probably adverse effects on productivity.

(4) Water rates: The longest-running policy proposal in the irrigation business is to increase water rates. So they have been, occasionally, though much less than the increase in the average value of the crop. Neither the Irrigation Department nor the mass of MLAs are enthusiastic about increasing water charges. Perhaps this lack of enthusiasm is not unrelated to a fear that farmers might be unwilling to pay both the official water charge at the higher rate and the unofficial charge at a rate no lower than before. If so, increasing the water rate would mean encroaching upon the flows of money through these alternative circuits, at cost to officers and politicians alike.

(5) Maintenance: Maintenance suffers badly, and hence so do both productivity and equity. (a) EEs and AEs make poor quality controllers, because they benefit from sub-standard work. (b) But the contractor has a further incentive to do sub-standard work, because on 'supplementary works' done to correct first-round mistakes he gets all the profit. (c) The contracts are divided into very small units (for example, one contract might be for maintenance of one mile, six furlongs of a long distributory), to keep good relations with as many contractors as possible, not least because the contractors are useful agents of the Irrigation Department in the villages for helping the AEs to raise money from the *ayacut*. (In other words, raising money 'from works' and 'from the *ayacut*' are not as distinct as the earlier discussion implied; the AE can use the promise of works to induce a contractor to help lever money 'from the *ayacut*', if need be.) Maintenance down the length of a distributory is often badly coordinated as a result. (d) The AE is empowered to sanction rather small 'emergency works' in certain circumstances, and these he makes use of to achieve revenue-raising objectives, as in (c). Again, patchwork, uncoordinated maintenance is the result. (e) Between 25 and 50 per cent of the resources meant to be spent on maintenance goes elsewhere. Off the main canal, sizeable distributories may not be maintained (except perhaps to replace broken structures) for 10 to 15 years at a time. The engineers say the government must give them more maintenance money.

(6) Effectiveness of new canal projects: Investigation of new canals, the preparation of project proposals to go for funding (perhaps to the World Bank) is being done by men whose chief aim is generally to get out of Investigations as fast as possible. The likely effect on the quality of project plans can readily be imagined. The quality of construction work is affected by the demand for rake-offs and lack of quality control. Add to this the politics of project approval—the exaggeration of expected irrigated area and the concealment of costs to raise the projected benefit/cost ratio high enough—and one has some of the reasons for the recurrent dismay of economists and farmers at the 'poor' performance of canal irrigation projects, in addition to all the factors described above at the O & M stage.

One should be careful, then, about the argument which says: corruption payments make a negligible difference to farmers' incentives, and help to make water allocation work more like a market. All the more should one be sceptical of the argument which says that corruption allows farmers to make government actions more predictable, and hence 'corruption can increase the rate of investment' [*Leff, 1970 (1964): 515*, speaking about the desirable economic effects of bribe payments by businessmen in Less Developed Countries].

There are, however, some points which have to qualify the generally adverse effects noted above. It would certainly be mistaken to advocate merely that corruption payments should be eliminated and the crop zoning pattern strictly followed; for the zoning itself not uncommonly makes no ecological sense. Second, in a political environment where politicians are interested less in long-term development goals than in the disbursement of short-term material benefits to those who support them, the consistent political commitment to irrigation investment, which in some Indian states accounts for over half the state's development budget yet has a gestation period of five to ten years or more, needs explaining. Perhaps the answer has something to do with the way in which irrigation investment *does* provide an abundant stream of short-term material benefits able to be profited from by both politicians and state officials. Thirdly, the elimination of officials' corruption incomes would generate pressures for salary increases, which if financed out of higher taxes would probably worsen income distribution.[49] These points are not intended as a comprehensive qualification of the adverse effects listed earlier, but only as an indication of the complexity of making an overall assessment of the economic effects.

IRRIGATION IN OTHER STATES

Several bits of evidence suggest that the practices described here are not confined to our particular state. A recent enquiry in another southern state indicates a similar mechanism of sale of irrigation posts there.[50] Pant's study of the Kosi canal system in Bihar reports that contractors normally give about 30 per cent of the bill to Supervisors and above, and 10 per cent to office staff; about 10 to 20 per cent they keep as their own profit, leaving only 40 to 50 per cent to be spent on the actual works [*1979: 127*]. The same study reports, without elaboration, 'Postings in places of choice or from non-work (design or investigations) to work units involve transactions of huge amounts of money' [*1979: 128*]. The *Report* of the Santhanam Committee, set up by Government of India to investigate ways of preventing corruption, states:

> We were told by a large number of witnesses that in all contracts of construction, purchase, sales, and other regular business on behalf of the Government, a regular percentage is paid by the parties to the transaction, and this is shared in agreed proportions among the various officials concerned. We were told that in the constructions of the Public Works Department [of which the states' Irrigation Departments are offshoots—RW], seven to eleven per cent was usually paid in this manner . . . . In all cases, failure to pay the percentage results invariably in difficulty and delay in getting the bills paid [*India, Government of, Ministry of Home Affairs, 1964: 10*].

One would expect the precise ways by which engineers raise revenue in O & M posts to depend on such things as crop type, the degree and location of water control made possible by the physical structures, rules for crop zoning (if any), extent of conjunctive use of canal and groundwater, and the character of political competition. The canals of Punjab-Haryana (often taken, mistakenly, to be the typical type of Indian canal in structure and operation) differ from those of the south in several relevant ways [*Reidinger, 1974*]:

(1) Crop zoning ('localization') is not used in the northwest, so the possibility of earning revenue from supplying out-of-zone land does not exist.

(2) There is more conjunctive use of groundwater (by private well) with canal water, so farmers are less dependent on public water supply authorities.

(3) Paddy has traditionally not been grown in the northwest; the main crops do not require such intensive irrigation and their yields are less adversely affected by a (smallish) shortfall of water supply below potential evapotranspiration level [*Levine, 1977*].

(4) Outlets on the northwestern canals are normally not gated—they are ungated 'proportional modules', which release a discharge proportional to the discharge in the canal, and so at outlet level there is less water control capacity and less scope for discrimination between outlet groups or villages [*Gustafson and Reidinger, 1971*]; in the southern uplands outlets are commonly gated.

(5) On the other hand, the Irrigation Departments in the northwest assess and collect water rates, while this is done by the Revenue Departments in the south.[51]

POLITICAL DIMENSIONS

It seems likely that long before elective political institutions became important irrigation staff not uncommonly used their power over water and contracts to multiply their own income and that of their bureaucratic superiors [*Krishnaswamy, 1980*]. If so, Marx's dictum, 'There have been in Asia, generally, from immemorial times, but three departments of Government: that of Finance, or the plunder of the interior; that of War, or the plunder of the exterior; and, finally, the department of Public Works' [*1853*], might plausibly have been still more damning. Perhaps the mechanism of public works plunder described here gives hints about the cyclical collapse of reigning dynasties in the hydraulic societies not only of India, but of Egypt, Mesopotamia, and China as well—about the ways by which an increase in bureaucratic corruption was translated into worse maintained canals and dikes, extra unreliability of water supply, and lower production.[52]

However, it is likely that elective institutions have amplified the pressures towards corruption and made it more systematic. Amplification has come especially because of the spiralling cost of fighting elections and nursing a constituency between elections. In our area it is said that a man needs to have at minimum one *lakh* rupees available before it is worth even thinking about contesting an MLA's seat (except perhaps in the case of seats reserved for a Scheduled Caste candidate). Votes are commonly purchased, especially from Low Caste and Scheduled Caste voters (voting within the politically dominant but numerically inferior castes is more likely to follow factional alignments). In the local government elections of 1981, a serious candidate even for village headship (*sarpanch*) would have to reckon on spending something of the order of Rs.30–50,000 in an average-sized village, if the election was contested.[53] And Ministers may have to pay the Chief Minister to get the portfolio they want (which is perhaps part of the reason for the expansion in ministerial portfolios). Money is not the only requirement, of course; favours for supporters must be obtained from the bureaucracy too, but there is no doubt that the rupee price of successful politics is very high.

Politicians have been able to make use of the bureaucracy to help meet the costs of electoral competition. We have seen how they do so in the case of Irrigation; and one would expect that Irrigation would be an especially valuable department to control, not only because it spends big money but also because its decisions greatly affect the political prospects of politicians and the economic prosperity of local communities. However, it is clear (though I shall not go into the matter here) that similar mechanisms operate in other government departments as well, including such apparently 'clean' ones as Agriculture and Labour Welfare.

The transfer is the politicians' basic weapon of control over the bureaucracy, and thus the lever for surplus-extraction from the clients of the bureaucracy. With the transfer weapon not only can the politicians raise money by direct sale; they can also remove someone who is not being responsive enough to their monetary demands or to their requests for favours to those from whom they get money and electoral support—in particular, contractors. One is thus led to visualise a special circuit of transactions, in which the bureaucracy acquires control of funds, partly (in this case) from farmers in the form of variable levies, and partly from the state's public works budget, then passes a portion to MLAs and especially Ministers, who in turn use the funds for distributing short-term material inducements in exchange for electoral support. These funds, it should be noticed, do flow through the public domain (in one sense); but they are neither open to public scrutiny nor available for public expenditure programmes [*Wade, forthcoming*].

This 'transfer model', with its systematic linkage between top-level and bottom-level corruption and between administrative and political corruption, is, I think, quite plausible once spelled out. One wonders whether the processes it describes are not more common in poor countries than its absence from the political science literature would suggest.[54]

POLICY RESPONSES

In the specific context of canal O & M, what should reformers press government to do to improve the situation? One line of solution which appeals to many economists is to institutionalise a market, as with some canals of Spain, Italy, and the United States [*Maass and Anderson, 1978; Wade, 1979*]. But the enforcement problem would be extremely difficult to overcome: Indian canals are typically many times bigger than where water markets are used (500 to 1,000 outlets in a typical canal system) and each outlet irrigates a much bigger area (perhaps 200 acres or more), belonging to many more farmers, who are much more unequal in wealth and power. At present canal managers are not able to deliver a *constant* discharge to each outlet down each distributory, let alone one which varies from outlet to outlet depending on demand. (With bribe or extortion payments, as we have seen, only a limited number of outlets or distributory offtakes need be controlled; the rest can get the residual.) Secondly, where paddy is a major crop, the response time—the time between when farmers ask for water and when it arrives—would have to be very short, because paddy yields fall off sharply if water supply is below potential evapotranspiration; and this would call for very high quality management and communications. Thirdly, in the first season, when canal water supplements rainfall, it is difficult for farmers to know the value of canal water much in advance, so the quantities demanded may fluctuate greatly within short periods depending on rainfall, making main system operation more difficult. Finally, one should remember that nowhere in Asia has volumetric pricing of water been adopted; not even in Taiwan where canal management and water use is said to be much more effective than in India [*Levine, 1977*].

A second line of solution is to inspect, audit, check and double-check the Irrigation Department, by giving the Indian Administrative Service more control over it and by giving stronger powers to the Anti-Corruption Bureau and Vigilance Cell; these measures would be coupled with stricter definition of the rights and duties of officials, and stronger complaints procedures before a strengthened Administrative Tribunal. Suffice it to say that this is a familiar direction of administrative reform in India, especially popular in the eyes of Indian Administrative Service officers; but on its own it is unlikely to make matters better and may make matters worse—a stronger Administrative Tribunal, for example, would quite possibly be engulfed in a mass of litigation which the Indian judicial process is ill-equipped to handle.

A third line of solution seems more promising. It would attempt to strengthen the user side of the irrigator-official relation, both by the familiar device of user organisation—councils of irrigators covering 20 or so villages, or a Section, for example—*and* by monitoring of the performance of each canal system by an independent monitoring organisation whose reports would be made public [*Wade, 1980a, 1982a; Seckler, 1981*]. Aerial or satellite photography could help to make the monitoring objective. Opportunities for the exercise of 'voice', if coupled with a non-partisan source of information, could be much more effective in curbing the arbitrary exercise of authority than the record of government-sponsored 'cooperatives' in India would lead one to expect.

This strengthening of the user side might be supplemented by two other sorts of measures, one of which has to do with the work motivation of canal managers. It is difficult to see how a closer link can be made between conscientious effort and reward than exists at present, especially because promotion and salary rules cannot be altered for the Irrigation Department as long as canals are run by civil servants, because of civil service parity issues. But at least canal managers can be given a clearer notion of what they should be doing by means of professional training—a training which should include not only engineering and agronomy but also management science, and which should aim to foster the development of an ethos of professional service around O & M work. At present, operational skills and professional norms in our state are so weak that the training prescription—often as ineffective a prescription for bureaucratic improvement as it is familiar—does seem pertinent in this particular case.

The other measure is technical: to build many more 'on-line' reservoirs along the length of a canal system, to provide storage intermediate between dam and fields. They would be filled according to a pre-determined, well-advertised schedule, and irrigators would themselves have more responsibility for allocating water to the fields (as they now do under 'tanks'). This solution is constrained by ecological and economic factors (for example, the cost of land acquisition); but arguments in its favour on engineering grounds are clearly reinforced by the argument of this paper.

Clearly though, one of the main reasons for the illicit payments system lies outside the irrigation sector, and reform of irrigation will be difficult without also reform of electoral competition. This is *not* to say that politicians should be prevented from interfering in irrigation—economists and others are too prone to accept at face value the engineers' own definition of political interference as a problem; merely to exclude politicians would in many cases expose irrigators to even worse extortion than they face at present. Nevertheless, some check on the cost of electoral competition would clearly be desirable. Electoral reform proposals in India have generally been based on the argument that India cannot afford such expensive elections, while the widespread ramifications of the politicians' drive to raise revenue have been inadequately recognised. Yet just because these ramifications are so wide, it is difficult to talk of electoral reform in isolation, without also talking of the need for political rejuvenation by means of one or more mass parties able to insist upon performance standards from the bureaucracy.[55]

NOTES

1. I assume a canal managed 'above the outlet' by a government department or parastatal agency, and 'below the outlet' by farmers, such as is normal throughout Asia for all but very small systems (say, less than 5,000 hectares irrigated area). I have applied this same dual perspective to irrigation in South Korea, in a way that encompasses both the technical characteristics of irrigation systems in that environment and, at the other extreme, the role of the bureaucracy in South Korea's rapid industrialisation [*Wade, 1982*]. For a comparison of South Korean and south Indian irrigation, which provides more detail on technical and organisational aspects of the south Indian case, see Wade [*1981a*]. For an analysis of the relevance of climate for understanding variations in irrigation institutions (including the incidence of corruption) see Wade [*1981b*].
2. Note the absence of such connections in two major works on corruption, Scott [*1972*] and Heidenheimer's selection of 58 readings [*1970*].

3. It proved difficult to get detailed information on such matters, though I tried at several points in the Irrigation Department. To the best of my knowledge, there is no organisation chart for the Department. The headquarters in the state capital has no information at all on how many field staff are employed throughout the state, and its aggregate information on number of employees above field staff level is, for AE and EE level, out of date and in any case available only for each rank as a whole, not broken into functional categories.
4. The figure excludes clerical staff, who may number about 50. The variation in staff numbers is less than in irrigated area, partly because Divisions with a relatively small irrigated area may be given more tank maintenance responsibilities, and partly because the crop zoning results in some canals having their irrigated area spread out in scattered non-contiguous blocks, with a relatively high ratio of channel length to irrigated area; such canals will need a higher density of staff per 10,000 irrigated acres.
5. I have checked the argument by presenting it in detail to two engineers, with experience in different parts of the state and of very different rank. I have also presented it in detail to an Indian economist long familiar with the state and its politics (his brother is closely involved in state and national politics). At the same time, it should be said that a few people from the sub-continent who have heard the paper in seminar have felt deeply affronted by the argument, and are not convinced it is not a tissue of exaggeration and half-truths. 'How many engineers did you interview, what percentage of them were corrupt?', they wanted to know. I hope that the earlier discussion shows why these questions are difficult to answer and why it is nevertheless worth making the argument.
6. The figure taken for irrigated area may be several years out of date—in 1980 the figure for 1974/75 was still being used.
7. One engineer said the division varies from half and half to one-third to contractor and two-thirds to officers; a retired engineer who since retirement had worked as a consultant to contractors said half and half was usual.
8. Even the formal stipulated procedures for quality control in the Irrigation Department are very weak—weaker than, for example, in the Roads and Buildings Department.
9. On big construction projects the percentage may well be lower. Over the summer of 1981 a Commission of Enquiry has been hearing evidence on the causes of the rupture of the Barna Dam, in Madhya Pradesh. A contractor has filed an affidavit alleging that contractors have to hand over 15 per cent of the contract value to the officers.
10. The percentage fluctuates, because increases in the maintenance grant and in field staff salaries do not occur at the same time.
11. It must be made clear that no engineer told me directly how much he was making. The income figures (as for the AE figures later) are arrived at indirectly, in the EE case from the size of the works budget, plus informants' statements about the way it is divided up. The income inferences can then be compared with what informants say about the price of posts (in specific instances, and in general). One can then see to what extent the figures tally.
12. This is the mid-point in the range, after the 1978 revision. The figure includes a cost-of-living allowance (Dearness Allowance) and a housing allowance.
13. In the case of big contracts, the *SE* is the payer of bills.
14. 'Speed' money is of course one of the oldest and most familiar forms of corruption. *The Northern India Patrika*, 30 July, 1981, reports that an EE of the Public Health Department of Uttar Pradesh was caught taking a Rs.1,000 bribe from a contractor; the contractor had complained to the Collector that the EE was demanding the bribe in return for paying a Rs.40,000 bill, and a trap was set up. Note that the bribe amounted to $2\frac{1}{2}$ per cent, the same as our EEs are said to get on 'savings on the estimates'.

    The speed money (as well as other types of payment which alter the allocation of benefits) is increasingly in the form of consumer durables. Krishnaswamy reports that a businessman told him that 'officials who have to pass bills ask for domestic durables to be purchased on the installment system in their names' [*1980*].
15. One EE related that he had been transferred early from being in charge of construction of a medium project for refusing to alter the accounts of a big contractor who turned out to have more influence with the Minister than he thought. Into his place was promoted his own AE, who though next in line for promotion would not usually have been given such a big responsibility immediately; but he had already demonstrated to the contractor his willingness to comply. Of course the Department could always argue that the AE's

experience with the project suggested he could proceed faster than could an older EE brought in from outside.

16. My guess is that on the coastal deltas the EE commonly is more actively involved in raising money from the *ayacut*, and that he has more direct ways of sharing in it than is the case on upland canals. If so, this might help explain why delta posts tend to be more 'expensive' (see below).
17. Biplab Dasgupta suggests (personal communication) that in many West Bengal villages such village-wide organisation would be difficult to achieve because of the greater degree of class-based organisation within villages than is normally the case in our state.
18. Occasionally incautious contractors are caught with huge sums of money on their hands, and such incidents may get small bylines in the press. For example, on 19 July 1980, *The Hindu* noted that the Income Tax Department had seized Rs.34 *lakh* from the residence of a contractor who owed even more in income tax arrears, plus another Rs.1½ *lakh* from the residence of a clerk of a private engineering college which bore the same name as the name of the contractor (the contractor comes from an adjacent state where private colleges have been permitted). I thank Jeremy Jackson for this reference.
19. These factors are relevant to variation over time and place within any canal command area. There is also variation between canals, especially between canals on the uplands and on the coastal deltas. Delta farmers tend to be prepared to pay more. When delta farmers come to the uplands (buying a bigger area with the proceeds of the sale of their delta land) they continue to be more willing to pay the irrigation staff—they become the 'price leaders'.

    A further qualification: Although the zoning of land for irrigation ('localisation') is intended to be once-and-for-all, some flexibility is permitted—villages can have their water rights changed. Such desired changes may well have to be paid for, and obtaining them may entail several trips by village representatives to the state capital, as well as to the Division and Sub-division offices. Their price would normally be several times the price of a one-season assurance; and even if the villagers are prepared to pay this sort of amount their request may not be granted.
20. The cross-bund increases the discharge through the sluice, thus reducing what is available for lower-down sluices.
21. This case occurred in 1977. The village was near a tail-end, so could be easily discriminated against; it had few families of the dominant caste of the region; and was clearly in the poorest quarter of villages in the district.
22. He actually said that rumour-mongering is one of the tricks of being a field staffer (banker or foreman); senior engineers are quite prepared to admit, in general terms, that the 'lower down fellows' accept bribes.
23. If the farmers lose confidence in the willingness or ability of a Supervisor or AE to deliver on promises, and also think him 'weak kneed', they will be more likely to resort to breaking the structures, by-passing the irrigation hierarchy. This checks the extent to which the officers can promise without delivering.
24. One engineer said there is what he called a 'vicious circle' between engineers and politicians: 'The engineer gives more water to the lands of a politician, that fellow obliges at the time of transfer'.
25. Assume conservatively that the wet season paddy area, about 160,000 acres or so, pays 1 kg/ac, and assume, as in the village where I lived, that each village gives about one-third to the Supervisor and AE, and two-thirds to the foremen and bankers who directly serve it. Then over the whole canal, if the 330 or so field staff divide the collections equally, they will each get about 320 kgs of paddy (which can be roughly valued at Rs.1.2 per kg), compared to a monthly salary of between Rs.300 and 700. Each Supervisor and AE will get roughly 2,000 kg (if they share equally—in practice the AE would get more, the Supervisor less), compared to an AE's average monthly salary of about Rs.1,900, and less for Supervisor. The plausibility of the assumptions is strengthened by the absence of rags-to-riches stories amongst field staff, and by the fact that the grain payments do not arouse anything like the same resentment amongst farmers that the money payments sometimes do (depending on what the payments are for, as well as on their level). In the dry season the grain payments are less common, less institutionalised, more at the discretion of individual households; and more of the dry season irrigated area is under non-food crops.
26. Rs.2,400,000 × 5% × 25% (to reduce to a Sub-division basis) × 50%.

27. See notes 11 and 12.
28. However, in states where private engineering colleges are now permitted, very large fees for a place in a private college are now common; and authorisation of private education in engineering and medicine is being opposed in some states by people who argue that the graduates of such colleges who get jobs in the public sector will have a strong incentive to recoup the fee on the job, perhaps in illicit ways.

    For some years in the late 1960s and first half of the 1970s the supply of graduates and diploma-holders wanting to join the Irrigation Department exceeded the expansion of places, and it is said that joining payments *did* then have to be made. The engineers of whom I speak all joined before this time.
29. The strategy varies from case to case depending on a whole range of factors, such as the political complexion at the place to which the engineer wishes to go, and the engineer's own 'influence'. What follows is a typical pattern, as I understand it.
30. I ignore the complication that (since the early 1970s) there are Ministers for each of Major Irrigation, Medium Irrigation and Minor Irrigation, and several Secretaries for different parts of Irrigation; one Minister and one Secretary are clearly senior to the others. I shall also ignore the role of the Secretary (who is an Indian Administrative Service officer) in the following discussion. I further ignore the distinction between members of the state legislature and members of the national legislature.
31. Two qualifications: If he can, the EE may take a very influential man with him to see the Minister, someone to whom the Minister will find it difficult to say no. This will help the negotiations. Second, on big construction projects the CE is in charge of several Circles, and is the sanctioning authority for EE transfers *within* this set of Circles.
32. This, at least, is how the engineers understand the matter—though given that political parties tend to be weak as corporate organisations, the distinction between personal use and party war-chests may not be sharp.
33. Normally only the one or two most powerful MLAs will be visited, though six or seven or more may have significant parts of their constituencies irrigated by the canal. In the state in which this study is set, the local government structure (*zilla parishad, panchayat samithi,* village *panchayat*) was more or less moribund from 1970 to 1981. In states where elective local government structures function, people like the *samithi* president may also be involved in transfers as well as the local MLAs.
34. Some Superintending Engineer posts on the deltas cost 12–15 *lakhs* (for what is normally a two-year term of office), or 38–48 times the average annual SE salary. Three specific posts are known to cost in this range, all within the area considered to be the nerve centre of state politics. It is common knowledge that the incumbents of these posts can 'make millions'. Building sumptuous retirement houses is a favourite use of the profits—a use much facilitated by engineers' privileged access to scarce cement at below free market prices. (One reason why engineers like canal-lining programmes is because, as one said, 'cement is a gold mine'.)
35. The relative authority of the CE and SE depends on whether the transfer is inter- or intra-Circle.
36. Three complications: In some areas there is a big farmer-contractor who, in the selection of the MLA, is known as the kingmaker; the AE may well visit him. Second, where excess water from an upland canal runs into a coastal reservoir, the MLAs and Ministers under that reservoir can have a distinct interest in having an AE who is sympathetic to their needs at the critical point of the upland canal where the amount of 'excess' is determined. In this way, interest in what goes on in one watershed is by no means confined to the people and politicians of that watershed, so the patterns of influence can be spatially quite complex. Third, the local MLA may be of different party, or different faction, to the Minister, and this again leads to more complex patterns of influence.
37. This figure comes from a canal where the EE's post cost about one *lakh* in the late 1970s; where the price of the EE's post is higher one would expect the payment to MLAs to be higher also. If however the man is of unusual influence he may not pay the MLAs—'they have to come to him, he does not have to go to them', said one informant describing an actual case. In this case, although the man had a great deal of influence—'he had four Ministers on his side'—he still had to pay a lot of money to get the post, but the payment went to senior officers, not to the Minister or MLAs.

38. It is said that if an AE wants to stay in the same place and in order to do so has to transfer to a separate Circle, he sometimes has to pay the SE of his own Circle, especially if it is an O & M Circle, for *release*.
39. They can appeal to the Administrative Tribunal, to which all service disputes relating to government employees may be referred; but the procedure is bothersome and the Tribunal's decision is not binding on the government, so it is little used by irrigation staff.
40. 'In the Food for Work programmes, inflated muster rolls with fictitious names, utilisation of foodgrain for purchase of crockery and furniture and upkeep of government buildings have come to light' [*Krishnaswamy, 1980*].
41. The three Supervisors who came in the first half of 1981 all reputedly had to pay this amount.
42. Well over 100 AEs found themselves having to take compulsory one-month holidays in order to share out the shortfall of posts, and presumably (since the normal ratio of Supervisors to AEs is 4: 1) well over 400 Supervisors. Occasional imbalances between the supply and demand for staff must be normal in any big construction organisation, and one wonders how they are handled in irrigation departments elsewhere in the world.
43. Hence farmers commonly do not want gates on their sluices, because if the sluices are ungated it is more difficult for the staff to cut off their water. On the other hand, farmers in tail-end locations *do* want upstream sluices to be gated, so that they can be closed and more water sent down to them. This sort of divergence between what irrigators want for themselves and what they want for the rest of the system is a fundamental feature of canal irrigation.
44. One has sympathy where the farmers could grow some crop other than paddy. But in some areas which are not zoned for paddy the land is too saturated by seepage from the canal, or from (zoned) paddy areas higher up, to grow any other crop; which reflects poor zoning, and failure to provide adequate drainage. In this case the engineers have much less justification.
45. A few engineers who reach SE or CE rank still find intolerable the pressures to be corrupt, to do a mediocre job and to keep quiet in the face of wrongdoing, and simply retire early. One SE appointed to a big new World Bank-aided project was appalled at the poor standard of design and construction, and said openly at meetings of engineers and senior government officials that if the minor distributories had been properly designed and constructed in the first place, the large amounts now having to be spent to upgrade them would have been unnecessary. He was harrassed so fiercely by his colleagues (it is said) that he retired early. I know at least one CE who did the same, for similar reasons. Both men were outstandingly talented and dynamic, and one suspects such people are more likely to take this course, depleting the Irrigation Department of a potential internal constituency for reform.
46. Collectors average less than two years in a place before being transferred. A correspondent, chiding me for not giving the Collector a central place in the checking mechanism, writes:

    > It is the Collector that would normally be expected to control the system. In some states he is very, very powerful—for instance in Maharashtra. It seems to me that his interests are overwhelmingly in *not* letting corruption get out of hand; the risk to him, if he is seen to knave at it, is enormous [loss of career and disgrace], and the gains from taking bribes himself are relatively small in this light.

    This is not my impression for the area I know; especially because of the distinction between what the Collector's interests are, and what he is able to do.
47. Betterment Levy is a levy on the increase in land values which the bringing of land under command is expected to result in.
48. This difference in the 'partial equilibrium' and 'general equilibrium' effects of the corrupt system in irrigation is similar to the probable effects of 'speed money' in the bureaucracy as a whole. Speed money, if common, probably has the effect of slowing down the overall work performance of the bureaucracy, as officials cut back their work effort in order to invite the payment of bribes, by means of which individuals are able to accelerate officials' effort from this reduced level to deal with their particular cases.
49. This holds because the higher taxes would likely fall on items of mass consumption, while bribery and extortion payments come disproportionately from the landed.
50. An agricultural economist with detailed knowledge of a large irrigation canal in the uplands of another southern state, to whom I put questions similar to those addressed in this paper, replied as follows:

> An AE working in the investigations or dam can get transfers in the canals by paying some amount or directly by political pressures through MLAs and then through concerned ministers. The money to be paid will be ranging from Rs.5,000 to 10,000 normally, depending upon the exact location in the canal system. In [his state], the political pressure is more dominant than direct influence through officials . . . . The staff in general are actually watching the vacancy position in different places and then get their transfer by giving money directly or through political pressures.
>
> Normally money is given by the farmers for certain benefits. The money thus received is invested in purchase of real estates in different places, purchase of lands for cultivation, starting up of business shops like fertiliser and pesticide shops where the engineers can control a sizeable number of farmers for the business. Most of the investments will be in the wives' names only, so as to avoid any legal complications if any one complains of malpractices in the canal system . . . . The engineers are normally getting more in kind and they will dispose of them through close businessmen for cash.

The figures he gives for AE transfers to canal O & M are lower than the orders of magnitude under our canals; but still come to a quarter to a half of an AE's average annual salary. And as far as one can judge, the basic mechanism is the same.

51. A British ex-Chief Engineer in Punjab related (personal communication, 1976) that prior to Independence his field staff used to make money with a pile of bricks: they would place the pile next to an outlet, the farmers came running with money to prevent 'remodernisation' (effectively, narrowing the outlet), and the pile was moved on to the next village or sluice, and so on; the next incumbent of the post repeated the procedure.
52. See, for example, Ch'ang Hu [*1955*]. The scale of corruption in the Yellow River Administration in China during the eighteenth and nineteenth centuries dwarfs the scale described here for a south Indian state. Ch'ang Hu reports that the YRA received about 10 per cent of the central state's total budget, and that 'hardly one tenth of the regular and extraordinary appropriations was spent for actual water conservancy' [*512*]. He quotes a top civil servant writing in 1812, 'The important river works are manipulated as a means of political favoritism, and treasury funds are either squandered or used as bribes; hence the river officials have become fops and dandies, while the sites of river work have become places of flower and wine' [*510*]. Ch'ang Hu links the decreasing effectiveness of the YRA directly to the collapse of the Ch'ing dynasty.
53. The figures in this paragraph come from conversations with farmers and others in the study area.
54. I am preparing a paper on the 'transfer' model which discusses it in a more general, non-irrigation-specific context.
55. International development agencies potentially have a role in reducing the mismanagement of development projects. But at present the official position of both the agencies and the recipient governments is that the agencies are to concern themselves with increasing the inputs to development, while it is for the host government to worry about the outputs from development projects. Indeed, there is perhaps no subject in the international development community so sensitive and suppressed as the mismanagement of development programmes (an observation for which I thank David Seckler).

REFERENCES

Ali, H., 1980, 'Practical experience of irrigation reform, India', Institute of Development Studies *Discussion Paper* No. 153, September.

Anderson, E. and P., 1967, *Political Institutions and Social Change in Continental Europe in the Nineteenth Century*, Berkeley: University of California Press, pp. 166–67, 206–19, 230–35. Reprinted in Heidenheimer, 1970.

Andreski, S., 1968, 'Kleptocracy or corruption as a system of government', in *The African Predicament*, New York: Atherton. Reprinted in Heidenheimer, 1970.

Bailey, F.G., 1957, *Caste and the Economic Frontier: A Village in Highland Orissa*, Manchester University Press.

Bayley, D., 1966, 'The effects of corruption in a developing nation', *Western Political Quarterly*, XIX(4). Reprinted in Heidenheimer, 1970.

Ch'ang Hu, 1955, 'The Yellow River Administration in the Ch'ing Dynasty', *Far Eastern Quarterly*, 14.

Epstein, T., 1962, *Economic Development and Cultural Change in South India,* Manchester University Press.
Gustafson, W. and R. Reidinger, 1971, 'Delivery of canal water in North India and West Pakistan', *Economic and Political Weekly* (Bombay), 6(50): A-157-162.
Heidenheimer, A., 1970, *Political Corruption: Readings in Comparative Analysis,* New York: Holt, Rinehart and Winston.
India, Government of, Ministry of Home Affairs, 1964, *Report of the Commission on the Prevention of Corruption* ('Santhanam Report'), New Delhi.
India, Government of, Ministry of Irrigation and Power, National Irrigation Commission, 1972, *Report* (4 vols.).
Krishnaswamy, S., 1980, 'Wide range of corruption', *The Hindu,* 30 August.
Leff, N., 1964, 'Economic development through bureaucratic corruption', *American Behavioral Scientist,* 8(3). Reprinted in Heidenheimer, 1970.
Levine, G., 1977, 'Management components in irrigation system design and operation', *Agricultural Administration,* Vol. 4, No. 1.
Levine, G., L. Chin, and S. Miranda, 1976, 'Requirements for the successful introduction and management of rotational irrigation', *Agricultural Water Management,* Vol. 1.
Maass, A. and R. Anderson, 1978, '*... and the Desert Shall Rejoice: Conflict, Growth, and Justice in Arid Environments',* Cambridge: MIT Press.
Marx, K., 1853, 'The British rule in India', reprinted in *Karl Marx and Frederick Engels, Selected Works,* Vol. One, Moscow: Progress Publishers, 1969.
Pant, N., 1979, 'Some aspects of irrigation administration (a case study of Kosi project)', mimeo, A.N.S. Institute of Social Studies, Patna, Bihar.
Ram, M., 1981, 'Ferreting out the black money', *Far Eastern Economic Review,* 6 Feb.
Reidinger, R., 1974, 'Institutional rationing of canal water in Northern India: conflict between traditional patterns and modern needs', *Economic Development and Cultural Change,* 23(1).
Scott, J., 1972, *Comparative Political Corruption,* Englewood Cliffs: Prentice-Hall.
Seckler, D., 1981, 'The new era of irrigation management in India', mimeo, Ford Foundation, New Delhi.
Shamasastry, R., 1967(1915), *Kautilya's Arthasastra,* Mysore: Mysore Printing and Publishing House.
Swart, K.W., 1949, *Sale of Offices in the Seventeenth Century,* The Hague: Martinus Nijhoff, pp. 112–127. Reprinted in Heidenheimer, 1970.
Wade, R., 1975, 'Water to the fields: India's changing strategy', *South Asian Review,* 8(4). Reprinted in E.W. Coward (ed.), 1980, *Irrigation and Agricultural Development in Asia: Perspectives from the Social Sciences,* Ithaca, N.Y.: Cornell University Press.
Wade, R., 1979, 'Collective responsibility in construction and management of irrigation canals: case of Italy', *Economic and Political Weekly,* Review of Agriculture, Vol. XIV, Nos. 51 & 52, Dec. 22–29.
Wade, R., 1980, 'Substituting management for water in canal irrigation: a South Indian case', *Economic and Political Weekly* (Bombay), Vol. XV, No. 52, Review of Agriculture, 27 Dec.
Wade, R., 1980a, 'Water users' associations: sociological principles and government practice', mimeo, Institute of Development Studies, University of Sussex.
Wade, R., 1981, 'The information problem of South Indian irrigation canals', *Water Supply and Management,* 5.
Wade, R., 1981a, 'Employment, water control and irrigation institutions: canal irrigation in South India and South Korea', paper prepared for the Asian Regional Team for Employment Promotion (ARTEP), International Labour Office, Bangkok.
Wade, R., 1981b, 'Climate and irrigation institutions', mimeo, Institute of Development Studies, University of Sussex.
Wade, R., forthcoming, 'The politics and economics of India's state accumulation policy: review of J. Toye, *Public Expenditure and Indian Development Policy 1960–1970', Economic Development and Cultural Change.*
Wade, R., 1982, *Irrigation and Agricultural Politics in South Korea,* Boulder: Westview Press.
Wade, R., 1982a, 'The World Bank and India's irrigation reform', *Journal of Development Studies,* Vol. 18, No. 2.
Wade, R. and R. Chambers, 1980, 'Managing the main system: canal irrigation's blind spot', *Economic and Political Weekly* (Bombay), Vol. 15, No. 39, Review of Agriculture.

Weber, M., 1968, *Economy and Society: An Outline of Interpretive Sociology*, Vol. III, New York: Bedminster Press.

Wertheim, W., 1963, 'Sociological aspects of corruption in Southeast Asia', *Sociologica Neerlandica*, 1(2). Reprinted in Heidenheimer, 1970.

Part VIII
Whistleblowing

[28]

Crime, Law & Social Change **22:** 381–390, 1995.

Whistleblowing and corruption control: The GE case *

LOUIS M. SEAGULL
Pace University, Lubin School of Business, New York, NY 10038, USA

Abstract. This paper focuses on the use of the amended False Claims Act to counter defense contract fraud against the U.S. government. The case deals with the scheme of a former Israeli Air Force General and a GE marketing specialist to divert funds, provided by the U.S. to Israel, for unauthorized and private usage, and with the actions of the GE whistleblower, Chester L. Walsh, in bringing suit against GE under FCA. The paper analyzes poses the ethical problem of providing an economic bounty for the whistleblower even while acknowledging the effectiveness of this practice in countering fraud.

This case mixes a brew of corruption and its containment combining bribery, misappropriation of funds, false claims and whistleblowing. It also highlights the role of economic incentive as a strategy in controlling the corruption of false claims against the federal government in the United States.

Blowing the whistle can apply to many different situations. But when an individual blows the whistle on a company for defrauding the federal government, the False Claims Act (FCA) may apply. The focus of the paper is on the FCA and defense contract fraud, which is one of the two major arenas of economic fraud against the U.S. government. The other is health care.

The false claims act and its amendment

First enacted during the Civil War to prosecute civil frauds against the government, since 1863 the False Claims Act has offered an economic bounty for citizen disclosure of fraud. This act was amended in 1986 to increase the economic incentive for citizen initiative in reporting such fraud and to offer increased protection for the whistleblower. However, the use of economic

* An earlier version of this paper was presented at The Third International Conference on Ethics in the Public Service, Jerusalem, Israel, June 6–11, 1993

reward for whistleblowing against false claims in the U.S. applies almost exclusively to federal fraud. Only two of the fifty states offer rewards and these are not large enough to have much impact.[1]

In its original 1863 form, the False Claims Act served to uncover and prosecute Civil War defense contractors who defrauded the government. In the Civil War period the frauds included selling old and useless muskets, boxes of sawdust supposed to contain muskets and ammunition, and horses and mules sold and resold to the government.[2] The original civil penalty, which stood until the 1986 amendment, was restitution of the amount of the fraud plus $ 2,000 penalty per claim issued. Informers providing information leading to the successful prosecution of the cases were awarded 10 percent of the funds paid to the government. This citizen initiative in revealing fraud is known as the *qui tam* provision and refers to suing for oneself and also for the government.

Between 1863 and 1986, the only major change in the FCA was a 1943 amendment that weakened it. Interestingly enough, it was military contractors who led the way in pushing through this change. The 1943 amendment was a response to "the parasitic lawsuit in which bounty hunters sued based on information already known to the Government to obtain money".[3]

The 1986 amendment to the FCA strengthened what had been weakened in 1943 and brought the penalties up to date. It increased penalties against those who defrauded the government, clarified the standards and procedures for suing, provided new incentives for private citizens to report suspected fraud and protected whistleblowers who reported it. The 1986 legislation raised the fine for violations from $2,000 to between $5,000 and $10,000 per claim. It required the defendants to pay triple the amount of damages sustained by the government, but allowed the judge to reduce the award to double the government's damages if the defendant could prove full cooperation with the government once fraud was detected. Its criminal provisions raised the term of imprisonment for a criminal violation from 5 to 10 years and increased criminal fines from $10,000 for individuals and corporations to $250,000 for individuals and $500,000 for corporations. Criminal prosecution applied when the Justice Department decided that the fraud was too serious for civil penalties alone.

Most important was the new incentive for the whistleblower. The Act provided the individual who initiated the suit with a damage award of between 15 and 25 percent if the government entered the case. If the government did not enter the case, the individual could receive at least 25 percent of the damage award but not more than 30 percent.[4]

Context for the fraud

The current U.S. military assistance program with Israel involves about $ 1.8 billion appropriated annually by the U.S. Congress with the stipulation that most of the funds be spent on weapons systems and support manufactured in the U.S. Consequently, over the years the Israel Defense Forces have purchased goods and services from General Electric and other U.S. defense contractors and have received reimbursement from the U.S. Foreign Military Financing Program. Therefore, any collusion and fraud between buyer and seller was also a fraud against the U.S. Treasury.

The particular mechanism by which the U.S. provides military assistance to Israel has contributed to the possibility of fraud. While the U.S. Congress appropriates the funds, the procurement negotiations occur between the recipient agency and U.S. defense contractors who are not monitored and controlled directly by the U.S. government. Israel is one of four nations where this looser form of control, or, indeed, absence of control, has prevailed.[5] Additionally, if fraud is suspected in the use of the funds, the receiver nation is obligated to cooperate with the U.S. investigators. Reluctance to cooperate in this regard once fraud was shown has been a source of tension between the U.S. and Israel.

The Dotan affair

In 1991 and 1992 a high-stakes corruption drama unfolded in Israel and the United States which joined personal, corporate, and international political intrigue on a grand scale. At its core, beginning in 1984, was a scheme led by former Israeli Air Force Brig. General Rami Dotan and former General Electric marketing specialist Herbert Steindler to divert U.S. funds earmarked for Israel's purchase of GE jet engines and support services for their own use and for unauthorized projects in Israel. Dotan was the commander of the Israeli Air Force's Quartermaster Corps.

A key player in unfolding the drama in the U.S. was the informer or whistleblower, Chester L. Walsh, a former GE manager in Israel, who provided crucial evidence and sued GE under the provisions of the amended False Claims Act.

Hearings on July 29, 1992, before the Subcommittee on Oversight and Investigations of the U.S. House Committee on Energy and Commerce provided the most thorough delineation of the fraud and surrounding criminal acts. As summed up by the committee chairperson, U.S. Rep. John Dingell, "What started innocently as aid to a valued and respected ally seems to have turned into a sordid tale of theft, bribery, money laundering, and attempted kidnapping or murder."[6]

Between 1984 and 1990, Dotan and Herbert Steindler, once GE's top employee in Israel, laundered approximately $40 million of U.S. military assistance funds through GE by writing vouchers for military equipment that was never delivered. Additionally, the price of other equipment was inflated. Approximately $35 million of these funds were funneled through a small company in New Jersey controlled by Steindler. Upon transfer to Israel, the funds were deployed to military base projects not authorized by the U.S. Government and to European bank accounts to which Dotan had access via his associate, Harold Katz. More than $11 million of the laundered funds were transferred to various European bank accounts and transferred repeatedly by personal courier to mask the transactions.

The detection of the fraud came from two sources, each of whom handled their whistleblowing in very different ways, with very different outcomes. The first was Opher P'ail, an Israeli Ministry of Defense employee in New York who wrote two letters to the Ministry of Defense in Israel detailing Dotan's procurement irregularities. Dotan must have been aware of these letters since he had $50,000 delivered to a hit man in the U.S. to "surveil, kidnap, beat, and possibly kill Mr. P'ail".[7] This letter led to investigations of General Dotan and to his arrest in October 1990.[8] He was later convicted in a military court and is serving 13 years in an Israeli military prison.

The second source of the fraud detection was in the evidence compiled by and presented by Walsh, who was nearing retirement age and has since retired to Sweden. During the period that the Israeli Ministry of Defense was investigating Dotan, Walsh contacted the U.S. House Subcommittee on Oversight and Investigations. Two weeks after Dotan's arrest filed his false claim suit against his former employer, General Electric, detailing the irregularities he had been witnessing over a period of several years, as was his right under the False Claims Act. This timing sequence was ultimately relevant to the U.S. government and was part of its rationale in its unsuccessful effort to reduce substantially the settlement Walsh was to receive.

Implications of a qui tam suit

The possibility of a *qui tam* suit is the legal framework for protecting and rewarding blowing the whistle on fraud against the government in the U.S. Under the amended False Claims Act, whistleblowers could claim up to 25 percent of the amount recovered by the government if the Justice Department entered the case and more if it did not. The actual amount of a whistleblower's award is decided by the Court after consideration of the value of a whistleblower's contribution to the recovery of funds. In Walsh's case, he claimed up to 25 percent of the amount the government collected from the civil charges.

In December 1992, Walsh and his co-plaintiff, Taxpayers Against Fraud, were awarded $13.4 million by U.S. District Judge Carl Rubin of Federal District Court in Cincinnati, Ohio for their *qui tam* suit.[9] This was 22.5 percent of the $ 59.5 million in civil damages collected from GE by the government. The criminal fines amounted to another $9.5 million, for a combined total of $69 million for GE's settlement with the government. The amount awarded by the Court here is almost the full 25 percent of the recovered civil damage to which the whistleblowers were entitled under the amended False Claims Act and is the current record for a qui tam plaintiff.

The size of this award was opposed by both GE and the U.S. Justice Department. Final approval of the whistleblower's award at $11.5 million came after the U.S. Justice Department dropped its effort to reduce substantially the award. The Justice Department had initially allied with the whistleblower but later opposed him in his quest for the full amount of the award.[10]

The opposition of the U.S. Government and of GE to the whistleblower's claim reveal the difficult position of the whistleblower who sues under the aegis of the FCA. Pleading in U.S. District Court before the award, the Department of Justice sought to reduce the amount Walsh and Taxpayers Against Fraud were to receive to below 10 percent or less than $4.5 million, rather than the more than $14 million sought by the plaintiffs. The government's position held that Israeli investigators discovered the fraud before Walsh did. The U.S. held that the False Claims Act provides for no more than a 10 percent return unless the whistleblower is an original source. The plaintiffs argued that the only standard in the FCA is whether the whistleblowers made a substantial contribution.[11]

GE opposed rewarding the plaintiffs because they claimed that Walsh participated in the fraud which escalated in scope as he was developing his case. As a matter of record, the government's damages grew by $27 million between June 1987, when Walsh first consulted counsel, and November 1990, when the suit was filed.[12]

The plaintiffs argued that under the amended False Claims Act they were entitled to receive between 15 and 25 percent of the amount recovered depending upon the extent of their contribution to the government's case. The plaintiffs argued that they contributed 80 key documents, detailed nine schemes by which the fraud took place, and that Walsh wore a wire through which taped conversations incriminating GE and Israeli officials were provided.[13]

Whistleblowing, therefore, played a role here. But the U.S. whistleblower differed in an important way from the stereotypical profile of the whistleblower as an "ethical resistor" who suffers materially or worse from violating the corporate or organizational ethic of loyalty, conformity, and obedience. Usually whistleblowing has been a selfless act whose consequences are not neutral to the whistleblowers who suffered financial losses, sidetracked careers and even blacklisting.[14] This is not what ultimately happened in the GE case. While not a certainty, and not an easy outcome to gain, Chester L. Walsh and his allied legal advocate, Taxpayers Against Fraud, were finally awarded the $11.5 million, which they split.[15] This was the largest bounty ever awarded to a whistleblower under the False Claims Act.

Whistleblowing and ethical considerations

Whistleblowing is the action of a person in an organization calling attention to the illegal or immoral behavior of others in the organization or of the organization itself. It encompasses a variety of behaviors that are dissimilar from a moral perspective.[16] The unequal moral standing stems from the fact that blowing the whistle, especially in a public way, rather than an internal one, also violates an employee's ethical obligation of loyalty to the organization. From the corporate perspective, the employee should report his or her concerns internally before or instead of "going public" with them. Thus, a very basic distinction is made between internal whistleblowing, which some do not even consider whistleblowing, and what Richard DeGeorge calls "nongovernmental, impersonal, external whistle blowing".[17] This is the form of whistleblowing which is discussed at length in the business ethics literature.

The exposures of Dotan by P'ail and Walsh reflect two different strategies in whistleblowing. P'ail reported his allegations internally; Walsh made his charges externally and filed a civil suit against his employer. Additionally, Walsh's course of action carried with it the potential of substantially greater financial reward than had been the case before. This is the special case of whistleblowing against defrauding the government in the United States. It also casts a different ethical light on whistleblowing than would be the case if there were no economic bounty to be gained. The Israeli whistleblower reported perceived irregularities within the organizational hierarchy while the GE informant went outside the corporate framework and instigated the *qui tam* suit, as was his right under the False Claims Act.

While whistleblowing played a role here, it is arguable that the fraud would have been caught despite Walsh's action. Dotan's activities were exposed by an Israeli Defense Ministry informer, Opher P'ail, not by Walsh's suit. Technically, however, the Israeli's action was not the form of whistleblowing which is viewed ambiguously in the business ethics literature because he did not go public with the charges. From the perspective of ethical theory P'ail did the right thing; Walsh did not.

The protection of whistleblowers from retaliation has always been as problematic as it has been necessary. The provision of incentives for their information has also been effective in countering fraud. Ethical purists, however, would fault their awards on ethical grounds and would certainly fault their claims to be acting only in the public interest.

Thus, blowing the whistle on illegal or immoral activity itself raises ethical questions.[18] The moral standing of the whistleblowers' actions themselves depend upon certain criteria and conditions. These include:

- the focus of the whistleblowing should be of serious, rather than trivial, consequence to the public;
- informers should present the charges and make their moral concerns known internally to their supervisor before going to higher authorities in the organization and ultimately to the public;
- informers must have verifiable evidence for the alleged charges;
- informers must have reason to believe that by going public the situation will be changed;
- informers must be motivated by moral concerns and not by revenge or personal gain.

Administrative process

The 1986 amendment of the FCA increased the incentive for citizens to blow the whistle on fraud against the government and also corrected a weakening of the act consequent to the 1943 amendment which abandoned the *qui tam* provision when and if the U.S. Justice Department refused to enter the case. The 1986 amendment restored and strengthened the qui tam provision and increased the reward for information leading to the recovery of funds and damages to between 15 and 25 percent if the government entered the case, and at least 25 percent but not more than 30 percent if the government did not enter the case.

The relationship between the Justice Department and whistleblowers has ranged from ambivalent to hostile. In the GE case the Justice Department initially joined the whistleblower's suit, but ultimately withdrew and sided with GE in opposing an award of the scale claimed. According to U.S. Senator Charles E. Grassley, one of the sponsors of the 1986 amendment to the False Claims Act, the Act has been successful in easing the restoration of millions to the Treasury despite the opposition of the Justice Department.[19] Grassley suggests that perhaps the Justice Department does not want to admit that it is unable to uncover all of the fraud that exists and resists sharing part of the government's recovered funds with those whose information makes the recovery possible.

Another and similar explanation is also very plausible. The U.S. Justice Department's greater preoccupation is with criminal rather than civil cases. The False Claims Act is designed to ease the recovery of funds to the government on a civil rather than a criminal case basis. The criteria for a civil case are less stringent than they are for a criminal one and the Act stipulates the recovery of double the damages if the company charged cooperates, or triple the amount if it does not. Given the vast scale of monetary fraud, it has been more valuable to the government to recover funds and assign penalties on a civil basis than to work to convict persons on a criminal basis and impose jail sentences. Dotan's jail sentence in Israel and GE's financial penalty in the U.S. provide an important outcome contrast in response to the same fraud.

Thus, this paper interweaves several lines of inquiry. The first deals with the facts of corruption in the case, the response of whistleblowing, and the reaction of corporate and governmental officials to the disclosures. The second deals with the character and potential of whistleblowing in the U.S. context, especially since 1986, and with the amended False Claims Act. Additional questions remain. These revolve around the fact that only parts of the diverted funds appear to have been personally appropriated by Dotan. The balances appear to have been applied to Israeli defense projects besides those authorized in contract with the United States, but the Israeli government has refused to cooperate in any investigation of this matter. Congressional hearings in the summer of 1992 raised this troublesome issue.[20] Interesting though these last questions are, they are not the focus of the paper.

Conclusion

Countering commercial fraud against the government has been more successful because of the strengthened False Claims Act. Whistleblowers in the U.S. still face great obstacles and odds, not the least of which is the seeming indifference or even hostility of the government that stands to gain from their efforts. Additionally, philosophers of business ethics should recognize the real risks and also high stakes in which whistleblowing takes place, and not insist on internal reporting of fraud before "going public". The central paradox remains: substantial economic incentive is a powerful weapon in countering fraud, even though it is an ethically questionable one.

References

Alert International, Inc., "Money Laundering Alert," August, 1992.

Black's Law Dictionary, sixth edition (St. Paul, Minn. West Publishing Co. (1990).

Boatright, John R., *Ethics and the Conduct of Business* (Englewood Cliffs, N.J.: Prentice–Hall, 1993).

Bowie, Norman E. and Ronald F. Duska, *Business Ethics*, second edition (Englewood Cliffs, N.J.: Prentice-Hall, 1990).

Bureau of National Affairs, Inc., "Federal Contracts Report" (November 16, 1992).

Congressional Quarterly Inc., *1986 C Q Almanac*, Washington D.C.

DeGeorge, Richard T., *Business Ethics*, second edition (New York: MacMillan, 1986).

Glazer, Myron P. and Penina M. Glazer, *The Whistle-Blowers: Exposing Corruption in Government and Industry* (New York: Basic Books, 1989).

Grassley, Charles E., "Abe Lincoln vs. the Justice Department," *The New York Times*, January 16, 1993.

Miceli, Marcia P. and Janet P. Near, *Blowing the Whistle: The Organizational and Legal Implications for Companies and Employees* (New York: Lexington Books, 1992).

Naj, Amal Kumar "Whistle-Blower at GE to Get $11.5 Million", *The Wall Street Journal*, April 26, 1993.

Stevenson, Richard W., "U.S. Accuses G.E. of Fraud in Israeli Deal," *The New York Times*, August 15, 1991.

—, "GE Guilty Plea in U.S. Aid to Israel," *The New York Times*, July 23, 1992.

The New York Times, March 28, 1991.

The Washington Post, December 20, 1990.

U.S. House of Representatives, 1986. Committee on the Judiciary, Subcommittee on Administrative Law and Governmental Relations, *Hearing*, Serial No. 48, "False Claim Act Amendments."

—, 1993. Committee on Energy and Commerce, Subcommittee on Oversight and Investigations, *Hearing*, Serial No. 102–165, "Illegal Military Assistance to Israel."

Notes

1. Marcia P. Miceli and Janet P. Near, *Blowing the Whistle: The Organizational and Legal Implications for Companies and Employees*, New York: Lexington Books, 1993, p. 248.
2. U.S. House of Representatives, "False Claims Act Amendments, 1986" p. 328; Glazer & Glazer, The Whistle-Blowers, 1989.
3. U.S. House, "False Claims Act Amendments," 1986, p. 118.
4. *C Q Almanac 1986*, p. 86.
5. *The Washington Post*, December 20, 1990.
6. U.S. House, "Illegal Military Assistance to Israel," 1993, p. 4.
7. U.S. House, "Illegal Military Assistance to Israel," p. 2.
8. U.S. House, "Illegal Military Assistance to Israel," 1993, p. 2.
9. Bureau of National Affairs, *Federal Contracts Report*, Nov. 16, 1992.
10. *The Wall Street Journal*, April 26, 1993, p. A3.
11. Bureau of National Affairs Inc., *Federal Contracts Report*, Nov. 16, 1992.
12. Bureau of National Affairs Inc., *Federal Contracts Report*, Nov. 16, 1992.
13. Bureau of National Affairs Inc., *Federal Contracts Report*, Nov. 16, 1992.
14. Glazer & Glazer, *The Whistle-Blowers*, 1989.
15. *The Wall Street Journal*, April 1993, p. A3.
16. Richard T. DeGeorge, *Business Ethics*, Second Ed., New York, MacMillan 1986, p. 223.
17. DeGeorge 1986, *Business Ethics*, p. 223.

18. DeGeorge, *Business Ethics*, 1986, pp. 226–235; Bowie and Duska, *Business Ethics*, 1990, pp. 74–77; Boatright, *Ethics and the Conduct of Business,* 1993, pp. 131–133.
19. Charles E. Grassley, "Abe Lincoln vs The Justice Department," *The New York Times*, Jan. 16, 1993, p. 21.
20. U.S. House, "Illegal Military Assistance to Israel," 1993, p. 3.

Corruption and Reform 2: 55–74 (1987)

Blowing the whistle on systematic corruption: On maximizing reform and minimizing retaliation

JUDITH A. TRUELSON
University of Southern California, USA

In this, no one ought to be excluded and no idea ignored. Bureaucratic revitalization by itself is insufficient; bureaucratic habits die hard. Simple remedies will not do. Contemporary administrative problems require new approaches, new organizational designs, new laws, new commitments, new relationships, new attitudes, new techniques, new inventions[1].

This article reports results of a study undertaken in 1984–85 on the dynamics of organizational retaliation against legitimate whistle-blowing[2]. The whistle-blowers under study protested acts of corruption, in the organizations in which they worked, which were verified by the FBI, General Accounting Office (GAO), and Congressional or criminal investigations as serious violations of law, regulations and/or professional standards. Sixteen of the protest issues involved life-threatening health or safety violations; nine other protest issues involved multi million dollar contract fraud. All of the whistle-blowers experienced retaliation, administered by individuals acting as organizational agents, which could not be explained without reference to the host organization as a social system in its own right. Retaliation against legitimate whistle-blowers is assumed in this study to be a deviant organizational act, reflective of systemic corruption in that it is contrary to societal norms and is known and supported by the dominant coalition in the organization.

This study is the first empirical analysis of retaliation as the organizational response to legitimate whistle-blowing. By studying cases of intense retaliation, this research moves beyond analysis of the whistle-blowing act itself to focus on the dynamics of the interaction among individual whistle-blowers, organizations, and their environments. As such, it addresses the critical question: how does the organizational retaliation process work? Exploration of this question can help to explain why existing whistle-blower protections are inadequate and why encouragement of responsible employee protest is falling behind expectations.

Whistle-blowing increased in the United States during the 1970s out of concern for the deterioration of morality. As a result of widespread post-Watergate belief in the endemic nature of official wrongdoing,

Congress enacted legislation prescribing a Code of Ethics for Government Service. Besides mandating honest, loyal and efficient service in the public interest, the code also requires that public servants 'expose corruption wherever discovered'[3].

Such expectations require a definition of corruption. While most people agree that the essence of corruption is abuse of a public role or trust for private gain, we cannot always agree on the nature of 'abuse'[4]. In the interest of precision and reliability, corruption is defined in this study in the formal-legal sense – as deliberate and knowing, unsanctioned deviations from the formal duties of an elective or appointive public role, involving the private-regarding use of public resources and goods by public servants. Corruption involves the breaking or bending of laws or other formal regulations, and can include failure to act as well as outright law-breaking deeds[5].

Although whistle-blowing is also subject to a variety of definitions, most authors agree that it involves a process in which an employee of an organization develops an awareness of a product or policy considered to be unethical, immoral, illegal or dangerous to the public. The employee expresses concern to the immediate supervisor, without obtaining satisfaction; expresses concern to supervisors higher up in the corporate or government hierarchy – still without satisfaction – and finally takes the concern outside of the organization, to the press or other support groups[6].

The Code of Ethics of Government Service seeks to incorporate whistle-blowing into policies designed to improve overall accountability of public agencies. But whistle-blowers frequently encounter severe damage to their careers and substantial economic loss as a result of exposing corruption. Congress thus concurrently enacted whistle-blower protection provisions in the Civil Service Reform Act of 1978 (CSRA), including the creation of the Office of the Special Counsel (OSC) and the Merit Systems Protection Board (MSPB)[7].

US Government employees, however, remain reluctant to blow the whistle. Congressional and GAO investigations indicate that the establishment of the OSC has not made federal employees more secure in speaking out[8]. Both the 1980 MSPB survey on whistle-blowing and its 1983 follow-up survey show that about 70% of federal employees claiming personal knowledge of corruption did not report it. An alarming increase in fear of retaliation, as reflected in Table 1, also emerges from comparison of the 1980 and 1983 survey responses.

Deficiencies in whistle-blower protection legislation may stem in part from assumptions that retaliation against legitimate whistle-blowing is purely an individual act. Evidence indicates, however, that such retaliation may instead be the systemic defense of a corrupt organization under attack.

Table 1. Whistle-blowers' fear of retaliation.

	% Response 1980 data (14 agencies)	% response 1983 data (14 agencies)
Received actual threats or reprisals	23%	22%
Feared reprisal from supervisor	27%	24%
Feared reprisal from upper management	26%	34%

Source: *Blowing the whistle in the Federal Government*, US MSPB, 1984: 39.

Most criminologists and organizational sociologists agree that organizations are real, independent, acting entities which can violate the law in their own right[10]. In order to understand government employee reluctance to blow the whistle, it is appropriate to investigate retaliation against whistle-blowers in environments of systemic corruption.

The process of systemic retaliation

The basic premise of this study is that retaliation is a correlate of blowing the whistle on systemic corruption. Although whistle-blowing is threatening to any organization because it challenges the legitimacy of top management's actions, organizations would seem least likely to retaliate against the whistle-blower whose case has been determined to have merit and thus some degree of public support. Research results conflict, however, indicating that employers retaliate both against whistle-blowers whose cases lack merit and who are relatively powerless, and against legitimate whistle-blowers who have public support[11]. The nature of systemic corruption itself suggests an explanation for retaliation against whistle-blowing which may account for this apparent contradiction.

'Systemic corruption' denotes a situation in which the goals of organizational loyalty and survival predominate over the public interest, in which behavior stemming from the notion of public responsibility and trust has become the exception, and in which wrongdoing becomes the norm[12]. As a result, whatever the merits of a whistle-blower's issue, the very act of whistle-blowing is an intolerable breach of the organization's de facto code of conduct. It thus incurs retaliation. Such retaliatory behavior is a form of bureaucratic corruption in that it is enacted by administrators in their official capacity, not in their personal or, where applicable, political capacity[13].

A growing body of literature suggests that such systemic corruption may be endemic to American governmental institutions[14]. When, for example, A. Ernest Fitzgerald blew the whistle on the Pentagon $2 billion cost overrun in the development of the Lockheed C5A transport plane, he exposed a prime example of systemic corruption[15]. Based on hundreds of hearings and federal reports, Hanrahan alleges that federal contracting abuses extending far beyond the Pentagon may also be described as systemic, ingrained, and immune to outside intervention[16]. Some large bureaucratized police organizations have also exemplified systemic corruption. As organizational rules become ends in themselves, the police can become an adjunct of the criminal world they are supposed to fight. Internal practices can encourage and protect violations of the external code of police practice[17].

Dynamics of systemic corruption

Caiden and Caiden argue that corrupt system displays the following features:

1. the organization professes an external code of ethics contradicted by internal practices;
2. internal practices encourage, aid, abet and hide violations of the external code;
3. nonviolators of the external code are penalized in that they lose the benefits of violation and offend those who indulge in violations;
4. violators are protected; and when exposed, they are treated leniently;
5. nonviolators, suffocating in the venal atmosphere, find no internal relief and often meet with external disbelief;
6. prospective whistle-blowers are intimidated and terrorized into silence;
7. courageous whistle-blowers have to be protected from retaliation;
8. violators become so accustomed to their practices and to the protection afforded them that when they are exposed, their surprise is genuine as is their complaint that they have been unfairly singled out;
9. collective guilt finds expression in rationalizations of the corrupt practices; there is no serious intention of ending them;
10. those formally responsible for investigating corruption rarely act, and when forced to do so by external pressure excuse the incidents as isolated rare occurrences;
11. following exposure, the organization makes gestures toward reform

and for a time gives the impression of cleansing itself, but once the publicity is over, it reverts to old practices[18].

Once whistle-blowers expose corrupt organizations to outside sanctions, those formally responsible for investigating corruption focus on the dysfunctionality of whistle-blowers, moving to expel them from the system. Even if they are subsequently reinstated, whistle-blowers find no internal relief from recurring intimidation and retaliation.

Method

This study employs the methodology of negative case analysis. Rooted in John Stuart Mill's 'method of difference', negative case analysis is based on the assumption that the perfect form of scientific knowledge is universal generalizations[19]. Using essentially the same steps in this research as Cressey used in his study of embezzlers, a rough definition and hypothetical explanation of the research problem was formulated. Each of 38 cases of whistle-blowing in large agencies plus (for purposes of proof) 2 cases involving intense retaliation in small organizations, was successively compared against a preliminary hypothesis. When a single negative case was found which disconfirmed the preliminary hypothesis, that hypothesis was revised to account for that case[20]. A thorough search is made for cases that might disconfirm the hypothesis. Although the search and the data collection are not routinized, nor do the data yield numbers that can be added or averaged, the procedure itself is systematic[21].

The sample

Aerospace engineer William Bush has become a veritable one-man whistle-blowing clearinghouse in the course of fighting his own protracted legal battles against retaliation for his revelations of age discrimination. For this study his 5,514 computerized case files were searched for cases of whistle-blowing which resulted in retaliation. The 575 cases thus selected were then scanned for cases which resulted in severe retaliation – defined as firing, forced resignation, transfer, demotion, harassment or blacklisting. Together with 15 cases gathered through personal contacts, a total population of 320 cases was constructed for this study. From this population 42 cases involving primarily public organizations of 1,000 or more employees were drawn, plus the two cases of intense retaliation in small organizations. All cases occurred in the US since 1960, and all could be documented on the following criteria: merit of the issue, intensiveness of retaliation, description of the whistle-blowing process, description of the support mechanisms used by the whistle-blower, and size of the organization.

Facts on the legitimacy of the whistle-blowing and the nature of organizational retaliation were verified through multiple sources including law cases, hearings, newspaper accounts, and case studies. Criteria for inclusion in William Bush's database include verification of data as to nature of dissent, employment sector of the whistle-blower, professional status of the whistle-blower, and nature of organizational retaliation, if any. In addition to the computer database, Bush has extensive files of backup data on these cases which were made available for this research. In 15 cases, documentation was supplemented by interviews modelled on pretested questionnaire items[22].

Interviews/questionnaire

These concerned respondents' perceptions of their organizations, of their jobs before they blew the whistle, of the whistle-blowing incidents themselves, of their reasons for reporting the incidents, of the retaliation experienced, and of their jobs after blowing the whistle. Interview information on the following variables was also documented in independent sources.

Whistle-blower's role influence

The role influence of a whistle-blower was assessed in terms of access to information, persons and organizational resources. The relationship of a role within its role set was used to determine the kinds of influence available to that role incumbent. Role influence was operationalized as tenure of functional expertise, tenure of boundary-spanning functions, tenure of functional independence in a role set, and tenure of auditing functions.

Merit of the issue

A whistle-blower's issue was considered meritorious if it was socially perceived as legitimate and salient. Indicators of merit of the issue included truth of the allegation, precedented grounds for legal action on the whistle-blower's issue, potential grounds for legal action on the whistle-blower's issue, and public acceptance of the moral grounds upon which a whistle-blower protested violation of social policy.

Intensity of the whistle-blowing process

Degree and duration of publicity were used as indicators of the intensity of the whistle-blowing process. Respondents were questioned as to their protest method (i.e, written, oral or both), the frequency of protest, the number of protest channels used within the organization, and the number of protest channels used outside the organization.

Intensity of retaliation against whistle-blowers

The operationalization of intensiveness of retaliation against whistle-blowers is crucial to the validity of this study. It is defined as an ongoing organizational response which is simultaneously comprehensive, involving upper management collusion and widespread collegial avoidance, threats, or refusal to support the whistle-blower; and severe retaliation, involving indirect or direct separation from the organization such as demotion, denial of promotion and dismissal. Comprehensiveness of retaliation included exclusion from staff meetings previously attended, loss of perquisites, receipt of less desirable work assignments, receipt of heavier work load, receipt of more stringent work criticisms, pressure to drop suit and co-worker avoidance of personal or social contact. Severity of retaliation included poor performance appraisal, suspension, transfer or reassignment to a different geographical location, demotion, denial of promotion, physical assault, or intimidation of whistle-blowers and/or their families.

Support used by the whistle-blower to combat retaliation

Assistance to whistle-blowers was considered to be supportive in that it afforded moral, financial, advisory, legal, and/or mediating support to the complainant. Respondents identified organizations such as unions, professional societies, consumer groups, environmental defense groups, civil liberties organizations, and other public interest groups as active supporters. Other indicators of support included statutory whistle-blower protection, Congressional support and grievance and appeal procedures.

Hypothesis

Since the organization focuses on making a scapegoat of the whistle-blower in retaliation for incurring unwelcome notoriety, internal organizational procedures rarely protect whistle-blowers and even more rarely discipline those who have retaliated against whistle-blowers. Actually, appeal mechanisms and dissent channels within corrupt systems such as 'open-door policies' have typically been captured by the very group whose conduct they were created to regulate. Since these channels are not segregated from the rest of the organization, they constitute no deterrent to organizational retaliation against whistle-blowing.

It is therefore predicted that:

> If the whistle-blower's issue is meritorious, the target organization is large and there is intense retaliation against the whistle-blower, there will be a positive relationship between the intensity of the whistle-blowing process, the supports used by the whistle-blower and the intensity of retaliation; there will be a negative relationship between the whistle-blower's role influence and the supports used by the whistle-blower process and the intensity of retaliation.

Corrupt systems display a preoccupation with secrecy, loyalty-security systems, and the segregation of clandestine operations. In such organizations, whistle-blowers who attract mass media coverage of their protests are immediately severed from continued access to organizational intelligence. If feasible, they will be expelled from the organization. In the event that expulsion is infeasible or delayed, they will be symbolically expelled through isolation from information, people and resources. Should the whistle-blowers persist in publicizing their protests – regardless of whether they are still positioned within the organization or are expelled from it – the organization will resort to defamation and even blacklisting in order to discredit adverse publicity.

The hypothesis above suggests a preliminary model of the retaliation process, as seen in Figs 1 and 2. The model assumes interaction among the individual, organizational and extra-organizational levels of activity. Although the stages within each level of activity are presented sequentially, it is understood that the stages may occur and interact simultaneously.

When an employee initiates stage 1 of the the retaliation process by blowing the whistle on a corrupt system, he or she triggers the retaliatory process. The severity of retaliation at this stage may be affected by the whistle-blower's ability to document the protest – which is a function of the extent to which a whistle-blower controls access to information, persons, and resources. Given the magnitude of the issue, a well documented protest also threatens to attract broad media attention and significant extra-organizational support. At this initial stage, the entire bureaucracy from top to bottom closes ranks against the whistle-blower – upper management backing their

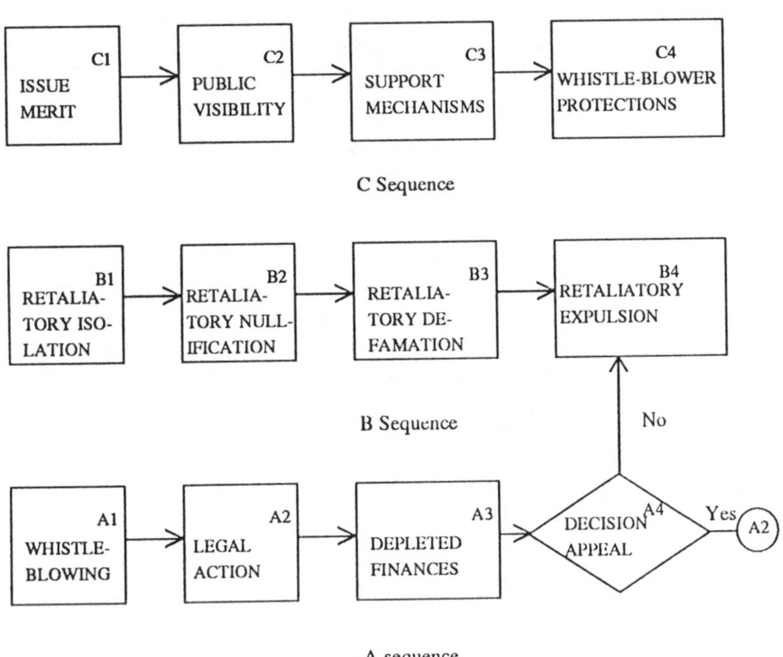

Fig. 1. Multi-level retaliation model. C Sequence = Focus at Extra-Organizational Level of Activity; B Sequence = Focus at the Organizational Level of Activity; A Sequence = Focus at the Individual Level of Activity.

subordinates' retaliatory actions; the subordinates covering up for upper management.

Demotion, expulsion and/or defamation of the whistle-blower initiates stage 2 of the retaliatory process by giving the whistle-blower grounds for appeal or legal action against the organization. Now, however, the employee is blowing the whistle on a different misdeed, that is, the alleged victimization. Invariably, appeals of retaliatory personnel actions are futile in that they are made through the chain of command to the very people who were the targets – directly or indirectly – of whistle-blowing and who allegedly retaliated against the whistle-blower. Nor do statutory whistle-blower protections afford much real protection against retaliation. In this legal environment, Congressional support is the best extra-organizational ally for the whistle-blower.

Deferred and prolonged lawsuits characterize stage 3 of the retaliation process. During both stages 2 and 3, the organization may pit its massive resources against the whistle-blower. The financial burden of whistle-

64

Stages of the retaliation process			
Stage 1	Stage 2	Stage 3	Stage 4
Employee blows whistle	Employee appeals/ takes legal action	Employee awaits legal decision	Employee's case is decided
Variables affecting outcomes of stages			
severity of retaliation, i.e. focus on expulsion	extent of continued retaliation i.e. focus on defamation	extent of continued retaliation, i.e. focus on defamation or concession	extent of continued retaliation, i.e. refocus on expulsion of reinstated employee
extent of issue documentation	extent of whistle-blower protections	depletion of financial resources	grounds for appeal of a lost case
extent of media exposure	extent of media exposure	extent of media exposure	extent of media exposure
impact of support mechanism	impact of support mechanism	impact of support mechanism	impact of support mechanism
	extent of financial resources		extent of financial resources

Fig. 2. The retaliation process.

blowing requires substantial financial resources. Legal services and court costs for private lawsuits are beyond the financial reach of the average employee and, therefore, are a continuing deterrent to cases which must be disentangled by expensive attorneys. Even if the legal assistance is available from a support group or public interest law firm, court costs may be prohibitive.

Delays also add significantly to costs. While an employee's appeal can be dismissed if it is not filed within a limited period, no such rules ensure that an appeals system or legal system will act promptly. The already substantial delay and expense associated with any litigation in today's courts is compounded for the whistle-blower by statutory loopholes such as the awarding of immunity in damages actions to public officials who have established reasonable belief in the legality of the actions for which they were sued. It is not unusual for whistle-blower suits to linger for years in the courts, only to be thrown out in the end on some pre-trial motion unrelated to the merits of the case.

Regardless of the court's decision, stage 4 in the retaliatory process can represent little or no victory for the whistle-blower. An award of reinstatement into a corrupt system only assures reactivation of the retaliatory process. Reinstatement settlements, if awarded, seldom allow for reimbursement of legal and court costs. Should an employee dismissed for whistle-blowing finally be reinstated, an award of back pay does little to compensate for the out-of-pocket expenses incurred.

A case of overpricing

The following case taken from the sample of 42 cases illustrates the model.

Stage 1: In 1983, a maintenance supply man in military service first attempted to report under the 'Zero Overpricing Program' that the service was paying $670.07 for an armrest which he claimed could be made on his base for less than $25. His report was ignored.

> The bottom line is that my suggestion didn't even make it past the first stage of evaluation in the base suggestion program and I never heard anything from the Zero Overpricing Program after submitting my suggestion.

He turned the suggestion in again, even supplying blueprints, yet it was still ignored. He estimated that his suggestion would save $1.5 million annually.

He then tried to report this overpricing issue to his immediate superior, the squadron commander, and even the base Inspector General (IG). He was told in that office that the suggestion had to be turned down three times before the IG would look at it.

The only person who would listen to him was the supply officer (also a case study in this research project). At the officer's suggestion, the supply man reported his overpricing concerns to a military watchdog support group – The Project for Military Procurement. He then joined the officer in answering the subpoena of the Senate Judiciary subcommittee and in testifying before it, under Congressional protection, on seven examples of excessive pricing. He also appeared on television on 'The Today Show', and got press coverage from the *San Francisco Chronicle*, the *New York Times* and the *Washington Post*.

Stage 2: When he returned to base, he was called into the colonel's office.

66

The colonel threatened to bring him up on AWOL charges and put him in another squadron – until the supply maintenance man showed the colonel the letter he had from the chairman of the Senate subcommittee, which outlined the penalties for retaliating against a Congressional witness.

Stage 3: The supply man was nonetheless severely criticized for attracting the attention of an IG investigation team, which was expected to arrive on the base within a matter of hours. The enlisted man was pressed into a crash program for cleaning up as much as possible all irregularities before the team arrived. He was interrogated by the IG team as to why he did not contact the base IG.

Stage 4: After the furor of the inspection team died down, he found himself stigmatized as a squealer and a stooge for Congress. He was finally given a cash award for his suggestion in the Zero Overpricing Program, although the suggestion was never implemented. Although he continued to do the same kind of work, he felt that he was being steered away from trouble areas. Near the end of his enlistment period at the time of the interview, he did not plan to re-enlist.

Despite strong support mechanisms and protection – an officer as co-testifier, support from a military watchdog support group, and Congressional protection – this whistle-blower still experienced comprehensive retaliation in terms of co-worker avoidance, threats and intimidation and severe retaliation in that his re-enlistment plans were affected.

The data

Review of the 40 cases, after six revisions to the preliminary hypothesis, suggests confirmation of the following:

> If the whistle-blower's issue is meritorious, if the target organization is large, and there is intense retaliation – at any point in the relationship between the whistle-blower and the target organization – the greater the public intensity of the whistle-blowing process, the greater the potential will be for use of effective, legal tactics and supports (particularly political and statutory ones); the more simultaneously these tactics and supports occur with the whistle-blowing process and the more energetically they are used, the more likely it is that the severity of intense retaliation will be regulated; the more the severity of intense retaliation is regulated by timely and energetic use of these tactics and supports, the more negative the relationship between the role influence of the whistle-blower and the intensity of retaliation.

Table 2. Effects of whistle-blowing in environments of intense retaliation (N=40).

	Effects on			
	Issue		Whistle-blower	
Issue	None	Token Action	Removed from org.	Diminished role in org.
Contract Fraud	8	3	5	6
Health/Safety	14	2	12	4
Illegality	1	4	2	3
Waste	1	2	2	1
Unfair Labor Practices	3	2	2	3
	27	13	23	17

The findings of this research correspond to the model of the retaliation process illustrated in Figs 1 and 2. Negative case analysis, however, has contributed a sense of the duration and intensity of the retaliation process.

The experiences of the whistle-blowers understudy reveal the destructive societal impact of systemic corruption. Table 2 shows that of the 23 whistle-blowers permanently separated from their organizations due to blowing the whistle, 16 were fired, six were forced to resign, and one was forced to retire. Ten of these 23 were blacklisted; six of those blacklisted have apparently never worked since in their profession. Among the remaining 17 whistle-blowers eight were transferred to positions which denied them access to continued information about their protest issue, two were permanently refused promotions and given less desirable work assignments, and seven were excluded from communication channels, avoided by co-workers and otherwise hampered in performing their assignments.

Institutional lawlessness and misuse of institutional power act as barriers to effective ethical behavior in an environment of systemic corruption. There is no indication that any of the studied whistle-blowers caused their organizations to abandon corruption. In more than 60% of the study cases, no change at all occured as a result of whistle-blowing. In the 13 cases where some action was taken – probably because of publicized direct evidence of statutory violation – reform was localized rather than systemic. For example, FBI exposure of systemic corruption among meat-graders resulted in removal of graders in a particular region – but not throughout the system.

68

Institutional lawlessness

The organizations involved in this study attacked the whistle-blowers from every side with accusations of insubordination, disloyalty, breach of confidence, poor performance appraisal – even mental instability – culminating in disgrace, reduction in role influence, and transfer, demotion or termination.

Since the 40 whistle-blowers found so little protection from reprisals, it appears that their organizations operate according to their own standards with their activities either beyond legal restriction or little penalized. The US legal structure itself helps to create an environment in which institutional lawlessness flourishes. Statutory antiretaliation provisions are both too broad and too narrow to afford protection to whistle-blowers. The law gives broad leeway to the Courts in the balancing of state and individual interests, and has thus resulted in precedents such as *Connick v. Myers* which upheld a restriction on first amendment rights in the interest of an organization's fulfillment of its responsibilities to the public[23]. Even if the government whistle-blower is allowed to press for damages and can prevail under the Supreme Court's balancing test, defendants may be able to assert the defense of immunity to their claims. Indeed, some officials carry out such controversial or far-reaching functions that they are accorded absolute immunity regardless of the legality of their actions. When acting in official capacity, for example, the President, judges, and prosecutors have all been accorded absolute immunity[24]. The protection of administrative policies and prerogatives so dominates the legal environment that the potential for retaliation against whistle-blowers is practically unrestricted.

The Merit Systems Protection Board, acting on behalf of whistle-blowers as an administrative court in prosecutions initiated by the Office of Special Counsel has taken an unduly technical view of its task – imposing unwarranted evidentiary burdens on whistle-blowers and expressing an unusually conservative interpretation of the First Amendment. As a result, whistle-blower reprisal complaints rarely qualify for Special Counsel protection. As of December 1984, 42% of all matters under active investigation were whistle-blower reprisal cases. Yet, an extremely small proportion of these complaints meet the legal standards required of OSC for a successful prosecution or a corrective or disciplinary action[25].

Table 3 shows that only about half of the whistle-blowers sought formal protection. Of the appeals, less than half were successful; eight of the whistle-blowers filed two appeals – several filed both an administrative and a civil suit. In all of the nine cases in which public employees won an appeal, reinstatement, back pay and benefits were the only reparation required of the organization.

Table 3. Effectiveness of whistle-blower statutory protections (N=40).

	Admin. Appeal		Union Appeal		Civil Suit	
Cause of Action	Won	Lost	Won	Lost	Won	Lost
Fired	4	9	–	2	4	4
Forced to resign	–	1	–	–	–	–
Transferred, Demoted	4	3	–	–	–	–
	8	13		2	4	4

Institutional staying power

Although none of the whistle-blowers in this study succeeded in avoiding retaliation, some of them such as the supply maintenance man were successful in regulating retaliation by enlisting outside support and by planning the timing and energy of response, and the duration of struggle. Yet, the study organizations had such complete control of their resources that they could impose at least some retaliation on whistle-blowers and sustain it indefinitely even in the face of outside support. In every case, the whistle-blower's organizational role influence, in terms of access to people, information and resources, was totally or essentially eliminated.

Table 4 presents data on the length of such struggles. Among the study group, 27 public employees invoked a combination of legal support and Congressional support sustained for at least two to three years. In nine cases, the struggle endured for more than five years. Despite considerable expenditures of time, money and other resources, these 27 battles resulted in only nine cases of reinstatement and one case of vindication.

Few of these reinstated whistle-blowers could attract enough support or could themselves afford the financial and psychological burden of renewed, protracted battles. Two of the nine reinstated employees are on stress-related disability leave; one resigned after five years of harassment; two others were reinstated to noncomparable jobs in which their failure was assured; one has been publicly labeled as 'paranoid'.

Table 4. Whistle-blowers' use of supports in combatting retaliation (N=33).

		Supports				Result
Length of Struggle	N	Law/ Reg.	Press/ Media	Congress	Legal Aid	Reinstated/ Vindicated
10+ yrs.	3	1	2	3	2	3
5–10 yrs.	6	4	2	4	3	3
2–5 yrs.	10	8	–	3	–	7
1–2 yrs.	7	3	5	4	1	3
–1 yr.	7	3	3	3	–	1
	33	19	12	17	6	17

Reform implications

In order to survive the experience of blowing the whistle on systemic corruption, statutory protections will certainly continue to be invoked. Yet, the law cannot stop systemic corruption. Unable to rely on mechanisms like conscience or threat of imprisonment or death which operate within individuals to repress or sublimate a certain amount of antisocial activity before it is even thought of, the law is limited to the application of minimal organizational penalties. Prosecutors such as the MSPB and the OSC must rely on weak disciplinary actions such as letters of reprimand and admonishment, and fines. Moreover, broadly written statutes such as the Civil Service Reform Act contain many administrative and procedural deficiences such as limited coverage of protected personnel actions. These problems are likely to persist: even if the controversial whistle-blower protection legislation which was recently proposed in the House, is passed, the benefits accruing from, for example, changing the standard of proof from 'preponderance of evidence' to 'substantial evidence' would be minimal[26].

The major problem in relying solely on the law as arbiter of organizational retaliation against whistle-blowers is that the law is primarily a reactive institution. Even if laws could be passed to effectively protect whistle-blowers until they are passed and enforced, a great deal of damage will be done. Blowing the whistle on systemic corruption may be better protected through increased political support generated through cultural and institutional changes.

Cultural change

Environmental social control seems to be an essential ingredient in the resocialization process. Scandal as a negative public reaction to systemic corruption can constitute a social control: a punitive sanction designed to deter further deviance. Labeling of the system as corrupt seems to hinge on public revelation of its managers' lack of interest in controlling the corrupt acts committed by its members[27].

Mobilization of scandal is used successfully in socialist countries, primarily in the Soviet Union and China[28]. Although mobilization of scandal may seem a return to the old predevelopment style of justice, it can be a productive means to supplement the inadequacy of whistle-blowing and formal legal systems in dealing with contemporary systemic corruption. The social reaction that constitutes scandal must be one of intense outrage and anger, rather than of mere disapproval. This outrage must be stimulated and sustained by the legislature, support group protests and intensive media exposure of corruption.

Inspections and investigations are also essential to the exploration of deviant behaviors as issues of social and community development. Review by peers or by higher authorities must serve as a forum for discussion of the moral stakes involved in particular decisions. Review procedures including those of formal complaints, hearings and appeals should also contribute to critical dialogue to revive commitment to agency ideals or personal standards of honesty.

Institutional change

The creation and support of dissent channels to permit expression of contrary views on policy issues is a critical ingredient of effective administrative reform. The concept of the ombudsman as an advocate for federal employee protest could be an innovative key to unlocking the virtually untapped reservoir of employee knowledge of corruption. Some ombudsman activities relating to employee protest might include: listening to the complaints of concerned employees and counseling them on procedures and possible outcomes for lodging protests, responding directly to some employee complaints and referring federal employees to the proper agency official or office to lodge their complaints[29].

Conclusions

While the number of study cases is small, the conclusions of this study are nonetheless indicative of directions for future research. The prospects for reform in the United States depend to a great extent on deepening the understanding of systemic retaliation against whistle-blowing. Continued research in the United States as well as crosscultural research on retaliation against legitimate whistle-blowing in other settings could provide valuable insights. Future comparative studies may also be in order to probe this study's assumption that although public and private organizations vary in important respects, the dynamics of retaliation against whistle-blowing are similar in both.

If we are seeking the evolution of civic virtue – the respect for publicness and community – we must endorse the mission of legitimate whistle-blowers. In addition to protection, we must guide whistle-blowers operating in an environment of systemic corruption. Codes of conduct are often too general and idealistic to be of much help. The reality of systemic corruption is relative – its subjective, political characteristics elude definition and agreement. Public servants cannot get 'up to code' in corrupt systems because systemic corruption has the power to effectively insulate the corrupt from denunciation and removal. Yet, the inability to adhere to codes of conduct adds to the ceaseless criticism of the public service.

Codes of conduct miss the mark because they are directed at the wrong target – the good public servants who follow them, not the corrupt ones[30]. The real target should be corrupt conduct. A new process of socialization, strengthened by well publicized corruption control guidelines, implemented within the civil service and among the public at large seems to be the best remedy for systemic corruption[31]. Codification of corruption would serve as a social reference point. For example, the New York City Police Department has devised an administrative manual which provides for the identification of corruption, including procedures for control, enforcement policy and accountability[32].

Clearly, to make inroads into systemic corruption, a genuine public service ideology must be cultivated. Bold and informed administrative and political initiatives and active if not violent dissent could make the prospects for administrative reform brighter than they have been for some decades[33].

Notes and references

1. G.E. Caiden, Postscript: 'Public Administration and Administrative Reform', in: G.E. Caiden and H. Siedentopf (eds), *Strategies for Administrative Reform*. Lexington, Massachusetts: Lexington Books, 1982: 231.

2. J.A. Truelson, *Blowing the Whistle on Systemic Corruption* (PhD dissertation). Los Angeles, California: School of Public Administration, University of Southern California, 1986.
3. Code of Conduct for Government Service, Public Law 96–303, October 1, 1980.
4. For discussions on the difficulties of defining corruption, see James C. Scott, *Comparative Political Corruption*. Englewood Cliffs, New Jersey: Prentice-Hall, 1972: 3–9; Susan Rose-Ackerman, *Corruption: A Study in Political Economy*. New York: Academic Press, 1978: 6–10; Arnold J. Heidenheimer (ed.), *Political Corruption: Readings in Comparative Analysis*. New York: Holt, Rinehart and Winston, 1970: 3–64: Michael Johnston, 'Systemic Origins of Fraud, Waste and Abuse', in: J.B. McKinney and M. Johnston (eds), *Fraud, Waste and Abuse in Government*. Philadelphia, Pennsylvania: ISHI Publications, 1986: 16–17.
5. G.E. Caiden, 'Public Maladministration and Bureaucratic Corruption', in: McKinney and Johnston (1986: 32); J.S. Nye, 'Corruption and Political Development: A Cost-Benefit Analysis', *American Political Science Review* 61: 416.
6. F.A. Elliston, 'Anonymity and Whistleblowing', *Journal of Business Ethics* 1: 168.
7. Civil Service Reform Act of 1978, 5 USC 2302, 1978.
8. US Congress, House Committee on Post Office and Civil Service, *Whistleblower Protection: Hearings before the House Subcommittee on Civil Service, 99th Congress, May 15, June 18, 26, 1985*. Washington, DC: US Government Printing Office, 1985: 16–21.
9. US Merit Systems Protection Board, Office of Merit Systems Review and Studies, *Blowing the Whistle in the Federal Government*. Washington, DC: US Government Printing Office, 1984: 39.
10. H.C. Finney and H.R. Lesieur, 'A Contingency Theory of Organizational Crime', in: S.B. Bacharach (ed.), *Research in Sociology of Organizations*, Vol. 1. Greenwich, Connecticut: JAI Press, 1982: 258.
11. M.A. Parmelee, J.P. Near and T.C. Jensen, 'Correlates of Whistleblowers' Perceptions of Organizational Retaliation', Administrative Science Quarterly 27: 30.
12. G.E. Caiden and N.J. Caiden, 'Administrative Corruption', Public Administration Review 37: 305–308.
13. G.E. Caiden, 'Public Maladministration and Bureaucratic Corruption', in: McKinney and Johnston (1986: 32).
14. See, for example, M.D. Ermann and R.J. Lundman, *Corporate and Governmental Deviance: Problems of Organizational Behavior in Contemporary Society*, (2nd edn). New York: Oxford University Press, 1982: 55–67; Rose-Ackerman (1978); L.W. Sherman, *Scandal and Reform: Controlling Police Corruption*. Berkeley, California: University of California Press, 1978.
15. R. Nader, P.J. Petkas and K. Blackwell (eds), *Whistle-Blowing; The Report of the Conference on Professional Responsibility*. New York: Grossman Publishers, 1972: 40.
16. J.D. Hanrahan, *Government by Contract* New York: W.W. Norton, 1983: 38–39.
17. G.E. Caiden, *Police Revitalization*. Lexington, Massachusetts: Lexington Books, 1977: 151–169.
18. G.E. Caiden and N.J. Caiden, op. cit. 306–307.
19. See D.R. Cressy, *Other People's Money*. Glencoe, Illinois: Free Press, 1953, for discussion of negative case analysis: see also 'Method of difference' in: John Stuart Mill, *A System of Logic*, Vol. 1. London: Longmans, Green, 1975: 452.
20. Cressey (1953: 16).
21. L.H. Kidder, *Selltiz, Wrightsman and Cook's Research Methods in Social Relations* (4th edn). New York: Holt, Rinehart and Winston, 1981: 105.
22. See US Merit Systems Protection Board, Office of Merit Systems Review and Studies, *Whistleblowing and the Federal Employee*. Washington, DC: US Government Printing Office, 1981, Appendix A; Kane, Parsons and Associates, *Engineers Survey*. New York, 1983: 1–16.
23. *Connick v. Myers*, 461 US 138 (1983).

24. P. Raven-Hansen, 'Protecting Whistleblowers: Can We and Should We?' First Wednesday Lecture, George Washington University National Law Center, June 1, 1983: 16–19.
25. US Government Accounting Office, *Whistleblower Complainants Rarely Qualify for Office of the Special Counsel*. Washington, DC: US Government Printing Office, GGD–85–33, May 10, 1985: 17.
26. 'Whistleblower Protection Opposed by Special Counsel, Justice', *BNA Government Employee Relations Report* Vol. 24, February 24, 1986, no. 1151.
27. Sherman (1978: 60–61).
28. S.B. Werner, 'New Directions in the Study of Administrative Corruption', Public Administration Review 43: 152.
29. J.A. Truelson, 'Protest is Not a Four Letter Word', *Bureaucrat* 14: 24.
30. G.E. Caiden, 'Public Service Ethics: What Should Be Done?', in: K. Kernaghan and O.P. Dwivedi (eds), *Ethics in the Public Service: Comparative Perspectives*. Brussels: International Institute of Administrative Sciences, 1983: 162.
31. Ibid., p. 168.
32. Ibid., p. 168–170.
33. G.E. Caiden, 'Reform and Revitalization in American Bureaucracy', in: R. Miewald and M. Steinman (eds), *Problems in Administrative Reform*. Chicago: Nelson-Hall, 1984: 264.

Name Index